FACTS ABOUT THE PRESIDENTS

Joseph Nathan Kane

FACTS ABOUT THE PRESIDENTS

A Compilation of Biographical and Historical Data

1976

ace books

A Division of Charter Communications Inc.
1120 Avenue of the Americas
New York, N.Y. 10036

FACTS ABOUT THE PRESIDENTS

Copyright © 1959, 1960, 1964, 1968, 1974, 1975
by Joseph Nathan Kane

New and Additional Material Copyright © 1976 by
Joseph Nathan Kane

First H. W. Wilson Company Edition 1959

Second Edition 1968

Third Edition 1974

First Ace printing: March 1976

An ACE Book,

by special arrangement with the author

Library of Congress Cataloging in Publication Data

Kane, Joseph Nathan
   Facts about the Presidents; a compilation of biographical
and historical data.

1. President–United States.   i. Title.
E176.1.K3 1974   973'.0992   74-5297
ISBN 0-8242-0538-3

Printed in the United States of America

PREFACE

The Presidents of the United States, from George Washington to Gerald Rudolph Ford, are subjects of continuing popular interest and scholarly research. About these thirty-seven men countless books have been published—individual biographies, collective biographies, academic studies, political analyses, pictorial histories. FACTS ABOUT THE PRESIDENTS is a compilation which presents, in one volume, data concerning their lives, their backgrounds, their tenure of office—and much about the office itself. It would not be possible, obviously, to cover in one book every known fact about every President, but the facts most likely to be sought by the general reader are included.

In Part I a chapter is devoted to each President in the chronological order in which he took office. The data in these chapters are arranged uniformly. A genealogical compilation presents vital material about the President's parents, brothers and sisters, wife, and children. Family history is followed by data on elections, congressional sessions, cabinet and Supreme Court appointments, and the Vice President, as well as highlights of the President's life and administration.

In Part II material is presented in comparative form, with collective data and statistics on the Presidents as individuals and on the office of the presidency.

The determination of correct dates—thousands in a work of this nature—has been a great problem, and it has been a major task to supply those dates which are buried in musty records. The inclusion of complete dates, rather than just the year or month, has made the task still more difficult. Where first-hand sources are not available and where discrepancies appear in secondary sources, the dates have been omitted.

It should also be noted that many dates disagree with those previously printed. Such discrepancies do not indicate that the dates herein presented are incorrect but rather that the others may be in error. Should further research bring primary sources to light to contradict any of the dates in FACTS ABOUT THE PRESIDENTS, we will appreciate hearing of these documents so that they may be examined to determine whether the new data should be included in future editions.

This first paperback edition includes the complete Third Edition of The H. W. Wilson Company and has been brought up to date as of January 1, 1976.

JOSEPH NATHAN KANE

March 1976

CONTENTS

Part I Biographical Data

George Washington — Gerald Rudolph Ford

PART II COMPARATIVE DATA

Facts About The Presidents

GEORGE WASHINGTON
1st PRESIDENT

Born–Feb. 22, 1732

Birthplace–Pope's Creek, Westmoreland County, Va.

College attended–None

Religious denomination–Episcopalian

Ancestry–English

Occupation–Surveyor, planter

Date and place of marriage–Jan. 6, 1759, Kent County, Va.

Age at marriage–26 years, 318 days

Years married–40 years, 342 days

Political party–Federalist

State represented–Virginia

Term of office–Apr. 30, 1789-Mar. 3, 1797

Term served–7 years, 308 days

Administration–1st, 2nd

Congresses–1st, 2nd, 3rd, 4th

Age at inauguration–57 years, 67 days

Lived after term–2 years, 285 days

Occupation after term–Planter and General of the Army

Date of death–Dec. 14, 1799

Age at death–67 years, 295 days

Place of death–Mount Vernon, Va.

Burial place–Family vault, Mount Vernon, Va.

PARENTS

Father–Augustine Washington

Born–1694, Westmoreland, Va.

Married (1)–Jane Butler, Apr. 20, 1715

Married (2)–Mary Ball, Mar. 6, 1730

Occupation–Farmer, planter

Died–Apr. 12, 1743, King George County, Va.

Age at death–About 49 years

First wife of father–Jane Butler Washington

Born–c. 1700

Married–Apr. 20, 1715

Died–Nov. 24, 1728, Stafford County, Va.

Mother–Mary Ball Washington

Born–1708, Lancaster County, Va.

Married–Mar. 6, 1730

Died–Aug. 25, 1789, near Fredericksburg, Va.

Age at death–81 years

BROTHERS AND SISTERS

Augustine Washington was the father of ten children, four by his first wife and six by his second wife. George Washington was his fifth child and the first-born of Mary Ball Washington.

Children of Jane Butler Washington and Augustine Washington

Butler Washington, b. 1716, d. 1716

Lawrence Washington, b. 1718, d. July 26, 1752

Augustine Washington, b. 1720, d. May 1762

Jane Washington, b. 1722, d. Jan. 17, 1735

Children of Mary Ball Washington and Augustine Washington

George Washington, b. Feb. 22, 1732, d. Dec. 14, 1799

Elizabeth ("Betty") Washington, b. June 20, 1733, d. Mar. 31, 1797

Samuel Washington, b. Nov. 16, 1734, d. Dec. 1781

John Augustine Washington, b. Jan. 13, 1736, d. Feb. 1787

Charles Washington, b. May 2,

For additional data see the end of this section and also specific subject headings in the index.

1738, d. May 3, 1799

Mildred Washington, b. June 21, 1739, d. Oct. 23, 1740

CHILDREN

None

MRS. GEORGE WASHINGTON

Name—Martha Dandridge Custis Washington

Born—June 21, 1731

Birthplace—New Kent County, Va.

Age at marriage to Washington—27 years, 199 days

Children by Washington—None

Mother—Frances Jones Dandridge

Father—Colonel John Dandridge

His occupation—Planter

Date of death—May 22, 1802

Age at death—70 years, 355 days

Place of death—Mount Vernon, Va.

Burial place—Mount Vernon, Va.

Years older than the President—246 days

Years she survived the President—2 years, 159 days

At the time of her marriage to Washington she was the widow of Daniel Parke Custis, by whom she had four children, two of whom died in infancy.

THE ELECTION OF 1789

When the first electors cast their ballots, there were no political organizations or political parties in existence. Each elector had to ballot for two persons. The one with the majority of votes was elected President and the next highest Vice President. No distinction was made between votes for President and Vice President until 1804.

The method of balloting and selecting the candidate is governed by Article 2, Section 1, Paragraph 3 of the Constitution:

The Electors shall meet in their respective States, and vote by Ballot for two persons, of whom one at least shall not be an Inhabitant of the same State with themselves. And they shall make a List of all the Persons voted for, and of the Number of Votes for each; which List they shall sign and certify, and transmit sealed to the Seat of the Government of the United States, directed to the President of the Senate. The President of the Senate shall, in the Presence of the Senate and the House of Representatives, open all the Certificates, and the Votes shall then be counted. The Person having the greatest Number of Votes shall be the President, if such a number be a Majority of the whole Number of Electors appointed; and if there be more than one who have such Majority, and have an equal number of Votes, then the House of Representatives shall immediately chuse by Ballot one of them for President; and if no Person has a Majority, then from the five highest on the List, the said House shall in like Manner chuse the President. But in chusing the President, the Votes shall be taken by States, the Representation from each State having one Vote; A quorum for this purpose shall consist of a Member or Members from two-thirds of the States, and a Majority of all the States shall be necessary to a Choice. In every Case, after the Choice of the President, the Person having the greatest Number of Votes of the Electors shall be the Vice President.

But if there should remain two or more who have equal Votes, the Senate shall chuse from them by Ballot the Vice President.

It was the intention of the Continental Congress that the newly formed government should convene on "the first Wednesday in March next" (March 4, 1789) at Federal Hall, New York City. Only eight of the twenty-six senators and thirteen of the sixty-five representatives presented themselves on that date and it was not until April 6, 1789, that a quorum was present. John Langdon, President of the Senate, received, opened, and counted the votes of the electors.

George Washington received one vote from each of the sixty-nine electors from the ten states and was the unanimous choice for President. The votes were cast by the states as follows: Massachusetts 10, Pennsylvania 10, Virginia 10, Connecticut 7, South Carolina 7, Maryland 6, New Jersey 6, Georgia 5, New Hampshire 5, and Delaware 3.

A committee from both houses was appointed to meet him: John Langdon of New Hampshire, Charles Carroll of Maryland, and William Samuel Johnson of Connecticut, representing the Senate; and Elias Boudinot of New Jersey, Richard Bland Lee of Virginia, Thomas Tudor Tucker of South Carolina, Egbert Benson of New York, and John Laurance of New York, representing the House.

Charles Thomson was appointed to notify George Washington that he had been elected President and Sylvanus Bourn was appointed to notify John Adams that he had been elected Vice President.

On April 14, 1789, Charles Thomson, secretary of the Continental Congress notified George Washington of his election, and on April 16, 1789, Washington left his home at Mount Vernon, Va., for the capital.

FULL ELECTORAL VOTE NOT CAST IN 1789

On February 4, 1789, the first presidential electors met in New York City. Ten states sent 69 electors. The electors of five states—Connecticut, Delaware, Georgia, New Jersey, and South Carolina—had been chosen by the state legislatures. Three states—Maryland, Pennsylvania, and Virginia—held popular elections. Massachusetts had a system combining popular election and appointment by the legislature. New Hampshire held a popular election, but none of the electors received a majority, and the electors finally chosen were those named by the state Senate.

Had all of the electors qualified, a total of 91 votes, instead of 69, would have been cast. New York had not yet chosen its 8 electors even though the seat of the new government was in New York. Consequently, New York's vote was not cast. The weather delayed the votes of 4 electors, 2 from Maryland and 2 from Virginia. Since North Carolina and Rhode Island had not yet ratified the Constitution, they did not cast their 7 and 3 votes respectively. Thus, 22 of the 91 possible votes were not cast.

ADAMS ELECTED VICE PRESIDENT

Each elector cast 1 of his 2 votes for Washington, who thus received 69 of the 138 votes. The other 69 went to 11 others; John Adams

of Massachusetts, the candidate with the greatest number, became
Vice President. The other candidates included John Jay of New York,
Robert Hanson Harrison of Maryland, John Rutledge of South Caro-
lina, John Hancock of Massachusetts, George Clinton of New York,
Samuel Huntington of Connecticut, John Milton of Georgia, James
Armstrong of Georgia, Edward Telfair of Georgia, and Benjamin Lin-
coln of Georgia.

Adams received 34 votes as follows: Conn. 5 (of the 7 votes); Mass.
10; N.H. 5; N.J. 1 (of the 6 votes);· Pa. 8 (of the 10 votes); Va. 5
(of the 10 votes).

The other candidates received the following votes:

Jay—Del. 3; N.J. 5 (of the 6 votes); Va. 1 (of the 10 votes)

Harrison—Md. 6

Rutledge—S.C. 6 (of the 7 votes)

Hancock—Pa. 2 (of the 10 votes); S.C. 1 (of the 7 votes); Va. 1
(of the 10 votes)

Clinton—Va. 3 (of the 10 votes)

Huntington—Conn. 2 (of the 7 votes)

Milton—Ga. 2 (of the 5 votes)

Armstrong—Ga. 1 (of the 5 votes)

Lincoln—Ga. 1 (of the 5 votes)

Telfair—Ga. 1 (of the 5 votes)

THE ELECTION OF 1792

Before the conclusion of George Washington's four-year term, it
was necessary to elect a President for the second administration.
George Washington and John Adams, who were known as Federalists,
were advocates of a strong central government. Those in accord with
their principles wanted them reelected for a second term of four years.

Naturally, not all of the ideas and plans advocated by them were
acceptable to everyone. Those who differed were known as Democratic Republicans or Republicans. As the Democratic Republicans
were a minority group, they realized the futility of organizing to oppose Washington's reelection, and did not oppose him.

On November 6, 1792, George Washington received 132 of the 264
electoral votes cast, a unanimous election. The second highest vote,
77 votes, was for John Adams of Massachusetts, who was reelected
Vice President. The balance of the 132 electoral votes was cast for
George Clinton of New York (50 votes), Thomas Jefferson of Virginia
(4 votes) and Aaron Burr of New York (l vote).

FIRST TERM
CABINET
March 4, 1789-March 3, 1793

State—John Jay, N.Y., Secretary for Foreign Affairs under the Confederation, continued to act at the request of President Washington
until Thomas Jefferson assumed office; Thomas Jefferson, Va.,
Sept. 26, 1789, entered upon duties, Mar. 22, 1790

Treasury—Alexander Hamilton, N.Y., Sept. 11, 1789

War—Henry Knox, Mass., Sept. 12, 1789

Attorney General–Edmund Randolph, Va., Sept. 26, 1789, entered upon duties Feb. 2, 1790

Postmaster General–Samuel Osgood, Mass., Sept. 26, 1789; Timothy Pickering, Pa., Aug. 12, 1791, entered upon duties Aug. 19, 1791

SECOND TERM
CABINET

March 4, 1793-March 3, 1797

State–Thomas Jefferson, Va., continued from preceding administration ; Edmund Randolph, Va., Jan. 2, 1794; Timothy Pickering, Pa. (secretary of war) ad interim August 20, 1795; Timothy Pickering, Pa., Dec. 10, 1795

Treasury–Alexander Hamilton, N.Y., continued from preceding administration; Oliver Wolcott, Jr., Conn. Feb. 2, 1795

War–Henry Knox, Mass., continued from preceding administration; Timothy Pickering, Pa., Jan. 2, 1795; Timothy Pickering, Pa. (secretary of state) ad interim Dec. 10, 1795 to Feb. 5, 1796; James McHenry, Md., Jan. 27, 1796, entered upon duties Feb. 6, 1796

Attorney General–Edmund Randolph, Va., continued from preceding administration; William Bradford, Pa., Jan. 27, 1794, entered upon duties Jan. 29, 1794; Charles Lee, Va., Dec. 10, 1795

Postmaster General–Timothy Pickering, Pa., continued from preceding administration; Timothy Pickering, Pa., recommissioned June 1, 1794; Joseph Habersham, Ga., Feb. 25, 1795

FIRST TERM
FIRST CONGRESS

March 4, 1789-March 3, 1791

First session–Mar. 4, 1789-Sept. 29, 1789 (210 days)
Second session–Jan. 4, 1790-Aug. 12, 1790 (221 days)
Third Session–Dec. 6, 1790-Mar. 3, 1791 (88 days)
Vice President–John Adams, Mass.
President pro tempore of the Senate–John Langdon, N.H., elected Apr. 6, 1789
Secretary of the Senate–Samuel Allyne Otis, Mass., elected Apr. 6, 1789
Speaker of the House–Frederick Augustus Conrad Muhlenberg, Pa., elected Apr. 1, 1789
Clerk of the House–John Beckley, Va., elected Apr. 1, 1789

SECOND CONGRESS

March 4, 1791-March 3, 1793

First session–Oct. 24, 1791-May 8, 1792 (197 days)
Second session–Nov. 5, 1792-Mar. 12, 1793 (119 days)
Special session of the Senate–Mar. 4, 1791 (1 day only)
Vice President–John Adams, Mass.
Presidents pro tempore of the Senate–Richard Henry Lee, Va., elected Apr. 18, 1792; John Langdon, N.H., elected Nov. 5, 1792, and Mar. 1, 1793

Secretary of the Senate—Samuel Allyne Otis, Mass.

Speaker of the House—Jonathan Trumbull, Conn., elected Oct. 24, 1791

Clerk of the House—John Beckley, Va., reelected Oct. 24, 1791

SECOND TERM

THIRD CONGRESS

March 4, 1793-March 3, 1795

First session—Dec. 2, 1793-June 9, 1794 (190 days)
Second session—Nov. 3, 1794-Mar. 3, 1795 (121 days)
Special session of the Senate—Mar. 4, 1793 (1 day only)
Vice President—John Adams, Mass.
Presidents pro tempore of the Senate—Ralph Izard, S. C., elected May 31, 1794; Henry Tazewell, Va., elected Feb. 20, 1795 (Samuel Livermore, N.H., was elected Feb. 20, 1795 but declined)
Secretary of the Senate—Samuel Allyne Otis, Mass.
Speaker of the House—Frederick Augustus Conrad Muhlenberg, Pa., elected Dec. 2, 1793
Clerk of the House—John Beckley, Va., reelected Dec. 2, 1793

FOURTH CONGRESS

March 4, 1795-March 3, 1797

First session—Dec. 7, 1795-June 1, 1796 (177 days)
Second session—Dec. 5, 1796-Mar. 3, 1797 (89 days)
Special session of the Senate—June 8, 1795-June 26, 1795 (19 days)
Vice President—John Adams, Mass.
Presidents pro tempore of the Senate—Henry Tazewell, Va., elected Dec. 7, 1795; Samuel Livermore, N.H., elected May 6, 1796; William Bingham, Pa., elected Feb. 16, 1797
Secretary of the Senate—Samuel Allyne Otis, Mass.
Speaker of the House—Jonathan Dayton, N.J., elected Dec. 7, 1795
Clerk of the House—John Beckley, Va., reelected Dec. 7, 1795

APPOINTMENTS TO THE SUPREME COURT

Chief Justices
John Jay, N.Y., Sept. 26, 1789
John Rutledge, S.C., July 1, 1795
Oliver Ellsworth, Conn., Mar. 4, 1796
John Rutledge, commissioned July 1, 1795 (in recess), presided at the August 1795 term. His nomination was rejected by the Senate on December 15, 1795.

Associate Justices
John Rutledge, S.C., Sept. 26, 1789
William Cushing, Mass., Sept. 27, 1789
Robert H. Harrison, Md., Sept. 28, 1789
James Wilson, Pa., Sept. 29, 1789
John Blair, Va., Sept. 30, 1789
James Iredell, N.C., Feb. 10, 1790

Thomas Johnson, Md., Aug. 5, 1791
William Paterson, N.J., Mar. 4, 1793
Samuel Chase, Md., Jan. 27, 1796
William Cushing was commissioned as Chief Justice on January 27, 1796, but declined to serve, continuing as Associate Justice.

ADMINISTRATION — IMPORTANT DATES

Apr. 1, 1789, first quorum, House of Representatives
Apr. 6, 1789, first quorum, U.S. Senate
June 1, 1789, first congressional act approved "to regulate the time and manner of administering certain oaths"
July 4, 1789, first tariff act, placing duties on imports to protect domestic industries
July 20, 1789, first federal navigation act, imposing duty on the tonnage of vessels
July 27, 1789, State Department created as Department of Foreign Affairs
Aug. 4, 1789, first federal bond issue authorized to fund domestic and state debt
Aug. 7, 1789, Department of War created
Sept. 2, 1789, Treasury Department established
Sept. 13, 1789, first loan to the U.S. Government negotiated by Alexander Hamilton with New York banks
Sept. 22, 1789, Post Office Department created
Sept. 24, 1789, Judiciary Act passed
Sept. 24, 1789, Office of Attorney General established
Sept. 25, 1789, first ten amendments to the Constitution enacted by Congress
Sept. 29, 1789, first Congress adjourned after 210-day session
Nov. 21, 1789, twelfth state ratified the Constitution
Feb. 1, 1790, first session of U.S. Supreme Court
Mar. 1, 1790, first U.S. census authorized
Apr. 10, 1790, first patent law passed
May 29, 1790, Rhode Island adopted Constitution (last of the original thirteen to sign)
May 31, 1790, first copyright law signed
July 16, 1790, Congress passed act locating future seat of government in District of Columbia
Aug. 9, 1790, *Columbia,* under Captain Robert Gray, returned to Boston, completing first trip around the world under U.S. flag
Jan. 10, 1791, Vermont ratified Constitution
Feb. 25, 1791, Bank of the United States chartered
Mar. 3, 1791, District of Columbia established
Mar. 3, 1791, first internal revenue act
Mar. 4, 1791, Vermont admitted as the 14th state
Mar. 4, 1791, Arthur St. Clair appointed commander-in-chief of federal troops
Apr. 7, 1791-June 12, 1791, George Washington made tour of the South

Nov. 4, 1791, General St. Clair surprised and defeated by Indians at Wabash River

Dec. 15, 1791, Bill of Rights, first ten amendments to the Constitution, ratified

Mar. 1, 1792, presidential succession bill enacted

Mar. 1, 1792, Secretary of State Jefferson announced the adoption of the first ten amendments

Apr. 2, 1792, U.S. Mint established; coinage of various denominations authorized

Apr. 5, 1792, Washington vetoed apportionment bill

June 1, 1792, Kentucky admitted as the 15th state

Sept. 27, 1792, peace treaty signed with Wabash and Illinois Indians

Oct. 13, 1792, cornerstone of White House laid

Mar. 4, 1793, second inauguration, held at Philadelphia, Pa.

Apr. 22, 1793, neutrality proclamation issued by Washington

Sept. 18, 1793, cornerstone of Capitol laid

Mar. 14, 1794, Eli Whitney patented cotton gin

July-Nov. 1794, Whisky Rebellion in western Pennsylvania

Aug. 20, 1794, General Wayne defeated Miami Indians at Fallen Timbers, Ohio

Nov. 19, 1794, Jay's Treaty with Great Britain signed to settle terms of peace, amity, commerce, navigation, boundaries, and extradition

Feb. 7, 1795, Eleventh Amendment to Constitution ratified

Sept. 5, 1795, treaty of peace and amity with Algiers signed

May 19, 1796, first national game law approved

May 31, 1796, treaty with Six Nations concluded

June 1, 1796, Tennessee admitted as the 16th state

Sept. 17, 1796, George Washington issued his Farewell Address

Nov. 4, 1796, treaty of peace, friendship, and navigation with Tripoli signed

IMPORTANT DATES IN HIS LIFE

1749, licensed as surveyor by College of William and Mary

July 20, 1749, official surveyor, Culpeper County, Va.

Nov. 6, 1752, appointed adjutant general of Virginia with rank of major

Mar. 15, 1754, lieutenant-colonel of Virginia regiment

June 5, 1754, colonel of Virginia regiment

May 10, 1755, appointed aide-de-camp (a volunteer position without rank) by General Braddock in French and Indian War

July 9, 1755, two horses were shot under him and four bullets pierced his coat in battle near Fort Duquesne, Pa.; withdrew remnants of Braddock's defeated army at the Monongahela to Fort Cumberland

Aug. 14, 1755, appointed by the legislature colonel of the Virginia regiment and commander-in-chief of the Virginia forces protecting the frontier against the French and Indians

1755-1758, engaged in recruiting and organizing troops for colonial defense

1758, commanded successful expedition to Fort Duquesne

July 24, 1758, elected to House of Burgesses from Frederick County

Dec. 1758, resigned commission as colonel of the Virginia regiment and commander-in-chief of the Virginia forces

1758, resided at Mount Vernon, Va.

Oct. 1770, justice of the peace for Fairfax County

Aug. 1773, delegate to the Williamsburg Convention

Aug. 1774, member, First Virginia Provincial Convention

Aug. 5, 1774, elected delegate to First Continental Congress

Sept. 5, 1774, attended first session of Continental Congress at Philadelphia, Pa.

Mar. 25, 1775, Second Virginia Provincial Congress selected Washington to attend Second Continental Congress

June 15, 1775, Congress elected Washington as General and Commander-in-Chief of the Army of the United Colonies

July 3, 1775, assumed command at Cambridge, Mass.

Mar. 17, 1776, Boston evacuated by the British

Aug. 27, 1776, Battle of Long Island

Oct. 28, 1776, Battle of White Plains

Dec. 25, 1776, recrossed Delaware River

Dec. 26, 1776, Battle of Trenton

Jan. 3, 1777, Battle of Princeton

Sept. 11, 1777, Battle of Brandywine

Oct. 4, 1777, Battle of Germantown

Dec. 19, 1777, winter headquarters established at Valley Forge

Oct. 19, 1781, Cornwallis surrendered at Yorktown, Va.

May 8, 1783, dinner with Lord Carleton after conference; Washington received seventeen-gun salute

June 19, 1783, elected President General of the Society of the Cincinnati

Sept. 3, 1783, Treaty of Peace signed

Nov. 2, 1783, issued Farewell Orders to the armies

Nov. 25, 1783, reoccupied New York City after British occupation

Dec. 4, 1783, bade farewell to his officers at Fraunces' Tavern

Dec. 23, 1783, surrendered his commission as commander-in-chief to Congress; returned to private life

May 25, 1787, delegate from Virginia to the Federal Convention; elected president unanimously

Feb. 4, 1789, unanimously elected President of the United States for 1789-1793 term

Apr. 30, 1789, inaugurated President at Federal Hall, New York City

June 1, 1789, signed first act of Congress

Aug. 25, 1789, his mother, Mary Ball Washington, died at Fredericksburg, Va.

Dec. 5, 1792, unanimously reelected President

Mar. 4, 1793, inaugurated at Philadelphia, Pa., as President of the United States for a second term

Sept. 18, 1793, laid cornerstone of the Capitol at Washington, D.C.

Sept. 17, 1796, issued Farewell Address

Mar. 3, 1797, expiration of his second term as President

July 11, 1798, President John Adams appointed him Lieutenant-Gen-

eral and Commander-in-Chief of all the armies of the United States
July 13, 1798, accepted appointment
Dec. 14, 1799, died at Mount Vernon, Va.

GEORGE WASHINGTON

___was the only President who was inaugurated in two cities (New
    York City, April 30, 1789, and Philadelphia, Pa., March 4, 1793).
___was the only President who did not live in Washington, D.C.
___was the first and only President unanimously elected, having re-
    ceived 69 of the 69 electoral votes cast.
___was the first President to refuse a third term.
___was the first President born in Virginia.
___was the first President whose mother was alive when he was inau-
    gurated.
___was the first President to marry a widow.
___was the first President whose mother was a second wife.
___was the first President to have stepbrothers.

WASHINGTON'S VICE PRESIDENT

Vice President—John Adams (1st V.P.)
Date of birth—Oct. 30, 1735
Birthplace—Braintree (now Quincy), Mass.
Political party—Federalist
State represented—Massachusetts
Term of office—Apr. 21, 1789-Mar. 3, 1797
Age at inauguration—53 years, 173 days
Occupation after term—President
Date of death—July 4, 1826
Age at death—90 years, 247 days
Place of death—Quincy, Mass.
Burial place—Quincy, Mass.
For further biographical information see John Adams, 2nd Pres-
ident.

ADDITIONAL DATA ON WASHINGTON

WASHINGTON WAS BORN ON FEBRUARY 11

George Washington was born on February 11, 1731, and celebrated
his first nineteen birthdays on February 11.

An act of the British Parliament in 1750 discarded the Julian calendar
and adopted the Gregorian calendar in its stead for Great Britain and
the colonies. In the Julian calendar, the first day of the year had been
March 25, but in the year 1751 the year ended on December 31 and
the days between January and March 24 were omitted from the calendar. This legal year contained only 282 days. The period from January
1 to March 24 was dated 1752.

Thus George Washington was nineteen years old on February 11,
1750, but his twentieth birthday was on February 11, 1752, not 1751.
Since the vernal equinox had been displaced by 11 days in the Julian

calendar, it was ordered that the difference be removed by the omission of 11 days from September 1752. There were no days dated September 3 to 13 inclusive; the day after September 2 was September 14. This required the addition of 11 days to compensate, and in 1753 George Washington celebrated his birthday on February 22 instead of on February 11.

BAPTISM

George Washington was baptized April 5, 1732 (1731 Old Style). His godfathers were Beverley Whiting and Captain Christopher Brooks and his godmother was Mrs. Mildred Gregory.

WASHINGTON OPERATED A FERRY

George Washington loaned $3,750 to Captain John Posey, who was unable to repay the amount and turned over his land, including a ferry and fishery, to Washington. Washington then ran the fishery, shipping fish in his own boats and selling them along the Atlantic seaboard.

The ferry, which he operated from 1769 to 1790, crossed the Potomac at a spot about a mile wide, landing at what is now Marshall Hall, Md. The schedule of rates as set up by the Virginia General Assembly was one shilling for an adult and a horse.

The rates were: for every coach, wagon, or chariot and driver, the same price as for six horses; for every four-wheeled chaise or phaeton and driver, the same price as for four horses; for every two-wheeled riding carriage, the same price as for two horses; for every hogshead of tobacco, the same price as for one horse; for every head of neat cattle, the same price as for one horse, and for every sheep, hog, goat or lamb, the same price as for one horse.

The ferry was abandoned in October 1790, a year and a half after Washington had become President. He submitted his reasons for discontinuing the service to the General Assembly which acceded to his request to be permitted to abandon the ferry service.

WASHINGTON ESCAPED KIDNAPPERS

Prior to George Washington's inauguration, while he was still commander-in-chief of the army, an attempt was made to kidnap or kill him. Involved in the conspiracy were the Tory governor of New York, William Tryon, the Tory mayor of New York City, David Matthews, and many others, including Thomas Hickey, one of Washington's bodyguards. Hickey was tried before a court-martial, which found him guilty. On June 28, 1776, Hickey was hanged on a field near the Bowery Lane in the presence of 20,000 persons.

The episode is recorded in General George Washington's orderly book on June 28, 1776, as follows: "The unhappy Fate of Thomas Hickey, executed this day for Mutiny, Sedition and Treachery; the General hopes will be a warning to every soldier, in the Army, to avoid those crimes and all others, so disgraceful to the character of a soldier and pernicious to his country, whose pay he receives and bread he eats."

WASHINGTON DISAPPROVED OF SWEARING

A General Order issued August 3, 1776, by General George Washington from his headquarters at New York stated:

The General is sorry to be informed that the foolish and wicked practice of profane cursing and swearing, a vice heretofore little known in an American army, is growing into fashion. He hopes the officers will, by example as well as influence, endeavor to check it, and that both they and the men will reflect, that we can have little hope of the blessing of Heaven on our arms, if we insult it by our impiety and folly. Added to this, it is a vice so mean and low, without any temptation, that every man of sense and character detests and despises it.

HONORARY DEGREES FOR WASHINGTON

The formal education of George Washington ceased before he was seventeen years of age; however, he did much studying on his own account. Although he lacked a college degree, five of the country's foremost colleges saw fit to confer honorary degrees upon him.

The first degree was the honorary degree of Doctor of Laws awarded by Harvard in 1776. Yale followed suit in 1781. The University of Pennsylvania made a similar award in 1783. Washington College of Chestertown, Md., and Brown University also conferred the honorary LL.D. degree in 1789 and 1790 respectively.

WASHINGTON REJECTED MONARCHY

The suggestion made by Colonel Lewis Nicola in a letter to General George Washington to the effect that Washington become king brought a stinging rebuke from the general. His answer from Newburgh, N.Y., dated May 22, 1782, follows:

With a mixture of great surprise and astonishment I have read with attention the Sentiments you have submitted to my perusal. Be assured Sir, no occurrence in the course of the War, has given me more painful sensations than your information of there being such ideas existing in the Army as you have expressed, and I must view with abhorrence, and reprehend with severity. For the present, the communication of them will rest in my bosom, unless some further agitation of the matter, shall make a disclosure necessary.

I am much at a loss to conceive what part of my conduct could have given encouragement to an address which to me seems big with the greatest mischiefs that can befall my Country.

If I am not deceived in the knowledge of myself, you could not have found a person to whom your schemes are more disagreeable; at the same time in justice to my own feelings I must add, that no Man possesses a more sincere wish to see ample justice done to the Army than I do, and as far as my powers and influence, in a constitutional way extend, they shall be employed to the utmost of my abilities to effect it, should there be any occasion. Let me conjure you then, if you have any regard for your Country, concern for yourself or posterity, or respect for me, to banish these thoughts from your Mind, and never communicate, as from yourself, or any one else, a sentiment of the like Nature.

WASHINGTON RAISED MULES

Although the exportation of full-blooded jacks from Spain was prohibited, Charles III of Spain sent George Washington two jacks and two jennets with a Spanish caretaker. They arrived at Boston on October 26, 1785. Only one of the jacks survived the trip; it was named Royal Gift by Washington and was used to breed heavy mules for draft purposes.

A Maltese jack sent by Lafayette to George Washington was named the Knight of Malta. It was used to breed lighter and nimbler mules for saddle and carriage use.

JOHN LANGDON, PRESIDENT OF THE SENATE PRO TEMPORE, NOTIFYING GEORGE WASHINGTON OF HIS ELECTION

New York, 6 April, 1789

Sir,

I have the honor to transmit to your Excellency the information of your unanimous election to the office of President of the United States of America. Suffer me, Sir, to indulge the hope, that so auspicious a mark of public confidence will meet your approbation, and be considered as a pledge of the affection and support you are to expect from a free and enlightened people.

I am, Sir, with sentiments of respect, &c.

JOHN LANGDON

GEORGE WASHINGTON'S LETTER TO JOHN LANGDON, PRESIDENT OF THE SENATE PRO TEMPORE, ACCEPTING THE OFFICE OF PRESIDENT OF THE UNITED STATES

Mount Vernon, Va.
April 14, 1789

Sir,

I had the honor to receive your official communication by the hand of Mr. Secretary Thomson, about one o'clock this day. Having concluded to obey the important and flattering call of my country, and having been impressed with an idea of the expediency of my being with Congress at as early a period as possible, I propose to commence my journey on Thursday morning which will be the day after tomorrow. I have the honor to be with sentiments of esteem, Sir,

Your most obedient servant,

G. WASHINGTON

WASHINGTON BORROWED MONEY TO GO TO HIS FIRST INAUGURATION

Although George Washington was one of the richest men of his time he was "land-poor" and was obliged to borrow money to finance his trip to New York. He received a loan of 600 pounds from Richard Conway of Alexandria, Va., to whom he had written the following letter on March 4, 1789 from his home at Mount Vernon:

DEAR SIR,

Never till within these two years have I experienced the want of money. Short crops, and other causes not entirely within my control, make me feel it now very sensibly. To collect money without the intervention of Suits (and these are tedious) seems impracticable—and Land, which I have offered for sale, will not command Cash at an undervalue, if at all. Under this statement, I am inclined to do what I never expected to be driven to, that is, to borrow money on Interest. Five hundred pounds would enable me to discharge what I owe in Alexandria, etc., and to leave the State (if it shall not be in my power to remain home in retirement) without doing this, would be exceedingly disagreeable to me. Having thus fully and candidly explained myself, permit me to ask if it is in your power to supply me with the above or smaller Sum. Any security you may best like I can give, and you may be assured, that it is no more my inclination than it can be yours, to let it remain long unpaid....

WASHINGTON ARRIVED IN NEW YORK BY BOAT

Thirteen pilots, all dressed in white sailor costume, rowed the barge which conveyed George Washington from Elizabeth Town, N.J., to New York City for his inauguration. The barge had a forty-seven-foot keel and carried two flags astern. It came out of the Kill van Kull into New York Bay, passed the Battery, and proceeded up the Hudson River to Murray's wharf at the foot of Wall Street.

A brief parade was held through Queen Street to the Franklin House. The order of march was as follows: 1, a troop of horse; 2, artillery and those remaining of the Legion under arms; 3, off-duty military officers in uniform; 4, The President's Guard, composed of the Grenadiers of the First Regiment; 5, The President, the governor and their suites; 6, the principal officers of the state; 7, the mayor of New York and the Corporation of New York; 8, the clergy; 9, the citizens.

FIRST INAUGURATION

George Washington took the oath of office as President of the United States on Thursday, April 30, 1789, out-of-doors on the balcony of the Senate Chamber at Federal Hall, Wall and Nassau Streets, New York City. The oath was administered by Robert R. Livingston, Chancellor of New York State. The Bible on which Washington took his oath was borrowed from St. John's Lodge, Free and Accepted Masons. His hand rested on Psalm 127:1 when he took the oath. He then proceeded to the Senate Chamber to deliver his inaugural address. After the ceremony, he was escorted to the President's House by a troop of cavalry, assistants, a committee of Representatives, a committee of the Senate and the gentlemen to be admitted to the Senate.

The evening celebration was opened and closed by thirteen skyrockets and thirteen cannon.

A weekly, the *U.S. Chronicle* of May 21, 1789, recorded:

The President of the United States on the day of his inauguration, appeared dressed in a complete suit of Homespun Cloaths; the cloth was of a fine fabric, and as handsomely finished, as any European superfine cloth. A circumstance, which must be considered as not only highly flattering to our manufacturers in particular, but interesting to our countrymen in general.

His Excellency the Vice President appeared also in a suit of American manufacture and several members of both Houses are distinguished by the same token of attention to the manufacturing interests of their country.

After Chancellor Robert R. Livingston administered the oath of office to George Washington on April 30, 1789, he proclaimed, "Long live George Washington, the President of the United States."

FIRST INAUGURAL BALL

The first inaugural ball was held Thursday, May 7, 1789, in the Assembly Rooms on the east side of Broadway, a little above Wall Street, New York City. It was attended by President Washington, Vice President Adams, the French and Spanish ministers, Chancellor Livingston, Baron von Steuben, General Knox, John Jay, Alexander Hamilton and the majority of the House of Representatives and the Senate. Fans decorated with a medallion portrait of President Washington in profile were presented as souvenirs to the ladies. Martha Washington did not attend as she did not arrive in the city until the end of May.

WASHINGTON'S FIRST TERM 57 DAYS SHORT

As George Washington did not take the oath of office until April 30, 1789, his first term was 57 days shorter than it would have been had the inauguration taken place on March 4 as originally intended.

THE FIRST PRESIDENTIAL MANSION

George Washington lived at No. 1 Cherry Street, New York City, from April 23, 1789, to February 23, 1790. This residence has been referred to as the first presidential mansion. Residences were not supplied for our earliest Presidents.

CONGRESS IN SESSION AT NEW YORK AND PHILADELPHIA

The only Congress to meet at New York City was the First Congress. It held two sessions, the first from March 4, 1789, to September 29, 1789 (210 days), the second from January 4, 1790, to August 12, 1790 (221 days). A quorum was not present, however, until April 6, 1789.

The first session of Congress to meet at Philadelphia, Pa., was the third session of the First Congress, which was held from December 6, 1790, to March 3, 1791 (88 days). The first session of the Sixth Congress from December 2, 1799, to May 14, 1800 (164 days) was the last Congress to meet at Philadelphia.

HIS HIGHNESS, GEORGE WASHINGTON?

The committee appointed by the United States Senate on Thursday, April 23, 1789, to decide on the proper form of address for the President of the United States, reported on Thursday, May 14, 1789 "that in the opinion of the committee it will be proper thus to address the President: "His Highness, the President of the United States of America, and Protector of their Liberties."

SENATORS' TERMS DETERMINED BY DRAWING LOTS

In accordance with the constitutional provision regarding senatorial terms (Article 1, section 3), the Senate decided on May 14, 1789, "that three papers of an equal size, numbered 1, 2 and 3, be, by the Secretary, rolled up and put into a box, and, drawn by Mr. Langdon, Mr. Wingate, Mr. Dalton, in behalf of the respective classes, in which each of them are placed; and that the classes shall vacate their seats in the Senate, according to the order of numbers drawn for them, beginning with Number 1.

"And that when Senators shall take their seats from States that have not yet appointed Senators, they shall be placed by lot in the foregoing classes, but in such manner as shall keep the classes as nearly equal as may be in numbers."

The senators in Class 1, who drew six-year terms, were John Langdon of New Hampshire, William Samuel Johnson of Connecticut, Robert Morris of Pennsylvania, John Henry of Maryland, Ralph Izard of South Carolina, and James Gunn of Georgia.

Those in Class 2, who drew four-year terms, were Paine Wingate of New Hampshire, Caleb Strong of Massachusetts, William Paterson of New Jersey, Richard Bassett of Delaware, Richard Lee of Virginia, Pierce Butler of South Carolina, and William Few of Georgia.

Those in Class 3, who drew two-year terms, were Tristram Dalton of Massachusetts, Oliver Ellsworth of Connecticut, Jonathan Elmer of New Jersey, William Maclay of Pennsylvania, George Read of Delaware, Charles Carroll of Maryland, and William Grayson of Virginia.

New York, North Carolina, and Rhode Island were not included in the original selection as their senators were still unrepresented at the time of the drawing.

THE FIRST ACT OF CONGRESS

"An Act to Regulate the Time and Manner of Administering Certain Oaths"

SECTION 1. Be it enacted by the Senate and Representatives of the United States of America in Congress assembled, That the Oath or Affirmation required by the sixth article of the Constitution of the United States, shall be administered in the form following, to wit, "I, A.B., do solemnly swear or affirm (as the case may be) that I will support the Constitution of the United States!" The said oath or affirmation shall be administered within three days after the passing of this act, by any one member of the Senate, to the President of the Senate, and by him to all the members, and to the Secretary; and by the Speaker of the House of Representatives to all members who have not taken a similar oath, by virtue of a particular resolution of the said House, and to the Clerk: And in case of the absence of any member from the service of either House, at the same time prescribed for taking said oath or affirmation, the same shall be administered to such member when he shall appear to take his seat.

Section 2. And be it further enacted, That at the first session of Congress after every general election of Representatives, the oath or affirmation aforesaid, shall be administered by any one member of the House of Representatives to the Speaker; and by him to all the members present, and to the Clerk, previous to entering on any other business; and to the members who shall afterward appear, previous to taking their seats. The President of the Senate for the time being, shall also administer the oath or affirmation to each Senator who shall hereafter be elected, previous to taking his seat; and in any future case of a President of the Senate, who shall not have taken said oath or affirmation, the same shall be administered to him by any one member of the Senate.

Section 3. And be it further enacted, That the members of the several State legislatures, at the next session of the said legislature respectively, and all executive and judicial officers of the several States, who have been heretofore chosen or appointed, or who shall be chosen or appointed, before the first day of August next, and who shall then be in office, shall within one month thereafter, take the same oath or affirmation, except where they shall have taken it before; which may be administered by any person authorized by the law of the State in which such office shall be holden, to administer oaths. And the members of the several State legislatures, and all executive and judicial officers of the several States, who shall be chosen or appointed after the said first day of August, shall, before they proceed to execute the duties of their respective offices, take the foregoing oath or affirmation which shall be administered by the person or persons who by the law of the State shall be authorized to administer the oath of office; and the person or persons so administering the oath hereby required to be taken, shall cause a record or certificate thereof to be made in the same manner as, by the law of the State, he or they shall be directed to record or certify the oath of office.

Section 4. And be it further enacted, That all officers appointed, or hereafter to be appointed, under the authority of the United States, shall, before they act in their respective offices, take the same oath or affirmation, which shall be administered by the person or persons who shall be authorized by law to administer to such officers their respective oaths of office; and such officers shall incur the same penalties in case of failure, as shall be imposed by law in case of failure in taking their respective oaths of office.

SECTION 5. And be it further enacted, That the Secretary of the Senate, and the Clerk of the House of Representatives for the time being, shall, at the time of taking the oath or affirmation aforesaid, each take an oath or affirmation in the words following, to wit, "I, A.B., Secretary of the Senate, or Clerk of the House of Representatives (as the case may be) of the United States of America, do solemnly swear or affirm that I will truly and faithfully discharge the duties of my office to the best of my knowledge and abilities."

FREDERICK AUGUSTUS MUHLENBERG
Speaker of the House of Representatives

JOHN ADAMS
Vice President of the United States
and President of the Senate

Approved June 1, 1789
GEORGE WASHINGTON
    President of the United States

(1 Stat. L. 23)

THE FIRST REJECTION OF A PRESIDENTIAL APPOINTEE

The first presidential appointee rejected by the Senate was Benjamin Fishbourn of Georgia, who was nominated by George Washington for the position of naval officer of the port of Savannah, Ga. Fishbourn had served valiantly in the storming of Stony Point and had held numerous important positions in Georgia. The Georgia senators preferred another for the job and on August 6, 1789, Washington nominated Lachlan McIntosh.

TEN CONSTITUTIONAL AMENDMENTS ENACTED

The first ten amendments to the Constitution, known as the Bill of Rights, were passed by Congress on September 25, 1789. As Vermont had become a state before the ratification of the Constitution was completed, it was necessary to have eleven of the fourteen states ratify the amendments. On December 15, 1791, Virginia became the eleventh state to ratify the first ten amendments.

THE FIRST PRESIDENTIAL TOURS

President George Washington made the first presidential tour through the New England states from October 15 to November 13, 1789. He traveled in a hired coach accompanied by Major William Jackson, his aide-de-camp; Tobias Leer, his private secretary; six servants; nine horses; and a luggage wagon. He went as far north as Kittery, Maine (then part of Massachusetts). As Rhode Island and Vermont had not joined the new government at that time, he did not visit those states. Washington's first tour of the southern states was made from April 7 to June 12, 1791, during which time he left Mount Vernon, Virginia, on his 1,887-mile trip which took him north through Philadelphia, south through Virginia and the Carolinas into Georgia, and back to Mount Vernon.

THE FIRST PRESIDENTIAL THANKSGIVING PROCLAMATION

By the President of the United States of America.

Whereas it is the duty of all nations to acknowledge the providence of Almighty God, to obey his will, to be grateful for his benefits, and humbly to implore his protection and favor—and Whereas both Houses of Congress have by their joint committee requested me "to recommend to the People of the United States a day of public thanksgiving and prayer, to be observed by acknowledging with grateful hearts the many signal favors of Almighty God, especially by affording them an opportunity to establish a form of government for their safety and happiness";

Now, therefore, I do recommend and assign Thursday, the 26th day of November next, to be devoted by the People of these States to the service of that great and glorious Being who is the beneficent Author of all the good that was, that is, or that will be—That we may then all unite in rendering unto him our sincere and humble thanks—for his kind care and protection of the People of this country previous to their becoming a Nation—for the signal and manifold mercies and the favorable interpositions of his providence, which we experienced in the course and conclusion of the late war—for the great degree of tranquillity, union and plenty, which we have since enjoyed—for the peaceful and rational manner in which we have been enabled to establish constitutions of government for our safety and happiness, and particularly the national One now lately instituted—for the civil and religious liberty with which we are blessed and the means we have of acquiring and diffusing useful knowledge; and in general for all the great and various favors which he hath been pleased to confer upon us.

And also that we may then unite in most humbly offering our prayers and supplications to the great Lord and Ruler of Nations, and beseech him to pardon our national and other transgressions—to enable us all, whether in public or private stations, to perform our several and relative duties properly and punctually—to render our national Government a blessing to all the People by constantly being a Government of wise, just, and constitutional laws, discreetly and faithfully executed and obeyed—to protect and guide all Sovereigns and Nations (especially such as have shown kindness to us) and to bless them with good Government, peace, and concord—to promote the knowledge and practice of true religion and virtue, and the increase of science among them and us—and generally to grant unto all mankind such a degree of temporal prosperity as he alone knows to be best.

Given under my hand at the City of New York the third day of October in the year of our Lord 1789.

GEORGE WASHINGTON

SECOND INAUGURATION

The Government having moved from New York City to Phila-

delphia, George Washington took the oath of office for his second
term on Monday, March 4, 1793, in the Senate Chamber, Federal
Hall, Philadelphia, Pa. Washington was the first President to be inaugurated at Philadelphia and the first inaugurated on March 4th. The
oath was administered by William Cushing of Massachusetts, Associate Justice of the Supreme Court.

THE FIRST PRESIDENTIAL VETO

During his two terms of office, George Washington vetoed only
two bills. His action on the first veto, dated April 5, 1792, was explained in the following letter to the members of the House of Representatives:

I have maturely considered the act passed by the two Houses
entitled "An act for an apportionment of Representatives among
the several States according to the first enumeration," and I return
it to your House, wherein it originated, with the following objections:

First. The Constitution has prescribed that Representatives shall
be apportioned among the several States according to their respective numbers, and there is no one proportion or divisor which,
applied to the respective numbers of the States, will yield the
number and allotment of representatives proposed by the bill.

Second. The Constitution has also provided that the number
of representatives shall not exceed 1 for every 30,000, which re-
striction is by the context and by fair and obvious construction
to be applied to the separate and respective numbers of the States;
and the bill has allotted to eight of the States more than 1 for
every 30,000.

His only other veto, dated February 28, 1797, rejected a bill to reduce
the cavalry force of the army.

WASHINGTON'S CONSULTATION OF THE CABINET

Washington, like the Presidents who succeeded him, made frequent
requests to the members of his cabinet for their opinions on the conduct of government affairs. One of his letters, from Philadelphia on
April 18, 1793, sent to his cabinet members, is reproduced herewith:

SIR,
The posture of affairs in Europe, particularly between France
and Great Britain, places the United States in a delicate situation,
and requires much consideration of the measures which will be
proper for them to observe in the war between those powers.
With a view to forming a general plan of conduct for the executive,
I have stated and enclosed sundry questions to be considered
preparatory to a meeting at my house to-morrow, where I shall
expect to see you at nine o'clock, and to receive the result of
your reflections thereon.
QUEST. 1. Shall a proclamation issue for the purpose of prevent-
ing interferences of the citizens of the United States between

France and Great Britain, &c.? Shall it contain a declaration of neutrality or not? What shall it contain?

2. Shall a minister from the republic of France be received?

3. If received, shall it be absolutely or with qualifications, and if with qualifications, of what kind?

4. Are the United States obliged by good faith to consider the treaties heretofore made with France as applying to the present situation of the parties? may they either renounce them or hold them suspended until the government of France shall be established?

5. If they have the right, is it expedient to do either? and which?

6. If they have an option, would it be a breach of neutrality to consider the treaties in operation?

7. If the treaties are to be considered as now in operation, is the guaranty in the treaty of alliance applicable to a defensive war only, or to a war, either offensive or defensive?

8. Does the war in which France is engaged appear to be offensive or defensive on her part? or of a mixed or equivocal character?

9. If of a mixed or equivocal character, does the guaranty in any event apply to such a war?

10. What is the effect of a guaranty, such as that to be found in the treaty of alliance between the United States and France?

11. Does any article in either of the treaties prevent ships of war, other than privateers, of the powers opposed to France, from coming into the ports of the United States to act as convoys to their own merchantmen? or does it lay any other restraints upon them more than would apply to the ships of war of France?

12. Should the future regent of France send a minister to the United States, ought he to be received?

13. Is it necessary or advisable to call together the two houses of Congress with a view to the present posture of European affairs? If it is, what should be the particular objects of such call?

THE FIRST PRESIDENTIAL COMMISSION

The first presidential commission was appointed by Washington to deal with the rebellious elements in Washington and Alleghany counties, Pennsylvania. In his proclamation to Congress on August 7, 1794, he said: "I do hereby command all persons, being insurgents as aforesaid, on or before the first day of September next to disperse and retire peacefully to their respective abodes." In his sixth annual report, on November 19, 1794, he declared: "The report of the commissioners marks their firmness and abilities, and must unite all virtuous men, by shewing that the means of conciliation have been exhausted."

WASHINGTON DECLINED A THIRD TERM

Washington's second term of office expired on March 3, 1797. On September 17, 1796, he issued his "Farewell Address," which was not delivered orally but released to the press. It was addressed "Friends and Fellow Citizens" and began

The period for a new election of a citizen to administer the

Executive Government of the United States being not far distant, and the time actually arrived when your thoughts must be employed in designating the person who is to be clothed with that important trust, it appears to me proper, especially as it may conduce to a more distinct expression of the public voice, that I should now apprise you of the resolution I have formed to decline being considered among the number of those out of whom a choice is to be made....

WASHINGTON APPOINTED LIEUTENANT-GENERAL

On July 11, 1798, Secretary of War James McHenry delivered a letter from President John Adams to George Washington appointing Washington, with the advice and consent of the Senate, "Lieutenant-General and Commander-in-Chief of all the armies raised or to be raised for the service of the United States."

Washington's reply, dated July 13, 1798, from Mount Vernon, Va., was read in the Senate on July 18. He accepted

with the reserve only that I shall not be called into the field until the Army is in a situation to require my presence, or it becomes indispensable by the urgency of circumstances. I take the liberty also to mention, that I must decline having my acceptance considered as drawing after it any immediate charge upon the public, or that I can receive any emoluments annexed to the appointment, before entering into a situation to incur expense.

WASHINGTON LEFT HUGE ESTATE

George Washington was one of our richest Presidents. His estate was valued at more than a half million dollars.

In his last will and testament, dated July 9, 1799, he listed his assets. His land holdings, exceeding 33,000 acres, consisted of 23,341 acres in Virginia, 5,000 acres in Kentucky, 3,051 acres in the Northwest Territory, 1,119 acres in Maryland, 1,000 acres in New York, 234 acres in Pennsylvania, and other property in Virginia and Washington, D.C., valued at $489,135. He also listed his stocks as worth $25,212. He valued his livestock, which consisted of 640 sheep, 329 cows, 42 mules, 20 working horses, pigs, etc., at $15,653. The value of these three items—acreage, stocks, and livestock was estimated at $530,000.

WASHINGTON OWNED LAND IN WASHINGTON, D.C.

On October 3, 1798, George Washington acquired two lots in the federal city (now Washington, D.C.). He described his purchase in his last will and testament as follows:

The two lots near the Capitol in Square 634, cost me $963 only, but in this price I was favoured on condition that I should build two brick houses, three storys high each:—without this reduction, the selling price of those lots would have cost me about $1,350. These lots with the buildings thereon when completed will stand me in $15,000 at least.

WASHINGTON'S SWORDS

In his will George Washington bequeathed five swords, one to each of his five nephews, with the admonition that none of these weapons should be unsheathed by the future owners for the purpose of shedding blood, "except it be for self-defence or in defence of their country and its rights and in the latter case to keep them unsheathed and prefer falling with them in their hands to the relinquishment thereof."

FIRST IN WAR, FIRST IN PEACE, FIRST IN THE HEARTS OF HIS COUNTRYMEN

This famous phrase was part of the "Funeral Oration Upon George Washington" delivered December 26, 1799, before the houses of Congress by General Henry Lee.

General Lee was familiarly known as "Light Horse Harry" and during the Revolutionary War commanded Lee's brigade, three troops of horses, which harassed and annoyed the British lines. He was the father of General Robert E. Lee, the Confederate general.

FIRST TOWN NAMED FOR WASHINGTON

The first town named for George Washington was Forks of Tar River, N.C., which changed its name to Washington in 1775. The town was originally formed November 20, 1771, by James Bonner, who owned all the land on which it was situated.

Washington, Ga., incorporated Jan. 23, 1780, was the first town incorporated with the name of Washington.

FIRST STAMP DEPICTING A PRESIDENT

The first president depicted on a United States postage stamp was George Washington, whose likeness appeared on the ten-cent black 1847, to take effect July 1, 1847. The stamps were produced by Rawdon, Wright, Hatch & Edson. The issue was declared invalid as of July 1, 1851. (Some of the local postmasters' provisional stamps, however, bore a likeness of Washington.)

MOUNT VERNON NEUTRAL TERRITORY

In the Civil War, George Washington's home at Mount Vernon (named for Admiral Vernon, under whom George's brother Lawrence served in the capture of Porto Bello) was treated as neutral territory by arrangement between both sides. No armed soldiers ever invaded the home.

THE FIRST LADY

The first lady of the land was Martha Washington, known as Lady Washington. She never occupied the Executive Mansion at Washington, D.C., as it had not been completed during George Washington's administration. The seat of the Government at the time of his first inauguration was at New York City; later it was moved to Philadelphia, Pa. The Government did not furnish the President's House and the expense of furnishing was borne by George Washington. Mrs. Washington's social affairs were very formal and reserved.

JOHN ADAMS
2nd PRESIDENT

Born–Oct. 30, 1735

Birthplace–Braintree (now Quincy), Mass.

College attended–Harvard College, Cambridge, Mass.

Date of graduation–July 16, 1755, four-year course, Bachelor of Arts

Religion–Unitarian

Ancestry–English

Occupation–Lawyer

Date and place of marriage–Oct. 25, 1764, Weymouth, Mass.

Age at marriage–28 years, 360 days

Years married–54 years, 3 days

Political party–Federalist

State represented–Massachusetts

Term of office–Mar. 4, 1797-Mar. 3, 1801

Term served–4 years

Administration–3rd

Congresses–5th, 6th

Age at inauguration–61 years, 125 days

Lived after term–25 years, 122 days

Occupation after term–Writer

Date of death–July 4, 1826

Age at death–90 years, 247 days

Place of death–Quincy, Mass.

Burial place–First Unitarian Church, Quincy, Mass.

PARENTS

Father–John Adams

Born–Feb. 8, 1691

Married–Oct. 31, 1734

Occupation–Farmer, cordwainer

Died–May 25, 1761

Age at death–70 years, 106 days

Mother–Susanna Boylston Adams

Born–March 5, 1699

Died–Apr. 17, 1797

Age at death–98 years, 43 days

BROTHERS

John Adams was the oldest in a family of three boys.

Children of John Adams and Susanna Boylston Adams

.John Adams, b. Oct. 30, 1735, d. July 4, 1826

Peter Boylston Adams, b. Oct. 16, 1738, d. June 2, 1823

Elihu Adams, b. May 29, 1741, d. Mar. 18, 1776

CHILDREN

Abigail Amelia Adams, b. July 14, 1765, Braintree, Mass.; m. June 12, 1786, William Stephens Smith; d. Aug. 15, 1813

John Quincy Adams, b. July 11, 1767, Braintree, Mass; m. July 26, 1797, Louisa Catherine Johnson; d. Feb. 23, 1848, Washington, D.C.

Susanna Adams, b. Dec. 28, 1768, Boston, Mass.; d. Feb. 4, 1770

Charles Adams, b. May 29, 1770, Boston, Mass.; m. Aug. 29, 1795, Sarah Smith; d. Nov. 30, 1800

Thomas Boylston Adams, b. Sept. 15, 1772, Quincy, Mass.; m. May 16, 1805, Ann Harod; d. Mar. 12, 1832

MRS. JOHN ADAMS

Name–Abigail Smith Adams

Date of birth–Nov. 11, 1744

Birthplace–Weymouth, Mass.

Age at marriage–19 years, 348 days

Children–3 sons, 2 daughters

Mother–Elizabeth Quincy Smith

For additional data see the end of this section and also specific subject headings in the index.

Father–William Smith
His occupation–Congregational minister
Date of death–Oct. 28, 1818
Age at death–73 years, 351 days

Place of death–Quincy, Mass.
Burial place–Quincy, Mass.
Years younger than the President–9 years, 12 days
Years the President survived her–7 years, 249 days

THE ELECTION OF 1796

After he had served his second four-year term, George Washington declined a third term for the presidency. This left the field wide open for numerous candidates.

The elections of 1788 and 1792 differed from the elections that followed; the early ones were contests between individuals rather than contests between political groups and factions. In 1796, the growth of political parties began.

The strong central-government contingent in Congress, to whom the designation "Federalists" was applied, had been in power eight years during Washington's two administrations. They met in a congressional caucus to discuss policy, plans and procedure. They pledged their support in the 1796 election to John Adams of Massachusetts and Thomas Pinckney of South Carolina, whose views coincided with theirs. Since the majority favored this selection, no balloting was undertaken.

At about the same time, the anti-Federalist group of congressmen convened and mutually agreed to support Jefferson and Burr. They were known as the Republicans, or Democratic-Republicans, and opposed the establishment of a central government more powerful than the states.

The Constitution did not provide for these congressional caucuses. The system, which flourished until 1824, was not typical or representative of the views of the country since it perpetuated the rule of those in power. Less important members of the factions had nothing to say about the selection of candidates and the people had no choice whatsoever.

Since the electors voted for the President and Vice President, they were the powerful influence in determining the presidential elections. As each state was sovereign unto itself, there was no uniform method of selecting the electors. Each state enacted its own law. Some electors were chosen by popular vote, some by designation of state legislatures, and some by other methods.

The electors, having been selected, were not legally bound to cast their ballot for a designated candidate, but none would dare break faith with the powers that placed them in nomination. At first, the votes of individuals were counted so that states could have had divided votes. Later, states voted as a unit, the political candidate with the greatest number of votes receiving the entire state electoral vote.

When the electoral vote of 1796 was counted, 16 states cast 276 votes, 138 for President and 138 for Vice President. As there was no distinction between the votes, a situation developed that had not been anticipated by the framers of the Constitution. John Adams received 71 votes, a majority, and was elected President of the United States. The candidate receiving the next highest number of votes was Thomas Jefferson of Virginia, who had 68 votes and was elected Vice President. Adams was a Federalist and Jefferson was a Democratic-Republican. The President represented one political party and his Vice President stood for a rival party.

The vote was cast as follows:

John Adams, Mass, 71
Thomas Jefferson, Va., 68
Thomas Pinckney, S.C., 59
Aaron Burr, N.Y., 30
Samuel Adams, Mass., 15
Oliver Ellsworth, Conn., 11
George Clinton, N.Y., 7
John Jay, N.Y., 5
James Iredell, N.C., 3
John Henry, Md., 2
Samuel Johnson, N.C., 2
George Washington, Va., 2
Charles Cotesworth Pinckney, S.C., 1

Total number of votes: 276

If the majority vote represented the will of the majority, the death of the President would have placed a minority-group candidate in the White House with presidential power. This inadequacy in the law was later corrected.

CABINET

March 4, 1797-March 3, 1801

State–Timothy Pickering, Pa., continued from preceding administration (requested to resign May 10, 1800, but declined to resign and was dismissed May 12, 1800); Charles Lee, Va. (Attorney General), ad interim, May 13, 1800; John Marshall, Va., May 13, 1800; entered upon duties June 6, 1800; John Marshall, Va., (Chief Justice of the United States), ad interim Feb. 4, 1801 to Mar. 3, 1801

Treasury–Oliver Wolcott, Jr., Conn., continued from preceding administration; Samuel Dexter, Mass., Jan. 1, 1801

War–James McHenry, Md., continued from preceding administration; Benjamin Stoddert, Md. (Secretary of the Navy), ad interim June 1, 1800, to June 12, 1800; Samuel Dexter, Mass., May 13, 1800; entered upon duties June 12, 1800; Samuel Dexter, Mass. (Secretary of the Treasury), ad interim Jan. 1, 1801

Attorney General–Charles Lee, Va., continued from preceding administration

Postmaster General–Joseph Habersham, Ga., continued from preceding administration

Navy–Benjamin Stoddert, Md., May 21, 1798; entered upon duties June 18, 1798

FIFTH CONGRESS

March 4, 1797-March 3, 1799

First session–May 15, 1797-July 10, 1797 (57 days)
Second session–Nov. 13, 1797-July 16, 1798 (246 days)
Third session–Dec. 3, 1798-Mar. 3, 1799 (91 days)
Special session of the Senate–Mar. 4, 1797 (one day only); July 17, 1798-July 19, 1798 (3 days)
Vice President–Thomas Jefferson, Va.
President pro tempore of the Senate–William Bradford, R.I., elected July 6, 1797; Jacob Read, S.C., elected Nov. 22, 1797; Theodore Sedgwick, Mass., elected June 27, 1798; John Laurance, N.Y., elected Dec. 6, 1798; James Ross, Pa., elected Mar. 1, 1799
Secretary of the Senate–Samuel Allyne Otis, Mass.
Speaker of the House–Jonathan Dayton, N.J., reelected May 15, 1797; George Dent, Md., elected speaker pro tempore for Apr. 20, 1798, and again for May 28, 1798
Clerks of the House–John Beckley, Va., Jonathan Williams Condy, Pa., elected May 15, 1797

SIXTH CONGRESS

March 4, 1799-March 3, 1801

First session–Dec. 2, 1799-May 14, 1800 (164 days)
Second session–Nov. 17, 1800-Mar. 3, 1801 (107 days)
Vice President–Thomas Jefferson, Va.
Presidents pro tempore of the Senate–Samuel Livermore, N.H., elected Dec. 2, 1799; Uriah Tracy, Conn., elected May 14, 1800; John Eager Howard, Md., elected Nov. 21, 1800; James Hillhouse, Conn., elected Feb. 28, 1801
Secretary of the Senate–Samuel Allyne Otis, Mass.
Speaker of the House–Theodore Sedgwick, Mass., elected Dec. 2, 1799
Clerks of the House–Jonathan Williams Condy, Pa., reelected Dec. 2, 1799, resigned Dec. 4, 1799; John Holt Oswald, Pa., elected Dec. 9, 1799

APPOINTMENTS TO THE SUPREME COURT

Chief Justice
John Marshall, Va., Jan. 31, 1801

Associate Justices
Bushrod Washington, Va., Sept. 29, 1798
Alfred Moore, N.C., Dec. 10, 1799

ADMINISTRATION — IMPORTANT DATES

May 10, 1797, first naval vessel, *United States,* launched, Philadelphia, Pa.
June 14, 1797, exportation of arms prohibited
Sept. 20, 1797, Frigate *Constitution* ("Old Ironsides") launched
Jan 8, 1798, Adams informed Congress that 11th amendment had been adopted
Apr. 7, 1798, Mississippi Territory created

Apr. 25, 1798, "Hail Columbia" first sung in theatre

Apr. 30, 1798, Navy Department created

June 25, 1798, Alien Act passed

July 1798, yellow fever epidemic in Philadelphia; many officials moved to Trenton, N.J.

July 9, 1798–Sept. 30, 1800, conflict with France

July 11, 1798, U.S. Marine Corps created

July 13, 1798, Lieutenant-General George Washington accepted office as commander-in-chief

July 14, 1798, Sedition Act passed

July 16, 1798, U.S. Public Health Service established

Oct. 2, 1798, treaty with Cherokee Indians

Nov. 16, 1798, governor of Kentucky signed law declaring the Alien and Sedition Acts unconstitutional

Dec. 21, 1798, Virginia resolution similarly declared the Alien and Sedition Act unconstitutional

Jan. 14, 1799, Senate impeachment trial of Senator William Blount of Tennessee concluded; charges dismissed for want of jurisdiction (first impeachment proceedings against a U.S. senator)

Feb. 25, 1799, first federal forestry legislation to acquire timber lands for the U.S. Navy

Dec. 14, 1799, death of George Washington

Apr. 4, 1800, federal bankruptcy act passed

Apr. 24, 1800, Library of Congress established

June 15, 1800, capital moved to District of Columbia

Sept. 3, 1800, treaty with Napoleon Bonaparte

Oct. 1, 1800, Spain ceded Louisiana back to France by secret treaty of San Ildefonso

Nov. 17, 1800, first session of Congress at Washington, D.C.

Jan. 31, 1801, John Marshall began thirty-four-year period as Chief Justice of the Supreme Court.

IMPORTANT DATES IN HIS LIFE

1755, taught school at Worcester, Mass.

1758, admitted to the bar, practiced at Boston, Mass.

1768, member of Massachusetts legislature

Sept. 5, 1774, delegate to First Continental Congress

Nov. 28, 1774, member of revolutionary Provincial Congress of Massachusetts

May 10, 1775, delegate to Second Continental Congress

1776, one of committee of five to draft the Declaration of Independence

Aug. 2, 1776, signed Declaration of Independence; head of War Department; proposed George Washington as leader of the American Army

Apr. 8, 1778, reached Paris as Commissioner to France, superseding Deane

Sept. 1, 1779, member of Massachusetts Constitutional Convention

Dec. 29, 1780, minister to the Netherlands; negotiated loan and Treaty of Amity and Commerce

May 14, 1785, minister to England (served until 1788)
Apr. 21, 1789, inaugurated Vice President of New York City
Mar. 4, 1793, inaugurated Vice President for a second term
Mar. 4, 1797-Mar. 3, 1801, President
Mar. 4, 1801, retired to Quincy, Mass.
Nov. 15, 1820, member of Second Constitutional Convention of Massachusetts.

JOHN ADAMS

____was the first President born in Massachusetts.

____was the only President whose son was inaugurated President.

____was the second President whose mother was alive when he was inaugurated.

____was the first President to reside at Washington, D.C. When he moved into the President's House on November 1, 1800, it was not completed and not a single apartment was finished.

____was the first President to have children. He had three sons and two daughters.

____was the first President to have a Justice of the Supreme Court administer the oath to him. He was sworn in on March 4, 1797, by Chief Justice Oliver Ellsworth.

____was the only President who was inaugurated at Philadelphia both as President and Vice President. On March 4, 1793, he was inaugurated as Vice President with George Washington as President, and on March 4, 1797, he was inaugurated President with Thomas Jefferson as his Vice President.

ADAMS' VICE PRESIDENT

Vice President–Thomas Jefferson (2nd V.P.)
Date of birth–Apr. 13, 1743
Birthplace–Shadwell, Va.
Political party–Democratic-Republican
State represented–Virginia
Term of office–Mar. 4, 1797-Mar. 3, 1801
Age at inauguration–53 years, 325 days
Occupation after term–President
Date of death–July 4, 1826
Place of death–Charlottesville, Va.
Age at death–83 years, 82 days
Burial place–Charlottesville, Va.

For further biographical information see Thomas Jefferson, 3rd President.

ADDITIONAL DATA ON ADAMS

ADAMS MARRIED BY FATHER-IN-LAW

The marriage of John Adams to Abigail Smith on October 25, 1764, at Weymouth, Mass., was performed by the father of the bride, the Reverend William Smith, a Congregational minister.

ADAMS SWORN IN AS WASHINGTON'S VICE PRESIDENT

John Adams entered upon his duties as Vice President of the United States on Tuesday, April 21, 1789, nine days before George Washington was inaugurated.

John Langdon of New Hampshire, who was president pro tempore of the Senate, introduced him to the senators as follows, "Sir; I have it in charge from the Senate to introduce you to the chair of this House; and, also to congratulate you on your appointment to the office of Vice President of the United States of America." He then conducted the Vice President to the chair, and John Adams addressed the Senate.

On Wednesday, June 3, 1789, the oath of office was administered to John Adams, who, in turn, administered the oath to the Senate members. The oath, "I . . . [name] do solemnly swear or affirm (as the case may be) that I will support the Constitution of the United States," was required by "an act to regulate the time and manner of administering certain oaths," June 1, 1789 (1 Stat. L. 23), Chapter One, Statute One.

The oath as administered at present is, "I do solemnly swear (or affirm) that I will support and defend the Constitution of the United States against all enemies, foreign and domestic; that I will bear true faith and allegiance to the same; that I take this obligation freely, without any mental reservation or purpose of evasion, and that I will well and faithfully discharge the duties of the office on which I am about to enter. So help me God."

Adams made an inaugural address. He spoke about the successful formation of the federal union, the adoption of the federal Constitution, and the auspicious circumstances under which the new government came into operation "under the presidency of him who had led the American armies to victory and conducted by those who had contributed to achieve Independence."

THE ELECTION OF 1796 — BROTHERS ASPIRED TO THE VICE PRESIDENCY

Washington announced that he would not be a candidate for a third term. The electors cast 276 ballots for 13 candidates for the presidency and the vice presidency. One of them was George Washington, who received two votes even though he was not a candidate. Two of the other twelve were brothers, Thomas Pinckney of South Carolina, who received 59 votes, Charles Cotesworth Pinckney, of South Carolina, who received 1 vote. Since 139 of the votes cast were for the President and were apportioned 71 to John Adams and 68 to Thomas Jefferson, the two Pinckney borthers were really vice presidential candidates.

INAUGURATION

John Adams, the first Vice President to be elevated to the presidency, was the only president besides George Washington to be inaugurated at Philadelphia. He was the first President to whom the oath of office was administered by a Chief Justice. On Saturday, March 4, 1797, in the Chamber of the House of Representatives in Federal

Hall, the oath was administered to John Adams by Oliver Ellsworth, Chief Justice of the United States. Adams was driven to the inauguration in a gilded coach drawn by six white horses.

ELEVENTH AMENDMENT ENACTED

The eleventh amendment to the Constitution, providing that the United States judicial power shall not extend to suits against a state by citizens of another state or subjects of any foreign state, was passed by Congress on March 4, 1794, and proposed to the legislatures of the several states by the Third Congress on March 5, 1794. The twelfth state to ratify, making the amendment effective, was Delaware. Although Delaware ratified it on January 23, 1795, it was not until January 8, 1798, that the Secretary of State certified that the amendment had been made a part of the Constitution. This was because the states were dilatory in notifying the central government.

SECRETARY OF THE NAVY APPOINTED BY ADAMS

The Secretary of War was in charge of both the army and the navy, until May 21, 1798, when President John Adams appointed Benjamin Stoddert as the first Secretary of the Navy.

APPOINTMENT OF A GENERAL AUTHORIZED

An act of May 28, 1798 (1 Stat. L. 558), "an act authorizing the President of the United States to raise a provisional army," empowered the President

to appoint, by and with the advice and consent of the Senate, a commander of the army which may be raised by virtue of this act, and who being commissioned as lieutenant-general may be authorized to command the armies of the united States, and shall be entitled to the following pay and emoluments, viz.: two-hundred-and-fifty dollars monthly pay, fifty dollars monthly allowance for forage, when the same shall not be provided by the United States, and forty rations per day, or money in lieu thereof at the current price, who shall have authority to appoint, from time to time, such number of aids not exceeding four, and secretaries not exceeding two, as he may judge proper, each to have the rank, pay and emoluments as a lieutenant-colonel.

CONGRESS IN SESSION AT WASHINGTON

The first Congress to meet at Washington, D.C., was the Sixth Congress; the second session opened on November 17, 1800, and lasted until March 3, 1801 (107 days). The House of Representatives did not have a quorum until November 18, and the Senate did not have a quorum until November 21. On November 22, 1800, President John Adams read his fourth annual address to Congress.

ADAMS APPOINTED "MIDNIGHT JUDGES"

On February 13, 1801, Congress passed "an act to provide for the more convenient organization of the Courts of the United States" (2 Stat. L. 89). It provided for the appointment of eighteen new judges.

President John Adams sat at his desk until midnight, March 3, 1801, signing the appointment of Federalists to public offices.

The law was repealed during Jefferson's term and the judges lost their offices. The act of April 29, 1802, "an act to amend the Judicial System of the United States," voided the appointments.

ADAMS DEFEATED FOR REELECTION

John Adams was the first President of the United States who was defeated for reelection. After completing his term, 1797-1801, John Adams hoped to be reelected but the electors decided otherwise.

Thomas Jefferson received 73 electoral votes and was elected President and Aaron Burr, who had the same number of votes, was elected Vice President. The decision was referred to the House of Representatives. John Adams received 65 electoral votes, Charles Cotesworth Pinckney 64 votes, and John Jay 1 vote.

ADAMS RECALLED SON

On January 31, 1801, John Adams recalled his son, John Quincy Adams, from his post as Minister to Prussia to prevent President-elect Thomas Jefferson from dismissing him. On April 26, 1801, the recall reached John Quincy Adams, who returned to Philadelphia, Pa., on September 4, 1801.

Adams' letter to Secretary of State John Marshall stated:

I request that you would cause to be prepared letters for me to sign, to the King of Prussia recalling Mr. John Quincy Adams as minister plenipotentiary from his court. . . . I wish you to make out one letter to go by the way of Hamburg, another by Holland, a third by France, a fourth through Mr. King in England, a fifth, if you please, by way of Bremen or Stettin, or any channel most likely to convey it soon. It is my opinion this minister ought to be recalled from Prussia.... Besides, it is my opinion that it is my duty to call him home.

ABSENCE AT INAUGURATION OF SUCCESSOR

John Adams started the precedent of not attending the inauguration of his successor. When Thomas Jefferson was inaugurated on March 4, 1801, Adams absented himself rather than witness the success of his political rival. His son, John Quincy Adams, likewise refused to attend the inauguration services for Andrew Jackson and other Presidents also followed this example.

FATHER AND SON PRESIDENTS

John Adams and John Quincy Adams were the only father and son to be inaugurated Presidents of the United States. They each served one term. John Adams lived to see his son sworn in as President.

ADAMS' LAST WORDS

The last words attributed to John Adams were made by him without a full knowledge of the facts. Adams' last words were reported to have been "Thomas Jefferson still survives." He had not learned, nor had he any means of knowing, that Thomas Jefferson had died the same morning at 9:50 A.M. on July 4, 1826, at Monticello, Va.

ADAMS SUPPLIED VITAL INFORMATION

In a letter dated March 11, 1809, from Quincy, Mass., in response to a request for biographical material, John Adams wrote to Skelton Jones:

I was born in Quincy on the 19th of October 1735. . . .

The Fourth of March 1801. The causes of my retirement are to be found in the writings of Freneau, Markoe, Ned Church, Andrew Brown, Paine, Callender, Hamilton, Cobbett and John Ward Fenno and many others, but more especially in the circular letters of Members of Congress from the southern and middle States. Without a complete collection of all these libels, no faithful history of the last twenty years can ever be written, nor any adequate account given of the causes of my retirement from public life.

I have one head, four limbs and five senses, like any other man, and nothing peculiar in any of them.

I have been married forty-four years.

To Miss Abigail Smith on the 25th of October 1764 in her father's house at Weymouth, the next town to his, and by her father who was a clergyman.

I have no miniature, and have been too much abused by painters ever to sit to any one again.

THE FIRST LADY AT THE EXECUTIVE MANSION

Mrs. John Adams, the first President's wife to live in the Executive Mansion, did not move to Washington, D.C., until November 1800, when the President's House was ready for occupancy. A New Year's reception was held there in 1801, the first reception at the White House. As Adams' term of office expired on March 3, 1801, Mrs. Adams resided at the Executive Mansion less than four months. She maintained the same strict etiquette as Martha Washington. She preferred the climate at Quincy, Mass., however, and she maintained her interests there, anticipating the time when her husband's term would be completed.

EXTRACT FROM FIRST LETTER FROM THE WHITE HOUSE BY A PRESIDENT (JOHN ADAMS TO HIS WIFE, ABIGAIL ADAMS)

President's House, Washington City
2 November, 1800

My Dearest Friend,

We arrived here last night, or rather yesterday, at one o'clock, and here we dined and slept. . . . Besides, it is fit and proper that you and I should retire together, and not one before the other. Before I end my letter, I pray heaven to bestow the best of blessings on this house, and on all that shall hereafter inhabit

it. May none but honest and wise men ever rule under this roof!
I shall not attempt a description of it. You will form the best
idea of it from inspection. . . .

I am, with unabated confidence and affection, yours,

JOHN ADAMS

MRS. ADAMS' IMPRESSION OF THE WHITE HOUSE (A LETTER TO HER DAUGHTER)

Washington, 21 November, 1800

MY DEAR CHILD:

I arrived here on Sunday last, and without meeting with any
accident worth noticing, except losing ourselves when we left Baltimore, and going eight or nine miles on the Frederick road, by
which means we were obliged to go the other eight through
woods, where we wandered two hours without finding a guide,
or the path. . . . The house is made habitable, but there is not
a single apartment finished, and all within-side, except the plas-
tering has been done since Briesler came. We have not the least
fence, yard, or other convenience, without, and the great unfinished audience room I make a drying-room of, to hang up the
clothes in. The principal stairs are not up, and will not be this
winter. . . .

Affectionately your mother
A. ADAMS

THOMAS JEFFERSON
3rd PRESIDENT

Born–Apr. 13, 1743

Birthplace–Shadwell, Goochland County, now Albermarle County, Va.

College attended–College of William and Mary, Williamsburg, Va.

Date of graduation–Apr. 25, 1762

Religion–No specific denomination

Ancestry–Welsh

Occupation–Lawyer, writer

Date and place of marriage–Jan. 1, 1772, Williamsburg, Va., at the Forest, the Wayles estate

Age at marriage–28 years, 263 days

Years married–10 years, 248 days

Political party–Democratic - Republican

State represented–Virginia

Term of office–Mar. 4, 1801-Mar. 3, 1809

Term served–8 years

Administration–4th, 5th

Congresses–7th, 8th, 9th, 10th

Age at inauguration–57 years, 325 days

Lived after term–17 years, 122 days

Occupation after term–Retired

Date of death–July 4, 1826

Age at death–83 years, 82 days

Place of death–Charlottesville, Va.

Burial place–Charlottesville, Va.

PARENTS

Father–Peter Jefferson

Born–Feb. 29, 1708

Married–Oct. 2, 1739

Occupation–Professor, planter, surveyor, land owner

Died–Aug. 17, 1757

Age at death–49 years, 170 days

Mother–Jane Randolph Jefferson

Born–Feb. 9, 1720, London, England

Died–Mar. 31, 1776

Age at death–56 years, 50 days

BROTHERS AND SISTERS

Thomas Jefferson was the third child in a family of ten.

Children of Peter Jefferson and Jane Randolph Jefferson

Jane Jefferson, b. June 27, 1740, d. Oct. 1, 1765

Mary Jefferson, b. Oct. 1, 1741, d. 1760

Thomas Jefferson, b. Apr. 13, 1743, d. July 4, 1826

Elizabeth Jefferson, b. Nov. 4, 1744, d. Feb. 1774

Martha Jefferson, b. May 29, 1746, d. Sept. 3, 1811

Peter Field Jefferson, b. Oct. 16, 1748, d. Nov. 29, 1748

____Jefferson (son), b. Mar. 9, 1750, d. Mar. 9, 1750

Lucy Jefferson, b. Oct. 10, 1752, d. 1811

Anna Scott Jefferson, twin, b. Oct. 1, 1755

Randolph Jefferson, twin, b. Oct. 1, 1755, d. Aug. 7, 1815

CHILDREN

Martha Washington Jefferson, b. Sept. 27, 1772, Monticello, Va.; m. Feb. 23, 1790, Thomas Mann Randolph; d. Oct. 10, 1836

Jane Randolph Jefferson, b. Apr. 3, 1774; d. Sept. 1775

____Jefferson (son), b. May 28, 1777; d. June 14, 1777

Mary ("Marie," "Polly") Jeffer-

For additional data see the end of this section and also specific subject headings in the index.

son, b. Aug. 1, 1778; m. Oct. 13, 1797, John Wayles Eppes; d. Apr. 17, 1804

Lucy Elizabeth Jefferson, b. Nov. 3, 1780, Richmond, Va.; d. Apr. 15, 1781

Lucy Elizabeth Jefferson, b. May 8, 1782; d. Nov. 17, 1785, Eppington, Va.

MRS. THOMAS JEFFERSON

Name—Martha Wayles Skelton Jefferson

Date of birth—Oct. 19, 1748

Birthplace—Charles City County, Va.

Age at marriage—23 years, 74 days

Children by Jefferson—5 daughters, 1 son

Mother—Martha Eppes Wayles

Father—John Wayles

His occupation—Lawyer, planter

Date of death—Sept. 6, 1782

Age at death—33 years, 322 days

Place of death—Monticello, Va.

Burial place—Monticello, Va.

Younger than the President—5 years, 189 days

Years the President survived her—43 years, 301 days

At the time of her marriage to Jefferson she was the widow of Bathurst Skelton, by whom she had one child—a son who was born November 7, 1767, and who died June 10, 1771.

THE ELECTION OF 1800

The fourth national election was held on November 4, 1800. It showed that the loosely knitted political groups had begun to organize. The Federalists, still advocating a strong central government with only such political power for the various states as was absolutely necessary, began to encounter apparent dissatisfaction with their policies. The Federalist congressmen, in a congressional caucus which met in a Senate chamber, decided to support Adams for a second term with Charles Cotesworth Pinckney of South Carolina as a running mate. Since both the President and the Vice President were elected by the same ballot, one faction of the Federalists hoped that Pinckney would receive the presidency and that Adams with the second greatest number of votes might become Vice President.

The Democratic-Republicans, believing that the states should yield to the federal government only that which was necessary, denounced the federal caucus but continued to work under it. At a congressional caucus held in Philadelphia, Pa., the Democratic-Republicans placed their hopes on Thomas Jefferson of Virginia and Aaron Burr of New York. At this caucus they adopted the first national platform ever formulated by a political party.

When the electoral votes of 1800 were counted, another unusual situation developed. The electors cast 276 votes. Of these, 73 were cast for Thomas Jefferson and 73 for Aaron Burr both Democratic-Republicans. The Federalists cast 65 votes for John Adams, 64 votes for Charles Cotesworth Pinckney, and 1 vote for John Jay of New York.

Inasmuch as both Jefferson and Burr had each received 73 votes and tied for first place, the election was referred to the House of Representatives to decide which candidate would be the President and which would be the Vice President. The outcome was not as critical as the election of 1796, since both candidates were members of the same political faction. The issue was not whether the Federalists or the Democratic-Republicans should be in power, but which Democratic-Republican should be elected, Jefferson or Burr. It was not a contest of political factions but of personalities.

The balloting to decide the tie took place on February 11, 1801. The representatives did not vote individually but by state groups, each state being entitled to one vote. On the first ballot, Jefferson had eight states and Burr six states, with Maryland and Vermont equally divided. As a majority was required, further ballots were taken. On February 17, the thirty-sixth ballot was taken to arrive at a choice. Ten states voted for Jefferson, four for Burr, and two voted blank. Jefferson was declared elected President and Burr his Vice President.

THE ELECTION OF 1804

In 1804, after Jefferson had served four years, the Democratic-Republicans found Vice President Aaron Burr no longer acceptable. His catering to the Federalists for their support had lowered his standing with his own party, and his killing of Alexander Hamilton in a duel had made him *persona non grata* with the public. When the congressional caucus was held on February 25, 1804, the Democratic-Republicans decided to support Jefferson for a second term as President. They withdrew their support of Burr and favored George Clinton, governor of New York for eighteen years, to supplant him as Vice President.

The Federalists, whose party strength was waning, held no congressional caucus and threw their support to Charles Cotesworth Pinckney of South Carolina for President and Rufus King of New York for Vice President.

Jefferson won a clear-cut victory and was elected President for a second term, carrying George Clinton with him as Vice President. He received 162 of the 176 electoral votes.

The election of November 6, 1804, was the first in which the President and the Vice President were voted for separately. This change in election procedure, authorized by the Twelfth Amendment to the Constitution, went into effect September 25, 1804, and superseded Article II, Section 1, paragraph three of the Constitution. The bill was passed by the Senate on December 3, 1803, by a vote of 22 yeas to 10 nays, and by the House of Representatives on December 9, 1803, by a vote of 83 yeas to 42 nays, with the speaker, Nathaniel Macon of North Carolina, casting the deciding vote to make the necessary two-thirds majority. The amendment was submitted to the states, was ratified by three fourths of them, and was declared in force on September 25, 1804. Connecticut, Delaware, Massachusetts, and New Hampshire rejected the amendment.

ELECTORAL VOTES (176-17 states)

Jefferson received 92.05 per cent (162 votes—15 states) as follows: Ga. 6; Ky. 8; Md. 9 (of the 11 votes); Mass. 19; N.H. 7; N.J. 8; N.Y. 19; N.C. 14; Ohio 3; Pa. 20; R.I. 4; S.C. 10; Tenn. 5; Vt. 6; Va. 24.

Pinckney received 7.95 per cent (14 votes—2 states) as follows: Conn. 9; Del. 3; Md. 2 (of the 11 votes).

FIRST TERM

CABINET

March 4, 1801-March 3, 1805

State–John Marshall, Va. (Chief Justice of the United States) for one day, Mar. 4, 1801, and for a special purpose; Levi Lincoln, Mass. (Attorney General) ad interim Mar. 5, 1801; James Madison, Va., Mar. 5, 1801; entered upon duties May 2, 1801

Treasury–Samuel Dexter, Mass., continued from preceding administration to May 6, 1801; Albert Gallatin, Pa., May 14, 1801

War–Henry Dearborn, Mass., Mar. 5, 1801

Attorney General–Levi Lincoln, Mass., Mar. 5, 1801 to Dec. 31, 1804

Postmaster General–Joseph Habersham, Ga., continued from preceding administration; Gideon Granger, Conn., Nov. 28, 1801

Navy–Benjamin Stoddert, Md., continued from preceding administration; Henry Dearborn, Mass. (Secretary of War) ad interim Apr. 1, 1801; Robert Smith, Md., July 15, 1801; entered upon duties July 27, 1801

SECOND TERM

CABINET

March 4, 1805-March 3, 1809

State–James Madison, Va., continued from preceding administration

Treasury–Albert Gallatin, Pa., continued from preceding administration

War–Henry Dearborn, Mass., continued from preceding administration; John Smith (chief clerk) ad interim Feb. 17, 1809

Attorney General–John Breckenridge, Ky., Aug. 7, 1805, died Dec. 14, 1806; Caesar Augustus Rodney, Del., Jan. 20, 1807

Postmaster General–Gideon Granger, Conn., continued from preceding administration

Navy–Robert Smith, Md., continued from preceding administration

FIRST TERM

SEVENTH CONGRESS

March 4, 1801-March 3, 1803

First session–Dec. 7, 1801-May 3, 1802 (148 days)

Second session–Dec. 6, 1802-Mar. 3, 1803 (88 days)

Special session–Mar. 4, 1801-Mar. 5, 1801 (2 days)

Vice President–Aaron Burr, N.Y.

Presidents pro tempore of the Senate–Abraham Baldwin, Ga., elected Dec. 7, 1801, Apr. 17, 1802; Stephen Row Bradley, Vt., elected Dec. 14, 1802, Feb. 25, 1803, Mar. 2, 1803

Secretary of the Senate–Samuel Allyne Otis, Mass.

Speaker of the House–Nathaniel Macon, N.C., elected Dec. 7, 1801

Clerks of the House–John Holt Oswald, Pa., John Beckley, Va., elected Dec. 7, 1801

EIGHTH CONGRESS

March 4, 1803-March 3, 1805

First session–Oct. 17, 1803-Mar. 27, 1804 (163 days)
Second session–Nov. 5, 1804-Mar. 3, 1805 (119 days)
Vice President–Aaron Burr, N.Y.
Presidents pro tempore of the Senate–John Brown, Ky., elected Oct. 17, 1803, Jan. 23, 1804; Jesse Franklin, N.C., elected Mar. 10, 1804; Joseph Anderson, Tenn., elected Jan. 15, 1805, Feb. 28, 1805, Mar. 2, 1805
Secretary of the Senate–Samuel Allyne Otis, Mass.
Speaker of the House–Nathaniel Macon, N.C., reelected Oct. 17, 1803
Clerk of the House–John Beckley, Va., reelected Oct. 17, 1803

SECOND TERM

NINTH CONGRESS

March 4, 1805-March 3, 1807

First session–Dec. 2, 1805-Apr. 21, 1806 (141 days)
Second session–Dec. 1, 1806-Mar. 3, 1807 (93 days)
Special session of the Senate–Mar. 4, 1805-Mar. 6, 1805 (3 days)
Vice President–George Clinton, N.Y.
President pro tempore of the Senate–Samuel Smith, Md., elected Dec. 2, 1805; Mar. 18, 1806; Mar. 2, 1807
Secretary of the Senate–Samuel Allyne Otis, Mass.
Speaker of the House–Nathaniel Macon, reelected Dec. 2, 1805
Clerk of the House–John Beckley, Va., reelected Dec. 2, 1805

TENTH CONGRESS

March 4, 1807-March 3, 1809

First session–Oct. 26, 1807-Apr. 25, 1808 (182 days)
Second session–Nov. 7, 1806-Mar. 3, 1809 (117 days
Vice President–George Clinton, N.Y.
Presidents pro tempore of the Senate–Samuel Smith, elected Apr. 16, 1808; Stephen Row Bradley, Vt., elected Dec. 28, 1808; John Milledge, Ga., elected Jan. 30, 1809
Secretary of the Senate–Samuel Allyne Otis, Mass.
Speaker of the House–Joseph Bradley Varnum, Mass., elected Oct. 26, 1807
Clerks of the House–John Beckley, Va.; Patrick Magruder, Md., elected Oct. 26, 1807

ADMINISTRATION — IMPORTANT DATES

June 10, 1801, Tripoli declared war against the United States
Feb. 6, 1802, war declared against Tripoli
Mar. 16, 1802, Army engineer corps created
Mar. 16, 1802, United States Military Academy authorized; opened July 4, 1802

Feb. 24, 1803, Marbury *vs.* Madison—Supreme Court decision declaring portion of Judiciary Act of 1789 unconstitutional

Mar. 1, 1803, Ohio admitted as 17th state

Apr. 30, 1803, Louisiana Purchase made from France for $15 million

May 2, 1803, Louisiana Purchase treaty signed

Oct. 31, 1803, Captain Bainbridge of the *Philadelphia* ran on a reef pursuing Tripoli cruiser and was captured

Dec. 30, 1803, France formally ceded Louisiana to United States

Feb. 3, 1804, Lieutenant Decatur, aboard the *Philadelphia,* defeated Tripolitans

Mar. 12, 1804, Judge John Pickering impeached and removed from office in trial begun Mar. 3, 1803 (first impeachment of a federal judge)

May 14, 1804, Lewis and Clark left St. Louis, Mo., on their expedition to the Pacific

July 12, 1804, Alexander Hamilton killed by Aaron Burr in a duel

Sept. 25, 1804, Twelfth Amendment to the Constitution ratified

Jan. 11, 1805, Michigan Territory created

Mar. 1, 1805, Supreme Court Justice Samuel Chase acquitted in impeachment trial begun Nov. 30, 1804 (first impeachment proceedings against a Supreme Court justice)

June 4, 1805, treaty of peace and amity signed with Tripoli

Nov. 15, 1805, Lewis and Clark reached Pacific Ocean

Mar. 29, 1806, Cumberland road construction to Ohio authorized

Nov. 13, 1806, Lieutenant Zebulon Pike discovered Colorado peak later named for him

Mar. 26, 1807, Territory of Orleans established

May 22, 1807-Oct. 20, 1807, trial of Aaron Burr at Richmond, Va., for conspiracy

June 1807, American ship *Chesapeake* fired upon by British *Leopard; Chesapeake* searched and British deserters seized

Aug. 7, 1807, Robert Fulton's steamboat *Clermont* made trip on Hudson River

Dec. 22, 1807, Embargo Act against international commerce

Jan. 1, 1808, law prohibiting importation of African slaves became effective

Nov. 10, 1808, Osage Treaty signed

Feb. 3, 1809, Illinois Territory established

Mar. 1, 1809, trade with Great Britain and France prohibited by non-intercourse act

APPOINTMENTS TO THE SUPREME COURT

Associate Justices

William Johnson, S.C., Mar. 26, 1804

Brockholst Livingston, N.Y., Nov. 10, 1806

Thomas Todd, Ky., Mar. 3, 1807

Levi Lincoln, Mass., Jan. 7, 1811 (declined to serve)

John Quincy Adams, Mass., Feb. 22, 1811 (declined to serve)

IMPORTANT DATES IN HIS LIFE

1757, inherited land and slaves on death of his father and took over responsibilities as head of the family

1760-1762 student, College of William and Mary

1767, admitted to the bar

1769 began building of home at Monticello

May 11, 1769, member of Virginia House of Burgesses (served until 1774)

Nov. 26, 1770, moved to Monticello

Apr. 1773, attended meeting of Committee of Correspondence

Mar. 1775, deputy delegate to Continental Congress, Philadelphia

June 21-July 31, Oct. 2-Dec. 28, 1775, delegate to Continental Congress

Aug. 1775, Virginia convention, Richmond

May 15-Sept. 2, 1776, delegate to Continental Congress

June 10-July 2, 1776, chairman of committee to prepare Declaration of Independence

Oct. 11- Dec. 14, 1776, Virginia General Assembly, Williamsburg

June 1, 1779, elected governor of Virginia

June 2, 1780, reelected governor

June 3, 1781, resigned governorship; offered post as Peace Commissioner by Continental Congress but declined appointment

June 15, 1781, empowered to negotiate treaty of peace with Great Britain

June 1783, drafted constitution for Virginia

May 7, 1784, appointed minister plenipotentiary to France

Mar. 10, 1785, elected by Congress to succeed Franklin as minister to France; presented credentials to King of France on May 14

June 1785, left Paris for London

1786-1787, diplomatic missions in Paris and London

Oct. 12, 1787, reelected minister for three-year term; appointment subject to revocation by Congress

1789, prepared Charter of Rights for France

Sept. 26, 1789, confirmed as secretary of state

Oct. 22-Nov. 23, 1789, returned from France on the *Clermont,* disembarking at Norfolk, Va.

Feb. 14, 1790-Dec. 31, 1793, secretary of state

Jan., 1797, elected president of Philosophical Society

1800, prepared *Parliamentary Manual*

Mar.4, 1801-Mar. 3, 1805, President (1st term)

May 2, 1803, Louisiana Purchase treaty signed

Mar. 4, 1805-Mar. 3, 1809, President (2nd term)

Sept. 1814, sold his library to Library of Congress

Mar. 29, 1819, rector of University of Virginia

Nov. 12, 1822, injured in fall (left forearm broken and wrist bones dislocated)

THOMAS JEFFERSON

_____was the second President born in Virginia.

____was the second President to marry a widow.

____was the first widower inaugurated President.

____was the first President inaugurated in Washington, D.C.

____was the first President who had been a governor of a state.

____was the first President to have served in a cabinet.

____was the first President whose parents had twins.

____was the first President elected by the House of Representatives.

____was the first President who had served as secretary of state.

JEFFERSON'S VICE PRESIDENTS

FIRST TERM

Vice President–Aaron Burr (3rd V.P.)
Date of birth–Feb. 6, 1756
Birthplace–Newark, N.J.
Political party–Democratic-Republican
State represented–New York
Term of office–Mar. 4, 1801-Mar. 3, 1805
Age at inauguration–45 years, 26 days
Occupation after term–Lawyer
Date of death–Sept. 14, 1836
Age at death–80 years, 220 days
Place of death–Staten Island, N.Y.
Burial place–Princeton Cemetary, Princeton, N.J.

Additional Data on Burr

1772, graduated from Princeton College, Princeton, N.J.

1733, studied theology at Litchfield, Conn. (He was the son of a clergy-man)

1775, joined Continental Army, distinguishing himself at Quebec, Monmouth, and New Haven

Mar. 10, 1779, resigned because of ill health

Apr. 17, 1782, admitted to the bar; practiced in Albany, N.Y.

1783, moved to New York City

1784, New York State Assembly

1789-1790, attorney general of New York

1791, commissioner on Revolutionary claims

Mar. 4, 1791-Mar. 3, 1797, U.S. Senate (from New York)

1798-1799, New York State Assembly

1801, New York State Consitutional Convention

1804, unsuccessful candidate for governor of New York

1804, killed Alexander Hamilton in duel (July 11); fled to South Carolina; completed term as Vice President

1807, arrested and tried for treason for attempting to form a republic in the Southwest of which he was to be the head; acquitted

1808, went to Europe

1812, resumed law practice, New York City.

SECOND TERM

Vice President–George Clinton (4th V.P.)

Date of birth–July 26, 1739
Birthplace–Little Britain, N.Y.
Political party–Democratic-Republican
State represented–New York
Term of office–Mar. 4, 1805-Mar. 3, 1809
Age at inauguration–65 years, 221 days
Occupation after term–Vice President under Madison; died in office
Date of death–Apr. 20, 1812
Age at death–72 years, 268 days
Place of death–Washington, D.C.
Burial place–Kingston, N.Y.

Additional Data on Clinton

1755, admitted to the bar; practiced in Little Britain, N.Y.
1758, lieutenant of Rangers in expedition against Fort Frontenac
1759, clerk of Court of Common Pleas
1765, district attorney; surveyor of New Windsor, N.Y.
1768, New York State Assembly
1774, New York Committee of Correspondence
May 13, 1775-July 8, 1776, Continental Congress
1775, brigadier-general of militia, appointed by George Washington
Mar. 25, 1777, brigadier-general, appointed by Congress
1777-1795, governor of New York
1788, president of state convention which ratified federal Constitution
1796, unsuccessful candidate for Vice President
1800-1801, New York State Assembly
1801-1804, governor of New York

VICE PRESIDENT CLINTON UNSUCCESSFUL IN THREE PREVIOUS ELECTIONS

George Clinton of New York, who was elected Vice President under Thomas Jefferson (second term, 1805-1809) and under James Madison (first term, 1809-1813) had been unsuccessful in three previous elections. In 1789 he received three votes for the vice presidency; in 1793 he received fifty electoral votes; and in 1797 he received seven electoral votes.

ADDITIONAL DATA ON JEFFERSON

JEFFERSON ADVOCATED RELIGIOUS FREEDOM

One of Jefferson's greatest achievements was the bill establishing religious freedom which was drawn up by him and enacted by the Legislature of Virginia in 1779.

Section 2 stated:

We the General Assembly of Virginia do enact that no man shall be compelled to frequent or support any religious worship, place, or ministry whatsoever, nor shall be enforced, restrained, molested, or burthened in his body or goods, or shall otherwise suffer, on account of his religious opinions or belief; but that all men shall be free to profess, and by argument to maintain, their opinions in matters of religion, and that the same shall in no wise diminish, enlarge, or affect their civil capacities.

JEFFERSON ADVOCATED DECIMAL SYSTEM OF CURRENCY

In April 1784 Thomas Jefferson wrote an important document entitled "Notes on the Establishment of a Money Unit and of a Coinage for the United States." The paper concluded:

My proposition then, is, that our notation of money shall be decimal, descending *ad libitum* of the person noting; that the Unit of this notation shall be a Dollar; that coins shall be accommodated to it from ten dollars to the hundredth of a dollar; and that, to set this on foot, the resolutions be adopted which were proposed in the notes only substituting *an enquiry into the fineness of the coins* in lieu of *an assay of them.*

GOVERNOR ELECTED PRESIDENT

Thomas Jefferson was the first governor of a state to be elected President. He was governor of Virginia from 1779 to 1781.

VICE PRESIDENT DEFEATED PRESIDENT

Thomas Jefferson was the first and last Vice President to defeat a President. In the election of 1800, Thomas Jefferson of Virginia and Aaron Burr of New York received 73 electoral votes, the election being decided in Jefferson's favor by the House of Representatives. Accordingly, Aaron Burr was made the Vice President. President John Adams received only 65 electoral votes and was defeated in his quest for re-election.

FIRST INAUGURATION

Thomas Jefferson was the first President to take the oath of office at Washington, D.C. It was a fair day and he walked to the Capitol from Mrs. Conrad's boarding house, one block away, accompanied by a group of riflemen, artillerymen, and civilians. The oath was administered on Wednesday, March 4, 1801, by Chief Justice John Marshall in the Senate Chamber in the Capitol. Only the north wing of the Capitol building had been completed and the center was unfinished. President John Adams drove out of the city at dawn, refusing to attend the inauguration of his successor to witness what he considered the dissolution of the republic.

JEFFERSON AT THE EXECUTIVE MANSION

The White House, which at the time of Jefferson's inauguration was called the President's House, was not fully completed. Jefferson described it as "a great stone house, big enough for two emperors, one pope and the grand lama in the bargain." Jefferson did not move into the official residence until March 19, 1801.

TROOPS REVIEWED FROM THE WHITE HOUSE

Thomas Jefferson held the first presidential review of military forces from his residence at the White House. On July 4, 1801, he reviewed the Marines, who were led by the Marine Band.

HAND-SHAKING INTRODUCED

On July 4, 1801, President Jefferson held a reception in the Blue Room at the White House which was attended by about one hundred guests. Jefferson introduced the custom of having the guests shake hands instead of bowing stiffly, a custom observed by Presidents Washington and Adams.

JEFFERSON SUBMITTED ANNUAL ADDRESS IN WRITING

When Thomas Jefferson prepared his first annual message to Congress, he sent it to that body on December 8, 1801, instead of addressing both houses in person as Washington and Adams had done. On the same date, he wrote the presiding officer of each house. The following letter was included with the message for the Senate:

Sir: The circumstances under which we find ourselves at this place rendering inconvenient the mode heretofore practiced of making by personal address the first communications between the legislative and executive branches, I have adopted that by message, as used on subsequent occasions through the session. In doing this I have had principal regard to the convenience of the Legislature, to the economy of their time, to their relief from the embarrassment of immediate answers on subjects not yet fully before them, and to the benefits thence resulting to the public affairs. Trusting that a procedure founded in these motives will meet their approbation, I beg leave through you, sir, to communicate the inclosed message, with the documents accompanying it, to the honorable the Senate, and pray you to accept for yourself and them the homage of my high respect and consideration.

TH. JEFFERSON

CHEESE PRESENTED TO JEFFERSON

On January 1, 1802, a cart pulled by six horses delivered a 1,235-pound cheese made at West Chester, Mass., to the White House. It was addressed "The greatest cheese in America for the greatest man in America."

UNITED STATES DOUBLED ITS AREA

The Louisiana Purchase contract, dated April 30, 1803, and signed on May 2, 1803, increased United States territory by approximately 846,000 square miles, practically doubling the area of the United States. Jefferson bought from Napoleon an area which was to become the entire states or substantial parts of Arkansas, Colorado, Iowa, Kansas, Louisiana, Minnesota, Missouri, Montana, Nebraska, North Dakota, Oklahoma, South Dakota, and Wyoming. The purchase price was $11,250,000, and the United States also assumed claims of Americans against France estimated at about $3,750,000.

TWELFTH AMENDMENT ENACTED

The Twelfth Amendment to the Constitution, altering the method of electing the President and the Vice President by the electoral college, was passed by Congress on December 9, 1803, and was proposed to the legislatures of the several states on December 12, 1803. Ratified by all the states except Connecticut, Delaware, Massachusetts, and New Hampshire, it was declared ratified by the Secretary of State on September 25, 1804.

The text of the amendment follows:

The electors shall meet in their respective states and vote by ballot for President and Vice-President, one of whom, at least, shall not be an inhabitant of the same state with themselves; they shall name in their ballots the persons voted for as President, and in distinct ballots the person voted for as Vice-President, and they shall make distinct lists of all persons voted for as President, and of all persons voted for as Vice-President, and of the number of votes for each, which lists they shall sign and certify, and transmit sealed to the seat of the government of the United States, directed to the President of the Senate;—The President of the Senate shall, in presence of the Senate and House of Representatives, open all the certificates and the votes shall then be counted;—The person having the greatest number of votes for President, shall be the President, if such number be a majority of the whole number of Electors appointed; and if no person have such majority, then from the persons having the highest numbers not exceeding three on the list of those voted for as President, the House of Representatives shall choose immediately, by ballot, the President. But in choosing the President, the votes shall be taken by states, the representation from each state having one vote; a quorum for this purpose shall consist of a member or members from two-thirds of the states, and a majority of all the states shall be necessary to a choice. (And if the House of Representatives shall not choose a President whenever the right of choice shall devolve upon them, before the fourth day of March next following, then the Vice-President shall act as President, as in the case of the death or other constitutional disability of the President.) The person having the greatest number of votes as Vice-President, shall be the Vice-President, if such number be a majority of the whole number of Electors appointed, and if no person have a majority, then from the two highest numbers on the list, the Senate shall choose the Vice-President; a quorum for the purpose shall consist of two-thirds of the whole number of Senators, and a majority of the whole number shall be necessary to a choice. But no person constitutionally ineligible to the office of President shall be eligible to that of Vice-President of the United States.

SECOND INAUGURATION

Thomas Jefferson took the oath of office for his second term on

Monday, March 4, 1805, in the Senate Chamber. Chief Justice John Marshall administered the oath. In the evening, a ceremony in the East Room of the Executive Mansion was attended by a large crowd which caused much disorder.

JEFFERSON ASSERTED PRESIDENT'S IMMUNITY TO COURTS

The lawyers defending Aaron Burr, who had been indicted for high treason, attempted to issue a *duces tecum* subpoena on June 10, 1807, on President Jefferson. In a letter to United States Attorney George Hay, dated June 20, 1807, President Jefferson wrote:

> Let us apply the Judge's own doctrine to the case of himself and his brethren. The Sheriff of Henrico summons him from the bench to quell a riot somewhere in his county. The Federal judge is by the general law a part of the *posse* of the state sheriff. Would the judge abandon major duties to perform lesser ones? Again, the court of Orleans or Maine commands by subpoenas the attendance of all judges of the Supreme Court. Would they abandon their posts as judges and the interest of millions committed to them to serve the purposes of a single individual? The leading principle of our constitution is the independence of the legislature, executive and judiciary of each other; and none are more jealous of this than the judiciary. But would the executive be independent of the judiciary if he were subject to the commands of the latter and to imprisonment for disobedience; if the several courts could bandy him from pillar to post, keep him constantly trudging from north to south, and east to west, and withdraw him entirely from his constitutional duties?

JEFFERSON SIGNED FIRST EMBARGO ACT

President Jefferson signed the first embargo act. It was passed December 22, 1807 (2 Stat. L. 451) by a vote of 82 to 44. Intended to prevent the United States from being drawn into the war between Britain and France, the act placed "an embargo on all ships and vessels in the ports and harbors of the United States" and required all American ships to refrain from international commerce. The act, signed by President Jefferson, stopped all foreign trade. It was repealed on March 1, 1809. A later act was substituted which stopped trade with England and France.

JEFFERSON WROTE HIS OWN EPITAPH

Thomas Jefferson wrote the epitaph to be placed over his grave. He made no mention of his presidency. The inscription reads: "Here was buried Thomas Jefferson, author of the Declaration of American Independence, of the statute of Virginia for religious freedom, and father of the University of Virginia."

FIRST WIDOWER TO BECOME PRESIDENT

Thomas Jefferson was the first widower to become President of the United States. His wife, Martha Wayles Skelton, died 18 years, 179 days before he was inaugurated. Jefferson never remarried and was a widower 35 years, 302 days. Four of his six children died before he became President.

HOSTESSES AT THE WHITE HOUSE

Thomas Jefferson had been a widower for about eighteen years when he entered the White House. The duties of mistress of the White House were assumed by his daughters; one was Martha Washington Jefferson, the wife of Thomas Mann Randolph, and the other was Marie Jefferson, the wife of John Wayles Eppes. The unhealthy condition of the city of Washington, which was low and marshy, engendered disease, and his daughters preferred not to bring their children to the capital city. Mrs. James Madison, wife of the Secretary of State, generally presided at functions in the absence of Jefferson's daughters. Jefferson opposed the levees, or official receptions, which he thought were not democratic.

FIRST CHILD BORN IN THE WHITE HOUSE

James Madison Randolph, the grandson of President Thomas Jefferson, was the first child born in the White House. He was born January 17, 1806, and died January 23, 1834. His parents were Thomas Mann Randolph and Martha Jefferson Randolph, the daughter of President Jefferson.

JAMES MADISON
4th PRESIDENT

Born–Mar. 16, 1751

Birthplace–Port Conway, Va.

College attended–College of New Jersey, now Princeton University, Princeton, N.J.

Date of graduation–Sept. 25, 1771, Bachelor of Arts (completed four-year course in three years)

Religion–Episcopalian

Ancestry–English

Occupation–Lawyer

Date and place of marriage–Sept. 15, 1794, Harewood, Jefferson County, Va.

Age at marriage–43 years, 183 days

Years married–41 years, 286 days

Political party–Democratic-Republican

State represented–Virginia

Term of office–Mar. 4, 1809-Mar. 3, 1817

Term served–8 years

Administration–6th, 7th

Congresses–11th, 12th, 13th, 14th

Age at inauguration–57 years, 353 days

Lived after term–19 years, 116 days

Occupation after term–Retired

Date of death–June 28, 1836

Age at death–85 years, 104 days

Place of death–Montpelier, Va.

Burial place–Family plot, Montpelier, Va.

PARENTS

Father–James Madison

Born–Mar. 27, 1723

Married–Sept. 15, 1749

Occupation–Justice of the peace, vestryman, land owner, farmer

Died–Feb. 27, 1801

Age at death–77 years, 337 days

Mother–Eleanor ("Nellie") Rose Conway Madison

Born–Jan. 9, 1731

Died–Feb. 11, 1829

Age at death–98 years, 33 days

BROTHERS AND SISTERS

James Madison was the oldest of twelve children.

Children of James Madison and Eleanor Rose Conway Madison

James Madison, b. Mar. 16, 1751, d. June 28, 1836

Francis Madison, b. June 18, 1753

Ambrose Madison, b. Jan. 27, 1755, d. Oct. 1793

Catlett Madison, b. Feb. 10, 1758, d. Mar. 18, 1758

Nellie Conway Madison, b. Feb. 14, 1760, d. 1802

William Madison, b. May 5, 1762, d. July 20, 1843

Sarah Madison, b. Aug. 17, 1764

Elizabeth Madison, b. Feb. 19, 1768

Reuben Madison, b. Sept. 19, 1771

Frances Taylor Madison, b. Oct. 4, 1774

_____Madison

Eli Madison

One child stillborn

CHILDREN

None

MRS. JAMES MADISON

Name–Dorothea ("Dolley," incorrectly "Dolly") Dandridge Payne Todd Madison

Date of birth–May 20, 1768

Birthplace–now Guilford County, N.C.

For additional data see the end of this section and also specific subject headings in the index.

Age at marriage–26 years, 118 days

Children by Madison–None

Mother–Mary Coles Payne

Father–John Payne

His occupation–Farmer, planter

Date of death–July 12, 1849

Age at death–81 years, 53 days

Place of death–Washington, D.C.

Burial place–Montpelier, Va.

Years younger than the President–17 years, 65 days

Years she survived the President–13 years, 14 days

At the time of her marriage to Madison she was the widow of John Todd, by whom she had two sons, one of whom died in infancy.

THE ELECTION OF 1808

After he had served two terms (1801-1809) as President, Jefferson carried out the policy established by George Washington and refused to be a candidate for a third term. Jefferson favored James Monroe of Virginia as his successor, but the Democratic-Republican caucus decided in favor of James Madison, also of Virginia.

The Federalists, again without a congressional caucus, put up the same candidate, Charles Cotesworth Pinckney of South Carolina, whom they had unsuccessfully run in 1804.

For the vice presidency the Democratic-Republican votes were split among four candidates: George Clinton of New York (who had served under Jefferson), John Langdon of New Hampshire, James Madison, and James Monroe.

The Federalist candidate for the vice presidency was Rufus King of New York, who had been Pinckney's running mate in 1804.

ELECTORAL VOTES (175 votes—17 states)

Madison received 69.71 per cent (122 votes—12 states) as follows: Ga. 6; Ky. 7; Md. 9 (of the 11 votes); N.J. 8; N.Y. 13 (of the 19 votes); N.C. 11 (of the 14 votes); Ohio 3; Pa. 20; S.C. 10; Tenn. 5; Vt. 6; Va. 24.

Pinckney received 26.86 per cent (47 votes—5 states) as follows: Conn. 9; Del. 3; Md. 2 (of the 11 votes); Mass. 19; N.H. 7; N.C. 3 (of the 14 votes); R.I. 4.

Clinton received 3.43 per cent (6 votes—of the 19 N.Y. votes).

For the vice presidency Clinton received 113 votes as follows: Ga. 6; Ky. 7; Md. 9 (of the 11 votes); N.J. 8; N.Y. 13 (of the 19 votes); N.C. 11 (of the 14 votes); Pa. 20; S.C. 10; Tenn. 5; Va. 24.

King, the Federalist, received 47 votes as follows: Conn. 9; Del. 3; Md. 2 (of the 11 votes); Mass. 19; N.H. 7; N C 3 (of the 14 votes); R.I. 4.

The other Democratic-Republican candidates for the vice presidency received the following votes:

Langdon—Ohio 3; Vt. 6

Madison—N.Y. 3 (of the 19 votes)

Monroe—N.Y. 3 (of the 19 votes)

THE ELECTION OF 1812

After James Madison had served one term, the Democratic-Republicans in May 1812 chose to support him for a second term. George Clinton had died on April 12 while serving as Vice President and the party favored John Langdon of New Hampshire for that office. Langdon, however, declined to run because of his age (71), and Elbridge Gerry of Massachusetts was then selected for the vice presidency.

The Federalists in caucus at New York City decided to support the nomination of De Witt Clinton of New York and Jared Ingersoll of Pennsylvania.

ELECTORAL VOTES (217 votes—18 states)

Madison received 58.99 per cent (128 votes—11 states) as follows: Ga. 8; Ky. 12; La. 3; Md. 6 (of the 11 votes); N.C. 15; Ohio 7; Pa. 25; S.C. 11; Tenn. 8; Vt. 8; Va. 25.

Clinton received 41.01 per cent (89 votes—7 states) as follows: Conn. 9; Del. 4; Md. 5 (of the 11 votes); Mass. 22; N.H. 8; N.J. 8; N.Y. 29; R.I. 4.

Gerry received 131 votes for the vice presidency as follows: Ga. 8; Ky. 12; La. 3; Md. 6 (of the 11 votes); Mass. 2 (of the 22 votes); N.H. 1 (of the 8 votes); N.C. 15; Ohio 7; Pa. 25; S.C. 11; Tenn. 8; Vt. 8; Va. 25.

Ingersoll received 86 votes for the vice presidency as follows: Conn. 9; Del. 4; Md. 5 (of the 11 votes); Mass. 20 (of the 22 votes); N.H. 7 (of the 8 votes); N.J. 8; N.Y. 29; R.I. 4.

FIRST TERM

CABINET

March 4, 1809-March 3, 1813

State–Robert Smith, Md., Mar. 6, 1809; James Monroe, Va., Apr. 2, 1811; entered upon duties Apr. 6, 1811

Treasury–Albert Gallatin, Pa., continued from preceding administration

War–John Smith (chief clerk), ad interim, continued from preceding administration; William Eustis, Mass., Mar. 7, 1809; entered upon duties Apr. 8, 1809; served to Dec. 31, 1812; James Monroe, Va. (Secretary of State), ad interim Jan. 1, 1813; John Armstrong, N.Y., Jan. 13, 1813; entered upon duties Feb. 5, 1813

Attorney General–Caesar Augustus Rodney, Del., continued from preceding administration, resigned Dec. 5, 1811; William Pinkney, Md., Dec. 11, 1811; entered upon duties Jan. 6, 1812

Postmaster General–Gideon Granger, Conn., continued from preceding administration

Navy–Robert Smith, Md., continued from preceding administration; Charles Washington Goldsborough (chief clerk), ad interim Mar. 8, 1809; Paul Hamilton, S.C., Mar. 7, 1809; entered upon duties May 15, 1809; served to Dec. 31, 1812; Charles Washington Goldsborough (chief clerk), ad interim Jan. 7, 1813 to Jan 18, 1813; William Jones, Pa., Jan. 12, 1813; entered upon duties Jan. 19, 1813

SECOND TERM

CABINET

March 4, 1813-March 3, 1817

State–James Monroe, Va., continued from preceding administration; James Monroe (Secretary of War), ad interim Oct. 1, 1814; James Monroe, Va., Feb. 28, 1815

Treasury–Albert Gallatin, Pa., continued from preceding administration; William Jones, Pa. (Secretary of the Navy), performed the duties of the Secretary of the Treasury during the absence of Gallatin in Europe (Apr. 21, 1813 to Feb. 9, 1814); George Washington Campbell, Tenn., Feb. 9, 1814; Alexander James Dallas, Pa., Oct. 6, 1814; entered upon duties Oct. 14, 1814; William Harris Crawford, Ga., Oct. 22, 1816

War–John Armstrong, N.Y., continued from preceding administration; James Monroe, Va. (Secretary of State), ad interim Aug. 30, 1814; James Monroe, Sept. 27, 1814; entered upon duties Oct. 1, 1814; James Monroe (Secretary of State), ad interim Mar. 1, 1815; Alexander James Dallas, Pa. (Secretary of the Treasury), ad interim Mar. 14, 1815 to Aug. 8, 1815; William Harris Crawford, Ga., Aug. 1, 1815; entered upon duties Aug. 8, 1815; George Graham (chief clerk), ad interim Oct. 22, 1816, to close of administration

Attorney General–William Pinkney, Md., continued from preceding administration; Richard Rush, Pa., Feb. 10, 1814, entered upon duties Feb. 11, 1814

Postmaster General–Gideon Granger, Conn., continued from preceding administration; Return Jonathan Meigs, Jr., Ohio, Mar. 17, 1814; entered upon duties Apr. 11, 1814

Navy–William Jones, Pa., continued from preceding administration; Benjamin Homans (chief clerk), ad interim Dec. 2, 1814; Benjamin Williams Crowninshield, Mass., Dec. 19, 1814; entered upon duties Jan. 16, 1815

FIRST TERM

ELEVENTH CONGRESS

March 4, 1809-March 3, 1811

First session–May 22, 1809-June 28, 1809 (38 days)
Second session–Nov. 27, 1809-May 1, 1810 (156 days)
Third session–Dec. 3, 1810-Mar. 3, 1811 (91 days)
Special session of the Senate–Mar. 4, 1809-Mar. 7, 1809 (4 days)
Vice President–George Clinton, N.Y.
Presidents pro tempore of the Senate–Andrew Gregg, Pa., elected June 26, 1809; John Gaillard, S.C., elected Feb. 28, 1810, reelected Apr. 17, 1810; John Pope, Ky., elected Feb. 23, 1811
Secretary of the Senate–Samuel Allyne Otis, Mass.
Speaker of the House–Joseph Bradley Varnum, Mass., reelected May 22, 1809
Clerk of the House–Patrick Magruder, Md., reelected May 22, 1809

TWELFTH CONGRESS

March 4, 1811-March 3, 1813

First session–Nov. 4, 1811-July 6, 1812 (245 days)
Second session–Nov. 2, 1812-Mar. 3, 1813 (122 days)
Vice President–George Clinton, N.Y., died Apr. 20, 1812
President pro tempore of the Senate–William Harris Crawford, Ga., elected Mar. 24, 1812
Secretary of the Senate–Samuel Allyne Otis, Mass.
Speaker of the House–Henry Clay, Ky., elected Nov. 4, 1811
Clerk of the House–Patrick Magruder, Md., reelected Nov. 4, 1811

SECOND TERM

THIRTEENTH CONGRESS

March 4, 1813-March 3, 1815

First session–May 24, 1813-Aug. 2, 1813 (71 days)
Second session–Dec. 6, 1813-Apr. 18, 1814 (134 days)
Third session–Sept. 19, 1814-Mar. 3, 1815 (166 days)
Vice President–Elbridge Gerry, Mass., died Nov. 23, 1814
Presidents pro tempore of the Senate–Joseph Bradley Varnum, Mass., elected Dec. 6, 1813; John Gaillard, S.C., elected Apr. 18, 1814; Nov. 25, 1814 upon the death of Vice President Elbridge Gerry
Secretaries of the Senate–Samuel Allyne Otis, Mass., died Apr. 22, 1814; Charles Cutts, N.H., elected Oct. 11, 1814
Speakers of the House–Henry Clay, Ky., reelected May 24, 1813; resigned from Congress Jan. 19, 1814; Langdon Cheves, S.C., elected Jan. 19, 1814
Clerks of the House–Patrick Magruder, Md., reelected May 24, 1813; resigned Jan. 28, 1815; Thomas Dougherty, Ky., elected Jan. 30, 1815

FOURTEENTH CONGRESS

March 4, 1815-March 3, 1817

First session–Dec. 4, 1815-Apr. 30, 1816 (148 days)
Second session–Dec. 2, 1816-Mar. 3, 1817 (92 days)
Vice President–Elbridge Gerry died during session of preceding Congress
President pro tempore of the Senate–John Gaillard, S.C.
Secretary of the Senate–Charles Cutts, N.H.
Speaker of the House–Henry Clay, Ky., elected Dec. 4, 1815
Clerk of the House–Thomas Dougherty, Ky., reelected Dec. 4, 1815

APPOINTMENTS TO THE SUPREME COURT

Associate Justices
Joseph Story, Mass., Nov. 18, 1811
Gabriel Duvall, Md., Nov. 18, 1811

ADMINISTRATION — IMPORTANT DATES

Sept. 30, 1809, General W. H. Harrison negotiated treaty with Indians for three million acres

1810-1811, British and French naval blockades during Napoleonic wars continued to harass American shipping

Oct. 1, 1811, arrival in New Orleans, La., of first steamboat to travel from Pittsburgh, Pa., to New Orleans

Nov. 7, 1811, General W. H. Harrison defeated Indian attackers at battle of Tippecanoe

Mar. 4, 1812, first war bond issue authorized

Apr. 8, 1812, Louisiana admitted as the 18th state

Apr. 20, 1812, death of George Clinton, first Vice President to die in office

June 4, 1812, Missouri Territory organized

June 18, 1812, war declared against Great Britain

June 30, 1812, first interest-bearing treasury notes authorized

Aug. 16, 1812, without firing a shot, General William Hull surrendered Detroit and Michigan Territory to the British under General Brock

Aug. 19, 1812, *Constitution,* under Captain Isaac Hull, defeated and burned the British *Guerrière* off Nova Scotia

Sept. 4, 1812, Captain Zachary Taylor defended Fort Harrison against Indian attack

Oct. 25, 1812, *United States,* under Captain Decatur, defeated the *Macedonian.*

Mar. 25, 1813, *Essex,* on cruise around Cape Horn, engaged in first U.S. naval encounter in the Pacific Ocean

June 1, 1813, Commander James Lawrence fatally wounded in combat between the *Chesapeake* and the British warship *Shannon*

Sept. 10, 1813, Oliver Hazard Perry's naval victory on Lake Erie

Aug. 25, 1814, British captured Washington, D.C.

Sept. 11, 1814, defeat of British on Lake Champlain

Sept. 13, 1814, "Star Spangled Banner" composed by Francis Scott Key as he watched the British attack on Fort McHenry at Baltimore

Dec. 24, 1814, peace treaty signed with Great Britain

1815, treaties with Algiers, Tripoli, and Tunis

Jan. 8, 1815, battle of New Orleans

Jan. 30, 1815, Thomas Jefferson's library purchased for Library of Congress

July 4, 1815, cornerstone of first monument to George Washington laid at Baltimore, Md.

1816, public debt of the United States exceeded $1 million for the first time

Dec. 11, 1816, Indiana admitted as the 19th state

Feb. 5, 1817, first gas light company incorporated, Baltimore, Md.

IMPORTANT DATES IN HIS LIFE

1763-1767, attended Donald Robertson's school, King and Queen County, Va.

1767-1768, private instruction from the Reverend Thomas Martin

1769-1772, student at Princeton (graduated 1771); one-year post-graduate course

17—, admitted to the bar
1772-1774, in ill-health, continued studies at home
Dec. 1774, member of "Committee of Safety"
May 6, 1776, delegate to Williamsburg convention which declared for independence and set up state government
1776, drafted Virginia guarantee of religious liberty
1776-1777, member of Virginia legislature
1777, elected to Virginia State Council
Jan 14, 1778, member of executive council to direct Virginia's activities in the Revolution
Dec. 14, 1779, elected by Virginia Legislature to Continental Congress
Mar. 20, 1780-Feb. 25, 1783, member of Continental Congress
1784-1786, member of Virginia legislature
1786-1788, member of Continental Congress
Feb.-Apr. 1787, attended Congress at New York
May 2, 1787, left for Federal Convention at Philadelphia
June 2, 1788, member of Virginia Ratification Convention
Mar. 4, 1789-Mar. 3, 1797, U.S. House of Representatives (from Virginia)
1794, declined Washington's invitation to join mission to France and position of Secretary of State
May 2, 1801-Mar. 3, 1809, Secretary of State under Jefferson
Mar. 4, 1809-Mar. 3, 1813, President (1st term)
Mar. 4, 1813-Mar. 3, 1817, President (2nd term)
1817, retired to estate at Montpelier, Va.
1826, Rector, University of Virginia
1829, delegate to Virginia Constitutional Convention

JAMES MADISON

_____was the third President born in Virginia.
_____was the third President whose mother was alive when he was inaugurated.
_____was the third President to marry a widow.
_____was the first President who had been a Congressman
_____was the first President regularly to wear trousers instead of knee breeches.
_____was the last surviving signer of the Constitution.

MADISON'S VICE PRESIDENTS

FIRST TERM

Vice President–George Clinton (4th V.P.)
Date of birth–July 26, 1739
Birthplace–Little Britain, N.Y.
Political party–Democratic-Republican
State represented–New York
Term of office–Mar. 4, 1809-Apr. 20, 1812
Age at inauguration–69 years, 221 days
Date of death–Apr. 20, 1812 (died in office)

Age at death–72 years, 268 days
Place of death–Washington, D.C.
Burial place–Kingston, N.Y.

For additional data on Clinton see Thomas Jefferson, 3rd President
—Jefferson's Vice Presidents.

SECOND TERM

Vice President–Elbridge Gerry (5th V.P.)
Date of birth–July 17, 1744
Birthplace–Marblehead, Mass.
Political party–Democratic-Republican
State represented–Massachusetts
Term of office–Mar. 4, 1813-Nov. 23, 1814
Age at inauguration–68 years, 230 days
Date of death–Nov. 23, 1814 (died in office)
Age at death–70 years, 129 days
Place of death–Washington, D.C.
Burial place–Washington, D.C.

Additional Data on Gerry

1762, graduated from Harvard College, Cambridge, Mass.
1772-1775, colonial House of Representatives
1776-1781, member of Continental Congress
1776, signer of Declaration of Independence
1782-1785, member of Continental Congress
1787, delegate to Constitutional Convention at Philadelphia
Mar. 4, 1789-Mar. 3, 1793, U.S. House of Representatives (from Massachusetts)
1797, diplomatic mission to France with Marshall and Pinckney
1801, unsuccessful candidate for governor of Massachusetts
1810-1811, governor of Massachusetts
1812, unsuccessful candidate for reelection as governor

ADDITIONAL DATA ON MADISON

FIRST INAUGURATION

James Madison took the oath of office on Saturday, March 4, 1809.
It was administered by Chief Justice John Marshall in the Chamber
of the House of Representatives. Madison was the first President
whose complete costume was made in the United States. He wore
a jacket of oxford cloth which came from Hartford, Conn., and merino
wool breeches fashioned from cloth made at the farm of Chancellor
Robert R. Livingston of New York. He wore silk stockings and black
shoes which were made in Massachusetts.

The inaugural ball, held at Long's Hotel on Capitol Hill, was the
first one at Washington, D.C. Dancing started at 7 P.M.

CONSCIENCE FUND ESTABLISHED

In 1811, during Madison's administration, the "Conscience Fund"
was started by an unknown person who sent an anonymous letter
containing five dollars, since he had, he claimed, defrauded the gov-

ernment of that sum. Other deposits received that year increased the total to $250. No further deposits were received until 1827 when $6 was forwarded anonymously. For statistical and accounting purposes, the funds are listed by the government as "miscellaneous receipts."

WHITE HOUSE WEDDING

The first wedding in the White House took place March 29, 1812, when Mrs. Lucy Payne Washington, a sister of Mrs. James Madison and the widow of George Steptoe Washington, was married to Justice Thomas Todd of the United States Supreme Court.

SECOND INAUGURATION

James Madison took his second oath of office on Thursday, March 4, 1813. It was administered by Chief Justice John Marshall in the Chamber of the House of Representatives. The inaugural ball was held at Long's Hotel.

JEWISH DIPLOMATIC REPRESENTATIVE APPOINTED

During James Madison's administration, Mordecai Manuel Noah, a Jew, was appointed United States Consul with diplomatic powers to Tunis. He served from 1813 to 1816 and was the first Jewish diplomatic representative of the United States.

MADISON AT SCENE OF BATTLE

President James Madison was the first President to face enemy gunfire while in office and the first and only President to exercise actively his authority as commander-in-chief.

On August 19, 1814, General Robert Ross, in command of British regulars, and Admiral George Cockburn, commanding the Marines, landed at Benedict, Md., on the Patuxent River. They started a forty-mile march to Washington, D.C. Five days later, at Bladensburg, Md., they encountered and routed the militia and marines under General William Henry Winder, who fled to Georgetown after a losing battle. President James Madison on August 25 assumed command of Commodore Joshua Barney's battery, known as "Barney's Battery," stationed a half-mile north of Bladensburg, Md., to forestall the capture of Washington by the British.

MADISON FLED FROM THE CAPITAL

On August 24, 1814, the British entered Washington, D.C., and found the officials of the government had fled. On August 24 and 25 the British burned the Capitol, the President's House, and numerous other buildings. The damage might have been more extensive had the British known how completely the defenders had been routed. Unable to understand the lack of defense at the Capitol, the British officers feared that they were being drawn too far away from their ships and supplies and were walking into a trap. Afraid of being cut off from their base, they returned, thus ending the holocaust.

MADISON MOVED TO OCTAGON HOUSE

After the British had burned the White House in 1814, Colonel John

Tayloe dispatched a courier offering President Madison the use of his home, the Octagon House. For more than a year, Madison made it his official residence. The building, known as the Octagon House, was not octagon-shaped. It had two rectangular wings connected by a circular tower.

MADISON'S VICE PRESIDENTS DIED IN OFFICE

James Madison was the only President whose administration suffered the death of two Vice Presidents.

George Clinton, who had served four years during the second term of Thomas Jefferson and three years and forty-seven days during the first term of James Madison, died in Washington, D.C., on April 20, 1812, at the age of 72.

On May 12, 1812, a Democratic-Republican caucus decided upon Senator John Langdon of New Hampshire as the party's vice presidential nominee. He received 64 of the 82 votes cast, but refused to accept the nomination because of his age (71). A second caucus nominated Elbridge Gerry of Massachusetts, who received 74 of the 77 votes cast. Gerry, who was over 68 and thus only 3 years younger than Langdon, was elected Vice President to serve during Madison's second term, 1813-1817. But he did not live to complete the term. He died on November 23, 1814, at the age of 70, having served one year and 264 days. (Langdon, who died September 18, 1819, at the age of 78, survived Gerry by almost five years.)

ONLY ONE VICE PRESIDENT BURIED AT WASHINGTON, D.C.

The only Vice President buried at Washington, D.C., was Elbridge Gerry. He was buried in the Washington Parish Burial Ground, better known as the Congressional Cemetery, comprising about thirty acres of ground on the north bank of the Anacostia River. He died November 23, 1814, at Washington, D.C.

THE GERRYMANDER

The only Vice President whose name has been adopted as part of the English language was Elbridge Gerry. On February 11, 1812, when he was the governor of the Commonwealth of Massachusetts, he signed an act which rearranged the senatorial districts so that the Federalists were massed together in one or two districts, leaving the other districts controlled by a safe majority of Democratic-Republicans.

It is claimed that when Gilbert Stuart, the painter, saw a colored map of the redistricting hanging in the Boston office of Benjamin Russell, Federalist editor of the *Columbian Centinel,* he added a few strokes and said, "This will do for a salamander." Russell said, "Call it a gerrymander." Thus the word was born which became a Federalist war cry. Ironically, however, Governor Gerry had not sponsored the bill and had signed it reluctantly.

THE FIRST LADY

When James Madison assumed the presidency in 1809, the duties of first lady fell upon his wife, Dolley, whose experience as hostess at White House social functions during Jefferson's administration had prepared her well for the task.

MRS. MADISON'S ACCOUNT OF THE BRITISH INVASION OF WASHINGTON

One of the most anxious periods in the life of a first lady is described by Dolley Madison in a letter to her sister:

Tuesday, August 23, 1814

Dear Sister:

My husband left me yesterday to join General Winder. He enquired anxiously whether I had the courage or firmness to remain in the President's House until his return, on the morrow, or succeeding day, and on my assurance that I had no fear but for him and the success of our army, he left me, beseeching me to take care of myself and of the Cabinet papers, public and private.

I have since received two dispatches from him, written with a pencil; the last is alarming, because he desires that I should be ready at a moment's warning, to enter my carriage and leave the city; that the enemy seemed stronger than had been reported, and that it might happen that they would reach the city with intention to destroy it. . . . I am accordingly ready; I have pressed as many Cabinet papers into trunks as to fill one carriage; our private property must be sacrificed, as it is impossible to procure wagons for its transportation. I am determined not to go myself, until I see Mr. Madison safe, and he can accompany me—as I hear of much hostility toward him. . . . Disaffection stalks around us. My friends and acquaintances are all gone, even Colonel C. with his hundred men, who were stationed as a guard in this enclosure. . . . French John (a faithful domestic) with his usual activity and resolution offers to spike the cannon at the gate, and lay a train of powder which would blow up the British, should they enter the house. To the last proposition, I positively objected, without being able, however, to make him understand why all advantages in war may not be taken.

Wednesday morning, twelve o'clock—Since sunrise, I have been turning my spyglass in every direction and watching with unwearied anxiety, hoping to discover the approach of my dear husband and his friends; but, alas, I can descry only groups of military wandering in all directions, as if there was a lack of arms, or of spirits, to fight for their own firesides.

Three o'clock. Will you believe it, my sister, we have had a battle, or a skirmish, near Bladensburg, and I am still here within sound of the cannon! Mr. Madison comes not; may God protect him! Two messengers, covered with dust, come to bid me fly; but I wait for him. . . . At this late hour a wagon has been procured; I have filled it with the plate and most valuable portable articles belonging to the house; whether it will reach its destination, the Bank of Maryland, or fall into the hands of British soldiery, events must determine. Our kind friend, Mr. Carroll, has come to hasten my departure, and is in a very bad humor with me because I insist on waiting until the large picture of General Washington is secured: and it requires to be unscrewed from the wall. This process was found too tedious for these perilous moments: I have ordered the frame to be broken and the canvas taken out; it is done, and the precious portrait placed in the hands of two gentlemen of New York for safe-keeping. And now, dear sister, I must leave this house or the retreating army will make me a prisoner in it, by filling up the road I am directed to take. When I shall again write to you, or where I shall be tomorrow, I cannot tell!

MADISON VOTED SEAT IN HOUSE OF REPRESENTATIVES

Dolley Madison was observed seated in the visitors' gallery of the House of Representatives. Romulus Saunders, a representative from North Carolina, introduced a resolution to grant 'Mrs. Madison a seat within the House. The measure was immediately and unanimously passed.

The widow of President Madison wrote a letter dated January 9, 1844, which was read in the House the following day. She stated:

Permit me to thank you, gentlemen, as the Committee on the part of the House of Representatives, for the great gratification you have this day conferred on me, by the delivery of the favor from that honorable body allowing me a seat within its hall. I shall be ever proud to recollect it, as a token of their remembrance, collectively and individually, of one who had gone before us.

JAMES MONROE
5th PRESIDENT

Born–Apr. 28, 1758
Birthplace–Westmoreland County, Va.
College attended–College of William and Mary, Williamsburg, Va.
Date of graduation–1776
Religion–Episcopalian
Ancestry–Scotch
Occupation–Lawyer
Date and place of marriage–Feb. 16, 1786, New York, N. Y.
Age at marriage–27 years, 294 days
Years married–44 years, 219 days
Political Party–Democratic-Republican
State represented–Virginia
Term of office–Mar. 4, 1817-Mar. 3, 1825
Term served–8 years
Administration–8th, 9th
Congresses–15th, 16th, 17th, 18th
Age at inauguration–58 years, 310 days
Lived after term–6 years, 122 days
Occupation after term–Writer
Date of death–July 4, 1831
Age at death–73 years, 67 days
Place of death–New York, N.Y.
Burial place–Marble Cemetery, New York, N.Y.; removed in 1858 to Hollywood Cemetery, Richmond, Va.

PARENTS

Father–Spence Monroe
Married–1752
Occupation–Circuit judge, farmer
Died–1774
Mother–Elizabeth Jones Monroe

BROTHERS AND SISTERS

James Monroe was the oldest of five children.

Children of Spence Monroe and Elizabeth Jones Monroe

James Monroe, b. Apr. 28, 1758, d. July 4, 1831
Andrew Monroe, d. 1826
Spence Monroe
Joseph Jones Monroe, b. 1764, d. Aug. 5, 1824
Elizabeth Monroe

CHILDREN

Eliza Kortright Monroe, b. Dec. 1786; m. Oct. 17, 1808, George Hay; d. 1835 (?)
——Monroe (son), b. May 1799; d. Sept 28, 1801
Maria Hester Monroe, b. 1803; m. Mar. 9, 1820, Samuel Lawrence Gouverneur in White House, Washington D.C.; d. 1850, Oak Hill, Va.

MRS. JAMES MONROE

Name–Elizabeth Kortright Monroe
Date of birth–June 30, 1768
Birthplace–New York, N.Y.
Age at marriage–17 years, 231 days
Children–2 daughters, 1 son
Mother–Hannah Aspinwall Kortright
Father–Captain Lawrence Kortright
His occupation–Former officer in British Army
Date of death–Sept. 23, 1830
Age at death–62 years, 85 days
Place of death–Oak Hill, Va.

For additional data see the end of this section and also specific subject headings in the index.

Burial place–Richmond, Va. **Years the President survived her**–
Years younger than the Pres-   284 days
  ident–10 years, 63 days

THE ELECTION OF 1816

After Madison had served two full terms, the Democratic-Republican party was divided between William Harris Crawford
and James Monroe, the latter securing the party endorsement by a
vote of 65 to 54. James Monroe's running mate was Daniel D. Tompkins of New York. Burr and other extremists denounced the caucus
system. They declared that Virginia was trying to dominate the presidential succession.

The Federalists made no nominations but supported Rufus King
of New York for the presidency. Their electoral vote for the vice presidency was split among four candidates—John Eager Howard of Maryland, James Ross of Pennsylvania, John Marshall of Virginia, and
Robert Goodloe Harper of Maryland.

ELECTORAL VOTES (217—19 states)

Monroe received 84.33 per cent (183 votes—16 states) as follows:
Ga. 8; Ind. 3; Ky. 12; La. 3; Md. 8; N.H. 8; N.J. 8; N.Y. 29; N.C.
15; Ohio 8; Pa. 25; R.I. 4; S.C. 11; Tenn. 8; Vt. 8; Va. 25.

King received 15.67 per cent (34 votes—3 states) as follows: Conn.
9; Del. 3; Mass. 22.

For the vice presidency Tompkins received 183 votes.

The Federalist candidates for the vice presidency received the following votes:

Howard—Mass. 22
Ross—Conn. 5 (of the 9 votes)
Marshall—Conn. 4 (of the 9 votes)
Harper—Del. 3

THE ELECTION OF 1820

James Monroe was so popular during his first term, 1817-1821, that
an "era of good feeling" swept the nation. All of the 232 electors,
with only one exception, voted for Monroe for a second term. William
Plumer, Sr., of New Hampshire, one of the electors, cast his vote
for John Quincy Adams in protest against a unanimous election. He
was not opposed to Monroe but felt that no one other than George
Washington should have the honor of a unanimous election. (Some
sources, however, maintain that he opposed the Virginia dynasty of
Presidents.)

The electoral vote for Vice President was split among five candi-
dates: Daniel D. Tompkins of New York (seeking reelection), Richard
Stockton of New Jersey, Daniel Rodney of Delaware, Robert Goodloe
Harper of Maryland, and Richard Rush of Pennsylvania.

The number of electors chosen was 235, but three electors died and
their respective states—Mississippi, Pennsylvania, and Tennessee—
did not replace them and as a result failed to cast full electoral votes
for President and Vice President.

ELECTORAL VOTES (235—24 states)

Monroe received 99.57 per cent (231 votes—24 states) as follows: Ala. 3; Conn. 9; Del. 4; Ga. 8; Ill. 3; Ind. 3; Ky. 12; La. 3; Me. 9; Md. 11; Mass 15; Miss. 2; Mo. 3; N.H. 7 (of the 8 votes); N.J. 8; N.Y. 29; N.C. 15; Ohio 8; Pa. 24; R.I. 4; S.C. 11; Tenn. 7; Vt. 8; Va. 25.

Adams received .43 per cent (1 vote—of the 9 N.H. votes).

For the vice presidency Tompkins received 218 votes as follows: Ala. 3; Conn. 9; Ga. 8; Ill. 3; Ind. 3; Ky. 12; La. 3; Me. 9; Md. 10 (of the 11 votes); Mass. 7 (of the 15 votes); Miss. 2; Mo. 3; N.H. 7 (of the 8 votes); N.J. 8; N.Y. 29; N.C. 15; Ohio 8; Pa. 24; R.I. 4; S.C. 11; Tenn. 7; Vt. 8; Va. 25.

The other candidates for the vice presidency received the following votes:

Stockton—Mass. 8 (of the 15 votes)
Rodney—Del. 4
Harper—Md. 1 (of the 11 votes)
Rush—N.H. 1 (of the 8 votes)

FIRST TERM

CABINET

March 4, 1817-March 3, 1821

State—John Graham (chief clerk), ad interim Mar. 4, 1817; Richard Rush, Pa. (Attorney General), ad interim Mar. 10, 1817; John Quincy Adams, Mass., Mar. 5, 1817; entered upon duties Sept. 22, 1817

Treasury—William Harris Crawford, Ga., recommissioned Mar. 5, 1817

War—George Graham (chief clerk), ad interim Mar. 4, 1817; John Caldwell Calhoun, S.C., Oct. 8, 1817; entered upon duties Dec. 10, 1817

Attorney General—Richard Rush, Pa., continued from preceding administration to Oct. 30, 1817; William Wirt, Va., Nov. 13, 1817; entered upon duties Nov. 15, 1817

Postmaster General—Return Jonathan Meigs, Jr., Ohio, continued from preceding administration

Navy—Benjamin Williams Crowninshield, Mass., continued from preceding administration; John Caldwell Calhoun (Secretary of War), ad interim Oct. 1, 1818; Smith Thompson, N.Y., Nov. 9, 1818; entered upon duties Jan. 1, 1819

SECOND TERM

CABINET

March 4, 1821-March 3, 1825

State—John Quincy Adams, Mass., continued from preceding administration

Treasury—William Harris Crawford, Ga., continued from preceding administration

War—John Caldwell Calhoun, S.C., continued from preceding administration

Attorney General–William Wirt, Va., continued from preceding administration

Postmaster General–Return Jonathan Meigs, Jr., Ohio, continued from preceding administration; John McLean, Ohio, commissioned June 26, 1823, commission to take effect July 1, 1823

Navy–Smith Thompson, N.Y., continued from preceding administration; John Rodgers (Commodore, United States Navy and President of the Board of Navy Commissioners) ad interim Sept. 1, 1823; Samuel Lewis Southard, N.J., Sept. 16, 1823

FIRST TERM
FIFTEENTH CONGRESS

March 4, 1817-March 3, 1819

First session–Dec. 1, 1817-Apr. 20, 1818 (141 days)
Second session–Nov. 16, 1818-Mar. 3, 1819 (108 days)
Special session of the Senate–Mar. 4, 1817 (one day only)
Vice President–Daniel D. Tompkins, N.Y.
Presidents pro tempore of the Senate–John Gaillard, S.C., elected Mar. 6, 1817, special session; Mar. 31, 1818; James Barbour, Va., elected Feb. 15, 1819
Secretary of the Senate–Charles Cutts, N.H.
Speaker of the House–Henry Clay, Ky., reelected Dec. 1, 1817
Clerk of the House–Thomas Dougherty, Ky., reelected Dec. 1, 1817

SIXTEENTH CONGRESS
March 4, 1819-March 3, 1821

First session–Dec. 6, 1819-May 15, 1820 (162 days)
Second session–Nov. 13, 1820-Mar. 3, 1821 (111 days)
Vice President–Daniel D. Tompkins, N.Y.
Presidents pro tempore of the Senate–James Barbour, Va., John Gaillard, S.C., elected January 25, 1820
Secretary of the Senate–Charles Cutts, N.H.
Speakers of the House–Henry Clay, Ky., reelected December 6, 1819; resigned as Speaker Oct. 28, 1820; John W. Taylor, N.Y., elected Nov. 15, 1820
Clerk of the House–Thomas Dougherty, Ky., reelected Dec. 6, 1819

SECOND TERM
SEVENTEENTH CONGRESS

March 4, 1821-March 3, 1823

First session–Dec. 3, 1821 May 8, 1822 (157 days)
Second session–Dec. 2, 1822-Mar. 3, 1823 (92 days)
Vice President–Daniel D. Tompkins, N.Y.
President pro tempore of the Senate–John Gaillard, S.C., elected Feb. 1, 1822; Feb. 19, 1823
Secretary of the Senate–Charles Cutts, N.H.
Speaker of the House–Philip Pendleton Barbour, Va., elected Dec. 4, 1821
Clerks of the House–Thomas Dougherty, Ky., reelected Dec. 4, 1821;

died 1822; Matthew St. Clair Clarke, Pa., elected December 3, 1822

EIGHTEENTH CONGRESS
March 4, 1823-March 3, 1825

First session–Dec. 1, 1823-May 27, 1824 (178 days)
Second session–Dec. 6, 1824-Mar. 3, 1825 (88 days)
Vice President–Daniel D. Tompkins, N.Y.
President pro tempore of the Senate–John Gaillard, S.C., elected May 21, 1824
Secretary of the Senate–Charles Cutts, N.H.
Speaker of the House–Henry Clay, Ky., elected Dec. 1, 1823
Clerk of the House–Matthew St. Clair Clarke, Pa., reelected Dec. 1, 1823

APPOINTMENT TO THE SUPREME COURT

Associate Justice
Smith Thompson, N.Y., Sept. 1, 1823

ADMINISTRATION — IMPORTANT DATES

July 4, 1817, Erie Canal construction began

Nov. 1817, first Seminole war bagan

Dec. 10, 1817, Mississippi admitted as the 20th state

Apr. 4, 1818, legislation established flag of the United States

May 28, 1818, Andrew Jackson captured Pensacola, Fla.

Oct. 19, 1818, treaty with Chickasaw Indians

Dec. 3, 1818, Illinois admitted as the 21st state

1819, financial panic

1819, McCulloch *vs.* Maryland and Dartmouth College cases—Supreme Court affirmed its power to set aside acts of state legislatures if unconstitutional

Feb. 22, 1819, Florida purchased from Spain

May 22, 1819, *Savannah,* first American steamship to cross the Atlantic Ocean, left Savannah, Ga.

Dec. 14, 1819, Alabama admitted as the 22nd state

Mar. 3, 1820, Missouri Compromise—Maine admitted as a separate state; Missouri admitted as slave state; slavery prohibited in Louisiana Purchase north of 36° 30'

Mar. 15, 1820, Maine admitted as the 23rd state

May 1820, first high school opened, Boston, Mass.

May 31, 1821, first Catholic cathedral dedicated, Baltimore, Md.

Aug. 10, 1821, Missouri admitted as the 24th state

Dec. 2, 1823, Monroe Doctrine proclaimed

1824, Clay's "American system" proposed—higher protective tariff and internal improvements in transportation

1824, Gibbons *vs.* Ogden case—Supreme Court declared a state law unconstitutional

Aug. 15, 1824, Lafayette landed in United States to begin tour

IMPORTANT DATES IN HIS LIFE

17—, pursued classical studies

17—, left College of William and Mary to join the army

Sept. 28, 1775, second lieutenant, Third Virginia Regiment, under General Hugh Mercer

June 24, 1776, first lieutenant

Sept. 16, 1776, wounded at Battle of Harlem Heights, N.Y.

Oct. 28, 1776, fought at White Plains, N.Y.

Dec. 26, 1776, wounded at Trenton, N.J.; promoted to rank of captain by General George Washington for "bravery under fire"

Sept. 11, 1777, fought at Brandywine, Pa.

Oct. 4, 1777, fought at Germantown, Pa.

Nov. 20, 1777, volunteer aide with rank of major on staff of General Lord Stirling

June 28, 1778, fought at Monmouth, N.J.

1780, military commissioner for Virginia, with rank of lieutenant colonel (appointed by Governor Thomas Jefferson)

Dec. 20, 1780, resigned

1780, elected to Virginia Legislature

1781-1783, on Governor Jefferson's council

Oct. 21, 1782, member of Virginia House of Delegates

Dec. 13, 1783-1786, member of Continental Congress

17—, resumed study of law in office of Thomas Jefferson

Oct. 1786, admitted to the bar of the Courts of Appeal and Chancery; practiced at Fredericksburg, Va.

1786, member of Virginia Assembly

June 2, 1788, delegate to Virginia state convention to ratify the Federal Constitution

Nov. 9, 1790-May 27, 1794, member of U.S. Senate (from Virginia); sworn in Dec. 6, 1790

May 28, 1794-Dec. 30, 1796, minister plenipotentiary to France (appointed by Washington)

1799-1803, governor of Virginia

Jan. 12-July 12, 1803, minister plenipotentiary to France (appointed by Jefferson)

Apr. 18, 1803, minister plenipotentiary to England

Feb. 14, 1804, headed diplomatic mission to Spain

May 21, 1805, left Spanish court for London

May 12, 1806, commissioner to negotiate treaty with England

1808, returned to the U.S.

1810, member of Virginia Assembly

1811, governor of Virginia

Apr. 6, 1811-Mar. 3, 1817, Secretary of State under Madison

Aug. 30, 1814, Secretary of War, ad interim

Sept. 27, 1814, Secretary of War

Mar. 1, 1815, Secretary of War, ad interim

Mar. 4, 1817-Mar. 3, 1821, President (1st term)

Mar. 4, 1821-Mar. 3, 1825, President (2nd term)

Mar. 1825, retired to his farm at Loudon County, Va.

1826, regent, University of Virginia, Charlottesville

Oct. 5, 1829, chairman of Virginia Constitutional Convention, Richmond

1831, moved to New York City

JAMES MONROE

____was the fourth President born in Virginia.

____was the first President who was inaugurated on March 5 (March 4 was a Sunday).

____was the first President who had been a senator.

____was the last of the Virginia regime of Presidents (Washington, Jefferson, Madison, Monroe).

____was the first President inaugurated outdoors.

____was the first President whose daughter was married in the White House.

MONROE'S VICE PRESIDENT

Vice President–Daniel D. Tompkins (6th V.P.)
Date of birth–June 21, 1774
Birthplace–Fox Meadows (now Scarsdale), N.Y.
Political party–Democratic-Republican
State represented–New York
Term of office–Mar. 4, 1817–Mar. 3, 1825
Age at inauguration–42 years, 256 days
Occupation after term–Lawyer
Date of death–June 11, 1825
Age at death–50 years, 355 days
Place of death–Tompkinsville, Staten Island, N.Y.
Burial place–New York City

Additional Data on Tompkins

1795, graduated from Columbia College
1797, admitted to bar; practiced in New York City
1801, delegate to New York State Constitutional Convention
1803, member of New York State Assembly
1804, elected to U.S. House of Representatives, but resigned before commencement of term to accept appointment as associate justice of New York Supreme Court
1807, resigned from Supreme Court
1807-1817, governor of New York
1821, president of New York State Constitutional Convention

ADDITIONAL DATA ON MONROE

FIRST INAUGURATION

James Monroe took his oath of office on Tuesday, March 4, 1817. It was administered by Chief Justice John Marshall on the platform erected on the east portico of the Capitol. As the result of a controversy between the Senate and the House of Representatives over the distribution of seats, it was decided that the inaugural be held outdoors. This was the first outdoor inaugural.

Monroe rode to the Capitol accompanied by an escort of citizens. After the ceremonies, he went to the Octagon House, at Eighteenth Street and New York Avenue, where he resided as the White House had been burned by the British during Madison's administration. He was accompanied by an escort of Marines, Georgia riflemen, artillerymen and two companies of infantry from Alexandria, Va.

In the evening a reception was held at Davis' Hotel.

MONROE RODE ON STEAMBOAT

The first President to ride on a steamboat was James Monroe, who sailed on the *Savannah* on May 11, 1819, on an all-day excursion to Tybee Light from Savannah, Ga. The *Savannah* was accompanied by the steamboat *Alatamaha* and two barges. Sails were used for part of the trip. The presidential party included John Caldwell Calhoun, Secretary of War; Major General Edmund Pendleton Gaines, Monroe's private secretary; General David Bradie Mitchell; Major General Floyd; General Benjamin Huger of South Carolina; General John M'Intosh; and Colonel James Marshall.

SECOND INAUGURATION

As March 4, 1821, fell on a Sunday, James Monroe did not take office until Monday, March 5. Because of snow and rain, Monroe took his oath of office in the Chamber of the Hall of Representatives. The oath was administered to him by Chief Justice John Marshall. This was the first postponement of an inauguration.

The Marine Band played, introducing a new trend followed in all later inaugurations.

SENATOR ELECTED PRESIDENT

James Monroe was the first senator to become President of the United States. He served as senator from Virginia from November 9, 1790, to May 27, 1794, filling the vacancy caused by the death of William Grayson on March 12, 1790.

THE MONROE DOCTRINE

Extract from President Monroe's Annual Message, Washington, D.C., December 2, 1823:

The citizens of the United States cherish sentiments the most friendly in favor of the liberty and happiness of their fellow-men on that side of the Atlantic. In the wars of the European powers, in matters relating to themselves, we have never taken any part, nor does it comport with our policy to do so. It is only when our rights are invaded, or seriously menaced, that we resent injuries or make preparations for our defence. With the movements in the hemisphere, we are, of necessity, more immediately connected, and by causes which must be obvious to all enlightened and impartial observers. The political system of the allied powers is essentially different, in this respect, from that of America. This difference proceeds from that which exists in their respective Governments. And to the defence of our own, which has been achieved by the loss of so much blood and treasure, and matured by the wisdom of their most enlightened citizens, and under which we have enjoyed unexampled felicity, this whole nation is devoted. . . .

We owe it, therefore, to candor and to the amicable relations existing between the United States and those powers, to declare, that we should consider any attempt on their part to extend their system to any portion of this hemisphere, as dangerous to our peace and safety.

With the existing colonies or dependencies of any European power, we have not interfered, and shall not interfere. But, with the Governments who have declared their independence, and maintained it, and whose independence we have, on great consideration, and on just principles, acknowledged, we could not view any interposition for the purpose of oppressing them, or controlling, in any other manner, their destiny, by any European power, in any other light than as the manifestation of an unfriendly dispositon towards the Unites States.

In the war between those new Governments and Spain, we declared our neutrality at the time of their recognition, and to this we have adhered, and shall continue to adhere, provided no change shall occur, which, in the judgement of the competent authorities of this Government, shall make a corresponding change on the part of the United States, indispensable to their security.

AFRICA HONORED MONROE

Upper Guinea, West Africa, was acquired by the American Colonization Society, founded in 1817 for the purpose of colonizing free Negroes from the United States. On August 15, 1824, the name of the country was changed to Liberia and its capital city was named Monrovia in honor of President James Monroe.

THE FIRST LADY

Mrs. Monroe had accompanied her husband to his posts in England and France and was familiar with political life. She became the first lady in 1817 and was an amiable hostess. Her health failed in later years, however, and she secluded herself from the throng. She discontinued the custom of returning calls.

JOHN QUINCY ADAMS
6th PRESIDENT

Born–July 11, 1767
Birthplace–Braintree (now Quincy), Mass.
College attended–Harvard College, Cambridge, Mass.
Date of graduation–July 18, 1787, Bachelor or Arts
Religion–Unitarian
Ancestry–English
Occupation–Lawyer
Date and place of marriage–July 26, 1797, London, England
Age at marriage–30 years, 15 days
Years married–50 years, 212 days
Political party–Democratic-Republican
State represented–Massachusetts
Term of office–Mar. 4, 1825-Mar. 3, 1829
Term served–4 years
Administration–10th
Congresses–19th, 20th
Age at inauguration–57 years, 236 days
Lived after term–18 years, 356 days
Occupation after term–Congressman
Date of death–Feb. 23, 1848
Age at death–80 years, 227 days
Place of death–Washington, D.C.
Burial place–First Unitarian Church, Quincy, Mass.

PARENTS

Father–John Adams
Born–Oct. 30, 1735, Braintree, Mass.
Married–Oct. 25, 1764
Occupation–Lawyer, President of the United States

Died–July 4, 1826, Quincy, Mass.
Age at death–90 years, 247 days
Mother–Abigail Smith Adams
Born–Nov. 11, 1744
Died–Oct. 28, 1818, Quincy, Mass.
Age at death–73 years, 351 days

BROTHERS AND SISTERS

John Quincy Adams was the second child in a family of five.

Children of John Adams and Abigail Smith Adams

Abigail Adams, b. July 14, 1765, d. Aug. 15, 1813

John Quincy Adams, b. July 11, 1767, d. Feb. 23, 1848

Susanna Adams, b. Dec. 28, 1768, d. Feb. 4, 1770

Charles Adams, b. May 29, 1770, d. Nov. 30, 1800

Thomas Boylston Adams, b. Sept. 15, 1772, d. Mar. 12, 1832

CHILDREN

George Washington Adams, b. April 13, 1801, Berlin, Germany; d. Apr. 30, 1829, on steamer in Long Island Sound, lost at sea

John Adams, b. July 4, 1803, Boston, Mass.; m. Feb. 25, 1828, Mary Catherine Hellen in the White House, Washington, D.C., d. Oct. 23, 1834, Washington, D.C.

Charles Francis Adams, b. Aug. 18, 1807, Boston, Mass.; m. Sept. 3, 1829, Abigail Brown Brooks; d. Nov. 21, 1886, Boston, Mass.

Louisa Catherine Adams, b. 1811, St. Petersburg, Russia; d. 1812

For additional data see the end of this section and also specific subject headings in the index.

MRS. JOHN QUINCY ADAMS
Name—Louisa Catherine Johnson Adams
Date of birth—Feb. 12, 1775
Birthplace—London, England
Age at marriage—22 years, 164 days
Children—3 sons, 1 daughter
Mother—Catherine Nuth Johnson
Father—Joshua Johnson

His occupation—U.S. Consul
Date of death—May 14, 1852
Age at death—77 years, 91 days
Place of death—Washington, D.C.
Burial place—Quincy, Mass.
Years younger than the President—7 years, 216 days
Years she survived the President—4 years, 80 days

THE ELECTION OF 1824

The last of the congressional caucuses met in 1824 in the chamber of the House of Representatives. William Harris Crawford of Georgia was chosen as the presidential candidate.

The selection was not popular with the various state legislatures, which asserted themselves and decided that they were no longer bound to endorse the congressional choices. The legislature of Tennessee placed Andrew Jackson in nomination on July 22, 1822, and other state legislatures proposed their choices.

The election of 1824 was a contest of individuals rather than political parties. There were four candidates—each representing a different faction of the Democratic-Republican Party.

ELECTION RESULTS, NOV. 2, 1824—PRESIDENTIAL CANDIDATES

Andrew Jackson, Tenn., 153,544
John Quincy Adams, Mass., 108,740
William Harris Crawford, Ga., 47,136
Henry Clay, Ky., 46,618

ELECTORAL VOTES (261-24 States)

Jackson received 37.93 per cent (99 votes—11 states) as follows: Ala. 5; Ill. 2 (of the 3 votes); Ind. 5; La. 3 (of the 5 votes); Md. 7 (of the 11 votes); Miss. 3; N.J. 8; N.Y. 1 (of the 36 votes); N.C. 15; Pa. 28; S.C. 11; Tenn. 11.

Adams received 32.18 per cent (84 votes—7 states) as follows: Conn 8; Del. 1 (of the 3 votes); Ill. 1 (of the 3 votes); La. 2 (of the 5 votes); Me. 9; Md. 3 (of the 11 votes); Mass. 15; N.H. 8; N.Y. 26 (of the 36 votes); R.I. 4; Vt. 7.

Crawford received 15.71 per cent (41 votes—3 states) as follows: Ga. 9; Del. 2 (of the 3 votes); Md. 1 (of the 11 votes); N.Y. 5 (of the 36 votes); Va. 24.

Clay received 14.18 per cent (37 votes—3 states) as follows: Ky. 14; Mo. 3; Ohio 16; N.Y. 4 (of the 36 votes).

As no candidate for the presidency received a majority of the electoral votes, it again devolved upon the House of Representatives to choose a President from the three leading contenders. Twenty-four tellers, one from each state, were appointed to examine the ballots. Clay's supporters threw their strength to Adams, with the result that

Adams was elected. Adams received 13 votes, Jackson 7 votes, and Crawford 4 votes.

VICE PRESIDENTIAL CANDIDATES

There were six vice presidential candidates: John Caldwell Calhoun of South Carolina, Nathan Sanford of New York, Nathaniel Macon of North Carolina, Andrew Jackson of Tennessee, Martin Van Buren of New York, and Henry Clay of Kentucky. Since one elector failed to cast his vote, the total number of votes was 260 instead of 261.

Calhoun received 182 votes as follows: Ala. 5; Del. 1 (of the 3 votes); Ill. 3; Ind. 5; Ky. 7 (of the 14 votes); La. 5; Md. 10 (of the 11 votes); Me. 9; Mass. 15; Miss. 3; N.H. 7; N.J. 8; N.Y. 29 (of the 36 votes); N.C. 15; Pa. 28; R.I. 3; S.C. 11; Tenn. 11; Vt. 7.

Sanford received 30 votes as follows: Ky. 7 (of the 14 votes); N.Y. 7 (of the 36 votes); Ohio 16.

Macon received the 24 Va. votes.

Jackson received 13 votes as follows: Conn. 8; Md. 1 (of the 11 votes); Mo. 3; N.H. 1.

Van Buren received the 9 Ga. votes.

Clay received 2 of the 3 Del. votes.

CABINET

March 4, 1825-March 3, 1829

State–Daniel Brent (chief clerk), ad interim Mar. 4, 1825; Henry Clay, Ky., Mar. 7, 1825

Treasury–Samuel Lewis Southard, N.J. (Secretary of the Navy), ad interim Mar. 7, 1825; Richard Rush, Pa., Mar. 7, 1825; entered upon duties Aug. 1, 1825

War–James Barbour, Va., Mar. 7, 1825; Samuel Lewis Southard, N.J., Secretary of the Navy, ad interim May 26, 1828; Peter Buell Porter, N.Y., May 26, 1828; entered upon duties June 21, 1828

Attorney General–William Wirt, Va., continued from preceding administration

Postmaster General–John McLean, Ohio, continued from preceding administration

Navy–Samuel Lewis Southard, N.J., continued from preceding administration

NINETEENTH CONGRESS

March 4, 1825-March 3, 1827

First session–Dec. 5, 1825-May 22, 1826 (169 days)

Second session–Dec. 4, 1826-Mar. 3, 1827 (90 days)

Special session of the Senate–Mar. 4, 1825-Mar. 9, 1825

Vice President–John Caldwell Calhoun, S.C.

Presidents pro tempore of the Senate–John Gaillard, S.C., elected Mar. 9, 1825, special session; Nathaniel Macon, N.C., elected May 20, 1826; Jan 2, 1827; and Mar. 2, 1827

Secretaries of the Senate–Charles Cutts, N.H.; Walter Lowrie, Pa., elected Dec. 12, 1825

Speaker of the House–John W. Taylor, N.Y., elected Dec. 5, 1825

Clerk of the House–Matthew St. Clair Clarke, Pa., reelected Dec. 5, 1825

TWENTIETH CONGRESS

March 4, 1827-March 3, 1829

First session–Dec. 3, 1827-May 26, 1828 (175 days)
Second session–Dec. 1, 1828-Mar. 3, 1829 (93 days)
Vice President–John Caldwell Calhoun, S.C.
President pro tempore of the Senate–Samuel Smith, Md., elected May 15, 1828
Secretary of the Senate–Walter Lowrie, Pa., reelected Dec. 10, 1827
Speaker of the House–Andrew Stevenson, Va., elected Dec. 3, 1827
Clerk of the House–Matthew St. Clair Clarke, Pa., reelected Dec. 3, 1827

APPOINTMENT TO THE SUPREME COURT

Associate Justice
Robert Trimble, Ky., May 9, 1826

ADMINISTRATION — IMPORTANT DATES

June 17, 1825, Bunker Hill Monument cornerstone laid by General Lafayette
Oct. 26, 1825, Erie Canal opened for traffic
Mar. 24, 1826, General Congress of South American States convened at Panama
July 4, 1826, John Adams and Thomas Jefferson died
1828, South Carolina Exposition on nullification of federal tariffs
July 4, 1828, construction of Baltimore and Ohio railroad begun

IMPORTANT DATES IN HIS LIFE

1778, attended school at Paris
Aug. 1779, returned to the United States
1780, made fourth trip across Atlantic
1780, attended school at Amsterdam, Holland; entered University of Leyden
July 1781, accompanied Francis Dana, minister to Russia, as his private secretary
1782, made a six-month trip alone to Sweden, Denmark, northern Germany, and France
Sept. 3, 1783, present at signing of Treaty of Paris
1785, secretary to his father, John Adams, minister to Great Britain
1785, returned to the United States
1786, entered Harvard College
1788, graduated from Harvard College; studied law in office of Theophilus Parsons
1791, admitted to the bar, practiced in Boston, Mass.
1791-17—, wrote pamphlets and articles under the pseudonyms of Publicola, Marcellus, Columbus, etc
May 30, 1794, appointed Minister to the Netherlands by George Washington

1796, minister plenipotentiary to Portugal

June 1, 1797, minister plenipotentiary to Prussia

Mar. 14, 1798, commissioned to make a commercial treaty with Sweden (mission terminated when Jefferson became President)

1801, resumed law practice, Boston, Mass.

1802, member of Massachusetts Senate

Mar. 4, 1803-June 8, 1808, U.S. Senate (from Massachusetts)

1805, professor of rhetoric and belles lettres, Harvard College

1808, resigned from Senate when Massachusetts legislature chose James Lloyd to succeed him

1809-1814, minister to Russia

1811, nominated to Supreme Court, but declined

1814, sent by President Madison to negotiate terms of peace with England (War of 1812); commissioners met at Ghent in Aug. 1814; signed Treaty of Ghent, Dec. 24, 1814

1815, Adams, Clay, and Gallatin negotiated a commercial treaty with England (completed July 13)

1815-1817, minister to England

Sept. 22, 1817-Mar. 3, 1825, Secretary of State

Mar. 4, 1825-Mar. 3, 1829, President

1828, unsuccessful candidate for reelection

1829, retired to farm

Mar. 4, 1831-Feb. 23, 1848, U.S. House of Representatives (from Massachusetts)

1834, unsuccessful candidate for governor of Massachusetts as nominee of the Anti-Masonic party

1846, paralysis; confined at home four months

1848, paralysis, second attack, in Speaker's Room, House of Representatives

JOHN QUINCY ADAMS

_____was the first President whose father had signed the Declaration of Independence.

_____was the only President whose father had been President.

_____was the second President born in Massachusetts.

_____was the first President who had been elected a member of Phi Beta Kappa.

_____was the first President to wear long trousers at his inauguration.

_____was the President least interested in clothes. It is said that he wore the same hat ten years.

_____was the first President elected without receiving the plurality of the popular votes.

_____was the first and only President to have a son whose given name was George Washington.

_____was the first President whose son was married in the White House.

_____was the first President who was married abroad.

ADAMS' VICE PRESIDENT

Vice President—John Caldwell Calhoun (7th V.P.)

Date of birth–Mar. 18, 1782
Birthplace–Abbeville District, S.C.
Political party–Democratic-Republican
State represented–South Carolina
Term of office–Mar. 4, 1825-Mar. 3, 1829
Age at inauguration–42 years, 351 days
Occupation after term–Vice President under Andrew Jackson
Date of death–Mar. 31, 1850
Age at death–68 years, 13 days
Place of death–Washington, D.C.
Burial place–Charleston, S.C.

Additional Data on Calhoun

1804, graduated from Yale College
1807, admitted to bar; practiced in Abbeville, S.C.
1808-1809, South Carolina House of Representatives
Mar. 4, 1811-Nov. 3, 1817, U.S. House of Representatives (from South Carolina)
Dec. 10, 1817-Mar. 3, 1825, Secretary of War
Dec. 29, 1832-Mar. 3, 1843, U.S. Senate (from South Carolina)
Mar. 6, 1844-Mar. 6, 1845, Secretary of State
Nov. 26, 1845-Mar. 31, 1850, U.S. Senate (from South Carolina)

ADDITIONAL DATA ON ADAMS

INAUGURATION

John Quincy Adams took the oath of office on Friday, March 4, 1825, at noon in the Hall of the House of Representatives (the same room in which he was to die on February 23, 1848). The oath was administered by Chief Justice John Marshall. Adams was accompanied to the Capitol by a military escort. After the ceremony, he returned to his residence at 1333 F Street, where a reception was held; later he went to the White House.

An inaugural ball was held that evening at Louis Carusi's Assembly Room, known also as the City Assembly Rooms.

ADAMS THE SON OF A PRESIDENT

John Quincy Adams was the only President whose father had also been a president. Like his father, he served only one term.

FORMER PRESIDENTS STILL LIVING

When John Quincy Adams took the oath of office as President of the United States on March 4, 1825, all of the former presidents, with the exception of George Washington, were living: John Adams, Thomas Jefferson, James Madison, and James Monroe.

ADAMS SUFFERED WORST DEFEAT

The most badly defeated presidential candidate, excluding those nominated by the minor parties, was John Quincy Adams. In the election of 1820, he received only one electoral vote, which was cast by an elector from New Hampshire, whereas James Monroe received 231 of the 232 electoral votes.

PRESIDENT BECAME CONGRESSMAN

After serving as President, John Quincy Adams became a congressman. He represented the Plymouth, Mass., district, serving as a Whig congressman in the Twenty-second and the eight succeeding congresses, from March 4, 1831, to February 23, 1848, when he died. He served ten days less than seventeen years.

FIRST VICE PRESIDENT BORN A CITIZEN OF THE UNITED STATES

John Caldwell Calhoun, Vice President under John Quincy Adams and Andrew Jackson, was the first Vice President not born a British subject. He was born March 18, 1782, near Calhoun Mills, Abbeville District, S.C.

VICE PRESIDENT RESIGNED TO BECOME SENATOR

John Caldwell Calhoun, Vice President from March 4, 1825, to December 28, 1832, resigned to become a senator from South Carolina. He had been elected to the United States Senate on December 12, 1832, to fill the vacancy caused by the resignation of Robert Young Hayne, who became governor of South Carolina. Calhoun was reelected in 1834 and 1840 and served from December 29, 1832, until his resignation, effective March 3, 1843. He later served as secretary of state and afterward was reelected to the Senate, where he served from November 26, 1845, until his death in Washington, D.C., on March 31, 1850.

THE FIRST LADY

The sixth in succession as lady of the Executive Mansion was Louisa Catherine Adams, who acted as hostess when her husbnad assumed the presidency in 1825. She ruled with little regard to politics and her hospitality was warm and sincere. The frugality and severity of the two previous administrations was replaced by an era of gracious living in which the choicest foods and the rarest wines were always served.

ANDREW JACKSON
7th PRESIDENT

Born–Mar. 15, 1767
Birthplace–Waxhaw, S.C.
College attended–None
Religion–Presbyterian
Ancestry–Scotch-Irish
Occupation–Soldier
Date and place of marriage–Aug. 1791, Natchez, Miss. (Jan. 17, 1794, Nashville, Tenn.—second ceremony)
Age at marriage–24 years
Years married–37 years
Political party–Democratic (Democratic-Republican)
State represented–Tennessee
Term of office–Mar. 4, 1829-Mar. 3, 1837
Term served–8 years
Administration–11th, 12th
Congresses–21st, 22nd, 23rd, 24th
Age at inauguration–61 years, 354 days
Lived after term–8 years, 96 days
Occupation after term–Retired
Date of death–June 8, 1845
Age at death–78 years, 85 days
Place of death–Nashville, Tenn.
Burial place–The Hermitage estate, Nashville, Tenn.

PARENTS

Father–Andrew Jackson
Born–Ireland
Occupation–Linen weaver (in Ireland), farmer
Died–Mar. 1767
Mother–Elizabeth Hutchinson Jackson
Born–Ireland
Died–1780, Charleston, S.C.

BROTHERS AND SISTERS

Andrew Jackson was the third child in a family of three.

Children of Andrew Jackson and Elizabeth Hutchinson Jackson

Hugh Jackson, b. 1762, d. May 29, 1780
Robert Jackson, b. 1765, d. Aug. 6, 1780
Andrew Jackson, b. Mar. 15, 1767, d. June 8, 1845

CHILDREN

None

MRS. ANDREW JACKSON

Name–Rachel Donelson Robards Jackson
Date of birth–June 15 (?), 1767
Birthplace–Halifax County, Va.
Age at marriage–24 years
Children–none
Mother–Rachel Stockley Donelson
Father–Colonel John Donelson
His occupation–Surveyor
Date of death–Dec. 22, 1828
Age at death–61 years, 190 days
Place of death–Nashville, Tenn.
Burial place–Nashville, Tenn.
Years younger than the President–92 days
Years the President survived her–16 years, 168 days

Rachel Donelson married Captain Lewis Robards March 1, 1785. In 1790 the legislature of Virginia granted Robards the right to sue for divorce-a grant which she mistakenly assumed

For additional data see the end of this section and also specific subject headings in the index.

was a divorce. She married Jackson in 1791, learned later that the proceeding had not been completed, and was remarried to Jackson in 1794 after Robards had received the divorce decree (September 27, 1793, Court of Quarter Sessions, Mercer County, Ky.).

THE ELECTION OF 1828

Jackson's supporters claimed that the caucus system defeated the purposes of the Constitution, which envisaged electors voting as they pleased, and that the power of selection had passed from the electors to an extra-legal body. They argued that the popular vote showed that the congressional caucus was not representative of the wishes of the people.

In 1828 a new policy was instituted. It was the first election in which the nominations were all made by the state legislatures instead of congressional caucuses. It was also the first in which the popular vote (November 4, 1828) was a real factor in the selection of electors.

The Democratic-Republicans, known also as Republicans or Democrats, were split into factions. Jackson's supporters (who tended more and more to call themselves Democrats) felt that he had been deprived of the election in 1825 and were determined to elect him in 1828. It was not only a personal matter, but a geographical struggle as well. The Adams-Clay adherents (who soon joined the remaining Federalists to form the National Republican Party) nominated two candidates from the North, Adams of Massachusetts and Rush of Pennsylvania. The Democrats nominated two from the South, Jackson of Tennessee and Calhoun of South Carolina. Jackson carried 15 of the 24 states.

ELECTION RESULTS, NOV. 4, 1828—PRESIDENTIAL AND VICE PRESIDENTIAL CANDIDATES

Jackson-Calhoun faction (Democratic Party) (647,286 votes)
Andrew Jackson, Tenn.
John Caldwell Calhoun, S.C.
Adams-Clay faction (Federalist or National Republican Party) (508,064 votes)
John Quincy Adams, Mass.
Richard Rush, Pa.

ELECTORAL VOTES (261— 24 states)

Jackson received 68.20 per cent (178 votes—15 states) as follows: Ala. 5; Ga. 9; Ill. 3; Ind. 5; Ky. 14; La. 5; Me. 1 (of the 9 votes); Md. 5 (of the 11 votes); Miss. 3; Mo. 3; N.Y. 20 (of the 36 votes); N.C. 15; Ohio 16; Pa. 28; S.C. 11; Tenn. 11; Va. 24.

For the vice presidency Calhoun received 171 votes and William Smith (also of South Carolina) received 7 votes.

Adams received 31.80 per cent (83 votes—9 states) as follows: Conn. 8; Del. 3; Me. 8 (of the 9 votes); Md. 6 (of the 11 votes); Mass. 15; N.H. 8; N.J. 8; N.Y. 16 (of the 36 votes); R.I. 4; Vt. 7.

For the vice presidency Rush received 83 votes.

THE ELECTION OF 1832

NOMINATIONS FOR TERM 1833-1837

Democratic (Democratic-Republican) Party Convention (1st)
May 21-23, 1832, The Athenaeum, Baltimore, Md.
Nominated for President-Andrew Jackson, Tenn.
Nominated for Vice President-Martin Van Buren, N.Y.
First ballot: Andrew Jackson, Tenn.

This convention was held by the "Republican Delegates from the Several States." The party which today bears the name Democratic was then known officially as the Republican Party (a name which had come down from the time of Jefferson) and popularly as the Democratic-Republican Party, or simply the Democratic Party. In the early national conventions, the designations "Democratic" and "Republican" were often used interchangeably, but in 1840 the designation "Republican" was dropped entirely and the official name of the party became the Democratic Party.

At the convention of 1832 a two-thirds majority was necessary for a choice. Since the Democrats were unanimous in the choice of Andrew Jackson for a second term, there was no opposition to his renomination. The sole purpose of this convention was to select a vice presidential candidate to replace John Caldwell Calhoun, who had resigned the vice presidency to serve in the Senate. Martin Van Buren of New York received 208 of the 283 votes cast and was elected Vice President on the first ballot. Other vice presidential nominees were Philip Pendleton Barbour of Virginia, who received 49 votes, and Richard Mentor Johnson of Kentucky, who received 26 votes.

National Republican Party Convention
December 12-15, 1831, The Athenaeum, Baltimore, Md.
Nominated for President-Henry Clay, Ky.
Nominated for Vice President-John Sergeant, Pa.
First ballot; Henry Clay, Ky.

This anti-Jackson political faction, although not fully crystallized as a political party, defined the issues of the campaign as the tariff, internal improvements, the renewal of the charter of the Bank of the United States, and the resettling of the Cherokee Indians. The National Republicans gradually began to call themselves Whigs, and by 1834 the name was in general use.

Independent Party Convention
November 20, 1832, Charleston, S.C.
Nominated for President-John Floyd, Va.
Nominated for Vice President-Henry Lee, Mass.

South Carolina cast its 11 electoral votes for this newly formed party—the nullification faction of the Democratic Party—which maintained that states had the right to veto or nullify federal legislation and executive orders.

Anti-Masonic Party Convention
Sept. 26-28, 1831, The Athenaeum, Baltimore, Md.

Nominated for President-William Wirt, Md.
Nominated for Vice President-Amos Ellmaker, Pa.

Wirt was nominated on the first ballot. Candidates for nomination and the votes they received:
William Wirt, Md., 108
Richard Rush, Pa., 1
Total number of votes: 111 (2 votes not cast)
Number necessary for nomination: 84
Nomination made unanimous

This was the first national nominating convention at which candidates were placed in nomination by delegates, a procedure which was later adopted by all political parties. The Anti-Masonic Party was formed in 1827 in western New York. A national convention, held at Philadelphia, Pa., September 11-18, 1830, was attended by 96 delegates from 10 states, but no nominations were made at that time.

ELECTION RESULTS, NOV. 6, 1832 — PRESIDENTIAL AND VICE PRESIDENTIAL CANDIDATES

Democratic (Democratic-Republican) Party (687,502 votes)

Andrew Jackson, Tenn.
Martin Van Buren, N.Y.

National Republican Party (530,189 votes)
Henry Clay, Ky.
John Sergeant, Pa.

Independent Party
John Floyd, Va.
Henry Lee, Mass.

Anti-Masonic Party William Wirt, Md.
Amos Ellmaker, Pa.

ELECTORAL VOTES (286—24 states)

Jackson received 76.57 per cent (219 votes—16 states) as follows: Ala. 7; Ga. 11; Ill. 5; Ind. 9; La. 5; Me. 10; Md. 3 (of the 8 votes); Miss. 4; Mo. 4; N.H. 7; N.J. 8; N.Y. 42; N.C. 15; Ohio 21; Pa. 30; Tenn. 15; Va. 23.

Clay received 17.13 per cent (49 votes—6 states) as follows: Conn. 8; Del. 3; Ky. 15; Md. 5 (of the 8 votes); Mass. 14; R.I. 4.

Floyd received 3.85 per cent (1 state): S.C. 11.

Wirt received 2.45 per cent (1 state): Vt. 7.

For the vice presidency Martin Van Buren received 189 votes and William Wilkins of Pennsylvania received 30 votes, the Democratic vote for the vice presidency being divided.

FIRST TERM

CABINET

March 4, 1829-March 3, 1833
State–James Alexander Hamilton, N.Y., ad interim Mar. 4, 1829; Mar-

tin Van Buren, N.Y., Mar. 6, 1829, entered upon duties Mar. 28, 1829; Edward Livingston, La., May 24, 1831

Treasury–Samuel Delucenna Ingham, Pa., Mar. 6, 1829; Asbury Dickins (chief clerk), ad interim June 21, 1831; Louis McLane, Del., Aug. 8, 1831

War–John Henry Eaton, Tenn., Mar. 9, 1829; Philip G. Randolph (chief clerk), ad interim June 20, 1831; Roger Brooke Taney, Md. (Attorney General), ad interim July 21, 1831; Lewis Cass, Ohio, Aug. 1, 1831, entered upon duties Aug. 8, 1831

Attorney General–John Macpherson Berrien, Ga., Mar. 9, 1829-June 22, 1831; Roger Brooke Taney, Md., July 20, 1831

Postmaster General–John McLean, Ohio, continued from preceding administration; William Taylor Barry, Ky., Mar. 9, 1829, entered upon duties Apr. 6, 1829

Navy–Charles Hay (chief clerk), ad interim Mar. 4, 1829; John Branch, N.C., Mar. 9, 1829; John Boyle (chief clerk), ad interim May 12, 1831; Levi Woodbury, N.H., May 23, 1831

SECOND TERM

CABINET

March 4, 1833-March 3, 1837

State–Edward Livingston, La., continued from preceding administration; Louis McLane, Del., May 29, 1833; John Forsyth, Ga., June 27, 1834, entered upon duties July 1, 1834

Treasury–Louis McLane, Del., continued from preceding administration; William John Duane, Pa., May 29, 1833, entered upon duties June 1, 1833; Roger Brooke Taney, Md., Sept. 23, 1833; McClintock Young (chief clerk), ad interim June 25, 1834; Levi Woodbury, N.H., June 27, 1834, entered upon duties July 1, 1834

War–Lewis Cass, Ohio, continued from preceding administration; Carey A. Harris, Tenn. (Commissioner of Indian Affairs), ad interim Oct. 5, 1836; Benjamin Franklin Butler, N.Y., commissioned Mar. 3, 1837, ad interim

Attorney General–Roger Brooke Taney, Md., continued from preceding administration to Sept. 23, 1833; Benjamin Franklin Butler, N.Y., Nov. 15, 1833; entered upon duties Nov. 18, 1833

Postmaster General–William Taylor Barry, Ky., continued from preceding administration; Amos Kendall, Ky., May 1, 1835

Navy–Levi Woodbury, N.H., continued from preceding administration; Mahlon Dickerson, N.J., June 30, 1834

FIRST TERM

TWENTY-FIRST CONGRESS

March 4, 1829-March 3, 1831

First session–Dec. 7, 1829-May 31, 1830 (176 days)

Second session–Dec. 6, 1830-Mar. 3, 1831 (88 days)

Special session of the Senate–Mar. 4, 1829-Mar. 17, 1829 (14 days)

Vice President–John Caldwell Calhoun, S.C.

President pro tempore of the Senate–Samuel Smith, Md., elected Mar. 13, 1829, special session; May 29, 1830; Mar. 1, 1831

Secretary of the Senate–Walter Lowrie, Pa., reelected Dec. 14, 1829

Speaker of the House–Andrew Stevenson, Va., reelected Dec. 7, 1829

Clerk of the House–Matthew St. Clair Clarke, Pa., reelected Dec. 7, 1829

TWENTY-SECOND CONGRESS

March 4, 1831-March 3, 1833

First session–Dec. 5, 1831-July 16, 1832 (225 days)

Second session–Dec. 3, 1832-Mar. 2, 1833 (91 days)

Vice President–John Caldwell Calhoun, S.C., resigned Dec. 28, 1832, having been elected senator

Presidents pro tempore of the Senate–Littleton Waller Tazewell, Va., elected July 9, 1832; Hugh Lawson White, Tenn., elected Dec. 3, 1832

Secretary of the Senate–Walter Lowrie, Pa., reelected Dec. 19, 1831

Speaker of the House–Andrew Stevenson, Va., reelected Dec. 5, 1831

Clerk of the House–Matthew St. Clair Clarke, Pa., reelected Dec. 5, 1831

SECOND TERM

TWENTY-THIRD CONGRESS

March 4, 1833-March 3, 1835

First session–Dec. 2, 1833-June 30, 1834 (211 days)

Second session–Dec. 1, 1834-Mar. 3, 1835 (93 days)

Vice President–Martin Van Buren, N.Y.

Presidents pro tempore of the Senate–Hugh Lawson White, Tenn.; George Poindexter, Miss., elected June 28, 1834; John Tyler, Va., elected Mar. 3, 1835

Secretary of the Senate–Walter Lowrie, Pa., reelected Dec. 9, 1833

Speakers of the House–Andrew Stevenson, Va., reelected Dec. 2, 1833; resigned from the House June 2, 1834; John Bell, Tenn., elected June 2, 1834

Clerks of the House–Matthew St. Clarke, Pa.; Walter S. Franklin, Pa., elected Dec. 2, 1833

TWENTY-FOURTH CONGRESS

March 4, 1835-March 3, 1837

First session–Dec. 7, 1835-July 4, 1836 (211 days)

Second session–Dec. 5, 1836-Mar. 3, 1837 (89 days)

Vice President–Martin Van Buren, N.Y.

President pro tempore of the Senate–William Rufus de Vane King, Ala., elected July 1, 1836; Jan 28, 1837

Secretaries of the Senate– Walter Lowrie, Pa., reelected Dec. 15, 1835; resigned Dec. 5, 1836; Asbury Dickens, N.C., elected Dec. 12, 1836

Speaker of the House–James Knox Polk, Tenn., elected Dec. 7, 1835

Clerk of the House–Walter S. Franklin, Pa., reelected Dec. 7, 1835

APPOINTMENTS TO THE SUPREME COURT

Chief Justice
Roger Brooke Taney, Md., Mar. 15, 1836

Associate Justices

John McLean, Ohio, Mar. 7, 1829
Henry Baldwin, Pa., Jan. 6, 1830
James Moore Wayne, Ga., Jan. 9, 1835
Philip Pendleton Barbour, Va., Mar. 15, 1836

ADMINISTRATION—IMPORTANT DATES

Aug. 9, 1829, "Stourbridge Lion," first locomotive for railroad use, in service

Oct. 17, 1829, Delaware River and Chesapeake Bay canal formally opened

1830, Webster-Hayne debates on states' rights

June 8, 1830, *Vincennes*, first warship to circumnavigate the world, returned to New York City

1832, Jackson vetoed renewal of charter of the Bank of the United States

Apr. 6, 1832, cholera epidemic broke out at New York City

July 4, 1832, "America" first sung publicly, Boston, Mass.

Aug. 2, 1832, Black Hawk War ended

Nov. 24, 1832, South Carolina declared federal tariff acts null and void; compromise reached to save Union sent to Charleston and action was suspended

Dec. 28, 1832, Vice President Calhoun resigned

1833, Jackson removed Government deposits from Bank of the United States

Mar. 20, 1833, treaty with Siam signed-first treaty with a Far Eastern nation

Sept. 3, 1833, first daily newspaper, *Sun*, New York City

Jan. 29, 1834, President ordered War Department to quell riot at Chesapeake and Ohio Canal, near Williamsport, Indiana

June 21, 1834, McCormick's reaper patented

June 24, 1834, appointment of Roger B. Taney as Secretary of the Treasury rejected by Senate-first rejection of cabinet appointee

Nov. 2, 1835, Second Seminole War begun by Osceola

Dec. 16, 1835, fire in New York City destroyed 600 buildings

Mar. 1, 1836, Texas declaration of independence

Mar. 6, 1836, slaughter of defenders of the Alamo

Apr. 21, 1836, Texans defeated Mexicans at San Jacinto battlefield

May 14, 1836, Wilkes expedition to the South Seas authorized

June 15, 1836, Arkansas admitted as the 25th state

July 4, 1836, Wisconsin Territory organized

July 11, 1836, Jackson issued specie circular requiring payment for public lands in coin

Jan. 26, 1837, Michigan admitted as the 26th state

IMPORTANT DATES IN HIS LIFE

1784, studied law, Salisbury, N.C.

1787, fought first duel (with Waightstill Avery)

Nov. 21, 1787, admitted to the bar (practiced in McLeanville, N.C., and Tennessee)

Oct. 1788, solicitor of western district of North Carolina (comprising what is now Tennessee)

Jan. 1796, delegate to Tennessee State Constitutional Convention, Knoxville

Dec. 5, 1796-Mar. 3, 1797, U.S. House of Representatives (from Tennessee)

Mar. 4, 1797-April 1798, U.S. Senate (from Tennessee)

1798-July 24, 1804, judge, Supreme Court of Tennessee

1801, major general of militia for western district of Tennessee

1804, moved to the Hermitage, near Nashville, Tenn.; engaged in planting and mercantile pursuits

May 30, 1806, killed Charles Dickinson in duel

1807, Tennessee state senator and lawyer

1812, commander of Tennessee militia; served against Creek Indians

1812-1814, major general of volunteers

Aug. 30, 1813, expedition against Creek Indians who massacred garrison at Fort Meigs, Ala.

Sept. 4, 1813, wounded in affray with the brothers Thomas Hart Benton and Jesse Benton

Mar. 27, 1814, defeated Creek Indians at Horseshoe Bend of the Tallapoosa

Apr. 19, 1814, commissioned brigadier general, U.S. Army

May 1, 1814, promoted to major general, U.S. Army

Aug. 9, 1814, negotiated treaty with the Creek Indians

Sept. 9, 1814, began first Florida compaign

Nov. 7, 1814, captured Pensacola and Fort Michael; British retreated

Jan. 8, 1815, defeated British under General Pakenham at Battle of New Orleans, not aware that a peace treaty had been signed at Ghent

Feb. 27, 1815, received thanks of Congress; awarded a gold medal by resolution

Mar. 24, 1815, fined $1,000 by Judge Dominick A. Hall for contempt of court

Dec. 26, 1817, ordered by Secretary of War Calhoun to attack the Seminoles

Mar. 1818, captured St. Marks, Fla., and defeated the Seminoles

Mar. 10-July 18, 1821, governor of Florida

July 20, 1822, nominated for President by Tennessee legislature

Mar. 4, 1823-Oct. 14, 1825, U.S. Senate (from Tennessee); resigned

1824, unsuccessful candidate for the presidency; won plurality of electoral votes, but House of Representatives chose John Quincy Adams

Mar. 4, 1829-Mar. 3, 1837, President

June 26, 1833, LL.D. degree conferred by Harvard

Mar. 28, 1834, censored by Senate resolution for removing public deposits from Bank of the United States

Mar. 16, 1837, Senate resolution expunging censure resolution of 1834

ANDREW JACKSON

____was the first President born in a log cabin.

____was the first President born in South Carolina.

____was the first President whose birthplace was in dispute. It was claimed that his birthplace was Union County, N.C.; Berkeley County, Va.; Augusta County, Va. (now W. Va.); York County, Pa.; England; Ireland; and on the high seas.

____was the first President born west of the Allegheny Mountains.

____was the first President to marry a woman who had been divorced.

____was the first President to receive a plurality of popular votes but fail to win the election (1824).

____was the second widower inaugurated President.

____was the first presidential candidate named by a national nominating convention.

____was the first President who was a resident of a state other than his native state.

____was the first President to ride on a railroad train. On June 6, 1833, he took the stagecoach from Washington, D.C., to Ellicott's Mill, Md., where he boarded a Baltimore and Ohio train for Baltimore, Md. It was a pleasure trip. (John Quincy Adams, however, had made a trip on the same line a few months earlier when he was no longer President.)

____could, most likely, have been elected for a third term, but as none of his predecessors had served more than two terms he refused to be a candidate again and supported Van Buren for the presidency.

JACKSON'S VICE PRESIDENTS

FIRST TERM

Vice President–John Caldwell Calhoun (7th V.P.)

Date of birth–Mar. 18, 1782

Birthplace–Abbeville District, S.C.

Political party–Democratic (Democratic-Republican)

State represented–South Carolina

Term of office–Mar. 4, 1829-Dec. 28, 1832

Age at inauguration–46 years, 351 days

Occupation after term–U.S. Senator

Date of death–Mar. 31, 1850

Age at death–68 years, 13 days

Place of death–Washington, D.C.

Burial place–Charleston, S.C.

For additional data on Calhoun see John Quincy Adams, 6th President-Adams' Vice President.

SECOND TERM

Vice President–Martin Van Buren (8th V.P.)
Date of birth–Dec. 5, 1782
Birthplace–Kinderhook, N.Y.
Political party–Democratic (Democratic-Republican)
State represented–New York
Term of office–Mar. 4, 1833-Mar. 3, 1837
Age at inauguration–50 years, 89 days
Occupation after term–President
Date of death–July 24, 1862
Age at death–79 years, 231 days
Place of death–Kinderhook, N.Y.
Burial place–Kinderhook, N.Y.

For further biographical information see Martin Van Buren, 8th President.

ADDITIONAL DATA ON JACKSON

ANDREW JACKSON, DUELIST

There are many estimates of the number of brawls and duels in which Andrew Jackson is believed to have participated. Some sources maintain that the figure approximates one hundred.

History records one duel in which Andrew Jackson killed his opponent. Charles Dickinson, one of the best pistol shots in the United States, made some derogatory remarks about Mrs. Jackson. Andrew Jackson challenged him to a duel. They met on May 30, 1806, at Harrison's Mills on Red River in Logan County, Ky. They stood twenty-four feet apart with pistols pointed downwards. At the signal, Dickinson fired first, breaking some of Jackson's ribs and grazing his breastbone. Jackson, without flinching, maintained his positon and fired. His shot proved mortal.

In 1812, Andrew Jackson was wounded in a gun battle at Knoxville, Tenn., by a bullet fired by Jesse Benton. It was feared that Jackson's arm would have to be amputated. In 1832, an operation was performed and the bullet which had been imbedded in Jackson's arm for twenty years was removed.

FIRST INAUGURATION

Like his father, John Adams, John Quincy Adams, the outgoing President, refused to participate in the inaugural ceremonies of his successor. Andrew Jackson took the oath of office on Wednesday, March 4, 1829, on the east portico of the White House. The oath was administered by Chief Justice John Marshall. The ceremonies ended with the firing of cannon.

It was a warm and spring-like day. Andrew Jackson was an imposing figure as he rode down Pennsylvania Avenue leading a parade which included war veterans, many of whom had fought in the Revolution. As Jackson was in mourning for his wife, who had died on December 22, 1828, no ceremonies were planned. In the evening a reception was held for the public at the White House. A crowd of twenty thousand people jammed the building, ruining rugs, furniture and glassware, and causing thousands of dollars' worth of damage. It was a boisterous reception. Jackson was a man of the people, the first President not descended from an old aristocratic family.

NOMINATION OF VAN BUREN NOT CONFIRMED BY THE SENATE

President Andrew Jackson's nomination of Martin Van Buren to the post of minister to Great Britain in August 1831 was not confirmed by the Senate. Van Buren therefore relinquished his post and returned from England.

CANDIDATES NOMINATED BY CONVENTIONS

The election of 1832 was the first in which all the candidates were nominated by national conventions. The Democratic Party chose Jackson and Van Buren, the National Republican Party Clay and Sergeant, and the Anti-Masonic Party Wirt and Ellmaker.

CONVENTION ENACTED TWO-THIRDS RULE

The two-thirds rule requiring nominees to obtain two thirds of the votes was enacted by the Democratic-Republican National Convention at Baltimore, Md., on May 22, 1832. The rule was an extension of the following provision adopted in 1831:

> Resolved: That each state be entitled, in the nomination to be made of a candidate for the vice presidency, to a number of votes equal to the number to which they will be entitled in the electoral college, under the new apportionment, in voting for President and Vice President; and that two thirds of the whole number of the votes in the convention shall be necessary to constitute a choice.

VICE PRESIDENT VAN BUREN NOMINATED AT A NATIONAL CONVENTION

As the nomination of President Andrew Jackson was assured at the Democratic-Republican Party Convention held May 21-23, 1832, at the Athenaeum, Baltimore, Md., the purpose of the convention was to select a vice presidential candidate to replace John Caldwell Calhoun, who had resigned the vice presidency to serve his state in the Senate. Richard Mentor Johnson received 26 votes, Philip Pendleton Barbour received 49 votes, and Martin Van Buren 208 votes of the 283 votes cast. This made Van Buren the running mate of Andrew Jackson and the first Vice President selected at a national convention.

JACKSON DENOUNCED NULLIFICATION ATTEMPT

South Carolina in convention assembled passed an ordinance which declared:

> The several acts and parts of acts of the Congress of the United States, purporting to be laws for the imposing of duties and imposts on the importation of foreign commodities, and now having actual operation and effect within the United States, and more

especially "two acts for the same purposes, passed on the 29th of May, 1828, and on the 14th of July, 1832," are unauthorized by the Constitution of the United States, and violate the true meaning and intent thereof, and are null and void, and no law.

President Jackson issued a proclamation on December 10, 1832, in which he stated, in part:

I consider, then, the power to annul a law of the United States, assumed by one state, incompatible with the existence of the Union, contradicted expressly by the letter of the Constitution, unauthorized by its spirit, inconsistent with every principle on which it was founded, and destructive of the great object for which it was formed.

The dispute ended in a compromise which provided for gradual reduction of the tariff, and South Carolina withdrew the ordinance.

SECOND INAUGURATION

Andrew Jackson took the oath of office for his second term on Monday, March 4, 1833, in the House of Representatives. John Marshall, the Chief Justice, administered the oath (the ninth presidential oath administered by him).

HARVARD CONFERRED LL.D. ON JACKSON

The honorary degree of LL.D. was conferred on President Andrew Jackson by Harvard, Cambridge, Mass.; on June 26, 1833. A distinguished alumnus, former President John Quincy Adams, expressed his disapproval of the award on June 18, to Josiah Quincy, President of Harvard College:

As myself an affectionate child of our alma mater, I would not be present to witness her disgrace in conferring her highest literary honors upon a barbarian who could not write a sentence of grammar and hardly could spell his own name.

THE PRESIDENT PROTESTED

The first presidential protest was signed April 15, 1834, by President Andrew Jackson. He protested against the following Senate resolution passed March 28, 1834, by a vote of 26 of the 46 senators present:

Resolved, That the President, in the late Executive proceedings in relation to the public revenue, has assumed upon himself authority and power not conferred by the Constitution and laws, but in derogation of both.

Jackson concluded his protest:

To the end that the resolution of the Senate may not be hereafter drawn into precedent with the authority of silent acquiescence on the part of the Executive department, and to the end also that my motives and views in the Executive proceedings denounced in that resolution may be known to my fellow-citizens, to the world, and to all posterity, I respectfully request that this message and protest may be entered at length on the journals of the Senate.

The Senate, however, ordered his message not to be entered in the journal.

SENATE REJECTED JACKSON CABINET APPOINTEE

The first cabinet appointee rejected by the Senate was Roger Brooke Taney of Frederick, Md., who was proposed by President Andrew Jackson for Secretary of the Treasury. He was rejected by a vote of 28 to 18 on June 24, 1834.

JACKSON ESCAPED ASSASSINATION

The first attempt upon the life of a President was made January 30, 1835, upon President Andrew Jackson in the rotunda of the Capitol while he attended the funeral services for Representative Warren Ransom Davis of South Carolina. As Jackson was about to go to the portico, Richard Lawrence, a mentally unbalanced house painter, fired two pistols at him from a distance of only six feet. Both weapons missed fire and Jackson was unhurt.

Lawrence was tried April 11, 1835, in the United States Circuit Court at Washington, D.C., and was committed to jail and mental hospitals for life. He suffered from chronic monomania and was found insane at the time of his act.

JACKSON APPOINTED CATHOLIC CHIEF JUSTICE

The first Catholic Chief Justice of the Supreme Court of the United States was Roger Brooke Taney of Frederick, Md., who was appointed on March 28, 1836, by President Andrew Jackson to succeed John Marshall as Chief Justice.

JACKSON REFUNDED TAXES

A surplus of $37 million accumulated during President Jackson's administration. On June 23, 1836, Congress voted to permit the government to disburse all but $5 million to the states in proportion to their representation in Congress. About $28 million was distributed in three installments. The panic of 1837 caused a sudden shift in government finances, and revenues decreased to such an extent that payments of the balance were discontinued.

JACKSON'S KITCHEN CABINET

Jackson had a coterie of advisers who met with him unofficially in the kitchen or rear of the White House to discuss public affairs. Referred to as "Jackson's kitchen cabinet," they held no government positions and had no official standing. Among those who were in this group were Andrew Jackson Donelson, his ward and private secretary; Amos Kendall of Kentucky, later postmaster general; General Duff Green, editor of the *United States Telegraph*, Francis P. Blair, editor of the Washington, D.C., *Globe*; Isaac Hill, Senator from New Hampshire; and Major William B. Lewis of Nashville, Tenn.

HOSTESSES AT THE WHITE HOUSE

As Rachel Donelson Robards Jackson had died of a heart attack before her husband was inaugurated and as they had no children,

President Jackson assigned the duties of hostess at the White House to Emily Donelson, his wife's niece, who was the wife of Andrew Jackson Donelson. Her four children were all born in the White House. She developed tuberculosis and in 1836 returned to her home in Tennessee. Also serving at various times as hostess was Sarah York Jackson, wife of Andrew Jackson's foster son.

EXTRACT FROM JACKSON'S WILL

June 7, 1843
The Hermitage

First, I bequeath my body to the dust whence it comes, and my soul to God who gave it, hoping for a happy immortality through the atoning merits of our Lord, Jesus Christ, the Saviour of the world. My desire is, that my body be buried by the side of my dear departed wife, in the garden at the Hermitage, in the vault prepared in the garden, and all expenses paid by my executor hereafter named. . . .

JACKSON WILLED HIS PISTOLS TO GENERAL ARMSTRONG

The famous pistols carried by Jackson are mentioned in his last will and testament:

As a memento of my high regard for Gen'l. Robert Armstrong as a gentleman, patriot and soldier, as well as for his meritorious military services under my command during the late British and Indian war, and remembering the gallant bearing of him and his gallant little band at Enotochopco Creek, when, falling desperately wounded, he called out—"My brave fellows, some may fall, but save the cannon"—as a memento of all these things, I give and bequeath to him my case of pistols and sword worn by me throughout my military career, well satisfied that in his hands they will never be disgraced—that they will never be used or drawn without occasion, nor sheathed but with honour.

JACKSON'S FINE RETURNED

On March 31, 1815, Judge Hall of the United States District Court at New Orleans fined Andrew Jackson $1,000 for contempt in declaring martial law during the defense of New Orleans. On January 8, 1844, the House of Representatives voted (158 to 28) to return the $1,000 with interest at 6 per cent.

MARTIN VAN BUREN
8th PRESIDENT

Born–Dec. 5, 1782
Birthplace–Kinderhook, N.Y.
College attended–None
Religious denomination–Dutch Reformed
Ancestry–Dutch
Occupation–Lawyer
Date and place of marriage–Feb. 21, 1807, Catskill, N.Y.
Age at marriage–24 years, 78 days
Years married–11 years, 349 days
Political party–Democratic (Democratic-Republican)
State represented–New York
Term of office–Mar. 4, 1837-Mar. 3, 1841
Term served–4 years
Administration–13th
Congresses–25th, 26th
Age at inauguration–54 years, 89 days
Lived after term–21 years, 142 days
Occupation after term–Retired; active in Free Soil Party
Date of death–July 24, 1862
Age at death–79 years, 231 days
Place of death–Kinderhook, N.Y.
Burial place–Kinderhook Cemetery, Kinderhook, N.Y.

PARENTS

Father–Abraham Van Buren
Born–Feb. 17, 1737, Albany, N.Y.
Married–1776
Occupation–Farmer, innkeeper, captain in 7th Regiment Albany County Militia
Died–Apr. 8, 1817
Age at death–80 years, 40 days
Mother–Maria Goes Hoes Van Alen Van Buren

Born–1747 (?) (baptized Jan. 16, 1747)
Died–Feb. 16, 1817 (or 1818)

BROTHERS AND SISTER

Martin Van Buren was the third child in a family of five.

Children of Abraham Van Buren and Maria Goes Hoes Van Alen Van Buren

Derike (or Dirckie) Van Buren, b. 1777, d. Oct. 18, 1865
Hannah (or Jannetje) Van Buren, baptized Jan. 16, 1780
Martin Van Buren, b. Dec. 5, 1782, d. July 24, 1862
Lawrence Van Buren, baptized Jan. 8, 1786, d. July 1, 1868
Abraham Van Buren, baptized May 11, 1788, d. Oct. 30, 1836
Mrs. Van Buren was the widow of Johannes Van Alen, by whom she had three children. The name of only one is known:
James Isaac Van Alen, b. 1776, d. Dec. 23, 1870(?)

CHILDREN

Abraham Van Buren, b. Nov. 27, 1807, Kinderhook, N.Y., m. Nov. 1838, Angelica Singleton; d. Mar. 15, 1873, New York, N.Y.
John Van Buren, b. Feb. 18, 1810, Hudson, N.Y., m. June 22, 1841, Elizabeth Van der Poel; d. Oct. 13, 1866, at sea
Martin Van Buren, b. Dec. 20, 1812, unmarried, d. Mar. 19, 1855, Paris
Smith Thompson Van Buren, b. Jan. 16, 1817, m. June 18, 1842,

For additional data see the end of this section and also specific subject headings in the index.

Ellen King James; m. Feb. 1, 1855, Henrietta Irving; d. 1876

Mother–Maria Quackenboss Hoes
Father–John Hoes
Date of death–Feb. 5, 1819
Age at death–35 years, 334 days
Place of death–Albany, N.Y.
Burial place–Kinderhook, N.Y.
Years younger than the President–93 days
Years the President survived her–43 years, 169 days

MRS. MARTIN VAN BUREN

Name–Hannah Hoes Van Buren
Date of birth–Mar. 8, 1783
Birthplace–Kinderhook, N.Y.
Age at marriage–23 years, 350 days
Children–4 sons

THE ELECTION OF 1836

NOMINATIONS FOR TERM 1837-1841

Democratic (Democratic-Republican) Party Convention (2nd)

May 20-22, 1835, First Presbyterian Church, Baltimore, Md.
Nominated for President-Martin Van Buren, N.Y.
Nominated for Vice President-Richard Mentor Johnson, Ky.
First ballot: 265, Martin Van Buren, N.Y.
Nomination made unanimous

Whig Party Convention (state convention)

December 14, 1835, Harrisburg, Pa.
Nominated for President-William Henry Harrison, Ohio
Nominated for Vice President-Francis Granger, N.Y.

The Anti-Masons and others opposed to Van Buren rallied to Harrison's support at this and other state conventions which confirmed Harrison's nomination. But the Whig Party (which had absorbed the short-lived National Republican Party) held no national convention and its electoral votes were divided among four presidential candidates.

ELECTION RESULTS, NOV. 1, 1836—PRESIDENTIAL AND VICE PRESIDENTIAL CANDIDATES

Democratic (Democratic-Republican) Party- (762,678 votes)
Martin Van Buren, N.Y.
Richard Mentor Johnson, Ky.

Whig Party (735, 561)

Presidential candidates
William Henry Harrison, Ohio
Hugh Lawson White, Tenn.
Daniel Webster, Mass.
Willie Person Mangum, N.C.

Vice presidential candidates
Francis Granger, N.Y.
John Tyler, Va.
William Smith, Ala.

ELECTORAL VOTES (294—26 states)

Van Buren received 57.82 per cent (170 votes—15 states) as follows: Ala. 7; Ark. 3; Conn. 8; Ill. 5; La. 5; Me. 10; Mich. 3; Miss. 4; Mo. 4; N.H. 7; N.Y. 42; N.C. 15; Pa. 30; R.I. 4; Va. 23.

Harrison received 24.83 per cent (73 votes—7 states) as follows: Del. 3; Ind. 9; Ky. 15; Md. 10; N.J. 8; Ohio 21; Vt. 7.

White received 8.85 per cent (26 votes—2 states) as follows: Ga. 11; Tenn. 15.

Webster received 4.76 per cent (1 state): Mass. 14.

Mangum received 3.74 per cent (1 state): S.C. 11.

For the vice presidency Johnson received 147 votes, Granger 77 votes, Tyler 47 votes, and Smith 23 votes. Since no candidate had a majority, the election devolved upon the Senate, and Johnson was elected by a vote of 33 to 16.

CABINET

March 4, 1837-March 3, 1841

State–John Forsyth, Ga., continued from preceding administration

Treasury–Levi Woodbury, N.H., continued from preceding administration

War–Benjamin Franklin Butler, N.Y., ad interim, continued from preceding administration; Joel Roberts Poinsett, S.C., Mar. 7, 1837; entered upon duties Mar. 14, 1837

Attorney General–Benjamin Franklin Butler, N.Y., continued from preceding administration; Felix Grundy, Tenn., July 5, 1838, to take effect Sept. 1, 1838; Henry Dilworth Gilpin, Pa., Jan. 11, 1840

Postmaster General–Amos Kendall, Ky., continued from preceding administration; John Milton Niles, Conn., May 19, 1840 to take effect May 25, 1840; entered upon duties May 26, 1840.

Navy–Mahlon Dickerson, N.J., continued from preceding administration; James Kirke Paulding, N.Y., June 25, 1838, to take effect "after the 30th instant," entered upon duties July 1, 1838

TWENTY-FIFTH CONGRESS

March 4, 1837-March 3, 1839

First session–Sept. 4, 1837-Oct. 16, 1837 (43 days)

Second session–Dec. 4, 1837-July 9, 1838 (218 days)

Third session–Dec. 3, 1838-Mar. 3, 1839 (91 days)

Special session of the Senate–Mar. 4, 1837-Mar. 10, 1837 (7 days)

Vice President–Richard Mentor Johnson, Ky.

President pro tempore of the Senate–William Rufus de Vane King, Ala., elected Mar. 7, 1837, special session; Oct. 13, 1837; July 2, 1838; Feb. 25, 1839

Secretary of the Senate–Asbury Dickens, N.C., reelected Sept. 11, 1837

Speaker of the House–James Knox Polk, Tenn., reelected Sept. 4, 1837

Clerks of the House–Walter S. Franklin, Pa., reelected Sept. 4, 1837, died Sept. 20, 1838; Hugh A. Garland, Va., elected Dec. 3, 1838

TWENTY-SIXTH CONGRESS

March 4, 1839-March 3, 1841

First session–Dec. 2, 1839-July 21, 1840 (231 days)
Second session–Dec. 7, 1840-Mar. 3, 1841 (87 days)
Vice President–Richard Mentor Johnson, Ky.
President pro tempore of the Senate–William Rufus de Vane King, Ala., reelected July 3, 1840; Mar. 3, 1841
Secretary of the Senate–Asbury Dickens, N.C., reelected Dec. 9. 1839
Speaker of the House–Robert Mercer Taliaferro Hunter, Va., elected Dec. 16, 1839
Clerk of the House–Hugh A. Garland, Va., reelected Dec. 21, 1839

APPOINTMENTS TO THE SUPREME COURT

Associate Justices
William Smith, Ala., Mar. 8, 1837 (declined to serve)
John Catron, Tenn., Mar. 8, 1837
John McKinley, Ala., Apr. 22, 1837
Peter Vivian Daniel, Va., Mar. 3, 1841

ADMINISTRATION—IMPORTANT DATES

Mar. 6, 1837, General Jessup concluded agreement with Seminole Indian chiefs
Mar. 17, 1837, Republic of Texas adopted constitution
Spring 1837, financial panic of 1837
June 17, 1837, rubber patent obtained by Charles Goodyear
July 29, 1837, Chippewa treaty signed
Aug. 25, 1837, Texas petition for annexation refused
Oct. 12, 1837, $10 million in Treasury notes authorized to relieve economic distress
Oct. 21, 1837, Osceola, Seminole chief, seized while under flag of truce
Dec. 25, 1837, Seminoles defeated by General Zachary Taylor at Okeechobee swamp
Jan. 5, 1838, Van Buren issued neutrality proclamation in Great Britain-Canada dispute
Jan. 8, 1838, Alfred Vail transmitted telegraph message using dots and dashes
Jan. 26, 1838, Osceola died in prison
Jan. 26, 1838, Tennessee forbade liquor sales
April 25, 1838, boundary treaty with Texas signed
June 12, 1838, Iowa territorial government authorized
Aug. 18, 1838, Charles Wilkes left Hampton Roads, Va., on scientific expedition to the South Seas
Feb. 23, 1839, express service organized, Boston, Mass.
Mar. 3, 1839, President authorized to send troops to Maine to protect frontiersmen in Aroostook war
Feb. 1, 1840, Baltimore College of Dental Surgery, first dental school, incorporated
July 4, 1840, independent treasury system created; subtreasuries estab-

lished in New York, Boston, Charleston, and St. Louis

IMPORTANT DATES IN HIS LIFE

1796-1802, worked in law office of Francis Sylvester

1802, studied law in New York City with William P. Van Ness

1803, admitted to the bar; practiced in Kinderhook, N.Y.

1807, counselor of Supreme Court, N.Y.

Feb. 20, 1808, appointed surrogate of Columbia County, N.Y. by Governor Tompkins (his first public office)

1809, moved to Hudson, N.Y.

1813-1820, New York State Senate

1815-1819, attorney general, New York State

Mar. 4, 1821-Dec. 20, 1828, U.S. Senate (from New York); resigned

Aug. 28, 1821, delegate to 3rd New York State constitutional convention

Jan. 1, 1829-Mar. 12, 1829, governor of New York; resigned

Mar. 28, 1829-May 23, 1831, secretary of state under Jackson; resigned

June 25, 1831, appointed minister to Great Britain

Jan. 25, 1832, Senate rejected his nomination; returned to U.S.

Mar. 4, 1833-Mar. 3, 1837, Vice President of the United States under Jackson

Mar. 4, 1837-Mar. 3, 1841, President

1840, unsuccessful Democratic nominee for reelection to the presidency; defeated in his own state

1844, unsuccessful Democratic candidate for nomination; received highest number of votes but not two-thirds majority

1848, unsuccessful Free Soil nominee for the presidency, not receiving any electoral votes; withdrew from public life; returned to his home, Lindenwald, at Kinderhook, N.Y.

MARTIN VAN BUREN

____was the first President born in New York.

____was the third widower inaugurated President.

____was the first President whose son died in a foreign country.

____was the eighth President and eighth Vice President of the United States.

____lived to see eight Presidents from eight different states succeed him.

____was the last Vice President to be elected to succeed the President under whom he served. The only other Vice Presidents similarly elected were John Adams in 1796 and Thomas Jefferson in 1800.

____brought his four sons with him when he went to the White House in 1837. They were 20, 25, 27, and 30 years of age.

VAN BUREN'S VICE PRESIDENT

Vice President–Richard Mentor Johnson (9th V.P.)

Date of birth–Oct. 17, 1780

Birthplace–Floyd's Station, Ky.

Political party–Democratic (Democratic-Republican)

State represented–Kentucky

Term of office–Mar. 4, 1837-Mar. 3, 1841
Age at inauguration–56 years, 138 days
Occupation after term–Retired; served in Kentucky legislature
Date of death–Nov. 19, 1850
Age at death–70 years, 33 days
Place of death–Frankfort, Ky.
Burial place–Frankfort, Ky.

Additional data on Johnson

1802, admitted to the bar; practiced at Great Crossings, Ky.

1804-1807, Kentucky House of Representatives

Mar. 4, 1807-Mar. 3, 1819, U.S. House of Representatives (from Kentucky)

1813, served during term as colonel in Kentucky Volunteers; commanded regiment under General William Henry Harrison in the expedition and engagements in lower Canada in 1813; participated in the Battle of the Thames, Oct. 5, 1813

Apr. 4, 1818, by resolution of Congress he was presented with a sword in recognition of "the daring and distinguised valor displayed by himself and the regiment of volunteers under his command in charging and essentially contributing to vanquish the combined British and Indian forces" in the battle

1819, Kentucky House of Representatives

Dec. 10, 1819-Mar. 3, 1829, U.S. Senate (from Kentucky)

Mar. 4, 1829-Mar. 3, 1837, U.S. House of Representatives (from Kentucky)

1836, elected Vice President by the Senate

Mar. 4, 1837-Mar. 3, 1841, Vice President

1840, unsuccessful candidate for Vice President

1841-1842, Kentucky House of Representatives

A monument in Frankfort, Ky., identifies Johnson as the slayer of Tecumseh, commander of the Indian confederate forces at the Battle of the Thames, Oct. 5, 1813.

ADDITIONAL DATA ON VAN BUREN

FIRST PRESIDENT BORN AN AMERICAN CITIZEN

The first President born a citizen of the United States and therefore never a British subject was Martin Van Buren, born December 5, 1782.

VAN BUREN CHANGED JOBS

In fourteen weeks Martin Van Buren held three important positions. On December 20, 1828, he gave up the office of United States senator. Eleven days later, he was governor of New York State. Sixty-four days later, he was made secretary of state under President Andrew Jackson, resigning the governorship on March 12 and assuming his new post on March 28.

INAUGURATION

Martin Van Buren took the oath of office on Saturday, March 4, 1837, on the east portico of the White House. Chief Justice Roger

Brooke Taney administered the oath. As Van Buren and Jackson rode to the Capitol in a beautiful phaeton built from wood obtained from the frigate *Constitution*, they were accompanied by cavalrymen and infantrymen, as well as delegations from political organizations.

For several hours crowds visited the White House to greet the new President and pay their respects to Andrew Jackson.

This inauguration was of great political importance. The Chief Justice of the United States Supreme Court, whose earlier appointments as Secretary of the Treasury and Associate Justice had not been confirmed by the Senate, swore in as President of the United States a man whose appointment as United States minister to Great Britain had likewise not been approved by the Senate.

VAN BUREN'S VICE PRESIDENT—FIRST VICE PRESIDENT ELECTED BY THE SENATE

In the election of 1836, Richard Mentor Johnson of Kentucky received 147 of the 294 electoral votes for the vice presidency; Francis Granger of New York, 77 votes; John Tyler of Virginia, 47 votes; and William Smith of Alabama, 23 votes. There was no choice for Vice President by the people; the election devolved upon the Senate of the United States. Johnson received 33 votes, Granger received 16 votes, and Johnson was declared elected Vice President.

The Twelfth Amendment to the Constitution provided that:

If no person have a majority, then from the two highest numbers on the list, the Senate shall choose the Vice President; a quorum for the purpose shall consist of two thirds of the whole number of Senators, and a majority of the whole number shall be necessary to a choice.

YOUNGEST SPEAKER OF THE HOUSE

The youngest Speaker of the House of Representatives was Robert Mercer Taliaferro Hunter of Virginia, who was 30 years and 7 months old when he became Speaker. He was elected Speaker of the First Session of the Twenty-sixth Congress on December 16, 1839.

VAN BUREN SOUGHT REELECTION

Martin Van Buren, who served as President from 1837 to 1841, made three unsuccessful attempts to be reelected. He was renominated by the Democrats in 1840 but was defeated by the Whig candidate, William Henry Harrison. Van Buren won in only seven of the twenty-six states.

In the 1844 convention, he received 146 of the 266 votes on the first nominating ballot, but the two-thirds rule was in effect and 177 votes were required for choice. He could not muster sufficient strength and the nomination was captured on the ninth ballot by a "dark horse," James Knox Polk.

The Democrats did not consider him as their candidate in 1848, but the antislavery faction of the party formed the Free Soil Party and ran Van Buren for President. In this election, his fourth candidacy, he received not a single electoral vote and less than 11 per cent of the popular vote.

HOSTESS AT THE WHITE HOUSE

Hannah Van Buren died about nineteen years before Martin Van Buren became President. The mistress of the White House during his administration was Angelica Van Buren, the wife of Abraham Van Buren, President Van Buren's son and private secretary.

THREE PRESIDENTS SERVED IN SAME YEAR

Martin Van Buren completed his four-year term on March 3, 1841. On March 4, 1841, William Henry Harrison was inaugurated. Harrison died on April 4, 1841, and on April 6, 1841, John Tyler was inaugurated President, the third President in one year.

WILLIAM HENRY HARRISON
9th PRESIDENT

Born–Feb. 9, 1773

Birthplace–Berkeley, Charles City County, Va.

College attended–Hampden-Sydney College, Hampden-Sydney, Va.

Date of graduation–None (attended college 1787-1790)

Religious denomination–Episcopalian

Ancestry–English

Occupation–Soldier

Date and place of marriage–Nov. 25, 1795, North Bend, Ohio

Age at marriage–22 years, 289 days

Years married–45 years, 130 days

Political party–Whig

State represented–Ohio

Term of office–Mar. 4, 1841-Apr. 4, 1841

Term served–32 days

Administration–14th

Congressess–27th

Age at inauguration–68 years, 23 days

Date of death–Apr. 4, 1841 (died in office)

Age at death–68 years, 54 days

Place of death–Washington, D.C.

Burial place–William Henry Harrison Memorial State Park, North Bend, Ohio

PARENTS

Father–Benjamin Harrison

Born–Apr. 5, 1726, Berkeley, Va.

Married–1748

Occupation–Politics, statesman

Died–Apr. 24, 1791, City Point, Va.

Age at death–65 years, 19 days

Mother–Elizabeth Bassett Harrison

Born–Dec. 13, 1730, Berkeley, Va.

Died–1792, Berkeley, Va.

Age at death–62 years

BROTHERS AND SISTER

William Henry Harrison was the seventh child in a family of seven.

Children of Benjamin Harrison and Elizabeth Bassett Harrison

Elizabeth Harrison, b. 1751

Ann Harrison, b. May 21, 1753, d. 1821

Benjamin Harrison, b. 1755, d. 1799

Lucy Harrison, d. 1809

Carter Bassett Harrison, d. Apr. 18, 1808

Sarah Harrison, b. 1770, d. 1812

William Henry Harrison, b. Feb. 9, 1773, d. Apr. 4, 1841

CHILDREN

Elizabeth Bassett Harrison, b. Sept. 29, 1796, Fort Washington, Ohio; m. June 29, 1814, John Cleves Short; d. Sept. 26, 1846

John Cleves Symmes Harrison, b. Oct. 28, 1798, Vincennes, Ind.; m. Sept. 29, 1819, Clarissa Pike; d. Oct. 30, 1830

Lucy Singleton Harrison, b. Sept. 1800, Richmond, Va.; m. Sept. 30, 1819, David K. Este; d. Apr. 7, 1826, Cincinnati, Ohio

William Henry Harrison, b. Sept. 3, 1802, Vincennes, Ind.; m. Feb. 18, 1824, Jane Findlay

For additional data see the end of this section and also specific subject headings in the index.

Irwin; d. Feb. 6, 1838, North Bend, Ohio

John Scott Harrison, b. Oct. 4, 1804, Vincennes, Ind.; m. 1824, Lucretia Knapp Johnson; m. Aug. 12, 1831, Elizabeth Ramsey Irwin; d. May 25, 1878, Point Farm, Ind.

Benjamin Harrison, b. 1806, Vincennes, Ind.; m. Louisa Bonner; m. Mary Raney; d. June 9, 1840

Mary Symmes Harrison, b. Jan. 22, 1809, Vincennes, Ind.; m. Mar. 5, 1829, John Henry Fitzhugh Thornton; d. Nov. 16, 1842

Carter Bassett Harrison, b. Oct. 26, 1811, Vincennes, Ind.; m. June 16, 1836, Mary Anne Sutherland; d. Aug. 12, 1839

Anna Tuthill Harrison, b. Oct. 28, 1813, Cincinnati, Ohio; m. June 16, 1836, William Henry Harrison Taylor; d. July 5, 1845

James Findlay Harrison, b. 1814, North Bend, Ohio; d. 1817, North Bend, Ohio

MRS. WILLIAM HENRY HARRISON

Name–Anna Tuthill Symmes Harrison

Born–July 25, 1775

Birthplace–Morristown, N.J.

Age at marriage–20 years, 123 days

Children–6 sons, 4 daughters

Mother–Susan Livingston Symmes

Father–John Cleves Symmes

His occupation–Judge, landowner

Date of death–Feb. 25, 1864

Age at death–88 years, 215 days

Place of death–North Bend, Ohio

Burial place–North Bend, Ohio

Years younger than the President–2 years, 166 days

Years she survived the President–22 years, 327 days

THE ELECTION OF 1840

NOMINATIONS FOR TERM 1841-1845

Whig Party Convention

Dec. 4-7, 1839, Zion Lutheran Church, Harrisburg, Pa.

Nominated for President–William Henry Harrison, Ohio

Nominated for Vice President–John Tyler, Va. Harrison was nominated on the second ballot.

Candidates for nomination and the votes they received on the first and second ballots:

Henry Clay, Ky., 103, 90

William Henry Harrison, Ohio, 94, 148

Winfield Scott, N.J., 57, 16

This was the first national convention to adopt the unit rule by which all the votes of a state delegation are cast for the candidate who receives a majority of the state's votes. There were 254 delegates from 22 states.

On May 4-5, 1840, the nomination was approved at a meeting of young Whigs at Baltimore, Md.

Democratic (Democratic-Republican) Party Convention (3rd)

May 5-7, 1840, Hall of the Musical Association, Baltimore, Md.

Nominated for President–Martin Van Buren, N.Y.

Nomination unanimous on the first ballot

The nomination for the vice presidency was not made at this convention. Each state proposed its own nominee. Candidates running on the Democratic ticket included the following:

Richard Mentor Johnson, Ky.

Littleton Waller Tazewell, Va.

James Knox Polk, Tenn.

The nomination was accorded to Johnson.

Liberty (Abolitionist) Party Convention

Nov. 13, 1839, Warsaw, N.Y.

Nominated for President—James Gillespie Birney, N.Y.

Nominated for Vice President—Francis Julius Lemoyne, Pa.

Both candidates declined the nomination, and on April 1, 1840, another nominating convention was held at Albany, N.Y.:

Nominated for President—James Gillespie Birney, N.Y.

Nominated for Vice President—Thomas Earle, Pa.

This newly formed political party advocated abolition of slavery in the District of Columbia, as well as abolition of interstate slave trade, and generally opposed slavery to the fullest extent within constitutional powers.

At this "national" convention, the name Liberty Party was adopted. The nominees declined the nomination but over 7,000 votes were cast for them in the popular election.

ELECTION RESULTS, NOV. 3, 1840—PRESIDENTIAL AND VICE PRESIDENTIAL CANDIDATES

Whig Party (1,275,016 votes)

William Henry Harrison, Ohio

John Tyler, Va.

Democratic (Democratic-Republican) Party (1,129,102 votes)

Martin Van Buren, N.Y.

Richard Mentor Johnson, Ky.

Liberty (Abolitionist) Party

James Gillespie Birney, N.Y.

Thomas Earle, Pa.

ELECTORAL VOTES (294—26 states)

Harrison received 79.60 per cent (234 votes-19 states) as follows: Conn. 8; Del. 3; Ga. 11; Ind. 9; Ky. 15; La. 5; Me. 10; Md. 10; Mass. 14; Mich. 3; Miss. 4; N.J. 8; N.Y. 42; N.C. 15; Ohio 21; Pa. 30; R.I. 4; Tenn. 15; Vt. 7.

Van Buren received 20.40 per cent (60 votes-7 states) as follows: Ala. 7; Ark. 3; Ill. 5; Mo. 4; N.H. 7; S.C. 11; Va. 23.

For the vice presidency the 60 Democratic votes were divided as follows: Johnson received 48 votes, Tazewell received 11 votes, and Polk received 1 vote.

CABINET

March 4, 1841-April 4, 1841

State–J. L. Martin (chief clerk), ad interim Mar. 4, 1841; Daniel Webster, Mass., Mar. 5, 1841

Treasury–McClintock Young (chief clerk), ad interim Mar. 4, 1841; Thomas Ewing, Ohio, Mar. 5, 1841

War–John Bell, Tenn., Mar. 5, 1841

Attorney General–John Jordan Crittenden, Ky., Mar. 5, 1841

Postmaster General–Selah Reeve Hobbie, N.Y. (first assistant postmaster general), ad interim Mar. 4, 1841; Francis Granger, N.Y., Mar. 6, 1841, entered upon duties Mar. 8, 1841

Navy–John D. Simms (chief clerk), ad interim Mar. 4, 1841; George Edmund Badger, N.C., Mar. 5, 1841

TWENTY-SEVENTH CONGRESS

March 4, 1841-Mar. 3, 1843

First session–May 31, 1841-Sept. 13, 1841 (106 days)

Second session–Dec. 6, 1841-Aug. 31, 1842 (269 days)

Third session–Dec. 5, 1842-Mar. 3, 1843 (89 days)

Special session of the Senate–Mar. 4, 1841-Mar. 15, 1841 (12 days)

Vice President–John Tyler, Va., succeeded to the presidency on the death of William Henry Harrison on Apr. 4, 1841

Presidents pro tempore of the Senate–William Rufus de Vane King, Ala., elected Mar. 4, 1841, special session; Samuel Lewis Southard, N.J., elected Mar. 11, 1841; Willie Person Mangum, N.C., elected May 31, 1842

Secretary of the Senate–Asbury Dickens, N.C., reelected June 7, 1841

Speaker of the House–John White, Ky., elected May 31, 1841

Clerks of the House–Hugh A. Garland, Va., continued from preceding Congress; Matthew St. Clair Clarke, Pa., elected May 31, 1841

ADMINISTRATION—IMPORTANT DATES

Mar. 9, 1841, decision by Supreme Court freed Negroes taken from Spanish ship *Amistad* after they had seized the ship (defense argued by John Quincy Adams)

Mar. 12, 1841, British minister made formal demand for release of Alexander McLeod, Canadian deputy sheriff involved in death of American citizen during Canadian rebellion (1837)

Mar. 17, 1841, Claims Convention signed with Peru

Mar. 27, 1841, steam fire-engine publicly tested, New York, N.Y.

IMPORTANT DATES IN HIS LIFE

1791, regularly enrolled in the Medical Department of the University of Pennsylvania

1791, left school to fight Indians

Aug. 16, 1791, commissioned ensign in the First Infantry by General George Washington

June 2, 1792, commissioned a second lieutenant

1793, aide-de-camp under General Anthony Wayne

1793, general orders issued thanking him and others for their part in expedition that erected Fort Recovery

June 30, 1794, served in Indian war

Aug. 20, 1794 fought in battle of Miami Rapids

May 15, 1797, promoted to captain; given command of Fort Washington

June 1, 1798, resigned with rank of captain

1798-1799, secretary of the Northwest Territory (appointed at $1,200 a year by President John Adams; resigned in Oct. 1799)

Mar. 4, 1799-May 14, 1800, U.S House of Representatives (delegate from the Territory Northwest of the River Ohio)

1801-1813, territorial governor of Indiana and superintendent of Indian Affairs (appointed by President John Adams; reappointed by Presidents Jefferson and Madison)

Nov. 7, 1811, defeated Indians under the Prophet, brother of Chief Tecumseh, at Tippecanoe, on the Wabash River (American casualties: 108 killed and wounded)

1811, complimented by President Madison; votes of thanks extended to him by legislatures of Kentucky and Indiana

Aug. 22, 1812, commissioned major general of Kentucky militia in War of 1812

Sept. 2, 1812, commissioned brigadier general in U.S. Army

Mar. 2, 1813, commissioned major general in chief command of the Northwest

Oct. 5, 1813, defeated the British and Indians in the battle of the Thames in which Tecumseh was killed

May 31, 1814, resigned from the Army

1814, appointed head commissioner to treat with the Indians

Oct. 8, 1816-Mar. 3, 1819, U.S. House of Representatives (from Ohio)

Mar. 24, 1818, received gold medal from Congress for his victory at the battle of the Thames

Dec. 6, 1819-1821, member of Ohio Senate

1822, unsuccessful candidate for U.S. House of Representatives

Mar. 4, 1825-May 20, 1828, U.S. Senate (from Ohio)

May 24, 1828-Sept. 26, 1829, envoy extraordinary and minister plenipotentiary to Colombia

1829, retired to his farm at North Bend, Ohio

1829-1836, county recorder, clerk of county court, president of county agricultural society

Nov. 8, 1836, unsuccessful Whig candidate for the presidency

Mar. 4-Apr. 4, 1841, President

WILLIAM HENRY HARRISON

_____was the first President to die in office. He died on April 4, 1841, in the White House.

_____was the second President who was a resident of a state other than his native state.

_____was the fifth President born in Virginia.

_____was the last President born before the American Revolution. He was born February 9, 1773.

_____was the second President whose father had been a signer of the Declaration of Independence.

_____was the oldest President inaugurated. He was 68 years and 23 days old when he took the oath of office.

_____was the first and only President who studied to become a doctor. He was regularly enrolled in the Medical Department of the University of Pennsylvania and completed sixteen weeks of a thirty-two-week course.

_____served the shortest term as President, from March 4, 1841, to April 4, 1841.

_____was the only President whose grandson (Benjamin Harrison) also became a President.

_____was the first President to lie in state in the White House.

HARRISON'S VICE PRESIDENT

Vice President–John Tyler (10th V.P.)
Born–March 29, 1790
Birthplace–Charles City County, Va.
Political party–Whig (originally Democratic)
State represented–Virginia
Term of office–Mar. 4, 1841-Apr. 6, 1841
Age at inauguration–50 years, 340 days
Occupation after term–President, Apr. 6, 1841-Mar. 3, 1845
Date of death–Jan. 18, 1862
Age at death–71 years, 295 days
Place of death–Richmond, Va.
Burial place–Richmond, Va.

For further biographical information see John Tyler, 10th President.

ADDITIONAL DATA ON HARRISON

HARRISON ARRIVED BY TRAIN

William Henry Harrison was the first President-elect to arrive by railroad at Washington, D.C., for his inauguration. Harrison left Baltimore, Md., February 9, 1841, on his sixty-eighth birthday. He boarded a Baltimore and Ohio Railroad train and arrived at Washington, D.C., where he registered at Gadsby's Hotel.

HARRISON'S PROPHETIC FAREWELL

In a speech delivered January 26, 1841, at Cincinnati, Ohio, Harrison said: "Gentlemen and fellow citizens. . . . Perhaps this may be the last time I may have the pleasure of speaking to you on earth or seeing you. I will bid you farewell, if forever, fare thee well."

INAUGURATION

William Henry Harrison, the oldest President inaugurated, took the oath of office on Thursday, March 4, 1841, on the east portico of the Capitol. The oath was administered by Chief Justice Taney. Harrison rode a white horse to the Capitol, refusing to wear hat or coat despite the cold and stormy weather. He read his 8,578-word inaugural address, the longest on record, taking about one hour and forty-five minutes.

After the ceremony, he led the inaugural parade to the White House. Numerous floats depicting log cabins and cider barrels were highlights of the parade. Great crowds flocked to the White House.

In the evening, Harrison attended three inaugural balls: one known as the "Native American Inaugural Ball"; another on Louisiana Avenue in a converted theatre known as the new Washington Assembly Room; and the third the People's Tippecanoe Ball at Carusi's Saloon between 10th and 11th Streets on C Street, attended by a thousand people who paid ten dollars each.

Harrison caught cold at the ceremonies and was prostrated by a chill on March 27, 1841. He died of pleurisy fever (pneumonia) at thirty minutes past one on Sunday morning April 4, 1841.

THE FIRST LADY

Anna Symmes Harrison, the wife of William Henry Harrison was taken ill one month before the inauguration and did not accompany her husband to Washington. Mrs. Harrison intended to follow later but was not able to go to Washington during her husband's brief term. Harrison's daughter-in-law, Mrs. Jane Irwin Harrison, the wife of Colonel William Henry Harrison, Jr., accompanied the President to Washington and acted temporarily as mistress of the White House. There was practically no social activity at the White House in the short time Harrison presided there.

HARRISON'S FAMILY IN OFFICE

Benjamin Harrison of Virginia, one of the signers of the Declaration of Independence and a menber of the Continental Congress from 1774 to 1778, was the father of William Henry Harrison.

Carter Bassett Harrison of Virginia, who served in the Third, Fourth, and Fifth Congresses from March 4, 1793, to March 3, 1799, was a brother of William Henry Harrison.

John Scott Harrison, a Whig representative from Ohio in the 34th and 35th Congresses from March 4, 1852, to March 3, 1857, was a son of William Henry Harrison.

Benjamin Harrison, a Republican senator from March 4, 1881, to March 3, 1887, and President of the United States from March 4, 1889, to March 3, 1893, was a grandson of William Henry Harrison.

JOHN TYLER
10th PRESIDENT

Born–Mar. 29, 1790

Birthplace–Charles City County, Va.

College attended–College of William and Mary, Williamsburg, Va.

Date of graduation–July 4, 1807

Religion–Episcopalian

Ancestry–English

Occupation–Lawyer

Date and place of first marriage–Mar. 29, 1813, New Kent County, Va.

Age at marriage–23 years

Years married–29 years, 165 days

Date and place of second marriage–June 26, 1844, New York, N.Y.

Age at second marriage–54 years, 89 days

Years married–17 years, 206 days

Political party–Whig (originally Democratic)

State represented–Virginia

Term of office–Apr. 6, 1841-Mar. 3, 1845 (Tyler succeeded to the presidency on the death of William Henry Harrison.)

Term served–3 years, 332 days

Administration–14th

Congresses–27th, 28th

Age at inauguration–51 years, 8 days

Lived after term–16 years, 320 days

Occupation after term–Lawyer

Date of death–Jan. 18, 1862

Age at death–71 years, 295 days

Place of death–Richmond, Va.

Burial place–Hollywood Cemetery, Richmond, Va.

PARENTS

Father–John Tyler

Born–Feb. 28, 1747, Yarmouth, James City County, Va.

Married–1776, Weyanoke, Va.

Occupation–Lawyer, judge, governor

Died–Jan. 6, 1813, Charles City County, Va.

Age at death–65 years, 312 days

Mother–Mary Marot Armistead Tyler

Born–1761

Died–Apr. 1797

Age at death–36 years

BROTHERS AND SISTERS

John Tyler was the sixth child in a family of eight.

Children of John Tyler and Mary Marot Armistead Tyler

Anne Contesse Tyler, b. 1778, d. June 12, 1803

Elizabeth Armistead Tyler, b. 1780, d. 1824

Martha Jefferson Tyler, b. 1782, d. 1855

Maria Henry Tyler, b. 1784, d. 1843

Wat Henry Tyler, b. 1788, d. July 1862

John Tyler, b. Mar. 29, 1790, d. Jan. 18, 1862

William Tyler, d. 1856

Christianna Booth Tyler, b. 1795, d. 1842

CHILDREN

By first wife, Letitia Christian Tyler

Mary Tyler, b. Apr. 15, 1815; m. Dec. 14, 1835, Henry Lightfoot Jones; d. June 17, 1848

Robert Tyler, b. Sept. 9, 1816; m. Sept. 12, 1839, Elizabeth Priscilla Cooper; d. Dec. 3, 1877

For additional data see the end of this section and also specific subject headings in the index.

John Tyler, b. Apr. 27, 1819; m. Oct. 25, 1838, Martha Rochelle; d. Jan. 26, 1896

Letitia Tyler, b. May 11, 1821; m. James A. Semple; d. Dec. 28, 1907

Elizabeth Tyler, b. July 11, 1823; m. Jan. 31, 1842, William Nevison Waller at the White House, Washington, D.C.; d. June 1, 1850

Anne Contesse Tyler, b. Apr. 1825; d. July 1825

Alice Tyler, b. Mar. 23, 1827; m. 1850, Rev. Henry Mandeville Denison; d. June 8, 1854

Tazewell Tyler, b. Dec. 6, 1830; m. Dec. 1857, Nannie Bridges; d. Jan. 8, 1874

By second wife, Julia Gardiner Tyler

David Gardiner Tyler, b. July 12, 1846, Charles City County, Va.; m. June 6, 1894, Mary Morris Jones; d. Sept. 5, 1927, Richmond, Va.

John Alexander Tyler, b. Apr. 7, 1848; m. Sarah Gardiner; d. Sept. 1, 1883

Julia Tyler, b. Dec. 25, 1849 (or 1850); m. June 26, 1869, William H. Spencer; d. May 8, 1871

Lachlan Tyler, b. Dec. 2, 1851; m. Georgia Powell; d. Jan. 26, 1902, New York, N.Y.

Lyon Gardiner Tyler, b. Aug. 1853, Charles City County, Va.; m. Nov. 14, 1878, Annie Baker Tucker; m. Sept. 12, 1923, Susan Ruffin; d. Feb. 12, 1935, Charles City County, Va.

Robert Fitzwalter Tyler, b. Mar. 12, 1856; m. Fannie Glinn; d. Dec. 30, 1927, Richmond, Va.

Pearl Tyler, b. June 20, 1860; m. Major William Mumford Ellis; d. June 30, 1947, Elliston, Va.

MRS. JOHN TYLER (first wife)

Name–Letitia Christian Tyler
Date of birth–Nov. 12, 1790
Birthplace–"Cedar Grove," New Kent County, Va.
Age at marriage–22 years, 137 days
Children–5 daughters, 3 sons
Mother–Mary Brown Christian
Father–Colonel Robert Christian
His occupation–Planter
Date of death–Sept. 10, 1842
Age at death–51 years, 302 days
Place of death–White House, Washington, D.C.
Burial place–Cedar Grove, Va.
Years younger than the President–228 days
Years the President survived her–19 years, 130 days

MRS. JOHN TYLER (second wife)

Name–Julia Gardiner Tyler
Date of birth–May 4, 1820
Birthplace–Gardiner's Island, N.Y.
Age at marriage–24 years, 53 days
Children–5 boys, 2 girls
Mother–Juliana McLachlen Gardiner
Father–David Gardiner
His occupation–Senator (New York)
Date of death–July 10, 1889
Age at death–69 years, 67 days
Place of death–Richmond, Va.
Burial place–Richmond, Va.
Years younger than the President–30 years, 36 days
Years she survived the President–27 years, 173 days

CABINET

April 6, 1841-March 3, 1845

State–Daniel Webster, Mass., continued from preceding administration; Hugh Swinton Legaré, S.C. (Attorney General), ad interim May 9, 1843; William S. Derrick (chief clerk), ad interim June 21, 1843; Abel Parker Upshur, Va. (Secretary of the Navy), ad interim June 24, 1843; John Nelson, Md. (Attorney General), ad interim Feb. 29, 1844; John Caldwell Calhoun, S.C., Mar. 6, 1844; entered upon duties Apr. 1, 1844

Treasury–Thomas Ewing, Ohio, continued from preceding administration; McClintock Young (chief clerk), ad interim Sept. 13, 1841; Walter Forward, Pa., Sept. 13, 1841; McClintock Young (chief clerk) ad interim Mar. 1, 1843; John Canfield Spencer, N.Y., Mar. 3, 1843; entered upon duties Mar. 8, 1843; McClintock Young (chief clerk), ad interim May 2, 1844; George Mortimer Bibb, Ky., June 15, 1844; entered upon duties July 4, 1844

War–John Bell, Tenn., continued from preceding administration; Albert M. Lea, Md. (chief clerk), ad interim Sept. 12, 1841; John Canfield Spencer, N.Y., Oct. 12, 1841; James Madison Porter, Pa., Mar. 8, 1843; William Wilkins, Pa., Feb. 15, 1844; entered upon duties Feb. 20, 1844

Attorney General–John Jordan Crittenden, Ky., continued from preceding administration; Hugh Swinton Legaré, S.C., Sept. 13, 1841; entered upon duties Sept. 20, 1841; John Nelson, Md., July 1, 1843

Postmaster General–Francis Granger, N.Y., continued from preceding administration; Selah Reeve Hobbie, N.Y. (first assistant), ad interim Sept. 14, 1841; Charles Anderson Wickliffe, Ky., Sept. 13, 1841; entered upon duties Oct. 13, 1841

Navy–George Edmund Badger, N.C., continued from preceding administration; John D. Simms (chief clerk), ad interim Sept. 11, 1841; Abel Parker Upshur, Va., Sept. 13, 1841; entered upon duties Oct. 11, 1841; David Henshaw, Mass., July 24, 1843; Thomas Walker Gilmer, Va., Feb. 15, 1844; entered upon duties Feb. 19, 1844; Lewis Warrington (captain, United States Navy), ad interim Feb. 29, 1844; John Young Mason, Va., Mar. 14, 1844; entered upon duties Mar. 26, 1844

TWENTY-EIGHTH CONGRESS

March 4, 1843-March 3, 1845

First session–Dec. 4, 1843-June 17, 1844 (196 days)
Second session–Dec. 2, 1844-Mar. 3, 1845 (92 days)
Vice President–Vice President John Tyler succeeded to the presidency on the death of William Henry Harrison on Apr. 4, 1841
President pro tempore of the Senate–Willie Person Mangum, N.C.
Secretary of the Senate–Asbury Dickens, N.C., reelected Dec. 11, 1843
Speaker of the House–John Winston Jones, Va., elected Dec. 4, 1843
Clerks of the House–Matthew St. Clair Clarke, Pa., Caleb J. McNulty, Ohio, elected Dec. 6, 1843; dismissed from office Jan. 18, 1845; Benjamin Brown French, N.H., elected Jan. 18, 1845

APPOINTMENT TO THE SUPREME COURT
Associate Justice
Samuel Nelson, N.Y., Feb. 13, 1845

ADMINISTRATION—IMPORTANT DATES

Aug. 13, 1841, independent treasury act repealed

Sept. 11, 1841, cabinet resigned, except secretary of state

1842, gold discovered, San Fernando Mission, Calif.

Feb. 1, 1842, Coast Guard commandant appointed

Feb. 15, 1842, adhesive postage stamps used, New York, N.Y.

Feb. 21, 1842, sewing machine patented, J. J. Greenough

Mar. 31, 1842, Henry Clay resigned after forty years in Congress

June 10, 1842, Wilkes Expedition returned

Aug. 9, 1842, Webster-Ashburton treaty with Great Britain signed, settling Maine boundary

Aug. 14, 1842, end of Seminole War announced by Colonel Worth

Aug. 22, 1842, Northeastern boundary treaty ratified by the Senate

Aug. 26, 1842, start of fiscal year changed from Jan. 1 to July 1

Aug. 30, 1842, tariff placed upon opium imports

Aug. 31, 1842, Bureau of Medicine and Surgery of the Navy authorized

Oct. 18, 1842, underwater cable laid in New York Harbor

Nov. 22, 1842, Mount Saint Helens, Wash., erupted

Mar. 3, 1843, Congress appropriated $30,000 to test the telegraph

May 2, 1843, organization of Oregon government attempted

June 17, 1843, Bunker Hill monument dedicated

Nov. 13, 1843, Mount Rainier, Wash., erupted

Feb. 28, 1844, explosion on warship *Princeton*

May 25, 1844, first news dispatch sent by telegraph to Baltimore *Patriot*

June 15, 1844, Charles Goodyear obtained patent on vulcanized rubber

July 3, 1844, treaty of peace, amity and commerce signed with China

Jan. 3, 1845, uniform election day established

Mar. 1, 1845, annexation of Texas by joint resolution of Congress

Mar. 3, 1845, first legislation passed over a presidential veto

Mar. 3, 1845, Florida admitted as the 27th state

IMPORTANT DATES IN HIS LIFE

1807, graduated from College of William and Mary, which he had entered at age of twelve

1809, admitted to the bar; practiced in Charles City County, Va.

1811-1816, member of Virginia House of Delegates

1813, captain of a military company

1816, member of Virginia Council of State

Dec. 16, 1817-Mar. 3, 1821, U.S. House of Representatives (from Virginia)

1820, declined renomination because of ill health

18—, rector and chancellor of College of William and Mary

1823-1825, Virginia House of Delegates

Dec. 1, 1825-1827, Governor of Virginia

Mar. 4, 1827-Feb. 29, 1836, member of U.S. Senate (from Virginia); resigned

1829, 1830, delegate to Virginia constitutional conventions

Mar. 3, 1835-July 1, 1836, president pro tempore of the Senate

1836, unsuccessful candidate for Vice President on Whig ticket

1838, president of Virginia African Colonization Society

1839, member of Virginia State House of Delegates

Mar. 4, 1841-Apr. 4, 1841, Vice President

Apr. 6, 1841-Mar. 3, 1845, President (took office on death of William Henry Harrison)

1844, proposed as presidential candidate by secessionist Democratic convention

1859, chancellor of College of William and Mary

Mar. 1, 1861, member of Virginia secession convention

July 20, 1861, delegate to Confederate Provisional Congress

JOHN TYLER

_____was the sixth President born in Virginia.

_____was the first President whose wife died while he was in office.

_____was the first Vice President elevated to the presidency through the death of a Chief Executive. He was elected as a Whig to the vice presidency and took office March 4, 1841. Upon the death of President William Henry Harrison, Tyler took the oath of office as President of the United States on April 6, 1841.

_____was the first President to marry while in office. He remarried on June 26, 1844.

_____was the first President to marry on his birthday.

_____was the first President whose father had been a governor of a state (Virginia).

ADDITIONAL DATA ON TYLER

SENATOR TYLER OPPOSED STATE MANDATE

Tyler refused to obey a resolution of the Virginia legislature demanding that he vote for the Benton resolution, and resigned his seat in the Senate on February 29, 1836.

President Jackson had removed Secretary of the Treasury Duane for refusing to check out the deposits in the United States Bank, and for this action he had been censured by the Senate. Senator Thomas Hart Benton of Missouri moved to have the Senate expunge the censure.

INAUGURATION

John Tyler was the first Vice President to succeed to the presidency through the death of a President. He was at Williamsburg, Va., when he received the news that President William Henry Harrison had died on April 4, 1841. Fletcher Webster, chief clerk of the Department of State and son of Daniel Webster, Secretary of State, delivered the note to Tyler at his home. Tyler returned to Washington, D.C., on April 6, 1841, at 4 A.M. At 12 noon on April 6 the oath was administered by William Cranch, Chief Justice of the United States Circuit

Court of the District of Columbia, at the Indian Queen Hotel, Washington, D.C. Tyler held a cabinet meeting in the afternoon. On April 14, 1841, he moved into the White House.

TYLER PROCLAIMED MEMORIAL FOR HARRISON

On April 13, 1841, one week after his succession to the presidency, John Tyler issued a proclamation recommending

to the people of the United States of every religious denomination that, according to their several modes and forms of worship, they observe a day of fasting and prayer by such religious services as may be suitable on the occasion; and I recommend Friday the 14th of May next, for that purpose. . . .

TYLER CABINET RESIGNED

On September 9, 1841, President Tyler vetoed a bill "to provide for the better collection, safekeeping, and disbursement of the public revenues by means of a corporation to be styled the Fiscal Corporation of the United States." This action was disapproved of by his cabinet and the secretaries of the Treasury, War, and Navy, as well as the Attorney General and the Postmaster General, resigned. The only cabinet member who retained his post was Secretary of State Daniel Webster:

PRESIDENTIAL COMMISSION OPPOSED

The first President requested by Congress to justify the creation of a presidential commission was John Tyler. The House of Representatives on February 7, 1842, passed a resolution

that the President of the United States inform this House under what authority the commission, consisting of George Poindexter and others, for the investigations of the concerns of the New York Customs House was raised, what were the purposes and objects of said commission . . . and out of what fund the said expenditures have been or are to be paid.

In a letter dated February 9. 1842, Tyler cited the

authority vested in the President of the United States "to take care that the laws be faithfully executed and to give to Congress from time to time information on the state of the Union."

TYLER'S GRANDDAUGHTER BORN IN WHITE HOUSE

The first girl born in the White House was Letitia Christian Tyler, the daughter of Robert Tyler, and the granddaughter of President John Tyler. She was born in 1842.

TYLER ESCAPED DEATH ABOARD THE PRINCETON

About four hundred visitors, including President Tyler, the members of the Cabinet, the diplomatic corps, members of Congress, and their families visited the U.S.S. *Princeton*, the first propeller-driven warship, on February 28, 1844. She proceeded from Alexandria, Va., down the Potomac River. Below Fort Washington, the ship's "Peacemaker," a ten-ton gun, fifteen feet long with a twelve-inch bore, fired a 225-pound ball.

On the return trip, when the ship was about fifteen miles below Washington, D.C., the gun was fired again, with a 25-pound charge. Although the gun had been tested at 49 pounds and had frequently been fired successfully with a 30-pound charge, it exploded and burst at the breech. Thomas Walker Gilmer, Secretary of the Navy; Abel Parker Upshur, Secretary of State; Commodore Kennon of the *Princeton*; David Gardiner, a former state senator of New York; Virgil Maxcy, a former United States chargé d'affaires in Belgium; and Tyler's Negro servant were killed. Seventeen seamen were wounded and many others were stunned, including Captain Robert Field Stockton of the *Princeton*. President Tyler was below decks, when the explosion took place.

The bodies were brought to the Executive Mansion and the coffins were placed in the East Room. Because the explosion was an accident the captain and the officers were exonerated from blame.

CONGRESS OVERRODE VETO

The first legislation passed over a President's veto was an act (S.66, 2 sess. 28 Cong.) "relating to revenue cutters and steamers." It provided that no revenue cutter could be built unless an appropriation was first made by law. President Tyler vetoed the bill, on the grounds a contract for two revenue cutters had already been let, one to a firm in Richmond, Va., and the other to a Pittsburgh, Pa., contractor. He vetoed the bill on February 20, 1845. It was reconsidered by the Senate and House on March 3, 1845. The former passed it without debate over his veto, 41 to 1, and the House by a vote of 127 to 30.

HOSTESSES AT THE WHITE HOUSE

Letitia Christian Tyler was still suffering from the effects of a paralytic attack when her husband became President. As she was unable to act as mistress of the White House, Priscilla Cooper Tyler, the wife of their eldest son, acted in that capacity.

During the seventeen months that Letitia Tyler was the first lady, she appeared in public at the White House only once. On January 31, 1842, she attended the marriage of her daughter, Elizabeth, to William Nevinson Waller. Less than eight months later, on September 10, 1842, Mrs. Tyler died.

ATTEMPT TO IMPEACH TYLER

John Minor Botts, representative from Virginia, introduced a resolution on January 10, 1843, charging "John Tyler, Vice President acting as President" of corruption, malconduct in office, high crimes and misdemeanors. The nine charges were rejected and the resolution was not accepted by a vote of 83 ayes to 127 nays. (*Congressional Globe*, Jan. 10, 1842)

PRESIDENT TYLER REMARRIED

John Tyler was the first President to marry while in office. After the death of his first wife, he remained a widower for a little over twenty-one months and then married Julia Gardiner on June 26, 1844, at the Church of the Ascension, New York, N.Y. She was the first lady of the land for a little over eight months until James Knox Polk became President.

TYLER PRESIDED AT PEACE CONFERENCE

Former President Tyler was president of the peace conference which met in secret session from February 4 to February 27, 1861, at Washington, D.C. a report presented to the delegates at the conference on February 15 was adopted February 26. The conference was attended by 133 commissioners from 22 states. The free states represented were Connecticut, Illinois, Indiana, Iowa, Kansas, Maine, Massachusetts, New Hampshire, New Jersey, New York, Ohio, Pennsylvania, Rhode Island, Vermont and Wisconsin; the slave states represented were Delaware, Kentucky, Maryland, Missouri, North Carolina, Tennessee and Virginia.

The report of the conference was submitted to Congress, which considered it and finally rejected it.

TYLER IN CONFEDERATE CONGRESS

John Tyler served as a member of the Confederate States Congress. On August 1, 1861, he was a delegate to the Provisional Congress of the Confederate States. He was elected a member of the House of Representatives of the permanent Confederate Congress on November 7, 1861, but never took his seat, as he died January 18, 1862, at Richmond, Va., before the Congress assembled.

TYLER'S DEATH IGNORED

When former President John Tyler died at Richmond, Va., on January 18, 1862, the government made no announcement or proclamation of his death and no official notice of his demise was taken.

GOVERNMENT AUTHORIZED TYLER MONUMENT FIFTY YEARS AFTER HIS DEATH

On March 4, 1911, Congress authorized the erection of a monument to Tyler's memory and on August 24, 1912, appropriated $10,000 for it. It was completed June 9, 1915, and dedicated October 12, 1915, at Hollywood Cemetery, Cherry and Albemarle Streets, Richmond, Va. Five senators and five congressmen represented the United States at the ceremonies.

TYLER HONORED HIS HORSE

In Sherwood, Charles City County, Va., John Tyler had a grave dug for his horse, "The General," over which was the following inscription:

Here lies the body of my good horse, "The General." For twenty years he bore me around the circuit of my practice, and in all that time he never made a blunder. Would that his master could say the same! John Tyler.

JAMES KNOX POLK
11th PRESIDENT

Born–Nov. 2, 1795
Birthplace–Near Pineville, Mecklenburg County, N.C.
College attended–University of North Carolina, Chapel Hill, N.C.
Date of graduation–June 4, 1818, Bachelor of Arts
Religion–Presbyterian
Ancestry–Scotch-Irish
Occupation–Lawyer
Date and place of marriage–Jan. 1, 1824, Murfreesboro, Tenn.
Age at marriage–28 years, 60 days
Years married–25 years, 165 days
Political party–Democratic
State represented–Tennessee
Term of office–Mar. 4, 1845-Mar. 3, 1849
Term served–4 years
Administration–15th
Congresses–29th, 30th
Age at inauguration–49 years, 122 days
Lived after term–103 days
Occupation after term–Retired because of illness
Date of death–June 15, 1849
Age at death–53 years, 225 days
Place of death–Nashville, Tenn.
Burial place–Polk Place, Nashville, Tenn.; remains removed in 1893 to the State Capitol Grounds, Nashville, Tenn.

PARENTS

Father–Samuel Polk
Born–July 5, 1772, Tryon, N.C.
Married–Dec. 25, 1794, Mecklenburg County, N.C.
Occupation–Planter, farmer

Died–Nov. 5, 1827, Maury County, Tenn.
Age at death–55 years, 123 days
Mother–Jane Knox Polk
Born–Nov. 15, 1776
Died–Jan. 11, 1852, Maury County, Tenn.
Age at death–75 years, 57 days

BROTHERS AND SISTERS

James Knox Polk was the oldest child in a family of ten.

Children of Samuel Polk and Jane Knox Polk

James Knox Polk, b. Nov. 2, 1795, d. June 15, 1849
Jane Maria Polk, b. Jan. 14, 1798, d. Oct. 11, 1876
Lydia Eliza Polk, b. Feb. 17, 1800, d. May 29, 1864
Franklin Ezekiel Polk, b. Aug. 23, 1802, d. Jan. 21, 1831
Marshall Tate Polk, b. Jan. 17, 1805, d. Apr. 12, 1831
John Lee Polk, b. Mar. 23, 1807, d. Sept. 28, 1831
Naomi Tate Polk, b. July 2, 1809, d. Aug. 6, 1836
Ophelia Clarissa Polk, b. Sept. 6, 1812, d. Apr. 18, 1851
William Hawkins Polk, b. May 24, 1815, d. Dec. 16, 1862
Samuel Wilson Polk, b. Oct. 17, 1817, d. Feb. 24, 1839

CHILDREN
None

MRS. JAMES KNOX POLK

Name–Sarah Childress Polk
Date of birth–Sept. 4, 1803
Birthplace–Murfreesboro, Tenn.
Age at marriage–20 years, 119 days

For additional data see the end of this section and also specific subject headings in the index.

Children–None
Mother–Elizabeth Childress
Father–Captain Joel Childress
His occupation–Planter
Date of death–Aug. 14, 1891
Age at death–87 years, 344 days

Place of death–Nashville, Tenn.
Burial place–Nashville, Tenn.
Years younger than the President–7 years, 306 days
Years she survived the President–42 years, 60 days

THE ELECTION OF 1844

NOMINATIONS FOR TERM 1845-1849

Democratic Party Convention (4th)

May 27-30, 1844, Odd Fellows' Hall, Baltimore, Md.
Nominated for President—James Knox Polk, Tenn.
Nominated for Vice President—George Mifflin Dallas, Pa.

Candidates for nomination and the votes they received on the first ballot:

Martin Van Buren, N.Y., 146
Lewis Cass, Mich., 83
Cave Johnson, Tenn., 24
John Caldwell Calhoun, S.C., 6
James Buchanan, Pa., 4
Levi Woodbury, N.H., 2
John Stewart, Conn., 1
Total number of votes: 266
Number necessary for nomination: 177

Polk received his first vote on the eighth ballot and was nominated unanimously on the ninth ballot.

Silas Wright of New York was nominated for the vice presidency, receiving 258 votes, while Levi Woodbury of New Hampshire received 8 votes. Wright declined the nomination and George Mifflin Dallas became the nominee.

Whig Party Convention

May 1, 1844, Universalist Church, Baltimore, Md.
Nominated for President—Henry Clay, Ky.
Nominated for Vice President—Theodore Frelinghuysen, N.J.

Clay was nominated on the first ballot by acclamation.

Liberty Party Convention

Aug. 30, 1843, Buffalo, N.Y.
Nominated for President—James Gillespie Birney, N.Y.
Nominated for Vice President—Thomas Morris, Ohio

National Democratic Tyler Convention

May 27-28, 1844, Calvert Hall, Baltimore, Md.
Nominated for President—John Tyler, Va.
Nominated for Vice President—None

A group of Democrats opposed to the nominations of the major parties endeavored to establish a separate ticket and party. A committee was appointed to nominate a vice presidential candidate.

ELECTION RESULTS, NOV. 5, 1844—PRESIDENTIAL AND VICE PRESIDENTIAL CANDIDATES

Democratic Party (1,337,243 votes)

James Knox Polk, Tenn.
George Mifflin Dallas, Pa.

Whig Party (1,299,062 votes)

Henry Clay, Ky.
Theodore Frelinghuysen, N.J.

Liberty Party (62,300 votes)

James Gillespie Birney, N.Y.
Thomas Morris, Ohio

ELECTORAL VOTES (275—26 states)

Polk received 61.82 per cent (170 votes—15 states) as follows:
Ala. 9; Ark. 3; Ga. 10; Ill. 9; Ind. 12; La. 6; Me. 9; Mich. 5; Miss.
6; Mo. 7; N.H. 6; N.Y. 36; Pa. 26; S.C. 9; Va. 17.

Clay received 38.18 per cent (105 votes—11 states) as follows: Conn.
6; Del. 3; Ky. 12; Md. 8; Mass. 12; N.J. 7; N.C. 11; Ohio 23; R.I.
4; Tenn. 13; Vt. 6.

CABINET

March 4, 1845-March 3, 1849

State–John Caldwell Calhoun, S.C., continued from preceding administration; James Buchanan, Pa., Mar. 6, 1845; entered upon duties Mar. 10, 1845

Treasury–George Mortimer Bibb, Ky., continued from preceding administration; Robert James Walker, Miss., Mar. 6, 1845; entered upon duties Mar. 8, 1845

War–William Wilkins, Pa., continued from preceding administration; William Learned Marcy, N.Y., Mar. 6, 1845; entered upon duties Mar. 8, 1845

Attorney General–John Nelson, Md., continued from preceding adminsitration; John Young Mason, Va., Mar. 6, 1845; entered upon duties Mar. 11, 1845; Nathan Clifford, Me., Oct. 17, 1846; resigned Mar. 18, 1848; Isaac Toucey, Conn., June 21, 1848; entered upon duties June 29, 1848

Postmaster General–Charles Anderson Wickliffe, Ky., continued from preceding administration; Cave Johnson, Tenn., Mar. 6, 1845

Navy–John Young Mason, Va., continued from preceding administration; George Bancroft, Mass., Mar. 10, 1845; John Young Mason, Va., Sept. 9, 1846

TWENTY-NINTH CONGRESS

March 4, 1845-March 3, 1847

First session–Dec. 1, 1845-Aug. 10, 1846 (253 days)
Second session–Dec. 7, 1846-Mar. 3, 1847 (87 days)
Special session of the Senate–Mar. 4, 1845-Mar. 20, 1845 (17 days)

Vice President–George Mifflin Dallas, Pa.

Presidents pro tempore of the Senate–Ambrose Hundley Sevier, Ark., served Dec. 27, 1845 (one day); David Rice Atchison, Mo., elected Aug. 8, 1846; Jan. 11, 1847; Mar. 3, 1847

Secretary of the Senate–Asbury Dickens, N.C., reelected Dec. 9, 1845

Speaker of the House–John Wesley Davis, Ind., elected Dec. 1, 1845

Clerk of the House–Benjamin Brown French, N.H., reelected Dec. 2, 1845

THIRTIETH CONGRESS

March 4, 1847-March 3, 1849

First session–Dec. 6, 1847-Aug. 14, 1848 (254 days)

Second session–Dec. 4, 1848-Mar. 3, 1849 (90 days)

Vice President–George Mifflin Dallas, Pa.

President pro tempore of the Senate–David Rice Atchison, Mo., elected Feb. 2, 1848; June 1, 1848; June 26, 1848; July 29, 1848; Dec. 26, 1848; Mar. 2, 1849

Secretary of the Senate–Asbury Dickens, N.C., reelected Dec. 13, 1847

Speaker of the House–Robert Charles Winthrop, Mass., elected Dec. 6, 1847

Clerks of the House–Benjamin Brown French, N.H., Thomas Jefferson Campbell, Tenn., elected Dec. 7, 1847

APPOINTMENTS TO THE SUPREME COURT

Associate Justices

Levi Woodbury, N.H., Sept. 20, 1845

Robert Cooper Grier, Pa., Aug. 4, 1846

ADMINISTRATION—IMPORTANT DATES

Oct. 10, 1845, United States Naval Academy opened

Dec. 29, 1845, Texas admitted as the 28th state

1846, Howe patented sewing machine

Jan. 23, 1846, uniform election day established

Mar. 4, 1846, Michigan legislature abolished death penalty (first state to do so)

Apr. 25, 1846, first skirmish in Mexican War

May 8, 1846, Battle of Palo Alto

May 9, 1846, Battle of Resaca de la Palma

May 13, 1846, United States formally declared war against Mexico

June 15, 1846, treaty concluded with Great Britain establishing Oregon boundary on the 49th parallel; in force Aug. 1846

Aug. 8, 1846, defeat in Senate of Wilmot proviso calling for exclusion of slavery from any territory acquired from Mexico

Sept. 24, 1846, Battle of Monterey

Dec. 28, 1846, Iowa admitted as the 29th state

1847, conquest of California by American forces

Feb. 23, 1847, Battle of Buena Vista

Mar. 29, 1847, General Winfield Scott captured Vera Cruz

Apr. 18, 1847, Battle of Cerro Gordo

May 5, 1847, American Medical Association organized
Sept. 8, 1847, Battle of Molino del Rey
Sept. 13, 1847, Battle of Chapultepec
Sept. 14, 1847, fall of Mexico City to General Scott
Jan. 24, 1848, gold discovered in California by James W. Marshall; beginning of gold rush which reached its height in 1849
Feb. 2, 1848, treaty of Guadalupe Hidalgo signed with Mexico; Mexico recognized Rio Grande as boundary and ceded, for $15 million, territory that became California, New Mexico, Arizona, Nevada, Utah, and parts of Colorado and Wyoming
Mar. 10, 1848, treaty of Guadalupe Hidalgo ratified by Senate
Mar. 25, 1848, treaty of Guadalupe Hidalgo ratified by Mexican government
May 29, 1848, Wisconsin admitted as the 30th state
May 30, 1848, treaty ratifications formally exchanged
June 12, 1848, American troops evacuated Mexico City
July 4, 1848, President Polk laid cornerstone of the Washington Monument
July 19-20, 1848, women's rights convention, Seneca Falls, N.Y.
Aug. 14, 1848, Oregon admitted as a territory
Mar. 3, 1849, Department of Interior created

IMPORTANT DATES IN HIS LIFE

1806, moved to Tennessee, settling in what is now Maury County
1818, graduated from the University of North Carolina
1820, admitted to the bar; practiced at Columbia, Tenn.
1821-1823, chief clerk of Tennessee Senate
1823-1825, Tennessee House of Representatives
Mar. 4, 1825-Mar. 3, 1839, U.S. House of Representatives (from Tennessee)
Dec. 7, 1835-Mar. 3, 1839, Speaker of the House of Representatives
1839-1841, governor of Tennessee
Mar. 4, 1845-Mar. 3, 1849, President
1849, declined to be a candidate for reelection; retired to Nashville

JAMES KNOX POLK

_____was the first President born in North Carolina.
_____was the third President who was a resident of a state other than his native state.
_____was the fourth President whose mother was alive when he was inaugurated.
_____was the first President who was survived by his mother.

POLK'S VICE PRESIDENT

Vice President—George Mifflin Dallas (11th V.P.)
Date of birth—July 10, 1792
Birthplace—Philadelphia, Pa.
Political party—Democratic
State represented—Pennsylvania
Term of office—Mar. 4, 1845-Mar. 3, 1849

Age at inauguration–52 years, 237 days
Occupation after term–Governmental positons
Date of death–Dec. 31, 1864
Place of death–Philadelphia, Pa.
Age at death–72 years, 174 days
Burial place–Philadelphia, Pa.

Additional data on Dallas

1810, graduated from Princeton
1813, admitted to the bar
1813, private secretary to U.S. minister to Russia, Albert Gallatin
1815-1817, solicitor of the U.S. Bank
1817, deputy attorney general of Philadelphia
1829, mayor of Philadelphia
1829-1831, U.S. district attorney, eastern district of Pennsylvania
Dec. 13, 1831-Mar. 3, 1833, U.S. Senate (from Pennsylvania)
1833-1835, attorney general of Pennsylvania
Mar. 7, 1837-July 29, 1839, minister to Russia
Mar. 4, 1845-Mar 3, 1849, Vice President
Feb. 4, 1856-May 16, 1861, minister to Great Britain

ADDITIONAL DATA ON POLK
NEWS OF POLK'S NOMINATION TELEGRAPHED

The first use of the telegraph in politics occurred on May 29, 1844, when news was flashed to Washington, D.C., from Baltimore, Md., that Polk had been nominated for the presidency on the Democratic ticket. The Washington *National Intelligencer* reported:

During the whole day, a crowd of persons, including a number of Members of Congress, were in attendance at the Capitol to receive the reports by telegraph of news from Baltimore, which were made at successive intervals with striking despatch and accuracy, and were received by the auditors, as the responses of the ancient Oracle may be supposed to have been, with emotions corresponding to the various and opposite sentiments of those comprising the assembly. Whatever variety of impression the news made upon the auditory, however, there was but one sentiment concerning the telegraph itself, which was that of mingled delight and wonder.

Twenty minutes after Polk had been nominated, a telegram was sent to the convention from Washington, D.C.:

The Democratic members of Congress to their Democratic brethren in convention assembled. Three cheers for James K. Polk.

POLK THE FIRST "DARK HORSE" ELECTED

Polk was not even considered as a candidate for the presidency at the Democratic national convention held at Odd Fellows' Hall, Baltimore, Md. from May 27 to May 30, 1844. His name was not mentioned during the first seven ballots and not a single vote was cast for him.

A stalemate existed between former President Martin Van Buren and Lewis Cass of Michigan. On the eighth ballot (May 29, 1844), Polk was suggested as a compromise candidate and received 44 votes, while Van Buren had 104 votes and Cass 114 votes. Two votes each were also cast for Buchanan and Calhoun. On the ninth ballot, amid indescribable confusion, the convention stampeded for Polk. State after state that had supported Van Buren or Cass cast its votes for Polk, and before the final tally his nomination was declared unanimous, as he had received 266 of the 266 votes cast.

INAUGURATION

James Knox Polk took the oath of office on Tuesday, March 4, 1845, on the east portico of the Capitol. Chief Justice Taney administered the oath. Although it rained, Polk delivered his inaugural address outdoors, and a large military parade took place. This was the first presidential inauguration reported by telegraph. Samuel F. B. Morse, using a telegraph key installed on the platform, sent the news by wire to Baltimore, Md. Two inaugural balls were held.

POLK THE FIRST PRESIDENT WHO HAD BEEN A SPEAKER OF THE HOUSE

James Knox Polk was the first Speaker of the House of Representatives who became a President of the United States. He served as Speaker of the 24th Congress (first session, December 7, 1835 to July 4, 1836, 211 days; second session, December 5, 1836 to March 3, 1837, 89 days). He also served as Speaker of the 25th Congress (first session, September 4, 1837 to October 16, 1837, 43 days; second session, December 4, 1837 to July 9, 1838, 218 days; an third session, December 3, 1838 to March 3, 1839, 91 days).

ELECTION DAY MADE UNIFORM

Originally, there was no uniform date for national elections. Each state could fix its own date, but all elections were required to be held at least thirty-four days before the first Wednesday in December, which was the date of the meeting of the presidential electors.

As a result, repeaters could go from state to state and vote. In 1844, the last year under this system, elections were held on the first Monday in November in Alabama, Arkansas, Connecticut, Georgia, Illinois, Indiana, Kentucky, Maine, Maryland, Michigan, Mississippi, Missouri, North Carolina, Rhode Island and Virginia. On the second Monday in November, elections were held in Massachusetts and New Hampshire. The first Tuesday in November was the date when elections were held in Delaware, Louisiana, Tennessee and Vermont. In New Jersey, election day was the first Tuesday in November and the next day. In New York, the day for election was the first Tuesday after the first Monday in November. Other dates were employed by Ohio, Pennsylvania, and South Carolina.

On January 23, 1845, an act was passed (5 Stat. L. 721) appointing the first Tuesday after the first Monday in November of every even-numbered year. As a result, the date has varied between November

2 and November 8. The law applied to all states except Maine, where the voting was earlier.

The first Tuesday after the first Monday was decided upon in order to eliminate the possibility of an Election Day falling on the first day of November, a day often inconvenient to merchants balancing their books for the month. Monday also was found objectionable as, prior to the establishment of good roads, it often took more than a day for the voter to reach the polling place. As this might have necessitated voters' leaving their homes on Sunday, the day of rest, it was found preferable to have Election Day fall on Tuesdays instead of on Mondays.

POLK RELIEVED AT CONCLUSION OF PRESIDENTIAL TERM

President Polk made the following notation in his diary on February 13, 1849:

I am heartily rejoiced that my term is so near its close. I will soon cease to be a servant and become a sovereign. As a private citizen, I will have no one but myself to serve, and will exercise a part of the sovereign power of the country. I am sure I will be happier in this condition than in the exalted station I now hold.

Under the date of Sunday, March 4, 1849, Polk wrote in his diary:

I feel exceedingly relieved that I am now free from all public cares. I am sure I shall be a happier man in my retirement than I have been during the four years I have filled the highest office in the gift of my countrymen.

THE FIRST LADY

As Sarah Childress Polk had no children, her interests were not divided and her entire time was devoted to her husband. She made a great effort to act as a capable mistress of the White House, but was grave and formal and maintained great dignity. A devout Presbyterian, she banned dancing and the serving of alcoholic refreshments, believing that they were not in keeping with the standards necessary in the White House. She carefully guarded the purse strings and did away with extravagance. Although the social set of Washington did not approve, the nation as a whole did not condemn her. Her policy was greatly admired by the strict religious elements in the nation.

POLK BAPTIZED A WEEK BEFORE HIS DEATH

Fullfilling a promise that he had made, Polk was baptized June 9, 1849, by the Reverend Mr. McFerren, a Methodist minister.

Polk died June 15, 1849, in the presence of the Reverend Dr. Edgar, a Presbyterian minister, and the Reverend Dr. Mack.

ZACHARY TAYLOR
12th PRESIDENT

Born–Nov. 24, 1784

Birthplace–Montebello, Orange County, Va.

College attended–None

Religion–Episcopalian

Ancestry–English

Occupation–Soldier

Date and place of marriage–June 21, 1810, near Louisville, Ky.

Age at marriage–25 years, 209 days

Years married–40 years, 18 days

Political party–Whig

State represented–Louisiana

Term of office–Mar. 4, 1849-July 9, 1850

Term served–1 year, 127 days

Administration–16th

Congresses–31st

Age at inauguration–64 years, 100 days

Date of death–July 9, 1850 (died in office)

Age at death–65 years, 227 days

Place of death–Washington, D.C.

Burial place–Springfield (near Louisville), Ky.

PARENTS

Father–Lieutenant Colonel Richard Taylor

Born–Apr. 3, 1744, Orange County, Va.

Married–Aug. 20, 1779

Occupation–Farmer, soldier

Died–Jan. 19, 1829, near Lexington, Ky.

Age at death–84 years, 291 days

Mother–Sarah Dabney Strother Taylor

Born–Dec. 14, 1760

Died–Dec. 13, 1822

Age at death–61 years, 364 days

BROTHERS AND SISTERS

Zachary Taylor was the third child in a family of nine.

Children of Richard Taylor and Sarah Dabney Strother Taylor

Hancock Taylor, b. Jan. 29, 1781, d. Mar. 20, 1841

William Dabney Strother Taylor, b. 1782, d. June 3, 1808

Zachary Taylor, b. Nov. 24, 1784, d. July 9, 1850

George Taylor, b. 1790, d. Sept. 1829

Elizabeth Lee Taylor, b. Jan. 14, 1792, d. Apr. 22, 1845

Joseph Pannill Taylor, b. May 4, 1796, d. June 29, 1864

Strother Taylor

Sarah Strother Taylor, b. June 11, 1799, d. Sept. 6, 1851

Emily Taylor, b. June 30, 1801, d. Nov. 30, 1842

CHILDREN

Anne Margaret Mackall Taylor, b. Apr. 9, 1811, Jefferson County, Ky.; m. Sept. 20, 1829, Robert Crooke Wood, Prairie du Chien, Michigan Territory; d. Dec. 2, 1875, Freiburg, Germany

Sarah Knox Taylor, b. Mar. 6, 1814, Fort Knox, Missouri Territory; m. June 17, 1835, Jefferson Davis, near Lexington, Ky.; d. Sept. 15, 1835, near St. Francisville, La.

Octavia Pannel Taylor, b. Aug. 16, 1816, Jefferson County, Ky.; d. July 8, 1820, Bayou Sara, La.

For additional data see the end of this section and also specific subject headings in the index.

Margaret Smith Taylor, b. July 27, 1819, Jefferson County, Ky.; d. Oct. 22, 1820, Bayou Sara, La.

Mary Elizabeth ("Betty") Taylor, b. Apr. 20, 1824, Jefferson County, Ky.; m. Dec. 5, 1848, William Wallace Smith Bliss, Baton Rouge, La.; m. Feb. 11, 1858, Philip Pendleton Dandridge; d. July, 26, 1909, Winchester, Va.

Richard Taylor, b. Jan. 27, 1826, near Louisville, Ky.; m. Feb. 10, 1851, Louise Marie Myrthé Bringier, New Orleans, La.; d. Apr. 12, 1879, New York, N.Y.

MRS. ZACHARY TAYLOR

Name–Margaret Mackall Smith Taylor

Date of birth–Sept. 21, 1788
Birthplace–Calvert County, Md.
Age at marriage–21 years, 273 days
Children–5 daughters, 1 son
Mother–Ann Mackall Smith
Father–Walter Smith
His occupation–Planter
Date of death–Aug. 18, 1852
Age at death–63 years, 331 days
Place of death–near Pascagoula, Miss.
Burial place–Springfield (near Louisville), Ky.
Years younger than the President–3 years, 301 days
Years she survived the President–2 years, 40 days

THE ELECTION OF 1848

NOMINATIONS FOR TERM 1849-1853

Whig Party Convention

June 7-9, 1848, Museum Building, Philadelphia, Pa.
Nominated for President—Zachary Taylor, La.
Nominated for Vice President—Millard Fillmore, N.Y.

Taylor was nominated on the fourth ballot. Candidates for nomination and the votes they received on the first and fourth ballots:
Zachary Taylor, La., 111, 171
Henry Clay, Ky., 97, 32
Winfield Scott, N.J., 43, 63
Daniel Webster, Mass., 22, 14
John Middleton Clayton, Del. 4, 0
John McLean, Ohio, 2, 0
Total number of votes:
    First ballot: 279
    Fourth ballot: 280
Number necessary for nomination: 140

Democratic Party Convention (5th)

May 22-26, 1848, Universalist Church, Baltimore, Md.
Nominated for President—Lewis Cass, Mich.
Nominated for Vice President—William Orlando Butler, Ky.

Cass was nominated on the fourth ballot. Candidates for nomination and the number of votes they received on the first and fourth ballots:
Lewis Cass, Mich., 125, 179

James Buchanan, Pa., 55, 33
Levi Woodbury, N.H., 53, 38
John Caldwell Calhoun, S.C., 9, 0
William Jenkins Worth, N.Y., 6, 1
George Mifflin Dallas, Pa., 3, 0
William Orlando Butler, Ky., 0, 3
Total number of votes:
   First ballot: 251
   Fourth ballot: 254
Number necessary for nomination: 168

Free Soil (Democratic) Party Convention

Aug. 9-10, 1848, Buffalo, N.Y.
Nominated for President—Matin Van Buren, N.Y.
Nominated for Vice President—Charles Francis Adams, Mass.
   Van Buren was nominated by acclamation on the first ballot.
First ballot:
Martin Van Buren, N.Y., 154
John Parker Hale, N.H., 129
   This party, formed by the antislavery element of the Democratic Party, was supported by the Liberty Party. Their campaign slogan was "Free Soil, Free Speech, Free Labor, Free Men." They were not abolitionists, but were opposed to the extension of slavery.

Free Soil (Barnburners—Liberty Party) Convention

Oct. 20, 1847, Buffalo, N.Y.
Nominated for President—John Parker Hale, N.H.
Nominated for Vice President—Leicester King, Ohio
   Later John Parker Hale relinquished the nomination.

National Liberty Party Convention

June 14-15, 1848, Buffalo, N.Y.
Nominated for President—Gerrit Smith, N.Y.
Nominated for Vice President—Charles C. Foote, Mich.
   Smith was nominated on the first ballot. Candidates for nomination and the votes they received:
Gerrit Smith, N.Y., 99
Beriah Green, N.Y., 2
Frederick Douglass, 1
Amos A. Sampson, 1
Charles C. Foote, Mich., 1

ELECTION RESULTS, NOV. 7, 1848 PRESIDENTIAL AND VICE PRESIDENTIAL CANDIDATES

Whig Party (1,360,099 votes)
Zachary Taylor, La.
Millard Fillmore, N.Y.

Democratic Party (1,220,544 votes)
Lewis Cass, Mich.
William Orlando Butler, Ky.

Free Soil (Democratic) Party (291,263 votes)

Martin Van Buren, N.Y.

Charles Francis Adams, Mass.

National Liberty Party (2,733 votes)

Gerrit Smith, N.Y.

Charles C. Foote, Mich.

ELECTORAL VOTES (290—30 states)

Taylor received 56.21 percent (163 votes—15 states) as follows: Conn. 6; Del. 3; Fla. 3; Ga. 10; Ky. 12; La. 6; Md. 8; Mass. 12; N.J. 7; N.Y. 36; N.C. 11; Pa. 26; R.I. 4; Tenn. 13; Vt. 6.

Cass received 43.79 per cent (127 votes—15 states) as follows: Ala. 9; Ark. 3; Ill. 9; Ind. 12; Iowa 4; Me. 9; Mich. 5; Miss. 6; Mo. 7; N.H. 6; Ohio 23; S.C. 9; Tex. 4; Va. 17; Wis. 4.

CABINET

March 4, 1849-July 9, 1850

State–James Buchanan, Pa., continued from preceding administration; John Middleton Clayton, Del., Mar. 7, 1849

Treasury–Robert James Walker, Miss., continued from preceding administration; McClintock Young (chief clerk), ad interim Mar. 6, 1849; William Morris Meredith, Pa., Mar. 8, 1849

War–William Learned Marcy, N.Y., continued from preceding administration; Reverdy Johnson, Md. (attorney general), ad interim Mar. 8, 1849; George Washington Crawford, Ga., Mar. 8, 1849; entered upon duties Mar. 14, 1849

Attorney General–Isaac Toucey, Conn., continued from preceding administration; Reverdy Johnson, Md., Mar. 8, 1849

Postmaster General–Cave Johnson, Tenn., continued from preceding administration; Selah Reeve Hobbie, N.Y. (first assistant postmaster general), ad interim Mar. 6, 1849; Jacob Collamer, Vt., Mar. 8, 1849

Navy–John Young Mason, Va., continued from preceding administration; William Ballard Preston, Va., Mar. 8, 1849

Interior–Thomas Ewing, Ohio, Mar. 8, 1849

THIRTY-FIRST CONGRESS

March 4, 1849-March 3, 1851

First session–Dec. 3, 1849-Sept. 30, 1850 (302 days)

Second Session–Dec. 2, 1850-Mar. 3, 1851 (92 days)

Special session of the Senate–Mar. 5, 1849-Mar. 23, 1849 (19 days)

Vice President–Millard Fillmore, N.Y., succeeded to the presidency on the death of Zachary Taylor on July 9, 1850

Presidents pro tempore of the Senate–David Rice Atchison, Mo., elected Mar. 5, 1849 and Mar. 16, 1849, special session; William Rufus De Vane King, Ala., elected May 6, 1850; July 11, 1850

Secretary of the Senate–Asbury Dickens, N.C.

Speaker of the House–Howell Cobb, Ga., elected Dec. 22, 1849

Clerks of the House–Thomas Jefferson Campbell, Tenn., reelected

Jan. 11, 1850; died Apr. 13, 1850; Richard Montgomery Young, Ill., elected Apr. 17, 1850

ADMINISTRATION—IMPORTANT DATES

Apr. 10, 1849, safety pin patented by Walter Hunt

May 22, 1849, Abraham Lincoln obtained a patent on inflated cylinders "for buoying vessels over shoals"

Dec. 20, 1849, treaty with Hawaiian Islands

1850, private mint authorized, Mt. Ophir, Calif.

Apr. 19, 1850, Clayton-Bulwer treaty with Great Britain ratified

July 2, 1850, gas mask patented by Benjamin J. Lane

Aug.-Sept. 1850, measures constituting Clay Compromise of 1850 passed, providing for admission of California as free state; formation of territories of New Mexico and Utah, with option on slavery at time of admission as states; abolition of slave trade in District of Columbia; drastic fugitive slave bill.

IMPORTANT DATES IN HIS LIFE

May 3, 1808, appointed first lieutenant, 7th Infantry

Nov. 30, 1810, appointed captain

July 1, 1811, in charge of Fort Knox at Vincennes in Indian territory

Sept. 1812, brevet rank of major conferred for gallant conduct at the defense of Fort Harrison

May 15, 1814, major, 26th Infantry

June 15, 1815, after the War of 1812, retained as captain of the 7th Infantry; declined and received honorable discharge

May 17, 1816, reinstated as major, 3rd Infrantry

Apr. 20, 1819, lieutenant colonel, 4th Infantry

1821, stationed at Cantonment Bay St. Louis, Miss.

Nov. 9, 1822, established Fort Jesup, La.

Dec. 1822, in charge of Cantonment Robertson near Baton Rouge, La.

May 1828, commanded Fort Snelling, unorganized territory, Minnesota

July 18, 1829, commanded Fort Crawford, Michigan territory (now Wisconsin)

Apr. 4, 1832, colonel, First Regiment

Aug. 2, 1832, Indians defeated at Bad Axe, ending the Black Hawk War

Dec. 25, 1837, brevet brigadier general for distinguished service at the battle of Okeechobee against the Seminole Indians

June 17, 1844, assumed command of Fort Jesup

Apr. 24, 1846, Mexicans crossed Rio Grande, clashed with a scouting party

May 8, 1846, Mexicans routed, battle of Palo Alto

May 9, 1846, Mexicans routed, Resaca de la Palma

May 18, 1846, Mexican army fled Matamoras, which was occupied without bloodshed

May 28, 1846, brevet major general for his zealous and distinguished services in Mexico

June 29, 1846, major general of the line

July 18, 1846, received thanks of Congress "for the fortitude, skill, enterprise and courage which have distinguished the recent operations on the Rio Grande"

Sept. 25, 1846, Monterey surrendered; Mexicans left city

Feb. 23, 1847, defeated Santa Anna at battle of Buena Vista (La Angostura)

July 18, 1848, nominated for the presidency by the Whigs

Jan. 31, 1849, resigned from the army

Mar. 4, 1849-July 9, 1850, President

ZACHARY TAYLOR

_____was the seventh President born in Virginia.

_____was the first President who had not served in the United States Congress or the Continental Congress.

_____was the second President inaugurated on March 5 (March 4 was a Sunday).

_____was the fourth President who was a resident of a state other than his native state.

_____was the second President to die in office.

_____was the second President to die in the White House.

TAYLOR'S VICE PRESIDENT

Vice President–Millard Fillmore (12th V.P.)

Date of birth–Jan. 7, 1800

Birthplace–Summerhill, Cayuga County, N.Y.

Political party–Whig

State represented–New York

Term of office–Mar. 4, 1849-July 9, 1950

Age at inauguration–49 years, 56 days

Occupation after term–President

Date of death–Mar. 8, 1874

Age at death–74 years, 60 days

Place of death–Buffalo, N.Y.

Burial place–Buffalo, N.Y.

For further biographical information see Millard Fillmore, 13th president.

ADDITIONAL DATA ON TAYLOR

TAYLOR THE THIRD PRESIDENT BORN AFTER REVOLUTION

Zachary Taylor was the third President born after the Revolutionary War. The two Presidents who preceded him in office were also born after the war and after Taylor.

The final draft of the treaty of peace was made on September 3, 1787. Taylor, the twelfth President, was born November 24, 1784, about six years before John Tyler (March 29, 1790), the tenth President, and about eleven years before James Knox Polk (November 2, 1795), the eleventh President.

TAYLOR THE FIRST PRESIDENT REPRESENTING A STATE WEST OF THE MISSISSIPPI

Zachary Taylor of Louisiana was the first President elected from a state west of the Mississippi River. He was, however, born in Virginia.

TAYLOR UNWITTINGLY REFUSED LETTER OF NOMINATION

The reason attributed to Zachary Taylor's not answering the letter sent by the Whigs notifying him at Baton Rouge, La., of his nomination for the presidency was that it arrived "postage due." Taylor refused to accept all unpaid mail. At that time, the Post Office carried "collect letters" which could be sent without the prepayment of postage.

BALLOTLESS PRESIDENT ELECTED

Zachary Taylor was too busy soldiering to vote. He served in the War of 1812, in the Indian wars against the Black Hawks and the Seminoles, and against the Mexicans. He never stayed in one place long enough to qualify as a voter, and being in the army, had not voted for forty years. His first vote was cast when he was sixty-two years of age.

CLAY TRIED FIFTH TIME FOR THE PRESIDENCY

Henry Clay's fifth attempt for the Whig Party nomination was made in 1848 at the Philadelphia convention. He failed to secure the necessary number of votes and the nomination was won by Zachary Taylor, who also won the election. At the Baltimore convention in 1840, Clay had tried in vain for the Whig Party nomination, the nominee that year being William Henry Harrison, who was elected President.

On three other occasions, Henry Clay was a presidential nominee, losing the election each time. He was defeated for the presidency in 1824 by John Quincy Adams, in 1832 by Andrew Jackson, and in 1844 by James Knox Polk.

Henry Clay made numerous speeches while he was a Senator from Kentucky stating that he was opposed to secession or separation from the union and advocating compromise measures. William Preston, a member of the Kentucky legislature, told Clay that his views would interfere with his chances of becoming President. Clay answered: "Sir, I would rather be right than be President."

TAYLOR'S SON-IN-LAW

Jefferson Davis, who eloped with and married Sarah Knox Taylor in 1835, had incurred the animosity of her father, Zachary Taylor, while serving under his military command. Davis, who had been promoted to the rank of first lieutenant in the First Dragoons on March 4, 1833, "for gallant service," was not the same hardbitten type of soldier as "Old Rough and Ready." In June 1846, after the outbreak of the Mexican War, Davis resigned from Congress, in which he represented Mississippi, and took command of the First Regiment of Mississippi Riflemen. He served under his father-in-law during the three-day siege of Monterey and greatly-distinguished himself, as he did later at Buena Vista.

INAUGURATION

Zachary Taylor took the oath of office on the east portico of the Capitol on Monday, March 5, 1849, as March 4 fell on a Sunday, the second time in inaugural history. One hundred marshals escorted the presidential carriage from Willard's Hotel to the Capitol. Thirty thousand persons witnessed the inauguration. After a parade lasting one hour, a reception was held in the afternoon at the White House. Three different inaugural balls were held, each attended by President Taylor.

HORSE PASTURED ON WHITE HOUSE LAWN

When Zachary Taylor moved into the White House, he had his favorite mount, Whitey, accompany him. The horse that had served the general in the Mexican War at Buena Vista, Palo Alto, and other battles was given the freedom of the White House lawn. When President Taylor was buried, old Whitey followed his master's body in the funeral procession.

INTERIOR DEPARTMENT ESTABLISHED

On March 3, 1849, "an act to establish the Home Department" was passed. On March 8, 1849, Thomas Ewing of Ohio was appointed Secretary; he served until July 23, 1850. The name of the department was later changed to the Department of Interior. It is concerned principally with the management, conservation, and development of the natural resources of the United States. These resources include the public lands and the federal range, water and power resources, oil, gas, and other mineral resources, certain foreign resources, fish and wildlife resources, and the national park system.

WAS ATCHISON PRESIDENT?

Many people have claimed that David Rice Atchison was President of the United States.

As March 4, 1849, fell on a Sunday, Zachary Taylor did not take his oath of office as President until Monday, March 5, 1849. Polk's four-year term constitutionally ended at noon on March 4, 1849. Vice President George Mifflin Dallas resigned as president of the Senate on Friday, March 2, 1849, and Senator David Rice Atchison of Missouri was elected president of the Senate pro tempore on March 2. He was nominated by Thomas Hart Benton.

Atchison presided over the Senate the following day and late into the night. On March 5, he was again elected president of the Senate pro tempore for the purpose of administering the oath of office to the senators-elect.

Article II of the Constitution contains the following provision:

In Case of the Removal of the President from Office, or of his Death, Resignation, or Inability to discharge the Powers and

Duties of said Office, the Same shall devolve on the Vice President, and the Congress may by Law provide for the Case of Removal, Death, Resignation or Inability, both of the President and the Vice President, declaring what Officer shall then act as President, and such Officer shall act accordingly, until the Disability be removed, or a President shall be elected.

Although Atchison was never a Vice President and never lived in the White House, and signed no acts of Congress, many insist that he was President of the United States for one day.

He died in 1886 and Missouri appropriated $15,000 for his monument, which bears this inscription: "David Rice Atchison, 1807-1886, President of U.S. one day. Lawyer, statesman and jurist."

THE FIRST LADY

Mrs. Margaret Smith Taylor refused to appear at public functions. She was about sixty-one years of age when her husband became President on March 4, 1849. She was in ill health and her youngest daughter, Mary Elizabeth, who was married to William Wallace Bliss, acted for her. Taylor became ill on July 4, 1850, and died five days later, having served about sixteen months. Mrs. Taylor, who had traveled from one military post to another during her husband's early years in the army, preferred to live a quiet, simple life, avoiding all gaiety and excitement.

MILLARD FILLMORE
13th PRESIDENT

Born–Jan. 7, 1800

Birthplace–Summerhill, Cayuga County, N.Y.

College attended–None

Religion–Unitarian

Ancestry–English

Occupation–Lawyer

Date and place of first marriage–Feb. 5, 1826, Moravia, N.Y.

Age at marriage–26 years, 29 days

Years married–27 years, 53 days

Date and place of second marriage–Feb. 10, 1858, Albany, N.Y.

Age at second marriage–58 years, 34 days

Years married–16 years, 36 days

Political party–Whig

State represented–New York

Term of office–July 10, 1850–Mar. 3, 1853 (Fillmore succeeded to the presidency on the death of Zachary Taylor.)

Term served–2 years, 236 days

Administration–16th

Congresses–31st, 32nd

Age at inauguration–50 years, 184 days

Lived after term–21 years, 4 days

Occupation after term–Chancellor of University of Buffalo

Date of death–Mar. 8, 1874

Age at death–74 years, 60 days

Place of death–Buffalo, N.Y.

Burial place–Forest Lawn Cemetery, Buffalo, N.Y.

PARENTS

Father–Nathaniel Fillmore

Born–Apr. 19, 1771, Bennington, Vt.

Married (1)–Phoebe Millard

Married (2)–Eunice Love

Occupation–Farmer, magistrate

Died–Mar. 28, 1863

Age at death–91 years, 343 days

Mother–Phoebe Millard Fillmore

Born–1780, Pittsfield, Mass.

Died–May 2, 1831

Age at death–About 51 years

Second wife of father–Eunice Love Fillmore

Married–May 2, 1834

BROTHERS AND SISTERS

Millard Fillmore was the second child in a family of nine.

Children of Nathaniel Fillmore and Phoebe Millard Fillmore

Olive Armstrong Fillmore, b. Dec. 16, 1797

Millard Fillmore, b. Jan. 7, 1800, d. Mar. 8, 1874

Cyrus Fillmore, b. Dec. 22, 1801

Almon Hopkins Fillmore, b. Apr. 13, 1806, d. Jan. 17, 1830

Calvin Turner Fillmore, b. July 9, 1810

Julia Fillmore, b. Aug. 29, 1812

Darius Ingraham Fillmore, b. Nov. 16, 1814, d. Mar. 9, 1837

Charles De Witt Fillmore, b. Sept. 23, 1817, d. 1854

Phoebe Maria Fillmore, b. Nov. 23, 1819, d. July 2, 1843

CHILDREN

By first wife, Abigail Powers Fillmore

Millard Powers Fillmore, b. Apr. 25, 1828, Aurora, N.Y.; d. Nov. 15, 1889, Buffalo, N.Y.

Mary Abigail Fillmore, b. Mar. 27, 1832, Buffalo, N.Y.; d. July 26, 1854, Aurora, N.Y.

For additional data see the end of this section and also specific subject headings in the index.

By second wife, Caroline Carmichael McIntosh Fillmore

None

MRS. MILLARD FILLMORE (first wife)

Name–Abigail Powers Fillmore
Date of birth–Mar. 13, 1798
Birthplace–Stillwater, N.Y.
Age at marriage–27 years, 329 days
Children–1 son, 1 daughter
Mother–Abigail Newland Powers
Father–Reverend Lemuel Powers
His occupation–Baptist clergyman
Date of death–Mar. 30. 1853
Age at death–55 years, 17 days
Place of death–Washington, D.C.
Burial place–Buffalo, N.Y.
Years older than the President–1 year, 300 days
Years the President survived her–20 years, 343 days

MRS. MILLARD FILLMORE (second wife)

Name–Caroline Carmichael McIntosh Fillmore
Date of birth–Oct. 21, 1813
Birthplace–Morristown, N.J.
Age at marriage–44 years, 112 days
Children–None
Mother–Temperance Blachley Carmichael
Father–Charles Carmichael
Date of death–Aug. 11, 1881
Age at death–67 years, 294 days
Place of death–Buffalo, N.Y.
Burial place–Buffalo, N.Y.
Years younger than the President–13 years, 287 days
Years she survived the President–7 years, 156 days

The second Mrs. Fillmore was the widow of Ezekiel C. McIntosh of Albany, N.Y.

CABINET

July 10, 1850-March 3, 1853

State–John Middleton Clayton, Del., continued from preceding administration; Daniel Webster, Mass., July 22, 1850 (died Oct. 24, 1852); Charles Magill Conrad, La. (secretary of war), ad interim Oct. 25, 1852; Edward Everett, Mass., Nov. 6, 1852

Treasury–William Morris Meredith, Pa., continued from preceding administration; Thomas Corwin, Ohio, July 23, 1850

War–George Washington Crawford, Ga., continued from preceding administration; Samuel J. Anderson (chief clerk), ad interim July 23, 1850; Winfield Scott (major general, U.S. Army), ad interim July 24, 1850; Charles Magill Conrad, La., Aug. 15, 1850

Attorney General–Reverdy Johnson, Md., continued from preceding administration; served to July 22, 1850; John Jordan Crittenden, Ky., July 22, 1850; entered upon duties Aug. 14, 1850

Postmaster General–Jacob Collamer, Vt., continued from preceding administration; Nathan Kelsey Hall, N.Y., July 23, 1850; Samuel Dickinson Hubbard, Conn., Aug. 31, 1852; entered upon duties Sept. 14, 1852

Navy–William Ballard Preston, Va., continued from preceding administration; Lewis Warrington (captain, U.S. Navy), ad interim July

23, 1850; William Alexander Graham, N.C., July 22, 1850; entered
upon duties Aug. 2, 1850; John Pendleton Kennedy, Md., July 22,
1852; entered upon duties July 26, 1852

Interior–Thomas Ewing, Md., continued from preceding administra-
tion; Daniel C. Goddard (chief clerk), ad interim July 23, 1850;
Thomas McKean Thompson McKennan, Pa., Aug. 15, 1850; Daniel
C. Goddard (chief clerk), ad interim Aug. 27, 1850; Alexander Hugh
Holmes Stuart, Va., Sept. 12, 1850; entered upon duties Sept. 16,
1850

THIRTY-SECOND CONGRESS

March 4, 1851-March 3, 1853

First session–Dec. 1, 1851-Aug. 31, 1852 (275 days)
Second session–Dec. 6, 1852-Mar. 3, 1853 (88 days)
Special session of the Senate–Mar. 4, 1851-Mar. 13, 1851 (10 days)
Vice President–Vice President Millard Fillmore succeeded to the presi-
dency on the death of Zachary Taylor on July 9, 1850
Presidents pro tempore of the Senate–William Rufus de Vane King,
Ala., resigned as president pro tempore on Dec. 20, 1852; David
Rice Atchison, Mo., elected Dec. 20, 1852
Secretary of the Senate–Asbury Dickens, N.C.
Speaker of the House–Linn Boyd, Ky., elected Dec. 1, 1851
Clerks of the House–Richard Montgomery Young, Ill.; John Wien
Forney, Pa., elected Dec. 1, 1851

APPOINTMENT TO THE SUPREME COURT

Associate Justice
Benjamin Robbins Curtis, Mass., Sept. 22, 1851

ADMINISTRATION — IMPORTANT DATES

Sept. 9, 1850, California admitted as the 31st state
Sept. 11, 1850, first American performance of Jenny Lind, "the Swed-
ish Nightingale," at New York City
Sept. 18, 1850, fugitive slave law enacted
July 4, 1851, cornerstone laid for the south House extension of the
Capitol
Dec. 5, 1851, General Louis Kossuth, Hungarian patriot, arrived; cele-
bration at New York City, Dec. 6
Dec. 24, 1851, Capitol at Washington, D.C., partly destroyed by fire
Nov. 1852, Commodore Matthew C. Perry sent on expedition to open
the ports of Japan to commerce
Mar. 2, 1853, Washington Territory created out of northern part of
Oregon
Mar. 3, 1853, federal assay office building authorized

IMPORTANT DATES IN HIS LIFE

18—, attended primitive rural schools and was self-instructed
1815, apprenticed to wool carder and cloth-dresser
1818, taught school at Scott, N.Y.
1823, admitted to the bar; practiced in East Aurora, N.Y.

1829-1831, New York State Assembly (Anti-Masonic party)

1830, moved to Buffalo, N.Y.

Mar. 4, 1833-Mar. 3, 1835, U.S. House of Representatives (from New York)

Mar. 4, 1837-Mar. 3, 1843, U.S. House of Representatives (from New York)

1842, declined to be a candidate for renomination

1844, unsuccessful Whig candidate for governor of New York

1846, commanded a corps of Home Guard during the Mexican War

1846, named chancellor of the University of Buffalo (served until his death)

Jan. 1, 1848-Feb. 20, 1849, New York State Controller

Mar. 4, 1849-July 9, 1850, Vice President

July 10, 1850-Mar. 3, 1853, President (took office on death of Zachary Taylor)

June 1852, unsuccessful aspirant for Whig presidential nomination

Nov. 1856, unsuccessful candidate for the presidency on the American ("Know-Nothing") Party and the Whig Party tickets

1862-1867, president of Buffalo Historical Society

MILLARD FILLMORE

_____was the second President born in New York.

_____was the second President whose father was alive when he was inaugurated.

_____was the second President to remarry.

_____was the fourth President to marry a widow.

_____was the first President to have a stepmother.

ADDITIONAL DATA ON FILLMORE

INAUGURATION

Millard Fillmore, succeeding President Zachary Taylor, who died on July 9, 1850, was the second Vice President to succeed to the presidency on the death of a President. At noon on Wednesday, July 10, 1850, Judge William Cranch, Chief Justice of the United States Circuit Court of the District of Columbia, administered the oath to Fillmore in the Hall of Representatives.

BOOKS FOR THE PRESIDENT

According to contemporary reports, when President Millard Fillmore took office, the White House had no books, not even a Bible. His wife, Abigail Powers Fillmore, a former schoolteacher and a voracious reader, converted a large room on the second floor into a library, and the appropriation act of March 3, 1851 (9 Stat. L. 613) authorized "for purchase of books for library at the Executive Mansion two hundred and fifty dollars to be expended under the direction of the President of the United States."

FILLMORE'S REPLY TO BIOGRAPHER

Fillmore wrote as follows to L. J. Cisti on January 4, 1855: "In compliance with your request I have frankly stated the facts connected with my early history, and as no man is responsible for the circumstances of his birth, they furnish nothing of which he should be ashamed or proud, and therefore while they require no apology they can justify no boasting. I need hardly add that this letter is not intended for publication."

FILLMORE DECLINED HONORARY DEGREE

Oxford University, through its chancellor, the Earl of Derby, offered to confer the honorary degree of Doctor of Civil Law (D.C.L.) on Millard Fillmore. He refused the honor, stating "I had not the advantage of a classical education and no man should, in my judgment, accept a degree he cannot read."

FILLMORE SOUGHT RENOMINATION AND REELECTION

Millard Fillmore served until the completion of the term ending March 3, 1853. He was an aspirant for the presidential nomination at the Whig convention held in Baltimore in June 1852, but the Whigs nominated General Winfield Scott.

Four years later, Fillmore was nominated for the presidency by the American Party (the "Know-Nothing" Party), but was defeated in the election. He received approximately 875,000 votes against 1,341,-000 for John Charles Fremont, the first presidential candidate of the newly formed Republican Party, and 1,838,000 for James Buchanan, the Democrat, who was elected.

The platform adopted by the American Party on February 21, 1856, at Philadelphia, Pa., contained the following sections:

Americans must rule America; and to this end *native-born* citizens should be selected for all state, federal, and municipal offices of government employment, in preference to all others.

A change in the laws of naturalization, making a continued residence of twenty-one years, of all not heretofore provided for, an indispensable requisite for citizenship hereafter, and excluding all paupers and persons convicted of crime from landing upon our shores; but no interference with the vested rights of foreigners.

THE FIRST LADY

Mrs. Abigail Powers Fillmore was an invalid when her husband succeeded to the presidency. Her daughter, Mary Abigail Fillmore, assumed the functions of first lady. Mrs. Fillmore died less than a month after her husband ended his term of office, having contracted a chill while attending the inauguration of President Franklin Pierce.

FRANKLIN PIERCE
14th PRESIDENT

Born–Nov. 23, 1804
Birthplace–Hillsborough, N.H. (now Hillsboro)
College attended–Bowdoin College, Brunswick, Me.
Date of graduation–Sept. 1, 1824, four-year course, Bachelor of Arts
Religion–Episcopalian
Ancestry–English
Occupation–Lawyer
Date and place of marriage–Nov. 10, 1834, Amherst, Mass.
Age at marriage–29 years, 352 days
Years married–29 years, 22 days
Political party–Democratic
State represented–New Hampshire
Term of office–Mar. 4, 1853-Mar. 3, 1857
Term served–4 years
Administration–17th
Congresses–33rd, 34th
Age at inauguration–48 years, 101 days
Lived after term–12 years, 218 days
Occupation after term–Retired; traveled
Date of death–Oct. 8, 1869
Age at death–64 years, 319 days
Place of death–Concord, N.H.
Burial place–Old North Cemetery, Concord, N.H.

PARENTS

Father–General Benjamin Pierce
Born–Dec. 25, 1757, Chelmsford, Mass.
Married (1)–Elizabeth Andrews
Married (2)–Anna Kendrick

Occupation–Soldier, farmer, tavern owner, governor
Died–Apr. 1, 1839
Age at death–81 years, 97 days
First wife of father–Elizabeth Andrews
Born–1768
Married–May 24, 1787
Died–Aug. 13, 1788
Age at death–20 years
Mother–Anna Kendrick Pierce
Born–1768
Married–Feb. 1, 1790
Died–Dec. 1838
Age at death–70 years

BROTHERS AND SISTERS

Franklin Pierce was the seventh child of his father, the sixth of eight children of a second marriage.

Children of Benjamin Pierce and Elizabeth Andrews Pierce

Elizabeth Andrews Pierce, b. Aug. 9, 1788, d. Mar. 27, 1855

Children of Benjamin Pierce and Anna Kendrick Pierce

Benjamin Kendrick Pierce, b. Aug. 29, 1790, d. Aug. 1, 1850

Nancy M. Pierce, b. Nov. 2, 1792, d. Aug. 27, 1837

John Sullivan Pierce, b. Nov. 5, 1796, d. Mar. 13, 1824

Harriet B. Pierce, b. 1800, d. Nov. 24, 1837

Charles Grandison Pierce, b. 1803, d. June 15, 1828

Franklin Pierce, b. Nov. 23, 1804, d. Oct. 8, 1869

Charlotte Pierce

Henry Dearborn Pierce, b. Sept. 19, 1812, d. 1880

For additional data see the end of this section and also specific subject headings in the index.

CHILDREN

Franklin Pierce, b. Feb. 2, 1836, Hillsborough, N.H., d. Feb. 5, 1836, Hillsborough, N.H.

Frank Robert Pierce, b. Aug. 27, 1839, Concord, N.H., d. Nov. 14, 1843, Concord, N.H.

Benjamin Pierce, b. Apr. 13, 1841, Concord, N.H.; d. Jan. 6, 1853, near Andover, Mass.

MRS. FRANKLIN PIERCE

Name—Jane Means Appleton Pierce

Date of birth—Mar. 12, 1806

Birthplace—Hampton, N.H.

Age at marriage—28 years, 243 days

Children—3 sons

Mother—Elizabeth Appleton

Father—Jesse Appleton

His occupation—Congregational minister

Date of death—Dec. 2, 1863

Age at death—57 years, 265 days

Place of death—Andover, Mass.

Burial place—Concord, N.H.

Years younger than the President—1 year, 109 days

Years the President survived her—5 years, 310 days

THE ELECTION OF 1852

NOMINATIONS FOR TERM 1853-1857

Democratic Party Convention (6th)

June 1-5, 1852, Maryland Institute Hall, Baltimore, Md.
Nominated for President—Franklin Pierce, N.H.
Nominated for Vice President—William Rufus De Vane King, Ala.
  Pierce was nominated on the forty-ninth ballot. Candidates for nomination and the votes they received on the first and forty-ninth ballots:
Lewis Cass, Mich., 116, 2
James Buchanan, Pa., 93, 0
William Learned Marcy, N.Y., 27, 0
Stephen Arnold Douglas, Ill., 20, 2
Joseph Lane, Ore., 13, 0
Samuel Houston, Tex., 8, 1
John B. Weller, Calif., 4, 0
Henry Dodge, Wis., 3, 0
William Orlando Butler, Ky., 2, 1
Daniel Stevens Dickinson, N.Y., 1, 1
Franklin Pierce, N.H., 0, 282
Total number of votes:
  First ballot: 287
  Forty-ninth ballot: 289

Whig Party Convention

June 17-20, 1852, Maryland Institute Hall, Baltimore, Md.
Nominated for President—Winfield Scott, N.J.
Nominated for Vice President—William Alexander Graham, N.C.
  Scott was nominated on the fifty-third ballot. Candidates for nomination and the votes they received on the first and fifty-third ballots:
Millard Fillmore, N.Y., 133, 112
Winfield Scott, N.J., 131, 159

Daniel Webster, Mass., 29, 21
Total number of votes:
First ballot: 293
Fifty-third ballot: 292

Free Soil (Democratic) Party Convention

Aug. 11, 1852, Pittsburgh, Pa.
Nominated for President—John Parker Hale, N.H.
Nominated for Vice President—George Washington Julian, Ind.

ELECTION RESULTS, NOV. 2, 1852—PRESIDENTIAL AND VICE PRESIDENTIAL CANDIDATES

Democratic Party (1,601,274 votes)

Franklin Pierce, N.H.
William Rufus De Vane King, Ala.

Whig Party (1,386,580 votes)

Winfield Scott, N.J.
William Alexander Graham, N.C.

Free Soil Party (155,825 votes)

John Parker Hale, N.H.
George Washington Julian, Ind.

ELECTORAL VOTES (296—31 states)

Pierce received 85.81 per cent (254 votes—27 states) as follows: Ala. 9; Ark. 4; Calif. 4; Conn. 6; Del. 3; Fla. 3; Ga. 10; Ill. 11; Ind. 13; Iowa 4; La. 6; Me. 8; Md. 8; Mich. 6; Miss. 7; Mo. 9; N.H. 5; N.J. 7; N.Y. 35; N.C. 10; Ohio 23; Pa. 27; R.I. 4; S.C. 8; Tex. 4; Va. 15; Wis. 5.

Scott received 14.19 per cent (42 votes—4 states) as follows: Ky. 12; Mass. 13; Tenn. 12; Vt. 5.

CABINET

March 4, 1853-March 3, 1857

State—William Hunter (chief clerk) ad interim Mar. 4, 1853; William Learned Marcy, N.Y., Mar. 7, 1853

Treasury—Thomas Corwin, Ohio, continued from preceding administration; James Guthrie, Ky., Mar. 7, 1853

War—Charles Magill Conrad, La., continued from preceding administration; Jefferson Davis, Miss., Mar. 7, 1853; Samuel Cooper (adjutant general, U.S. Army), ad interim Mar. 3, 1857

Attorney General—John Jordan Crittenden, Ky., continued from preceding administration; Caleb Cushing, Mass., Mar. 7, 1853

Postmaster General—Samuel Dickinson Hubbard, Conn., continued from preceding administration; James Campbell, Pa., Mar. 7, 1853

Navy—John Pendleton Kennedy, Md., continued from preceding administration; James Cochran Dobbin, N.C., Mar. 7, 1853

Interior—Alexander Hugh Holmes Stuart, Va., continued from preceding administration; Robert McClelland, Mich., Mar. 7, 1853

THIRTY-THIRD CONGRESS

March 4, 1853-March 3, 1855

First session—Dec. 5, 1853-Aug. 7, 1854 (246 days)
Second session—Dec. 4, 1854-Mar. 3, 1855 (90 days)
Special session of the Senate—Mar. 4, 1853-Apr. 11, 1853 (38 days)
Vice President—William Rufus De Vane King, Ala., (died Apr. 18, 1853)
Presidents pro tempore of the Senate—David Rice Atchison, Mo., elected Mar. 4, 1853; Lewis Cass, Mich., elected Dec. 4, 1854 for one day only; Jesse David Bright, Ind., elected Dec. 5, 1854
Secretary of the Senate—Asbury Dickens, N.C.
Speaker of the House—Linn Boyd, Ky., reelected Dec. 5, 1853
Clerk of the House—John Wien Forney, Pa., reelected Dec. 5, 1853

THIRTY-FOURTH CONGRESS

March 4, 1855-March 3, 1857

First session—Dec. 3, 1855-Aug. 18, 1856 (260 days)
Second session—Aug. 21, 1856-Aug. 30, 1856 (10 days)
Third session—Dec. 1, 1856-Mar. 3, 1857 (93 days)
Vice President—William Rufus De Vane King died Apr. 18, 1853 (Thirty-third Congress)
Presidents pro tempore of the Senate—Jesse David Bright, Ind., reelected June 11, 1856; Charles Edward Stuart, Mich., served June 5, 1856; elected June 9, 1856; resigned June 11, 1856; James Murray Mason, Va., served Jan. 5, 1856, elected Jan. 6, 1857
Secretary of the Senate—Asbury Dickens, N.C.
Speaker of the House—Nathaniel Prentice Banks, Mass., elected Feb. 2, 1856
Clerks of the House—John Wien Forney, Pa.; William Cullom, Tenn., elected Feb. 4, 1856

APPOINTMENT TO THE SUPREME COURT

Associate Justice
John Archibald Campbell, Ala., Mar. 22, 1853

ADMINISTRATION — IMPORTANT DATES

May 31, 1853, Elisha Kent Kane expedition to Arctic left New York City
June 1853, first stamped envelopes issued
July 14, 1853, President Pierce opened Crystal Palace Exposition, New York, N.Y.
Sept. 19, 1853, patent on sleeping car issued to H. B. Myer
Mar. 8, 1854, Perry's treaty with Japan ratified
May 22, 1854, Congress enacted Kansas-Nebraska Act permitting state option on slavery, nullifying the Missouri Compromise
June 30, 1854, Gadsden Purchase treaty proclaimed; United States acquired border territory from Mexico
Oct. 1854, Ostend Manifesto, issued by U.S. ministers to England,

France, and Spain, urged American acquisition of Cuba from Spain by purchase or force

1855, first postal directory published

Aug. 19, 1856, Gail Borden obtained condensed milk patent

Sept. 4, 1856, first American flag flown in Japan by Consul General Townsend Harris

1857, financial panic

Feb. 24, 1857, first perforated postage stamps used

IMPORTANT DATES IN HIS LIFE

18—, attended the academies of Hancock and Francestown, N.H.

18—, prepared for college at Exeter

Sept. 1, 1824, graduated from Bowdoin College, Brunswick, Me.

1827, admitted to the bar; practiced at Hillsborough, N.H.

June 3, 1829-1833, New Hampshire House of Representatives

1832, speaker, New Hampshire House of Representatives

Mar. 4, 1833-Mar. 3, 1837, U.S. House of Representatives (from New Hampshire)

Mar. 4, 1837-Feb. 28, 1842, U.S. Senate (from New Hampshire)

1842, resigned to practice law at Concord, N.H.

1846, declined appointment as U.S. Attorney General under President Polk

1847 enlisted as private in Mexican War

Feb. 16, 1847, became colonel of 9th Regiment, Infantry

Mar. 3, 1847, commissioned brigadier general

Apr. 12, 1847, served at Cerro Gordo

May 27, 1847, sailed for Mexico City

June 27, 1847, landed in Mexico

Aug. 19, 1847, injured at Contreras when horse took fright

Sept.-Dec., 1847, in Mexico City

Sept. 13, 1847, served at Chapultepec

Mar. 20, 1848, resigned from army

18—, declined senatorial appointment made by the governor of New Hampshire

18—, declined to run as governor of New Hampshire

Nov. 6, 1850, member and president of New Hampshire Fifth State Constitutional Convention

1852, Democratic nominee for the presidency

Mar. 4, 1853-Mar. 3, 1857, President

1856, unsuccessful candidate for Democratic nomination for the presidency

Nov. 1857, made European tour, visiting Portugal, Spain, France, Switzerland, Italy, Austria, Germany, Belgium, and England

May 1860, received one complimentary vote at Democratic convention

FRANKLIN PIERCE

——was the first President born in New Hampshire.

——was the first President born in the nineteenth century (November 23, 1804).

_____was the first President who did not read his inaugural address but instead delivered it as an oration.

PIERCE'S VICE PRESIDENT

Vice President–William Rufus De Vane King (13th V.P.)
Date of birth–Apr. 7, 1786
Birthplace–Sampson County, N.C.
Political party–Democratic
State represented–Alabama
Term of office–Mar. 4, 1853-Apr. 18, 1853
Age at inauguration–66 years, 331 days
Occupation after term–Died in office
Date of death–Apr. 18, 1853
Age at death–67 years, 11 days
Place of death–Cahaba, Ala.
Burial place–Selma, Ala.

Additional data on King

1803, graduated from the University of North Carolina, Chapel Hill, N.C.

1806, admitted to bar; practiced in Clinton, N.C.

1807-1809, North Carolina State House of Commons

1810, city Solicitor, Wilmington, N.C.

Mar. 4, 1811-Nov. 4, 1816, U.S. House of Representatives (from North Carolina)

1816, secretary of U.S. legation, Naples, Italy

18—, secretary of U.S. legation, St. Petersburg, Russia

Dec. 14, 1819-Apr. 15, 1844, U.S. Senate (from Alabama)

1844-1846, minister to France

July 1, 1848-Dec. 20, 1852, U.S. Senate (from Alabama)

ADDITIONAL DATA ON PIERCE

PIERCE A "DARK HORSE" CANDIDATE

Franklin Pierce, the Democratic nominee for President in 1852, was not considered as a candidate until the thirty-fifth ballot, when Virginia cast fifteen votes for him. On the forty-eighth ballot, he received 55 votes. On the forty-ninth ballot, there was a sudden surge in his favor and he received 283 of the 289 votes cast, thereby winning the nomination.

PIERCE DEFEATED GENERAL SCOTT

Franklin Pierce carried 27 of the 31 states and defeated General Winfield Scott, the Whig party nominee. Pierce, a brigadier general in the Mexican War, served under General Scott and was with him during his march to and capture of Mexico City on September 14, 1847. Pierce enlisted in the war as a private and was enrolled in a company of volunteers organized at Concord, N.H. He was commissioned a colonel in the Ninth Regiment and on March 3, 1847, was commissioned a brigadier in the volunteer army.

INAUGURATION

Franklin Pierce was inaugurated on Friday, March 4, 1853, and took the oath of office on the east portico of the Capitol. A raw northeasterly wind blew over the fast melting snow.

The oath was administered by Chief Justice Taney. In taking the oath Pierce availed himself of an option provided in Article Two, section one of the Constitution. Instead of the usual "I do solemnly swear," he said, "I do solemnly affirm," the only President to "affirm" instead of "swear."

Pierce delivered his 3,319-word inaugural address without reference to notes and was the first President to deliver his speech as an oration instead of reading it. Over eighty thousand spectators flocked to Washington, but as it commenced to snow during the ceremonies, only about fifteen thousand remained to hear the address.

The cost of putting up and taking down the grandstand in front of the Capitol was $322, including the pay of sixteen extra policemen.

A reception was held at the White House. The inaugural ball at Jackson Hall was canceled since Pierce was in mourning for his son, who had been killed in a railroad accident on January 6. Mrs Pierce did not go to Washington for the inauguration.

PIERCE NOT RENOMINATED

Pierce has the dubious distinction of being the only President elected to office who was not renominated by his party for a second term. The Democratic Party convention held in Cincinnati, Ohio, June 2-6, 1856, did not endorse Pierce. He was named on the first ballot but more votes were received by James Buchanan. On the seventeenth ballot, Buchanan received the nomination which was declared unanimous.

FULL CABINET RETAINED

Franklin Pierce was the only President to retain the same cabinet for four years without any changes, replacements, resignations, or vacancies due to illness or death. His seven cabinet members remained in office until the completion of his term on March 3, 1857.

VICE PRESIDENT KING NEVER SERVED

William Rufus De Vane King, who was elected Vice President of the United States in 1852 under Franklin Pierce, had the oath of office administered to him in Havana, Cuba, by William L. Sharkey, United States Consul at Havana. This was permitted by a special act of Congress. Of all the Presidents and Vice Presidents, King was the first and only one to take the oath in a foreign country.

King died April 18, 1853, and as the first session of the Thirty-third Congress was not held until December 5, 1853, he never performed any of the duties of his office and therefore never presided over the Senate.

VICE PRESIDENT KING SERVED IN BOTH HOUSES AND REPRESENTED TWO STATES

King was the only Vice President of the United States to serve in both houses of Congress. In each house he represented a different state. He was a representative from North Carolina from March 4, 1811, to November 4, 1816, and a senator from Alabama from December 14, 1819; to April 15, 1844, and again from July 1, 1848, to December 20, 1852.

133 BALLOTS TO ELECT SPEAKER

The Thirty-fourth Congress assembled on Monday, December 3, 1855, to elect a Speaker of the House of Representatives. It was not until the 133rd ballot, on February 2, 1856, that Nathaniel Prentice Banks of Massachusetts was elected Speaker.

THE FIRST LADY

When Jane Appleton Pierce became mistress of the White House on March 4, 1853, she entered upon her duties with a troubled heart. Less than two months before the inauguration, her third and youngest son had been killed in a railroad accident. Her three children died before they had reached their teens. Her grief was so great that she lost interest in other matters. She always dressed in black while in the White House.

The second wife of Mrs. Pierce's uncle, Mrs. Abby Kent Means, acted as White House hostess.

JAMES BUCHANAN
15th PRESIDENT

Born–Apr. 23, 1791
Birthplace–Cove Gap, Pa.
College attended–Dickinson College, Carlisle, Pa.
Date of graduation–Sept. 27, 1809, two-year course
Religion–Presbyterian
Ancestry–Scotch-Irish
Occupation–Lawyer
Marital status–Bachelor
Political party–Democratic
State represented–Pennsylvania
Term of office–Mar. 4, 1857-Mar. 3, 1861
Term served–4 years
Administration–18th
Congresses–35th, 36th
Age at inauguration–65 years, 315 days
Lived after term–7 years, 89 days
Occupation after term–Writing
Date of death–June 1, 1868
Age at death–77 years, 39 days
Place of death–Lancaster Pa.
Burial place–Woodward Hill Cemetery, Lancaster, Pa.

PARENTS

Father–James Buchanan
Born–1761, County Donegal, Ireland
Married–Apr. 16, 1788

Occupation–Merchant, farmer
Died–June 11, 1821
Age at death–60 years
Mother–Elizabeth Speer Buchanan
Born–1767
Died–May 14, 1833, Greensburg, Pa.
Age at death–66 years

BROTHERS AND SISTERS

James Buchanan was the second child in a family of eleven.

Children of James Buchanan and Elizabeth Speer Buchanan

Mary Buchanan, b. 1789, d. 1791
James Buchanan, b. Apr. 23, 1791, d. June 1, 1868
Jane Buchanan, b. 1793, d. 1839
Maria Buchanan, b. 1795, d. 1849
Sarah Buchanan, b. 1798, d. 1825
Elizabeth Buchanan, b. 1800, d. 1801
Harriet Buchanan, b. 1802, d. 1840
John Buchanan, b. 1804, d. 1804
William Speer Buchanan, b. Nov. 14, 1805, d. Dec. 19, 1826
George Washington Buchanan, b. 1808, d. Nov. 13, 1832
Edward Young Buchanan, b. May 30, 1811, d. Jan. 20, 1895

THE ELECTION OF 1856

NOMINATIONS FOR TERM 1857-1861

Democratic Party Convention (7th)

June 2-6, 1856, Smith and Nixon's Hall, Cincinnati, Ohio
Nominated for President—James Buchanan, Pa.
Nominated for Vice President—John Cabell Breckinridge, Ky.

Buchanan was nominated on the seventeenth ballot, receiving all of the 296 votes cast. Candidates for nomination and the votes they

For additional data see the end of this section and also specific subject headings in the index.

received on the first ballot:
James Buchanan, Pa., 135$^1/_2$
Franklin Pierce, N.H., 122$^1/_2$
Stephen Arnold Douglas, Ill., 33
Lewis Cass, Mich., 5
Nomination made unanimous

Republican Party Convention (1st)
June, 17-19, 1856, Music Fund Hall, Philadelphia, Pa.
Nominated for President—John Charles Fremont, Calif.
Nominated for Vice President—William Lewis Dayton, N.J.
    Fremont was nominated on the first official ballot. Candidates for
nomination and the votes they received on the first informal and the
first official ballots:
John Charles Fremont, Calif., 359, 520
John McLean, Ohio, 190, 37
Charles Sumner, Mass., 2, 0
Nathaniel Prentice Banks, Mass., 1, 0
William Henry Seward, N.Y., 1, 1
Total number of votes:
    First informal ballot: 553
    First official ballot: 558
Nomination made unanimous

    The antislavery factions of the Whigs and the Free Democratic par-
ties formed the Republican Party. (The name "Republican" had been
applied to the earlier Democratic-Republican Party, which developed
into the present Democratic Party.)

American (Know-Nothing) Party Convention

Feb. 22, 1856, National Hall, Philadelphia, Pa.
Nominated for President—Millard Fillmore, N.Y.

Nominated for Vice President—Andrew Jackson Donelson, Tenn.
    The American Party started as more of a secret society than a politi-
cal party. Membership was divided into three degrees. The first included members who were American-born and were wholly uncon-
nected with the Roman Catholic Church. They were obliged to vote
as the society dictated. The second degree included members who
were permitted to hold office inside the organization. The third degree
was composed of members who were eligible for office outside the
organization. At this convention, the secret features were eliminated
and nominations were made.

Whig Party (the "Silver Grays") Convention

Sept. 17, 1856, Baltimore, Md.
Nominated for President—Millard Fillmore, N.Y.
Nominated for Vice President—Andrew Jackson Donelson, Tenn.
    The Whig Party lost its power in 1852. Its few remaining adherents
—conservative "Old-Line" Whigs known as "Silver Grays"—supported the candidates of the American Party in 1856. Most of the

southern Whigs had joined the Democrats, and most of the antislavery northern Whigs eventually joined the Republican Party.

North American Party Convention

June 12, 1856, New York, N.Y.
Nominated for President—Nathaniel Prentice Banks, Mass.
Nominated for Vice President—William Freame Johnson, Pa.

The North Americans broke away from the American Party. Their nominees later declined and their support was given to the Republican party.

ELECTION RESULTS, NOV. 4, 1856—PRESIDENTIAL AND VICE PRESIDENTIAL CANDIDATES

Democratic Party (1,838,169 votes)
James Buchanan, Pa.
John Cabell Breckinridge, Ky.

Republican Party (1,341,264 votes)
John Charles Fremont, Calif.
William Lewis Dayton, N.J.

American Party (874,534 votes)
Millard Fillmore, N.Y.
Andrew Jackson Donelson, Tenn.

ELECTORAL VOTES (296—31 states)

Buchanan received 58.79 per cent (174 votes—19 states) as follows: Ala. 9; Ark. 4; Calif. 4; Del. 3; Fla. 3; Ga. 10; Ill. 11; Ind. 13; Ky. 12; La. 6; Miss. 7; Mo. 9; N.J. 7; N.C. 10; Pa. 27; S.C. 8; Tenn. 12; Tex. 4; Va. 15.

Fremont received 38.51 per cent (114 votes—11 states) as follows: Conn. 6; Iowa 4; Me. 8; Mass. 13; Mich. 6; N.H. 5; N.Y. 35; Ohio 23; R.I. 4; Vt. 5; Wis. 5.

Fillmore received 2.70 per cent (1 state): Md. 8.

CABINET

March 4, 1857-March 3, 1861

State–William Learned Marcy, N.Y., continued from preceding administration; Lewis Cass, Mich., Mar. 6, 1857; William Hunter (chief clerk), ad interim Dec. 15, 1860; Jeremiah Sullivan Black, Pa., Dec. 17, 1860

Treasury–James Guthrie, Ky., continued from preceding administration; Howell Cobb, Ga., Mar. 6, 1857; Isaac Toucey, Conn. (secretary of the Navy), ad interim Dec. 10, 1860; Philip Francis Thomas, Md., Dec. 12, 1860; John Adams Dix, N.Y., Jan. 11, 1861; entered upon duties Jan. 15, 1861

War–Samuel Cooper (adjutant-general, U.S. Army), ad interim Mar. 4, 1857; John Buchanan Floyd, Va., Mar. 6, 1857; Joseph Holt, Ky. (postmaster general), ad interim Jan. 18, 1861

Attorney General–Caleb Cushing, Mass., continued from preceding administration; Jeremiah Sullivan Black, Pa., Mar. 6, 1857; entered upon duties Mar. 11, 1857; Edwin McMasters Stanton, Pa., Dec. 20, 1860; entered upon duties Dec. 22, 1860

Postmaster General–James Campbell, Pa., continued from preceding administration; Aaron Venable Brown, Tenn., Mar. 6, 1857; died Mar. 8, 1859; Horatio King, Me. (first assistant postmaster general), ad interim Mar. 9, 1859; Joseph Holt, Ky., Mar. 14, 1859; Horatio King, Me. (first assistant postmaster general), ad interim Jan. 1, 1861; Horatio King, Me., Feb. 12, 1861

Navy–James Cochran Dobbin, N.C., continued from preceding administration; Isaac Toucey, Conn., Mar. 6, 1857

Interior–Robert McClelland, Mich., continued from preceding administration; Jacob Thompson, Miss., Mar. 6, 1857; entered upon duties Mar. 10, 1857; Moses Kelly (chief clerk), ad interim Jan. 10, 1861

THIRTY-FIFTH CONGRESS

March 4, 1857-March 3, 1859

First session–Dec. 7, 1857-June 14, 1858 (189 days)

Second session–Dec. 6, 1858-Mar. 3, 1859 (88 days)

Special sessions of the Senate–Mar. 4, 1857-Mar. 14, 1857 (11 days); June 15, 1858-June 16, 1858 (2 days)

Vice President–John Cabell Breckinridge, Ky.

Presidents pro tempore of the Senate–James Murray Mason, Va., elected Mar. 4, 1857, special session; Thomas Jefferson Rusk, Tex., elected Mar. 14, 1857, special session; Benjamin Fitzpatrick, Ala., elected Dec. 7, 1857; Mar. 29, 1858; June 14, 1858; Jan. 25, 1859

Secretary of the Senate–Asbury Dickens, N.C.

Speaker of the House–James Lawrence Orr, S.C., elected Dec. 7, 1857

Clerks of the House–William Cullom, Tenn.; James Cameron Allen, Ill., elected Dec. 7, 1857

THIRTY-SIXTH CONGRESS

March 4, 1859-March 3, 1861

First session–Dec. 5, 1859-June 25, 1860 (202 days)

Second session–Dec. 3, 1860-Mar. 3, 1861 (93 days)

Special sessions of the Senate–Mar. 4, 1859-Mar. 10, 1859 (7 days); June 26, 1860-June 28, 1860 (3 days)

Vice President–John Cabell Breckinridge, Ky.

Presidents pro tempore of the Senate–Benjamin Fitzpatrick, Ala., elected Mar. 9, 1859, special session; Dec. 19, 1859; Feb. 20, 1860; June 26, 1860, special session; Jesse David Bright, Ind., elected June 12, 1860; Solomon Foot, Vt., elected Feb. 16, 1861

Secretary of the Senate–Asbury Dickens, N.C.

Speaker of the House–William Pennington, N.J., elected Feb. 1, 1860

Clerks of the House–James Cameron Allen, Ill.; John Wien Forney, Pa., elected Feb. 3, 1860

APPOINTMENT TO THE SUPREME COURT
Associate Justice
Nathan Clifford, Me., Jan. 12, 1858

ADMINISTRATION — IMPORTANT DATES
Mar. 6, 1857, Chief Justice Taney announced Dred Scott decision rendering the Missouri Compromise unconstitutional

May 11, 1858, Minnesota admitted as the 32nd state

Aug.-Oct. 1858, Lincoln-Douglas debates

Aug. 5, 1858, Atlantic cable completed

Aug. 16, 1858, James Buchanan and Queen Victoria exchanged greetings by means of the Atlantic cable

Feb. 14, 1859, Oregon admitted as the 33rd state

Aug. 27, 1859, oil discovered in Pennsylvania

Oct. 16, 1859, Harper's Ferry, Va., raided by John Brown

Apr. 3, 1860, Pony Express service began between St. Joseph, Mo., and Sacramento, Calif.

Sept. 20, 1860, Prince of Wales arrived at Detroit, Mich., from Canada, traveling as Baron Renfrew

Dec. 1860-Feb. 1861, futile compromise attempts to save the Union

Dec. 20, 1860, South Carolina seceded from the Union

Dec. 26, 1860, Major Robert Anderson, commander of troops in Charleston Harbor, S.C., removed his garrison from Fort Moultrie to Fort Sumter

Jan.-Feb. 1861, secession of Mississippi, Florida, Alabama, Georgia, Louisiana, Texas

Jan. 9, 1861, *Star of the West* fired on by Confederate troops from Morris Island and Fort Moultrie as the unarmed Union supply ship attempted to enter Charleston Harbor

Jan. 29, 1861, Kansas admitted as the 34th state

Feb. 4, 1861, Confederate States of America organized

Feb. 8, 1861, delegates from seceding states met at Montgomery, Ala.

IMPORTANT DATES IN HIS LIFE
1807, entered junior class Dickinson College

Nov. 17, 1812, admitted to the bar; practiced at Lancaster, Pa.

1814, served in company of dragoons under Major Charles Sterret Ridgely of Baltimore in War of 1812

Dec. 6, 1814-Oct. 1815, Pennsylvania House of Representatives

1816, unsuccessful candidate for U.S. House of Representatives

18—, became a Jacksonian Democrat when Federalist Party went out of existence

Mar. 4, 1821-Mar. 3, 1831, U.S. House of Representatives (from Pennsylvania)

Jan. 4, 1832-Aug. 5, 1833, U.S. Minister to Russia

Dec. 6, 1834-Mar. 5, 1845, U.S. Senate (from Pennsylvania)

May 29, 1844, unsuccessful aspirant to Democratic presidential nomination

Mar. 6, 1845-Mar. 6, 1849, secretary of state in cabinet of President Polk

May 25, 1848, unsuccessful aspirant to Democratic presidential nomination

1849, retired to Wheatland, his twenty-two-acre estate near Lancaster, Pa.

June 4, 1852, unsuccessful aspirant to Democratic presidential nomination

Apr. 11, 1853, envoy extraordinary and minister plenipotentiary to Great Britain

Mar. 4, 1857-Mar. 3, 1861, President

JAMES BUCHANAN

____was the first president born in Pennsylvania.

____was the only President to remain a bachelor.

BUCHANAN'S VICE PRESIDENT

Vice President–John Cabell Breckinridge (14th V.P.)

Date of birth–Jan. 21, 1821

Birthplace–near Lexington, Ky.

Political party–Democratic

State represented–Kentucky

Term of office–Mar. 4, 1857-Mar. 3, 1861

Age at inauguration–36 years, 42 days

Occupation after term–Military service in Confederate Army, lawyer

Date of death–May 17, 1875

Age at death–54 years, 116 days

Place of death–Lexington, Ky.

Burial place–Lexington, Ky.

Additional data on Breckenridge

1839, graduated from Centre College, Danville, Ky.

1840, admitted to the bar; practiced at Lexington, Ky.

1847-1848, major, Third Kentucky Volunteers, in Mexican War

1849, Kentucky State House of Representatives

Mar. 4, 1851-Mar. 3, 1855, U.S. House of Representatives (from Kentucky)

1860, unsuccessful candidate for President on the Southern Democratic ticket

Mar. 4, 1861-Dec. 4, 1861, U.S. Senate (from Kentucky); expelled by resolution

1862, served in Confederate Army as brigadier general at Bowling Green; later major general

May 18-July 27, 1862, defended Vicksburg

Jan. 1863, at battle of Murfreesboro

May 14, 1863, at battle of Jackson, Miss.

Jan.-Apr. 1865, secretary of war in cabinet of Confederate States

1865, escaped to Europe

1867, returned to Lexington, Ky., from Europe; resumed law practice

ADDITIONAL DATA ON BUCHANAN

BUCHANAN WAS ENGAGED TO MARRY

In the summer of 1819, James Buchanan, twenty-eight, was engaged to twenty-three-year-old Ann Caroline Coleman, the daughter of Robert Coleman of Lancaster, Pa. While on a visit in Philadelphia, Pa., she took an overdose of laudanum and died there on December 9, 1819. She was buried December 12, 1819, in the St. James Episcopal churchyard at Lancaster, Pa.

BACHELOR ELECTED PRESIDENT

James Buchanan was the first bachelor elected President of the United States and the only one to remain unmarried.

Grover Cleveland, also a bachelor, was elected as the twenty-second President, but on June 2, 1886, he married his ward, Frances Folsom, in a ceremony performed in the White House.

INAUGURATION

James Buchanan was inaugurated on Wednesday, March 4, 1857, the oath of office being administered by Chief Justice Taney on the east portico of the Capitol.

A big parade containing impressive floats attracted great crowds. Models of battleships, the Goddess of Liberty, and historical scenes were depicted on the floats.

A special building to accommodate six thousand persons was erected at a cost of $15,000 on Judiciary Square for the inaugural ball. The building, which contained two rooms, one for dancing and one for the supper, was 235 feet long, 77 feet wide, and 20 feet high, and had a white ceiling studded with gold stars. The walls were red, white, and blue. The music was furnished by an orchestra of 40. Food was lavishly served. At the supper, 400 gallons of oysters were consumed, 60 saddles of mutton, 4 saddles of venison, 125 tongues, 75 hams, 500 quarts of chicken salad, 500 quarts of jellies, 1200 quarts of ice cream, and a cake four feet high. Over $3,000 was spent for wine.

FIRST NATIONAL REPUBLICAN PLATFORM ADOPTED DURING BUCHANAN'S ADMINISTRATION

This convention of delegates, assembled in pursuance of a call addressed to the people of the United States, without regard to past political differences or divisions, who are opposed to the repeal of the Missouri Compromise, to the policy of the present administration, to the extension of slavery into free territory; in favor of admitting Kansas as a free State, of restoring the action of the Federal Government to the principles of Washington and Jefferson, and who purpose to unite in presenting candidates for the offices of President and Vice President, do resolve as follows:

RESOLVED, that the maintenance of the principles promulgated in the Declaration of Independence and embodied in the Federal Constitution is essential to the preservation of our republican institutions, and that the Federal Constitution, the rights of the States, and the Union of the States, shall be preserved.

RESOLVED, That with our Republican fathers we hold it to be a self-evident truth that all men are endowed with the inalienable rights to life, liberty, and the pursuit of happiness, and that the primary object and ulterior designs of our Federal Government were to secure these rights to all persons within its exclusive jurisdiction; that as our Republican fathers, when they had abolished slavery in all of our national territory, ordained that no person should be deprived of life, liberty, or property without due process of law, it becomes our duty to maintain this provision of the Constitution against all attempts to violate, for the purpose of establishing slavery in any territory of the United States, by positive legislation, prohibiting its existence or extension therein. That we deny the authority of Congress, or of a territorial Legislature, of any individual or association of individuals, to give legal existence to slavery in any Territory of the United States, while the present Constitution shall be maintained.

RESOLVED, That the Constitution confers upon Congress sovereign power over the Territories of the United States for their government, and that in the exercise of this power it is both the right and the duty of Congress to prohibit in the Territories those twin relics of barbarism—polygamy and slavery.

RESOLVED, That while the Constitution of the United States was ordained and established by the people in order to form a more perfect union, establish justice, insure domestic tranquillity, provide for the common defense, and secure the blessings of liberty, and contains ample provision for the protection of the life, liberty and property of every citizen, the dearest constitutional rights of the people of Kansas have been fraudulently and violently taken from them; their territory has been invaded by an armed force; spurious and pretended legislative, judicial, and executive officers have been set over them, by whose usurped authority, sustained by the military power of the Government, tyrannical and unconstitutional laws have been enacted and enforced; the rights of the people to keep and bear arms have been infringed; test oaths of an extraordinary and entangling nature have been imposed as a condition of exercising the right of suffrage and holding office; the right of an accused person to a speedy and public trial by an impartial jury has been denied; the right of the people to be secure in their persons, houses, papers, and effects against unreasonable searches and seizures has been violated; they have been deprived of life, liberty, and property without due process of law; the freedom of speech and of the press has been abridged; the right to choose their representatives has been made of no effect; murders, robberies, and arsons have been instigated and encouraged, and the offenders have been allowed to go unpunished;—that all of these things have been done with the knowledge, sanction, and procurement of the present administration, and that for this high crime against the Constitution, the Union, and humanity, we arraign the administration, the President, his advisers, agents, supporters, apologists, and accessories, either before or after the facts, before the country and before the world, and that it is our fixed purpose to bring the actual perpetrators of these atrocious outrages and their accomplices to a sure and condign punishment hereafter.

RESOLVED, That Kansas should be immediately admitted as a State of the Union, with her present free Constitution, as at once the most effectual way of securing to her citizens the enjoyment of the rights and privileges to which they are entitled, and of ending the civil strife now raging in her territory.

RESOLVED, That the highwayman's plea, that "might makes right," embodied in the Ostend circular, was in every respect unworthy of American diplomacy, and would bring shame and dishonor upon any government or people that gave it their sanction.

RESOLVED, That a railroad to the Pacific Ocean by the most central and practicable route, is imperatively demanded by the interests of the whole country and that the Federal Government ought to render immediate and efficient aid in its construction, and, as an auxiliary thereto, the immediate construction of an emigrant route on the line of the railroad.

RESOLVED, That appropriations by Congress for the improvement of rivers and harbors, of a national character, required for the accommodation and security of our existing commerce, are authorized by the Constitution, and justified by the obligation of Government to protect the lives and property of its citizens.

BUCHANAN TIRED OF PRESIDENCY

Buchanan, in a letter to Mrs. James Knox Polk on September 19, 1859, wrote:

I am now in my sixty-ninth year and am heartily tired of my position as president. I shall leave it in the beginning of March 1861, should a kind Providence prolong my days, until that period, with much greater satisfaction than when entering on the duties of the office.

YOUNGEST VICE PRESIDENT

John Cabell Breckinridge of Kentucky, who served as Vice President under President James Buchanan, was the youngest man to become Vice President. He was inaugurated on March 4, 1857, when he was 36 years, 1 month, and 11 days old.

HOSTESS AT THE WHITE HOUSE

Since James Buchanan was a bachelor, Harriet Lane, the daughter of his sister Jane Lane, served as mistress of the White House during his administration. Her mother had died when she was seven and her father when she was nine. During her uncle's presidential term, she married Henry Elliott Johnson of Baltimore, Md.

ABRAHAM LINCOLN
16th PRESIDENT

Born–Feb. 12, 1809

Birthplace–Hodgenville, Hardin County (now Larue County), Ky.

College attended–None

Religion–No specific denomination

Ancestry–English

Occupation–Lawyer

Date and place of marriage–Nov. 4, 1842, Springfield, Ill.

Age at marriage–33 years, 265 days

Years married–22 years, 162 days

Political party–Republican

State represented–Illinois

Term of office–Mar. 4, 1861-Apr. 15, 1865

Term served–4 years, 42 days

Administrations–19th, 20th

Congresses–37th, 38th, 39th

Age at inauguration–52 years, 20 days

Lived after term–Died in office

Date of death–Apr. 15, 1865

Age at death–56 years, 62 days

Place of death–Washington, D.C.

Burial place–Oak Ridge Cemetery, Springfield, Ill.

PARENTS

Father–Thomas Lincoln

Born–Jan. 6, 1778, Rockingham County, Va.,

Married (1)–Nancy Hanks

Married (2)–Sarah Bush Johnston

Occupation–Farmer, carpenter, wheelwright

Died–Jan. 17, 1851, Coles County, Ill.

Age at death–73 years, 11 days

Mother–Nancy Hanks Lincoln

Born–Feb. 5, 1784, Campbell County, Va.

Married–June 12, 1806, Beechland, Ky.

Died–Oct. 5, 1818, Spencer County, Ind.

Age at death–34 years, 242 days

Second wife of father–Sarah Bush Johnston Lincoln

Born–Dec. 12, 1788, Hardin County, Ky.

Married–Dec. 2, 1819, Elizabethtown, Ky.

Died–Apr. 10, 1869, Charleston, Ill.

Age at death–80 years, 119 days

At the time of her marriage to Thomas Lincoln, Sarah Bush Johnston was the widow of Daniel Johnston, by whom she had four children. Her marriage to Johnston took place Mar. 13, 1806, and his death Oct. 1818.

BROTHERS AND SISTERS

Abraham Lincoln was the second child of his father's first wife.

Children of Thomas Lincoln and Nancy Hanks Lincoln

Nancy (called Sarah) Lincoln, b. Feb. 10, 1807, d. Jan. 20, 1828

Abraham Lincoln, b. Feb. 12, 1809, d. Apr. 15, 1865

Thomas Lincoln, b. 1811, d. 1813

CHILDREN

Robert Todd Lincoln, b. Aug. 1, 1843, Springfield, Ill.; m. Sept. 24, 1868, Mary Harlan, Washington, D.C.; d. July 25, 1926, Manchester, Vt.

Edward Baker Lincoln, b. Mar.

For additional data see the end of this section and also specific subject headings in the index.

10, 1846, Springfield, Ill.; d.
Feb. 1, 1850, Springfield, Ill.

William Wallace Lincoln, b. Dec.
21, 1850, Springfield, Ill.; d.
Feb. 20, 1862, at the White
House, Washington, D.C.

Thomas (Tad) Lincoln, b. Apr. 4,
1853 Springfield, Ill.; d. July
15, 1871, Chicago, Ill.

MRS. ABRAHAM LINCOLN

Name–Mary Todd Lincoln
Date of birth–Dec. 13, 1818
Birthplace–Lexington, Ky.
Age at marriage–23 years, 326
days

Children–4 sons
Mother–Eliza Ann Parker Todd
Father–Robert Smith Todd
His occupation–Banker, manu-
facturer, merchant, farmer

Date of death–July 16, 1882
Age at death–63 years, 215 days
Place of death–Springfield, Ill.
Burial place–Springfield, Ill.

Years younger than the President–9 years, 304 days
Years she survived the President–
17 years, 92 days

THE ELECTION OF 1860
NOMINATIONS FOR TERM 1861-1865
Republican Party Convention (2nd)

May 16-18, 1860, the Wigwam, Chicago, Ill.

Nominated for President—Abraham Lincoln, Ill.

Nominated for Vice President—Hannibal Hamlin, Me.

Lincoln was nominated on the third ballot.

Candidates for nomination and the votes they received on the first
and third ballots:

William Henry Seward, N.Y., 173$^1/_2$, 180
Abraham Lincoln, Ill., 102, 231$^1/_2$
Simon Cameron, Pa., 50$^1/_2$, 0
Salmon Portland Chase, Ohio, 49, 24$^1/_2$
Edward Bates, Mo., 48, 22
William Lewis Dayton, N.J., 14, 1
John McLean, Ohio, 12, 5
Jacob Colamer, Vt., 10, 0
Benjamin Franklin Wade, Ohio, 3, 0
John Charles Fremont, Calif., 1,0
John M. Read, Pa., 1, 0
Charles Sumner, Mass., 1, 0
Cassius Marcellus Clay, Ky., 0, 1

Total number of votes: 465

Number necessary for nomination: 233

Before the third ballot was completed, a shift in votes brought Lincoln's total to 364 votes.

Democratic Party Convention (8th)

April 23-28, 30, and May 1-3, 1860, the Hall of the South Carolina
Institute, Charleston, S.C.

Nominated for President—No nomination made

Nominated for Vice President—No nomination made

Candidates for nomination and the votes they received on the first
and fifty-seventh ballots:

Stephen Arnold Douglas, Ill., 145$^1/_2$, 151$^1/_2$
Robert Mercer Taliaferro Hunter, Va., 42, 16
James Guthrie, Ky., 35, 65$^1/_2$
Andrew Johnson, Tenn., 12, 0
Daniel Stevens Dickinson, N.Y., 7, 4
Joseph Lane, Ore., 6, 14
Isaac Toucey, Conn., 2$^1/_2$, 0
Jefferson Davis, Miss., 1$^1/_2$, 1
Franklin Pierce, N.H., 1, 0
Total number of votes:
  First ballot: 252$^1/_2$
  Fifty-seventh ballot: 252
Number necessary for nomination: 202
  Unable to reach a decision on the fifty-seventh ballot, the convention adjourned to meet at Baltimore, Md., on June 18, 1860.

Democratic Party Convention (Northern or Douglas Democrats)

June 18-23, 1860, Front Street Theatre, Baltimore, Md.
Nominated for President—Stephen Arnold Douglas, Ill.
Nominated for Vice President—Herschel Vespasian Johnson, Ga.
  Douglas was nominated on the second ballot. Candidates for nomination and the votes they received on the first and second ballots:
Stephen Arnold Douglas, Ill., 173$^1/_2$, 181$^1/_2$
James Guthrie, Ky., 9, 5$^1/_2$
John Cabell Breckinridge, Ky., 5, 7$^1/_2$
Horatio Seymour, N.Y., 1, 0
Thomas Stanhope Bocock, Va., 1, 0
Daniel Stevens Dickinson, N.Y., $^1/_2$, 0
Henry Alexander Wise, Va., $^1/_2$, 0
Total number of votes:
  First ballot: 190$^1/_2$
  Second ballot: 194$^1/_2$
Nomination made unanimous

National Democratic Party Convention (Independent Democratic Party)

June 23, 1860, Maryland Institute Hall, Baltimore, Md.
Nominated for President—John Cabell Breckinridge, Ky.
Nominated for Vice President—Joseph Lane, Ore.
  Breckinridge was nominated on the first ballot. Candidates for nomination and the votes they received:
John Cabell Breckinridge, Ky., 81
Daniel Stevens Dickinson, N.Y., 24
Total number of votes: 105
Nomination made unanimous
  This segment seceded from the Democratic Party and pledged the new party to a Pacific railroad, the acquisition of Cuba, the enforcement of the Fugitive Slave Law, and the admission of territories as states when their populations were adequate, with or without slavery as their constitutions provided.

Southern Democratic Party Convention (Southern or Breckinridge Democrats)

June 28, 1860, Market Hall, Baltimore, Md.
Nominated for President—John Cabell Breckinridge, Ky.
Nominated for Vice President—Joseph Lane, Ore.

This party declared that it was the right and duty of Congress to protect slavery in the territories whenever the owners chose to take slaves to the territories.

Constitutional Union Party Convention (formerly the American Party)

May 9-10, 1860, Presbyterian Church, Baltimore, Md.
Nominated for President—John Bell, Tenn.
Nominated for Vice President—Edward Everett, Mass.

Bell was nominated on the second ballot. Candidates for nomination and the votes they received on the first and second ballots:

John Bell, Tenn., 68$^1/_2$, 138
Samuel Houston, Tex., 57, 69
John Jordan Crittenden, Ky., 28, 1
Edward Everett, Mass., 25, 9$^1/_2$
William Alexander Graham, N.C., 24, 18$^1/_2$
John McLean, Ohio, 19, 1
William Cabell Rives, Va., 13, 0
John Minor Botts, Va., 9$^1/_2$, 5$^1/_2$
William Lewis Sharkey, 7, 8$^1/_2$
William Leftwich Goggin, Va., 3, 2
Total number of votes:
   First ballot: 254
   Second ballot: 253
Number necessary for nomination: 138

This party tried to ignore the slavery question. It favored "the constitution of the country, the union of the states and the enforcement of the laws."

ELECTION RESULTS, NOV. 6, 1860—PRESIDENTIAL AND VICE PRESIDENTIAL CANDIDATES

Republican Party (1,866,452 votes)

Abraham Lincoln, Ill.
Hannibal Hamlin, Me.

Democratic Party (Northern Democrats) (1,375,157 votes)

Stephen Arnold Douglas, Ill.
Herschel Vespasian Johnson, Ga.

Democratic Party (Southern Democrats) (847,953 votes)

John Cabell Breckinridge, Ky.
Joseph Lane, Ore.

Constitutional Union Party (590,631 votes)

John Bell, Tenn.
Edward Everett, Mass.

ELECTORAL VOTES (303—33 states)

Lincoln received 59.41 per cent (180 votes—18 states) as follows: Calif. 4; Conn. 6; Ill. 11; Ind. 13; Iowa 4; Me. 8; Mass. 13; Mich. 6; Minn. 4; N.H. 5; N.J. 4 (of the 7 votes); N.Y. 35; Ohio 23; Ore. 3; Pa. 27; R.I. 4; Vt. 5; Wis. 5.

Breckinridge received 23.76 per cent (72 votes—11 states) as follows: Ala. 9; Ark. 4; Del. 3; Fla. 3; Ga. 10; La. 6; Md. 8; Miss. 7; N.C. 10; S.C. 8; Tex. 4.

Bell received 12.87 per cent (39 votes—3 states) as follows: Ky. 12, Tenn. 12; Va. 15.

Douglas received 3.96 per cent (12 votes—2 states) as follows: Mo. 9; N.J. 3 (of the 7 votes).

THE ELECTION OF 1864

NOMINATIONS FOR TERM 1865-1869

Republican Party Convention (National Union Convention) (3rd)

June 7-8, 1864, Front Street Theatre, Baltimore, Md.
Nominated for President—Abraham Lincoln, Ill.
Nominated for Vice President—Andrew Johnson, Tenn.

Abraham Lincoln was nominated on the first ballot. Candidates for nomination and the votes they received:

Abraham Lincoln, Ill., 484
Ulysses Simpson Grant, Ill., 22
Total number of votes: 506
Nomination made unanimous

Democratic Party Convention (9th)

August 29-31, 1864, the Amphitheatre, Chicago, Ill.
Nominated for President—George Brinton McClellan, N.Y.
Nominated for Vice President—George Hunt Pendleton, Ohio

George Brinton McClellan was nominated on the first ballot. Candidates for nomination and the votes they received:

George Brinton McClellan, N.J., 202$^1/_2$
Thomas Hart Seymour, Conn., 23$^1/_2$
Total number of votes: 226
Number necessary for nomination: 151
Nomination made unanimous

Independent Republican Party Convention

May 31, 1864, Cleveland, Ohio
Nominated for President—John Charles Fremont, Calif.
Nominated for Vice President—John Cochrane, N.Y.

A one-term principle was advocated by this faction of the Republican Party. Later, the candidates withdrew and supported the Republican Party nominations.

ELECTION RESULTS, NOV. 8, 1864—PRESIDENTIAL AND VICE PRESIDENTIAL CANDIDATES

Republican Party (2,213,635 votes)

Abraham Lincoln, Ill.
Andrew Johnson, Tenn.

Democratic Party (1,805,237 votes)

George Brinton McClellan, N.Y.

George Hunt Pendleton, Ohio

ELECTORAL VOTES (233—25 states)

Lincoln received 90.99 per cent (212 votes—22 states) as follows: Calif. 5; Conn. 6; Ill. 16; Ind. 13; Iowa 8; Kan. 3; Me. 7; Md. 7; Mass. 12; Mich. 8; Minn. 4; Mo. 11; Nev. 2; N.H. 5; N.Y. 33; Ohio 21; Ore. 3; Pa. 26; R.I. 4; Vt. 5; W.Va. 5; Wis. 8.

McClellan received 9.01 per cent (21 votes—3 states) as follows: Del. 3; Ky. 11; N.J. 7.

Eleven Confederate states with 80 votes did not vote: Ala. 8; Ark. 5; Fla. 3; Ga. 9; La. 7; Miss. 7; N.C. 9; S.C. 6; Tenn. 10; Tex. 6; Va. 10.

FIRST TERM

CABINET

March 4, 1861-March 3, 1865

State–Jeremiah Sullivan Black, Pa., continued from preceding administration; William Henry Seward, N.Y., Mar. 5, 1861

Treasury–John Adams Dix, N.Y., continued from preceding administration; Salmon Portland Chase, Ohio, Mar. 5, 1861; entered upon duties Mar. 7, 1861; George Harrington, D.C. (assistant secretary), ad interim July 1, 1864; William Pitt Fessenden, Me., July 1, 1864; entered upon duties July 5, 1864

War–Joseph Holt, Ky., continued from preceding administration; Simon Cameron, Pa., Mar. 5, 1861; entered upon duties Mar. 11, 1861; Edwin McMasters Stanton, Pa., Jan. 15, 1862; entered upon duties Jan. 20, 1862

Attorney General–Edwin McMasters Stanton, Pa., continued from preceding administration; Edward Bates, Mo., Mar. 5, 1861; James Speed, Ky., Dec. 2, 1864; entered upon duties Dec. 5, 1864

Postmaster General–Horatio King, Me.; continued from preceding administration; Montgomery Blair, D.C., Mar. 5, 1861; entered upon duties Mar. 9, 1861; William Dennison, Ohio, Sept. 24, 1864; entered upon duties Oct. 1, 1864

Navy–Isaac Toucey, Conn., continued from preceding administration; Gideon Welles, Conn., Mar. 5, 1861; entered upon duties Mar. 7, 1861

Interior–Moses Kelly (chief clerk), ad interim Mar. 4, 1861; Caleb Blood Smith, Ind., Mar. 5, 1861; John Palmer Usher, Ind. (assistant secretary), ad interim Jan. 1, 1863; John Palmer Usher, Ind. Jan. 8, 1863

SECOND TERM

CABINET

March 4, 1865-April 15, 1865

State–William Henry Seward, N.Y., continued from preceding administration

Treasury–George Harrington, D.C. (assistant secretary), ad interim Mar. 4, 1865; Hugh McCulloch, Ind., Mar. 7, 1865; entered upon duties Mar. 9, 1865

War–Edwin McMasters Stanton, Pa., continued from preceding administration

Attorney General–James Speed, Ky., continued from preceding administration

Postmaster General–William Dennison, Ohio, continued from preceding administration

Navy–Gideon Welles, Conn., continued from preceding administration

Interior–John Palmer Usher, Ind., continued from preceding administration

FIRST TERM

THIRTY-SEVENTH CONGRESS

March 4, 1861-March 3, 1863

First session–July 4, 1861-Aug. 6, 1861 (34 days)
Second session–Dec. 2, 1861-July 17, 1862 (228 days)
Third session–Dec. 1, 1862-Mar. 3, 1863 (93 days)
Special session of the Senate–Mar. 4, 1861-Mar. 28, 1861 (24 days)
Vice President–Hannibal Hamlin, Me.
President pro tempore of the Senate–Solomon Foot, Vt., elected Mar. 23, 1861; July 18, 1861; Jan. 15, 1862; Mar. 31, 1862; June 19, 1862; Feb. 18, 1863
Secretaries of the Senate–Asbury Dickens, N.C.; John Wien Forney, Pa., elected July 15, 1861; William Hickey (chief clerk), appointed Mar. 22, 1861, "to serve during the present infirmity of the secretary"
Speaker of the House–Galusha Aaron Grow, Pa., elected July 4, 1861
Clerks of the House–John Wien Forney, Pa., Emerson Etheridge, Tenn., elected July 4, 1861

THIRTY-EIGHTH CONGRESS

March 4, 1863-March 3, 1865

First session–Dec. 7, 1863-July 4, 1864 (209 days)
Second session–Dec. 5, 1864-Mar. 3, 1865 (89 days)
Special session of the Senate–Mar. 4, 1863-Mar. 14, 1863 (11 days)
Vice President–Hannibal Hamlin, Me.
Presidents pro tempore of the Senate–Solomon Foot, Vt. elected Mar. 4, 1863, special session; Dec. 18, 1863; Feb. 23, 1864; Mar. 11, 1864; Apr. 11, 1864; Daniel Clark, N.H., elected Apr. 26, 1864; Feb. 9, 1865
Secretary of the Senate–John Wien Forney, Pa.
Speaker of the House–Schuyler Colfax, Ind., elected Dec. 7, 1863
Clerks of the House–Emerson Etheridge, Tenn., Edward McPherson, Pa., elected Dec. 8, 1863

SECOND TERM

THIRTY-NINTH CONGRESS

March 4, 1865-March 3, 1867

First session–Dec. 4, 1865-July 28, 1866 (237 days)
Second session–Dec. 3, 1866-Mar. 3, 1867 (91 days)
Special session of the Senate–Mar. 4, 1865-Mar. 11, 1865 (8 days)
Vice President–Andrew Johnson, Tenn., succeeded to the presidency on the death of Abraham Lincoln on Apr. 15, 1865
Presidents pro tempore of the Senate–Lafayette Sabine Foster, Conn., elected Mar. 7, 1865, special session, "to serve in the absence of the Vice President"; Benjamin Franklin Wade, Ohio, elected Mar. 2, 1867.
Secretary of the Senate–John Wien Forney, Pa.
Speaker of the House–Schuyler Colfax, Ind., reelected Dec. 4, 1865
Clerk of the House–Edward McPherson, Pa., reelected Dec. 4, 1865

APPOINTMENTS TO THE SUPREME COURT

Chief Justice
Salmon Portland Chase, Ohio, Dec. 6, 1864

Associate Justices
Noah Haynes Swayne, Ohio, Jan. 24, 1862
Samuel Freeman Miller, Iowa, July 16, 1862
David Davis, Ill., Oct. 17, 1862
Stephen Johnson Field, Calif., Mar. 10, 1863

ADMINISTRATION — IMPORTANT DATES

Feb. 1861, plot to assassinate President-elect Lincoln at Baltimore, Md.
Apr.-June 1861, secession of Virginia, Arkansas, North Carolina, Tennessee
Apr. 12, 1861, first attack in Civil War at Fort Sumter, S.C.
Apr. 15, 1861, President Lincoln issued call for 75,000 volunteers
Apr. 19, 1861, riot at Baltimore, Md.
May 3, 1861, call for 42,034 volunteers for three years
June 3, 1861, first bloodshed in Civil War, Philippi, W.Va.
July 21, 1861, First battle of Bull Run
Aug. 16, 1861, proclamation prohibiting intercourse between loyal and seceding states
Nov. 8, 1861, *Trent* affair—Confederate agents Mason and Slidell taken from British steamer *Trent* by Union ship
Mar. 9, 1862, battle between *Monitor* and *Merimac*
Mar. 11, 1862, President Lincoln assumed command of the Army and the Navy
Apr. 6-7, 1862, battle of Shiloh
Apr. 16, 1862, slavery abolished in the District of Columbia
May 15, 1862, act to establish Department of Agriculture approved
May 20, 1862, Homestead Act approved
July 2, 1862, Morrill land-grant college act approved

Aug. 30, 1862, Second Battle of Bull Run

Sept. 17, 1862, Battle of Antietam

Sept. 22, 1862, preliminary Emancipation Proclamation issued

Jan. 1, 1863, Emancipation Proclamation issued

Feb. 25, 1863, national banking system created

May 1-4, 1863, Battle of Chancellorsville

June 1863, occupation of Mexico by French troops led to American protests

June 19, 1863, West Virginia admitted as the 35th state

July 1-3, 1863, Battle of Gettysburg

July 4, 1863, Surrender of Vicksburg

Sept. 19-20, 1863, Battle of Chickamauga

Nov. 19, 1863, Lincoln delivered Gettysburg Address

Nov. 24-25, 1863, Battle of Chattanooga

May 5-7, 1864, Battle of the Wilderness

June 19, 1864, U.S. warship *Kearsarge* sank the British-built Confederate ship *Alabama,* which had preyed upon American vessels

Sept. 2, 1864, General Sherman captured Atlanta

Oct. 31, 1864, Nevada admitted as the 36th state

Nov. 15, 1864, burning of Atlanta; beginning of Sherman's march to the sea

Apr. 3, 1865, evacuation of Richmond

Apr. 9, 1865, General Robert E. Lee surrendered to General Ulysses S. Grant at Appomattox Courthouse, Va.

IMPORTANT DATES IN HIS LIFE

1816, family moved from Kentucky to Indiana

July 1827, hired to operate a ferry across the Anderson River in Spencer County, Ind.

Apr. 1828, hired to pilot a flatboat from Rockport, Ind., to New Orleans, La.

Mar. 1, 1830, family moved from Indiana to Illinois

Mar. 1831, hired to build a flatboat at Sangamon Town, Ill., and take a load of produce to New Orleans

1832, volunteer, Sangamon Rifle Co., Richland, Ill.; reenlisted as private; mustered out June 16; returned to New Salem, Ill.; unsuccessful in general merchandise business with partner

Aug. 6, 1832, unsuccessful candidate for Illinois House of Representatives

Mar. 6, 1833, received saloon license to dispense liquor at Springfield, Ill. (Berry and Lincoln)

May 7, 1833, appointed postmaster, New Salem, Ill.

Dec. 7, 1835-Feb. 7, 1836, Illinois General Assembly

1837, moved to Springfield, Ill.

Mar. 1, 1837, admitted to the bar

Mar. 4, 1847-Mar. 3, 1849, U.S. House of Representatives (from Illinois) (only Whig elected from Illinois)

Feb. 8, 1855, unsuccessful candidate for senator from Illinois on Whig ticket

June 19, 1856, unsuccessful aspirant to the Republican vice presidential nomination

Aug.-Oct. 1858, Lincoln-Douglas debates in Illinois (senatorial campaign)

Nov. 2, 1858, unsuccessful candidate for senator from Illinois on Republican ticket

May 18, 1860, nominated for the presidency

Nov. 6, 1860, elected as first Republican President

Mar. 4, 1861-Mar. 3, 1865, President (first term)

Nov. 19, 1863, delivered Gettysburg Address

Nov. 8, 1864, reelected President

Mar. 4, 1865, inaugurated President for second term ending Mar. 3, 1869

Apr. 14, 1865, assassinated at Ford's Theater, Washington D.C.; died at 7:22 A.M., Apr. 15

ABRAHAM LINCOLN

____was the first President born in Kentucky.

____was the third President to die in office.

____was the first President assassinated.

____was the fifth President who was a resident of a state other than his native state.

LINCOLN'S VICE PRESIDENTS

FIRST TERM

Vice President–Hannibal Hamlin (15th V.P.)

Date of birth–Aug. 27, 1809

Birthplace–Paris, Me.

Political party–Republican (after 1856)

State represented–Maine

Term of office–Mar. 4, 1861-Mar. 3, 1865

Age at inauguration–51 years, 189 days

Occupation after term–U.S. senator, minister to Spain

Date of death–July 4, 1891

Age at death–81 years, 311 days

Place of death–Bangor, Me.

Burial place–Bangor, Me.

Additional data on Hamlin

18—, attended local schools and Hebron Academy; worked on farm until of age

18—, served one year as compositor

1833, admitted to bar; practiced in Hampden, Penobscot County, Me.

1836-1840, Maine House of Representatives; served as Speaker 1837, 1839, and 1840

1840, unsuccessful candidate for U.S. House of Representatives

Mar. 4, 1843-Mar. 3, 1847, U.S. House of Representatives (from Maine)

1846, unsuccessful Anti-slavery Democratic candidate for U.S. Senate (from Maine)

1848, Maine House of Representatives
June 8, 1848-Jan. 7, 1857, U.S. Senate (from Maine)
Jan. 8, 1857-Feb. 20, 1857, governor of Maine
Mar. 4, 1857-Jan. 17, 1861, U.S. Senate
1864, enlisted as a private in Maine State Guard for sixty-day period
1865-1866, collector of the port of Boston; resigned
Mar. 4, 1869-Mar. 3, 1881, U.S. Senate
1881-1882, U.S. Minister to Spain
1882, engaged in agricultural pursuits

SECOND TERM

Vice President–Andrew Johnson (16th V.P.)
Date of birth–Dec. 29, 1808
Birthplace–Raleigh, N.C.
Political party–Democratic (elected Vice President on Republican ticket)
State represented–Tennessee
Term of office–Mar. 4, 1865-Apr. 15, 1865
Age at inauguration–56 years, 65 days
Occupation after term–President
Date of death–July 31, 1875
Age of death–66 years, 214 days
Place of death–Carter's Station, Tenn.
Burial place–Greeneville, Tenn.

For further biographical information see Andrew Johnson, 17th President.

ADDITIONAL DATA ON LINCOLN

FIRST PRESIDENT BORN OUTSIDE ORIGINAL THIRTEEN STATES

Abraham Lincoln was the first President born beyond the boundaries of the original thirteen states. He was born near Hodgenville, in Hardin County, now Larue County, Ky.

LINCOLN ENLISTED AS A SOLDIER

On April 16, 1832, Governor John Reynolds called the Illinois militia to duty. When the notice reached New Salem on April 19, 1832, Lincoln gave up his job as a clerk and enlisted. On April 21, 1832, he was elected captain of his company.

The call for troops was issued as follows:

Your Country Requires Your Services

The Indians have assumed a hostile attitude and have invaded the State in violation of the treaty of last summer. The British band of Sacs and other hostile Indians, headed by Black Hawk, are in possession of the Rock River country, to the great terror of the frontier inhabitants. . . . No citizen ought be remain inactive when his country is invaded and the helpless part of the community are in danger.

His company was enrolled at Beardstown, Ill., in the state service on April 28 and into federal service on May 9. When mustered out on May 27, Lincoln reenlisted as a private in Captain Elijah Iles's company. This enlistment expired June 16, while Lincoln was at Fort Wilbourn, and he reenlisted in the company under the command of Captain Jacob M. Early. On July 10, he was mustered out of service at White Water, Wis.

LINCOLN A PATENTEE

On March 10, 1849, Abraham Lincoln of Springfield, Ill., applied for a patent on "a new and improved manner of combining adjustable buoyant air chambers with a steamboat or other vessel for the purpose of enabling their draught of water to be readily lessened to enable them to pass over bars, or through shallow water, without discharging their cargoes."

A waterproof fabric or India-rubber cloth in the form of a cylinder was placed at the sides of a vessel. When inflated with air, the buoyant cylinder chamber expanded and increased the size of the hull, decreasing the relative proportionate weight of the boat. When not inflated, the cylinder contracted and occupied little space.

The Patent Office awarded Lincoln U.S. Patent No. 6,469 on May 22, 1849, for "buoying vessels over shoals."

This was the first and only patent obtained by a President. It was never put into practical use.

"LINCOLN'S LOST SPEECH"

The Kansas-Nebraska Bill which became a law May 30, 1854, provided that the two new territories could determine whether they wanted to be free states or slave states. This act repealed the Missouri Compromise, an act of Congress passed in February 1820, which had admitted Missouri as a slave state and prohibited the extension of slavery to the remainder of the Louisiana territory north of the 36° 30' line.

Slavery agitators sacked the town of Lawrence, Kan., on May 21, 1856. Lives were lost, homes burned, printing presses destroyed. The slavery question aroused the nation and when the Illinois Republican Party held its first convention at Bloomington, Ill. on May 29, 1856, Lincoln was called upon to speak. His denunciation of slavery thrilled the newspaper reporters, and they listened instead of taking notes. As no verbatim account exists, this speech is known as "Lincoln's Lost Speech."

LINCOLN DEFEATED IN RACE FOR VICE PRESIDENTIAL NOMINATION

On June 19, 1856, at the first Republican Party convention, held at Philadelphia, Pa., Abraham Lincoln ran for the vice presidential nomination. He received 110 votes (Illinois 33, Indiana 26, California 12, Pennsylvania 11, New Hampshire 8, Massachusetts 7, Michigan 5, New York 3, Ohio 2, Rhode Island 2 and Maine 1). He was defeated on the first ballot, as William Lewis Dayton of New Jersey received 253 votes. Another candidate for the office of Vice President was Nathaniel Prentice Banks of Massachusetts, who received 46 votes.

LINCOLN'S MODESTY

Some authorities have claimed that Abraham Lincoln, by his own admission, was not fit to be President, an opinion based upon Lincoln's letter to Thomas J. Pickett, of Rock Island, Ill., dated April 16, 1859. Lincoln wrote him: "I do not think myself fit for the Presidency. I certainly am flattered, and grateful that some partial friends think of me in that connection."

FIRST CONVENTION BUILDING ERECTED

The first building especially constructed to house a political convention was the "Wigwam" on Lake Street, Chicago, Ill., built for the second Republican Party convention, which met May 16, 17, and 18, 1860. The main floor was reserved for delegates. A balcony was provided for spectators. The building was equipped with telegraph equipment. The Wigwam, decorated with flags, flowers, evergreens, and statuary, accommodated ten thousand persons. William Boyington was the architect.

LINCOLN SUPPORTERS PACKED THE WIGWAM

The Republican convention of 1860 was the first to which the general public was admitted. While the supporters of William Henry Seward of New York were parading through the city with a brass band prior to the time set for nominating, the followers of Abraham Lincoln of Illinois filled the spectators' seats in the convention hall, leaving only a few places for the thousands of Seward followers seeking admission.

LINCOLN NOT EXPECTED TO WIN NOMINATION

Reporting the prospects of the various candidates at the Republican convention of 1860, the Washington, D.C., *Evening Star* of May 16, 1860, said "Lincoln is urged by the delegates from Illinois, but his alleged want of administrative ability is the objection raised against him. After a complimentary vote for him, Illinois will likely go for [Edward] Bates."

KENTUCKY IGNORED FAVORITE SONS

Kentucky cast its twelve electoral votes in the election of 1860 for John Bell of Tennessee despite the fact that the two other presidential candidates, Abraham Lincoln and John Cabell Breckinridge, were born in Kentucky.

LINCOLN'S BEARD

Abraham Lincoln was the first President to wear a beard, which he began to grow shortly after his election in 1860. Many of his supporters had suggested that he would look more dignified with a beard, and while he was campaigning he received the following letter:

Westfield, Chautauqua Co., N.Y.
October 15, 1860

Hon. A B Lincoln
Dear Sir

I am a little girl 11 years old, but want you should be President of the United States very much so I hope you wont think me very bold to write to such a great man as you are.

Have you any little girls about as large as I am if so give them my love and tell her to write me if you cannot answer this letter. I have got four brothers and part of them will vote for you any way and if you will let your whiskers grow I will try to get the rest of them to vote for you. You would look a great deal better for your face is so thin. All the ladies like whiskers and they would tease their husbands to vote for you and then you would be President.

GRACE BEDELL

Lincoln replied to her letter as follows:

Private
Springfield, Ill.
Oct. 19, 1860

Miss Grace Bedell
Westfield, N.Y.
My dear little Miss:

Your very agreeable letter of the 15th is received. I regret the necessity of saying I have no daughters. I have three sons, one seventeen, one nine, and one seven years of age. They, with their mother, constitute my whole family. As to the whiskers, having never worn any, do you not think people would call it a piece of silly affectation if I were to begin it now?"

Your very sincere well-wisher,

A. LINCOLN

When the train bearing Lincoln to the White House stopped at a station near Westfield, Lincoln told the assembled crowd about his correspondent. He asked if she was present. When she came forward, he picked her up, kissed her, and told the crowd, "She wrote me that she thought I'd look better if I wore whiskers."

LINCOLN'S ADIEU TO SPRINGFIELD, ILLINOIS

On February 11, 1861, from the rear of the railroad car transporting him to Washington, D.C., for his inauguration, President-elect Lincoln made a prophetic speech to his fellow Springfield townsfolk who had gathered in the morning rain to bid him farewell. His speech as reported follows:

My friends: No one, not in my situation, can appreciate my feeling of sadness at this parting. To this place, and the kindness of these people, I owe everything. . . . Here my children have been born, and one is buried. I now leave, not knowing when or whether I may return, with a task before me greater than that which rested on Washington.

ATTEMPT MADE TO ASSASSINATE LINCOLN IN 1861

An attempt to assassinate Lincoln was made in 1861. Lincoln's inaugural train left Springfield, Ill., on February 11, 1861, bound for Washington, D.C., and conspirators planned to kill him at the Calvert Street Depot, Baltimore, Md. A commotion was to be staged that would engage the attention of the police, during which time the assassin would carry out his plan. The plot was discovered and the crime prevented by Allan Pinkerton, a detective assigned to guard Lincoln. He arrived in Washington nine days before the inauguration.

FIRST INAUGURATION

Abraham Lincoln was inaugurated on Monday, March 4, 1861, on the east portico of the Capitol. It was the seventh time that Chief Justice Taney administered the oath of office to a President.

Former President Buchanan greeted the incoming President by saying, "If you are as happy, my dear sir, on entering this house as I am on leaving it and returning home, you are the happiest man on earth."

Lincoln was the first President whose military escort was really a guard instead of an honorary escort.

The intense feeling between the North and the South marred the occasion, but a large military parade seemed to lend assurance to the nervous populace. After the ceremonies, Lincoln returned to the White House to watch the parade. One of the floats carried thirty-four young girls, each one representing a state of the union. As the float passed in front of Lincoln, the girls rushed over to him and he kissed all of them.

Lincoln did not attend the inaugural ball, which was held in a frame building called, for the occasion, "the White Muslin Palace of Aladdin."

FIVE FORMER PRESIDENTS ALIVE WHEN LINCOLN WAS INAUGURATED

When President Abraham Lincoln took the oath of office on March 4, 1861, as the sixteenth President of the United States, five former Presidents of the United States were alive: Martin Van Buren, John Tyler, Millard Fillmore, Franklin Pierce, and James Buchanan.

KENTUCKY PRESIDENTS OF 1861

Abraham Lincoln, inaugurated President of the United States on March 4, 1861, was born in Hodgenville, Hardin County, Ky., on February 12, 1809.

Jefferson Davis, chosen President of the Confederate States of America by the provisional Confederate congress on February 18, 1861, was born in Fairview, Todd County (formerly Christian County), Ky., on June 3, 1808.

CONFEDERATE STATES ADOPT CONSTITUTION

During President Lincoln's first term, the first formal attempts of a united secession government were made when the Constitution of the Confederate States of America was adopted by the seceding southern states on March 11, 1861, at Montgomery, Ala. It contained the following preamble:

We, the people of the Confederate States, each State acting in its sovereign and independent character, in order to form a permanent federal government, establish justice, insure domestic tranquillity, and secure the blessings of liberty to ourselves and our posterity—invoking the favor and guidance of Almighty God —do ordain and establish this Constitution for the Confederate States of America.

CHARLES FRANCIS ADAMS APPOINTED AMBASSADOR TO ENGLAND

President Lincoln appointed Charles Francis Adams as envoy extraordinary and minister plenipotentiary to England on March 20, 1861. Adams was the third member of his family to receive this coveted appointment. His father, President John Quincy Adams, and his grandfather, President John Adams, had also served as ambassadors to Great Britain.

LINCOLN'S FIRST CALL FOR TROOPS, APRIL 15, 1861

Whereas, the laws of the United States have been for some time past, and now are, opposed, and the execution thereof obstructed, in the States of South Carolina, Georgia, Alabama, Florida, Mississippi, Louisiana, and Texas, by combinations too powerful to be suppressed by the ordinary course of judicial proceedings, or by the powers vested in the marshals by law; now, therefore, I, Abraham Lincoln, President of the United States, in virtue of the power in me vested by the Constitution and the laws, have thought fit to call forth the Militia of the several States of the Union to the aggregate number of 75,000, in order to suppress said combinations, and to cause the laws to be duly executed.

The details for this object will be immediately communicated to the State authorities through the War Department. I appeal to all loyal citizens to favor, facilitate, and aid, this effort to maintain the honor, the integrity, and existence, of our national Union, and the perpetuity of popular government, and to redress wrongs already long enough endured. I deem it proper to say that the first service assigned to the forces hereby called forth will probably be to repossess the forts, places, and property which have been seized from the Union; and in every event the utmost care will be observed, consistently with the objects aforesaid, to avoid any devastation, any destruction of, or interference with property, or any disturbance of peaceful citizens of any part of the country; and I hereby command the persons composing the combinations aforesaid, to disperse and retire peacefully to their respective abodes, within twenty days from this date.

Deeming that the present condition of public affairs presents an extraordinary occasion, I do hereby, in virtue of the power in me vested by the Constitution, convene both houses of Congress. The Senators and Representatives are, therefore, summoned to assemble at their respective chambers at twelve o'clock, noon, on Thursday, the fourth day of July next, then and there to consider and determine such measures as, in their wisdom, the public safety and interest may seem to demand.

In witness whereof, I have hereunto set my hand, and caused the seal of the United States to be affixed.

Done at the City of Washington, this fifteenth day of April, in the year of our Lord, one thousand eight hundred and sixty-one, of the Independence of the United States the eighty-fifty.

FIRST PRESIDENTIAL EXECUTIVE ORDER

The first presidential executive order to be numbered was Order No. 1 signed by President Lincoln on October 20, 1862. This order established a provisional court in Louisiana. It was not the first executive order issued by a President, but the first one in the files of the Department of State.

THE EMANCIPATION PROCLAMATION

The Emancipation Proclamation, issued by President Lincoln as a war measure, did not free all the slaves. The complete abolition of slavery everywhere in the United States was brought about by the Thirteenth Amendment, ratified on December 18, 1865.

Lincoln's preliminary proclamation of September 22, 1862, declared that slavery was to be abolished in those states which should be in rebellion against the government on January 1, 1863. The seceding states controlled by the Confederate armies (Alabama, Arkansas, Florida, Georgia, Mississippi, North Carolina, South Carolina, Texas, and parts of Louisiana and Virginia) of course ignored the warning, and on January 1, 1863, Lincoln issued his Emancipation Proclamation.

The document, which freed the slaves in all Confederate territory occupied by Union troops—it did not affect loyal districts and could not be enforced in Confederate-held areas—proclaimed the policy of the United States on the question of slavery:

Whereas, on the twenty-second day of September, in the year of our Lord, one thousand eight hundred and sixty-two, a Proclamation was issued by the President of the United States, containing among other things the following, to wit;

"That on the first day of January, in the year of our Lord one thousand eight hundred and sixty-three, all persons held as slaves within any State, or designated part of a State, the people whereof shall then be in rebellion against the United States, shall be then, thenceforth and forever free, and the Executive Government of the United States, including the military and naval authorities thereof, will recognize and maintain the freedom of such persons, and will do no act or acts to repress such persons, or any of them, in any efforts they may make for their actual freedom.

"That the Executive will, on the first day of January aforesaid, by proclamation, designate the States and parts of States, if any, in which the people thereof respectively shall then be in rebellion against the United States, and the fact that any State, or the people thereof, shall on that day be in good faith represented in the

Congress of the United States by members chosen thereto at elections wherein a majority of the qualified voters of such State shall have participated, shall, in the absence of strong countervailing testimony, be deemed conclusive evidence that such State and the people thereof are not then in rebellion against the United States."

Now, therefore, I, Abraham Lincoln, President of the United States, by virtue of the power in me vested as Commander-in-Chief of the Army and Navy of the United States in time of actual armed rebellion against the authority and government of the United States, and as a fit and necessary war measure for suppressing said rebellion, do, on this first day of January, in the year of our Lord, one thousand eight hundred and sixty-three, and in accordance with my purpose so to do, publicly proclaim for the full period of one hundred days from the day of first above mentioned order, and designate, as the States and parts of States wherein the people thereof respectively are this day in rebellion against the United States the following, to wit:

ARKANSAS, TEXAS, LOUISIANA (except the Parishes of St. Bernard, Plaquemines, Jefferson, St. John, St. Charles, St. James, Ascension, Assumption, Terre Bonne, Lafourche, St. Mary, St. Martin, and Orleans, including the City of New Orleans), MISSISSIPPI, ALABAMA, FLORIDA, GEORGIA, SOUTH CAROLINA, NORTH CAROLINA AND VIRGINIA (except the forty-eight counties designated as West Virginia, and also the counties of Berkeley, Accomac, Northampton, Elizabeth City, York, Princess Anne, and Norfolk, including the cities of Norfolk and Portsmouth), and which excepted parts are, for the present, left precisely as if this Proclamation were not issued.

And by virtue of the power and for the purpose aforesaid, I do order and declare that ALL PERSONS HELD AS SLAVES within said designated States and parts of States ARE, AND HENCEFORWARD SHALL BE FREE! and that the Executive Government of the United States, including the military and naval authorities thereof, will recognize and maintain the freedom of said persons.

And I hereby enjoin upon the people so declared to be free, to abstain from all violence, unless in necessary self-defense, and I recommend to them that in all cases, when allowed, they labor faithfully for reasonable wages.

And I further declare and make known that such persons of suitable condition will be received into the armed service of the United States to garrison forts, positions, stations and other places, and to man vessels of all sorts in said service.

And upon this act, sincerely believed to be an act of justice, warranted by the Constitution, upon military necessity, I invoke the considerate judgment of mankind and the gracious favor of Almighty God.

In testimony whereof I have hereunto set my name, and caused the seal of the United States to be affixed.

Done at the City of Washington, this first day of January, in the year of our Lord one thousand eight hundred and sixty-three, and of the Independence of the United States the eighty-seventy.

ABRAHAM LINCOLN

By the President
  WILLIAM H. SEWARD
  Secretary of State

LINCOLN PROCLAIMED ANNUAL THANKSGIVING DAY

Thanksgiving Day proclamations had been issued on numerous earlier occasions. Governor William Bradford in 1621 proclaimed a day for the Massachusetts colonists to offer thanks to God for their lives, their food, their clothing, etc. During the Revolutionary War, numerous days of thanksgiving were appointed for prayer and fasting by the Continental Congress. November 26, 1789, was set aside by President Washington to thank God for the newly formed government and the blessings which accompanied it. Other Thanksgiving days were set aside to commemorate special occasions such as the conclusion of a war.

The first of the national Thanksgiving Day proclamations was issued by Abraham Lincoln in 1863, on October 3, the month and day of George Washington's first Thanksgiving Day proclamation. President Andrew Johnson continued the custom, which was followed by the succeeding Presidents until President Franklin Delano Roosevelt made a change.

An extract from Lincoln's Thanksgiving Day proclamation of October 3, 1863, follows:

I do, therefore, invite my fellow-citizens in every part of the United States, and also those who are at sea and those who are sojourning in foreign lands, to set apart and observe the last Thursday of November next [November 26] as a day of thanksgiving and praise to our beneficent Father who dwelleth in the heavens. And I recommend to them that, while offering up the ascriptions justly due to Him for singular deliverances and blessings, they do also, with humble penitence for our national perverseness and disobedience, commend to His tender care all those who have become widows, orphans, mourners, or sufferers in the lamentable civil strife in which we are unavoidably engaged, and fervently implore the interposition of the almighty hand to heal the wounds of the nation, and to restore it, as soon as may be consistent with the Divine purposes, to the full enjoyment peace, harmony, tranquillity, and union.

LINCOLN'S GETTYSBURG ADDRESS

Delivered on November 19, 1863, this immortal address commemorated the battle fought at Gettysburg, July 1-3, 1863:

Fourscore and seven years ago our fathers brought forth on this continent a new nation, conceived in liberty, and dedicated to the proposition that all men are created equal.

Now we are engaged in a great civil war, testing whether that nation, or any nation so conceived and so dedicated, can long endure. We are met on a great battlefield of that war. We have come to dedicate a portion of that field as a final resting place for those who here gave their lives that the nation might live. It is altogether fitting and proper that we should do this.

But, in a larger sense we cannot dedicate—we cannot consecrate —we cannot hallow—this ground. The brave men, living and dead, who struggled here, have consecrated it far above our poor power to add or detract. The world will little note nor long remember what we say here, but it can never forget what they did here. It is for us, the living, rather, to be dedicated here to the unfinished work which they who fought here have thus far so nobly advanced. It is rather for us to be here dedicated to the great task remaining before us—that from these honored dead we take increased devotion to that cause for which they gave the last full measure of devotion; that we here highly resolve that these dead shall not have died in vain; that this nation, under God, shall have a new birth of freedom; and that government of the people, by the people, for the people, shall not perish from the earth.

FIRST AMNESTY PROCLAMATION

The first amnesty proclamation to citizens was issued by President Abraham Lincoln on December 8, 1863. He issued a similar proclamation on March 26, 1864.

President Andrew Johnson issued supplementary proclamations on May 29, 1865; September 27, 1867; July 4, 1868; and December 25, 1868.

REPUBLICAN FACTION DISAPPROVED OF SECOND TERM

Although Lincoln was chosen unanimously on the first ballot at the Republican convention of 1864, not all the Republicans had favored his candidacy for a second term. A group of Republican dissenters held a convention at Cleveland, Ohio, on May 31, 1864, and nominated John Charles Fremont for the presidency and John Cochrane of New York for the vice presidency. Both nominees withdrew on September 21, 1864, urging the reelection of Abraham Lincoln.

LINCOLN WATCHED CIVIL WAR BATTLE

On July 12, 1864, Lincoln visited Fort Stevens, Washington, D.C., which was being defended by three brigades (6th Corps) of the Army of the Potomac under Major General Horatio Gates Wright against an attack led by Lieutenant General Jubal Anderson Early of the 2nd Corps, Army of the Confederacy. Captain Oliver Wendell Holmes acted as the President's guide. Lincoln watched the battle from the parapet of the fort, heedless of the danger. Three additional brigades reinforced the defenders and the tide of battle changed.

LINCOLN WON 1864 SOLDIER VOTE

In the 1864 election, Lincoln received 77.5 per cent of the soldier vote, compared with 22.5 per cent cast for Major General George Brinton McClellan, general-in-chief of the armies of the United States and commander of the Army of the Potomac. The vote was 116,887 for Lincoln and 33,748 for McClellan.

The states which provided for soldier votes were California, Iowa, Kentucky, Maine, Maryland, Michigan, New Hampshire, Ohio, Pennsylvania, Vermont, and Wisconsin. No provision was made allowing the soldiers to vote in Connecticut, Delaware, Illinois, Indiana, Massachusetts, Missouri, Nevada, New Jersey, New York, Oregon, Rhode Island, and West Virginia. The votes of Kansas and Minnesota soldiers were not counted as they arrived too late.

The 1864 election was the first in which the army vote was tabulated.

LINCOLN'S LETTER TO MRS. BIXBY

Perhaps the most famous letter in American literature was Lincoln's letter to Mrs. Lydia Bixby of Boston, written at the request of Governor Andrew of Massachusetts. The letter, dated November 21, 1864, was sent to Adjutant General Schouler, who delivered it on November 25 to Mrs. Bixby. It reads:

> I have been shown in the files of the War Department a statement of the Adjutant General that you are the mother of five sons who have died gloriously on the field of battle. I feel how weak and fruitless must be any word of mine which should attempt to beguile you from the grief of a loss so overwhelming. But I cannot refrain from tendering you the consolation that may be found in the thanks of the republic they died to save. I pray that our Heavenly Father may assuage the anguish of your bereavement, and leave you only the cherished memory of the loved and lost, and the solemn pride that must be yours to have laid so costly a sacrifice upon the altar of freedom.
>
> Yours very sincerely and respectfully,
>
> A. Lincoln

The reports upon which Lincoln based his consoling letter were inaccurate. Charles N. Bixby was killed at the second battle of Fredericksburg, May 3, 1863. Henry Cromwell Bixby, first reported missing and later as killed, was captured and honorably discharged on December 19, 1864. Edward Bixby deserted from Company C, 1st Massachusetts Heavy Artillery, and went to sea to escape the penalty of desertion. Oliver Cromwell Bixby was killed in action in the Crater fight before Petersburg, Va., on July 30, 1864. George Way Bixby was captured on July 30, 1864, and deserted to the enemy at Salisbury, N.C.

THIRTEENTH AMENDMENT ENACTED

The Thirteenth Amendment to the Constitution, prohibiting slavery, was passed by Congress on January 31, 1865. It was proposed to the legislatures of the several states by the Thirty-eighth Congress on February 1, 1865. It was rejected by Delaware and Kentucky and was conditionally ratified by Alabama and Mississippi. Texas took no action. The twenty-seventh state to ratify, making it effective, was Georgia on December 6, 1865. The amendment was declared ratified by the Secretary of State on December 18, 1865.

This amendment was the first of the three Civil War amendments.

LINCOLN MET CONFEDERATE COMMISSIONERS

The conference of February 3, 1865, between President Lincoln and the Confederate peace commissioners, Alexander Hamilton Stephens, vice president of the Confederate States, Robert Mercer Taliaferro Hunter, Confederate States senator, and John Archibald Campbell, assistant secretary of war of the Confederate States, was held at Hampton Roads, Va., aboard the *River Queen,* a steamer of 536 tons, hired by the Quartermaster General of the War Department from Georgia N. Power at $241 per day. A second conference was held on March 23, 1865, aboard the same steamer.

SECOND INAUGURATION

Abraham Lincoln was inaugurated on Saturday, March 4, 1865, on the east portico of the Capitol. The oath was administered by Chief Justice Salmon Portland Chase. The morning was stormy, but the weather cleared by afternoon.

This was the first inauguration in which Negroes participated. Negro civic associations and a battalion of Negro soldiers formed part of the Lincoln escort. For security reasons, Lincoln did not ride in the military procession to the Capitol. Enthusiasm gripped the people as the war was drawing to a close.

At the inaugural ball, held on Monday, March 6, Mrs. Lincoln wore a white silk and lace dress with a headdress, an ensemble that cost over $2,000.

LINCOLN ASSASSINATED

The first assassination of a President was the murder of Lincoln on Good Friday, April 14, 1865, by John Wilkes Booth, an actor and Southern sympathizer. President Lincoln drove to Ford's Theatre on Tenth Street, between E and F streets, Washington D.C., with Mrs. Lincoln, Major Henry Reed Rathbone, and Clara Harris, Rathbone's fiancée. They were viewing a performance of *Our American Cousin,* a three-act comedy by Tom Taylor starring Laura Keene, when at about 10:30 P.M. Booth fired the fatal shot. Lincoln was carried across the street to William Peterson's boarding house at 453 Tenth Street, and put in the room of William Clark, a boarder. He died at 21 minutes 55 seconds past 7 A.M. on April 15, 1865.

Booth, who had fled after the crime, was shot April 26, 1865, in a barn by Sergeant Boston Corbett.

FUNERAL PROCESSION AND INTERMENT

Abraham Lincoln was the first President to lie in state at the United States Capitol retunda. His body was taken first to the White House, where it remained from April 15 to April 18, after which it was removed to the Capitol rotunda, where it was displayed from April 19 to April 20. On April 21, it was taken to the railroad station, where it was conveyed to Springfield, Ill.

The funeral procession took twelve days, stops along the route being made at Baltimore, Harrisburg, Philadelphia, New York City, Albany, Utica, Syracruse, Cleveland, Columbus, Indianapolis, and Chicago, where people paid their respects before the train arrived at Springfield, Ill. Lincoln was buried on May 4, 1865, in Oakland Cemetery, Springfield.

Lincoln was moved seventeen times from the night of April 14, 1865, when he was carried from Ford's Theatre to the Peterson house across the street, until his body was finally laid to rest in a solid block of concrete in the Lincoln tomb at Springfield in 1901.

THE FIRST LADY

Mary Todd Lincoln served as hostess of the White House in a very simple and quiet manner. The war years placed a pall on social functions. Much of her time was devoted to war work.

LINCOLN'S WIFE AND THE SOUTH

Lincoln's wife, Mary Todd Lincoln, born in Lexington, Ky., was the subject of much speculation. Her patriotism was questioned by many.

Her brother, George Rogers Clark Todd, was a surgeon in the Confederate army.

Her half-brother, Samuel Briggs Todd, a soldier in the Confederate army, was killed at the battle of Shiloh, Tenn., April 6-7, 1862. Another half-brother, David H. Todd, an officer, died from wounds received at Vicksburg, Miss., and another, Alexander H. Todd, was killed at Baton Rouge, La., August 20, 1862.

The husband of Emilie, her half-sister, was Confederate Brigadier General Ben Hardin Helm, killed September 20, 1863, at Chickamauga, Ga.

Two other brothers-in-law were also in the Confederate service.

President Lincoln appeared before the Senate members of the Committee on the Conduct of the War, and made this statement:

I, Abraham Lincoln, President of the United States, appear on my own volition before this committee of the Senate, to say I, of my own knowledge, know that it is untrue that any of my family hold treasonable relations with the enemy.

MRS. LINCOLN COMMITTED

In 1875 a Court of Inquest ordered that Mrs. Lincoln "be committed to a state hospital for the insane." She was confined to the Bellevue Place Sanatorium, a private institution at Batavia, Ill., from May 20, 1875, to September 10, 1875.

THIEVES TRIED TO STEAL LINCOLN'S BODY

On November 7, 1876, a gang of thieves and counterfeiters broke into Lincoln's tomb at Springfield, Ill., tore open the sarcophagus and partially pulled out the Lincoln casket. They intended to cart the casket by wagon, bury it in the sand dunes of Indiana, and demand $200,000 for its return. They intended also to demand the freedom of Benjamin Boyd, an engraver of counterfeit plates, who was confined in the penitentiary at Joliet, Ill. A Pinkerton detective to whom they had confided their plans agreed to help them. Instead he notified the Secret Service, worked with the conspirators and gave the signal which enabled the Secret Service to make the arrests. As there was no penalty at that time for such an offense, they were charged with breaking the lock and sentenced to serve a year in the penitentiary. The next legislature enacted a law which made body-stealing punishable by imprisonment for from one to ten years.

LINCOLN'S SON AT THE SCENE OF THREE ASSASSINATIONS

Robert Todd Lincoln, Lincoln's oldest son, who was in Washington, D.C., the night his father was shot at Ford's Theatre, was summoned to the house across the street to which the wounded President was carried.

On July 2, 1881, Lincoln, then secretary of war in President Garfield's cabinet, went to the railroad station at Washington to tell the President that pressure of business prevented him from accompanying the President to Elberon, N.J. When Lincoln arrived at the station, Garfield had just been shot by Charles J. Guiteau.

Twenty years later, Lincoln received an invitation from President William McKinley to meet him on September 6, 1901, at the Pan American Expositon at Buffalo, N.Y. When Lincoln arrived there, he saw a group gathered about the President, who had just been mortally wounded by Leon Czolgosz.

ANDREW JOHNSON
17th PRESIDENT

Born–Dec. 29, 1808
Birthplace–Raleigh, N.C.
College attended–None
Religion–No specific denomination
Ancestry–English
Occupation–Tailor, legislator
Date and place of marriage–May 5, 1827, Greeneville, Tenn.
Age at marriage–18 years, 127 days
Years married–48 years, 87 days
Political party–Democratic (elected Vice President on Republican [National Union] ticket)
State represented–Tennessee
Term of office–Apr. 15, 1865-Mar. 3, 1869 (Johnson succeeded to the presidency on the death of Abraham Lincoln.)
Term served–3 years, 323 days
Administration–20th
Congresses–39th, 40th
Age at inauguration–56 years, 107 days
Lived after term–6 years, 149 days
Occupation after term–U.S. senator
Date of death–July 31, 1875
Age at death–66 years, 214 days
Place of death–Carter's Station, Tenn.
Burial place–Andrew Johnson National Cemetery, Greeneville, Tenn.

PARENTS

Father–Jacob Johnson
Born–Apr. 1778
Married–Sept. 9, 1801 (date of marriage bond)
Occupation–Sexton, porter, constable
Died–Jan. 4, 1812, Raleigh, N.C.
Age at death–33 years
Mother–Mary McDonough Johnson
Born–July 17, 1783
Died–Feb. 13, 1856
Age at death–72 years, 211 days

After the death of Jacob Johnson, Mary McDonough Johnson married Turner Dougherty of Raleigh, N.C.

BROTHERS AND SISTER

Andrew Johnson was the third child in a family of three.

Children of Jacob Johnson and Mary McDonough Johnson

William Johnson, b. 1804
____Johnson (daughter), d. in infancy
Andrew Johnson, b. Dec. 29, 1808, d. July 31, 1875

CHILDREN

Martha Johnson, b. Oct. 25, 1828, Greeneville, Tenn.; m. Dec. 13, 1855, David Trotter Patterson, Greeneville, Tenn.; d. July 10, 1901, Greeneville, Tenn.

Charles Johnson, b. Feb. 19, 1830, Greeneville, Tenn.; d. Apr. 4, 1863, near Nashville, Tenn.

Mary Johnson, b. May 8, 1832, Greeneville, Tenn.; m. Apr. 7, 1852, Daniel Stover; m. William R. Brown; d. Apr. 19, 1883, Bluff City, Tenn.

Robert Johnson, b. Feb. 22, 1834, Greeneville, Tenn.; d. Apr. 22, 1869, Greeneville, Tenn.

For additional data see the end of this section and also specific subject headings in the index.

Andrew Johnson, b. Aug. 5, 1852, Greeneville, Tenn.; m. Bessie May Rumbough; d. Mar. 12, 1879, Elizabethtown, Tenn.

MRS. ANDREW JOHNSON
Name–Eliza McCardle Johnson
Date of birth–Oct. 4, 1810
Birthplace–Leesburg, Tenn.
Age at marriage–16 years, 213 days
Children–3 sons, 2 daughters

Mother–Sarah Phillips McCardle
Father–John McCardle
His occupation–Shoemaker
Date of death–Jan. 15, 1876
Age at death–65 years, 103 days
Place of death–Greene County, Tenn.
Burial place–Greeneville, Tenn.
Years younger than the President–1 year, 279 days
Years she survived the President–168 days

CABINET

April 15, 1865-March 3, 1869

State–William Henry Seward, N.Y., continued from preceding administration

Treasury–Hugh McCulloch, Ind., continued from preceding administration

War–Edwin McMasters Stanton, Pa., continued from preceding administration; suspended Aug. 12, 1867; Ulysses Simpson Grant (General of the Army), ad interim Aug. 12, 1867; Edwin McMasters Stanton, Pa., reinstated Jan. 13, 1868 to May 26, 1868; John McAlister Schofield, Ill., May 28, 1868; entered upon duties June 1, 1868

Attorney General–James Speed, Ky., continued from preceding administration; J. Hubley Ashton, Pa. (assistant attorney general), acting, July 17, 1866; Henry Stanbery, Ohio, July 23, 1866; Orville Hickman Browning, Ill. (secretary of the interior), ad interim Mar. 13, 1868; William Maxwell Evarts, N.Y., July 15, 1868; entered upon duties July 20, 1868

Postmaster General–William Dennison, Ohio, continued from preceding administration; Alexander Williams Randall, Wis. (first assistant postmaster general), ad interim July 17, 1866; Alexander Williams Randall, Wis., July 25, 1866

Navy–Gideon Welles, Conn., continued from preceding administration

Interior–John Palmer Usher, Ind., continued from preceding administration; James Harlan, Iowa, May 15, 1865; Orville Hickman Browning, Ill., July 27, 1866, appointment to take effect Sept. 1, 1866

FORTIETH CONGRESS

March 4, 1867-March 3, 1869

First session–Mar. 4, 1867-Mar. 30, 1867; July 3, 1867-July 20, 1867; Nov. 21, 1867-Dec. 1, 1867 (274 days)

Second session–Dec. 2, 1867-July 27, 1868; Sept. 21, 1868, for 1 day only; Oct. 16, 1868, for 1 day only; Nov. 10, 1868, for 1 day only (345 days)

Third session–Dec. 7, 1868-Mar. 3, 1869 (87 days)

Special session of the Senate—Apr. 1, 1867-Apr. 20, 1867 (20 days)

Vice President—Vice President Andrew Johnson succeeded to the presidency on the death of Abraham Lincoln on Apr. 15, 1865

President pro tempore of the Senate—Benjamin Franklin Wade, Ohio

Secretaries of the Senate—John Wien Forney, Pa., resigned, effective June 4, 1868; George Congdon Gorham, Calif., elected June 4, 1868

Speaker of the House—Schuyler Colfax, Ind., reelected Mar. 4, 1867; resigned Mar. 3, 1869, having been elected Vice President; Theodore Medad Pomeroy, N.Y., elected Mar. 3, 1869

Clerk of the House—Edward McPherson, Pa., reelected Mar. 4, 1867

ADMINISTRATION—IMPORTANT DATES

Apr. 26, 1865, General Joseph E. Johnston surrendered at Durham Station, N.C., to General William T. Sherman

May 10, 1865, Confederate President Jefferson Davis captured by federal troops

May 26, 1865, General Edmund Kirby-Smith, commander of Trans-Mississippi Department, surrendered at New Orleans, La., to Major General E. S. Canby (last major Confederate commander to surrender)

Dec. 18, 1865, Thirteenth Amendment to the Constitution ratified, abolishing slavery

1867, Reconstruction Acts passed despite President Johnson's opposition

Mar. 1, 1867, Nebraska admitted as the 37th state

Mar. 30, 1867, Territory of Alaska ceded by treaty with Russia

May 16, 1868, July 28, 1898 President Johnson acquitted at impeachment trial before U.S. Senate

July 28, 1868, Fourteenth Amendment to the Constitution ratified, establishing rights of citizens

IMPORTANT DATES IN HIS LIFE

Feb. 18, 1822, bound out as an apprentice to a tailor, James J. Shelby, Wake County, N.C.

1824, opened tailor shop, Laurens, S.C.

1828, became leader of a workingmen's party which he organized; elected alderman of Greeneville, Tenn.; reelected in 1829

1830-1833, mayor of Greeneville, Tenn. (three terms)

1833, trustee of Rhea Academy

Oct. 5, 1835, nominated himself for the Tennessee legislature; elected; served two years

1837, opposed bond issue and was defeated for reelection

1839, reelected to legislature

Oct. 4, 1841, elected to Tennessee Senate

Mar. 4, 1843-Mar. 3, 1853, U.S. House of Representatives (from Tennessee)

Oct. 3, 1853, elected governor of Tennessee

1855, reelected governor

Oct. 8, 1857-Mar. 4, 1862, U.S. Senate (from Tennessee)

Mar. 4, 1862-Mar. 3, 1865, military governor of Tennessee with rank
   of brigadier general of volunteers (appointed by President Lincoln)
1864, nominated as vice presidential candidate by National Union
   Party at Baltimore, Md.
Mar. 4, 1865-April 15, 1865, Vice President
Apr. 15, 1865-Mar. 3, 1869, President (took office on death of Abraham
   Lincoln)
Mar. 13, 1868, impeachment trial in U.S. Senate
May 26, 1868, acquitted
1868, unsuccessful candidate for nomination to the presidency on the
   Democratic ticket
1869, unsuccessful candidate for U.S. Senate (from Tennessee)
1872, unsuccessful candidate for U.S. House of Representatives (from
   Tennessee)
1874, elected to U.S. Senate
Mar. 4-July 31, 1875, U.S. Senate

ANDREW JOHNSON

____was the second President born in North Carolina.

____was the sixth President who was a resident of a state other than
   his native state.

____married at a younger age than any other President.

____was the first and only President against whom impeachment pro-
   ceedings were instituted.

____was the first President whose early background was not military
   or legal.

ADDITIONAL DATA ON JOHNSON

JOHNSON TAUGHT ABC'S BY HIS WIFE

Andrew Johnson never attended school and was scarely able to read
when he met Eliza McCradle, whom he married on May 5, 1827.
He was about seventeen years of age when she taught him how to
write.

JOHNSON DEFIED ENEMIES

Several threats were made against the life of Andrew Johnson while
he was campaigning for a second term as governor of Tennessee.
While addressing an enthusiastic crowd, Johnson, it is recorded, drew
a pistol and laid it on the table so that everyone could see it. He
addressed his audience as follows:

Fellow-citizens, I have been informed that part of the business
to be transacted on the present occasion is the assassination of
the individual who now has the honor of addressing you. I beg
respectfully to propose that this be the first business in order.
Therefore if any man has come here tonight for the purpose indicated, I do not say to him let him speak, but let him shoot.

JOHNSON DEFENDED THE UNION

Senator Andrew Johnson of Tennessee made a stirring pro-Union
speech on the floor of the Senate on December, 18, 1860. He said:

I am in the Union, and intend to stay in it. I intend to hold on to the Union, and the guarantees under which the Union has grown; and I do not intend to be driven from it, nor out of it, by. . .unconstitutional enactments.

The following day, Johnson said:

Then, let us stand by the Constitution; and in preserving the Constitution we shall save the Union; and in saving the Union we save this, the greatest government on earth.

"WHAT WILL THE ARISTOCRATS DO?"

When Andrew Johnson was told that he, a former tailor, had been nominated on the same ticket with Abraham Lincoln, a former rail splitter, it is reported that he said, "What will the aristocrats do?"

JOHNSON INAUGURATED VICE PRESIDENT

One of the most unusual events in American history occurred on March 4, 1865, when Andrew Johnson was inaugurated Vice President of the United States. Not fully recovered from the effects of typhoid fever, he had doctored himself with intoxicating liquor. He walked arm-in-arm with Hannibal Hamlin, the former Vice President, into the stuffy Senate Chamber, the galleries of which were packed with guests.

His face was flushed and his balance unsteady. Before taking the vice presidential oath, he delivered a peculiar harangue in which he stressed his lowly origin. The liquor had gone to his head. Although this was the most humiliating event that had ever occurred at an inauguration, Johnson was not disgraced. Even his enemies forgave him since it was known Johnson was not a drinking man.

OATH OF OFFICE

The death of Lincoln profoundly shocked the nation. The oath of office as Lincoln's successor was quietly administered to Andrew Johnson at 10 A.M., on Saturday, April 15, 1865, at the Kirkwood House, Washington, D.C. Chief Justice Chase went to Johnson's suite to administer the oath. The following is an extract from Johnson's inaugural address:

I have long labored to ameliorate and elevate the condition of the great mass of the American people. Toil and an honest advocacy of the great principles of free government have been my lot. Duties have been mine; consequences are God's. This has been the foundation of my political creed, and I feel that in the end the government will triumph and that these great principles will be permanently established.

DAY OF MOURNING FOR LINCOLN

On April 25, 1865, President Johnson issued the following proclamation:

Thursday, the 25th of May next, [is] to be observed, wherever in the United States the flag of the country may be respected, as a day of humiliation and mourning, and I recommend my fellow-citizens then to assemble in their respective places of worship, there to unite in solemn service to Almighty God in memory of the good man who has been removed, so that all shall be occupied at the same time in contemplation of his virtues and in sorrow for his sudden and violent end.

On April 29, 1865, President Johnson issued a further proclamation changing the date to Thursday, June 1, 1865, as his attention had since been called to "the fact that the day aforesaid is sacred to large numbers of Christians as one of rejoicing for the ascension of the Saviour."

GOVERNMENT OFFERED REWARDS FOR ARREST

On May 2, 1865, President Andrew Johnson issued a proclamation offering rewards for the arrest of the persons presumed to be connected with the assassination of President Lincoln and the attempted assassination of William H. Seward, secretary of state. The rewards were $100,000 for Jefferson Davis, $25,000 for Clement C. Clay, $25,000 for Jacob Thompson, $25,000 for George N. Sanders, $25,000 for Beverley Tucker, and $10,000 for William C. Cleary.

AMNESTY PROCLAMATION

On May 29, 1865, President Andrew Johnson issued the following amnesty proclamation:

I hereby grant to all persons who have, directly or indirectly, participated in the existing rebellion, except as hereinafter excepted, amnesty and pardon, with restoration of all rights of property, except as to slaves and except in cases where legal proceedings under the laws of the United States providing for the confiscation of property of persons engaged in rebellion have been instituted; but upon the condition, nevertheless, that every such person shall take and subscribe the following oath (or affirmation) and thenceforward keep and maintain said oath inviolate, and which oath shall be registered for permanent preservation and shall be of the tenor and effect following, to wit: "I, . . ., do hereby solemnly swear (or affirm), in presence of Almighty God, that I will henceforth faithfully support, protect, and defend the Constitution of the United States and the Union of the States thereunder, and that I will in like manner abide by and faithfully support all laws and proclamations which have been made during the existing rebellion with reference to the emancipation of slaves. So help me God."

EXTRACT OF PROCLAMATION OF PEACE, APRIL 2, 1866

Whereas there now exists no organized armed resistance of misguided citizens or others to the authority of the United States in the States of Georgia, South Carolina, Virginia, North Carolina, Tennessee, Alabama, Louisiana, Arkansas, Mississippi, and Florida, and the laws can be sustained and enforced therein by the proper civil authority, State or Federal, and the people of said

States are well and loyally disposed and have conformed or will conform in their legislation to the condition of affairs growing out of the amendment to the Constitution of the United States prohibiting slavery within the limits and jurisdiction of the United States; and . . .

Whereas the people of the several beforementioned States have, in the manner aforesaid, given satisfactory evidence that they acquiesce in this sovereign and important resolution of national unity; and

Whereas it is believed to be a fundamental principle of government that people who have revolted and who have been overcome and subdued must either be dealt with so as to induce them voluntarily to become friends or else they must be held by absolute military power or devastated so as to prevent them from ever again doing harm as enemies, which last-named policy is abhorrent to humanity and to freedom; and . . .

Whereas the observance of political equality, as a principle of right and justice, is well calculated to encourage the people of the aforesaid States to be and become more and more constant and persevering in their renewed allegiance; and . . .

Whereas the policy of the Government of the United States from the beginning of the insurrection to its overthrow and final suppression has been in conformity with the principles herein set forth and enumerated:

Now, therefore, I, Andrew Johnson, President of the United States, do hereby proclaim and declare that the insurrection which heretofore existed in the States of Georgia, South Carolina, Virginia, North Carolina, Tennessee, Alabama, Louisiana, Arkansas, Mississippi, and Florida is at an end and is henceforth to be so regarded.

CIVIL RIGHTS LEGISLATION ENACTED

The first session of the Thirty-ninth Congress passed an "act to protect all persons in the United States in their Civil Rights and furnish the means of their vindication" on April 9, 1866 (14 Stat. L. 27).

This first civil rights act provided that "citizens of every race and color, without regard to any previous condition of slavery or involuntary servitude...shall have the same right, in every State and Territory in the United States to make and enforce contracts, to sue, be parties, and give evidence, to inherit, purchase, lease, sell, hold and convey real and personal property and to full and equal benefit of all laws and proceedings for the security of person and property, as in enjoyed by white citizens, and shall be subject to like punishment, pains and penalties, and to none other, any law, statute, ordinance, regulation or custom, to the contrary notwithstanding."

Indians were not covered by the legislation.

FOURTEENTH AMENDMENT ENACTED

The Fourteenth Amendment to the Constitution, decreeing citizenship "for all persons born or naturalized in the United States" and declaring that states shall not deprive any person of "life, liberty, or property without due process of law," was passed by Congress June 13, 1866. It was proposed to the legislatures of the several states by the Thirty-ninth Congress on June 16, 1866. It received the support of twenty-three Northern states. California took no action. It was rejected by Delaware, Kentucky, Maryland, and ten Southern states, which later ratified it. The twenty-eighth state to ratify it, making if effective, was Louisiana, which ratified it on July 9, 1868 (the same day on which South Carolina ratified it). The amendment was declared ratified by the Secretary of State on July 28, 1868.

VISIT OF A QUEEN

Andrew Johnson was the first President to receive the visit of a queen. Queen Emma, widow of King Kamehameha IV of the Sandwich Islands (Hawaii), sailed from England on the Cunard ship *Java* and arrived in New York City on August 8, 1866. She was received on August 14, 1866, by President Johnson and introduced to his official family.

IMPEACHMENT PROCEEDINGS

Johnson's attempt to carry out Lincoln's policies of reconstruction and reconciliation brought him into bitter conflict with the Radical Republicans in Congress.

The Tenure of Office Act of March 2, 1867, prohibited the President from removing a cabinet officer without Senate approval. On August 12, 1867, in defiance of this act, President Johnson dismissed a cabinet officer, Secretary of War Edwin McMasters Stanton, a Radical Republican. The President appointed General of the Army Ulysses Simpson Grant to act ad interim.

The Senate declared Stanton's removal from office illegal and in its session of January 13, 1868, ordered Stanton reinstated. Grant returned to his army duties and Stanton again returned to head the War Department.

On February 21, 1868, President Johnson replaced Stanton by Brevet Major General Lorenzo Thomas, to whom he wrote: "You are hereby authorized and empowered to act as Secretary of War ad interim, and will immediately enter upon the discharge of the duties pertaining to that office."

Impeachment proceedings were instituted against President Johnson by the House of Representatives on February 24, 1868, with the following resolution: "Resolved: that Andrew Johnson be impeached of high crimes and misdemeanors." The charges brought against him were usurpation of the law, corrupt use of the veto power, interference at elections, and misdemeanors.

The trial began formally on March 13, 1868, with Chief Justice Salmon Portland Chase of the Supreme Court of the United States presiding in the Senate chambers.

Associate Justice Samuel Nelson of the Supreme Court administered the following oath to the Chief Justice: "I do solemnly swear that in all things appertaining to the trial of the impeachment of Andrew Johnson, President of the United States, now pending, I will do impartial justice according to the Constitution and laws. So help me God." This oath was then administered by the Chief Justice to the fifty-four members of the Senate.

The vote on the eleventh article was guilty 35, not guilty 19 (May 16, 1868). The vote on the second article was guilty 35, not guilty 19 (May 26, 1868). The proceedings terminated on May 26, 1868, with the acquittal of Johnson by one vote, a two-thirds vote being necessary for conviction.

JOHNSON'S FEUD WITH GRANT

President Johnson wrote an angry letter to General Grant, who had given up his ad interim appointment as Secretary of War and returned to his army duties, thereby allowing Stanton to return to the War Department. Johnson accused Grant of violating his word.

Grant replied that he considered Congress the final authority and that he had never given the President any intimation that he would disobey the law. He concluded his letter dated February 3, 1868, by stating:

> And now, Mr. President, when my honor as a soldier and integrity as a man have been so violently assailed, pardon me for saying that I can but regard this whole matter from beginning to end as an attempt to involve me in a resistance of law for which you hesitated to assume the responsibility, and thus destroy my character before the country.

When Grant was inaugurated President of the United States on March 4, 1869, Johnson refused to ride with him to his inaugural and therefore did not witness Grant's induction into office.

PRESIDENT BECOMES SENATOR

The first President to become a senator after his term of office was Andrew Johnson. He was elected senator from Tennessee and served from March 4, 1875, until his death on July 31, 1875. He had made an unsuccessful attempt to become a senator in 1869, and another unsuccessful attempt in 1872 to win a seat as a representative in the 43rd Congress.

When Johnson took his seat in the 44th Congress he was one of seventy-four senators. Only fourteen of these senators had taken part in his trial of 1868. Twelve of them had voted "guilty" and two of them "not guilty."

THE FIRST LADY

Eliza McCardle Johnson was an invalid when Andrew Johnson became President on April 15, 1865. Their daughter, Martha Johnson Patterson, the wife of Senator David Trotter Patterson, acted as White House hostess. Another daughter, Mary Johnson Stover, the wife of David Stover, also acted in this capacity.

ULYSSES SIMPSON GRANT

18th PRESIDENT

Born–Apr. 27, 1822 (Given name —Hiram Ulysses Grant)

Birthplace–Point Pleasant, Ohio

College attended–U.S. Military Academy, West Point, N.Y.

Date of graduation–July 1, 1843, four-year course

Religion–Methodist

Ancestry–English, Scotch

Occupation–Soldier

Date and place of marriage–Aug. 22, 1848, St. Louis, Mo.

Age at marriage–26 years, 117 days

Years married–36 years, 335 days

Political party–Republican

State represented–Illinois

Term of office–Mar. 4, 1869-Mar. 3, 1877

Term served–8 years

Administration–21st, 22nd

Congresses–41st, 42nd, 43rd, 44th

Age at inauguration–46 years, 311 days

Lived after term–8 years, 141 days

Occupation after term–Traveling and writing

Date of death–July 23, 1885

Age at death–63 years, 87 days

Place of death–Mount McGregor, N.Y.

Burial place–Grant's Tomb, New York, N.Y.

PARENTS

Father–Jesse Root Grant

Born–Jan. 23, 1794, near Greensburgh, Pa.

Married–June 24, 1821, Point Pleasant, Ohio

Occupation–Leather tanner, factory manager

Died–June 29, 1873, Covington, Ky.

Age at death–79 years, 157 days

Mother–Hannah Simpson Grant

Born–Nov. 23, 1798, Montgomery County, Pa.

Died–May 11, 1883, Jersey City, N.J.

Age at death–84 years, 169 days

BROTHERS AND SISTERS

Ulysses Simpson Grant was the oldest child in a family of six.

Children of Jesse Root Grant and Hannah Simpson Grant

Ulysses Simpson Grant, b. Apr. 27, 1822, d. July 23, 1885

Samuel Simpson Grant, b. Sept. 23, 1825, d. Sept. 13, 1861

Clara Rachel Grant, b. Dec. 11, 1828, d. Mar. 6, 1865

Virginia Paine Grant, b. Feb. 20, 1832, d. Mar. 28, 1881

Orville Lynch Grant, b. May 15, 1835, d. Aug. 5, 1881

Mary Frances Grant, b. July 30, 1839, d. Jan. 23, 1898

CHILDREN

Frederick Dent Grant, b. May 30, 1850, St. Louis, Mo.; m. Oct. 20, 1874, Ida Maria Honoré, Chicago, Ill.; d. Apr. 11, 1912, New York, N.Y.

Ulysses Simpson Grant, b. July 22, 1852, Bethel, Ohio; m. Nov. 1, 1880, Fannie Josephine Chaffee, New York, N.Y.; m. July 12, 1913, America Workman Wills, San Diego, Calif.; d. Sept. 25, 1929, San Diego, Calif.

Ellen (Nellie) Wrenshall Grant, b. July 4, 1855, Wistonwisch,

For additional data see the end of this section and also specific subject headings in the index.

Mo.; m. May 21, 1874, Algernon Charles Frederick Sartoris at the White House, Washington, D.C.; m. July 4, 1912, Franklin Hatch Jones, Cobourg, Ontario, Canada; d. Aug. 30, 1922, Chicago, Ill.

Jesse Root Grant, b. Feb. 6, 1858, St. Louis, Mo.; m. Sept. 21, 1880, Elizabeth Chapman, San Francisco, Calif.; m. Aug. 26, 1918, Lillian Burns Wilkins, New York, N.Y.; d. June 8, 1934, Los Altos, Calif.

MRS. ULYSSES SIMPSON GRANT

Name–Julia Boggs Dent Grant

Date of birth–Jan. 26, 1826
Birthplace–St. Louis, Mo.
Age at marriage–22 years, 208 days
Children–3 sons, 1 daughter
Mother–Ellen Wrenshall Dent
Father–Frederick Dent
His occupation–Judge
Date of death–Dec. 14, 1902
Age at death–76 years, 322 days
Place of death–Washington, D.C.
Burial place–New York, N.Y.
Years younger than the President–3 years, 274 days
Years she survived the President–17 years, 144 days

THE ELECTION OF 1868

NOMINATIONS FOR TERM 1869-1873

Republican Party Convention (4th) (Union-Republican Party)

May 20-21, 1868, Crosby's Opera House, Chicago, Ill.
Nominated for President—Ulysses Simpson Grant, Ill.
Nominated for Vice President—Schuyler Colfax, Ind.
First ballot: Ulysses Simpson Grant, Ill., 650
Nomination made unanimous

Democratic Party Convention (10th)

July 4-9, 1868, Tammany Hall, New York City
Nominated for President—Horatio Seymour, Ind.
Nominated for Vice President—Francis Preston Blair, Jr., Mo.

Forty-seven nominations were made. Seymour was nominated on the twenty-second ballot; the nomination was declared unanimous before the final vote was recorded. Candidates for nomination and the votes they received on the first ballot:

George Hunt Pendleton, Ohio, 105
Andrew Johnson, Tenn., 65
Sanford Elias Church, N.Y., 34
Winfield Scott Hancock, Pa., 33$\frac{1}{2}$
Asa Packer, Pa., 26
James Edward English, Conn., 16
James Rood Doolittle, Wis., 13
Joel Parker, N.J., 13
Reverdy Johnson, Md., 8$\frac{1}{2}$
Thomas Andrews Hendricks, Ind., 2$\frac{1}{2}$
Francis Preston Blair, Mo., $\frac{1}{2}$
Total number of votes: 317
Number necessary for nomination: 212

ELECTION RESULTS, NOV. 3, 1868—PRESIDENTIAL AND VICE PRESIDENTIAL CANDIDATES

Republican Party (3,012, 833 votes)

Ulysses Simpson Grant, Ill.
Schuyler Colfax, Ind.

Democratic Party (2,703,249 votes)

Horatio Seymour, Ind.
Francis Preston Blair, Jr., Mo.

ELECTORAL VOTES (294—34 states)

Grant received 72.79 per cent (214 votes—26 states) as follows: Ala. 8; Ark, 5; Calif. 5; Conn. 6; Fla. 3; Ill. 16; Ind. 13; Iowa 8; Kan. 3; Me. 7; Mass. 12; Mich. 8; Minn. 4; Mo. 11; Neb. 3; Nev. 3; N.H. 5; N.C. 9; Ohio 21; Pa. 26; R.I. 4; S.C. 6; Tenn. 10; Vt. 5; W.Va. 5; Wis. 8.

Seymour received 27.21 per cent (80 votes—8 states) as follows: Del. 3; Ga. 9; Ky. 11; La. 7; Md. 7; N.J. 7; N.Y. 33; Ore. 3.

Three states with 26 votes were not represented in the balloting: Miss. 10; Tex. 6; Va. 10.

THE ELECTION OF 1872

NOMINATIONS FOR TERM 1873-1877

Republican Party Convention (5th)

June 5-6, 1872, Academy of Music, Philadelphia, Pa.
Nominated for President—Ulysses Simpson Grant, Ill.
Nominated for Vice President—Henry Wilson, Mass.
First ballot: Ulysses Simpson Grant, Ill., 752
Nomination made unanimous

Liberal Republican Party Convention

May 1, 1872, Industrial (Music) Hall, Cincinnati, Ohio
Nominated for President—Horace Greeley, N.Y.
Nominated for Vice President—Benjamin Gratz Brown, Mo.

Greeley was nominated on the sixth ballot. Candidates for nomination and the votes they received on the first and sixth ballots:

Charles Francis Adams, Mass., 203, 187
Horace Greeley, N.Y., 147, 482
Lyman Trumbull, Ill., 108, 21
David Davis, Ill., 92$^1/_2$, 6
Benjamin Gratz Brown, Mo., 95, 0
Andrew Gregg Curtin, Pa., 62, 0
Salmon Portland Chase, Ohio, 2$^1/_2$, 0
Total number of votes:

First ballot: 689
Sixth ballot: 682

The Liberal Republicans recognized the equality of all men; pledged the party to union, enfranchisement; demanded amnesty for former

Confederates, states' rights, reform of the civil service, a modest tariff, and maintenance of public credit.

Independent Liberal Republican Party Convention (Opposition Party)

June 21, 1872, Fifth Avenue Hotel, New York, N.Y.
Nominated for President—William Slocum Groesbeck, Ohio
Nominated for Vice President—Frederick Law Olmsted, N.Y.

This nomination was made by members of the Liberal Republican Party opposed to the nomination of Greeley and Brown.

Democratic Party Convention (11th)

July 9-10, 1872, Ford's Opera House, Baltimore, Md.
Nominated for President—Horace Greeley, N.Y.
Nominated for Vice President—Benjamin Gratz Brown, Mo.

Greeley was nominated on the first ballot. Candidates for nomination and the votes they received:

Horace Greeley, N.Y., 686
Jeremiah Sullivan Black, Pa., 21
James Asheton Bayard, Del., 16
William Slocum Groesbeck, Ohio, 2
Total number of votes: 725
Blank votes: 7
Nomination made unanimous

Straight-out Democratic Party Convention

Sept. 3, 1872, Louisville, Ky.
Nominated for President—Charles O'Conor, N.Y.
Nominated for Vice President—Charles Francis Adams, Mass.

This party was opposed to the fusion of the Democrats with the Liberal Republicans. O'Conor declined the nomination but was not permitted to withdraw.

Prohibition Party Convention (1st)

Feb. 22, 1872, Opera House, Columbus, Ohio
Nominated for President—James Black, Pa.
Nominated for Vice President—John Russell, Mich.

This party, formed in 1869 at Chicago, Ill., endorsed prohibition, woman suffrage, a direct popular vote for President and Vice President, sound currency, the encouragement of immigration, and a reduction in transportation rates.

People's Party Convention (Equal Rights Party)

May 10, 1872, Appollo Hall, New York, N.Y.
Nominated for President—Victoria Claflin Woodhull, N.Y.
Nominated for Vice President—Frederick Douglass

This party was formed by unauthorized delegates, seceders, and others who bolted from the National Woman Suffrage Association convention. The Equal Rights Party convention was attended by 500 delegates from 26 states and 4 territories.

Labor Reform Party Convention

Feb. 21-22, 1872, Columbus, Ohio
Nominated for President—David Davis, Ill.
Nominated for Vice President—Joel Parker, N.J.

Davis was nominated on the third ballot. Candidates for nomination and the votes they received on the first and third ballots:

John White Geary, Pa., 69, 0
Horace H. Day, N.Y., 59, 3
David Davis, Ill., 47, 201
Wendell Phillips, Mass., 13, 0
John McCauley Palmer, Ill., 8, 0
John Parker, N.J., 7, 0
George Washington Julian, Ind., 6,0
Both of the candidates declined the nominations.

Liberal Republican Convention of Colored Men

Sept. 25, 1872, Weissiger Hall, Louisville, Ky.
Nominated for President—Horace Greeley, N.Y.
Nominated for Vice President—Benjamin Gratz Brown, Mo.

National Working Men's Convention

May 23, 1872, New York, N.Y.
Nominated for President—Ulysses Simpson Grant, Ill.
Nominated for Vice President—Henry Wilson, Mass.
Delegates from thirty-one states attended.

ELECTION RESULTS, NOV. 5, 1872—PRESIDENTIAL AND VICE PRESIDENTIAL CANDIDATES

Republican Party (3,597,132 votes)

Ulysses Simpson Grant, Ill.
Henry Wilson, Mass.

Democratic Party and Liberal Republican Party (2,834,079 votes)

Horace Greeley, N.Y.
Benjamin Gratz Brown, Mo.

Straight-Out Democrats (29,489 votes)

Charles O'Conor, N.Y.
Charles Francis Adams, Mass.

Prohibition Party (5,608 votes)

James Black, Pa.
John Russell, Mich.

ELECTORAL VOTES (352—35 states)

The returns of two states—Arkansas and Louisiana—were disputed and not counted.

Grant received 81.205 per cent (286 votes—29 states) as follows:
Ala. 10; Calif. 6; Conn. 6; Del. 3; Fla. 4; Ill. 21; Ind. 15; Iowa 11;
Kan. 5; Me. 7; Mass. 13; Mich. 11; Minn. 5; Miss. 8; Neb. 3; Nev.

3; N.H. 5; N.J. 9; N.Y. 35; N.C. 10; Ohio 22; Ore. 3; Pa. 29; R.I. 4; S.C. 7; Vt. 5; Va. 11; W. Va. 5; Wis. 10.

Greeley died on November 29, 1872, three weeks after the election. The six states he had carried—Georgia, Kentucky, Maryland, Missouri, Tennessee, and Texas—split their electoral votes among the following: Thomas Andrew Hendricks of Illinois, Benjamin Gratz Brown of Missouri, Charles Jones Jenkins of Georgia, and David Davis of Illinois.

Hendricks received 11.93 per cent (42 votes—4 states) as follows: Ky. 8 (of the 12 votes); Md. 8; Mo. 6 (of the 15 votes); Tenn. 12; Tex. 8.

Brown received 5.14 per cent (18 votes—2 states) as follows: Ga. 6 (of the 11 votes); Ky. 4 (of the 12 votes); Mo. 8 (of the 15 votes).

Jenkins received 2 votes (of the 11 Ga. votes).

Davis received 1 vote (of the 15 Mo. votes).

Greeley received 3 votes (of the 11 Ga. votes), but by House resolution they were not counted.

The electoral vote for the vice presidency was divided, as the party lines were not solidly for one candidate. Nine individuals received electoral votes: Henry Wilson of Massachusetts, Benjamin Gratz Brown of Missouri, Alfred Holt Colquitt of Georgia (Democrat), George Washington Julian of Indiana (Liberal Republican), John McCauley Palmer of Illinois (Democrat), Thomas E. Bramlette of Kentucky (Democrat), William Slocum Groesbeck of Ohio (Democrat), Willis Benson Machen of Kentucky (Democrat), and Nathaniel Prentiss Banks of Massachusetts (Liberal Republican).

Wilson received 81.25 per cent (286 votes—29 states) as follows: Ala. 10; Calif. 6; Conn. 6; Del. 3; Fla. 4; Ill. 21; Ind. 15; Iowa 11; Kan. 5; Me. 7; Mass. 13; Mich. 11; Minn. 5; Miss. 8; Neb. 3; Nev. 3; N.H. 5; N.J. 9; N.Y. 35; N.C. 10; Ohio 22; Ore. 3; Pa. 29; R.I. 4; S.C. 7; Vt. 5; Va. 11; W.Va. 5; Wis. 10.

Brown received 13.35 per cent (47 votes—4 states) as follows: Ga. 5 (of the 11 votes); Ky. 8 (of the 12 votes); Md. 8; Mo. 6 (of the 15 votes); Tenn. 12; Tex. 8.

Colquitt received 5 votes (of the 11 Ga. votes).

Julian received 5 votes (of the 15 Mo. votes).

Palmer received 3 votes (of the 15 Mo. votes).

Bramlette received 3 votes (of the 12 Ky. votes).

Groesbeck received 1 vote (of the 15 Mo. votes).

Machen received 1 vote (of the 12 Ky. votes).

Banks received 1 vote (of the 11 Ga. votes).

FIRST TERM

CABINET

March 4, 1869-March 3, 1873

State—William Henry Seward, N.Y., continued from preceding administration; Elihu Benjamin Washburne, Ill., Mar. 5, 1869; Hamilton Fish, N.Y., Mar. 11, 1869; entered upon duties Mar. 17, 1869

Treasury–Hugh McCulloch, Ind., continued from preceding administration; John F. Hartley, Me. (assistant secretary), ad interim Mar. 5, 1869; George Sewall Boutwell, Mass., Mar. 11, 1869.

War–John McAllister Schofield, Ill., continued from preceding administration; John Aaron Rawlins, Ill., Mar. 11, 1869; William Tecumseh Sherman, Ohio, Sept. 9, 1869; entered upon duties Sept. 11, 1869; William Worth Belknap, Iowa, Oct. 25, 1869; entered upon duties Nov. 1, 1869

Attorney General–William Maxwell Evarts, N.Y., continued from preceding administration; J. Hubley Ashton, Pa. (assistant attorney general), acting, Mar. 5, 1869; Ebenezer Rockwood Hoar, Mass., Mar. 5, 1869; entered upon duties Mar. 11, 1869; Amos Tappan Akerman, Ga., June 23, 1870; entered upon duties July 8, 1870; George Henry Williams, Ore., Dec. 14, 1871; to take effect Jan. 10, 1872

Postmaster General–St. John B. L. Skinner, N.Y. (first assistant postmaster general), ad interim Mar. 4, 1869; John Angel James Creswell, Md., Mar. 5, 1869

Navy–William Faxon, Conn. (assistant secretary), ad interim Mar. 4, 1869; Adolph Edward Borie, Pa., Mar. 5, 1869; entered upon duties Mar. 9, 1869; George Maxwell Robeson, N.J., June 25, 1869

Interior–William Tod Otto, Ind. (assistant secretary), ad interim Mar. 4, 1869; Jacob Dolson Cox, Ohio, Mar. 5, 1869; entered upon duties Mar. 9, 1869; Columbus Delano, Ohio, Nov. 1, 1870

SECOND TERM
CABINET
March 4, 1873–March 3, 1877

State–Hamilton Fish, N.Y., continued from preceding administration; recommissioned Mar. 17, 1873

Treasury–George Sewall Boutwell, Mass., continued from preceding administration; William Adams Richardson, Mass., Mar. 17, 1873; Benjamin Helm Bristow, Ky., June 2, 1874; entered upon duties June 4, 1874; Charles F. Conant, N.H. (assistant secretary), ad interim June 21, 1876–June 30, 1876; Lot Myrick Morrill, Me., June 21, 1876; entered upon duties July 7, 1876

War–William Worth Belknap, Iowa, continued from preceding administration; recommissioned Mar. 17, 1873; George Maxwell Robeson, N.J. (secretary of the Navy), ad interim Mar. 2, 1876; Alphonso Taft, Ohio, Mar. 8, 1876; entered upon duties Mar. 11, 1876; James Donald Cameron, Pa., May 22, 1876; entered upon duties June 1, 1876

Attorney General–George Henry Williams, Ore., continued from preceding administration; recommissioned Mar. 17, 1873; Edward Pierrepont, N.Y., Apr. 26, 1875; to take effect May 15, 1875; Alphonso Taft, Ohio, May 22, 1876; entered upon duties June 1, 1876

Postmaster General–John Angel James Creswell, Md., continued from preceding administration; recommissioned Mar. 17, 1873; James William Marshall, Va., July 3, 1874; entered upon duties July 7,

1874; Marshall Jewell, Conn., Aug. 24, 1874; entered upon duties Sept. 1, 1874; James Noble Tyner, Ind., July 12, 1876

Navy–George Maxwell Robeson, N.J., continued from preceding administration; recommissioned Mar. 17, 1873

Interior–Columbus Delano, Ohio, continued from preceding administration; recommissioned Mar. 17, 1873; Benjamin Rush Cowen, Ohio (assistant secretary), ad interim Oct. 1, 1875; Zachariah Chandler, Mich., Oct. 19, 1875

FIRST TERM
FORTY-FIRST CONGRESS

March 4, 1869-March 3, 1871

First session–Mar. 4, 1869-Apr. 10, 1869 (38 days)
Second session–Dec. 6, 1869-July 15, 1870 (222 days)
Third session–Dec. 5, 1870-Mar. 3, 1871 (89 days)
Special session of the Senate–Apr. 12, 1869-Apr. 22, 1869 (11 days)
Vice President–Schuyler Colfax, Ind.
President pro tempore of the Senate–Henry Bowen Anthony, R.I., elected Mar. 23, 1869; Apr. 9, 1869; May 28, 1870; July 1, 1870; July 14, 1870
Secretary of the Senate–George Congdon Gorham, Calif.
Speaker of the House–James Gillespie Blaine, Me., elected Mar. 4, 1869
Clerk of the House–Edward McPherson, Pa., reelected Mar. 5, 1869

FORTY-SECOND CONGRESS

March 4, 1871-March 3, 1873

First session–Mar. 4, 1871-Apr. 20, 1871 (48 days)
Second session–Dec. 4, 1871-June 10, 1872 (190 days)
Third session–Dec. 2, 1872-Mar. 3, 1873 (92 days)
Special session of the Senate–May 10, 1871-May 27, 1871 (18 days)
Vice President–Schuyler Colfax, Ind.
President pro tempore of the Senate–Henry Bowen Anthony, R.I., elected Mar. 10, 1871; Apr. 17, 1871; May 23, 1871, special session; Dec. 21, 1871; Feb. 23, 1872; June 8, 1872; Dec. 4, 1872; Dec. 13, 1872; Dec. 20, 1872; Jan. 24, 1873
Secretary of the Senate–George Congdon Gorham, Calif.
Speaker of the House–James Gillespie Blaine, Me., reelected Mar. 4, 1871
Clerk of the House–Edward McPherson, Pa., reelected Mar. 4, 1871

SECOND TERM
FORTY-THIRD CONGRESS

March 4, 1873-March 3, 1875

First session–Dec. 1, 1873-June 23, 1874 (204 days)
Second session–Dec. 7, 1874-Mar. 3, 1875 (87 days)
Special session of the Senate–Mar. 4, 1873-Mar. 26, 1873 (22 days)
Vice President–Henry Wilson, Mass.

Presidents pro tempore of the Senate–Matthew Hale Carpenter, Wis., elected Mar. 12, 1873; Mar. 26, 1873, special session; Dec. 11, 1873; Dec. 23, 1874; Henry Bowen Anthony, R.I., elected Jan. 25, 1875; Feb. 15, 1875

Secretary of the Senate–George Congdon Gorham, Calif.

Speaker of the House–James Gillespie Blaine, Me., reelected Dec. 1, 1873

Clerk of the House–Edward McPherson, Pa., reelected Dec. 1, 1873

FORTY-FOURTH CONGRESS

March 4, 1875-March 3, 1877

First session–Dec. 6, 1875-Aug. 15, 1876 (254 days)

Second session–Dec. 4, 1876-Mar. 3, 1877 (90 days)

Special session of the Senate–Mar. 5, 1875-Mar. 24, 1875 (20 days)

Vice President–Henry Wilson, Mass.; died Nov. 22, 1875

President pro tempore of the Senate–Thomas White Ferry, Mich., elected Mar. 9, 1875, special session; Dec. 20, 1875

Secretary of the Senate–George Congdon Gorham, Calif.

Speakers of the House–Michael Crawford Kerr, Ind., elected Dec. 6, 1875; died Aug. 19, 1876; Samuel Jackson Randall, Pa., elected Dec. 4, 1876

Clerks of the House–Edward McPherson, Pa.; George Madison Adams, Ky., elected Dec. 6, 1875

APPOINTMENTS TO THE SUPREME COURT

Chief Justice
Morrison Remick Waite, Ohio, Jan. 21, 1874

Associate Justices
Edwin McMasters Stanton, Pa., Dec. 20, 1869 (did not serve)
William Strong, Pa., Feb. 18, 1870
Joseph Philo Bradley, N.J., Mar. 21, 1870
Ward Hunt, N.Y., Dec. 11, 1872

ADMINISTRATION — IMPORTANT DATES

Apr. 13, 1869, George Westinghouse received patent on air-brake

May 10, 1869, ceremonies at Promontory, Utah, to celebrate junction of Pacific railroads and start of transcontinental service

Sept. 24, 1869, Black Friday financial panic

Dec. 9, 1869, Knights of Labor formed at Philadelphia, Pa.

Mar. 30, 1870, Fifteenth Amendment to the Constitution ratified

June 22, 1870, Department of Justice created

May 8 , 1871, Treaty of Washington signed with Great Britain to provide for settlement of boundary and fishery disputes and *Alabama* claims

Dec. 14, 1871, Chicago fire; 200 killed, 70,000 homeless

1872, revelation of Crédit Mobilier stock scandal involving several members of Congress

Jan. 1, 1872, Civil Service Act became effective

Aug. 25, 1872, international commission, in Geneva Award, directed Great Britain to pay United States $15.5 million to compensate for damages caused by Confederate *Alabama*, built in England despite British neutrality

Feb. 1873, Congress demonetized silver, causing a drop in the value of silver

Sept. 18, 1873, start of financial panic of 1873

Nov. 18, 1874, National Woman's Christian Temperance Union organized at Cleveland, Ohio

Mar. 10. 1876, Bell transmitted sound of the human voice on telephone

May 10, 1876, International Centennial Exposition opened, Philadelphia, Pa. (to Nov. 10)

June 25, 1876, General Custer's command destroyed by Indians under Sitting Bull at Little Big Horn River, Mont.

Aug. 1, 1876, Colorado admitted as the 38th state

IMPORTANT DATES IN HIS LIFE

1829-1839, worked on his father's farm

July 1, 1839-July 1, 1843, U.S. Military Academy

July 1, 1843, graduated from U.S. Military Academy (21st in class of 39); brevet second lieutenant, 4th Infantry

1846, served under Generals Zachary Taylor and Winfield Scott in Mexican War

Sept. 8, 1847, brevet first lieutenant for gallant and meritorious conduct in battle of Molino del Rey

Sept. 13, 1847, brevet captain for gallant conduct in the battle of Chapultepec

Sept. 16, 1847, commissioned first lieutenant of Fourth Infantry

Aug. 5, 1853, commissioned captain of Fourth Infantry

July 31, 1854, resigned from army

1854, farming and real estate business, St. Louis, Mo.

1860, worked in father's hardware and leather store, Galena, Ill.

April 19, 1861, commander of a company of Illinois volunteers

May 17, 1861, brigadier general, U.S. Volunteers

June 17, 1861, commissioned by Governor Yates of Illinois as colonel of the 21st Illinois Infantry Regiment

Feb. 16, 1862, major general, U.S. Volunteers

July 4, 1863, captured Vicksburg; major general, U.S. Army

Nov. 24-25, 1863, received thanks of Congress and a gold medal

June 8, 1864, unsuccessful candidate for the Republican nomination for President

Apr. 9, 1865, received General Lee's surrender at Appomattox, Va.

Mar. 9, 1866, commissioned lieutenant general, U.S. Army

July 25, 1866, commissioned general of the army by Congress

Aug. 12, 1867-Jan. 13, 1868, secretary of war, ad interim

Mar. 4, 1869-Mar. 3, 1873, President (first term)

Mar. 4, 1873-Mar. 3, 1877, President (second term)

1877-1879, toured the world

1880, visited the South, Cuba, and Mexico

1880, unsuccessful candidate for the presidential nomination on the Republican ticket

Dec. 24, 1883, injured hip in fall; afterwards always walked with cane

1884, failure of Grant and Ward, New York bankers, wiped out his fortune

1885, wrote his *Memoirs*, which were completed four days before he died; family derived about $500,000 from royalties

Apr. 2, 1885, baptized a Methodist by the Reverend John Philip Newman

ULYSSES SIMPSON GRANT

____was the first President born in Ohio.

____was the seventh President who was a resident of a state other than his native state.

____was the first President whose parents were both alive when he was inaugurated.

GRANTS VICE PRESIDENTS

FIRST TERM

Vice President–Schuyler Colfax (17th V.P.)
Date of birth–Mar. 23, 1823
Birthplace–New York, N.Y.
Political party–Republican
State represented–Indiana
Term of office–Mar. 4, 1869-Mar. 3, 1873
Age at inauguration–45 years, 346 days
Occupation after term–Retired; lecturer
Date of death–Jan. 13, 1885
Age at death–61 years, 296 days
Place of death–Mankato, Minn.
Burial place–South Bend, Ind.

Additional data on Colfax

1836, moved to Indiana

1841, appointed deputy auditor of St. Joseph County, Ind.

1845, acquired interest in South Bend *Free Press*, changed its name to St. Joseph Valley *Register*

1850, member, Indiana state constitutional convention

1850, unsuccessful Whig candidate for Congress

Mar. 4, 1855-Mar. 3, 1869, U.S. House of Representatives (from Indiana)

Dec. 7, 1863-Mar. 3, 1869, speaker, U.S. House of Representatives

1872, unsuccessful candidate for vice presidential renomination

1873, charged with corruption, in Crédit Mobilier scandal, but completely exonerated

SECOND TERM

Vice President–Henry Wilson (18th V.P.)
Date of birth–Feb. 16, 1812
Birthplace–Farmington, N.H.
Political party–Republican
State represented–Massachusetts
Term of office–Mar. 4, 1873-Nov. 22, 1875

Age at inauguration–61 years, 16 days
Occupation after term–Died in office
Date of death–Nov. 22, 1875
Age at death–63 years, 279 days
Place of death–Washington, D.C.
Burial place–Natick, Mass.

Additional data on Wilson

18—, educated in common schools

1822-33, worked on farm

1833, adopted name of Henry Wilson legally (Former name: Jeremiah Jones Colbaith)

1833, moved to Massachusetts; learned shoemaker's trade

1841-1842, Massachusetts House of Representatives

1844-1846, Massachusetts Senate

1848-1851, owner and editor of Boston *Republican*

1850-1852, Massachusetts Senate

1852, president of Free Soil National Convention at Pittsburgh, Pa.; unsuccessful candidate for Congress on Free Soil ticket

1853, delegate to Massachusetts state constitutional convention

Jan. 31, 1855- Mar. 3, 1873, U.S. Senate (from Massachusetts)

1861, commanded Twenty-second Regiment, Massachusetts Volunteer Infantry

ADDITONAL DATA ON GRANT

GRANT CHANGED HIS NAME

Ulysses Simpson Grant was given the name Hiram Ulysses Grant when he was born. He transposed it to Ulysses Hiram Grant. When he applied to Representative Thomas Lyon Hamer in 1839 for an appointment to West Point, the congressman made an error and listed Grant as Ulysses Simpson Grant. Grant accepted this accidental change in his name.

GRANT RECEIVED CIGARS

General Grant is reputed to have smoked twenty cigars daily. The cigar habit was acquired after the battle at Fort Donelson, Tenn., February 13-16, 1862. It is reported that General Grant gave the following explanation to General Horace Porter:

I had been a light smoker previous to the attack on Donelson. . . . In the accounts published in the papers, I was represented as smoking a cigar in the midst of the conflict; and many persons, thinking, no doubt, that tobacco was my chief solace, sent me boxes of the choicest brands. . . . As many as ten thousand were soon received. I gave away all I could get rid of, but having such a quantity on hand I naturally smoked more than I would have done under ordinary circumstances, and I have continued the habit ever since.

GRANT ACQUIRED NICKNAME

General Grant's letter to Confederate General Simon Bolivar Buckner dated February 16, 1862, dictating the terms for the surrender of Fort Donelson, earned him the nickname "Unconditional Surrender" Grant. Grant wrote:

> Yours of this date proposing armistice, and appointment of commissioners to settle terms of capitulation is just received. No terms except an unconditional and immediate surrender can be accepted. I propose to move immediately upon your works.

LINCOLN PROMOTED GRANT

On March 9, 1864, President Lincoln in the presence of the entire cabinet in the cabinet chamber at the Executive Mansion presented Grant, then a major general, with his commission as lieutenant general in command of all the Union armies. Lincoln spoke briefly and Grant replied with a short prepared speech.

On July 25, 1866, Grant was appointed a general with four stars, a rank he relinquished when he became President.

SURRENDER OF LEE ANNOUNCED BY GRANT

On April 9, 1865, the surrender of General Lee was announced in the following terse communication to the secretary of war by General Grant:

> Hon. E. M. Stanton,
> Secretary of War,
> Washington.
> General Lee surrendered the Army of Northern Virginia this afternoon on terms proposed by myself. The accompanying additional correspondence will show the conditions fully.
>   U.S. Grant, Lt. Gen.

GRANT'S RELUCTANT OPPONENT

Horatio Seymour, the Democratic presidential nominee in 1868, was perhaps the most reluctant candidate ever nominated. He knew that the standard bearer of the party would be blamed for the Civil War and that the opposition candidate was Grant, the most popular hero of the war. Seymour refused to be a candidate, but on the twenty-second ballot he was unanimously chosen. He received 80 electoral votes compared with 214 for Grant.

FIRST INAUGURATION

Ulysses Simpson Grant took the oath of office on Thursday, March 4, 1869, on the east portico of the Capitol. Eight full divisions of troops participated in the parade, the most impressive inauguration that had yet been seen.

Retiring President Johnson refused to attend the inauguration. He stayed with his cabinet until noon and then left the city.

The inaugural ball was held in a newly finished section of the Treasury Building. Errors in the checking room caused guests to wait hours to reclaim their possessions. It was reported that costly jewels were stolen.

COLFAX PRESIDED OVER BOTH HOUSES

The first officer to preside over both houses of Congress was Schuyler Colfax of Indiana, who served as Speaker of the House of Representatives in the 38th, 39th, and 40th Congresses (December 7, 1863-November 10, 1868). As Vice President under President Grant he presided over the Senate from March 4, 1869 to March 3, 1873.

FIFTEENTH AMENDMENT RATIFIED

The Fifteenth Amendment to the Consitution, which declares that the right of suffrage shall not be denied to citizens "on account of race, color or previous condition of servitude," was passed by Congress February 26, 1869. It was proposed to the legislatures of the several states by the Fortieth Congress on February 27, 1869. It was not acted on by Tennessee and was rejected by California, Delaware, Kentucky, Maryland, and Oregon. New York rescinded its ratification of January 5, 1870. New Jersey rejected it in 1870, but ratified it in 1871. The twenty-eighth state to ratify it, making it effective, was Georgia, on February 2, 1870. The amendment was declared ratified by the secretary of state on March 30, 1870.

WOMAN PRESIDENTIAL CANDIDATE

The first woman presidential candidate was Victoria Claflin Woodhull, who was nominated May 10, 1872, at a convention held at Apollo Hall, New York City, by a group of seceders and unauthorized delegates attending the National Woman Suffrage Association convention at Steinway Hall, New York City. The group adopted the name Equal Rights Party. Judge Carter of Cincinnati, Ohio, nominated Mrs. Woodhull.

Members of the group were known as People's Party and also as the National Radical Reformers. About five hundred delegates, representing twenty-six states and four territories, were present at the convention.

NEGRO VICE PRESIDENTIAL CANDIDATE

The first Negro vice presidential candidate was Frederick Douglass, who was nominated with Victoria Claflin Woodhull at the Equal Rights Party convention held May 10, 1872, at Apollo Hall, New York City.

CATHOLIC NOMINATED FOR PRESIDENCY

Charles O'Conor of New York, a Catholic, was nominated for the presidency at the Democratic convention at Louisville, Ky., by a wing of the Democrats who refused to accept the nomination of Horace Greeley made at Baltimore, Md. O'Conor declined the nomination on August 31, 1872, but his name, nevertheless, was listed as a candidate and he received approximately thirty thousand votes from twenty-three states.

SECOND INAUGURATION

Ulysses Simpson Grant took the oath of office for his second term on Tuesday, March 4, 1873. The oath was administered by Chief Justice Chase. The parade was marred by a near-blizzard. The thermometer registered zero, causing marchers great discomfort, and several West Point cadets lost consciousness because of the cold. The inaugural ball was held at Judiciary Square in a temporary building so cold that the guests wore their coats while dancing. The valves on the musicians' instruments froze and the violinists had difficulty manipulating their violins. The ice cream and the champagne were frozen solid.

GRANT RECEIVED HAWAIIAN KING

The first reigning king to visit the United States was David Kalakaua, king of the Sandwich Islands (Hawaii), who was received by President Ulysses Simpson Grant at the White House on December 15, 1874. Congress tendered him a reception on December 18, 1874. Grant arranged for a treaty of reciprocity, which was concluded January 30, 1875, with ratification being effected at Washington, D.C., on June 3, 1875. The king came to the United States on the U.S.S. *Benicia* and returned on the U.S.S. *Pensacola*.

GRANT REINSTATED AS GENERAL

General Grant suffered great financial reverses after his term of office and was almost destitute. To relieve this situation, Congress passed legislation restoring former President Grant to his old military status as general. On March 3, 1885, Congress passed an act (23 Stat. L. 434) to authorize an additional appointment on the retired list of the Army—from among those who had been generals commanding the armies of the United States or generals-in-chief of said army—of one person with the rank and full pay of general.

GRANT WROTE "BEST SELLER"

One of the best-paying books of its time and still high on the all-time list was President Grant's *Memoirs*. Royalties amounted to an estimated $500,000. He never saw his book in type, as he died four days after he had completed the manuscript. The book was published in 1885.

WHY GRANT WAS BURIED IN NEW YORK CITY

Grant was born in Ohio, represented Illinois, served eight years in Washington, D.C., and spent many years in military service. On June 24, 1885, shortly before his death, Grant wrote a note in long hand (he was unable to speak) and handed it to his son, who crumpled and disposed of it. The note said, in effect: I would prefer this (West Point) above others but for the fact that my wife could not be placed beside me there. Galena, or some place in Illinois, because from that state I received my first general commission. New York City, because the people of that city befriended me in my need.

On June 16, 1885, Grant went from New York City to Mount McGregor, N.Y., where he died on July 23, 1885. He was buried Saturday, August 8, 1885, in Riverside Park, New York City. On April 27, 1897, his tomb was dedicated.

WANT OF MUSICAL KNOWLEDGE

President Grant claimed that he knew only two tunes. One was "Yankee Doodle" and the other wasn't.

THE FIRST LADY

Julia Dent Grant, wife of President Grant, was very much admired as a White House hostess.

RUTHERFORD BIRCHARD HAYES

19th PRESIDENT

Born–Oct. 4, 1822

Birthplace–Delaware, Ohio

College attended–Kenyon College, Gambier, Ohio

Date of graduation–Aug. 3, 1842, Bachelor of Arts

Religion–Attended Methodist Church

Ancestry–Scotch

Occupation–Lawyer

Date and place of marriage–Dec. 30, 1852, Cincinnati, Ohio

Age at marriage–30 years, 87 days

Years married–40 years, 18 days

Political party–Republican

State represented–Ohio

Term of office–Mar. 4, 1877-Mar. 3, 1881

Term served–4 years

Administration–23rd

Congresses–45th, 46th

Age at inauguration–54 years, 151 days

Lived after term–11 years, 319 days

Occupation after term–Philanthropic activities

Date of death–Jan. 17, 1893

Age at death–70 years, 105 days

Place of death–Fremont, Ohio

Burial place–Spiegel Grove State Park, Fremont, Ohio

PARENTS

Father–Rutherford Hayes

Born–Jan. 4, 1787, Brattleboro, Vt.

Married–Sept. 13, 1813

Occupation–Storekeeper

Died–July 20, 1822, Delaware, Ohio

Age at death–35 years, 197 days

Mother–Sophia Birchard Hayes

Born–Apr. 15, 1792, Wilmington, Vt.

Died–Oct. 30, 1866, Columbus, Ohio

Age at death–74 years, 198 days

BROTHERS AND SISTERS

Rutherford Birchard Hayes was the fifth child in a family of five.

Children of Rutherford Hayes and Sophia Birchard Hayes

————Hayes (son), b. Aug. 14, 1814, d. Aug. 14, 1814

Lorenzo Hayes, June 9, 1815, d. Jan. 20, 1825

Sarah Sophia Hayes, b. July 10, 1817, d. Oct. 9, 1821

Fanny Arabella Hayes, b. Jan. 20, 1820, d. July 16, 1856

Rutherford Birchard Hayes, b. Oct. 4, 1822, d. Jan. 17, 1893

CHILDREN

Birchard Austin Hayes, b. Nov. 4, 1853, Cincinnati, Ohio; m. Dec. 30, 1886, Mary Nancy Sherman, Norwalk, Ohio; d. Jan. 24, 1926, Toledo, Ohio

James Webb Cook Hayes, b. Mar. 20, 1856, Cincinnati, Ohio; m. Sept. 30, 1912, Mary Otis Miller, Fremont, Ohio; d. July 26, 1934, Fremont, Ohio

Rutherford Platt Hayes, b. June 24, 1858, Cincinnati, Ohio; m. Oct. 24, 1894, Lucy Hayes Platt, Columbus, Ohio; d. July 31, 1927, Tampa. Fla.

Joseph Thompson Hayes, b. Dec. 21, 1861, Cincinnati,

For additional data see the end of this section and also specific subject headings in the index.

Ohio; d. June 24, 1863, near Charleston, W.Va.

George Crook Hayes, b. Sept. 29, 1864, Chillicothe, Ohio; d. May 24, 1866, Chillicothe, Ohio

Fanny Hayes, b. Sept. 2, 1867, Cincinnati, Ohio; m. Sept. 1, 1897, Harry Eaton Smith, Fremont, Ohio; d. Mar. 18, 1950, Lewiston, Me.

Scott Russell Hayes, b. Feb. 8, 1871, Columbus, Ohio; m. Sept. 1912, Maude Anderson; d. May 6, 1923, Croton-on-the-Hudson, N.Y.

Manning Force Hayes, b. Aug. 1, 1873, Fremont, Ohio; d. Aug. 28, 1874, Fremont, Ohio.

MRS. RUTHERFORD BIRCHARD HAYES

Name–Lucy Ware Webb Hayes
Date of birth–Aug. 28, 1831
Birthplace–Chillicothe, Ohio
Age at marriage–21 years, 124 days
Children–7 sons, 1 daughter
Mother–Maria Cook Webb
Father–James Webb
His occupation–Physician
Date of death–June 25, 1889
Age at death–57 years, 301 days
Place of death–Fremont, Ohio
Burial place–Fremont, Ohio
Years younger than the President–8 years, 328 days
Years the President survived her–3 years, 206 days

THE ELECTION OF 1876

NOMINATIONS FOR TERM 1877-1881

Republican Party Convention (6th)

June 14-16, 1876, Exposition Hall, Cincinnati, Ohio
Nominated for President—Rutherford Birchard Hayes, Ohio
Nominated for Vice President—William Almon Wheeler, N.Y.

Hayes was nominated on the seventh ballot. Candidates for nomination and the votes they received on the first and seventh ballots:

James Gillespie Blaine, Me., 285, 351
Oliver Hazard Perry Throck Morton, Ind., 124, 0
Benjamin Helm Bristow, Ky., 113, 21
Roscoe Conkling, N.Y., 99, 0
Rutherford Birchard Hayes, Ohio, 61, 384
John Frederick Hartranft, Pa., 58, 0
Marshall Jewell, Conn., 11, 0
William Almon Wheeler, N.Y., 3, 0
Total number of votes

First ballot: 754
Seventh ballot: 756

Number necessary for nomination: 379

Democratic Party Convention (12th)

June 27-29, 1876, Merchant's Exchange, St. Louis, Mo.
Nominated for President—Samuel Jones Tilden, N.Y.
Nominated for Vice President—Thomas Andrews Hendricks, Ind.

Tilden was nominated on the second ballot. Candidates for nomination and the votes they received on the first and second ballots:

Samuel Jones Tilden, N.Y., 403$\frac{1}{2}$, 508
Thomas Andrews Hendricks, Ind., 133$\frac{1}{2}$, 85
Winfield Scott Hancock, Pa., 77, 60
William Allen, Ohio, 56, 54
Thomas Francis Bayard, Del., 31, 11
Joel Parker, N.J., 18, 18
James Overton Broadhead, Mo., 16, 0
Allen Granberry Thurman, Ohio, 3, 2
Total number of votes: 738
Number necessary for nomination: 492

Greenback Party Convention (Independent Party)

May 16-18, 1876, Academy of Music, Indianapolis, Ind.
Nominated for President—Peter Cooper, N.Y.
Nominated for Vice President—Samuel Fenton Cary, Ohio

The Greenback Party was organized November 25, 1874 at Indianapolis. It advocated withdrawal of all national and state bank currency and substitution of paper currency issued by the government. Newton Booth, Calif., was nominated for the vice presidency, but declined.

Prohibition Party Convention (2nd) (National Prohibition Reform Party)

May 17, 1876, Halle's Hall, Cleveland, Ohio
Nominated for President—Green Clay Smith, Ky.
Nominated for Vice President—Gideon Tabor Stewart, Ohio

American National Party Convention

June 9, 1875, Pittsburgh, Pa.
Nominated for President—James B. Walker, Ill.
Nominated for Vice President—Donald Kirkpatrick, N.Y.

ELECTION RESULTS, NOV. 7, 1876—PRESIDENTIAL AND VICE PRESIDENTIAL CANDIDATES

Republican Party (4,036,298 votes)

Rutherford Birchard Hayes, Ohio
William Almon Wheeler, N.Y.

Democratic Party (4,300,590 votes)

Samuel Jones Tilden, N.Y.
Thomas Andrews Hendricks, Ind.

Greenback Party (81,737 votes)

Peter Cooper, N.Y.
Samuel Fenton Cary, Ohio

Prohibition Party (9,522 votes)

Green Clay Smith, Ky.
Gideon Tabor Stewart, Ohio

American National Party (2,636 votes)

James B. Walker, Ill.
Donald Kirkpatrick, N.Y.

DISPUTED ELECTION DECIDED BY ELECTORAL COMMISSION

It was not until March 2, 1877, that the nation knew who would be inaugurated President of the United States on Monday, March 5, 1877.

Tilden had won a majority of the popular votes, but neither candidate had the requisite 185 electoral votes—Tilden had 184 and Hayes had 165. Twenty votes were in dispute: the votes of three southern states with "carpetbag" governments (Florida, Louisiana, and South Carolina) were claimed by both parties, and an elector of a fourth state (Oregon) was found ineligible. When the electoral college met in December 1876 there was a conflict as to which electors should be certified. The Constitution provided that the votes should be counted in the presence of both houses of Congress. But the Republican-controlled Senate and the Democratic-controlled House could not agree on how the votes were to be counted. To end the deadlock congressional leaders suggested a compromise: decision by a bipartisan electoral commission consisting of seven Republicans, seven Democrats, and one independent. Unexpectedly, the independent (Supreme Court Justice David Davis) retired, and a Republican (Justice Bradley) was substituted.

The count, begun on February 1, was not completed until March 2. The commission, which voted strictly on partisan lines (eight to seven in favor of all Hayes electors), consisted of the following members:

Justices of the Supreme Court
Nathan Clifford (President of the Commission), Me., Democrat; Samuel Freeman Miller, Iowa, Republican; Stephen Johnson Field, Calif., Democrat; William Strong, Pa., Republican; Joseph Philo Bradley, N.J., Republican

U.S. Senators (appointed by the Vice President)
George Franklin Edmunds, Vt., Republican; Oliver Hazard Perry Thock Morton, Ind., Republican; Frederick Theodore Frelinghuysen, N.J., Republican; Thomas Francis Bayard, Del., Democrat; Allen Granberry Thurman, Ohio, Democrat

U.S. Representatives (appointed by the Speaker)
Henry B. Payne, Ohio, Democrat; Eppa Hunton, Va., Democrat; Josiah Gardner Abbott, Mass., Democrat; James Abram Garfield, Ohio, Republican; George Frisbie Hoar, Mass., Republican

According to most historians, the Democrats agreed to accept the decision of the electoral commission only in return for a promise that all troops would be withdrawn from the carpetbag states, thereby ending the Reconstruction governments and giving the Democrats control in the South.

ELECTORAL VOTES (369—38 states)

Hayes received 50.14 per cent (185 votes—21 states) as follows: Calif. 6; Colo. 3; Fla. 4; Ill. 21; Iowa 11; Kans. 5; La. 8; Me. 7;

Mass. 13; Mich. 11; Minn. 5; Neb. 3; Nev. 3; N.H. 5; Ohio 22; Ore. 3; Pa. 29; R.I. 4; S.C. 7; Vt. 5; Wis. 10.

Tilden received 49.86 per cent (184 votes—17 states) as follows: Ala. 10; Ark. 6; Conn. 6; Del. 3; Ga. 11; Ind. 15; Ky. 12; Md. 8; Miss. 8; Mo. 15; N.J. 9; N.Y. 35; N.C. 10; Tenn. 12; Tex. 8; Va. 11; W.Va. 5.

CABINET

March 4, 1877-March 3, 1881

State–Hamilton Fish, N.Y., continued from preceding administration; William Maxwell Evarts, N.Y., Mar. 12, 1877

Treasury–Lot Myrick Morrill, Me., continued from preceding administration; John Sherman, Ohio, Mar. 8, 1877; entered upon duties Mar. 10, 1877

War–James Donald Cameron, Pa., continued from preceding administration; George Washington McCrary, Iowa, Mar. 12, 1877; Alexander Ramsey, Minn., Dec. 10, 1879; entered upon duties Dec. 12, 1879

Attorney General–Alphonso Taft, Ohio, continued from preceding administration; Charles Devens, Mass., Mar. 12, 1877

Postmaster General–James Noble Tyner, Ind., continued from preceding administration; David McKendree Key, Tenn., Mar. 12, 1877, resigned June 1, 1880; served to Aug. 24, 1880; Horace Maynard, Tenn., June 2, 1880, entered upon duties Aug. 25, 1880

Navy–George Maxwell Robeson, N.J. continued from preceding administration; Richard Wigginton Thompson, Ind., Mar. 12, 1877; Alexander Ramsey, Minn. (secretary of war), ad interim Dec. 20, 1880; Nathan Goff, Jr., W.Va., Jan. 6, 1881

Interior–Zachariah Chandler, Mich., continued from preceding administration; Carl Schurz, Mo., Mar. 12, 1877

FORTY-FIFTH CONGRESS

March 4, 1877-March 3, 1879

First session–Oct. 15, 1877-Dec. 3, 1877 (50 days)
Second session–Dec. 3, 1877-June 20, 1878 (200 days)
Third session–Dec. 2, 1878-Mar. 3, 1879 (92 days)
Special session of the Senate–Mar. 5, 1877-Mar. 17, 1877 (13 days)
Vice President–William Almon Wheeler, N.Y.
President pro tempore of the Senate–Thomas White Ferry, Mich., elected Mar. 5, 1877, special session of the Senate; Feb. 26, 1878; Apr. 17, 1878; Mar. 3, 1879
Secretary of the Senate–George Congdon Gorham, Calif.
Speaker of the House–Samuel Jackson Randall, Pa., reelected Oct. 15, 1877
Clerk of the House–George Madison Adams, Ky., reelected Oct. 15, 1877

FORTY-SIXTH CONGRESS

March 4, 1879-March 3, 1881

First session–Mar. 18, 1879-July 1, 1879 (106 days)
Second session–Dec. 1, 1879-June 16, 1880 (199 days)
Third session–Dec. 6, 1880-Mar. 3, 1881 (88 days)
Vice President–William Almon Wheeler, N.Y.
President pro tempore of the Senate–Allen Granberry Thurman, Ohio
Secretaries of the Senate–George Congdon Gorham, Mass., John C. Burch, Tenn., elected Mar. 24, 1879
Speaker of the House–Samuel Jackson Randall, Pa., reelected Mar. 18, 1879
Clerk of the House–George Madison Adams, Ky., reelected Mar. 18, 1879

APPOINTMENTS TO THE SUPREME COURT

Associate Justices
John Marshall Harlan, Ky., Nov. 29, 1877
William Burnham Woods, Ga., Dec. 21, 1880

ADMINISTRATION — IMPORTANT DATES

Feb. 12, 1877, first news dispatch telephoned to Boston *Globe*

Apr. 24, 1877, President Hayes withdrew federal troops from New Orleans

May 10, 1877, opening ceremonies of the Permanent Exhibition, Philadelphia, Pa.

July 21, 1877, troops from Philadelphia, Pa., attacked by railroad strikers at Pittsburgh, Pa.

Oct. 4, 1877, surrender of Chief Joseph ended war with Idaho Indians

Feb. 19, 1878, Thomas Alva Edison obtained phonograph patent

Feb. 21, 1878, first telephone directory issued at New Haven, Conn.

Feb. 28, 1878, Bland-Allison Act passed over presidential veto permitting limited coinage of silver

Oct. 4, 1878, first Chinese embassy officials received by President Hayes

Jan. 1, 1879, resumption of specie payment—redemption of paper money in coin

Feb. 15, 1879, act passed to permit women to practice before U.S. Supreme Court

Mar. 3, 1879, Belva Ann Lockwood, first woman admitted to practice before U.S. Supreme Court

Mar. 3, 1879, office of U.S. Geological Survey director authorized

Oct. 21, 1879, first electric incandescent lamp of practical value invented by Edison

Nov. 1, 1879, Indian school opened at Carlisle, Pa.

Nov. 4, 1879, James and John Ritty granted patent on cash register

1880, New York City (not including Brooklyn) the first city with population of a million (1,206,299 shown in the 1880 census report)

Mar. 10, 1880, first Salvation Army services held by Commissioner George Scott Railton and seven women at New York City

July 20, 1880, Egyptian obelisk, "Cleopatra's Needle," arrived at New York City

IMPORTANT DATES IN HIS LIFE

18—, attended elementary schools, the Methodist Academy at Norwalk, Ohio, and the Webb Preparatory School, Middletown, Conn.

Aug. 4(?), 1842, graduated from Kenyon College

Jan. 1845, graduated from Harvard Law School, L.L.B. degree

Mar. 10, 1845, admitted to the bar, Marietta, Ohio; practiced in Sandusky (now Fremont), Ohio

1849, moved to Cincinnati; practiced law

1857-1859, city solicitor of Cincinnati

June 27, 1861, commissioned major, 23rd Regiment, Ohio Volunteer Infantry

Sept. 19, 1861, appointed judge advocate general

Oct. 24, 1861, lieutenant colonel

Sept. 14, 1862, wounded in left arm at South Mountain

1862, detailed to act as brigadier general in command of Kanawha division

July 1863, checked Confederate raid led by John Morgan

1864, commanded brigade under General Crook

July 1864, with Colonel Milligan ordered to charge superior force; Milligan fell and Hayes conducted retreat

Sept. 1864, second battle of Winchester

Sept. 22, 1864, routed enemy at Fisher's Hill

Oct. 9, 1864, brigadier general of volunteers

Oct. 19, 1864, Battle of Cedar Creek; badly stunned when his horse was killed

Oct. 24, 1862, colonel

Mar. 3, 1865, breveted major general of volunteers "for gallant and distinguished services during the campaign of 1864 in West Virginia and particularly at the battles of Fisher's Hill and Cedar Creek."

Mar. 4, 1865-July 20, 1867, U.S. House of Representatives (from Ohio)

June 8, 1865, resigned from Army

Jan. 13, 1868, governor of Ohio

1872, unsuccessful candidate for election to Congress; declined appointment as U.S. treasurer at Cincinnati

Jan. 10, 1876-Mar. 2, 1877, governor of Ohio

Mar. 4, 1877-Mar. 3, 1881, President

1880, declined to run for a second term

RUTHERFORD BIRCHARD HAYES

_____was the second President born in Ohio.

_____was the first president sworn in on March 3 in a private ceremony at the White House.

_____was the third President inaugurated on March 5.

HAYES' VICE PRESIDENT

Vice President–William Almon Wheeler (19th V.P.)
Date of birth–June 30, 1819
Birthplace–Malone, N.Y.
Political party–Republican

State represented–New York
Term of office–Mar. 4, 1877-Mar. 3, 1881
Age at inauguration–57 years, 247 days
Occupation after term–Lawyer
Date of death–June 4, 1887
Age at death–67 years, 339 days
Place of death–Malone, N.Y.
Burial place–Malone, N.Y.

Additional data on Wheeler

1838, student, University of Vermont, Burlington, Vt.
1845, admitted to the bar; practiced in Malone, N.Y.
1846-1849, district attorney for Franklin County, N.Y.
1850-1851, New York State Assembly
1858-1859, New York State Senate
Mar. 4, 1861-Mar. 3, 1863, U.S. House of Representatives (from New York)
1867-1868, delegate to state constitutional conventions
Mar. 4, 1869-Mar. 3, 1877, U.S. House of Representatives (from New York)
1877, resumed law practice

ADDITIONAL DATA ON HAYES

INAUGURATION

Rutherford Birchard Hayes took the oath of office on Monday, March 5, 1877, the oath being administered by Chief Justice Morrison Remick Waite at the east end of the Capitol.

As March 4 for the third time in the history of the republic fell on a Sunday, and as this was the most disputed election in history, Hayes took the oath of office privately on Saturday, March 3, in the Red Room of the White House. This was the first time that a president-elect had taken the oath in the White House.

A torchlight parade was held Monday night and a reception followed at the Willard Hotel, Washington, D.C. No inaugural parade or inaugural ball was held.

SILVER WEDDING ANNIVERSARY AT WHITE HOUSE

President Hayes celebrated his silver wedding anniversary on December 31, 1877, in the White House. Reverend Dr. Lorenzo Dow McCabe of Ohio Wesleyan University, who had united Lucy Webb and Rutherford Birchard Hayes on December 30, 1852, reenacted the ceremony at their silver wedding.

ABOLITION OF SEX DISCRIMINATION IN LAW PRACTICE BEFORE SUPREME COURT

President Hayes on February 15, 1879, signed "an act to relieve certain legal disabilities of women." It provided that any woman member of the bar of good moral character who had practiced for three years before a state Supreme Court was eligible for admittance to practice before the Supreme Court of the United States. The first woman admitted to practice before the Supreme Court was Belva Ann Bennett Lockwood.

HAYES VISITED THE WEST COAST

The first President in office to visit the west coast was Hayes. He attended a reunion of the Twenty-third Ohio Regiment on September 1, 1880, at the Opera House, Canton, Ohio, and left from there for the west coast. On September 8, 1880, he arrived at San Francisco, Calif. He stopped at the Palace Hotel in the same suite occupied by former President Grant on September 20, 1879, on his return from his world tour. He returned to his home in Fremont, Ohio, on November 1, 1880. On the tour he was accompanied by his wife, his sons Birchard and Rutherford, General Sherman and his daughter, General and Mrs. Mitchell, and other friends.

HAYES CONTENT ON RETIREMENT

President Hayes wrote a letter to Guy Bryan on January 1, 1881, in which he said, "Nobody ever left the Presidency with less regret, less disappointment, fewer heartburnings, or more general content with the result of his term (in his own heart, I mean) than I do." (Guy Bryan of Texas, a descendant of Stephen F. Austin, had been a classmate of Hayes at Kenyon College.)

HAYES ESCAPED INJURY

After President Garfield's inauguration on March 4, 1881, former President Hayes left Washington on a special train of the Baltimore and Potomac Railroad. A few miles out of Baltimore, Md., his train collided with another and the former President was thrown several feet out of his chair. Two people were killed and twenty were seriously injured in the collision. The train was delayed twenty-four hours. Hayes was with a party of friends in the fifth car. The three preceding cars contained the Cleveland City Troop, which had marched in the inaugural parade.

THE FIRST LADY

Lucy Webb Ware, the wife of President Hayes, acquired the nickname "Lemonade Lucy" while she was first lady of the land because of her habit of serving lemonade and other soft drinks instead of liquor at White House receptions. Both the President and his wife were total abstainers.

JAMES ABRAM GARFIELD

20th PRESIDENT

Born–Nov. 19, 1831
Birthplace–Orange, Ohio
College attended–Williams College, Williamstown, Mass.
Date of graduation–Aug. 6, 1856, four-year course
Religious denomination– Disciples of Christ
Ancestry–English
Occupation–Teacher
Date and place of marriage–Nov. 11, 1858, Hiram, Ohio
Age at marriage–26 years, 357 days
Years married–22 years, 312 days
Political party–Republican
State represented–Ohio
Term of office–Mar. 4, 1881-Sept. 19, 1881
Term served–199 days
Administration–24th
Congresses–47th
Age at inauguration–49 years, 105 days
Lived after term–Died in office
Date of death–Sept. 19, 1881
Age at death–49 years, 304 days
Place of death–Elberon, N.J.
Burial place–Lake View Cemetery, Cleveland, Ohio

PARENTS

Father–Abram Garfield
Born–Dec. 28, 1799
Married–Feb. 3, 1820, Zanesville, Ohio
Occupation–Farmer, canal constructor
Died–May 8, 1833, Otsego County, Ohio
Age at death–33 years, 126 days
Mother–Eliza Ballou Garfield

Born–Sept. 21, 1801, Richmond, N.H.
Died–Jan. 21, 1888, Mentor, Ohio
Age at death–86 years, 122 days

BROTHERS AND SISTERS

James Abram Garfield was the fifth child in a family of five.

Children of Abram Garfield and Eliza Ballou Garfield

Mehitabel Garfield, b. Jan. 28, 1821
Thomas Garfield, b. Oct. 16, 1822
Mary Garfield, b. Oct. 19, 1824, d. Nov. 4, 1884
James Ballou Garfield, b. Oct. 21, 1826, d. Jan. 8, 1829
James Abram Garfield, b. Nov. 19, 1831, d. Sept. 19, 1881

CHILDREN

Eliza Arabella Garfield, b. July 3, 1860, Hiram, Ohio; d. Dec. 3, 1863, Hiram, Ohio
Harry Augustus Garfield, b. Oct. 11, 1863, Hiram, Ohio; m. June 14, 1888, Belle Hartford Mason, Williamstown, Mass.; d. Dec. 12, 1942, Williamstown, Mass.
James Rudolph Garfield, b. Oct. 17, 1865, Hiram, Ohio; m. Dec. 30, 1890, Helen Newell, Chicago, Ill.; d. Mar. 24, 1950, Cleveland, Ohio
Mary ("Molly") Garfield, b. Jan. 16, 1867, Washington, D.C.; m. June 14, 1888, Joseph Stanley-Brown, Mentor, Ohio; d. Dec. 30, 1947, Pasadena, Calif.
Irvin McDowell Garfield, b. Aug. 3, 1870, Hiram, Ohio; m. Oct.

For additional data see the end of this section and also specific subject headings in the index.

16, 1906, Susan Emmons, Falmouth, Mass.; d. July 18, 1951, Boston, Mass.

Abram Garfield, b. Nov. 21, 1872, Washington, D.C.; m. Oct. 14, 1897, Sarah Granger Williams, Cleveland, Ohio; m. Apr. 12, 1947, Helen Grannis Matthews, Cleveland, Ohio; d. Oct. 16, 1958, Cleveland, Ohio

Edward Garfield, b. Dec. 25, 1874, Hiram, Ohio; d. Oct. 25, 1876, Washington, D.C.

MRS. JAMES ABRAM GARFIELD

Name—Lucretia Rudolph Garfield

Date of birth—Apr. 19, 1832

Birthplace—Hiram, Ohio

Age at marriage—26 years, 206 days

Children—5 sons, 2 daughters

Mother—Arabella Green Mason Rudolph

Father—Zebulon Rudolph

His occupation—Farmer

Date of death—Mar. 14, 1918

Age at death—85 years, 329 days

Place of death—Pasadena, Calif.

Burial place—Cleveland, Ohio

Years younger than the President—151 days

Years she survived the President—36 years, 176 days

THE ELECTION OF 1880

NOMINATIONS FOR TERM 1881-1885

Republican Party Convention (7th)

June 2-5, 7-8, 1880, Exposition Hall, Chicago, Ill.

Nominated for President—James Abram Garfield, Ohio

Nominated for Vice President—Chester Alan Arthur, N.Y.

Garfield was nominated on the thirty-sixth ballot. Candidates for nomination and the votes they received on the first and thirty-sixth ballots:

Ulysses Simpson Grant, Ill., 304, 306

James Gillespie Blaine, Me., 284, 42

John Sherman, Ohio, 93, 3

George Franklin Edmunds, Vt., 34, 0

Elihu Benjamin Washburne, Ill., 30, 5

William Windom, Minn., 10, 0

James Abram Garfield, Ohio, 0, 339

Total number of votes: 755

Number necessary for nomination: 378

Democratic Party Convention (13th)

June 22-24, 1880, Music Hall, Cincinnati, Ohio

Nominated for President—Winfield Scott Hancock, Pa.

Nominated for Vice President—William Hayden English, Ind.

Hancock was nominated on the second ballot. Candidates for nomination and the votes they received on the first and second ballots:

Winfield Scott Hancock, Pa., 171, 705

Thomas Francis Bayard, Del., 153$\frac{1}{2}$, 2

Henry B. Payne, Ohio, 81, 0

Allen Granberry Thurman, Ohio, 68$\frac{1}{2}$, 0

Stephen Johnson Field, Calif., 65, 0

William Ralls Morrison, Ill., 62, 0
Thomas Andrews Hendricks, Ind., 49$^1/_2$, 30
Samuel Jones Tilden, N.Y., 38, 1
Thomas Ewing, Ohio, 10, 0
Horatio Seymour, N.Y., 8, 0
Samuel Jackson Randall, Pa., 6, 0
William Austin Hamilton Loveland, Colo., 5, 0
Joseph Ewing McDonald, Ind., 2, 0
George Brinton McClellan, N.J., 2, 0
Jeremiah Sullivan Black, Pa., 1, 0
James Edward English, Conn., 1, 0
Hugh Judge Jewett, Ohio, 1, 0
George Van Ness Lothrop, Mich., 1, 0
Joel Parker, N.J., 1, 0
Total number of votes
  First ballot: 726$^1/_2$
  Second ballot: 738
Number necessary for nomination: 492

Greenback Labor Party Convention (National Party)

June 9-11, 1880, Exposition Hall, Chicago, Ill.
Nominated for President—James Baird Weaver, Iowa
Nominated for Vice President—Benjamin J. Chambers, Tex.
  Weaver was nominated on the first ballot. Candidates for nomination and the votes they received:
James Baird Weaver, Iowa, 224$^1/_2$
Hendrick Bradley Wright, Pa., 126$^1/_2$
Stephen Devalson Dillaye, N.Y., 119
Benjamin Franklin Butler, Mass., 95
Solon Chase, Me., 89
Edward Phelps Allis, Wis., 41
Alexander Campbell, Ill., 21
Total number of votes: 716
Nomination made unanimous

Prohibition Party Convention (3rd) (National Prohibition Reform Party)

June 17, 1880, Halle's Hall, Cleveland, Ohio
Nominated for President—Neal Dow, Me.
Nominated for Vice President—Henry Adams Thompson, Ohio
Candidates nominated by acclamation

American Party

Nominated for President—John Wolcott Phelps, Vt.
Nominated for Vice President—Samuel Clarke Pomeroy, Kan.
  This was an Anti-Masonic party.

ELECTION RESULTS, NOV. 2, 1880—PRESIDENTIAL AND VICE PRESIDENTIAL CANDIDATES

Republican Party (4,454,416 votes)

James Abram Garfield, Ohio
Chester Alan Arthur, N.Y.

Democratic Party (4,444,952 votes)

Winfield Scott Hancock, Pa.
William Hayden English, Ind.

Greenback Labor Party (National Party) (308,578 votes)

James Baird Weaver, Iowa
Benjamin J. Chambers, Tex.

Prohibition Party (10,305 votes)

Neal Dow, Me.
Henry Adams Thompson, Ohio

American Party (700 votes)

John Wolcott Phelps, Vt.
Samuel Clarke Pomeroy, Kan.

ELECTORAL VOTES (369—38 states)

Garfield received 57.99 per cent (214 votes—19 states) as follows:
Calif. 1 (of the 6 votes); Colo. 3; Conn. 6; Ill. 21; Ind. 15; Iowa
11; Kan. 5; Me. 7; Mass. 13; Mich. 11; Minn. 5; Neb. 3; N.H. 5;
N.Y. 35; Ohio 22; Ore. 3; Pa. 29; R.I. 4; Vt. 5; Wis. 10.

Hancock received 42.01 per cent (155 votes—19 states) as follows:
Ala. 10; Ark. 6; Calif. 5 (of the 6 votes); Del. 3; Fla. 4; Ga. 11; Ky.
12; La. 8; Md. 8; Miss. 8; Mo. 15; Nev. 3; N.J. 9; N.C. 10; S.C.
7; Tenn. 12; Tex. 8; Va. 11; W.Va. 5.

CABINET

March 4, 1881-September 19, 1881

State—William Maxwell Evarts, N.Y., continued from preceding administration; James Gillespie Blaine, Me., Mar. 5, 1881; entered upon duties Mar. 7, 1881

Treasury—Henry Flagg French, Mass. (assistant secretary), ad interim Mar. 4, 1881; William Windom, Minn., Mar. 5, 1881; entered upon duties Mar. 8, 1881

War—Alexander Ramsey, Minn., continued from preceding administration; Robert Todd Lincoln, Ill., Mar. 5, 1881; entered upon duties Mar. 11, 1881

Attorney General—Charles Devens, Mass., continued from preceding administration, Wayne McVeagh, Pa., Mar. 5, 1881; entered upon duties Mar. 7, 1881

Postmaster General—Horace Maynard, Tenn., continued from preceding administration; Thomas Lemuel James, N.Y., Mar. 5, 1881; entered upon duties Mar. 8, 1881

Navy—Nathan Goff, Jr., W.Va., continued from preceding administration; William Henry Hunt, La., Mar. 5, 1881; entered upon duties Mar. 7, 1881

Interior–Carl Schurz, Mo., continued from preceding administration; Samuel Jordan Kirkwood, Iowa, Mar. 5, 1881; entered upon duties Mar. 8, 1881

FORTY-SEVENTH CONGRESS

March 4, 1881-March 3, 1883

First session–Dec. 5, 1881-Aug. 8, 1882 (247 days)

Second session–Dec. 4, 1882-Mar. 3, 1883 (90 days)

Special sessions of the Senate–Mar. 4, 1881-May 20, 1881 (77 days); Oct. 10, 1881-Oct. 29, 1881 (20 days)

Vice President–Chester Alan Arthur, N.Y., succeeded to the presidency on the death of James Abram Garfield on Sept. 19, 1881

Presidents pro tempore of the Senate–Thomas Francis Bayard, Del., elected Oct. 10, 1881; David Davis, Ill., elected Oct. 13, 1881, resigned Mar. 3, 1883; George Franklin Edmunds, Vt., elected Mar. 3, 1883

Secretaries of the Senate–John C. Burch, Tenn., died July 28, 1881; Francis Edwin Shober (chief clerk), N.C., appointed acting secretary by resolution of Oct. 24, 1881

Speaker of the House–Joseph Warren Keifer, Ohio, elected Dec. 5, 1881

Clerks of the House–George Madison Adams, Ky., Edward McPherson, Pa., elected Dec. 5, 1881

APPOINTMENTS TO THE SUPREME COURT

Associate Justice
Stanley Matthews, Ohio, May 12, 1881

ADMINISTRATION — IMPORTANT DATES

Apr. 9, 1881, Post Office Department discovery of fraudulent payments for mail service caused several resignations

May 16, 1881, Senators Roscoe Conkling and Thomas Collier Platt of New York resigned because of a disagreement with President Garfield over federal appointments in New York

May 21, 1881, American Red Cross organized

IMPORTANT DATES IN HIS LIFE

1841, worked on farm; supported widowed mother

18—, attended district school three months every winter

1848, driver, helmsman, carpenter on Ohio canals

Mar. 6, 1849, entered Geauga Seminary, Chester, Ohio

1849, taught one term in district school in Solon, Geauga County, Ohio

1851, attended Geauga Seminary (name later changed to Western Reserve Eclectic Institute and on Feb. 20, 1867, to Hiram College)

1854-1856, attended Williams College

1857-1861, president of Western Reserve Eclectic Institute; taught Latin, Greek, higher mathematics, history, philosophy, English literature and English rhetoric

1859, member, Ohio state senate

1860, admitted to the bar

Aug. 21, 1861, commissioned lieutenant colonel of 42nd Regiment, Ohio Volunteer Infantry

Nov. 27, 1861, promoted to colonel

Dec. 14, 1861, ordered into field at Big Sandy Valley (in charge of 18th Brigade)

Jan. 10, 1862, defeated Confederate forces under General Marshall at Paintville, Ky.

Jan. 11, 1862, promoted to brigadier general of volunteers

1862, commanded brigade at Shiloh but was not ordered into fighting until the second day, when the battle was over

1862, developed camp fever; relieved of command and given leave to recuperate

Feb. 1863, appointed chief of staff under General Rosecrans

Mar. 4, 1863-Nov. 8, 1880, U.S. house of Representatives (from Ohio) (elected in 1862 while in military service)

Sept. 19, 1863, promoted to major general of volunteers

Dec. 5, 1863, resigned from army to take seat in House of Representatives

1877, moved to Mentor, Ohio

1877, member of the Electoral Commission created by act of Congress approved Jan. 29, 1877, to decide the contests in the various states in the disputed election of 1876

Jan. 13, 1880, elected by Ohio legislature to U.S. Senate for term beginning Mar. 4, 1881

June 8, 1880, nominated for the presidency at the Republican convention at Chicago

Nov. 4, 1880, elected President

Nov. 8, 1880, resigned from House of Representatives

Dec. 23, 1880, declined senatorial election, having been elected President

Mar. 4, 1881-Sept. 19, 1881, President

July 2, 1881, shot by Charles J. Guiteau while passing through the railroad depot, Washington, D.C.

Sept. 19, 1881, died from effects of the wound at Elberon, N.J.

JAMES ABRAM GARFIELD

____was the third President born in Ohio.

____was the first President whose mother was present at his inauguration.

____was the fourth President to die in office.

____was the second President assassinated.

____was the sixth President whose mother was alive when he was inaugurated.

____was the first President to review an inaugural parade from a stand in front of the White House.

____was the second President who was survived by his mother.

____was the first left-handed President.

GARFIELD'S VICE PRESIDENT

Vice President–Chester Alan Arthur (20th V.P.)
Date of birth–Oct. 5, 1830
Birthplace–Fairfield, Vt.
Political party–Republican
State represented–New York
Term of office–Mar. 4, 1881-Sept. 19, 1881
Age at inauguration–50 years, 150 days
Occupation after term–President
Date of death–Nov. 18, 1886
Age at death–56 years, 44 days
Place of death–New York, N.Y.
Burial place–Rural Cemetery, Albany, N.Y.

For further biographical information see Chester Alan Arthur, 21st President.

ADDITIONAL DATA ON GARFIELD

GARFIELD DISPERSED HECKLERS

In 1863 General James Abram Garfield, speaking in favor of abolition at Chestertown, Md., was besieged by a barrage of eggs thrown by a rebel sympathizer. Garfield stopped his speech and said, "I have just come from fighting brave rebels at Chickamauga; I shall not flinch before cowardly rebels." He continued his speech and his opponents dispersed.

GARFIELD CALMED THE MOB

Fifty thousand angry citizens answered a call to assemble at the Custom House, New York City, on April 15, 1865, ready to take the law into their own hands to avenge the death of President Lincoln. Two men in the crowd who expressed sentiments against the martyred President were attacked; one was killed, the other severely injured. About ten thousand people prepared to march to the office of the New York *World* crying "Vengeance!" A telegram that arrived from Washington stating "Seward is dying" stopped the march for a moment. Garfield, then visiting New York as a member of Congress, lifted his arm and in a loud voice addressed the mob:

Fellow-citizens! Clouds and darkness are round about Him! His pavilion is dark waters and thick clouds of the skies! Justice and judgment are the establishment of His throne! Mercy and truth shall go before His face! Fellow-citizens! God reigns and the Government at Washington still lives!

The crowd was deeply moved by Garfield's words and the threatened riot never occurred.

NOMINATION OF GARFIELD

At the Republican convention of 1880, on the first ballot, not one vote was cast for Garfield. On the second, third, fourth, and fifth ballots, a delegate from Pennsylvania cast his vote for Garfield. A delegate from Alabama joined him on the sixth and seventh ballots.

On the eighth ballot, Garfield lost the Alabama vote. The ninth, tenth, and eleventh ballots saw delegates from Massachusetts and one from Pennsylvania casting their votes for Garfield. The Massachusetts delegate did not vote for Garfield on the twelfth and thirteenth ballots but the Pennsylvania delegate still voted for Garfield. The next five ballots saw Garfield dropped from the running. He did not receive a single vote in the fourteenth, fifteenth, sixteenth, seventeenth, or eighteenth ballots.

The delegate from Pennsylvania brought Garfield back into the running, casting one vote for him in the nineteenth, twentieth, twenty-first, and twenty-second ballots. The next eight ballots, the twenty-third to the thirtieth, saw Garfield's strength double. Instead of one vote from Pennsylvania, he received two. The next three ballots, the thirty-first to the thirty-third, witnessed a drop in Garfield's strength. He managed to keep only one vote, that from Pennsylvania.

The thirty-fourth vote showed that the persistent delegate from Pennsylvania was a great strategist, because Wisconsin added sixteen votes to his, giving Garfield seventeen votes. The next ballot, the thirty-fifth, showed Garfield with fifty votes; on the next ballot he received 399 of the 756 votes, which gave him the Republican nomination for the presidency. This was the largest number of ballots cast at a Republican convention up to that time.

Garfield was the only presidential nominee who was present in the convention hall to see himself nominated. Garfield was the leader of the Ohio delegation, which originally supported Secretary of the Treasury John Sherman for the presidency.

GARFIELD CAMPAIGNED IN GERMAN AS WELL AS IN ENGLISH

Garfield studied Latin and Greek at Williams College and chose German as an elective study. The latter language was of great help to him in his campaign for the German-American vote. On October 18, 1880, a delegation of about five hundred German-Americans from Cleveland, Ohio, visited General Garfield at Mentor, Ohio. He welcomed them in German, "Wilkommen alle," and often used the German language in campaigning.

TEN THOUSAND VOTES DETERMINED THE PRESIDENCY

A plurality of about one tenth of one per cent of the popular vote enabled Garfield to become President of the United States. Garfield received 4,454,416 votes; Hancock, the Democratic candidate, received 4,444,952 votes. With a plurality of 9,464 votes Garfield won 214 of the electoral votes, as compared with 155 for Hancock.

GARFIELD QUALIFIED FOR THREE FEDERAL POSITIONS AT THE SAME TIME

On November 2, 1880, Garfield qualified for three federal positions. He was a congressman from Ohio, having taken office in the House of Representatives on March 4, 1863, and having served in the 38th Congress and the eight succeeding Congresses. On January 13, 1880, while he was serving in the House of Representatives, he was elected by the legislature of Ohio to serve in the United States Senate for the term beginning March 4, 1881. On November 2, 1880, Garfield was elected President of the United States. On that date, he was president-elect, senator-elect, and member of the House of Representatives (the first member elected President while serving in the House).

As the senatorial and presidential terms began on the same day, Garfield surrendered his seat and never sat in the Senate. (John Sherman served in his place.) On November 8, 1880, Garfield resigned from the House and on March 4, 1881, he was inaugurated President of the United States.

INAUGURATION

James Abram Garfield took the oath of office on Friday, March 4, 1881. Chief Justice Morrison Remick Waite administered the oath.

A heavy snowstorm, accompanied by strong winds, and the damp, penetrating cold kept the crowds down to a minimum. Despite the weather, about fifteen to twenty thousand people were in the two-and-a-half-hour parade. In the evening, a fireworks display thrilled the city.

The inaugural ball was held in the Hall of the Smithsonian Institution. An electric lamp, which was a great attraction to many of the guests, hung over the main entrance. The music was supplied by 150 musicians, members of the German Orchestra of Philadelphia under the direction of William Stoll, Jr., and the United States Marine Band under John Philip Sousa.

Those who attended the inaugural ball for President Garfield held at the Smithsonian Institution paid five dollars for tickets. Those who paid one dollar extra were entitled to a supper, which was served in a temporary building. The bill of fare consisted of pickled oysters, chicken salad, roast turkey, roast ham. roast beef, beef tongues, ice cream, water ices, assorted cakes, jellies, rolls, bread and butter, tea, coffee, lemonade, fruits, and relishes.

The caterers prepared 50 hams, 1,500 pounds of turkey, 100 gallons of oysters, 200 gallons of chicken salad, 150 gallons of ice cream, 50 gallons of water ices, 50 gallons of jelly, 350 pounds of butter, 15,000 cakes, 200 gallons of coffee, and 2,000 biscuits.

GARFIELD'S MOTHER WITNESSED INAUGURATION

Mrs. Elizabeth Ballou Garfield was the first mother of a President to witness the inauguration of her son. The first act of President Garfield after his inauguration was to kiss his mother. Mrs. Garfield was also the first mother of a President to live at the White House.

GARFIELD JUDGES GARFIELD

Garfield said:

I do not care what others say and think about me. But there is one man's opinion which I very much value, and that is the opinion of James Garfield. Others I need not think about. I can get away from them, but I have to be with him all the time. He is with me when I rise up and when I lie down; when I eat and talk; when I go out and come in. It makes a great difference whether he thinks well of me or not.

GARFIELD ASSASSINATED

Garfield was shot on July 2, 1881, at the Baltimore and Potomac Railway Depot, Washington, D.C., by Charles Julius Guiteau, a disappointed office-seeker who had wanted to be appointed United States consul at Paris. The President survived eighty days, during which time his only official act was the signing of an extradition paper. On September 6, 1881, Garfield was taken to Elberon, N.J., to recuperate, but he died there of blood poisoning on September 19, 1881. He had three funerals, one at Elberon, N.J., another at Washington, D.C., where his body rested in state for three days, and the third at Cleveland, Ohio, where he was buried.

Guiteau was tried on November 14, 1881. The verdict was rendered on January 25, 1882 and he was hanged at the jail at Washington, D.C., on June 30, 1882.

PRESIDENT GARFIELD'S LAST LETTER

August 11, 1881

Dear Mother:
Don't be disturbed by conflicting reports about my condition. It is true I am still weak and on my back, but I am gaining every day and need only time and patience to bring me through. Give my love to all the relatives and friends and especially to sisters Hetty and Mary.

Your loving son,
JAMES ABRAM GARFIELD

MRS. ELIZA GARFIELD,
HIRAM, OHIO.

THE FIRST LADY

Lucretia ("Crete") Rudolph Garfield was first lady of the land for less than seven months, her husband meeting an untimely death at the hand of the assassin Guiteau.

CHESTER ALAN ARTHUR
21st PRESIDENT

Born–Oct. 5, 1830
Birthplace–Fairfield, Vt.
College attended–Union College, Schenectady, N.Y.
Date of graduation–July 1848
Religion–Episcopalian
Ancestry–Scotch-Irish
Occupation–Lawyer
Date and place of marriage–Oct. 25, 1859, New York, N.Y.
Age at marriage–29 years, 20 days
Years married–20 years, 79 days
Political party–Republican
State represented–New York
Term of office–Sept. 20, 1881-Mar. 3, 1885 (Arthur succeeded to the presidency on the death of James Abram Garfield.)
Term served–3 years, 166 days
Administration–24th
Congresses–47th, 48th
Age at inauguration–50 years, 350 days
Lived after term–1 year, 260 days
Occupation after term–Lawyer
Date of death–Nov. 18, 1886
Age at death–56 years, 44 days
Place of death–New York, N.Y.
Burial place–Rural Cemetery, Albany, N.Y.

PARENTS

Father–William Arthur
Born–Dec. 5, 1796, Antrim County, Ireland
Married–Apr. 12, 1821, Dunham, Quebec
Occupation–Baptist clergyman
Died–Oct. 27, 1875, Newtonville, N.Y.
Age at death–78 years, 326 days
Mother–Malvina Stone Arthur

Born–Apr. 29, 1802, Berkshire, Vt.
Died–Jan. 16, 1869, Newtonville, N.Y.
Age at death–66 years, 262 days

BROTHERS AND SISTERS

Chester Alan Arthur was the fifth child and the oldest son in a family of nine.

Children of William Arthur and Malvina Stone Arthur

Regina Malvina Arthur, b. Mar. 8, 1822, d. Nov. 15, 1910
Jane Arthur, b. Mar. 14, 1824, d. Apr. 15, 1842
Almeda Arthur, b. Jan. 22, 1826, d. Mar. 26, 1899
Ann Eliza Arthur, b. Jan. 1, 1828, d. Apr. 10, 1915
Chester Alan Arthur, b. Oct. 5, 1830, d. Nov. 18, 1886
Malvina Arthur, b. 1832, d. Jan. 16, 1920
William Arthur, b. May 28, 1834, d. Feb. 27, 1915
George Arthur, b. May 24, 1836, d. Mar. 8, 1838
Mary Arthur, b. June 5, 1841, d. Jan. 8, 1917

CHILDREN

William Lewis Herndon Arthur, b. Dec. 10, 1860, New York, N.Y.; d. July 7, 1863, Englewood, N.J.
Chester Alan Arthur, b. July 25, 1864, New York, N.Y.; m. May 8, 1900, Myra Townsend Fithian Andrews, Montreux, Switzerland; m. Nov. 3, 1934, Mrs. Rowena Dashwood Graves, Colorado Springs, Colo.; d.

For additional data see the end of this section and also specific subject headings in the index.

July 17, 1937, Colorado Springs, Colo.

Ellen Herndon Arthur, b. Nov. 21, 1871; m. Charles Pinkerton; d. Sept. 6, 1915, Mount Kisco, N.Y.

MRS. CHESTER ALAN ARTHUR

Name–Ellen Lewis Herndon Arthur

Date of birth–Aug. 30, 1837

Birthplace–Fredericksburg, Va.

Age at marriage–22 years, 56 days

Children–2 sons, 1 daughter

Mother–Frances Elizabeth Hansbrough Herndon

Father–William Lewis Herndon

His occupation–Captain, U.S. Navy

Date of death–Jan. 12, 1880

Age at death–42 years, 135 days

Place of death–New York, N.Y.

Burial place–Albany, N.Y.

Years younger than the President–6 years, 329 days

Years the President survived her–6 years, 310 days

CABINET

September 20, 1881-March 3, 1885

State–James Gillespie Blaine Me., continued from preceding administration; Frederick Theodore Frelinghuysen, N.J., Dec. 12, 1881; entered upon duties Dec. 19, 1881

Treasury–William Windom, Minn., continued from preceding administration; Charles James Folger, N.Y., Oct. 27, 1881; entered upon duties Nov. 14, 1881; died Sept. 4, 1884; Charles E. Coon, N.Y. (assistant secretary), ad interim Sept. 4, 1884; Henry Flagg French, Mass. (assistant secretary), ad interim Sept. 8, 1884; Charles E. Coon, N.Y. (assistant secretary), ad interim Sept. 15, 1884; Walter Quintin Gresham, Ind., Sept. 24, 1884; Henry Flagg French, Mass. (assistant secretary), ad interim Oct. 29, 1884; Hugh McCulloch, Ind., Oct. 28, 1884; entered upon duties Oct. 31, 1884

War–Robert Todd Lincoln, Ill., continued from preceding administration

Attorney General–Wayne MacVeagh, Pa., continued from preceding administration; Samuel Field Phillips, N.C. (solicitor general), ad interim Nov. 14, 1881; Benjamin Harris Brewster, Pa., Dec. 19, 1881; entered upon duties Jan. 3, 1882

Postmaster General–Thomas Lemuel James, N.Y., continued from preceding administration; recommissioned Oct. 27, 1881; Timothy Otis Howe, Wis., Dec. 20, 1881; entered upon duties Jan. 5, 1882, died Mar. 25, 1883; Frank Hatton, Iowa (first assistant postmaster general), ad interim Mar. 26, 1883; Walter Quintin Gresham, Ind., Apr. 3, 1883; entered upon duties Apr. 11, 1883; Frank Hatton, Iowa (first assistant postmaster general), ad interim Sept. 25, 1884; Frank Hatton, Iowa, Oct. 14, 1884

Navy–William Henry Hunt, La., continued from preceding administration; William Eaton Chandler, N.H., Apr. 12, 1882; entered upon duties Apr. 17, 1882

Interior–Samuel Jordan Kirkwood, Iowa, continued from preceding administration; Henry Moore Teller, Colo., Apr. 6, 1882; entered upon duties Apr. 17, 1882

FORTY-EIGHTH CONGRESS

March 4, 1883-March 3, 1885

First session–Dec. 3, 1883-July 7, 1884 (218 days)

Second session–Dec. 1, 1884-Mar. 3, 1885 (93 days)

Vice President–Vice President Chester Alan Arthur succeeded to the presidency on the death of James Abram Garfield on Sept. 19, 1881

President pro tempore of the Senate–George Franklin Edmunds, Vt., reelected Jan. 14, 1884

Secretaries of the Senate–Francis Edwin Shober (chief clerk), N.C.; Anson George McCook, N.Y., elected Dec. 18, 1883

Speaker of the House–John Griffin Carlisle, Ky., elected Dec. 3, 1883

Clerks of the House–Edward McPherson, Pa., John Bullock Clark, Jr., Mo., elected Dec. 4, 1883

APPOINTMENTS TO THE SUPREME COURT

Associate Justices

Horace Gray, Mass., Dec. 20, 1881

Roscoe Conklin, N.Y., Feb. 1882 (declined appointment)

Samuel Blatchford, N.Y., Mar. 22, 1882

ADMINISTRATION — IMPORTANT DATES

May 22, 1882, treaty of peace, amity, commerce, and navigation signed with Korea

Aug. 5, 1882, exclusion act passed restricting Chinese immigration

Mar. 9, 1883, Civil Service Commission organized

Nov. 18, 1883, standard time adopted

1884, United States granted exclusive right to establish coaling and repair station at Pearl Harbor, Oahu, Hawaii by Hawaiian king

May 17, 1884, establishment of territorial government in Alaska (formed from territory ceded to the United States by Russia by treaty of March 30, 1867)

Dec. 1884, treaty with Nicaragua for construction of a canal

Dec. 16, 1884, President Arthur pressed a button at Washington, D.C., to open the World's Industrial and Cotton Centennial Exposition at New Orleans, La.

Feb. 21, 1885, Washington monument dedicated, Washington, D.C.

IMPORTANT DATES IN HIS LIFE

18—, attended public school

18—, taught penmanship at Pownal, Vt., to earn tuition

1848, graduated from Union College

1851, principal of academy in North Pownal, Vt.

1848-1853, taught school, studied law

1854, admitted to the bar; practiced at New York, N.Y.

1857, judge advocate of Second Brigade, New York State Militia

1860, appointed engineer-in-chief on the staff of Governor Morgan with the rank of brigadier-general, New York State Militia

July 10-Dec. 31, 1862, quartermaster-general with the rank of brigadier-general

1863, resumed practice of law at New York, N.Y.

Nov. 24, 1871-July 11, 1878, collector of the Port of New York (appointed by President Grant)

July 11, 1878, removed as collector by executive order issued by President Hayes

1878, resumed practice of law at New York, N.Y.

1880, delegate from New York to Republican National Convention at Chicago to name Grant for a third term

Nov. 5, 1880, nominated for the vice presidency

Mar. 4, 1881, inaugurated Vice President

Sept. 20, 1881-Mar. 3, 1885, President (succeeded to the presidency on the death of James Abram Garfield)

June 6, 1884, unsuccessful candidate for presidential nomination on the Republican ticket

CHESTER ALAN ARTHUR

____was the first President born in Vermont.

____was the eighth President who was a resident of a state other than his native state.

____was the fourth widower inaugurated President.

ADDITIONAL DATA ON ARTHUR

THREE PRESIDENTS IN ONE YEAR

In 1881, for the second time in American history, there were three Presidents in one year. Rutherford Birchard Hayes concluded his term on March 3, 1881. On March 4, 1881, James Abram Garfield was inaugurated President. Garfield died September 19, 1881, on which date Chester Alan Arthur, his Vice President, became President.

In 1841, the three Presidents of the United States had been Martin Van Buren, William Henry Harrison, and John Tyler.

OATH OF OFFICE

Chester Alan Arthur, who succeeded to the presidency upon the death of President Garfield, took the oath of office at his residence, 123 Lexington Avenue, New York, N.Y., at 2 A.M. on September 20, 1881. Garfield had died at 10:30 P.M. on September 19.) The oath was administered by New York Supreme Court Justice John R. Brady.

The oath was repeated on Thursday, September 22, 1881, in the Vice President's room at the Capitol, where it was administered by Chief Justice Morrison Remick Waite in the presence of former Presidents Hayes and Grant.

HOSTESS AT THE WHITE HOUSE

President Arthur's wife, Ellen Herndon Arthur, died on January 12, 1880, before her husband succeeded to the presidency. As Arthur's only daughter, Ellen, was only ten years of age, the duties of mistress of the White House were assumed by Mary Arthur McElroy (Mrs. John McElroy) of Albany, the President's sister.

GROVER CLEVELAND
22nd PRESIDENT

Born–Mar. 18, 1837 (Given name —Stephen Grover)

Birthplace–Caldwell, N.J.

College attended–None

Religion–Presbyterian

Ancestry–English-Irish

Occupation–Lawyer, sheriff

Date and place of marriage–June 2, 1886, Washington, D.C.

Age at marriage–49 years, 76 days

Years Married–22 years, 22 days

Political party–Democratic

State represented–New York

Term of office–Mar. 4, 1885-Mar. 3, 1889

Term served–4 years

Administration–25th

Congresses–49th, 50th

Age at inauguration–47 years, 351 days

Lived after term–19 years, 112 days

Occupation after term–Reelected President in 1892

Date of death–June 24, 1908

Age at death–71 years, 98 days

Place of death–Princeton, N.J.

Burial place–Princeton, N.J.

PARENTS

Father–Richard Falley Cleveland

Born–June 19, 1804, Norwich, Conn.

Married–Sept. 10, 1829, Baltimore, Md.

Occupation–Congregational minister

Died–Oct. 1, 1853, Holland Patent, N.Y.

Age at death–49 years, 104 days

Mother–Anne Neal Cleveland

Born–Feb. 4, 1806, Baltimore, Md.

Died–July 19, 1882, Holland Patent, N.Y.

Age at death–76 years, 165 days

BROTHERS AND SISTERS

Grover Cleveland was the fifth child in a family of nine.

Children of Richard Falley Cleveland and Anne Neal Cleveland

Anna Neal Cleveland, b. July 9, 1830, d. 1909

William Neal Cleveland, b. Apr. 7, 1832, d. Jan. 15, 1906

Mary Allen Cleveland, b. Nov. 16, 1833, d. July 28, 1914

Richard Cecil Cleveland, b. July 31, 1835, d. Oct. 22, 1872

(Stephen) Grover Cleveland, b. Mar. 18, 1837, d. June 24, 1908

Margaret Louise Falley Cleveland, b. Oct. 28, 1838, d. Mar. 5, 1932

Lewis Frederick Cleveland, b. May 2, 1841, d. Oct. 22, 1872

Susan Sophia Cleveland, b. Sept. 2, 1843, d. Nov. 4, 1938

Rose Elizabeth Cleveland, b. June 13, 1846, d. Nov. 26, 1918

CHILDREN

Ruth Cleveland, b. Oct. 3, 1891, New York, N.Y.; d. Jan. 7, 1904, Princeton, N.J.

Esther Cleveland, b. Sept. 9, 1893, in White House, Washington, D.C., m. Mar. 14, 1918, William Sydney Bence Bosanquet, London, England

Marion Cleveland, b. July 7, 1895, Buzzards Bay, Mass.; m. Nov. 28, 1917, William Stanley Dell, Princeton, N.J.; m. July 25, 1926, John Harlan Amen, Tamworth, N.H.

For additional data see the end of this section and also specific subject headings in the index.

Richard Folson Cleveland, b. Oct. 28, 1897, Princeton, N.J.; m. June 20, 1923, Ellen Douglas Gailor, Memphis, Tenn.; m. 1943, Jessie Maxwell Black; d. Jan. 10, 1974, Baltimore, Md.

Francis Grover Cleveland, b. July 18, 1903, Buzzards Bay, Mass.; m. June 20, 1925, Alice Erdman, Princeton, N.J.

MRS. GROVER CLEVELAND

Name–Frances Folson Cleveland
Date of birth–July 21, 1864
Birthplace–Buffalo, N.Y.

Age at marriage–21 years, 316 days
Children–3 daughters, 2 sons
Mother–Emma Cornelia Harmon Folson
Father–Oscar Folsom
His occupation–Lawyer
Date of death–Oct. 29, 1947
Age at death–83 years, 100 days
Place of death–Baltimore, Md.
Burial place–Princeton, N.J.
Years younger than the President–27 years, 125 days
Years she survived the President–39 years, 137 days

THE ELECTION OF 1884

NOMINATION FOR TERM 1885-1889

Democratic Party Convention (14th)

July 8-11, 1884, Expositon Hall, Chicago, Ill.
Nominated for President—Grover Cleveland, N.Y.
Nominated for Vice President—Thomas Andrews Hendricks, Ind.

Cleveland was nominated on the second ballot. Candidates for nomination and the votes they received on the first and second ballots:
Grover Cleveland, N.Y., 392, 683
Thomas Francis Bayard, Del., 170, 81$^1/_2$
Allen Granberry Thurman, Ohio, 88, 4
Samuel Jackson Randall, Pa., 78, 4
Joseph Ewing McDonald, Ind., 56, 2
John Griffin Carlisle, Ky., 27, 0
Roswell Pettibone Flower, N.Y., 4, 0
George Hoadly, Ohio, 3, 0
Thomas Andrews Hendricks, Ind., 1, 45$^1/_2$
Samuel Jones Tilden, N.Y., 1, 0
Total number of votes: 820
Number necessary for nomination: 547

Republican Party Convention (8th)

June 3-6, 1884, Exposition Hall, Chicago, Ill.
Nominated for President—James Gillespie Blaine, Me.
Nominated for Vice President—John Alexander Logan, Ill.

Blaine was nominated on the fourth ballot. Candidates for nomination and the votes they received on the first and fourth ballots:
James Gillespie Blaine, Me., 334$^1/_2$, 541
Chester Alan Arthur, N.Y., 278, 207
George Franklin Edmunds, Vt., 93, 41
John Alexander Logan, Ill. 63$^1/_2$, 7
John Sherman, Ohio, 30, 0

Joseph Roswell Hawley, Conn., 13, 15
Robert Todd Lincoln, Ill., 4, 2
William Tecumseh Sherman, Mo., 2, 0
Total number of votes:

First ballot: 818
Fourth ballot: 813
Number necessary for nomination: 411

Anti-Monopoly Party

May 14, 1884, Hershey Music Hall, Chicago, Ill.
Nominated for President—Benjamin Franklin Butler, Mass.
Nominated for Vice President—Absolom Madden West, Miss.
Butler was nominated on the first ballot. Candidates for nomination and the votes they received:
Benjamin Franklin Butler, Mass., 124
Allen Granberry Thurman, Ohio, 7
Solon Chase, Me., 1
This political group was formed as The Anti-Monopoly Organization of the United States. West was not nominated at the convention. His nomination was decided by a committee appointed to negotiate with other political parties.

Greenback Party Convention (National Greenback Labor Party)

May 28-29, 1884, English's Opera House, Indianapolis, Ind.
Nominated for President—Benjamin Franklin Butler, Mass.
Nominated for Vice President—Absolom Madden West, Miss.
Butler was nominated on the first ballot. Candidates for nomination and the votes they received:
Benjamin Franklin Butler, Mass., 323
Jesse Harper, Ill., 98
Solon Chase, Me., 2
Edward Phelps Allis, Wis., 1
Total number of votes: 424
The Greenback and Anti-Monopoly parties endorsed the same candidates.

Prohibition Party Convention (4th)

July 23-24, 1884, Lafayette Hall, Pittsburgh, Pa.
Nominated for President—John Pierce St. John, Kan.
Nominated for Vice President—William Daniel, Md.

American Prohibition Party Convention

June 19, 1884, Chicago, Ill.
Nominated for President—Samuel Clarke Pomeroy, Kan.
Nominated for Vice President—John A. Conant, Conn.

Equal Rights Party

September 20, 1884, San Francisco, Calif.
Nominated for President—Belva Ann Bennett Lockwood, D.C.
Nominated for Vice President—Marietta Lizzie Bell Stow, Calif.

This convention was held by the Woman's Rights Party or Female Suffragettes. Suffrage for women was its principal aim, but it also endorsed equal property rights for women, the discouragement of trade in liquor, and the distribution of public lands to settlers only.

ELECTION RESULTS, NOV. 4, 1884—PRESIDENTIAL AND VICE PRESIDENTIAL CANDIDATES

Democratic Party (4,874,986 votes)

Grover Cleveland, N.Y.
Thomas Andrews Hendricks, Ind.

Republican Party (4,851,981 votes)

James Gillespie Blaine, Me.
John Alexander Logan, Ill.

Greenback Party and Anti-Monopoly Party (175,370 votes)

Benjamin Franklin Butler, Mass.
Absolom Madden West, Miss.

Prohibition Party (150,369 votes)

John Pierce St. John, Kan.
William Daniel, Md.

ELECTORAL VOTES (401—38 states)

Cleveland received 54.61 per cent (219 votes—20 states) as follows: Ala. 10; Ark. 7; Conn. 6; Del. 3; Fla. 4; Ga. 12; Ind. 15; Ky. 13; La. 8; Md. 8; Miss. 9; Mo. 16; N.J. 9; N.Y. 36; N.C. 11; S.C. 9; Tenn. 12; Tex. 13; Va. 12; W.Va. 6.

Blaine received 45.39 per cent (182 votes—18 states) as follows: Calif. 8; Colo. 3; Ill. 22; Iowa 13; Kan. 9; Me. 6; Mass. 14; Mich. 13; Minn. 7; Neb. 5; Nev. 3; N.H. 4; Ohio 23; Ore. 3; Pa. 30; R.I. 4; Vt. 4; Wis. 11.

CABINET

March 4, 1885-March 3, 1889

State–Frederick Theodore Frelinghuysen, N.J., continued from preceding administration; Thomas Francis Bayard, Del., Mar. 6, 1885

Treasury–Hugh McCulloch, Ind., continued from preceding administration; Daniel Manning, N.Y., Mar. 6, 1885; entered upon duties Mar. 8, 1885; Charles Stebbins Fairchild, N.Y., Apr. 1, 1887

War–Robert Todd Lincoln, Ill., continued from preceding administration; William Crowninshield Endicott, Mass., Mar. 6, 1885

Attorney General–Benjamin Harris Brewster, Pa., continued from preceding administration; Augustus Hill Garland, Ark., Mar. 6, 1885; entered upon duties Mar. 9, 1885

Postmaster General–Frank Hatton, Iowa, continued from preceding administration; William Freeman Vilas, Wis., Mar. 6, 1885; Donald McDonald Dickinson, Mich., Jan. 16, 1888

Navy–Wiliam Eaton Chandler, N.H., continued from preceding administration; William Collins Whitney, N.Y., Mar. 6, 1885

Interior–Merritt L. Joslyn, Ill. (assistant secretary), ad interim Mar. 4, 1885; Lucius Quintus Cincinnatus Lamar, Miss., Mar. 6, 1885; Henry Lowndes Muldrow, Miss. (first assistant secretary), ad interim Jan. 11, 1888; William Freeman Vilas, Wis., Jan. 16, 1888

Agriculture–Norman Jay Colman, Mo., Feb. . 13, 1889

FORTY-NINTH CONGRESS

March 4, 1885-March 3, 1887

First session–Dec. 7, 1885-Aug. 5, 1886 (242 days)

Second session–Dec. 6, 1886-March 3, 1887 (88 days)

Special session of the Senate–Mar. 4, 1885-Apr. 2, 1885 (30 days)

Vice President–Thomas Andrews Hendricks, Ind., died Nov. 25, 1885

Presidents pro tempore of the Senate–John Sherman, Ohio; elected Dec. 7, 1885; resigned effective Feb. 26, 1887; John James Ingalls, Kan., elected Feb. 25, 1887

Secretary of the Senate–Anson George McCook, N.Y.

Speaker of the House–John Griffin Carlisle, Ky., reelected Dec. 7, 1885

Clerk of the House–John Bullock Clark, Mo., reelected Dec. 7, 1885

FIFTIETH CONGRESS

March 4, 1887-March 3, 1889

First session–Dec. 5, 1887-Oct. 20, 1888 (321 days)

Second session–Dec. 3, 1888-Mar. 3, 1889 (91 days)

Vice President–Thomas Andrews Hendricks, Ind., died Nov. 25, 1885

President pro tempore of the Senate–John James Ingalls, Ky.

Secretary of the Senate–Anson George McCook, N.Y.

Speaker of the House–John Griffin Carlisle, Ky., reelected Dec. 5, 1887

Clerk of the House–John Bullock Clark, Jr., Mo., reelected Dec. 5, 1887

APPOINTMENTS TO THE SUPREME COURT

Chief Justice
Melville Weston Fuller, Ill., July 20, 1888

Associate Justice
Lucius Quintus Cincinnatus Lamar, Miss., Jan. 16, 1888

ADMINISTRATION — IMPORTANT DATES

Apr. 8, 1885, U.S. marines landed at Panama

May 17, 1885, Apache chief Geronimo on warpath in Arizona and New Mexico

Sept. 3, 1885, Naval War College opened at Newport, R.I.

Jan. 19, 1886, Presidential Succession Act approved

Mar. 22, 1886, first Interstate Commerce Commission appointed

May 17, 1886, act passed providing for commissioning of graduates of U.S. Military Academy as second lieutenants

Oct. 28, 1886, dedication of the Statue of Liberty

Dec. 1886, American Federation of Labor organized

Feb. 4, 1887, Interstate Commerce Act approved

Feb. 23, 1887, importation of opium from China prohibited

Aug. 9, 1887, Colorado troops battled Ute Indians

May 30, 1888, Massachusetts first state to adopt the Australian ballot

Feb. 1889, Department of Agriculture established as executive department

IMPORTANT DATES IN HIS LIFE

18—, clerk at store, Clinton, N.Y.

Oct. 5, 1853, assistant teacher, New York Institution for the Blind

Aug. 1855, clerk and copyist for a Buffalo, N.Y., law firm, at no salary, then at $4 a week

1858, salary raised to $500 a year

1859, admitted to the bar

1861, helped edit a book about cattle

Nov. 1862, elected ward supervisor, Buffalo

1863-1865, assistant district attorney of Erie County, N.Y.

1865, unsuccessful candidate for district attorney

1871-1873, sheriff of Erie County

1882, mayor of Buffalo

Jan. 1, 1883-Jan. 6, 1885, governor of New York

July 11, 1884 nominated for the presidency by the Democratic convention at Chicago, Ill.

Mar. 4, 1885-Mar. 3, 1889, President (first term)

June 5, 1888, nominated for the presidency by the Democratic convention at St. Louis, Mo.

Nov. 6, 1888, defeated in election by Republican candidate, Benjamin Harrison

Mar. 4, 1889, returned to law practice

June 2, 1892, nominated for the presidency by the Democratic convention at Chicago, Ill.

Mar. 4, 1893-Mar. 3, 1897, President (second term)

Oct. 15, 1901, trustee of Princeton University

GROVER CLEVELAND

____was the first President born in New Jersey.

____was the only President who was defeated for reelection and later reelected, thus serving two nonconsecutive terms (March 4, 1885-March 3, 1889 and March 4, 1893-March 3, 1897).

____was the second President married while in office.

____was the only President married in the White House.

____was the ninth President who was a resident of a state other than his native state.

____was the first President elected after the Civil War who had not taken an active part in the conflict.

____was the first Democratic President elected after the Civil War.

CLEVELAND'S VICE PRESIDENT

Vice President–Thomas Andrews Hendricks (21st V.P.)

Date of birth–Sept. 7, 1819

Birthplace–Muskingum County, Ohio
Political party–Democratic
State represented–Indiana
Term of office–Mar. 4, 1885-Nov. 25, 1885
Age at inauguration–65 years, 178 days
Occupation after term–Died in office
Date of death–Nov. 25, 1885
Age at death–66 years, 79 days
Place of death–Indianapolis, Ind.
Burial place–Indianapolis, Ind.

Additional data on Hendricks

1841, graduated from Hanover College, Hanover, Ind.
1843, admitted to bar; practiced at Shelbyville, Ind.
1848, Indiana State House of Representatives
1849, Indiana State Senate
1851, member, Indiana State Constitutional Convention
Mar. 4, 1851-Mar. 3, 1885, U.S. House of Representatives (from Indiana)
1854, unsuccessful candidate for reelection
1855-1859, commissioner, General Land Office
1860, unsuccessful candidate for governor of Indiana
Mar. 4, 1863-Mar. 3, 1869, U.S. Senate (from Indiana)
1876, unsuccessful candidate for Vice President on Democratic ticket with Tilden
1883-1887, governor of Indiana

ADDITIONAL DATA ON CLEVELAND

CLEVELAND CHANGED NAME

Grover Cleveland was orginally named Stephen Grover Cleveland, for Stephen Grover, the minister of the First Presbyterian Church at Caldwell, N.J., from 1787 to 1837. This was the position to which Cleveland's father was appointed. Cleveland dropped his first name, Stephen, in his youth.

CLEVELAND HANGED CRIMINALS

On January 1, 1871, Grover Cleveland took office as sheriff of the Erie County Jail, Buffalo, N.Y. Instead of delegating disagreeable tasks, such as hangings, to others, he personally carried out the duties of his office. On September 6, 1872, he superintended the hanging of Patrick Morrissey, convicted of stabbing his mother.

The Buffalo *Express* on September 7, 1872, reported that "the sheriff [Cleveland] stood at the gallows with his right hand on the rod attached to the trap bolt, and at fourteen minutes past twelve, Mr. Emerick gave the signal."

On February 14, 1873, Cleveland took charge also of the hanging of Jack Gaffney, a gambler, convicted of shooting and killing a man during a card game at Buffalo.

CLEVELAND'S TWO BROTHERS PERISHED IN FIRE AT SEA

On October 22, 1872, the S.S. *Missouri* of the Atlantic Mail Line bound from New York City to Havana, Cuba, burned at sea. Over eighty lives were lost, including Cleveland's two brothers: Richard Cecil Cleveland, aged 37, and Lewis Frederick Cleveland, aged 31. Grover Cleveland at that time was sheriff of Erie County.

RELIGIOUS ISSUE IN THE CAMPAIGN OF 1884

A few days before the election, on October 29, 1884, a delegation of Protestant clergymen met the Republican candidate at the Fifth Avenue Hotel in New York City. One of the ministers, Dr. Samuel Dickinson Burchard, made a speech in which he referred to the Democrats as the party of "rum, Romanism, and rebellion." In his reply, Blaine failed to disavow this insult to the Catholic Church and the Democratic party, and his subsequent denials of anti-Catholic bigotry came too late. As a result Blaine lost many votes in New York, which had been expected to vote Republican, and he failed to carry that key state. Since a few hundred more votes would have carried the state for Blaine—Cleveland's New York plurality was under twelve hundred—the religious issue played a significant part in the election.

FIRST INAUGURATION

Grover Cleveland took the oath of office on his mother's Bible on Wednesday, March 4, 1885, on the east portico of the Capitol. The oath was administered by Chief Justice Morrison Remick Waite. The President reviewed the parade from the White House.

PRESIDENT MARRIED IN WHITE HOUSE

James Buchanan and Grover Cleveland were the only bachelors elected President. Buchanan remained a bachelor but Cleveland married his ward, Frances Folsom (the daughter of his deceased law partner), on June 2, 1886, in a ceremony performed in the White House. Before his marriage the President's sister, Rose Elizabeth Cleveland, acted as White House hostess.

THE FIRST LADY

Frances Folsom Cleveland, who was 21 years and 316 days old when she married Grover Cleveland, was the youngest President's wife in the White House.

BENJAMIN HARRISON
23rd PRESIDENT

Born–Aug. 20, 1833

Birthplace–North Bend, Ohio

College attended–Miami University, Oxford, Ohio

Date of graduation–June 24, 1852, two-year course, Bachelor of Arts

Religious denomination–Presbyterian

Ancestry–English

Occupation–Lawyer

Date of first marriage–Oct. 20, 1853

Age at marriage–20 years, 61 days

Years married–39 years, 5 days

Date and place of second marriage–Apr. 6, 1896, New York, N.Y.

Age at second marriage–62 years, 229 days

Years married–4 years, 341 days

Political party–Republican

State represented–Indiana

Term of office–Mar. 4, 1889-Mar. 3, 1893

Term served–4 years

Administration–26th

Congresses–51st, 52nd

Age at inauguration–55 years, 196 days

Lived after term–8 years, 9 days

Occupation after term–Lawyer, teacher

Date of death–Mar. 13, 1901

Age at death–67 years, 205 days

Place of death–Indianapolis, Ind.

Burial place–Crown Hill Cemetery, Indianapolis, Ind.

PARENTS

Father–John Scott Harrison

Born–Oct. 4, 1804, Vincennes, Ind.

Married (1)–Lucretia Knapp Johnson

Married (2)–Elizabeth Ramsey Irwin

Occupation–Farmer, U.S. congressman

Died–May 25, 1878, North Bend, Ohio

Age at death–73 years, 233 days

First wife of father–Lucretia Knapp Johnson Harrison

Born–Sept. 16, 1804

Married–1824

Died–Feb. 6, 1830

Age at death–25 years, 143 days

Mother–Elizabeth Ramsey Irwin Harrison

Born–July 18, 1810, Mercersburg, Pa.

Married–Aug. 12, 1831

Died–Aug. 15, 1850

Age at death–40 years, 28 days

BROTHERS AND SISTERS

Benjamin Harrison was the fifth of his father's thirteen children, the second of ten children of a second marriage.

Children of John Scott Harrison and Lucretia Knapp Johnson Harrison

Elizabeth Short Harrison, b. 1825, d. May 12, 1904

William Henry Harrison, b. Mar. 9, 1827, d. Sept. 15, 1829

Sarah Lucretia Harrison, b. 1829

Children of John Scott Harrison and Elizabeth Ramsey Irwin Harrison

Archibald Irwin Harrison, b. June 9, 1832, d. Dec. 16, 1870

For additional data see the end of this section and also specific subject headings in the index.

Benjamin Harrison, b. Aug. 20, 1833, d. Mar. 13, 1901

Mary Jane Irwin Harrison, b. July 5, 1835, d. Sept. 14, 1867

Anna Symmes Harrison, b. Aug. 23, 1837, d. Aug. 26, 1838

John Irwin Harrison, b. June 25, 1839, d. Oct. 25, 1839

Carter Bassett Harrison, b. Sept. 26, 1840, d. Dec. 6, 1905

Anna Symmes Harrison, b. Nov. 4, 1842, d. Mar. 26, 1926

John Scott Harrison, b. Nov. 16, 1844, d. Jan. 10, 1926

James Friedlay Harrison, b. Feb. 14, 1847, d. Jan. 3, 1848

James Irwin Harrison, b. Oct. 7, 1849, d. Aug. 25, 1850

CHILDREN

By first wife, Carolina Lavinia Scott Harrison

Russell Benjamin Harrison, b. Aug. 12, 1854, Oxford, Ohio; m. Jan 9, 1884, Mary Angeline Saunders, Omaha, Neb.; d. Dec. 13, 1936, Indianapolis, Ind.

Mary Scott Harrison, b. Apr. 3, 1858; m. Nov. 5, 1884, James Robert McKee, Indianapolis, Ind.; d. Oct. 28, 1930, Greenwich, Conn.

By second wife, Mary Scott Lord Dimmick Harrison

Elizabeth Harrison, b. Feb. 21, 1897, Indianapolis, Ind.; m. Apr. 6, 1921, James Blaine Walker, N.Y.

MRS. BENJAMIN HARRISON (first wife)

Name–Caroline Lavinia Scott Harrison

Born–Oct. 1, 1832

Birthplace–Oxford, Ohio

Age at marriage–21 years, 19 days

Children–1 son, 1 daughter

Mother–Mary Potts Neal Scott

Father–John Witherspoon Scott

His occupation–Presbyterian minister

Date of death–Oct. 25, 1892

Age at death–60 years, 24 days

Place of death–Washington, D.C.

Burial place–Indianapolis, Ind.

Years older than the President–323 days

Years the President survived her–8 years, 139 days

MRS. BENJAMIN HARRISON (second wife)

Name–Mary Scott Lord Dimmick Harrison

Born–Apr. 30, 1858

Birthplace–Honesdale, Pa.

Age at marriage–37 years, 341 days

Children–1 daughter

Mother–Elizabeth Scott Lord

Father–Russell Farnham Lord

His occupation–Engineer and manager, Delaware and Hudson Canal Co.

Date of death–Jan. 5, 1948

Age at death–89 years, 250 days

Place of death–New York, N.Y.

Burial place–Indianapolis, Ind.

Years younger than the President–24 years, 253 days

Years she survived the President–46 years, 298 days

The second Mrs. Harrison was the widow of Walter Erskine Dimmick, who died Jan. 14, 1882. She married Benjamin Harrison after the expiration of his term as President.

THE ELECTION OF 1888

NOMINATIONS FOR TERM 1889-1893

Republican Party Convention (9th)

June 19-23, 25, 1888, Civic Auditorium, Chicago, Ill.
Nominated for President—Benjamin Harrison, Ind.
Nominated for Vice President—Levi Parsons Morton, N.Y.

Harrison was nominated on the eighth ballot. Candidates for nomination and the votes they received on the first and eighth ballots:

John Sherman, Ohio, 229, 118
Walter Quintin Gersham, Ind., 107, 59
Chauncey Mitchell Depew, N.Y., 99, 0
Benjamin Harrison, Ind., 85, 544
Russell Alexander Alger, Mich., 84, 100
William Boyd Allison, Iowa, 72, 0
James Gillespie Blaine, Me., 35, 5
John James Ingalls, Kan., 28, 0
Darwin Phelps, Pa., 25, 0
Jeremiah McLain Rusk, Wis., 25, 0
Edwin Henry Fitler, Pa., 24, 0
Joseph Roswell Hawley, N.C., 13, 0
Robert Todd Lincoln, Ill., 3, 0
William McKinley, Ohio, 2, 4
Total number of votes:
    First ballot: 831
    Eighth ballot: 830
Number necessary for nomination: 416

Democratic Party Convention (15th)

June 5-7, 1888, Exposition Building, St. Louis, Mo.
Nominated for President—Grover Cleveland, N.Y.
Nominated for Vice President—Allen Granberry Thurman, Ohio
First ballot: 822, Grover Cleveland, N.Y.; Nominated by acclamation

Prohibition Party Convention (5th)

May 30-31, 1888, Tomlinson Hall, Indianapolis, Ind.
Nominated for President—Clinton Bowen Fisk, N.J.
Nominated for Vice President—John Anderson Brooks, Mo.

Fisk was nominated by acclamation.

Union Labor Party

May 16, 1888, Cincinnati, Ohio
Nominated for President—Alson Jenness Streeter, Ill.
Nominated for Vice President—Charles E. Cunningham, Ark.

The Union Labor Party was organized February 24, 1887, at Cincinnati, Ohio.

Delegates to the convention came from the Knights of Labor, Agricultural Wheelers, Corngrowers, Homesteadry, Farmers' Alliances, Greenbackers, and Grangers.

United Labor Party

May 15-17, 1888, Grand Opera House, Cincinnati, Ohio
Nominated for President—Robert Hall Cowdrey, Ill.
Nominated for Vice President—William H. T. Wakefield, Kan.
This party, an outgrowth of the Henry George movement of 1886, nominated its first national ticket in 1888.

American Party

Aug. 14-15, 1888, Grand Army Hall, Washington, D.C.
Nominated for President—James Langdon Curtis, N.Y.
Nominated for Vice President—Peter Dinwiddie Wigginton, Calif.
Curtis was nominated on the first ballot. Candidates for nomination and the votes they received:
James Langdon Curtis, N.Y., 45
Abram Stevens Hewitt, N.Y., 15
James Scott Negley, Pa., 4
Nomination made unanimous

James R. Greer of Tennessee was nominated for Vice President but declined.

Equal Rights Party

May 15, 1888, Des Moines, Iowa
Nominated for President—Belva Ann Bennett Lockwood, D.C.
Nominated for Vice President—Alfred Henry Love, Pa.
Love declined the nomination and Charles Stuart Wells was substituted.

Industrial Reform Party

Feb. 22-23, 1888, Washington, D.C.
Nominated for President—Albert E. Redstone, Calif.
Nominated for Vice President—John Colvin, Kan.

ELECTION RESULTS, NOV. 6, 1888—PRESIDENTIAL AND VICE PRESIDENTIAL CANDIDATES

Democratic Party (5,540,309 votes)

Grover Cleveland, N.Y.
Allen Granberry Thurman, Ohio

Republican Party (5,444,337 votes)

Bejamin Harrison, Ind.
Levi Parsons Morton, N.Y.

Prohibition Party (249,506 votes)

Clinton Bowen Fisk, N.J.
John Anderson Brooks, Mo.

Union Labor Party (146,935 votes)

Alson Jenness Streeter, Ill.
Charles E. Cunningham, Ark.

United Labor Party (2,818 votes)

Robert Hall Cowdrey, Ill.
William H. T. Wakefield, Kan.

American Party (1,612 votes)

James Langdon Curtis, N.Y.
Peter Dinwiddie Wigginton, Calif.

ELECTORAL VOTES (401—38 states)

Harrison received 58.10 per cent (233 votes—20 states) as follows:
Calif. 8; Colo. 3; Ill. 22; Ind. 15; Iowa 13; Kan. 9; Me. 6; Mass.
14; Mich. 13; Minn. 7; Neb. 5; Nev. 3; N.H. 4; N.Y. 36; Ohio 23;
Ore. 3; Pa. 30; R.I. 4; Vt. 4; Wis. 11.

Cleveland received 41.90 per cent (168 votes—18 states) as follows:
Ala. 10; Ark. 7; Conn. 6; Del. 3; Fla. 4; Ga. 12; Ky. 13; La. 8; Md.
8; Miss. 9; Mo. 16; N.J. 9; N.C. 11; S.C. 9; Tenn. 12; Tex. 13; Va.
12; W.Va. 6.

CABINET

March 4, 1889-March 3, 1893

State–Thomas Francis Bayard, Del., continued from preceding administration; James Gillespie Blaine, Me., Mar. 5, 1889, entered upon
duties Mar. 7, 1889; William Fisher Wharton, Mass. (assistant secretary) ad interim June 4, 1892; John Watson Foster, Ind., June 29,
1892; William Fisher Wharton, Mass. (assistant secretary) ad interim Feb. 23, 1893

Treasury–Charles Stebbins Fairchild, N.Y., continued from preceding
administration; William Windom, Minn., Mar. 5, 1889, entered
upon duties Mar. 7, 1889; Alvred Bayard Nettleton, Minn. (assistant
secretary) ad interim Jan. 30, 1891; Charles Foster, Ohio, Feb. 24,
1891

War–William Crowninshield Endicott, Mass., continued from preceding administration; Redfield Proctor, Vt., Mar. 5, 1889; Lewis Addison Grant, Minn. (assistant secretary) ad interim Dec. 6, 1891;
Stephen Benton Elkins, W.Va., Dec. 22, 1891, entered upon duties
Dec. 24, 1891

Attorney General–Augustus Hill Garland, Ark., continued from preceding administration; William Henry Harrison Miller, Ind., Mar.
5, 1889

Postmaster General–Donald McDonald Dickinson, Mich., continued
from preceding administration; John Wanamaker, Pa., Mar. 5, 1889

Navy–William Collins Whitney, N.Y., continued from preceding administration; Benjamin Franklin Tracy, N.Y., Mar. 5, 1889

Interior–William Freeman Vilas, Wis., continued from preceding administration; John Willock Noble, Mo., Mar. Mar. 5, 1889, entered
upon duties Mar. 7, 1889

Agriculture–Norman Jay Colman, Mo., continued from preceding administration; Jeremiah McLain Rusk, Wis., Mar. 5, 1889, entered
upon duties Mar. 7, 1889

FIFTY-FIRST CONGRESS

March 4, 1889-March 3, 1891

First session–Dec. 2, 1889-Oct. 1, 1890 (304 days)
Second session–Dec. 1, 1890-Mar. 2, 1891 (93 days)
Special session of the Senate–Mar. 4, 1889-Apr. 2, 1889 (30 days)
Vice President–Levi Parsons Morton, N.Y.
Presidents pro tempore of the Senate–John James Ingalls, Kan., elected Mar. 7, 1889 and Apr. 2, 1889, special sessions of the Senate; Feb. 28, 1890 and Apr. 3, 1890; Charles Frederick Manderson, Neb., elected Mar. 2, 1891
Secretary of the Senate–Anson George McCook, N.Y.
Speaker of the House–Thomas Brackett Reed, Me., elected Dec. 2, 1889
Clerks of the House–John Bullock Clark, Jr., Mo., Edward McPherson, Pa., elected Dec. 2, 1889

FIFTY-SECOND CONGRESS

March 4, 1891-March 3, 1893

First session–Dec. 7, 1891-Aug. 5, 1892 (251 days)
Second session–Dec. 5, 1892-Mar. 3, 1893 (89 days)
Vice President–Levi Parsons Morton, N.Y.
President pro tempore of the Senate–Charles Frederick Manderson, Neb.
Secretary of the Senate–Anson George McCook, N.Y.
Speaker of the House–Charles Frederick Crisp, Ga., elected Dec. 8, 1891
Clerks of the House–Edward McPherson, Pa., continued from preceding Congress; James Kerr, Pa., elected Dec. 8, 1891

APPOINTMENTS TO THE SUPREME COURT

Associate Justices
David Josiah Brewer, Kan., Dec. 18, 1889
Henry Billings Brown, Mich., Dec. 29, 1890
George Shiras, Jr., Pa., July 26, 1892
Howell Edmunds Jackson, Tenn., Feb. 18, 1893

ADMINISTRATION — IMPORTANT DATES

Apr. 22, 1889, Oklahoma opened to settlers
May 31, 1889, Johnstown flood
Oct. 2, 1889, Pan American Conference
Nov. 2, 1889, North Dakota and South Dakota admitted to the Union as the 39th and 40th states
Nov. 8, 1889, Montana admitted as the 41st state
Nov. 11, 1889, Washington admitted as the 42nd state
July 2, 1890, Sherman Anti-trust Act enacted
July 3, 1890, Idaho admitted as the 43rd state
July 10, 1890, Wyoming admitted as the 44th state
July 14, 1890, Sherman Silver Purchase Act passed

IMPORTANT DATES IN HIS LIFE

1853, admitted to the bar, practiced at Cincinnati, Ohio

1854, moved to Indiana

1855, received A.M. degree

1860, reported of decisions, Indiana Supreme Court

July 14, 1862, commissioned second lieutenant of Indiana Volunteers

July 1862-June 1865, formed Company A of the 70th Regiment, Indiana Volunteer Infantry, and was made captain; at the organization of the regiment was commissioned colonel; went with regiment to Kentucky and served until June 1865

1864-1868, served as reporter of Indiana Supreme Court while still in military service

Jan. 23, 1865, breveted brigadier general

June 8, 1865, honorable discharge from army

1876, unsuccessful candidate for governor of Indiana

1879, member, Mississippi River Commission

Mar. 4, 1881-Mar. 3, 1887, U.S. Senate (from Indiana)

Mar. 4, 1889-Mar. 3, 1893, President

1892, unsuccessful candidate for a second term—defeated by Cleveland

1900, practiced law, served in Paris as chief attorney for the Republic of Venezuela in the Venezuela-Great Britain boundary dispute

BENJAMIN HARRISON

_____was the fourth President born in Ohio.

_____was the tenth President who was a resident of a state other than his native state.

_____was the third President to remarry.

_____was the fifth President to marry a widow.

_____was the second President whose wife died while he was in office.

HARRISON'S VICE PRESIDENT

Vice President–Levi Parsons Marton (22nd V.P.)

Born–May 16, 1824

Birthplace–Shoreham, Vt.

Political party–Republican

State represented–New York

Term of office–Mar. 4, 1889-Mar. 3, 1893

Age at inauguration–64 years, 292 days

Occupation after term–Governor of New York, 1895-1897

Date of death–May 16, 1920

Age at death–96 years

Place of death–Rhinebeck, N.Y.

Burial place–Rhinebeck, N.Y.

Additional data on Morton

1838-1840, clerk, general store, Enfield, Mass.

1840-1841, taught school, Boscawen, N.H.

1845, mercantile pursuits, Hanover, N.H.

1854, dry goods business, New York City

1863, banker, New York City

1876, unsuccessful candidate for U.S. Congress
1878, Commissioner, Paris Exposition
Mar. 4, 1879-Mar. 21, 1881, U.S. House of Representatives (from New York)
Aug. 5, 1881-May 14, 1885, U.S. minister to France

ADDITIONAL DATA ON HARRISON

GRANDSON OF A PRESIDENT

Benjamin Harrison was the only grandson of a President to become President. The twenty-third President was a grandson of William Henry Harrison, the ninth President, who took office on March 4, 1841 and died on April 4, 1841.

INAUGURATION

Benjamin Harrison took the oath of office on Monday, Mar. 4, 1889. The oath was administered by Chief Justice Melville Weston Fuller on the east portico of the Capitol. Despite the torrential rains and strong winds, Harrison rode to the Capitol in an open carriage and delivered his inaugural address.

A parade that continued after dark was marred by the inclement weather. The fireworks exhibition scheduled for the evening was abandoned.

The inaugural ball, attended by more than 12,000 persons, was held in the Pension Office, 5th and F Streets, Washington, D.C. An orchestra of one hundred provided the music. The menu included blue points on ice. The hot foods consisted of bouillon in cups, steamed oysters, oysters à la poulette, chicken croquettes, sweetbread pâté à la reine, and terrapin, Philadelphia style. The cold foods were assorted roll sandwiches, mayonnaise of chicken, lobster salad, cold tongue en Bellevue, cold ham à la Montmorency, boned turkey à la Américaine, breast of quail à la Cicéron, pâté de foie gras à la Harrison, terrine of game à la Morton. The desserts were assorted ice cream, orange water ice, Roman punch, pyramid of nougat renaissance, beehive of bon-bons Republican, Pavilion Rustic, and assorted fancy cakes. Fruits, other desserts, and coffee were also available.

A one-hour fireworks display was held on the Monument grounds, the concluding display being a set piece representing the Capitol and the White House.

HARRISON PRECEDED AND FOLLOWED BY CLEVELAND

Benjamin Harrison was the only President who was preceded and succeeded by the same man. When Grover Cleveland retired from office on March 4, 1889, Harrison was sworn in and when Harrison retired on March 4, 1893, Grover Cleveland took the oath of office for a second time.

TWO CABINET OFFICERS WITH SAME NAME

Benjamin Harrison was the only President who had two secretaries in his cabinet with the same last name. For a period of eight months, from June 29, 1892, to February 23, 1893, he had two secretaries named

Foster. One was Charles Foster of Ohio, Secretary of the Treasury from February 24, 1891, to March 3, 1893; the other was John Watson Foster of Indiana, Secretary of State from June 29, 1892, to February 23, 1893.

SIX STATES ADMITTED

More states were admitted into the United States during Benjamin Harrison's administration than in any other. The states were (39-40) North Dakota and South Dakota, November 2, 1889; (41) Montana, November 8, 1889; (42) Washington, November 11, 1889; (43) Idaho, July 3, 1890, and (44) Wyoming, July 10, 1890.

HARRISON HAD FIRST BILLION-DOLLAR CONGRESS

The first congress to appropriate a billion dollars was the 52nd Congress (March 4, 1891 to March 3, 1893) which appropriated $507,376,397.52 in the first session for the fiscal year 1893, and $519,535,293.31 in the second session for the fiscal year 1894. The appropriations included the postal service items payable from postal revenues and estimated permanent annual appropriations including sinking-fund requirements.

HARRISON'S FIRST WIFE

Caroline Scott Harrison was the first President General of the National Society of the Daughters of the American Revolution. The society was organized on October 11, 1890, and incorporated on June 8, 1891.

HARRISON'S SECOND WIFE

Mary Scott Lord Dimmick Harrison, the second wife of Benjamin Harrison, never was mistress of the White House in her own right, although she lived at the White House two years. She was a niece of Caroline Scott Harrison, the President's first wife. She lived at the White House for two years, taking charge of the social functions as Mrs. Harrison had become an invalid. She married the President after the completion of his term of office. They were married at St. Thomas's Protestant Episcopal Church, New York City, by the Reverend J. Wesley Brown.

HARRISON'S DAUGHTER WAS YOUNGER THAN HIS GRAND-CHILDREN

On February 21, 1897, Mary Scott Lord Dimmick Harrison, Harrison's second wife, bore the former President a daughter. The child was younger than Harrison's four grandchildren. Harrison's son, Russell Benjamin Harrison, had two children: Marthena, born January 18, 1888, and William Henry, born August 10, 1896. His daughter, Mary Scott Harrison McKee, had two children: Benjamin Harrison McKee, born in 1887, and Mary Lodge McKee, born in 1888.

GROVER CLEVELAND
24th PRESIDENT

Term of office–Mar. 4, 1893–Mar. 3, 1897

Administration–27th

Congresses–53rd, 54th

Age at inauguration–55 years, 351 days

Lived after term–11 years, 112 days

THE ELECTION OF 1892

NOMINATIONS FOR TERM 1893-1897

Democratic Party Convention (16th)

June 21-23, 1892, in specially constructed building, Chicago, Ill.

Nominated for President—Grover Cleveland, N.Y.

Nominated for Vice President—Adlai Ewing Stevenson, Ill.

Cleveland was nominated on the first ballot. Candidates for nomination and the votes they received:

Grover Cleveland, N.Y., 617^1/$_3$

David Bennett Hill, N.Y., 114

Horace Boies, Iowa, 103

Arthur Pue Gorman, Md., 36^1/$_2$

Adlai Ewing Stevenson, Ill., 16^2/$_3$

John Griffin Carlisle, Ky., 14

William Ralls Morrison, Ill., 3

James Edwin Campbell, Ohio, 2

Robert Emory Pattison, Pa., 1

William Eustis Russell, Mass., 1

William Collins Whitney, N.Y., 1

Total number of votes: 909^1/$_2$

Number necessary for nomination: 607

Nomination made unanimous

Republican Party Convention (10th)

June 7-10, 1892, Industrial Exposition Building, Minneapolis, Minn.

Nominated for President—Benjamin Harrison, Ind.

Nominated for Vice President—Whitelaw Reid, N.Y.

Harrison was nominated on the first ballot. Candidates for nomination and the votes they received:

Benjamin Harrison, Ind., 535^1/$_6$

James Gillespie Blaine, Me., 182^1/$_6$

William McKinley, Ohio, 182

Thomas Brackett Reed, Me., 4

Robert Todd Lincoln, Ill., 1

Total number of votes: 904^1/$_3$

Number necessary for nomination: 453

For additional data see the end of this section and also specific subject headings in the index.

People's Party of America Convention

July 2-5, 1892, Convention Hall Coliseum, Omaha, Neb.
Nominated for President—James Baird Weaver, Iowa
Nominated for Vice President—James Gaven Field, Va.
   Weaver was nominated on the first ballot. Candidates for nomination and the votes they received:
James Baird Weaver, Iowa, 995
James Henderson Kyle, S.D., 265
Seymour Frank Norton, Ill., 1
____Page, 1
____Stanford, 1
Total number of votes: 1,263
Nomination made unanimous
   The People's Party (formed by members of the Farmers' Alliance and other industrial unions) was organized May 19, 1891, at a national convention at Cincinnati, Ohio. The first presidential candidates were nominated in 1892. The People's Party later developed into the Populist Party.

Prohibition Party Convention (6th)

June 29-30, 1892, Music Hall, Cincinnati, Ohio
Nominated for President—John Bidwell, Calif.
Nominated for Vice President—James Britton Cranfill, Tex.
   Bidwell was nominated on the first ballot. Candidates for the nomination and the votes they received:
John Bidwell, Calif., 590
Gideon Stewart, Ohio, 179
W. Jennings Demarest, N.Y., 139
Total number of votes: 908

Socialist Labor Party Convention (1st)

Aug. 28, 1892, New York City
Nominated for President—Simon Wing, Mass.
Nominated for Vice President—Charles Horatio Matchett, N.Y.
   The Social Democratic Workmen's Party of North America, which was formed July 4, 1874, changed its name to the Socialist Labor Party of North America in 1877, at which time it held a national convention at Newark, N.J. No presidential candidates were nominated until 1892 when the party appeared on the ballot in six states.

ELECTION RESULTS, NOV. 8, 1892—PRESIDENTIAL AND VICE PRESIDENTIAL CANDIDATES

Democratic Party (5,556,918 votes)

Grover Cleveland, N.Y.
Adlai Ewing Stevenson, Ill.

Republican Party (5,176,108 votes)

Benjamin Harrison, Ind.
Whitelaw Reid, N.Y.

People's Party (Populists) (1,041,028 votes)

James Baird Weaver, Iowa
James Gaven Field, Va.

Prohibition Party (264,138 votes)

John Bidwell, Calif.
James Britton Cranfill, Tex.

Socialist Labor Party (21,512 votes)

Simon Wing, Mass.
Charles Horatio Matchett, N.Y.

ELECTORAL VOTES (444—44 states)

Cleveland received 62.39 per cent (277 votes—23 states) as follows: Ala. 11; Ark. 8; Calif. 8 (of the 9 votes); Conn. 6; Del. 3; Fla. 4; Ga. 13; Ill. 24; Ind. 15; Ky. 13; La. 8; Md. 8; Mich. 5 (of the 14 votes); Miss. 9; Mo. 17; N.J. 10; N.Y. 36; N.C. 11; N.D. 1 (of the 3 votes); Ohio 1 (of the 23 votes); S.C. 9; Tenn. 12; Tex. 15; Va. 12; W. Va. 6; Wis. 12.

Harrison received 32.66 per cent (145 votes—16 states) as follows: Calif. 1 (of the 9 votes); Iowa 13; Me. 6; Mass. 15; Mich. 9 (of the 14 votes); Minn. 9; Mont. 3; Neb. 8; N.H. 4; N.D. 1 (of the 3 votes); Ohio 22 (of the 23 votes); Ore. 3 (of the 4 votes); Pa. 32; R.I. 4; S. D. 4; Vt. 4; Wash. 4; Wyo. 3.

Weaver received 4.95 per cent (22 votes—4 states) as follows: Colo. 4; Idaho 3; Kan. 10; Nev. 3; N.D. 1 (of the 3 votes); Ore. 1 (of the 4 votes).

The North Dakota vote was divided evenly among the three candidates.

CABINET

March 4, 1893-March 3, 1897

State–William Fisher Wharton, Mass. (assistant secretary), ad interim, continued from preceding administration; Walter Quintin Gresham, Ill., Mar. 6, 1893 (died May 28, 1895); Edwin Fuller Uhl. Mich. (assistant secretary), ad interim May 28, 1895; Alvey Augustus Adee, District of Columbia (second assistant secretary), ad interim May 31, 1895; Edwin Fuller Uhl, Mich. (assistant secretary), ad interim June 1, 1895; Richard Olney, Mass., June 8, 1895; entered upon duties June 10, 1895

Treasury–Charles Foster, Ohio, continued from preceding administration; John Griffin Carlisle, Ky., Mar. 6, 1893

War–Stephen Benton Elkins, W. Va., continued from preceding administration; Daniel Scott Lamont, N.Y., Mar. 6, 1893

Attorney General–William Henry Harrison Miller, Ind., continued from preceding administration; Richard Olney, Mass., Mar. 6, 1893; Judson Harmon, Ohio, June 8, 1895; entered upon duties June 11, 1895

Postmaster General–John Wanamaker, Pa., continued from preceding administration; Wilson Shannon Bissell, N.Y., Mar. 6, 1893; William Lyne Wilson, W.Va., Mar. 1, 1895; entered upon duties April 4, 1895

Navy–Benjamin Franklin Tracy, N.Y., continued from preceding administration; Hilary Abner Herbert, Ala., Mar. 6, 1893

Interior–John Willock Noble, Mo., continued from preceding administration; Hoke Smith, Ga., Mar. 6, 1893; John Merriman Reynolds, Pa., (assistant secretary), ad interim Sept. 1, 1896; David Rowland Francis, Mo., Sept. 1, 1896; entered upon duties Sept. 4, 1896

Agriculture–Jeremiah McLain Rusk, Wis., continued from preceding administration; Julius Sterling Morton, Neb., Mar. 6, 1893

FIFTY-THIRD CONGRESS

March 4, 1893-March 3, 1895

First session–Aug. 7, 1893-Nov. 3, 1893 (89 days)
Second session–Dec. 4, 1893-Aug. 28, 1894 (268 days)
Third session–Dec. 3, 1894-Mar. 3, 1895 (97 days)
Special session of the Senate–Mar. 4, 1893-Apr. 15, 1893 (43 days)
Vice President–Adlai Ewing Stevenson, Ill.
Presidents pro tempore of the Senate–Charles Frederick Manderson, Neb., resigned as president pro tempore Mar. 22, 1893; Isham Green Harris, Tenn., elected Mar. 22, 1893; Matt Whitaker Ransom, N.C., elected Jan. 7, 1895, resigned as president pro tempore Jan. 10, 1895; Isham Green Harris, Tenn., elected Jan. 10, 1895
Secretaries of the Senate–Anson George McCook, N.Y., William Ruffin Cox, N.C., elected Apr. 6, 1893
Speaker of the House–Charles Frederick Crisp, Ga., reelected Aug. 7, 1893
Clerk of the House–James Kerr, Pa., reelected Aug. 7, 1893

FIFTY-FOURTH CONGRESS

March 4, 1895-March 3, 1897

First session–Dec. 2, 1895-June 11, 1896 (193 days)
Second session–Dec. 7, 1896-Mar. 3, 1897 (87 days)
Vice President–Adlai Ewing Stevenson, Ill.
President pro tempore of the Senate–William Pierce Frye, Me., elected Feb. 7, 1896
Secretary of the Senate–William Ruffin Cox, N.C.
Speaker of the House–Thomas Brackett Reed, Me., elected Dec. 2, 1895
Clerks of the House–James Kerr, Pa., Alexander McDowell, Pa., elected Dec. 2, 1895

APPOINTMENTS TO THE SUPREME COURT

Associate Justices
Edward Douglass White, La., Feb. 19, 1894
Rufus William Peckham, N.Y., Dec. 9, 1895

ADMINISTRATION—IMPORTANT DATES

1893, financial panic

May 1, 1893, World's Columbian Exposition (Chicago World's Fair) opened by President Cleveland

Oct. 30, 1893, Sherman Silver Purchase Act repealed

May 1894, President Cleveland sent federal troops to Chicago to stop obstruction of mails by Pullman Company strikers

July 4, 1894, Hawaii made a republic

Aug. 18, 1894, Carey Act passed, providing for land reclamation by irrigation

Feb. 24, 1895, Cuban revolt began

May 20, 1895, income tax declared unconstitutional

Dec. 17, 1895, Cleveland's message to Congress denounced Great Britain's refusal to arbitrate with Venezuela in territorial dispute between Venezuela and British Guinea

Jan. 4, 1896, Utah admitted as the 45th state

CLEVELAND'S VICE PRESIDENT

Vice President–Adlai Ewing Stevenson (23rd V.P.)
Date of birth–Oct. 23, 1835
Birthplace–Christian County, Ky.
Political party–Democratic
State represented–Illinois
Term of office–Mar. 4, 1893-Mar. 3, 1897
Age at inauguration–57 years, 132 days
Occupation after term–Politics
Date of death–June 14, 1914
Age at death–78 years, 234 days
Place of death–Chicago, Ill.
Burial place–Bloomington, Ill.

Additional data on Stevenson

1852, moved to Bloomington, Ill.

1858, admitted to the bar, practiced in Metamora, Ill.

1860, master in chancery, four years

1865, District Attorney, three years

Mar. 4, 1875-Mar. 3, 1877, U.S. House of Representatives (from Illinois)

1876, unsuccessful candidate for reelection to Congress

Mar. 4, 1879-Mar. 3, 1881, U.S. House of Representatives

1880, unsuccessful candidate for reelection to Congress

1885-1889, first assistant postmaster general

1900, unsuccessful candidate for Vice President

1908, unsuccessful candidate for governor of Illinois; retired from public and political activities

ADDITIONAL DATA ON CLEVELAND
CLEVELAND STAGED COMEBACK

Grover Cleveland was inaugurated on March 4, 1885, as the twenty-second President. He was a candidate for reelection in 1888 for the 1889-1893 term but was defeated by Benjamin Harrison, who received 233 of the 401 electoral votes. In 1892 Harrison was a candidate for reelection for the 1893-1897 term but he was defeated by Cleveland, who received 277 of the 444 electoral votes. Cleveland was inaugurated on March 4, 1893. As Cleveland served two non consecutive terms, he is referred to by most authorities as the twenty-second and the twenty-fourth President.

CLEVELAND RECEIVED PLURALITY VOTE THREE TIMES

In the 1884 election Cleveland received 4,874,986 votes while Blaine received 4,851,981. In 1888 Cleveland received 5,540,309 votes, about 100,000 more than Harrison, but Cleveland was not elected as the electoral vote was in Harrison's favor. In 1892 Cleveland received the popular vote plurality for the third time—5,556,918 votes compared with 5,176,108 for Harrison. As he also received the greater electoral vote he was elected President for the second time.

SECOND INAUGURATION

Grover Cleveland took the oath of office on Saturday, March 4, 1893, on the east protico of the Capitol. Chief Justice Melville Weston Fuller administered the oath.

On March 3, 1893, it rained, and at midnight snow and rain began to fall. March 4 was clear, but the ground was covered with one inch of moist snow. Cleveland made an address before taking the oath of office. The inaugural parade lasted about six hours. An inaugural ball was held at the Pension Office, but the fireworks display was postponed until March 6.

CLEVELAND AND THE GEORGE WASHINGTONS

When Grover Cleveland looked over the roster of the 53rd Congress, which took office with him on March 4, 1893, he found that eight congressmen had *George Washington* as their given names:

George Washington Smith, Murphysboro, Ill.
George Washington Fithian, Newton, Ill.
George Washington Ray, Norwich, N.Y.
George Washington Houk, Dayton, Ohio
George Washington Hulick, Batavia, Ohio
George Washington Wilson, London, Ohio
George Washington Shell, Laurens, S.C.
George Washington Murray, Sumter, S.C.

SURGERY PERFORMED ON CLEVELAND

In 1893 President Cleveland was afflicted with cancer of the mouth, the growth necessitating the removal of his upper left jaw. The operation was performed without any publicity on July 1, 1893, aboard Commodore E. C. Benedict's yacht *Oneida* on Long Island Sound. Dr.

Joseph Decatur Bryant was the chief surgeon. In a second secret operation, on July 17, other parts of the growth were removed and the President was fitted with an artificial jaw of vulcanized rubber. By August 7 he had recovered sufficiently to address Congress.

PRESIDENT'S DAUGHTER BORN IN WHITE HOUSE

The first child of a President to be born in the White House was Esther Cleveland, the second child of President and Mrs. Grover Cleveland. She was born on September 9, 1893.

FEDERAL TROOPS DISPATCHED TO MAINTAIN ORDER

Without the request of Governor John Peter Altgeld of Illinois, President Cleveland dispatched federal troops from Fort Sheridan to Chicago, Ill., on July 4, 1894, to maintain order and insure the transportation of mail during the strike of the employees of the Pullman Palace Car Company and the sympathetic strike of railway workers.

THE FIRST LADY

When Grover Cleveland was reelected for a second, nonconsecutive term, Frances Folsom Cleveland, with an experienced hand, resumed her duties as first lady of the land.

FIRST PRESIDENT'S WIFE TO REMARRY

On February 10, 1913, President Cleveland's widow, Frances Folsom Cleveland, married Thomas Jex Preston, Jr., a professor of archeology at Princeton University. (Grover Cleveland had died on June 24, 1908.)

WILLIAM McKINLEY

25th PRESIDENT

Born–Jan. 29, 1843
Birthplace–Niles, Ohio
College attended–Allegheny College, Meadville, Pa.
Date of graduation–Left before graduation
Religion–Methodist
Ancestry–Scotch-Irish
Occupation–Lawyer
Date and place of marriage–Jan. 25, 1871, Canton, Ohio
Age at marriage–27 years, 361 days
Years married–30 years, 232 days
Political party–Republican
State represented–Ohio
Term of office–Mar. 4, 1897-Sept. 14, 1901
Term served–4 years, 194 days
Administration–28th, 29th
Congresses–55th, 56th, 57th
Age at inauguration–54 years, 34 days
Lived after term–Died in office
Date of death–Sept. 14, 1901
Age at death–58 years, 228 days
Place of death–Buffalo, N.Y.
Burial place–Adjacent to Westlawn Cemetery, Canton, Ohio

PARENTS

Father–William McKinley
Born–Nov. 15, 1807, Pine Township, Pa.
Married–Jan. 6, 1829
Occupation–Iron manufacturer
Died–Nov. 24, 1892, Canton, Ohio
Age at death–85 years, 9 days
Mother–Nancy Campbell Allison McKinley
Born–Apr. 22, 1809, near Lisbon, Ohio
Died–Dec. 12, 1897, Canton, Ohio
Age at death–88 years, 234 days

BROTHERS AND SISTERS

William McKinley was the seventh child in a family of nine

Children of William McKinley and Nancy Campbell Allison McKinley

David Allison McKinley, b. 1829, d. Sept. 18, 1892
Anna McKinley, b. 1832, d. July 29, 1890
James McKinley, d. Oct. 11, 1889
Mary McKinley
Helen Minerva McKinley
Sarah Elizabeth McKinley
William McKinley, b. Jan. 29, 1843, d. Sept. 14, 1901
Abbie Celia McKinley
Abner McKinley, b. Nov. 27, 1849, d. June 11, 1904

CHILDREN

Katherine McKinley, b. Jan. 25, 1872, d. July 25, 1875
Ida McKinley, b. Mar. 31, 1873, d. Aug. 22, 1873

MRS. WILLIAM McKINLEY

Name–Ida Saxton McKinley
Date of birth–June 8, 1847
Birthplace–Canton, Ohio
Age at marriage–23 years, 231 days
Children–2 daughters
Mother–Catherine Dewalt Saxton
Father–James Asbury Saxton
His occupation–Banker

For additional data see the end of this section and also specific subject headings in the index.

Date of death–May 26, 1907
Age at death–59 years, 352 days
Place of death–Canton, Ohio
Burial place–Canton, Ohio

Years younger than the President–4 years, 130 days
Years she survived the President–5 years, 254 days

THE ELECTION OF 1896

NOMINATIONS FOR TERM 1897-1901

Republican Party Convention (11th)

June 16-18, 1896, at a specially built auditorium, St. Louis, Mo.
Nominated for President—William McKinley, Ohio
Nominated for Vice President—Garret Augustus Hobart, N.J.
McKinley was nominated on the first ballot. Candidates for nomination and the votes they received:
William McKinley, Ohio, 666 1/2
Thomas Brackett Reed, Me., 84 1/2
Matthew Stanley Quay, Pa., 61 1/2
Levi Parsons Morton, N.Y., 58
William Boyd Allison, Iowa, 35 1/2
James Donald Cameron, Pa., 1
Total number of votes: 907
Nomination made unanimous

Democratic Party Convention (17th)

July 7-11, 1896, the Coliseum, Chicago, Ill.
Nominated for President—William Jennings Bryan, Neb.
Nominated for Vice President—Arthur Sewall, Me.
Bryan was nominated on the fifth ballot. Candidates for nomination and the votes they received on the first and fifth ballots:
Richard Parks Bland, Mo., 235,11
William Jennings Bryan, Neb., 137,652
Robert Emory Pattison, Pa., 97,95
Joseph Clay Stiles Blackburn, Ky., 82, 0
Horace Boies, Iowa, 67, 0
John McLean, Ohio, 54, 0
Claude Matthews, Ind., 37, 0
Benjamin Ryan Tillman, S.C., 17, 0
Sylvester Pennoyer, Ore., 8, 0
Henry Moore Teller, Colo., 8, 0
Adlai Ewing Stevenson, Ill., 6, 8
William Eustis Russell, Mass., 2, 0
James Edwin Campbell, Pa., 1, 0
David Bennett Hill, N.Y., 1, 1
David Turpie, Ind., 0, 1
Total number of votes:
    First ballot: 752
    Fifth ballot: 768
Number necessary for nomination:512
Nominated by acclamation

Populist Party Convention (People's Party, Middle-of-the-Road Party)

July 22-25, 1896, the Auditorium, St. Louis, Mo.
Nominated for President—William Jennings Bryan, Neb.
Nominated for Vice President—Thomas Edward Watson, Ga.
    Bryan was nominated on the first ballot. Candidates for nomination and the votes they received:
William Jennings Bryan, Neb., 1042
Seymour Frank Norton, Ill., 321
Eugene Victor Debs, Ind., 8
Ignatius Donnelly, Minn., 3
Jacob Sechler Coxey, Ohio, 1
    At this convention, the nomination for Vice President was made before the nomination for President

National Democratic Party Convention (Sound Money Democratic Party)

Sept. 2-3, 1896, Indianapolis, Ind.
Nominated for President—John McAuley Palmer, Ill.
Nominated for Vice President—Simon Bolivar Buckner, Ky.
    Palmer was nominated on the first ballot. Candidates for nomination and the votes they received:
John McAuley Palmer, Ill., $763^1/_4$
Edward Stuyvesant Bragg, Wis., $124^1/_2$

Prohibition Party Convention (7th)

May 27-28, 1896, Exhibition Hall, Pittsburgh, Pa.
Nominated for President—Joshua Levering, Md.
Nominated for Vice President—Hale Johnson, Ill.

Socialist Labor Party Convention (2nd)

July 4-10, 1896, Grand Central Palace, New York, N.Y.
Nominated for President—Charles Horatio Matchett, N.Y.
Nominated for Vice President—Matthew Maguire, N.J.

National Party Convention

May 28, 1896, Pittsburgh, Pa.
Nominated for President—Charles Eugene Bentley, Neb.
Nominated for Vice President—James Haywood Southgate, N.C.
    This group bolted from the Prohibition Party and formed a new party advocating a financial plan favoring the free and unlimited coinage of both silver and gold at a ratio of 16 to 1.

National Silver Party Convention (Bi-Metallic League)

July 23-25, 1896, Exposition Building, St. Louis, Mo.
Nominated for President—William Jennings Bryan, Neb.
Nominated for Vice President—Arthur Sewall, Me.
Nominated by acclamation

ELECTION RESULTS, NOV. 3, 1896—PRESIDENTIAL AND VICE PRESIDENTIAL CANDIDATES

Republican Party (7,104,779 votes)

William McKinley, Ohio
Garret Augustus Hobart, N.J.

Democratic Party (6,502,925 votes)

William Jennings Bryan, Neb.
Arthur Sewall, Me.

Populist Party (People's Party) (222,583 votes)

William Jennings Bryan, Neb.
Thomas Edward Watson, Ga.

National Democratic Party (133,148 votes)

John McAuley Palmer, Ill.
Simon Bolivar Buckner, Ky.

Prohibition Party (132,007 votes)

Joshua Levering, Md.
Hale Johnson, Ill.

Socialist Labor Party (36,274 votes)

Charles Horatio Matchett, N.Y.
Matthew Maguire, N.J.

National Party (13,969 votes)

Charles Eugene Bentley, Neb.
James Haywood Southgate, N.C.

ELECTORAL VOTES (447—45 states)

McKinley received 60.63 per cent (271 votes—23 states) as follows: Calif. 8 (of the 9 votes); Conn. 6; Del. 3; Ill. 24; Ind. 15; Iowa 13; Ky. 12 (of the 13 votes); Me. 6; Md. 8; Mass. 15; Mich. 14; Minn. 9; N.H. 4; N.J. 10; N.Y. 36; N.D. 3; Ohio 23; Ore. 4; Pa. 32; R.I. 4; Vt. 4; W. Va. 6; Wis. 12.

Bryan received 39.37 per cent (176 votes—22 states) as follows: Ala. 11; Ark. 8; Calif. 1 (of the 9 votes); Colo. 4; Fla. 4; Ga. 13; Idaho 3; Kan. 10; Ky. 1 (of the 13 votes); La. 8; Miss. 9; Mo. 17; Mont. 3; Neb. 8; Nev. 3; N.C. 11; S.C. 9; S.D. 4; Tenn. 12; Tex. 15; Utah 3; Va. 12; Wash. 4; Wyo. 3.

For the vice presidency the electoral votes were divided as follows:
Hobart, McKinley's Republican running-mate, received 271 votes.
Sewall, Bryan's Democratic running-mate, received 149 votes.
Watson, Bryan's Populist running-mate, received 27 votes.

THE ELECTION OF 1900
NOMINATIONS FOR TERM 1901-1905

Republican Party Convention (12th)

June 19-21, 1900, Exposition Auditorium, Philadelphia, Pa.

Nominated for President—William McKinley, Ohio
Nominated for Vice President—Theodore Roosevelt, N.Y.
First ballot: William McKinley, Ohio, 926
Nomination made unanimous

Democratic Party Convention (18th)

July 4-6, 1900, Convention Hall, Kansas City, Mo.
Nominated for President—William Jennings Bryan, Neb.
Nominated for Vice President—Adlai Ewing Stevenson, Ill.
First ballot: William Jennings Bryan, Neb., 936
Nomination made unanimous

Prohibition Party Convention (8th)

June 27-28, 1900, Chicago, Ill.
Nominated for President—John Granville Woolley, Ill.
Nominated for Vice President—Henry Brewer Metcalf, R.I.
Woolley was nominated on the first ballot. Candidates for nomination and the votes they received:
John Granville Woolley, Ill., 380
Silas Comfort Swallow, Pa., 329

Social-Democratic Party Convention (1st)

Mar. 6-7, 1900, Indianapolis, Ind.
Nominated for President—Eugene Victor Debs, Ind.
Nominated for Vice President—Job Harriman, Calif.
This party was later known as the Socialist Party.

People's Party Convention (Populists—Middle-of-the-road, Anti-Fusionist faction)

May 9-10, 1900, Robinson's Opera House, Cincinnati, Ohio
Nominated for President—Wharton Barker, Pa.
Nominated for Vice President—Ignatius Donnelly, Minn.
Barker was nominated on the second ballot. Candidates for nomination and the votes they received on the first and second ballots:
Milford Wryarson Howard, Ala., 326 6/10, 336
Wharton Barker, Pa., 323 4/10, 370
Ignatius Donnelly, Minn., 70, 7
Seymour Frank Norton, Ill., 3, 2
Total number of votes:
First ballot: 723
Second ballot: 715
Nomination made unanimous

Socialist Labor Party Convention

June 2-8, 1900, Grand Central Palace, New York City
Nominated for President—Joseph Francis Malloney, Mass.
Nominated for Vice President—Valentine Remmel, Pa.
Malloney was nominated on the first ballot. Candidates for nomination and the votes they received:
Joseph Francis Malloney, Mass., 60
VaLENTINE Remmel, Pa., 17

W. B. Hammond, Minn., 1

Union Reform Party

Sept. 3, 1900, Baltimore, Md.
Nominated for President—Seth Hockett Ellis, Ohio
Nominated for Vice President—Samuel T. Nicholson, Pa.

This party was organized Mar. 1, 1899, at Cincinnati, Ohio, by Silver
Republicans, Populists, Socialist Labor Party members, Liberty Party
members, and others.

United Christian Party Convention

May 1-2, 1900, Rock Island, Ill.
Nominated for President—Jonah Fitz Randolph Leonard, Iowa
Nominated for Vice President—David H. Martin, Pa.

The original nominees, Silas Comfort Swallow, Pa., and John Granville Woolley, Ill., declined the nominations.

People's Party Convention (Populists—Fusionist faction)

May 9-10, 1900, in a tent, Sioux Falls, S.D.
Nominated for President—William Jennings Bryan, Neb.
Nominated for Vice President—Adlai Ewing Stevenson, Ill.
Nominated by acclamation

Silver Republican Party Convention

July 5-6, 1900, the Auditorium, Kansas City, Mo.
Nominated for President—William Jennings Bryan, Neb.
Nominated for Vice President—Adlai Ewing Stevenson, Ill.
Charles Arnette Towne was nominated Vice President but declined
the nomination.

This party favored bimetallism, a graduated income tax, and the
direct election of senators. It opposed the importation of Oriental
labor.

National Party Convention

Sept. 5, 1900, Carnegie Lyceum, New York, N.Y.
Nominated for President—Donelson Caffery, La.
Nominated for Vice President—Archibald Murray Howe, Mass.
Both candidates refused the nomination.

ELECTION RESULTS, NOV. 6, 1900—PRESIDENTIAL AND VICE PRESIDENTIAL CANDIDATES

Republican Party (7,207,923 votes)

William McKinley, Ohio
Theodore Roosevelt, N.Y.

Democratic Party (6,358,138 votes)

William Jennings Bryan, Neb.
Adlai Ewing Stevenson, Ill.

Prohibition Party (208,914 votes)

John Granville Woolley, Ill.

Henry Brewer Metcalf, Ohio

Social-Democratic Party (87,814 votes)

Eugene Victor Debs, Ind.
Job Harriman, Calif.

People's Party (Populists—Middle-of-the-Road, Anti-Fusionist faction) (50,373 votes)

Wharton Barker, Pa.
Ignatius Donnelly, Minn.

Socialist Labor Party (39,739 votes)

Joseph Francis Malloney, Mass.
Valentine Remmel, Pa.

Union Reform Party (5,700 votes)

Seth Hockett Ellis, Ohio
Samuel T. Nicholson, Pa.

United Christian Party (5,500 votes)

Jonah Fitz Randolph Leonard, Iowa
David H. Martin, Pa.

ELECTORAL VOTES (447—45 states)

McKinley received 65.33 per cent (292 votes—28 states) as follows: Calif. 9; Conn. 6; Del. 3; Ill. 24; Ind. 15; Iowa 13; Kan. 10; Me. 6; Md. 8; Mass. 15; Mich. 14; Minn. 9; Neb. 8; N.H. 4; N.J. 10; N.Y. 36; N.D. 3; Ohio 23; Ore. 4; Pa. 32; R.I. 4; S.D. 4; Utah 3; Vt. 4; Wash. 4; W. Va. 6; Wis. 12; Wyo. 3.

Bryan received 34.67 per cent (155—17 states) as follows: Ala. 11; Ark. 8; Colo. 4; Fla. 4; Ga. 13; Idaho 3; Ky. 13; La. 8; Miss. 9; Mo. 17; Mont. 3; Nev. 3; N.C. 11; S.C. 9; Tenn. 12; Tex. 15; Va. 12.

FIRST TERM

CABINET
March 4, 1897-March 3, 1901

State—Richard Olney, Mass., continued from preceding administration; John Sherman, Ohio, Mar. 5, 1897; William Rufus Day, Ohio, Apr. 26, 1898; entered upon duties Apr. 28, 1898; Alvey Augustus Adee (second assistant secretary), ad interim Sept. 17, 1898; John Hay, D. C., Sept. 20, 1898; entered upon duties Sept. 30, 1898

Treasury—John Griffin Carlisle, Ky., continued from preceding administration; Lyman Judson Gage, Ill., Mar. 5, 1897

War—Daniel Scott Lamont, N.Y., continued from preceding administration; Russell Alexander Alger, Mich., Mar. 5, 1897; Elihu Root, N.Y., Aug. 1, 1899

Attorney General—Judson Harmon, Ohio, continued from preceding administration; Joseph McKenna, Calif., Mar. 5, 1897; entered upon duties Mar. 7, 1897; John Kelvey Richards, Ohio (solicitor general), ad interim Jan. 26, 1898; John William Griggs, N.J., Jan. 25, 1898; entered upon duties Feb. 1, 1898

Postmaster General–William Lyne Wilson, W. Va., continued from preceding administration; James Albert Gary, Md., Mar. 5, 1897; Charles Emory Smith, Pa., Apr. 21, 1898

Navy–Hilary Abner Herbert, Ala., continued from preceding administration; John Davis Long, Mass., Mar. 5, 1897

Interior–David Rowland Francis, Mo., continued from preceding administration; Cornelius Newton Bliss, N.Y., Mar. 5, 1897; Ethan Allen Hitchcock, Mo., Dec. 21, 1898; entered upon duties Feb. 20, 1899

Agriculture–Julius Sterling Morton, Neb., continued from preceding administration; James Wilson, Iowa, Mar. 5, 1897

SECOND TERM

CABINET

March 4, 1901-September 14, 1901

State–John Hay, D.C., continued from preceding administration; recommissioned Mar. 5, 1901

Treasury–Lyman Judson Gage, Ill., continued from preceding administration; recommissioned Mar. 5, 1901

War–Elihu Root, N.Y., continued from preceding administration; recommissioned Mar. 5, 1901

Attorney General–John William Griggs, N.J., continued from preceding administration; recommissioned Mar. 5, 1901; John Kelvey Richards, Ohio (solicitor general), ad interim Apr. 1, 1901; Philander Chase Knox, Pa., Apr. 5, 1901; entered upon duties Apr. 10, 1901

Postmaster General–Charles Emory Smith, Pa., continued from preceding administration; recommissioned Mar. 5, 1901

Navy–John Davis Long, Mass., continued from preceding administration; recommissioned Mar. 5, 1901

Interior–Ethan Allen Hitchcock, Mo., continued from preceding administration; recommissioned Mar. 5, 1901

Agriculture–James Wilson, Iowa, continued from preceding administration; recommissioned Mar. 5, 1901

FIRST TERM

FIFTY-FIFTH CONGRESS

March 4, 1897-March 3, 1899

First session–Mar. 15, 1897-July 24, 1897 (131 days)
Second session–Dec. 6, 1897-July 8, 1898 (215 days)
Third session–Dec. 5, 1898-Mar. 3, 1899 (89 days)
Special session of the Senate–Mar. 4, 1897-Mar. 10, 1897 (7 days)
Vice President–Garret Augustus Hobart, N.J.
President pro tempore of the Senate–William Pierce Frye, Me.
Secretary of the Senate–William Ruffin Cox, N.C.
Speaker of the House–Thomas Brackett Reed, Me., reelected Mar. 15, 1897
Clerk of the House–Alexander McDowell, Pa., reelected Mar. 15, 1897

FIFTY-SIXTH CONGRESS

March 4, 1899-March 3, 1901

First session–Dec. 4, 1899-June 7, 1900 (186 days)
Second session–Dec. 3, 1900-Mar. 3, 1901 (91 days)
Vice President–Garret Augustus Hobart, N.J., died Nov. 21, 1899
President pro tempore of the Senate–William Pierce Frye, Me.
Secretaries of the Senate–William Ruffin Cox, N.C.; Charles Goodwin
   Bennett, N.Y., elected Jan. 29, 1900
Speaker of the House–David Bremner Henderson, Iowa, elected Dec.
   4, 1899
Clerk of the House–Alexander McDowell, Pa., reelected Dec. 4, 1899

SECOND TERM

FIFTY-SEVENTH CONGRESS

March 4, 1901-March 3, 1903

First session–Dec. 2, 1901-July 1, 1902 (212 days)
Second session–Dec. 1, 1902-March 3, 1903 (93 days)
Special session of the Senate–Mar. 4, 1901-Mar. 9, 1901 (6 days)
Vice President–Theodore Roosevelt, N.Y., succeeded to the presidency
   on the death of William McKinley on Sept. 14, 1901
President pro tempore of the Senate–William Pierce Frye, Me., ree-
   lected Mar. 7, 1901
Secretary of the Senate–Charles Goodwin Bennett, N.Y.
Speaker of the House–David Bremner Henderson, Iowa, elected Dec.
   1, 1901
Clerk of the House–Alexander McDowell, Pa., elected Dec. 2, 1901

APPOINTMENTS TO THE SUPREME COURT

Associate Justice
Joseph McKenna, Calif., Jan. 21, 1898

ADMINISTRATION—IMPORTANT DATES

Feb. 15, 1898, battleship U.S.S. *Maine* blown up in Havana harbor
Apr. 23, 1898, President McKinley issued call for 125,000 volunteers
   to serve two years
Apr. 25, 1898, United States declared war in Spain
May 1, 1898, Commodore Dewey, commander of Asiatic squadron,
   destroyed Spanish fleet at Manila Bay in the Philippines
July 1, 1898, United States Expeditionary Force at Manila
July 1, 1898, first balloon destroyed by enemy gunfire, Santiago, Cuba
July 7, 1898, Hawaii annexed to the United States by act of Congress
   (first island territory annexed)
Aug. 12, 1898, peace protocol signed
Nov. 8, 1898, South Dakota voters approved initiative and referendum
Dec. 10, 1898, Treaty of Paris signed: Spain freed Cuba and ceded
   Puerto Rico, Guam, and the Philippines to the United States, receiv-
   ing $20 million in payment for the Philippines; the United States
   established as a world power
Feb. 4, 1899, Filipino insurgents started unsuccessful guerrilla war

against United States to gain recognition of independence

Mar. 3, 1899, George Dewey made Admiral of the Navy

Apr. 11, 1899, Philippines, Puerto Rico, and Guam formally acquired by the United States

Dec. 2, 1899, American Samoa acquired by treaty

Sept. 8, 1900, Galveston tornado

Nov. 3-10, 1900, first automobile show, New York City

IMPORTANT DATES IN HIS LIFE

18—, attended public schools, Poland Academy, and Allegheny College

1859, taught school near Poland, Ohio

June 11, 1861, enlisted as a private in the 23rd Regiment, Ohio Volunteer Infantry

Sept. 10, 1861, Battle of Carnifax Ferry, his first engagement

Apr. 15, 1862, promoted to commissary sergeant

Sept. 17, 1862, Battle of Antietam

Sept. 24, 1862, commissioned second lieutenant

Feb. 7, 1863, promoted to first lieutenant

July 25, 1864, promoted to captain

Mar. 13, 1865, brevet major of volunteers for gallant and meritorious services at battles of Opequan, Fisher's Hill, and Cedar Creek

July 26, 1865, honorable discharge with rank of captain

1865-1867, studied law

1867, admitted to the bar; practiced at Canton County, Ohio

1869-1871, prosecuting attorney, Stark County, Ohio

Mar. 4, 1877-Mar. 3, 1883, U.S. House of Representatives (from Ohio)

Mar. 4, 1883, presented credentials as a member-elect to the 48th Congress (served to May 27, 1884, when he was succeeded by Jonathan Hasson Wallace, who contested his election)

Mar. 4, 1885-Mar. 3, 1891, U.S. House of Representatives (from Ohio)

June 1888, received two complimentary votes for nomination to the presidency on the Republican ticket

1890, unsuccessful candidate for reelection to Congress

Jan. 11, 1892-Jan. 13, 1896, governor of Ohio

June 1892, unsuccessful candidate for Republican nomination for the presidency

Nov. 1896, nominated as presidential candidate on Republican ticket

Mar. 4, 1897-Mar. 3, 1900, President (first term)

Mar. 4, 1901, inaugurated President (second term)

Sept. 6, 1901, shot by anarchist while attending Pan American Exposition, Buffalo, N.Y.

Sept. 14, 1901, died from wound

WILLIAM McKINLEY

_____was the fifth President born in Ohio.

_____was the seventh President whose mother was alive when he was inaugurated.

_____was the fifth President to die in office.

_____was the third President assassinated.

_____was the second Ohio-born President to be assassinated.

_____was the fifth Ohio-born President elected within twenty-eight years.

McKINLEY'S VICE PRESIDENTS

FIRST TERM

Vice President–Garret Augustus Hobart (24th V.P.)
Date of birth–June 3, 1844
Birthplace–Long Branch, N.J.
Political party–Republican
State represented–New Jersey
Term of office–Mar. 4, 1897–Nov. 21, 1899
Age at inauguration–52 years, 274 days
Occupation after term–Died in office
Date of death–Nov. 21, 1899
Age at death–55 years, 171 days
Place of death–Paterson, N.J.
Burial place–Paterson, N.J.

Additional data on Hobart
1863, graduated from Rutgers College, New Brunswick, N.J.
18—, taught school
1865, clerk for grand jury, Passaic County, N.J.
1869, admitted to the bar; practiced in Paterson, N.J.
1871-1872, city counsel, Paterson, N.J.
1872, counsel, Board of Freeholders
1872-1876, New Jersey State Assembly
1874, speaker, New Jersey State Assembly
1876-1882, New Jersey State Senate
1881-1882, president, New Jersey State Senate

SECOND TERM

Vice President–Theodore Roosevelt (25th V.P.)
Date of birth–Oct. 27, 1858
Birthplace–New York, N.Y.
Political party–Republican
State represented–New York
Term of office–Mar. 4, 1901-Sept. 14, 1901
Age at inauguration–42 years, 128 days
Occupation after term–President
Date of death–Jan. 6, 1919
Age at death–60 years, 71 days
Place of death–Oyster Bay, N.Y.
Burial place–Young's Memorial Cemetery, Oyster Bay, N.Y.

For further biographical information see Theodore Roosevelt, 26th President.

ADDITIONAL DATA ON McKINLEY

McKINLEY CAMPAIGNED BY TELEPHONE

William McKinley was the first President to use the telephone for campaign purposes. In 1896 he telephoned thirty-eight of his campaign managers in as many states from his residence at Canton, Ohio, on matters pertaining to his campaign.

FIRST INAUGURATION

William McKinley took the oath of office on Thursday, March 4, 1897, on the east portico of the Capitol. The oath was administered by Chief Justice Melville Weston Fuller. The ceremonies were climaxed by an impressive parade.

SECOND INAUGURATION

President McKinley took his second oath of office on Monday, March 4, 1901, on the east portico of the Capitol. Chief Justice Melville Weston Fuller administered the oath. The inaugural parade was even larger than the one held during his first inauguration.

Drenched by showers, many spectators left to avoid the downpour. The fireworks scheduled for the evening were postponed because of the rain.

McKINLEY ASSASSINATED

President McKinley was shot on September 6, 1901, at the Pan American Exposition, Buffalo, N.Y., by Leon Czolgosz, a factory worker who was an anarchist. Czolgosz fired two shots from a pistol hidden in his handkerchief. McKinley died on September 14, 1901. Czolgosz was tried in the Supreme Court of New York and was convicted. He was electrocuted on October 29, 1901, at Auburn State Prison, Auburn, N.Y.

THE FIRST LADY

Ida Saxton McKinley had been an invalid for many years before coming to the White House. She was an epileptic and had a seizure at the second inaugural ball. The President was noted for his tender affection for and great devotion to his ailing wife.

THEODORE ROOSEVELT
26th PRESIDENT

Born–Oct. 27, 1858

Birthplace–New York, N.Y.

College attended–Harvard College, Cambridge, Mass.

Date of graduation–June 30, 1880, four-year course, Bachelor of Arts

Religious denomination–Dutch Reformed Church

Ancestry–Dutch

Occupation–Rancher, writer, public official

Date and place of first marriage–Oct. 27, 1880, Brookline, Mass.

Age at marriage–22 years

Years married–3 years, 110 days

Date and place of second marriage–Dec. 2, 1886, London, England

Age at second marriage–28 years, 36 days

Years married–32 years, 35 days

Political party–Republican

State represented–New York

Term of office–Sept. 14, 1901-Mar. 3, 1909 (Roosevelt succeeded to the presidency on the death of William McKinley)

Term served–7 years, 171 days

Administration–29th, 30th

Congresses–57th, 58th, 59th, 60th

Age at inauguration–42 years, 322 days

Lived after term–9 years, 309 days

Occupation after term–Writer, big-game hunter, political leader

Date of death–Jan. 6, 1919

Age at death–60 years, 71 days

Place of death–Oyster Bay, N.Y.

Burial place–Young's Memorial Cemetery, Oyster Bay, N.Y.

PARENTS

Father–Theodore Roosevelt

Born–Sept. 22, 1831, New York, N.Y.

Married–Dec. 22, 1853, Roswell, Ga.

Occupation–Glass importer, merchant

Died–Feb. 9, 1878, New York, N.Y.

Age at death–46 years, 140 days

Mother–Martha Bulloch Roosevelt

Born–July 8, 1834, Hartford, Conn.

Died–Feb. 14, 1884, New York, N.Y.

Age at death–49 years, 221 days

BROTHERS AND SISTERS

Theodore Roosevelt was the second of four children

Children of Theodore Roosevelt and Martha Bulloch Roosevelt

Anna Roosevelt, b. Jan. 7, 1855, d. Aug. 25, 1931

Theodore Roosevelt, b. Oct. 27, 1858, d. Jan. 6, 1919

Elliott Roosevelt, b. Feb. 28, 1860, d. Aug. 14, 1894

Corinne Roosevelt, b. Sept. 17, 1861, d. Feb. 17, 1933

CHILDREN

By First Wife, Alice Lee Roosevelt

Alice Lee Roosevelt, b. Feb. 12, 1884, New York, N.Y.; m. Feb. 17, 1906, Nicholas Longworth, at the White House, Washington, D.C.

By Second Wife, Edith Kermit

For additional data see the end of this section and also specific subject headings in the index.

Carow Roosevelt

Theodore Roosevelt, b. Sept. 13, 1887, Oyster Bay, N.Y.; m. June 20, 1910, Eleanor Butler Alexander, New York, N.Y.; d. July 12, 1944, Normandy, France

Kermit Roosevelt, b. Oct. 10, 1889, Oyster Bay, N.Y.; m. June 11, 1914, Belle Wyatt Willard, Madrid, Spain; d. June 4, 1943, on active military duty in Alaska

Ethel Carow Roosevelt, b. Aug. 13, 1891, Oyster Bay, N.Y.; m. Apr. 4, 1913, Dr. Richard Derby, Oyster Bay, N.Y.

Archibald Bulloch Roosevelt, b. Apr. 9, 1894, Washington, D.C.; m. Apr. 14, 1917, Grace Stackpole Lockwood, Boston, Mass.

Quentin Roosevelt, b. Nov. 19, 1897, Washington, D.C.; d. July 14, 1918, shot down in aerial combat in France

MRS. THEODORE ROOSEVELT (first wife)

Name–Alice Hathaway Lee Roosevelt

Date of birth–July 29, 1861

Birthplace–Chestnut Hill, Mass.

Age at marriage–19 years, 82 days

Children–1 daughter

Mother–Caroline Haskell Lee

Father–George Cabot Lee

Date of death–Feb. 14, 1884

Age at death–22 years, 192 days

Place of death–New York, N.Y.

Burial place–Cambridge, Mass.

Years younger than the President–2 years, 283 days

Years the President survived her–34 years, 326 days

MRS. THEODORE ROOSEVELT (second wife)

Name–Edith Kermit Carow Roosevelt

Date of birth–Aug. 6, 1861

Birthplace–Norwich, Conn.

Age at marriage–25 years, 118 days

Children–4 sons, 1 daughter

Mother–Gertrude Elizabeth Tyler Carow

Father–Charles Carow

Date of death–Sept. 30, 1948

Age at death–87 years, 45 days

Place of death–Oyster Bay, N.Y.

Burial place–Oyster Bay, N.Y.

Years younger than the President–2 years, 293 days

Years she survived the President–29 years, 267 days

THE ELECTION OF 1904

NOMINATIONS FOR TERM 1905-1909

Republican Party Convention (13th)

June 21-23, 1904, the Coliseum, Chicago, Ill.

Nominated for President—Theodore Roosevelt, N.Y.

Nominated for Vice President—Charles Warren Fairbanks, Ind.

First ballot: Theodore Roosevelt, N.Y., 994

Nomination made unanimous

Democratic Party Convention (19th)

July 6-9, 1904, the Coliseum, St. Louis, Mo.

Nominated for President—Alton Brooks Parker, N.Y.

Nominated for Vice President—Henry Gassaway Davis, W. Va.

Parker was nominated on the first ballot. Candidates for nomination and the votes they received:

Alton Brooks Parker, N.Y., 679
William Randolph Hearst, N.Y., 181
Francis Marion Cockrell, Mo., 42
Richard Olney, Mass., 38
Edward C. Wall, Wis., 27
George Gray, Del., 12
John Sharp Williams, Miss., 8
Robert Emory Pattison, Pa., 4
Nelson Appleton Miles, Mass., 3
George Brinton McClellan, N.J., 3
Charles Arnette Towne, Minn., 2
Bird Sim Coler, N.Y., 1
Total number of votes: 1,000
Number necessary for nomination: 667
Nomination made unanimous

Socialist Party Convention

May 1-6, 1904, Brand's Hall, Chicago, Ill.
Nominated for President—Eugene Victor Debs, Ind.
Nominated for Vice President—Benjamin Hanford, N.Y.
  Debs was nominated by acclamation on the first ballot.
  This was the first nominating convention of the Socialist Party,
which was formed March 25, 1900, at Indianapolis, Ind., by a group
of secessionists from the Socialist Labor Party.

Prohibition Party Convention (9th)

June 30, 1904, Indianapolis, Ind.
Nominated for President—Silas Comfort Swallow, Pa.
Nominated for Vice President—George W. Carroll, Tex.

People's Party (Populists)

July 4, 1904, Springfield, Ill.
Nominated for President—Thomas Edward Watson, Ga.
Nominated for Vice President—Thomas Henry Tibbles, Neb.

Socialist Labor Party Convention

July 2-8, 1904, New York, N.Y.
Nominated for President— Charles Hunter Corregan, N.Y.
Nominated for Vice President—William Wesley Cox, Ill.

Continental Party

Aug. 31, 1904, Chicago, Ill.
Nominated for President—Austin Holcomb, Ga.
Nominated for Vice President—A. King, Mo.

United Christian Party Convention

May 2, 1904, St. Louis, Mo.
  A platform was adopted, but no nominations were made for President or Vice President.

274 THEODORE ROOSEVELT

ELECTION RESULTS, NOV. 8, 1904—PRESIDENTIAL AND VICE PRESIDENTIAL CANDIDATES

Republican Party (7,623,486 votes)

Theodore Roosevelt, N.Y.
Charles Warren Fairbanks, Ind.

Democratic Party (5,077,911 votes)

Alton Brooks Parker, N.Y.
Henry Gassaway Davis, W. Va.

Socialist Party (402,283 votes)

Eugene Victor Debs, Ind.
Benjamin Hanford, N.Y.

Prohibition Party (258,536 votes)

Silas Comfort Swallow, Pa.
George W. Carroll, Tex.

People's Party (117,183 votes)

Thomas Edward Watson, Ga.
Thomas Henry Tibbles, Neb.

Socialist Labor Party (31,249 votes)

Charles Hunter Corregan, N.Y.
William Wesley Cox, Ill.

Continental Party (1,000 votes)

Austin Holcomb, Ga.
A. King, Mo.

ELECTORAL VOTES (476—45 states)

Roosevelt received 70.60 per cent (336 votes—32 states) as follows:
Calif. 10; Colo. 5; Conn. 7; Del. 3; Idaho 3; Ill. 27; Ind. 15; Iowa
13; Kan. 10; Me. 6; Md. 1 (of the 8 votes); Mass. 16; Mich. 14;
Minn. 11; Mo. 18; Mont. 3; Neb. 8; Nev. 3; N.H. 4; N.J. 12; N.Y.
39; N.D. 4; Ohio 23; Ore. 4; Pa. 34; R.I. 4; S.D. 4; Utah 3; Vt.
4; Wash. 5; W. Va. 7; Wis. 13; Wyo. 13.

Parker received 29.40 per cent (140 votes—13 states) as follows:
Ala. 11; Ark. 9; Fla. 5; Ga. 13; Ky. 13; La. 9; Md. 7 (of the 8 votes);
Miss. 10; N.C. 12; S.C. 9; Tenn. 12; Tex. 18; Va. 12.

FIRST TERM

CABINET

September 14, 1901-March 3, 1905

State–John Hay, D.C., continued from preceding administration
Treasury–Lyman Judson Gage, Ill., continued from preceding administration; Leslie Mortier Shaw, Iowa, Jan. 9, 1902; entered upon duties Feb. 1, 1902
War–Elihu Root, N.Y., continued from preceding administration; William Howard Taft, Ohio, Jan. 11, 1904, to take effect Feb. 1, 1904

Attorney General–Philander Chase Knox, Pa., continued from preceding administration; recommissioned Dec. 16, 1901; William Henry Moody, Mass., July 1, 1904

Postmaster General–Charles Emory Smith, Pa., continued from preceding administration; Henry Clay Payne, Wis., Jan. 9, 1902; Robert John Wynne, Pa., Oct. 10, 1904

Navy–John Davis Long, Mass., continued from preceding administration; William Henry Moody, Mass., Apr. 29, 1902; entered upon duties May 1, 1902; Paul Morton, Ill., July 1, 1904

Interior–Ethan Allen Hitchcock, Mo., continued from preceding administration

Agriculture–James Wilson, Iowa, continued from preceding administration

Commerce and Labor–George Bruce Cortelyou, N.Y., Feb. 16, 1903; Victor Howard Metcalf, Calif., July 1, 1904

SECOND TERM

CABINET

March 4, 1905-March 3, 1909

State–John Hay, D.C., continued from preceding administration; recommissioned Mar. 6, 1905; died July 1, 1905; Francis Butler Loomis, Ohio (assistant secretary), ad interim July 1-18, 1905; Elihu Root, N.Y., July 7, 1905; entered upon duties July 19, 1905; Robert Bacon, N.Y., Jan. 27, 1909

Treasury–Leslie Mortier Shaw, Iowa, continued from preceding administration; recommissioned Mar. 6, 1905; George Bruce Cortelyou, N.Y., Jan. 15, 1907, to take effect Mar. 4, 1907

War–William Howard Taft, Ohio, continued from preceding administration; recommissioned Mar. 6, 1905; Luke Edward Wright, Tenn., June 29, 1908; entered upon duties July 1, 1908

Attorney General–William Henry Moody, Mass., continued from preceding administration; recommissioned Mar. 6, 1905; Charles Joseph Bonaparte, Md., Dec. 12, 1906; entered upon duties Dec. 17, 1906

Postmaster General–Robert John Wynne, Pa., continued from preceding administration; George Bruce Cortelyou, N.Y., Mar. 6, 1905; George von Lengerke Meyer, Mass., Jan 15, 1907, to take effect Mar. 4, 1907

Navy–Paul Morton, Ill., continued from preceding administration; recommissioned Mar. 6, 1905; Charles Joseph Bonaparte, Md., July 1, 1905; Victor Howard Metcalf, Calif., Dec. 12, 1906; entered upon duties Dec. 17, 1906; Truman Handy Newberry, Mich., Dec. 1, 1908

Interior–Ethan Allen Hitchcock, Mo., continued from preceding administration; recommissioned Mar. 6, 1905; James Rudolph Garfield, Ohio, Jan. 15, 1907, to take effect Mar. 4, 1907

Agriculture–James Wilson, Iowa, continued from preceding administration; recommissioned Mar. 6, 1905

Commerce and Labor–Victor Howard Metcalf, Calif., continued from preceding administration; recommissioned Mar. 6, 1905; Oscar Solomon Straus, N.Y., Dec. 12, 1906; entered upon duties Dec. 17, 1906

FIRST TERM

FIFTY-EIGHTH CONGRESS

March 4, 1903-March 3, 1905

First session–Nov. 9, 1903-Dec. 7, 1903 (29 days)
Second session–Dec. 7, 1903-May 7, 1904 (144 days)
Third session–Dec. 5, 1904–Mar. 3, 1905 (89 days)
Special session of the Senate–Mar. 5, 1903–Mar. 19, 1903 (14 days)
Vice President–Vice President Theodore Roosevelt succeeded to the presidency on the death of William McKinley on Sept. 14, 1901
President pro tempore of the Senate–William Pierce Frye, Me.
Secretary of the Senate–Charles Goodwin Bennett, N.Y.
Speaker of the House–Joseph Gurney Cannon, Ill., elected Nov. 9, 1903
Clerk of the House–Alexander McDowell, Pa., reelected Nov. 9, 1903

SECOND TERM

FIFTY-NINTH CONGRESS

March 4, 1905-March 3, 1907

First session–Dec. 4, 1905-June 30, 1906 (209 days)
Second session–Dec. 3, 1906-Mar. 3, 1907 (91 days)
Special session of the Senate–Mar. 4, 1905-Mar. 18, 1905 (14 days)
Vice President–Charles Warren Fairbanks, Ind.
President pro tempore of the Senate–William Pierce Frye, Me.
Secretary of the Senate–Charles Goodwin Bennett, N.Y.
Speaker of the House–Joseph Gurney Cannon, Ill., reelected Dec. 4, 1905
Clerk of the House–Alexander McDowell, Pa., reelected Dec. 4, 1905

SIXTIETH CONGRESS

March 4, 1907-March 3, 1909

First session–Dec. 2, 1907-May 30, 1908 (181 days)
Second session–Dec. 7, 1908-Mar. 3, 1909 (87 days)
Vice President–Charles Warren Fairbanks, Ind.
President pro tempore of the Senate–William Frye, Me., reelected Dec. 5, 1907
Secretary of the Senate–Charles Goodwin Bennett, N.Y.
Speaker of the House–Joseph Gurney Cannon, Ill., reelected Dec. 2, 1907
Clerk of the House–Alexander McDowell, Pa., reelected Dec. 2, 1907

APPOINTMENTS TO THE SUPREME COURT

Associate Justices

Oliver Wendell Holmes, Mass., Dec. 4, 1902

William Rufus Day, Ohio, Feb. 23, 1903
William Henry Moody, Mass., Dec. 12, 1906

ADMINISTRATION—IMPORTANT DATES

Sept. 18, 1901, commission form of government adopted, Galveston, Tex.

Dec. 11, 1901, first wireless signal received from Europe

May 12, 1902, Pennsylvania coal strike begun

May 20, 1902, Cuban republic inaugurated

June 17, 1902, Newlands conservation act passed

Dec. 14, 1902, laying of Pacific cable began at San Francisco, Calif.

Dec. 19, 1902, U.S. intervention in Venezuelan dispute with European nations

Feb. 14, 1903, Department of Commerce and Labor created

Mar. 19, 1903, reciprocity treaty with Cuba ratified

Oct. 17, 1903, Alaska boundary award made

Nov. 6, 1903, Republic of Panama recognized

Nov. 18, 1903, Isthmian Canal Convention; Panama ceded Canal Zone strip ten miles wide through lease and sale to United States

Dec. 17, 1903, Wright brothers' airplane flight, Kitty Hawk, N.C.

Feb. 26, 1904, Panama Canal Zone formally acquired by the United States

Apr. 30, 1904, President Roosevelt opened Louisiana Purchase Exposition, St. Louis, Mo.

Dec. 2, 1904, President Roosevelt issued corollary to the Monroe Doctrine, defending American intervention in Latin America to stop European aggression

Sept. 5, 1905, Russo-Japanese peace treaty signed, Portsmouth, N.H.

Apr. 18-20, 1906, San Francisco earthquake

June 30, 1906, federal Food and Drug Act passed 1907, financial panic

Oct. 18, 1907, Fourth Hague Convention signed by 32 nations

Nov. 16, 1907, Oklahoma admitted as the 46th state

Dec. 16, 1907, American battleships left on around-the-world cruise

1907-1908, "gentlemen's agreement" with Japan—Japanese declared they would issue no passports to laborors wishing to emigrate to the United States

Feb. 9, 1909, first narcotic prohibition act passed

IMPORTANT DATES IN HIS LIFE

18—, attended public schools

1880, graduated from Harvard

1880-1881, studied law

1882-1884, New York State Assembly

1884-1886, at his North Dakota ranch

1886, returned to New York City; unsuccessful candidate for mayor

May 13, 1889-1895, U.S. Civil Service Commission (appointed by President Harrison)

May 6, 1895, president of New York City Board of Police Commissioners

Apr. 19, 1897, appointed assistant secretary of the Navy

1898, resigned Navy post; organized first regiment U.S. volunteer cavalry, known as "Roosevelt's Rough Riders"

May 6, 1898, lieutenant colonel

July 11, 1898, colonel

Sept. 15, 1898, mustered out of service

1899-1901, governor of New York

1900, nominated as vice presidential candidate on Republican ticket

Mar. 4, 1901, inaugurated Vice President

Sept. 14, 1901, succeeded to the presidency on the death of President McKinley; took oath of office at Buffalo, N.Y.

1904, nominated for another term as President on the Republican ticket

Mar. 4, 1905-Mar. 3, 1909, President (second term)

1906, awarded Nobel Prize for services in connection with Russo-Japanese peace treaty

June 1908, received three complimentary votes at Republican nominating convention

1909, on African hunting and scientific expedition outfitted by the Smithsonian Institution

1910, special ambassador from the United States at the funeral of King Edward VII of England

June 1912, unsuccessful candidate for Republican nomination for the presidency

Aug. 1912, organized Progressive ("Bull Moose") Party; nominated for presidency

Oct. 1913-May 1914, explored River of Doubt in South America

1916, declined nomination by the Progressive Party as presidential candidate

1916-1919, engaged in literary pursuits

THEODORE ROOSEVELT

_____was the third President born in New York

_____was the fourth President to remarry.

_____was the first President to win a Nobel peace prize.

_____was the youngest President at the time he took office.

ROOSEVELT'S VICE PRESIDENT

Vice President–Charles Warren Fairbanks, (26th V.P.)

Date of birth–May 11, 1852

Birthplace–Unionville Center, Ohio

Political party–Republican

State represented–Indiana

Term of office–Mar. 4, 1905-Mar. 3, 1909

Age at inauguration–52 years, 297 days

Occupation after term–lawyer

Date of death–June 4, 1918

Age at death–66 years, 24 days

Place of death–Indianapolis, Ind.

Burial place–Indianapolis, Ind.

Additional data on Fairbanks

1872, graduated from Ohio Wesleyan University, Delaware, Ohio

1874, admitted to the bar in Ohio; practiced in Indianapolis, Ind.

1892, unsuccessful candidate for election to U.S. Senate (from Indiana)

Mar. 4, 1897-Mar. 3, 1905, U.S. Senate (from Indiana)

1916, unsuccessful candidate for vice presidency on Republican ticket headed by Charles Evans Hughes

1916, resumed law practice, Indianapolis, Ind.

ADDITIONAL DATA ON ROOSEVELT

DOUBLE TRAGEDY IN THE ROOSEVELT FAMILY

Thursday, February 14, 1884, was a day of tragedy for Assemblyman Theodore Roosevelt. On that day, at Roosevelt's home in New York City, his mother died of typhoid fever and his wife, Alice, died of Bright's disease.

On February 16, 1884, two hearses were driven from his mother's residence in New York City to the Fifth Avenue Presbyterian Church, where services were conducted by Rev. John Hall, prior to interment in Greenwood Cemetery, Brooklyn, N.Y.

FIRST OATH OF OFFICE

After death of President McKinley, Theodore Roosevelt took the oath of office on Saturday, September 14, 1901, at 3:32 P.M., at the residence of Ansley Wilcox at Buffalo, N.Y. The oath was administered by Judge John R. Hazel of the United States District Court.

THE YOUNGEST PRESIDENT

Theodore Roosevelt was the youngest man to take the oath of office as Chief Executive. He was a little over forty-two years and ten months old when sworn in.

ROOSEVELT RODE IN AUTOMOBILE AND AIRPLANE

The first President to ride in an automobile was Theodore Roosevelt, who was a passenger in a purple-lined Columbia Electric Victoria on a trip through Hartford, Conn., on August 22, 1902. Twenty carriages followed the presidential automobile during its tour of the city.

After his term of office, Roosevelt again pioneered when he took a ride in an airplane on October 11, 1910, at St. Louis, Mo. He was a passenger in an airplane piloted by Archie Hoxsey. Roosevelt was the first of the Presidents to fly in an airplane.

ROOSEVELT APPOINTED COMMERCE AND LABOR SECRETARY

On February 16, 1903, Theodore Roosevelt appointed George B. Cortelyou Secretary of Commerce and Labor, the first man to hold that office.

INAUGURATION IN 1905

Theodore Roosevelt took the oath of office Saturday, March 4, 1905, on the east portico of the Capitol. Chief Justice Melville Weston Fuller administered the oath. A spectacular parade from 3:00 P.M. to 6:15 P.M. was witnessed by more than 200,000 visitors. Although it was very windy, Roosevelt delivered his inaugural address bareheaded, the first President to do so.

LINCOLN'S RING WORN BY ROOSEVELT

Prior to the inauguration, Secretary of State John Hay gave the President a ring that had been worn by Abraham Lincoln and taken off his hand after his death. After the ceremonies, Roosevelt returned the ring to Hay. (John Hay had been Lincoln's private secretary.)

ROOSEVELT VISITED A FOREIGN COUNTRY

Theodore Roosevelt was the first President to visit a foreign country during his term of office. He traveled to Panama on the U.S.S. *Louisiana*. After visiting Panama from November 14 to 17, 1906, he went to Puerto Rico.

PEACE PRIZE TO ROOSEVELT

The first American recipient of a Nobel Prize was Theodore Roosevelt, to whom the $40,000 prize was awarded in 1906 for his services in concluding the treaty of peace between Russia and Japan at the end of the Russo-Japanese War.

ROOSEVELT SUBMERGED IN SUBMARINE

Theodore Roosevelt was the first President to submerge in a submarine. On Friday, August 25, 1905, he went aboard the submarine *Plunger,* commanded by Lieutenant Charles Preston Nelson, in Long Island Sound, off Oyster Bay, N.Y. The *Plunger* submerged to a depth of twenty feet in water from thirty to forty feet deep, remaining stationary for about fifty-five minutes. Roosevelt operated the controls. At one time, the lights were turned off and the *Plunger* operated in complete darkness.

ASSASSINATION OF ROOSEVELT ATTEMPTED

When President Roosevelt was leaving the Hotel Gilpatrick in Milwaukee, Wis., on October 14, 1912, about 8 P.M., en route to the Auditorium to make a speech during the presidential campaign, John Nepomuk Schrank, a saloon keeper, attempted to assassinate him. Roosevelt was shot in the chest. The assassin was opposed to Roosevelt's attempt to capture a third term.

Although the bullet tore through his coat and his shirt was covered with blood, Roosevelt said, " I will deliver this speech or die, one or the other." He began, "Friends, I shall ask you to be very quiet and please excuse me from making you a very long speech. I'll do my best, but you see, there is a bullet in my body. But, it's nothing. I'm not hurt badly." He spoke about fifty minutes and then went to the hospital.

Five alienists decided Schrank was suffering from insane delusions, and on November 13, 1912, he was declared insane. He was committed to the Northern State Hospital for the Insane at Oshkosh, Wis., and died September 15, 1943, at Central State Hospital, Waupun, Wis.

THE PRESIDENT'S FAMILY

When Theodore Roosevelt succeeded to the presidency, Edith Kermit Carow, Roosevelt's second wife, became the first lady, of the land. The White House was a lively place because of the activities of the President's children—four sons and two daughters. During Roosevelt's administration, Alice Lee Roosevelt, the daughter of the President by his first wife, Alice Lee, was married to Nicholas Longworth at the White House.

WILLIAM HOWARD TAFT
27th PRESIDENT

Born–Sept. 15, 1857

Birthplace–Cincinnati, Ohio

College attended–Yale College, New Haven, Conn.

Date of graduation–June 27, 1878

Religion–Unitarian

Ancestry–English

Occupation–Lawyer

Date and place of marriage–June 19, 1886, Cincinnati, Ohio

Age at marriage–28 years, 277 days

Years married–43 years, 262 days

Political party–Republican

State represented–Ohio

Term of office–Mar. 4, 1909-Mar. 3, 1913

Term served–4 years

Administration–31st

Congresses–61st, 62nd

Age at inauguration–51 years, 170 days

Lived after term–17 years, 4 days

Occupation after term–Associate Justice, U.S. Supreme Court

Date of death–Mar. 8, 1930

Age at death–72 years, 174 days

Place of death–Washington, D.C.

Burial place–Arlington National Cemetery, Arlington, Va.

PARENTS

Father–Alphonso Taft

Born–Nov. 5, 1810, East Townshend, Vt.

Married (1)–Fanny Phelps

Married (2)–Louise Maria Torrey

Occupation–Lawyer, U.S. Secretary of War

Died–May 21, 1891, San Diego, Calif.

Age at death–80 years, 197 days

First wife of father–Fanny Phelps Taft

Born–Mar. 28, 1823, West Townshend, Vt.

Married–Aug. 29, 1841, Townshend, Vt.

Died–June 2, 1852, Cincinnati, Ohio

Age at death–29 years, 66 days

Mother–Louise Maria Torrey Taft

Born–Sept. 11, 1827, Boston, Mass.

Married–Dec. 26, 1853, Millbury, Mass.

Died–Dec. 8, 1907, Millbury, Mass.

Age at death–80 years, 88 days

BROTHERS AND SISTERS

William Howard Taft was the seventh of his father's ten children, the second of five children of a second marriage.

Children of Alphonso Taft and Fanny Phelps Taft

Charles Phelps Taft, b. Dec. 21, 1843, d. Dec. 31, 1929

Peter Rawson Taft, b. May 12, 1846, d. June 4, 1889

Mary Taft, b. 1848 (died in infancy)

Alphonso Taft, b. 1850, d. June 2, 1851

Alphonso Taft, b. 1851, d. 1852

Children of Alphonso Taft and Louise Maria Torrey Taft

Samuel Davenport Taft, b. Feb. 1855, d. Apr. 8, 1856

William Howard Taft, b. Sept 15, 1857, d. Mar. 8, 1930

Henry Waters Taft, b. May 27, 1859, d. Aug. 11, 1945

For additional data see the end of this section and also specific subject headings in the index.

Horace Dutton Taft, b. Dec. 28, 1861, d. Jan. 28, 1843

Frances Louise Taft, b. July 18, 1865, d. Jan. 5, 1950

CHILDREN

Robert Alphonso Taft, b. Sept. 8, 1889, Cincinnati, Ohio; m. Oct. 17, 1914, Martha Wheaton Bowers, Washington, D.C.; d. July 31, 1953, New York, N.Y.

Helen Herron Taft, b. Aug. 1, 1891, Cincinnati, Ohio; m. July 19, 1920, Frederick Johnson Manning, Murray Bay, Canada

Charles Phelps Taft, b. Sept. 20, 1897, Cincinnati, Ohio; m. Oct. 16, 1917, Eleanor Kellogg Chase, Waterbury, Conn.

MRS. WILLIAM HOWARD TAFT

Name–Helen Herron Taft
Date of birth–Jan. 2, 1861
Birthplace–Cincinnati, Ohio
Age at marriage–25 years, 168 days
Children–2 sons, 1 daughter
Mother–Harriet Collins Herron
Father–John Williamson Herron
His occupation–Judge
Date of death–May 22, 1943
Age at death–82 years, 140 days
Place of death–Washington, D.C.
Burial place–Arlington National Cemetery, Arlington, Va.
Years younger than the President–3 years, 109 days
Years she survived the President–13 years, 75 days

THE ELECTION OF 1908

NOMINATIONS FOR TERM 1909-1913

Republican Party Convention (14th)

June 16-19, 1908, the Coliseum, Chicago, Ill.
Nominated for President—William Howard Taft, Ohio
Nominated for Vice President—James Schoolcraft Sherman, N.Y.
 Taft was nominated on the first ballot. Candidates for nomination and the votes they received:
William Howard Taft, Ohio, 702
Philander Chase Knox, Pa., 68
Charles Evans Hughes, N.Y., 67
Joseph Gurney Cannon, Ill., 58
Charles Warren Fairbanks, Ind., 40
Robert Marion La Follette, Wis., 25
Joseph Benson Foraker, Ohio, 16
Theodore Roosevelt, N.Y., 3
Total number of votes: 979
Nomination made unanimous

Democratic Party Convention (20th)

July 8-10, 1908, Civic Auditorium, Denver, Colo.
Nominated for President—William Jennings Bryan, Neb.
Nominated for Vice President—John Worth Kern, Ind.
 Bryan was nominated on the first ballot. Candidates for nomination and the votes they received:
William Jennings Bryan, Neb., 888

George Gray, Del., 59
John Albert Johnson, Minn., 46
Total number of votes: 993

Socialist Party Convention

May 10-17, 1908, Brand's Hall, Chicago, Ill.
Nominated for President—Eugene Victor Debs, Ind.
Nominated for Vice President—Benjamin Hanford, N.Y.
  Debs was nominated on the first ballot. Candidates for nomination and the votes they received:
Eugene Victor Debs, Ind., 159
James F. Carey, Mass., 16
Carl D. Thompson, Wis., 14
A.M. Simons, Ill., 9
Nomination made unanimous

Prohibition Party Convention (10th)

July 15-16, 1908, Columbus, Ohio
Nominated for President—Eugene Wilder Chafin, Ill.
Nominated for Vice President—Aaron Sherman Watkins, Ohio
  Chafin was nominated on the third ballot. Candidates for nomination and the votes they received on the third ballot:
Eugene Wilder Chafin, Ill., 636
William B. Palmer, Mo., 451

Independence Party Convention

July 29, 1908, Chicago, Ill.
Nominated for President—Thomas Louis Hisgen, Mass.
Nominated for Vice President—John Temple Graves, Ga.
  Hisgen was nominated on the third ballot. Candidates for nomination and the votes they received on the third ballot:
Thomas Louis Hisgen, Mass., 83
Milford W. Howard, Ala., 38
John Temple Graves, Ga., 7
William Randolph Hearst, N.Y., 2

People's Party (Populist Party)

Apr. 2-3, 1908, St. Louis, Mo.
Nominated for President—Thomas Edward Watson, Ga.
Nominated for Vice President—Samuel Williams, Ind.
  Watson was nominated on the first ballot.

Socialist Labor Party Convention

July 2-5, 1908, New York, N.Y.
Nominated for President—August Gillhaus, N.Y.
Nominated for Vice President—Donald L. Munro, Va.
  Martin R. Preston of Nevada, convicted of killing a man in 1905 and serving a twenty-five-year term in a Nevada penitentiary, was unanimously nominated even though he was also ineligible as he was under constitutional age. Gillhaus was selected later.

United Christian Party Convention

May 1, 1908, Rock Island, Ill.
Nominated for President—Daniel Braxton Turner, Ill.
Nominated for Vice President—Lorenzo S. Coffin, Iowa

ELECTION RESULTS, NOV. 3, 1908—PRESIDENTIAL AND VICE PRESIDENTIAL CANDIDATES

Republican Party (7,678,908 votes)

William Howard Taft, Ohio
James Schoolcraft Sherman, N.Y.

Democratic Party (6,409,104 votes)

William Jennings Bryan, Neb.
John Worth Kern, Ind.

Socialist Party (420,793 votes)

Eugene Victor Debs, Ind.
Benjamin Hanford, N.Y.

Prohibition Party (253,840 votes)

Eugene Wilder Chafin, Ill.
Aaron Sherman Watkins, Ohio

Independence Party (82,872 votes)

Thomas Louis Hisgen, Mass.
John Temple Graves, Ga.

People's Party (Populist Party) (29,100 votes)

Thomas Edward Watkins, Ga.
Samuel Williams, Ind.

Socialist Labor Party (14,021 votes)

August Gillhaus, N.Y.
Donald L. Munro, Va.

United Christian Party (400 votes)

Daniel Braxton Turney, Ill.
Lorenzo S. Coffin, Iowa

ELECTORAL VOTES (483-46 states)

Taft received 66.46 per cent (321 votes—29 states) as follows: Calif. 10; Conn. 7; Del. 3; Idaho 3; Ill. 27; Ind. 15; Iowa 13; Kan. 10; Me. 6; Md. 2 (of the 8 votes); Mass. 16; Mich. 14; Minn. 11; Mo. 18; Mont. 3; N.H. 4; N.J. 12; N.Y. 39; N.D. 4; Ohio 23; Ore. 4; Pa. 34; R.I. 4; S.D. 4; Utah 3; Vt. 4; Wash. 5; W. Va. 7; Wis. 13; Wyo. 3.

Bryan received 33.54 per cent (162 votes—17 states) as follows: Ala. 11; Ark. 9; Colo. 5; Fla. 5; Ga. 13; Ky. 13; La. 9; Md. 6 (of the 8 votes); Miss. 10; Neb. 8; Nev. 3; N.C. 12; Okla. 7; S.C. 9; Tenn. 12; Tex. 18; Va. 12.

CABINET

March 4, 1909-March 3, 1913

State–Robert Bacon, N.Y., continued from preceding administration; Philander Chase Knox, Pa., Mar. 5, 1909

Treasury–George Bruce Cortelyou, continued from preceding administration; Franklin MacVeagh, Ill., Mar. 5, 1909; entered upon duties Mar. 8, 1909

War–Luke Edward Wright, Tenn., continued from preceding administration; Jacob McGavock Dickinson, Tenn., Mar. 5, 1909, entered upon duties Mar. 12, 1909; Henry Lewis Stimson, N.Y., May 16, 1911; entered upon duties May 22, 1911

Attorney General–Charles Joseph Bonaparte, Md., continued from preceding administration; George Woodward Wickersham, N.Y., Mar. 5, 1909

Postmaster General–George von Lengerke Meyer, Mass., continued from preceding administration; Frank Harris Hitchcock, Mass., Mar. 5, 1909

Navy–Truman Handy Newberry, Mich., continued from preceding administration; George von Lengerke Meyer, Mass., Mar. 5, 1909

Interior–James Rudolph Garfield, Ohio, continued from preceding administration; Richard Achilles Ballinger, Wash., Mar. 5, 1909; Walter Lowrie Fisher, Ill., Mar. 7, 1911

Agriculture–James Wilson, Iowa, continued from preceding administration; recommissioned Mar. 5, 1909

Commerce and Labor–Oscar Solomon Straus, N.Y., continued from preceding administration; Charles Nagel, Mo., Mar. 5, 1909

SIXTY-FIRST CONGRESS

March 4, 1909-March 3, 1911

First session–Mar. 15, 1909-Aug. 5, 1909 (144 days)
Second session–Dec. 6, 1909-June 25, 1910 (202 days)
Third session–Dec. 5, 1910-Mar. 3 1911 (89 days)
Special session of the Senate–Mar. 4, 1909-Mar. 6, 1909 (3 days)
Vice President–James Schoolcraft Sherman, N.Y.
President pro tempore of the Senate–William Pierce Frye, Me.
Secretary of the Senate–Charles Goodwin Bennett, N.Y.
Clerk of the House–Alexander McDowell, Pa., reelected Mar. 15, 1909
Speaker of the House–Joseph Gurney Cannon, Ill.

SIXTY-SECOND CONGRESS

March 4, 1911-March 3, 1913

First session–Apr. 4, 1911-Aug. 22, 1911 (141 days)
Second session–Dec. 4, 1911-Aug. 26, 1912 (267 days)
Third session–Dec. 2, 1912-Mar. 3, 1913 (92 days)
Vice President–James Schoolcraft Sherman, N.Y., died Oct. 30, 1912

Presidents pro tempore of the Senate–William Pierce Frye, Me., resigned as president pro tempore Apr. 27, 1911; Charles Curtis, Kan., elected to serve Dec. 4-12, 1911; Augustus Octavius Bacon, Ga., elected to serve Jan. 15-17, Mar. 11-12, Apr. 8, May 10, May 30-June 3, June 13-July 5, Aug. 1-10, and Aug. 27-Dec. 15, 1912; Jan. 5-18 and Feb. 2-15, 1913; Jacob Harold Gallinger, N.H., elected to serve Feb. 12-14, Apr. 26-27, May 7, July 6,31, Aug. 12-26, 1912, Dec. 16, 1912-Jan. 4, 1913, Jan. 19-Feb. 1 and Feb. 16-Mar. 3, 1913; Henry Cabot Lodge, Mass., elected to serve Mar. 25-26, 1912; Frank Bosworth Brandegee, Conn., elected to serve May 25, 1912

Secretary of the Senate–Charles Goodwin Bennett, N.Y.

Speaker of the House–Champ Clark, Mo. elected Apr. 4, 1911

Clerks of the House–Alexander McDowell, Pa., South Trimble, Ky., elected Apr. 4, 1911

APPOINTMENTS TO THE SUPREME COURT

Chief Justice
Edward Douglass White, La., Dec. 19, 1910 (served as Associate Justice, 1894-1910)

Associate Justices
Horace Harmon Lurton, Tenn., Dec. 20, 1909
Charles Evans Hughes, N.Y., May 2, 1910
Willis Van Devanter, Wyo., Dec. 16, 1910
Joseph Rucker Lamar, Ga., Dec. 17, 1910
Mahlon Pitney, N.J., Mar. 13, 1912

ADMINISTRATION—IMPORTANT DATES

Apr. 6, 1909, Peary discovered the North Pole
July 30, 1909, Army officer, B. D. Foulois, made first transcontinental flight
Aug. 2, 1909, U.S. purchased its first airplane
Aug. 11, 1909, first radio SOS from an American ship
Feb. 8, 1910, Boy Scouts of America incorporated
June 1, 1910, Atlantic fisheries dispute settled by the Hague
June 25, 1910, postal savings bank authorized
Jan 3, 1911, postal banks established
Jan. 6, 1911, "Flying Fish," first successful hydroplane, flown
Feb. 15, 1911, U.S. Commerce Court opened
Oct. 18, 1911, keel of *Jupiter,* first electrically propelled vessel of U.S. Navy, laid
Jan. 6, 1912, New Mexico admitted as the 47th state
Feb. 14, 1912, Arizona admitted as the 48th state
Aug. 24, 1912, parcel post service authorized
Nov. 25, 1912, American College of Surgeons incorporated
Jan. 1, 1913, parcel post service began

Feb. 25, 1913, Sixteenth Amendment to the Constitution ratified, giving Congress the power to collect taxes on income

Mar. 4, 1913, Department of Commerce and Labor reorganized as two departments

IMPORTANT DATES IN HIS LIFE

June 5, 1874, graduated from Woodward High School, Cincinnati, Ohio

June 27, 1878, graduated from Yale

May 1, 1880, graduated from Cincinnati Law School

May 5, 1880, admitted to the bar

1880-1881, law reporter on Cincinnati newspapers

1881-1882, assistant prosecuting attorney, Cincinnati, Ohio

1887, assistant city solicitor, Cincinnati

Mar. 7, 1887-Feb., 1890, judge, Superior Court of Cincinnati

Feb. 4, 1890-1892, U.S. Solicitor General

Mar. 17, 1892-1900, U.S. Federal Circuit Court

1896-1900, dean, University of Cincinnati Law School

Mar. 13, 1900-1901, president of Philippines Commission

July 4, 1901, appointed governor-general of Philippine Islands

1902, arranged with Pope Leo XIII for the purchase of Roman Catholic lands in the Philippines

Feb. 1, 1904-June 1908, secretary of war

1907, government mission to Cuba, Panama, and Philippine Islands

1907, provisional governor of Cuba

June 22, 1912, nominated for the presidency by the Republican Party

Apr. 1, 1913-1921, professor of law, Yale

June 30, 1921-Feb. 3, 1930, chief justice, U.S. Supreme Court

WILLIAM HOWARD TAFT

_____was the sixth President born in Ohio.

_____was the first President to become chief justice of the United States Supreme Court.

_____was the first President who had been a member of a cabinet after the Civil War.

_____was the first cabinet member other than a secretary of state to become President.

TAFT'S VICE PRESIDENT

Vice President–James Schoolcraft Sherman (27th V.P.)

Date of birth–Oct. 24, 1855

Birthplace–Utica, N.Y.

Political party–Republican

State represented–New York

Term of office–Mar. 4, 1909-Oct. 30, 1912

Age at inauguration–53 years, 131 days
Occupation after term–Died in office
Date of death–Oct. 30, 1912
Age at death–57 years, 6 days
Place of death–Utica, N.Y.
Burial place–Utica, N.Y.

Additional data on Sherman

1878, graduated from Hamilton College, Clinton, N.Y.

1880, admitted to the bar; practiced in Utica, N.Y.

1884, mayor of Utica, N.Y.

Mar. 4, 1887-Mar. 3, 1891, U.S. House of Representatives (from New York)

1890, unsuccessful candidate for reelection

Mar. 4, 1893-Mar. 3, 1909, U.S. House of Representatives (from New York)

1912, Republican nominee for Vice President

ADDITIONAL DATA ON TAFT

TAFT AT YALE

William Howard Taft stood second in scholarship in the Yale class of 1878, which consisted of 132 graduates. On graduation day, he was 20 years and 285 days old. He was 5 feet $10^3/_4$ inches tall and weighed 225 pounds. The average weight of classmates was 151 pounds.

INAUGURATION

William Howard Taft took the oath of office on Thursday, March 4, 1909, in the Senate Chamber. The oath was to have been administered on the east portico of the Capitol, but as a blizzard was raging the ceremonies were held indoors. The oath was administered by Chief Justice Melville Weston Fuller. It was the sixth time Justice Fuller officiated in this capacity.

Ice forming on trees cracked branches and made transportation so hazardous that incoming trains were prevented from entering the city. Most of the inaugural parade was disbanded; only a small part of the planned parade was held. Mrs. Taft set a precedent by riding to the White House with her husband.

Instead of riding back to the White House with the new President, former President Roosevelt went directly to the railroad station from which he left the city.

SIXTEENTH AMENDMENT ENACTED

The Sixteenth Amendment to the Constitution, granting income tax power to the Federal Government "without apportionment among the several states and without regard to census," was passed by Congress on July 12, 1909, and was ratified by all the states except Connecticut, Florida, Pennsylvania, Rhode Island, Utah, and Virginia. Delaware, New Mexico, and Wyoming all ratified it on February 3, 1913, making it effective. The amendment was declared ratified by the Secretary of State on February 25, 1913.

JAPANESE CHERRY TREES PLANTED

In 1909 Mrs. Taft was instrumental in securing eighty Japanese cherry trees from various nurseries, all that were available at that time. These were planted along the banks of the Potomac River in West Potomac Park.

On December 10, 1909, a shipment of two thousand additional trees, the gift of the City of Tokyo to the City of Washington, reached Seattle, Washington. They were transported to Washington, D.C., where they were destroyed by burning after inspection by the United States Department of Agriculture showed them to be infected with insect pests and fungus diseases. A second consignment of three thousand trees replaced them. The first of these trees was planted by Mrs. Taft on March 27, 1912, the second by Viscountess Chinda, the wife of the Japanese ambassador. The trees were planted around the Tidal Basin and along Riverside Drive in East and West Potomac Parks.

TAFT OPENED BASEBALL SEASON

William Howard Taft was the first President to pitch a ball to open the baseball season. On April 14, 1910, he tossed the baseball which opened the American League game between Washington and Philadelphia. A crowd of 12,226 broke all previous attendance records.

SILVER WEDDING CELEBRATION

President and Mrs. Taft celebrated their silver wedding anniversary at the White House with a night garden party on June 19, 1911, for about five thousand guests. The members of the House of Representatives presented them with a $1,700 solid silver service and the members of the Senate gave them compote dishes.

FIRST PRESIDENT OF FORTY-EIGHT STATES

The forty-eighth state admitted to the United States was Arizona, which became a state on February 14, 1912, during the Taft administration. President Taft thus became the first President of the forty-eight states which comprised the Union until 1959.

VICE PRESIDENT RENOMINATED BUT DIED BEFORE ELECTION

James Schoolcraft Sherman of New York was elected Vice President to serve with President Taft from March 4, 1909 to March 3, 1913. In June 1912 he was renominated by the Republicans for a second term, but he died on October 30, 1912, six days before the election. The eight electoral votes which would have been cast for him had he lived were transferred to Nicholas Murray Butler, nominated by the Republican National Committee.

THE FIRST LADY

As Helen Herron Taft was ill during part of Taft's administration, her sister, Mrs. Louis More, often acted as White House hostess.

PRESIDENT BECAME CHIEF JUSTICE

President Taft was the first and only President of the United States to become a chief justice of the Supreme Court of the United States. Taft was appointed by President Warren G. Harding on June 30, 1921, and he resigned on February 3, 1930, a few weeks before his death.

TAFT BURIED IN ARLINGTON CEMETERY

The first President buried in the National Cemetery at Arlington, Va., was William Howard Taft, interred March 11, 1930.

WOODROW WILSON

28th PRESIDENT

Born–Dec. 28, 1856 (Given name —Thomas Woodrow)

Birthplace–Staunton, Va.

College attended–Princeton University, Princeton, N.J.

Date of graduation–June 18, 1879, B.A.

Religion–Presbyterian

Ancestry–Scotch-Irish

Occupation–Teacher, governor

Date and place of first marriage–June 24, 1885, Savannah, Ga.

Age at marriage–28 years, 178 days

Years married–29 years, 43 days

Date and place of second marriage–Dec. 18, 1915, Washington, D.C.

Age at second marriage–58 years, 355 days

Years married–8 years, 47 days

Political party–Democratic

State represented–New Jersey

Term of office–Mar. 4, 1913-Mar. 3, 1921

Term served–8 years

Administration–32nd, 33rd

Congresses–63rd, 64th, 65th, 66th

Age at inauguration–56 years, 66 days

Lived after term–2 years, 337 days

Occupation after term–Lawyer

Date of death–Feb. 3, 1924

Age at death–67 years, 37 days

Place of death–Washington, D.C.

Burial place–National Cathedral, Washington, D.C.

PARENTS

Father–Joseph Ruggles Wilson

Born–Feb. 28, 1822, Steubenville, Ohio

Married–June 7, 1849, Chillicothe, Ohio

Occupation–Presbyterian minister

Died–Jan. 21, 1903, Princeton, N.J.

Age at death–80 years, 327 days

Mother–Jessie Janet Woodrow Wilson

Born–Dec. 20, 1826, Carlisle, England

Died–Apr. 15, 1888, Clarksville, Tenn.

Age at death–61 years, 116 days

BROTHERS AND SISTERS

Woodrow Wilson was the third child in a family of four.

Children of Joseph Ruggles Wilson and Jessie Janet Woodrow Wilson

Marion Wilson, b. 1850

Annie Josephine Wilson, b. 1854, d. Sept. 15, 1916

(Thomas) Woodrow Wilson, b. Dec. 28, 1856, d. Feb. 3, 1924

Joseph Ruggles Wilson, b. 1866

CHILDREN

By First Wife, Ellen Louise Axson Wilson

Margaret Woodrow Wilson, b. Apr. 30, 1886, Gainesville, Ga.; d. Feb. 12, 1944, Pondicherry, India

Jessie Woodrow Wilson, b. Aug. 28, 1887, Gainesville, Ga.; m. Nov. 25, 1913, Francis Bowes Sayre; at the White House, Washington, D.C.; d. Jan. 15, 1933, Cambridge, Mass.

For additional data see the end of this section and also specific subject headings in the index.

Eleanor Randolph Wilson, b. Oct. 16, 1889, Middletown, Conn.; m. May 7, 1914, William Gibbs McAdoo, at the White House, Washington, D.C.; d. Apr. 5, 1967. Montecito, Calif.

By Second Wife, Edith Bolling Galt Wilson
None

MRS. WOODROW WILSON (first wife)

Name–Ellen Louise Axson Wilson
Date of birth–May 15, 1860
Birthplace–Savannah, Ga.
Age at marriage–25 years, 40 days
Children–3 daughters
Mother–Margaret Hoyt Axson
Father–Samuel Edward Axson
His occupation–Presbyterian minister
Date of death–Aug. 6, 1914
Age at death–54 years, 83 days
Place of death–Washington, D.C.
Burial place–Rome, Ga.
Years younger than the President–3 years, 138 days

Years the President survived her–9 years, 181 days

MRS. WOODROW WILSON (second wife)

Name–Edith Bolling Galt Wilson
Date of birth–Oct. 15, 1872
Birthplace–Wytheville, Va.
Age at marriage–43 years, 64 days
Children–None
Mother–Sallie White Bolling
Father–William Holcombe Bolling
His occupation–Judge
Date of death–Dec. 28, 1961
Age at death–89 years, 64 days
Place of death–Washington, D.C.
Burial place–Washington, D.C.
Years younger than the President–15 years, 291 days
Years she survived the President–37 years, 328 days

At the time of her marriage to President Wilson she was the widow of Norman Galt, whom she had married at Wytheville, Ga., on April 30, 1896, and who had died on January 28, 1908.

THE ELECTION OF 1912

NOMINATIONS FOR TERM 1913-1917

Democratic Party Convention (21st)

June 25-29, July 1-2, 1912, Fifth Maryland Regiment Armory, Baltimore, Md.
Nominated for President—Woodrow Wilson, N.J.
Nominated for Vice President—Thomas Riley Marshall, Ind.

Wilson was nominated on the forty-sixth ballot. Candidates for nomination and the votes they received on the first and forty-sixth ballots:

Champ Clark, Mo., 440½, 84
Woodrow Wilson, N.J., 324, 990
Judson Harmon, Ohio, 148, 0
Oscar Wilder Underwood, Ala., 117½, 12
Thomas Riley Marshall, Ind. 31, 0

Simeon Eben Baldwin, Conn., 22, 0
George Sebastian Silzer, N.J., 2, 0
William Jennings Bryan, Neb., 1, 0
Total number of votes: 1,086
Number necessary for nomination: 545

Progressive Party Convention ("Bull Moose" Party)

Aug. 5-7, 1912, the Coliseum, Chicago, Ill.
Nominated for President—Theodore Roosevelt, N.Y.
Nominated for Vice President—Hiram Warren Johnson, Calif.
    Roosevelt was nominated by acclamation on the first ballot.
    The Progressive Party was organized June 19, 1912, by Roosevelt
supporters who seceded from the Republican party after the nomination of Taft. The nickname "Bull Moose" was derived from Roosevelt's
comparison of his own strength with that of a bull moose.

Republican Party Convention (15th)

June 18-22, 1912, the Coliseum, Chicago, Ill.
Nominated for President—William Howard Taft, Ohio
Nominated for Vice President—James Schoolcraft Sherman, N.Y.
    Taft was nominated on the first ballot. Candidates for nomination
and the votes they received:
William Howard Taft, Ohio, 561
Theodore Roosevelt, N.Y., 107
Robert Marion La Follette, Wis., 41
Albert Baird Cummins, Iowa, 17
Charles Evans Hughes, N.Y., 2
Total number of votes: 728
Of the 1,078 delegates present, 344 did not vote.

Socialist Party Convention

May 12-18, 1912, Tomlinson Hall, Indianapolis, Ind.
Nominated for President—Eugene Victor Debs, Ind.
Nominated for Vice President—Emil Seidel, Wis.
    Debs was nominated on the first ballot. Candidates for nomination
and the votes they received:
Eugene Victor Debs., Ind. 163
Emil Seidel, Wis., 56
Charles Edward Russell, 54
Nomination made unanimous

Prohibition Party Convention (11th)

July 10-12, 1912, Atlantic City, N.J.
Nominated for President—Eugene Wilder Chafin, Ill.
Nominated for Vice President—Aaron Sherman Watkins, Ohio
    Chafin was nominated by acclamation on the first ballot.

Socialist Labor Party Convention

Apr. 7-10, 1912, New York, N.Y.
Nominated for President—Arthur Elmer Reimer, Mass.
Nominated for Vice President—August Gillhaus, N.Y.

ELECTION RESULTS, NOV. 5, 1912—PRESIDENTIAL AND VICE PRESIDENTIAL CANDIDATES

Democratic Party (6,293,454 Votes)

Woodrow Wilson, N.J.
Thomas Riley Marshall, Ind.

Progressive Party (4,119,538 votes)

Theodore Roosevelt, N.Y.
Hiram Warren Johnson, Calif.

Republican Party (3,484,980 votes)

William Howard Taft, Ohio
James Schoolcraft Sherman, N.Y. (votes transferred to Nicholas Murray Butler, N.Y., after the death of Sherman on Oct. 30, 1912)

Socialist Party (900,672 votes)

Eugene Victor Debs. Ind.
Emil Seidel, Wis.

Prohibition Party (206,275 votes)

Eugene Wilder Chafin, Ill.
Aaron Sherman Watkins, Ohio

Socialist Labor Party (28,750)

Arthur Elmer Reimer, Mass.
August Gillhaus, N.Y.

ELECTORAL VOTES (531—48 states)

Wilson received 81.92 per cent (435 votes—40 states) as follows: Ala. 12; Ariz. 3; Ark. 9; Calif. 2 (of the 13 votes); Colo. 6; Conn. 7; Del. 3; Fla. 6; Ga. 14; Idaho 4; Ill. 29; Ind. 15; Iowa 13; Kan. 10; Ky. 13; La. 10; Me. 6; Md. 8; Mass. 18; Miss. 10; Mo. 18; Mont. 4; Neb. 8; Nev. 3; N.H. 4; N.J. 14; N.M. 3; N.Y. 45; N.C. 12; N.D. 5; Ohio 24; Okla. 10; Ore. 5; R.I. 5; S.C. 9; Tenn. 12; Tex. 20; Va. 12; W.Va. 8; Wis. 13; Wyo. 3.

Roosevelt received 16.57 per cent (88 votes—6 states) as follows: Calif. 11 (of the 13 votes); Mich. 15; Minn. 12; Pa. 38; S.D. 5; Wash. 7.

Taft received 1.51 per cent (8 votes—2 states) as follows: Utah 4; Vt. 4.

The Republican electoral votes for the vice presidency were transferred to Butler after the death of Sherman.

THE ELECTION OF 1916

NOMINATIONS FOR TERM 1917-1921

Democratic Party Convention (22nd)

June 14-16, 1916, the Coliseum, St. Louis, Mo.
Nominated for President—Woodrow Wilson, N.J.
Nominated for Vice President—Thomas Riley Marshall, Ind.
First ballot: Woodrow Wilson, N.J., 1,093

Nominated by acclamation

Republican Party Convention (16th)

June 7-10, 1916, the Coliseum, Chicago, Ill.
Nominated for President—Charles Evans Hughes, N.Y.
Nominated for Vice President—Charles Warren Fairbanks, Ind.
   Hughes was nominated on the third ballot. Candidates for nomination and the votes they received on the first and third ballots:
Charles Evans Hughes, N.Y., 253$^1/_2$, 949$^1/_2$
John Wingate Weeks, Mass., 105, 3
Elihu Root. N.Y., 103, 0
Albert Baird Cummins, Iowa, 85, 0
Theodore Elijah Burton, Ohio, 77$^1/_2$, 0
Charles Warren Fairbanks, Ind., 74$^1/_2$, 0
Laurence Yates Sherman, Ill., 66, 0
Theodore Roosevelt, N.Y., 65, 18$^1/_2$
Philander Chase Knox, Pa., 36, 0
Henry Ford, Mich., 32, 0
Martin Grove Brumbaugh, Pa., 29, 0
Robert Marion La Follette, Wis., 25, 3
William Howard Taft, Ohio, 14, 0
Thomas Coleman Du Pont, Del., 12, 5
Frank Bartlett Willis, Ohio, 4, 0
William Edgar Borah, Idaho, 2, 0
Samuel Walker McCall, Mass., 1, 0
Henry Cabot Lodge, Mass., 0, 7
Total number of votes:
   First ballot: 984$^1/_2$
   Third ballot: 986

Socialist Party

Mar. 10-11, 1916, Chicago, Ill.
Nominated for President—Allan Louis Benson, N.Y.
Nominated for Vice President—George Ross Kirkpatrick, N.J.
   Ballots sent by mail to state organizations were counted at this meeting, which served in place of a national convention. The ballots were cast as follows:
Allan Louis Benson, N.Y., 16,639
James Hudson Maurer, Pa., 12,264
Arthur Lesueur, N.D., 3,495

Prohibition Party Convention

July 19-21, 1916, St. Paul, Minn.
Nominated for President—James Franklin Hanly, Ind.
Nominated for Vice President—Ira Landrith, Tenn.

Socialist Labor Party Convention

Apr. 29-30, May 1-3, 1916, New York, N.Y.
Nominated for President—Arthur Elmer Reimer, Mass.
Nominated for Vice President—Caleb Harrison, Ill.

Progressive Party Convention

June 7-10, 1916, Auditorium, Chicago, Ill.
Nominated for President—Theodore Roosevelt, N.Y.
Nominated for Vice President—John Milliken Parker, La.

Roosevelt declined the nomination. In accord with his wishes, the Republican candidate, Hughes, was endorsed. The Progressive Party went out of existence before the election.

ELECTION RESULTS, NOV. 7, 1916—PRESIDENTIAL AND VICE PRESIDENTIAL CANDIDATES

Democratic Party (9,129,606 votes)

Woodrow Wilson, N.J.
Thomas Riley Marshall, Ind.

Republican Party (8,538,221 votes)

Charles Evans Hughes, N.Y.
Charles Warren Fairbanks, Ind.

Socialist Party (585,113 votes)

Allan Louis Benson, N.Y.,
George Ross Kirkpatrick, N.J.

Prohibition Party (220,506 votes)

James Franklin Hanly, Ind.
Ira Landrith, Mass.

Socialist Labor Party (13,403 votes)

Arthur Elmer Reimer, Mass.
Caleb Harrison, Ill.

ELECTORAL VOTES (531—48 states)

Wilson received 52.17 per cent (277 votes—30 states) as follows: Ala. 12; Ariz. 3; Ark. 9; Calif. 13; Colo. 6; Fla. 6; Ga. 14; Idaho 4; Kan. 10; Ky. 13; La. 10; Md. 8; Miss. 10; Mo. 18; Mont. 4; Neb. 8; Nev. 3; N.H. 4; N.M. 3; N.C. 12; N.D. 5; Ohio 24; Okla. 10; S.C. 9; Tenn. 12; Tex. 20; Utah 4; Va. 12; Wash. 7; W.Va. 1 (of the 8 votes); Wyo. 3.

Hughes received 47.83 per cent (254 votes—18 states) as follows: Conn. 7; Del. 3; Ill. 29; Ind. 15; Iowa 13; Me. 6; Mass. 18; Mich. 15; Minn. 12; N.J. 14; N.Y. 45; Ore. 5; Pa. 38; R.I. 5; S.D. 4; Vt. 4; W.Va. 7 (of the 8 votes); Wis. 13.

FIRST TERM

CABINET

March 4, 1913-March 3, 1917

State—Philander Chase Knox, Pa., continued from preceding administration; William Jennings Bryan, Neb., Mar. 5, 1913; Robert Lansing, N.Y. (counselor), ad interim June 9, 1915; Robert Lansing, N.Y., June 23, 1915

Treasury–Franklin MacVeagh, Ill., continued from preceding administration; William Gibbs McAdoo, N.Y., Mar. 5, 1913; entered upon duties Mar. 6, 1913

War–Henry Lewis Stimson, N.Y., continued from preceding administration; Lindley Miller Garrison, N.J., Mar. 5, 1913; Hugh Lenox Scott (United States Army), ad interim Feb. 12, 1916; served Feb. 11-Mar. 8, 1916; Newton Diehl Baker, Ohio, Mar. 7, 1916; entered upon duties Mar. 9, 1916

Attorney General–George Woodward Wickersham, N.Y., continued from preceding administration; James Clark McReynolds, Tenn., Mar. 5, 1913; entered upon duties Mar. 6, 1913; Thomas Watt Gregory, Tex., Aug. 29, 1914; entered upon duties Sept. 3, 1914

Postmaster General–Frank Harris Hitchcock, Mass., continued from preceding administration; Albert Sidney Burleson, Tex., Mar. 5, 1913

Navy–George von Lengerke Meyer, Mass., continued from preceding administration; Josephus Daniels, N.C., Mar. 5, 1913

Interior–Walter Lowrie Fisher, Ill., continued from preceding administration; Franklin Knight Lane, Calif., Mar. 5, 1913

Agriculture–James Wilson, Iowa, continued from preceding administration; David Franklin Houston, Mo., Mar. 5, 1913; entered upon duties Mar. 6, 1913

Commerce–Charles Nagel, Mo. (secretary of commerce and labor), continued from preceding administration; William Cox Redfield, N.Y., Mar. 5, 1913

Labor–Charles Nagel, Mo. (secretary of commerce and labor), continued from preceding administration; William Bauchop Wilson, Pa., Mar. 5, 1913

SECOND TERM

CABINET

March 4, 1917-March 3, 1921

State–Robert Lansing, N.Y., continued from preceding administration; Frank Lyon Polk, N.Y. (under secretary), ad interim Feb. 14, 1920-Mar. 13, 1920; Bainbridge Colby, N.Y., Mar. 22, 1920; entered upon duties Mar. 23, 1920

Treasury–William Gibbs McAdoo, N.Y., continued from preceding administration; Carter Glass, Va., Dec. 6, 1918; entered upon duties Dec. 16, 1918; David Franklin Houston, Mo., Jan. 31, 1920; entered upon duties Feb. 2, 1920

War–Newton Diehl Baker, Ohio, continued from preceding administration

Attorney General–Thomas Watt Gregory, Tex., continued from preceding administration; Alexander Mitchell Palmer, Pa., Mar. 5, 1919

Postmaster General–Albert Sidney Burleson, Tex., continued from preceding administration; recommissioned Jan. 24, 1918

Navy–Josephus Daniels, N.C., continued from preceding administration

Interior–Franklin Knight Lane, Calif., continued from preceding administration; John Barton Payne, Ill., Feb. 28, 1920, entered upon duties Mar. 13, 1920

Agriculture–David Franklin Houston, Mo., continued from preceding administration; Edwin Thomas Meredith, Iowa, Jan. 31, 1920; entered upon duties Feb. 2, 1920

Commerce–William Cox Redfield, N.Y., continued from preceding administration; Joshua Willis Alexander, Mo., Dec. 11, 1919; entered upon duties Dec. 16, 1919

Labor–William Bauchop Wilson, Pa., continued from preceding administration

FIRST TERM

SIXTY-THIRD CONGRESS

March 4, 1913-March 3, 1915

First Session–Apr. 7, 1913-Dec. 1, 1913 (239 days)
Second session–Dec. 1, 1913-Oct. 24, 1914 (328 days)
Third session–Dec. 7, 1914-Mar. 3, 1915 (87 days)
Special session of the Senate–Mar. 4, 1913-Mar. 17, 1913 (13 days)
Vice President–Thomas Riley Marshall, Ind.
President pro tempore of the Senate–James Paul Clarke, Ark., elected Mar. 13, 1913
Secretaries of the Senate–Charles Goodwin Bennett, N.Y., James Marion Baker, S.C., elected Mar. 13, 1913
Speaker of the House–Champ Clark, Mo., reelected Apr. 7, 1913
Clerk of the House–South Trimble, Ky., reelected Apr. 7, 1913

SIXTY-FOURTH CONGRESS

March 4, 1915-March 3, 1917

First session–Dec. 6, 1915-Sept. 8, 1916 (278 days)
Second session–Dec. 4, 1916-Mar. 3, 1917 (90 days)
Vice President–Thomas Riley Marshall, Ind.
Presidents pro tempore of the Senate–James Paul Clarke, Ark., reelected Dec. 6, 1915, died Oct. 1, 1916; Willard Saulsbury, Del., elected Dec. 14, 1916
Secretary of the Senate–James Marion Baker, S.C.
Speaker of the House–Champ Clark, Mo., reelected Dec. 6, 1915
Clerk of the House–South Trimble, Ky., reelected Dec. 6, 1915

SECOND TERM

SIXTY-FIFTH CONGRESS

March 4, 1917-March 3, 1919

First session–Apr. 2, 1917-Oct. 6, 1917 (188 days)
Second session–Dec. 3, 1917-Nov. 21, 1918 (354 days)
Third session–Dec. 2, 1918-Mar. 3, 1919 (92 days)
Special session of the Senate–Mar. 5, 1917-Mar. 16, 1917
Vice President–Thomas Riley Marshall, Ind.

President pro tempore of the Senate–Willard Saulsbury, Del.
Secretary of the Senate–James Marion Baker, S.C.
Speaker of the House–Champ Clark Mo., reelected Apr. 2, 1917
Clerk of the House–South Trimble, Ky., reelected Apr. 2, 1917

SIXTY-SIXTH CONGRESS

March 4, 1919-March 3, 1921

First session–May 19, 1919-Nov. 19, 1919 (185 days)
Second session–Dec. 1, 1919-June 5, 1920 (188 days)
Third session–Dec. 6, 1920-Mar. 3, 1921 (88 days)
Vice President–Thomas Riley Marshall, Ind.
President pro tempore of the Senate–Albert Baird Cummins, Iowa, elected May 19, 1919
Secretaries of the Senate–James Marion Baker, S.C.; George Andrew Sanderson, Ill., elected May 19, 1919
Speaker of the House–Frederick Huntington Gillett, Mass., elected May 19, 1919
Clerks of the House–South Trimble, Ky.; William Tyler Page, Md., elected May 19, 1919

APPOINTMENTS TO THE SUPREME COURT

Associate Justices
James Clark McReynolds, Tenn., Aug. 29, 1914
Louis Dembitz Brandeis, Mass., June 1, 1916
John Hessin Clarke, Ohio, July 24, 1916

ADMINISTRATION — IMPORTANT DATES

May 31, 1913, Seventeenth Amendment to the Constitution ratified (direct election of senators)
Dec. 23, 1913, Federal Reserve Act.
Apr. 22, 1914, Vera Cruz taken by U.S. Navy
Aug. 15, 1914, Panama Canal admitted commercial traffic
Sept. 26, 1914, Federal Trade Commission established
Oct. 15, 1914, Clayton Anti-trust Act passed
Nov. 23, 1914, U.S. troops withdrawn from Vera Cruz
Jan. 25, 1915, New York to San Francisco trans continental telephone demonstration
Feb. 20, 1915, Panama-Pacific Exposition opened, San Francisco, Calif.
May 7, 1915, sinking of *Lusitania* by German submarine
Oct. 19, 1915, United States recognized de facto government of Carranza in Mexico
Feb. 28, 1916, treaty signed with Haitian government for United States to assume protectorate over Haiti
Mar. 1916, General Pershing with 6,000 troops sent to Mexico in pursuit of revolutionary bandit Francisco ("Pancho") Villa
July 17, 1916, Federal Farm Loan Act signed
Aug. 4, 1916, Danish West Indies (Virgin Islands) bought from Denmark for $25 million
Sept. 1, 1916, Keating-Owen Child Labor Act signed

Sept. 3, 1916, Adamson Act established eight-hour day on railroads

Sept. 7, 1916, Senate ratified treaty to purchase Danish West Indies (Virgin Islands)

Nov. 1916, Jeannette Rankin of Montana elected as first congresswoman

Mar. 19, 1917, Supreme Court ruled that Congress has the power to deal with wages and hours of work of railroad employees in interstate commerce

Apr. 6, 1917, United States declared war against Germany

June 8, 1917, advance unit of American Expeditionary Force landed at Liverpool, England

July 28, 1917, War Industries Board created

Dec. 7, 1917, United States declared war against Austria-Hungary

Dec. 26, 1917, railroads placed under government operation

Jan 1, 1918, government operation of railroads

Jan. 8, 1918, Wilson outlined his "fourteen points" to Congress

Nov. 11, 1918, armistice signed at 11 A.M.

Jan. 29, 1919, Eighteenth Amendment to the Constitution ratified (prohibition of liquor manufacture, sale, and transportation)

June 28, 1919, Treaty of Versailles signed

Nov. 19, 1919, Treaty of Versailles rejected by the Senate

Jan. 13, 1920, first meeting of League of Nations called; United States not represented

June 10, 1920, Federal Water Power Act approved

Aug. 26, 1920, Nineteenth Amendment to the Constitution ratified (woman suffrage)

Feb. 22, 1921, first transcontinental airmail flight from San Francisco to New York

IMPORTANT DATES IN HIS LIFE

1856, family moved to Augusta, Ga.

1870, family moved to Columbia, S.C.

1873, entered Davidson College, Davidson, N.C.

1874, withdrew from college because of ill health

Sept. 1875, entered the College of New Jersey (now Princeton)

June 18, 1879, graduated from Princeton

Oct. 2, 1879, entered University of Virginia Law School

1880, left school because of ill health

June 30, 1881, graduated from law school

1882, admitted to the bar

1882-1883, practiced law at Atlanta, Ga., with partner, Edward I. Renick

1885, taught history and political science at Bryn Mawr College, Bryn Mawr, Pa.

June 1886, received Ph.D. degree in political science from Johns Hopkins University

1888-1890, taught at Wesleyan University, Middletown, Conn.

1890-1902, professor of jurisprudence and political economy, Princeton University

June 9, 1902, unanimously elected president of Princeton University
Oct. 25, 1902-Oct. 23, 1910, president of Princeton University
Sept. 15, 1910, nominated by the Democrats as candidate for governor of New Jersey
Jan. 7, 1911-Mar. 1, 1913, governor of New Jersey
July 2, 1912, nominated by the Democrats for the presidency
Nov. 5, 1912, elected President of the United States
Mar. 4, 1913-Mar. 3, 1921, President
Dec. 8, 1915, married Edith Bolling Galt at Washington, D.C.
Dec. 4, 1918, sailed for Europe to attend Peace Conference at Paris
Jan. 18, 1919, addressed opening session of Paris Peace Conference
Feb. 1919, returned to United States
Mar. 1919, sailed for Europe
June 28, 1919, signed peace treaty with Germany at Versailles, France
July 8, 1919, returned to United States
Sept. 26, 1919, collapsed; suffered paralytic stroke at Pueblo, Colo.
Oct. 2, 1919, stroke paralyzed his left arm and leg
Oct. 4, 1919, complete physical breakdown
Dec. 10, 1920, awarded Nobel Peace Prize
Mar. 4, 1921, after inauguration of his successor retired to his Washington, D.C., residence, where his health continued to deteriorate

WOODROW WILSON

_____was the eighth President born in Virginia.

_____was the second Democratic President since the Civil War.

_____was the first President who majored in history and government at college.

_____was the first President who had been president of a major university.

_____was the fourth President inaugurated on March 5, (March 4 was a Sunday).

_____was the eleventh President who was a resident of a state other than his native state.

_____was the third President whose wife died while he was in office.

_____was the fifth President to remarry.

_____was the sixth President to marry a widow.

_____was the third President married while in office.

_____was the only President who had two daughters who married in the White House.

WILSON'S VICE PRESIDENT

Vice President–Thomas Riley Marshall (28th V.P.)
Date of birth–Mar. 14, 1854
Birthplace–North Manchester, Ind.
Political party–Democratic
State represented–Indiana
Term of office–Mar. 4, 1913-Mar. 3, 1921
Age at inauguration–58 years, 355 days
Occupation after term–Lawyer and writer

Date of death–June 1, 1925
Age at death–71 years, 79 days
Place of death–Washington, D.C.
Burial place–Indianapolis, Ind.

Additional data on Marshall

1873, graduated from Wabash College, Crawfordsville, Ind.
1875, admitted to the bar; practiced at Columbia City, Ind.
1909-1913, governor of Indiana
1922-1923, member of Federal Coal Commission

ADDITIONAL DATA ON WILSON

EXTRAORDINARY POLITICAL RISE OF WILSON

Within two years and 170 days, Woodrow Wilson rose from a citizen who had never held public office to President of the United States. Wilson had never been a candidate for political office until September 15, 1910, when the Democrats nominated him for governor of New Jersey. He took office on January 17, 1911, and served two years. On July 2, 1912, he was nominated as the Democratic candidate for the presidency; on November 5, 1912, he was elected; and on March 4, 1913, he took office as President.

THREE PRESIDENTIAL RIVALS

The three men who served as Presidents of the United States from September 14, 1901, to March 3, 1921, were all candidates for the presidency on November 5, 1912, each representing a different political party. The candidates were Theodore Roosevelt, Progressive, who served from September 14, 1901, to March 3, 1909, William Howard Taft, Republican, who served from March 4, 1909, to March 3, 1913; and Woodrow Wilson, Democrat, who was to serve from March 4, 1913, to March 3, 1921.

Taft received 3,484,980 popular votes, and Roosevelt received 4,119,538 votes; their combined total was 7,604,518 votes. Wilson, who had 6,293,454 votes, had a plurality. He was elected with 435 electoral votes to Roosevelt's 88 votes and Taft's 8 votes. Wilson was the only President who silmultaneously defeated two other Presidents in one election.

FIRST INAUGURATION

Woodrow Wilson took the oath of office on Tuesday, March 4, 1913, on the east portico of the Capitol. The oath was administered by Chief Justice Edward Douglass White. The day was cold and disagreeable.

WILSON APPOINTED NAMESAKE TO CABINET

Woodrow Wilson was the only President who had a cabinet member with the same last name as his own—Secretary of Labor William Bauchop Wilson of Pennsylvania, who took office on March 5, 1913.

WILSON APPOINTED FIRST SECRETARY OF LABOR

The work of Secretary of Commerce and Labor was divided into two separate departments with the passing of a law by the Sixty-second Congress. On March 5, 1913, President Wilson appointed William Cox Redfield as Secretary of Commerce and William Bauchop Wilson as Secretary of Labor.

WILSON HELD FIRST PRESS CONFERENCE

The first presidential press conference was held on March 15, 1913, eleven days after his inauguration, by President Wilson at the Executive Offices in the White House. Newsmen who covered White House news were invited, and about 125 attended. The meeting was suggested by Joseph Patrick Tumulty, Wilson's private secretary. Previously news conferences had been limited to selected and favored newsmen.

WILSON EARNED DOCTORATE

Woodrow Wilson was the first President who had earned a doctoral degree. His thesis, *Congressional Government, a Study in American Politics,* earned him his doctorate from Johns Hopkins University in 1886. The work contained 333 pages and was published October 7, 1884, by Houghton Miffin Company, Boston, Mass. It ran into fifteen editions.

SEVENTEENTH AMENDMENT ENACTED

The Seventeenth Amendment to the Constitution, providing for direct election of United States senators, was passed by Congress on May 13, 1912. It was proposed to the legislatures of the several states by the Sixty-second Congress on May 16, 1912, and adopted by all the states except Alabama, Delaware, Florida, Georgia, Kentucky, Louisiana, Maryland, Mississippi, Rhode Island, South Carolina, Utah and Virginia. The thirty-sixth state to ratify, making it effective, was Connecticut, on April 8, 1913. The amendment was declared ratified by the Secretary of State on May 31, 1913.

WILSON APPOINTED BRANDEIS

The first Jewish associate justice of the Supreme Court was Louis Dembitz Brandeis, appointed on January 28, 1916, by President Woodrow Wilson. The nomination was confirmed by the Senate on June 1, 1916, and Brandeis was sworn in on June 3, 1916. He served until February 13, 1939.

WILSON INTENDED TO RESIGN

Wilson wrote to Secretary of State Robert Lansing on November 5, 1916, two days prior to his reelection:

What would it be my duty to do were Mr. [Charles Evans] Hughes to be elected? Four months would elapse before he could take charge of the affairs of the government, and during those four months I would be without such moral backing from the nation as would be necessary to steady and control our relations with other governments. I would be known to be the rejected, not the accredited, spokesman of the country; and yet the accredited spokesman would be without legal authority to speak for the nation. Such a situation would be fraught with the gravest dangers. The direction of the foreign policy of the government would in effect have been taken out of my hands and yet its new definition would be impossible until March.

I feel that it would be my duty to relieve the country of the perils of such a situation at once. The course I have in mind is dependent upon the consent and cooperation of the Vice President; but if I could gain his consent to the plan, I would ask your permission to invite Mr. Hughes to become Secretary of State and would then join the Vice President in resigning, and thus open to Mr. Hughes the immediate succession to the presidency.

The election of Woodrow Wilson and Thomas Riley Marshall for a second term made this drastic action unnecessary.

FINAL COUNT CHANGED RESULTS

The early returns of the election of November 7, 1916, indicated that Wilson had been defeated and that Charles Evans Hughes had been elected President. Many newspapers carried the news of Wilson's defeat. When the votes of California were finally tabulated, Hughes lost the state by approximately 4,000 votes—a loss which insured the election of Wilson.

SECOND INAUGURATION

Woodrow Wilson took the oath of office Monday, March 5, 1917, as March 4 fell on Sunday for the fifth time in the history of the country. Chief Justice Edward Douglass White again administered the oath to him.

WILSON'S FOURTEEN POINTS

The fourteen points which President Wilson announced to Congress in January 1918 as necessary for world peace were the following:

1. Open treaties openly arrived at through international diplomacy
2. Freedom of the seas
3. Free international trade
4. Reduction of national armaments
5. Impartial adjustment of colonial claims
6. Evacuation of Russian territory
7. Evacuation of Belgium
8. Evacuation of French territory and return of Alsace-Lorraine to France
9. Readjustment of Italian frontiers
10. Autonomy for Austria and Hungary
11. Evacuation of Rumania, Serbia, and Montenegro, and security for the Balkan States
12. Self-determination for the peoples of the Turkish empire
13. Independence for Poland
14. Formation of a "general association of nations"

WILSON VISITED EUROPE

Woodrow Wilson was the first President of the United States to cross the Atlantic while in office. He left Washington, D.C., December 4, 1918, and sailed on the transport S.S. *George Washington* from Hoboken, N.J. He arrived at Brest, France, on December 13, 1918. He left there on February 15, 1919, and landed at Boston, Mass., on February 24, 1919.

Wilson made a second trip, leaving Hoboken, N.J., on March 5, 1919, arriving March 13, 1919, at Brest, from which city he sailed on June 29, 1919, returning to Hoboken on July 8, 1919.

The trips were made to further the peace negotiations after World War I.

EIGHTEENTH AMENDMENT ENACTED

The Eighteenth Amendment to the Constitution, prohibiting the manufacture, sale, or transportation of intoxicating liquors, was passed by Congress on December 18, 1917, and proposed to the legislatures of the several states by the Sixty-fifth Congress. It was ratified by a total of thirty-six states on January 16, 1919, when Missouri, Nebraska, and Wyoming voted approval. On January 29, 1919, it was declared by the Secretary of State to have been ratified and on January 16, 1920, it went into effect. It was repealed December 5, 1933, by ratification of the Twenty-first Amendment.

NINETEENTH AMENDMENT ENACTED

More than forty years before the adoption of the woman suffrage amendment, a resolution in favor of suffrage for women had been introduced by Senator Aaron Augustus Sargent of California. The resolution, introduced on June 10, 1878, at the request of Susan Brownell Anthony, had failed to pass.

The Nineteenth Amendment to the Constitution, guaranteeing suffrage for women, was passed by Congress on June 4, 1919. It was proposed to the legislatures of the several states on June 5, 1919, by the Sixty-sixth Congress. There was no action by Alabama, Florida, or North Carolina. It was rejected by Delaware, Georgia, Louisiana, Maryland, Mississippi, South Carolina, and Virginia. The thirty-sixth state to ratify, making it effective, was Tennessee, on August 18, 1920. Later, the Tennessee House rescinded its ratification. The amendment was declared ratified by the Secretary of State on August 26, 1920. Connecticut ratified it later, on September 14, 1920, and Vermont on February 8, 1921.

CABINET MEETINGS NOT CALLED

After his paralytic stroke on September 26, 1919, Wilson issued no calls for cabinet meetings. The first cabinet meeting he held after September 2, 1919, was called on April 13, 1920, the meeting taking place in the President's study in the White House instead of the cabinet room. The cabinet, however, met unofficially without call.

WILSON APPOINTED WOMAN AS SUB-CABINET MEMBER

Wilson created a precedent when he appointed a woman as a sub-cabinet member. On June 26, 1920, he appointed Annette Abbott Adams as assistant attorney general, a post which she held until August 15, 1921.

ELECTION RETURNS BROADCAST

Election returns were broadcast for the first time on August 31, 1920, when WWJ of Detroit, Mich., broadcast the results of congressional and county primaries.

WILSON THE SECOND PRESIDENT TO RECEIVE NOBEL PRIZE

Woodrow Wilson was the second President to receive the Nobel Prize for Peace, the first having been awarded to President Theodore Roosevelt. On December 10, 1920, at Christiania, Norway, the 1919 prize was presented to President Wilson and received by Albert Schmedeman, the American Minister to Norway. The prize carried with it a gift of 150,000 kroner, then worth about $29,100.

THE FIRST LADIES

Ellen Louis Axson Wilson died on August 6, 1914, having served only seventeen months as first lady of the land. A daughter, Margaret, took over the functions of hostess of the White House, serving until December 18, 1915, when President Wilson married Edith Bolling Galt. After Wilson suffered a paralytic attack on September 26, 1919, social activities at the White House were suspended for the balance of his term.

WILSON BURIED IN WASHINGTON, D.C.

The only President buried in Washington, D.C., is Woodrow Wilson, interred February 5, 1924, in the National Cathedral (the Protestant Episcopal Cathedral of Saints Peter and Paul).

WARREN GAMALIEL HARDING

29th PRESIDENT

Born–Nov. 2, 1865
Birthplace–Corsica, Ohio
College attended–Ohio Central College, Iberia, Ohio
Years attended–1879-1882
Religion–Baptist
Ancestry–English, Dutch
Occupation–Editor
Date and place of marriage–July 8, 1891, Marion, Ohio
Age at marriage–25 years, 248 days
Years married–32 years, 25 days
Political party–Republican
State represented–Ohio
Term of office–Mar. 4, 1921-Aug. 2, 1923
Term served–2 years, 151 days
Administration–34th
Congresses–67th
Age at inauguration–55 years, 122 days
Lived after term–Died in office
Date of death–Aug. 2, 1923
Age at death–57 years, 273 days
Place of death–San Francisco, Calif.
Burial place–Marion Cemetery, Marion, Ohio (His body and that of his wife were reinterred Dec. 21, 1927.)

PARENTS

Father–George Tryon Harding
Born–June 12, 1843, Blooming Grove (now Corsica), Ohio
Married (1)–Phoebe Elizabeth Dickerson
Married (2)–Eudora Adella Kelley Luvisi
Married (3)–Alice Severns

Occupation–Physician
Died–Nov. 19, 1928, Santa Ana, Calif.
Age at death–84 years, 160 days
Mother–Phoebe Elizabeth Dickerson Harding
Born–Dec. 21, 1843, near Blooming Grove, Ohio
Married–May 7, 1864, Galion, Ohio
Died–May 20, 1910
Age at death–66 years, 159 days
Second wife of father–Eudora Adella Kelley Luvisi Harding
Born–Sept. 25, 1868, near Bartonia, Ind.
Married–Nov. 23, 1911, Anderson, Ind.
Divorced–1916
Died–July 24, 1955, Union City, Ind.
Third wife of father–Alice Severns Harding
Born–Nov. 13, 1869, Acosta (now New Bloomington, Ohio)
Married–Aug. 11, 1921, Monroe, Mich.
Died–Nov. 24, 1964, Marion, Ohio

BROTHERS AND SISTERS

Warren Gamaliel Harding was the oldest of eight children.

Children by George Tryon Harding and Phoebe Elizabeth Dickerson Harding

Warren Gamaliel Harding, b. Nov. 2, 1865, d. Aug. 2, 1923
Charity Malvina Harding, b. Mar. 1, 1867, d. Nov. 2, 1951
Mary Clarissa Harding b. Apr. 26,

For additional data see the end of this section and also specific subject headings in the index.

1868, d. Oct. 29, 1913

Eleanor Priscilla Harding, b. Nov. 1 , 1872, d. Nov. 9, 1878

Charles Alexander Harding, b. Apr. 8, 1874, d. Nov. 9, 1878

Abigail Victoria Harding, b. May 31, 1875, d. Mar. 21, 1935

George Tryon Harding, b. Mar. 11, 1878, d. Jan. 13, 1934

Phoebe Caroline Harding, b. Oct. 21, 1879, d. Oct. 21, 1951

CHILDREN

None

MRS. WARREN GAMALIEL HARDING

Name–Florence Kling De Wolfe Harding

Date of birth–Aug. 15, 1860

Birthplace–Marion, Ohio

Age at marriage–30 years, 327 days

Children–None

Mother–Louisa M. Bouton Kling

Father–Amos H. Kling

His occupation–Banker, merchant

Date of death–Nov. 21, 1924

Age at death–64 years, 98 days

Place of death–Marion, Ohio

Burial place–Marion, Ohio

Years older than the President–5 years, 79 days

Years she survived the President–1 year, 111 days

Florence Kling De Wolfe was divorced in 1885 from Henry De Wolfe, whom she had married in 1880. They had one son, Marshall Eugene De Wolfe.

THE ELECTION OF 1920

NOMINATIONS FOR TERM 1921-1925

Republican Party Convention (17th)

June 8-12, 1920, the Coliseum, Chicago, Ill.

Nominated for President—Warren Gamaliel Harding, Ohio

Nominated for Vice President—Calvin Coolidge, Mass.

Harding was nominated on the tenth ballot. Candidates for nomination and the votes they received on the first and tenth ballots:

Leonard Wood, Mass., 287$^1/_2$, 156

Frank Orren Lowden, Ill., 211$^1/_2$, 11

Hiram Johnson, Calif., 133$^1/_2$, 80$^4/_5$

William Cameron Sproul, Pa., 84, 0

Nicholas Murray Butler, N.Y., 69$^1/_2$, 2

Warren Gamaliel Harding, Ohio, 65$^1/_2$, 692$^1/_5$

Calvin Coolidge, Mass., 34, 5

Robert Marion La Follette, Wis., 24, 24

Peter Conley Pritchard, Tenn., 21, 0

Miles Poindexter, Wash., 20, 0

Howard Sutherland, W.Va., 17, 0

Thomas Coleman Du Pont, Del., 7, 0

Herbert Clark Hoover, Calif., 5$^1/_2$, 9$^1/_2$

William Edgar Borah, Idaho, 2, 0

Charles Beecher Warren, Mich., 1, 0

William Harrison Hays, Ind., 0, 1

Irving Luther Lenroot, Wis., 0, 1

Philander Chase Knox, Pa., 0, 1

Total number of votes: 984
Nomination made unanimous

Democratic Party Convention (23rd)

June 28-30, July 1-3, 5-6, 1920, Civic Auditorium, San Francisco, Calif.
Nominated for President—James Middleton Cox, Ohio
Nominated for Vice President—Franklin Delano Roosevelt, N.Y.

Cox was nominated on the forty-fourth ballot. Candidates for nomination and the votes they received on the first and forty-fourth ballots:

William Gibbs McAdoo, Calif., 266, 267
Alexander Mitchell Palmer, Pa., 256, 1
James Middleton Cox, Ohio, 134, $732^1/_2$
Alfred Emanuel Smith, N.Y., 109, 0
Edward Irving Edwards, N.J., 42, 0
Thomas Riley Marshall, Ind., 37, 52
Robert Latham Owen, Okla., 33, 34
John William Davis, W.Va., 32, 0
Edwin Thomas Meredith, Iowa, 27, 0
Carter Glass, Va., $26^1/_2$, $1^1/_2$
Homer Stille Cummings, Conn., 25, 1
Furnifold McLendel Simmons, N.C., 24, 0
James Watson Gerard, N.Y., 21, 0
John Sharp Williams, Miss., 20, 0
Gilbert Monell Hitchcock, Neb., 18, 0
Champ [James Beauchamp] Clark, Mo., 9, 0
Francis Burton Harrison, N.Y., 6, 0
Alfred M. Wood, Mass., 4, 0
William Jennings Bryan, Neb., 1, 0
Bainbridge Colby, N.Y., 1, 0
Josephus Daniels, N.C., 1, 0
William Randolph Hearst, N.Y., 1, 0
Oscar Wilder Underwood, Ala., $^1/_2$, 0
Total number of votes: 1094
Number necessary for nomination: 729

On the forty-fourth ballot the rules were suspended and Cox was declared nominated unanimously.

Socialist Party Convention

May 8-14, 1920, Finnish Socialist Hall, New York, N.Y.
Nominated for President—Eugene Victor Debs, Ind.
Nominated for Vice President—Seymour Stedman, Ill.

Farmer Labor Party Convention

July 13-15, 1920, Carmen's Hall, Chicago, Ill.
Nominated for President—Parley Parker Christensen, Utah
Nominated for Vice President—Maximilian Sebastian Hayes, Ohio

Christensen was nominated on the second ballot. Candidates for nomination and the votes they received on the first and second ballots:
Dudley Field Malone, N.Y., 166 $^8/_{10}$, 174 $^6/_{10}$

Parley Parker Christensen, Utah, 121 $^1/_{10}$, 193 $^5/_{10}$
Eugene Victor Debs, Ind., 68, 0
Henry Ford, Mich., 12 $^3/_{10}$
Lynn Joseph Frazier, N.D., 12 $^3/_{10}$, 9
Herbert Bigelow, $^1/_2$, 0
Louis Freeland Post, Ill., 1 $^2/_{10}$, 0

The Farmer Labor Party was formed July 13, 1920 at Chicago, Ill., from the National Labor Party.

Prohibition Party Convention (13th)

July 21-22, 1920, Lincoln, Neb.
Nominated for President—Aaron Sherman Watkins, Ohio
Nominated for Vice President—David Leigh Colvin, N.Y.

Socialist Labor Party Convention

May 5-10, 1920, New York, N.Y.
Nominated for President—William Wesley Cox, Mo.
Nominated for Vice President—August Gillhaus, N.Y.

Single Tax Party Convention

July 12-14, 1920, Chicago, Ill.
Nominated for President—Robert Colvin Macauley, Pa.
Nominated for Vice President—R. G. Barnum, Ohio

American Party

Nominated for President—James Edward Ferguson, Tex.

The American Party was formed August 14, 1919, at Fort Worth, Tex., by a group of Democrats. On April 21, 1920, former Governor Ferguson announced his candidacy at Temple, Tex.

ELECTION RESULTS, NOV. 2, 1920—PRESIDENTIAL AND VICE PRESIDENTIAL CANDIDATES

Republican Party (16,152,200 votes)

Warren Gamaliel Harding, Ohio
Calvin Coolidge, Mass.

Democratic Party (9,147,353 votes)

James Middleton Cox, Ohio
Franklin Delano Roosevelt, N.Y.

Socialist Party (919,799 votes)

Eugene Victor Debs, Ind.
Seymour Stedman, Ill.

Farmer Labor Party (265,411 votes)

Parley Parker Christensen, Utah
Maximilian Sebastian Hayes, Ohio

Prohibition Party (189,408 votes)

Aaron Sherman Watkins, Ohio
David Leigh Colvin, N.Y.

Socialist Labor Party (31,715 votes)

William Wesley Cox, Mo.

August Gillhaus, N.Y.

Single Tax Party (5,837 votes)

Robert Colvin Macauley, Pa.

R. G. Barnum, Ohio

ELECTORAL VOTES (531—48 states)

Harding received 76.08 per cent (404 votes—37 states) as follows: Ariz. 3; Calif. 13; Colo. 6; Conn. 7; Del. 3; Idaho 4; Ill. 29; Ind. 15; Iowa 13; Kan. 10; Me. 6; Md. 8; Mass. 18; Mich. 15; Minn. 12; Mo. 18; Mont. 4; Neb. 8; Nev. 3; N.H. 4; N.J. 14; N.M. 3; N.Y. 45; N.D. 5; Ohio 24; Okla. 10; Ore. 5; Pa. 38; R.I. 5; S.D. 5; Tenn. 12; Utah 4; Vt. 4; Wash. 7; W.Va. 8; Wis. 13; Wyo. 3.

Cox received 23.92 per cent (127 votes—11 states) as follows: Ala. 12; Ark. 9; Fla. 6; Ga. 14; Ky. 13; La. 10; Miss. 10; N.C. 12; S.C. 9; Tex. 20; Va. 12.

CABINET

March 4, 1921-August 2, 1923

State–Bainbridge Colby, N.Y., continued from preceding administration; Charles Evans Hughes, N.Y., Mar. 4, 1921, entered upon duties Mar. 5, 1921

Treasury–David Franklin Houston, Mo., continued from preceding administration; Andrew William Mellon, Pa., Mar. 4, 1921; entered upon duties Mar. 5, 1921

War–Newton Diehl Baker, Ohio, continued from preceding administration; John Wingate Weeks, Mass., Mar. 4, 1921

Attorney General–Alexander Mitchell Palmer, Pa., continued from preceding administration; Harry Micajah Daugherty, Ohio, Mar. 5, 1921

Postmaster General–Albert Sidney Burleson, Tex., continued from preceding administration; William Harrison Hays, Ind., Mar. 5, 1921; Hubert Work, Colo., Mar. 4, 1922; Harry Stewart New, Ind., Feb. 27, 1923; entered upon duties Mar. 5, 1923

Navy–Josephus Daniels, N.C., continued from preceding administration; Edwin Denby, Mich., Mar. 5, 1921

Interior–John Barton Payne, Ill., continued from preceding administration; Albert Bacon Fall, N.M., Mar. 5, 1921; Hubert Work, Colo., Feb. 27, 1923; entered upon duties Mar. 5, 1923

Agriculture–Edwin Thomas Meredith, Iowa, continued from preceding administration; Henry Cantwell Wallace, Iowa, Mar. 5, 1921

Commerce–Joshua Willis Alexander, Mo., continued from preceding administration; Herbert Clark Hoover, Calif., Mar. 5, 1921

Labor–William Bauchop Wilson, Pa., continued from preceding administration; James John Davis, Pa., Mar. 5, 1921

SIXTY-SEVENTH CONGRESS

March 4, 1921-March 3, 1923

First session–Apr. 11, 1921-Nov. 23, 1921 (227 days) (in recess Aug. 24, 1921-Sept. 21, 1921)

Second session–Dec. 5, 1921-Sept. 22, 1922 (292 days) (The House of Representatives was in recess June 30, 1922-Aug. 15, 1922)

Third session–Nov. 20, 1922-Dec. 4, 1922 (15 days)

Fourth session–Dec. 1922-Mar. 3, 1923 (90 days)

Special session of the Senate–Mar. 4, 1921-Mar. 15, 1921

Vice President–Calvin Coolidge, Mass.

President pro tempore of the Senate–Albert Baird Cummins, Iowa, reelected Mar. 7, 1921

Secretary of the Senate–George Andrew Sanderson, Ill., reelected Mar. 7, 1921

Speaker of the House–Frederick Huntington Gillett, Mass., reelected Apr. 11, 1921

Clerk of the House–William Tyler Page, Md.

SIXTY-EIGHTH CONGRESS

March 4, 1923-March 3, 1925

First session–Dec. 3, 1923-June 7, 1924 (188 days)

Second session–Dec. 1, 1924-Mar. 3, 1925 (93 days)

Vice President–Calvin Coolidge, Mass., succeeded to the presidency on the death of Warren Gamaliel Harding on Aug. 2, 1923

President pro tempore of the Senate–Albert Baird Cummins, Iowa

Secretary of the Senate–George Andrew Sanderson, Ill., reelected Dec. 17, 1923

Speaker of the House–Frederick Huntington Gillett, Mass.

Clerk of the House–William Tyler Page, Md.

APPOINTMENTS TO THE SUPREME COURT

Chief Justice
William Howard Taft, Ohio, June 30, 1921

Associate Justices
George Sutherland, Utah, Sept. 5, 1922
Pierce Butler, Minn., Dec. 21, 1922
Edward Terry Sanford, Tenn., Jan. 29, 1923

ADMINISTRATION — IMPORTANT DATES

Mar. 28, 1921, Nevada first state to authorize executions by lethal gas

Apr. 11, 1921, Iowa enacted first state cigarette tax

May 3, 1921, West Virginia approved first state sales tax

May 19, 1921, first immigration quota act passed

June 10, 1921, U.S. Budget Bureau created

June 20, 1921, first congresswoman to preside over the House of Representatives, Mrs. Alice M. Robertson of Oklahoma, announced the vote on an appropriation

June 27, 1921, U.S. Comptroller General appointed

July 21, 1921, battleship sunk by an airplane in demonstration at Hampton Roads, Va.

Nov. 11, 1921, dedication of the Tomb of the Unknown Soldier at Arlington, Va.

Nov. 12, 1921, conference on the limitation of armaments at Washington, D.C.; nine nations represented

Mar. 29, 1922, Five-power Limitation on Naval Armaments Treaty (France, Great Britain, Italy, Japan, United States)

June 16, 1922, helicopter flight by H. A. Berliner demonstrated to U.S. Bureau of Aeronautics

Oct. 3, 1922, first woman senator, Rebecca L. Felton of Georgia, appointed

Oct. 27, 1922, Navy Day celebrated for the first time as an annual holiday

Jan. 23, 1923, first woman elected to Congress to serve in the place of her husband, Mrs. Mae Ella Nolan of California, took office

IMPORTANT DATES IN HIS LIFE

1879-1882, attended Ohio Central College (originally Iberia College), Iberia, Ohio

18—, studied law

1882, taught school

1883, in insurance business

Nov. 26, 1884, with two others purchased Marion, Ohio, *Star* for $300

1895, county auditor, Marion, Ohio, (his first political office)

1899-1903, Ohio Senate

1904-1905, lieutenant-governor of Ohio

1910, unsuccessful Republican candidate for governor of Ohio

Mar. 4, 1915-Jan. 13, 1921, U.S. Senate (from Ohio)

Mar. 4, 1921-Aug. 2, 1923, President

WARREN GAMALIEL HARDING

____was the seventh President born in Ohio.

____was the sixth President elected from Ohio.

____was the second President elected while a senator.

____was the sixth President to die in office.

____was the fourth Ohioan to die in office.

____was the first newspaper publisher elected to the presidency.

____was the second President to marry a woman who had been divorced.

____was the fourth President whose father was alive when he was inaugurated

____was the first President who was survived by his father.

____was the first President to ride to his inauguration in an automobile.

HARDING'S VICE PRESIDENT

Vice President–Calvin Coolidge (29th V.P.)

Date of birth–July 4, 1872

Birthplace–Plymouth, Vt.
Political party–Republican
State represented–Massachusetts
Term of office–Mar. 4, 1921-Aug. 3, 1923
Age at inauguration–48 years, 243 days
Occupation after term–President
Date of death–Jan. 5, 1933
Age at death–60 years, 185 days
Place of death–Northampton, Mass.
Burial place–Hillside Cemetery, Plymouth, Vt.

For further biographical information see Calvin Coolidge, 30th President.

ADDITIONAL DATA ON HARDING

THE SMOKE-FILLED ROOM

The 1920 Republican convention in Chicago was unable to decide upon a candidate after the first day of balloting (June 11, 1920), and it did not seem likely that an amicable decision would be reached by the contenders and their adherents. On June 12, 1920, Senator Harding received 692$\frac{1}{5}$ votes on the tenth ballot, a total which won him the nomination.

On Sunday, June 13, 1920, the New York *Times* carried the headline "Prophesied How Harding Would Win—Daugherty, His Campaign Manager, Said Fifteen Tired Mem Would Put Him Over." The story stated that Harry Micajah Daugherty, the Ohio lawyer and politician who managed Harding's campaign, had said shortly before the presidential primaries in Ohio:

At the proper time after the Republican National Convention meets some fifteen men, bleary-eyed with loss of sleep and perspiring profusely with the excessive heat, will sit down in seclusion around a big table. I will be with them and will present the name of Senator Harding to them, and before we get through they will put him over.

In the early hours of the morning of June 12 a group of senators and party leaders met in a room at the Blackstone Hotel. Daugherty's prediction had come true.

THREE NEWSPAPERMEN PRESIDENTIAL NOMINEES IN 1920

Three of the presidential candidates in 1920 were active newspapermen. Warren Gamaliel Harding, the Republican candidate, was the editor and publisher of the Marion, Ohio, *Star.* James Middleton Cox, the Democratic candidate, became the owner and publisher of the Dayton, Ohio, *Daily News* in 1898 and later acquired other newspapers. Robert C. Macauley, the candidate for the Single Tax party, was a reporter on the Philadelphia *Inquirer.*

PRESIDENTIAL ELECTION RETURNS BROADCAST

Presidential election returns were communicated by radio for the first time on November 2, 1920, when Leo H. Rosenberg of station

KDKA, Pittsburgh, Pa., broadcast the results of the Harding-Cox election.

HARDING ELECTED WHILE SERVING IN THE SENATE

Warren Gamaliel Harding of Ohio, elected to the presidency on November 2, 1920, was the first senator in office to be elected President. He resigned from the Senate on January 13, 1921.

INAUGURATION

Warren Gamaliel Harding took the oath of office on Friday, March 4, 1921, on the east portico of the Capitol. Chief Justice Edward Douglass White administered the oath.

Accompanied by outgoing President Woodrow Wilson, he rode to the Capitol in an automobile, the first President to ride thus to his inaugural. This inauguration was also the first one described over radio. Another innovation was the use of an amplifying public address system so that the assembled crowds could hear the proceedings.

HARDING HAD A RADIO

Warren Gamaliel Harding was the first President to have a radio. On February 8, 1922, he had a vacuum tube detector and two-state amplifier receiving set installed in a bookcase in his study on the second floor of the White House.

HARDING BROADCAST SPEECH

The first President to broadcast over the radio was Warren Gamaliel Harding, whose speech at the dedication of the Francis Scott Key Memorial at Fort McHenry, Baltimore, Md., on June 14, 1922, was transmitted by WEAR (now WFBR), Baltimore, Md. His voice was carried over telephone wires to the studio from which it was broadcast. President Harding's World Court speech on June 21, 1923, at St. Louis, Mo., was transmitted over KSD, St. Louis, Mo., and WEAF, New York, N.Y.

On November 5, 1921, a message from President Harding had been broadcast from Washington, D.C., to twenty-eight countries. It was sent in code over the RCA 25,000-volt station at Rocky Point, N.Y.

HARDING VISITED ALASKA AND CANADA

President Harding was the first President to visit Alaska and Canada during his term of office. He sailed on the U.S.S. *Henderson,* a naval transport, and visited Metlakahtla, Alaska, on July 8, 1923, and Vancouver, British Columbia, on July 26, 1923.

CABINET MEMBER CONVICTED IN TEAPOT DOME CASE

The first cabinet member convicted of a crime was Albert Bacon Fall, Secretary of the Interior during the Harding administration. On October 25, 1929, after a trial in the District of Columbia Supreme Court, Fall was found guilty by Justice William Hitz of having received and accepted a bribe of $100,000 from Edward Laurence Doheny in connection with the Elk Hills Naval Oil Reserve in California. The bribe had been given v.ith a view to influencing Fall to grant valuable oil leases to Doheny's Pan-American Petroleum and Transport Company. Also involved were the Teapot Dome oil reserves in Wyoming, which Fall had secretly leased to Harry F. Sinclair. On November 1, 1929, Fall was sentenced to one year in prison and a $100,000 fine.

THE FIRST LADY

Although not in good health, Florence Kling Harding went to the West Coast, Canada, and Alaska with her husband, who died in San Francisco on the return trip.

DEATH AND BURIAL

The first and only time that both a President and his wife died during the period for which the President had been elected was the term of March 4, 1921-March 3, 1925. President Harding died August 2, 1923, and his wife died November 21, 1924. On December 20, 1927, their bodies were removed from the vault in Marion Cemetery to an $800,000 mausoleum ($500,000 for the memorial, $300,000 for the ground and landscaping). The mausoleum was dedicated on June 16, 1931.

CALVIN COOLIDGE
30th PRESIDENT

Born–July 4, 1872 (Given name—John Calvin)

Birthplace–Plymouth, Vt.

College attended–Amherst College, Amherst, Mass.

Date of graduation–June 26, 1895, four-year course, Bachelor of Arts

Religion–Congregationalist

Ancestry–English

Occupation–Governor, lawyer

Date and place of marriage–Oct. 4, 1905, Burlington, Vt.

Age at marriage–33 years, 92 days

Years married–27 years, 93 days

Political party–Republican

State represented–Massachusetts

Term of office–Aug. 3, 1923-Mar. 3, 1929 (Coolidge succeeded to the presidency on the death of Warren Gamaliel Harding.)

Term served–5 years, 214 days

Administration–34th, 35th

Congresses–68th, 69th, 70th

Age at inauguration–51 years, 30 days

Lived after term–3 years, 307 days

Occupation after term–Writer, columnist

Date of death–Jan. 5, 1933

Age at death–60 years, 185 days

Place of death–Northampton, Mass.

Burial place–Notch Cemetery, Plymouth Notch, Plymouth, Vt.

PARENTS

Father–John Calvin Coolidge

Born–Mar. 31, 1845, Plymouth, Vt.

Married (1)–Victoria Josephine Moor

Married (2)–Caroline A. Brown

Occupation–Farmer, storekeeper, notary public

Died–Mar. 18, 1926, Plymouth, Vt.

Age at death–80 years, 352 days

Mother–Victoria Josephine Moor Coolidge

Born–Mar. 14, 1846, Pinney Hollow, Vt.

Married–May 6, 1868, Plymouth, Vt.

Died–Mar. 14, 1885, Plymouth, Vt.

Age at death–39 years

Second wife of father–Caroline Athelia Brown Coolidge

Born–Jan. 22, 1857

Married–Sept. 9, 1891

Died–May 18, 1920, Plymouth, Vt.

Age at death–63 years, 116 days

BROTHERS AND SISTERS

Calvin Coolidge was the older of two children of his father's first marriage.

Children of John Calvin Coolidge and Victoria Josephine Moor Coolidge

Calvin Coolidge, b. July 4, 1872, d. Jan. 5, 1933

Abigail Gratia Coolidge b. Apr. 15, 1875, d. Mar. 6, 1890

CHILDREN

John Coolidge, b. Sept. 7, 1906, Northampton, Mass., m. Sept. 23, 1929, Florence Trumbull, Plainville, Conn.

Calvin Coolidge, b. Apr. 13 1908,

For additional data see the end of this section and also specific subject headings in the index.

Northampton, Mass., d. July 7, 1924, Washington, D.C.

MRS. CALVIN COOLIDGE

Name—Grace Anna Goodhue Coolidge
Date of birth—Jan. 3, 1879
Birthplace—Burlington, Vt.
Age at marriage—26 years, 274 days
Children—2 sons
Mother—Lemira Barnett Goodhue

Father—Andrew Isaachar Goodhue
Date of death—July 8, 1957
Age at death—78 years, 186 days
Place of death—Northampton, Mass.
Burial place—Plymouth, Vt.
Years younger than the President—6 years, 183 days
Years she survived the President—24 years, 184 days

THE ELECTION OF 1924

NOMINATIONS FOR TERM 1925-1929

Republican Party Convention (18th)

June 10-12, 1924, Municipal Auditorium, Cleveland, Ohio
Nominated for President—Calvin Coolidge, Mass.
Nominated for Vice President—Charles Gates Dawes, Ill.
    Coolidge was nominated on the first ballot. Candidates for nomination and the votes they received:
Calvin Coolidge, Mass., 1065
Robert Marion La Follette, Wis., 34
Hiram Johnson, Calif., 10
Total number of votes: 1109
Nomination made unanimous

Democratic Party Convention (24th)

June 24-28, 30, July 1-5, 7-9, 1924, Madison Square Garden, New York, N.Y.
Nominated for President—John William Davis, W.Va.
Nominated for Vice President—Charles Wayland Bryan, Neb.
    Davis was nominated on the one hundred and third ballot. Candidates for nomination and the votes they received on the first and one hundred and third ballots:
William Gibbs McAdoo, Calif., 431$^1/_2$, 11$^1/_2$
Alfred Emanuel Smith, N.Y., 241, 7$^1/_2$
James Middleton Cox, Ohio, 59, 0
Byron Patrick Harrison, Miss., 43$^1/_2$, 0
Oscar Wilder Underwood, Ala., 42$^1/_2$, 102$^1/_2$
George Sebastian Silzer, N.J., 38, 0
John William Davis, W.Va., 31, 844
Samuel Moffett Ralston, Ind., 30, 0
Woodbridge Nathan Ferris, Mich., 30, 0
Carter Glass, Va., 25, 23
Albert Cabell Ritchie, Md., 22$^1/_2$, 0
Joseph Taylor Robinson, Ark., 21, 20
Jonathan McMillan Davis, Kan., 20, 0
Charles Wayland Bryan, Neb., 18, 0

Fred Herbert Brown, N.H., 17, 0
William Ellery Sweet, Colo., 12, 0
Willard Saulsbury, Del., 7, 0
John Benjamin Kendrick, Wyo., 6, 0
Houston Thompson, 1, 0
Thomas James Walsh, Mont., 0, 58
Edwin Thomas Meredith, Iowa, 0, 15$\frac{1}{2}$
James Watson Gerard, N.Y., 0, 7
Cordell Hull, Tenn., 0, 1
Total number of votes:
   First ballot: 1096
   One hundred and third ballot: 1090
Number necessary for nomination: 731

This was the longest nominating convention of a major political party. Sixty candidates were nominated for the presidency.

Progressive Party Convention

July 4, 1924, Municipal Auditorium, Cleveland, Ohio
Nominated for President—Robert Marion La Follette, Wis.
Nominated for Vice President—Burton Kendall Wheeler, Mont.

Prohibition Party Convention (14th)

June 4-6, 1924, Columbus, Ohio
Nominated for President—Herman Preston Faris, Mo.
Nominated for Vice President—Marie Caroline Brehm, Calif.
   Faris was nominated on the first ballot. Candidates for nomination and the votes they received:
Herman Preston Faris, Mo., 82
A. P. Gouttey, Wash., 40
William Frederick Varney, N.Y., 2
A. P. Gouttey was nominated for the vice presidency but declined.

Socialist Labor Party Convention

May 10-13, 1924, New York, N.Y.
Nominated for President—Frank T. Johns, Ore.
Nominated for Vice President—Verne L. Reynolds, N.Y.

Socialist Party Convention

July 6-8, 1924, Cleveland, Ohio
Nominated for President—Robert Marion La Follette, Wis.
Nominated for Vice President—Burton Kendall Wheeler, Mont.
   The national committee was authorized at this convention to name a suitable vice presidential candidate at a later date. Wheeler was endorsed on July 22, 1924.

Workers Party (Communist Party) Convention

July 11, 1924, St. Paul, Minn.
Nominated for President—William Zebulon Foster, Ill.
Nominated for Vice President—Benjamin Gitlow, N.Y.

American Party Convention

June 3-4, 1924, Columbus, Ohio
Nominated for President—Gilbert Owen Nations, D.C.
Nominated for Vice President—Charles Hiram Randall, Calif.

Commonwealth Land Party Convention

Feb. 9, 1924, Engineering Society Building, New York, N.Y.
Nominated for President—William J. Wallace, N.J.
Nominated for Vice President—John Cromwell Lincoln, Ohio

Farmer Labor Party Convention

June 17-19, 1924, Convention Hall, St. Paul, Minn.
Nominated for President—Duncan McDonald, Ill.
Nominated for Vice President—William Bouck, Wash.
  Both candidates withdrew in July and the party supported the candidates of the Communist Party.

Greenback Party Convention

July 9, 1924, Indianapolis, Ind.
Nominated for President—John Zahnd, Ind.
Nominated for Vice President—Roy M. Harrop, Neb.

ELECTION RESULTS, NOV. 4, 1924—PRESIDENTIAL AND VICE PRESIDENTIAL CANDIDATES

Republican Party (15,725,016 votes)
Calvin Coolidge, Mass.
Charles Gates Dawes, Ill.

Democratic Party (8,386,503 votes)
John William Davis, W.Va.
Charles Wayland Bryan, Neb.

Progressive Party (4,822,856 votes)
Robert Marion La Follette, Wis.
Burton Kendall Wheeler, Mont.

Prohibition Party (57,520 votes)
Herman Preston Faris, Mo.
Marie Caroline Brehm, Calif.

Socialist Labor Party (36,428 votes)
Frank T. Johns, Ore.
Verne L. Reynolds, N.Y.

Workers Party (Communist Party) (36,386 votes)
William Zebulon Foster, Ill.
Benjamin Gitlow, N.Y.

American Party (23,967 votes)
Gilbert Owen Nations, D.C.
Charles Hiram Randall, Calif.

Commonwealth Land Party (1,582 votes)

William J. Wallace, N.J.

John Cromwell Lincoln, Ohio

ELECTORAL VOTES (531—48 states)Coolidge received 71.94 per cent (382 votes—35 states) as follows: Ariz. 3; Calif. 13; Colo. 6; Conn. 7; Del. 3; Idaho 4; Ill. 29; Ind. 15; Iowa 13; Kan. 10; Ky. 13; Me. 6; Md. 8; Mass. 18; Mich. 15; Minn. 12; Mo. 18; Mont. 4; Neb. 8; Nev. 3; N.H. 4; N.J. 14; N.M. 3; N.Y. 45; N.D. 5; Ohio 24; Ore. 5; Pa. 38; R.I. 5; S.D. 5; Utah 4; Vt. 4; Wash. 7; W.Va. 8; Wyo. 3.

Davis received 25.61 per cent (136 votes—12 states) as follows: Ala. 12; Ark. 9; Fla. 6; Ga. 14; La. 10; Miss. 10; N.C. 12; Okla. 10; S.C. 9; Tenn. 12; Tex. 20; Va. 12.

La Follette received 2.45 per cent (1 state): Wis. 13.

FIRST TERM

CABINET

August 3, 1923-March 3, 1925

State–Charles Evans Hughes, N.Y., continued from preceding administration

Treasury–Andrew William Mellon, Pa., continued from preceding administration

War–John Wingate Weeks, Mass., continued from preceding administration

Attorney General–Harry Micajah Daugherty, Ohio, continued from preceding administration; Harlan Fiske Stone, N.Y., Aprl. 7, 1924; entered upon duties Apr. 9, 1924

Postmaster General–Harry Stewart New, Ind., continued from preceding administration

Navy–Edwin Denby, Mich., continued from preceding administration; Curtis Dwight Wilbur, Calif., Mar. 18, 1924

Interior–Hubert Work, Colo., continued from preceding administration

Agriculture–Henry Cantwell Wallace, Iowa, continued from preceding administration, died Oct. 25, 1924; Howard Mason Gore, W.Va. (assistant secretary), ad interim Oct. 26, 1924 to Nov. 22, 1924; Howard Mason Gore, W.Va., Nov. 21, 1924; entered upon duties Nov. 22, 1924

Commerce–Herbert Clark Hoover, Calif., continued from preceding administration

Labor–James John Davis, Pa., continued from preceding administration

SECOND TERM

CABINET

March 4, 1925-March 3, 1929

State–Charles Evans Hughes, N.Y., continued from preceding administration; Frank Billings Kellogg, Minn., Feb. 16, 1925; entered upon duties Mar. 5, 1925

Treasury–Andrew William Mellon, Pa., continued from preceding administration

War–John Wingate Weeks, Mass., continued from preceding administration; Dwight Filley Davis, Mo., Oct. 13, 1925; entered upon duties Oct. 14, 1925

Attorney General–James Montgomery Beck, Pa., (solicitor general), ad interim Mar. 4, 1925 to Mar. 16, 1925; John Garibaldi Sargent, Vt., Mar. 17, 1925; entered upon duties Mar. 18, 1925

Postmaster General–Harry Stewart New, Ind., continued from preceding administration; recommissioned Mar. 5, 1925

Navy–Curtis Dwight Wilbur, Calif., continued from preceding administration

Interior–Hubert Work, Colo., continued from preceding administration; Roy Owen West, Ill, ad interim July 25, 1928, to Jan. 21, 1929; Roy Owen West, Ill., Jan. 21, 1929

Agriculture–Howard Mason Gore, W.Va., continued from preceding administration; William Marion Jardine, Kan., Feb. 18, 1925; entered upon duties Mar. 5, 1925

Commerce–Herbert Clark Hoover, Calif., continued from preceding administration; William Fairfield Whiting, Mass., ad interim Aug. 21, 1928 to Dec. 11, 1928; William Fairfield Whiting, Mass., Dec. 11, 1928

Labor–James John Davis, Pa., continued from preceding administration

SECOND TERM

SIXTY-NINTH CONGRESS
March 4, 1925-March 3, 1927

First session–Dec. 7, 1925-July 3, 1926 (209 days); Nov. 10, 1926 (The Senate met subsequent to adjournment for the purpose of sitting as a court of impeachment; adjourned sine die the same day; court of impeachment adjourned to Dec. 13, 1926, when, on request of House managers, impeachment proceedings were dismissed.)

Second session–Dec. 6, 1926-March 3, 1927 (88 days)

Special session of the Senate–Mar. 4, 1925-Mar. 18, 1925

Vice President–Charles Gates Dawes, Ill.

Presidents pro tempore of the Senate–Albert Baird Cummins, Iowa; George Higgins Moses, N.H., elected Mar. 6, 1925

Secretaries of the Senate–George Andrew Sanderson, Ill., reelected Mar. 6, 1925; died Apr. 24, 1925; Edwin Pope Thayer, Ind., elected Dec. 7, 1925

Speaker of the House–Nicholas Longworth, Ohio, elected Dec. 7, 1925

Clerk of the House–William Tyler Page, Md., reelected Dec. 7, 1925

SEVENTIETH CONGRESS
March 4, 1927-March 3, 1929

First session–Dec. 5, 1927-May 29, 1928 (177 days)

Second session–Dec. 3, 1928-Mar. 3, 1929 (91 days)

Vice President–Charles Gates Dawes, Ill.

President pro tempore of the Senate–George Higgins Moses, N.H., reelected Dec. 15, 1927

Secretary of the Senate–Edwin Pope Thayer, Ind., reelected Dec. 15, 1927

Speaker of the House–Nicholas Longworth, Ohio, reelected Dec. 5, 1927

Clerk of the House–William Tyler Page, Md., reelected Dec. 5, 1927

APPOINTMENT TO THE SUPREME COURT

Associate Justice
Harlan Fiske Stone, N.Y., Feb. 5, 1925

ADMINISTRATION — IMPORTANT DATES

1923-1924, Teapot Dome oil scandal of Harding administration revealed in Senate investigation

May 15, 1924, soldier bonus bill vetoed, later passed over veto by both Houses of Congress

May 26, 1924, immigration bill signed reducing quotas established in 1921

June 2, 1924, citizenship granted to non-citizen American Indians born in the United States

July 1, 1924, airmail transcontinental through regular service established

July 1, 1924, U.S. Foreign Service created

Dec. 17, 1924, diesel electric locomotive placed in service

Jan. 5, 1925, first woman governor, Nellie Tayloe Ross, took office in Wyoming

Mar. 23, 1925, Tennessee enacted law making it unlawful to teach theory of evolution

Mar. 16, 1926, liquid fuel rocket flown

Apr. 6, 1926, Tacna-Arica Conference between Chile and Peru held at Washington, D.C.

May 9, 1926, Richard E. Byrd and Floyd Bennett made first flight over North Pole

May 31, 1926, Sesquicentennial Exposition opened, Philadelphia, Pa.

June 14, 1926, Board of Mediation appointed to succeed Railroad Labor Board

July 2, 1926, Distinguished Flying Cross authorized

Feb. 23, 1927, U.S. Radio Commission created

May 20, 1927, Lindbergh's transatlantic solo flight

Jan. 15, 1929, Kellogg-Briand peace pact ratified by U.S. Senate

IMPORTANT DATES IN HIS LIFE

June 26, 1895, graduated from Amherst College

July 2, 1897, admitted to the bar; practiced in Northampton, Mass.

1899, City Council, Northampton, Mass.

1900-1901, city solicitor, Northampton, Mass.

June 1903-Jan. 1, 1904, clerk of the courts, Hampshire County, Northampton, Mass.

1907-1908, Massachusetts House of Representatives
1909, resumed law practice, Northampton, Mass.
1910-1911, mayor, Northampton, Mass.
1912-1915, Massachusetts Senate
1914-1915, president of Massachusetts Senate
1916-1918, lieutenant governor of Massachusetts
Nov. 27, 1918, president of Nonotuck Savings Bank, Northampton, Mass.
1919-1920, governor of Massachusetts
1919, settled Boston police strike
Mar. 4, 1921, inaugurated Vice President
Aug. 3, 1923, succeeded to the presidency on the death of President Harding
Nov. 1924, nominated for another term as President on the Republican ticket
Mar. 4, 1925-Mar. 3, 1929, President (second term)
1928, declined to be a candidate for renomination
19—, chairman of Nonpartisan Railroad Commission
1929, published his *Autobiography*
1930-32, president of American Antiquarian Society
1930, conducted syndicated newspaper column

CALVIN COOLIDGE

_____was the second President born in Vermont.
_____was the twelfth President who was a resident of a state other than his native state.
_____was the fifth President whose father was alive when he was inaugurated.
_____was the first President sworn in by his father.
_____was the first President whose inaugural ceremonies were broadcast.
_____was the first President sworn in by a former President.

COOLIDGE'S VICE PRESIDENT

Vice President–Charles Gates Dawes (30th V.P.)
Date of birth–Aug. 27, 1865
Birthplace–Marietta, Ohio
Political party–Republican
State represented–Illinois
Term of office–Mar. 4, 1925-Mar. 3, 1929
Age at inauguration–59 years, 189 days
Occupation after term–Banker
Date of death–Apr. 23, 1951
Age at death–85 years, 239 days
Place of death–Evanston, Ill.
Burial place–Chicago, Ill.

Additional data on Dawes

1884, graduated from Marietta College, Marietta, Ohio
1886, admitted to the bar; practiced in Lincoln, Neb.
1892, published *The Banking System of the United States*

1898-1901, U.S. comptroller of the currency

1902-1925, officer, Chicago, Ill., banks

June 11, 1917, commissioned major of Seventeenth Engineers, U.S. Army

July 16, 1917, commissioned lieutenant colonel

Sept. 27, 1917, chief of supply procurement on staff of commander-in-chief of American Expeditionary Forces

Jan. 16, 1918, commissioned colonel

Oct. 15, 1918, commissioned brigadier general

1918, member, Liquidation Commission, American Expeditionary Forces

Aug. 31, 1919, resigned from Army

1919, awarded Distinguished Service Medal of the United States for "exceptionally meritorious and distinguished services"; French Legion of Honor and Croix de Guerre with Palm; British Order of the Bath; Italian Order of St. Maurice and St. Lazarus; Belgian Order of Leopold

June 1920, unsuccessful candidate for Republican presidential nomination

1921, director of the U.S. Bureau of the Budget

1921-1926, brigadier general, Officers' Reserve Corps

1923, president of German reparations commission, which worked out the "Dawes Plan"

1925, recipient, with Sir Austen Chamberlain, of Nobel Peace Prize

19—, wrote musical compositions, including one played by Fritz Kreisler

June 1928, received four votes for Republican presidential nomination

1929-1932, ambassador to Great Britain

1930, delegate, London Naval Conference

Feb.-June 1932, president, Reconstruction Finance Corporation

June 1932, resumed banking business

June 1932, received one vote for Republican presidential nomination

1939, wrote *Journal as Ambassador to Great Britain*

1950, wrote *A Journal of the McKinley Years*

ADDITIONAL DATA ON COOLIDGE

COOLIDGE BORN ON INDEPENDENCE DAY

Calvin Coolidge was born on July 4, 1872, at Plymouth, Vt., on the ninety-sixth anniversary of the Declaration of Independence.

FIRST OATH OF OFFICE

Calvin Coolidge, who succeeded to the presidency on the death of President Harding, took the oath of office as President at the family homestead at Plymouth, Vt., at 2:47 A.M. on August 3, 1923. The oath was administered to him by his father, Colonel John Calvin Coolidge, a notary public and justice of the peace. The ceremony, which took place in the sitting room by the light of a kerosene lamp, was witnessed by Mrs. Coolidge, Senator Dale Porter Hinman, and Coolidge's stenographer and Chauffeur.

The oath was repeated on Tuesday, August 21, 1923, by Calvin Coolidge in his suite at the Willard Hotel, Washington, D.C. It was administered by Justice Adolph August Hoehling of the District of Columbia Supreme Court.

PRESIDENTIAL CANDIDATES POSED FOR NEWSREELS

The first films of presidential candidates were seen by movie spectators in September 1924. On August 11, 1924, Theodore W. Case and Lee de Forest took motion pictures on the grounds of the White House of President Calvin Coolidge, Republican candidate for reelection. On the same day they photographed Senator Robert Marion La Follette, Progressive Party candidate, who posed on the steps of the Capitol. Later, movies were taken of John William Davis, Democratic presidential nominee, at Locust Valley, N.Y.

INAUGURATION IN 1925

Calvin Coolidge took the oath of office on Wednesday, March 4, 1925, on the east portico of the Capitol. The oath was administered by Chief Justice William Howard Taft. This was the first time that a former President administered the oath to a President-elect.

The forty-one-minute inaugural speech was broadcast by twenty-five radio stations and heard by an audience estimated at 22,800,000.

THE PRESIDENT'S FAMILY

Mrs. Grace Goodhue Coolidge was not given to much social entertainment. During the Coolidges' residence at the White House, their son Calvin Coolidge, Jr., died. President Coolidge's father also died less than two years later, with the result that White House social functions were greatly curtailed.

LIKENESS OF COOLIDGE ON COINS

The first coin bearing the likeness of a living President was the 1926 Sesquicentennial half dollar, the obverse of which bore the heads of Presidents George Washington and Calvin Coolidge. The reverse depicted the Liberty Bell. The net coinage was 141,120 pieces struck at the mint at Philadelphia, Pa.

HERBERT CLARK HOOVER
31st PRESIDENT

Born–Aug. 10, 1874

Birthplace–West Branch, Iowa

College attended–Stanford University, Stanford, Calif.

Date of graduation–May 29, 1895, four-year course, Bachelor of Arts

Religious denomination–Society of Friends (Quaker)

Ancestry–Swiss-German

Occupation–Engineer

Date and place of marriage–Feb. 10, 1899, Monterey, Calif.

Age at marriage–24 years, 184 days

Years married–44 years, 331 days

Political party–Republican

State represented–California

Term of office–Mar. 4, 1929-Mar. 3, 1933

Term served–4 years

Administration–36th

Congresses–71st, 72nd

Age at inauguration–54 years, 206 days

Lived after term–31 years, 231 days

Occupation after term–Special reorganization commissions, writing

Date of death–Oct. 20, 1964

Age at death–90 years, 71 days

Place of death–New York, N.Y.

Burial place–West Branch, Iowa

PARENTS

Father–Jesse Clark Hoover

Born–Sept. 2, 1846, West Milton, Ohio

Married–Mar. 12, 1870

Occupation–Blacksmith, farm implement business

Died–Dec. 13, 1880, West Branch, Iowa

Age at death–34 years, 112 days

Mother–Hulda Randall Minthorn Hoover

Born–May 4, 1848, Burgersville, Ontario, Canada

Died–Feb. 22, 1884, West Branch, Iowa

Age at death–35 years, 294 days

BROTHERS AND SISTERS

Herbert Clark Hoover was the second child in a family of three.

Children of Jesse Clark Hoover and Hulda Randall Minthorn Hoover

Theodore Jesse Hoover, b. Jan. 28, 1871; d. Feb. 4, 1955

Herbert Clark Hoover, b. Aug. 10, 1874; d. Oct. 20, 1964

Mary (May) Hoover, b. Sept. 1, 1876; d. June 7, 1953

CHILDREN

Herbert Clark Hoover, Jr., b. Aug. 4, 1903, London, England; m. June 25, 1925, Margaret Eva Watson, Palo Alto, Calif.; d. July 9, 1969, Pasadena, Calif.

Allan Henry Hoover, b. July 17, 1907, London, England; m. Mar. 17, 1937, Margaret Coberly, Los Angeles, Calif.

MRS. HERBERT CLARK HOOVER

Name–Lou Henry Hoover

Date of birth–Mar. 29, 1875

Birthplace–Waterloo, Iowa

Age at marriage–23 years 318 days

For additional data see the end of this section and also specific subject headings in the index.

Children–2 sons
Mother–Florence Ida Week Henry
Father–Charles Delano Henry
His occupation–Banker
Date of death–Jan. 7, 1944
Age at death–68 years, 284 days

Place of death–New York, N.Y.
Burial place–Alta Mesa Cemetery, Stanford, Calif.; reinterred Nov. 1, 1966, West Branch, Iowa
Years younger than the President–231 days

THE ELECTION OF 1928

NOMINATIONS FOR TERM 1929-1933

Republican Party Convention (19th)

June 12-15, 1928, Civic Auditorium, Kansas City, Mo.
Nominated for President—Herbert Clark Hoover, Calif.
Nominated for Vice President—Charles Curtis, Kan.

Hoover was nominated on the first ballot. Candidates for nomination and the votes they received:

Herbert Clark Hoover, Calif., 837
Frank Orren Lowden, Ill., 74
Charles Curtis, Kan., 64
James Eli Watson, Ind., 45
George William Norris, Neb., 24
Guy Despard Goff, W.Va., 18
Calvin Coolidge, Mass., 17
Charles Gates Dawes, Ill., 4
Charles Evans Hughes, N.Y., 1
Total number of votes: 1089
Nomination made unanimous

Democratic Party Convention (25th)

June 26-29, Sam Houston Hall, Houston, Tex.
Nominated for President—Alfred Emanuel Smith, N.Y.
Nominated for Vice President—Joseph Taylor Robinson, Ark.

Smith was nominated on the first ballot. Candidates for nomination and the votes they received:

Alfred Emanuel Smith, N.Y., $849^2/_3$
Walter Franklin George, Ga., $52^1/_2$
James Alexander Reed, Mo., 52
Cordell Hull, Tenn., $50^5/_6$
Jesse Holman Jones, Tex., 43
Richard Cannon Watts, S.C., 18
Byron Patton Harrison, Miss., $8^1/_2$
Evans Woollen, Ind. 7
Alvin Victor Donahey, Ohio, 5
William Augustus Ayres, Kan., 3
Atlee Pomerene, Ohio, 3
Gilbert Monell Hitchcock, Neb., 2
Theodore Gilmore Bilbo, Miss., 1
Total number of votes: $1,097^1/_2$

Number necessary for nomination: 733
Nomination made unanimous

Socialist Party Convention

Apr. 13-17, 1928, Finnish Socialist Hall and Manhattan Opera House, New York, N.Y.
Nominated for President—Norman Mattoon Thomas, N.Y.
Nominated for Vice President—James Hudson Maurer, Pa.

Workers Party (Communist Party)

May 25-26, 1928, Mecca Temple and Central Opera House, New York, N.Y.
Nominated for President—William Zebulon Foster, Ill.
Nominated for Vice President—Benjamin Gitlow, N.Y.

Socialist Labor Party Convention

May 12-14, 1928, New York, N.Y.
Nominated for President—Verne L. Reynolds, Mich.
Nominated for Vice President—Jeremiah D. Crowley, N.Y.
   Frank T. Johns of Oregon was nominated for the presidency, but lost his life endeavoring to effect a rescue. On May 22, 1928, Reynolds was nominated in his place.

Prohibition Party Convention (15th)

July 10-12, 1928, Chicago, Ill.
Nominated for President—William Frederick Varney, N.Y.
Nominated for Vice President—James Arthur Edgerton, Va.
   Varney was nominated on the second ballot. Candidates for nomination and the votes they received on the first and second ballots:
William Frederick Varney, N.Y., 52, 68
Herbert Clark Hoover, Calif., 42, 45

Farmer Labor Party Convention

July 10-11, 1928, Chicago, Ill.
Nominated for President—Frank Elbridge Webb, Calif.
Nominated for Vice President—Will Vereen, Ga.
   Senator George William Norris of Nebraska was nominated for the presidency, but declined the nomination.

Greenback Party

Nominated for President—John Zahnd, Ind.
Nominated for Vice President—Wesley Henry Bennington, Ohio
   The party filed no ticket. The candidates were write-in candidates.

ELECTION RESULTS, NOV. 6, 1928—PRESIDENTIAL AND VICE PRESIDENTIAL CANDIDATES

Republican Party (21,392,190 votes)
Herbert Clark Hoover, Calif.
Charles Curtis, Kan.

Democratic Party (15,016,443 votes)

Alfred Emanuel Smith, N.Y.
Joseph Taylor Robinson, Ark.

Socialist Party (267,420 votes)

Norman Mattoon Thomas, N.Y.
James Hudson Maurer, Pa.

Workers Party (Communist Party) (48,770 votes)

William Zebulon Foster, Ill.
Benjamin Gitlow, N.Y.

Socialist Labor Party (21,603 votes)

Verne L. Reynolds, N.Y.
Jeremiah D. Crowley, N.Y.

Prohibition Party (20,106 votes)

William Frederick Varney, N.Y.
James Arthur Edgerton, Va.

Farmer Labor Party (6,390 votes)

Frank Elbridge Webb, Calif.
Will Vereen, Ga.

ELECTORAL VOTES (531—48 states)

Hoover received 83.62 per cent (444 votes—40 states) as follows:
Ariz. 3; Calif. 13; Colo. 6; Conn. 7; Del. 3; Fla. 6; Idaho 4; Ill. 29;
Ind. 15; Iowa 13; Kan. 10; Ky. 13; Me. 6; Md. 8; Mich. 15; Minn.
12; Mo. 18; Mont. 4; Neb. 8; Nev. 3; N.H. 4; N.J. 14; N.M. 3; N.Y.
45; N.C. 12; N.D. 5; Ohio 24; Okla. 10; Ore. 5; Pa. 38; S.D. 5;
Tenn. 12; Tex. 20; Utah 4; Vt. 4; Va. 12; Wash. 7; W. Va. 8; Wis. 13;
Wyo. 3.

Smith received 16.38 per cent (87 votes—8 states) as follows: Ala.
12; Ark. 9; Ga. 14; La. 10; Mass. 18; Miss. 10; R.I. 5; S.C. 9.

CABINET

March 4, 1929-March 3, 1933

State—Frank Billings Kellogg, Minn., continued from preceding administration; Henry Lewis Stimson, N.Y., Mar. 4, 1929; entered upon duties Mar. 29, 1929

Treasury—Andrew William Mellon, Pa., continued from preceding administration; Ogden Livingston Mills, N.Y., Feb. 10, 1932; entered upon duties Feb. 13, 1932

War—Dwight Filley Davis, Mo., continued from preceding administration; James William Good, Ill., Mar. 5, 1929; entered upon duties Mar. 6, 1929; Patrick Jay Hurley, Okla., Dec. 9, 1929

Attorney General—John Garibaldi Sargent, Vt., continued from preceding administration; William De Witt Mitchell, Minn., Mar. 5, 1929; entered upon duties Mar. 6, 1929

Postmaster General–Harry Stewart New, Ind., continued from preceding administration; Walter Folger Brown, Ohio, Mar. 5, 1929; entered upon duties Mar. 6, 1929

Navy–Curtis Dwight Wilbur, Calif., continued from preceding administration; Charles Francis Adams, Mass., Mar. 5, 1929

Interior–Roy Owen West, Ill., continued from preceding administration: Ray Lyman Wilbur, Calif., Mar. 5, 1929

Agriculture–William Marion Jardine, Kan., continued from preceding administration; Arthur Mastick Hyde, Mo., Mar. 5, 1929; entered upon duties Mar. 6, 1929

Commerce–William Fairfield Whiting, Mass., continued from preceding administration; Robert Patterson Lamont, Ill.,Mar. 5, 1929; Roy Dikeman Chapin, Mich., ad interim Aug. 8, 1932-Dec. 14, 1932; Roy Dikeman Chapin, Mich., Dec. 14, 1932

Labor–James John Davis, Pa., continued from preceding administration; William Nuckles Doak, Va., Dec. 8, 1930; entered upon duties Dec. 9, 1930

SEVENTY-FIRST CONGRESS

March 4, 1929-March 3, 1931

First session–Apr. 15, 1929-Nov. 22, 1929 (222 days)
Second session–Dec. 2, 1929-July 3, 1930 (214 days)
Third session–Dec. 1, 1930-Mar. 3, 1931 (93 days)
Special sessions of the Senate–Mar. 4, 1929-Mar. 5, 1929 (2 days); July 7, 1930-July 21, 1930 (15 days)
Vice President–Charles Curtis, Kan.
President pro tempore of the Senate–George Higgins Moses, N.H.
Secretary of the Senate–Edwin Pope Thayer, Ind.
Speaker of the House–Nicholas Longworth, Ohio, reelected Apr. 15, 1929
Clerk of the House–William Tyler Page, Md., reelected Apr. 15, 1929

SEVENTY-SECOND CONGRESS

March 4, 1931-March 3, 1933

First session–Dec. 7, 1931-July 16, 1932 (223 days)
Second session–Dec. 5, 1932-Mar. 3, 1933 (89 days)
Vice President–Charles Curtis, Kan.
President pro tempore of the Senate–George Higgins Moses, N.H.
Secretary of the Senate–Edwin Pope Thayer, Ind.
Speaker of the House–John Nance Garner, Tex., elected Dec. 7, 1931
Clerk of the House–South Trimble, Ky., elected Dec. 7, 1931

APPOINTMENTS TO THE SUPREME COURT

Chief Justice
Charles Evans Hughes, N.Y., Feb. 13, 1930

Associate Justices
Owen Josephus Roberts, Pa., May 20, 1930
Benjamin Nathan Cardozo, N.Y., Mar. 2, 1932

ADMINISTRATION — IMPORTANT DATES

Mar. 16, 1929, Indiana taxed chain stores

May 16, 1929, first Moving Picture Academy "Oscars" awarded

June 15, 1929, Agricultural Marketing Act established Farm Board to encourage cooperatives and dispose of surpluses

July 10, 1929, new small-size dollar bills issued

Oct. 25, 1929, former cabinet member A. B. Fall convicted

Oct. 29, 1929, stock market panic preceding depression

Nov. 19-27, 1929, White House conference on depression

Nov. 28, 1929, Richard Byrd made South Pole flight

Feb. 10, 1930, Grain Stabilization Corporation authorized

Mar. 26, 1930, Inter-American highway appropriation bill enacted

July 1, 1930, streamlined submarine *Nautilus* commissioned

July 21, 1930, Veterans Administration created

Feb. 14, 1931, Airmail Flyer's Medal of Honor authorized

Mar. 3, 1931, "Star Spangled Banner" adopted as national Anthem

June 1931, Hoover moratorium on German debts arranged

July 1, 1931, Harold Gatty and Wiley Post completed airplane flight around the world

Sept. 26, 1931, keel laid for the *Ranger,* first aircraft carrier

Dec. 15, 1931, Maria Norton of New Jersey appointed chairman of House committee (first woman to head congressional committee)

Jan. 12, 1932, Hattie Caraway of Arkansas elected senator (first woman to hold Senate office by election rather than appointment)

Jan. 22, 1932, Reconstruction Finance Corporation created

May 21, 1932, Amelia Earhart Putnam completed first transatlantic solo flight by a woman

July 1932, bonus army march on Washington, D.C., by unemployed veterans

Feb. 6, 1933, Twentieth ("Lame Duck") Amendment to the Constitution ratified

IMPORTANT DATES IN HIS LIFE

1884, moved to Newberg, Ore.

1891, enrolled at Leland Stanford University

1895, graduated from Leland Stanford University

1895-1913, mining engineer, consultant in North America, Europe, Asia, Africa, and Australia

1899, went to China with his bride

1900, took part in defense of Tientsin in Boxer outbreak

1914-1915, chairman of American Relief Committee in London

1915-1918, chairman of Commission for Relief in Belgium

Aug, 1917-June 1919, U.S. food administrator

1919, chairman of Supreme Economic Conference, Paris

1920, chairman of European Relief Council

1920, complimentary votes at Republican nominating convention

1921-1928, secretary of commerce under Presidents Harding and Coolidge

1922, coal administration

June 14, 1928, nominated for the presidency by the Republican convention at Kansas City, Mo.

Mar. 4, 1929-Mar. 3, 1933, President

Nov. 8, 1932, defeated for reelection by Democratic candidate, Franklin Delano Roosevelt

1946, appointed coordinator of European food program by President Truman

1947-1949, 1953-1955, chairman of Commission on Organization of the Executive Branch of the Government (Hoover Commission on administrative reform)

HERBERT CLARK HOOVER

_____was the first President born in Iowa.

_____was the thirteenth President who was a resident of a state other than his native state.

_____was the first President to have served in a cabinet other than as secretary of state or war.

_____was the last President whose term of office ended on March 3.

HOOVER'S VICE PRESIDENT

Vice President–Charles Curtis (31st V.P.)

Date of birth–Jan. 25, 1860

Birthplace–Topeka, Kan.

Political party–Republican

State represented–Kansas

Term of office–Mar. 4, 1929-Mar. 3; 1933

Age at inauguration–69 years, 38 days

Occupation after term–Lawyer

Date of death–Feb. 8, 1936

Age at death–76 years, 14 days

Place of death–Washington, D.C.

Burial place–Topeka, Kan.

Additional data on Curtis

1881, admitted to the bar; practiced in Topeka, Kan.

1885-1889, prosecuting attorney, Shawnee County, Kan.

Mar. 4, 1893-Jan. 28, 1907, U.S. House of Representatives (from Kansas)

Jan. 29, 1907-Mar. 3, 1913, U.S. Senate (from Kansas)

Dec. 4-12, 1911, president pro tempore of the Senate

1912, unsuccessful candidate for reelection to Senate

Mar. 4, 1915-Mar. 3 1929, U.S. Senate

1924, elected majority leader of the Senate

1932, unsuccessful candidate for reelection as Vice President

1933-1936, practiced law in Washington, D.C.

ADDITIONAL DATA ON HOOVER

FIRST PRESIDENT BORN WEST OF THE MISSISSIPPI

Herbert Clark Hoover, born August 10, 1874, at West Branch, Iowa, was the first President born west of the Mississippi River. His wife,

Lou Henry Hoover, born March 29, 1875, at Waterloo, Iowa, was the first President's wife born west of the Mississippi.

ASTEROID NAMED FOR HOOVER

The first asteroid named for an American President was Hooveria. It was discovered in March 1920 by Professor Johann Palisan of the University of Vienna, Austria, and named for Herbert Hoover. At that time, Hoover was not yet President; he was engaged in providing food for distressed European countries.

NOTIFICATION OF NOMINATION TELEVISED

Presidential nomination notification ceremonies were televised for the first time at the Assembly Chamber, Albany, N.Y. on Wednesday, August 22, 1928, when Democratic candidate Alfred Emanuel Smith was notified of his nomination. The pictures were transmitted by television to Schenectady, N.Y., and sent out by short wave over 2XAF and 2XAD by the General Electric Company.

INAUGURATION

Herbert Clark Hoover took his oath of office on Monday, March 4, 1929, on the east portico of the Capitol. A crowd of about fifty thousand witnessed the ceremony.

At 1:08 P.M. Chief Justice William Howard Taft administered the oath of office. Twenty years before, on Monday March 4, 1909, the same oath had been administered to Taft by Chief Justice Edward Douglass White.

The dirigible *Los Angeles,* four blimps, and thirty airplanes flew over the city. Rain fell in the afternoon. At 8 P.M. a fireworks display thrilled the crowds. At 9 P.M. the largest inaugural ball up to that time was held at the Washington Auditorium. The ball was opened by an Indian orchestra from Tulsa, Okla. The reigning woman at the ball was Mrs. Gann, sister of Vice President Curtis.

HUGHES REAPPOINTED TO SUPREME COURT

President Hoover established a precedent when he appointed as Chief Justice of the Supreme Court Charles Evans Hughes, who served February 13, 1930, to July 1, 1941. This was Hughes' second appointment to the Court, a distinction accorded no other person. He was appointed an associate justice of the Supreme Court by President Taft, serving from May 2, 1910, to June 10, 1916, when he resigned. He became the Republican nominee for President in 1916 and was defeated by Woodrow Wilson. Afterward he served as secretary of state (1921-1925), as a member of the Hague Tribunal (1926-1930), and as a judge on the Permanent Court of International Justice (1928-1930).

ABSOLUTE MONARCH VISITED HOOVER

The first absolute monarch to visit the United States was King Prajadhipok of Siam. He arrived in New York City, April 1931, accompanied by his wife, Queen Rambai Barni, and the royal entourage. President Hoover received them on April 29, 1931. They crossed into the United States on April 19, 1931 at Portal, N.D., from Canada. This was not, however, the king's first visit to the United States. As a prince he had arrived at New York City from England on September 22, 1924, for a short visit.

TWENTIETH AMENDMENT ENACTED

The Twentieth Amendment to the Constitution, known as the "lame duck amendment," which provided that "the terms of the President and the Vice President shall end at noon on the 20th day of January," was proposed to the states on March 2, 1932, by the Seventy-second Congress. Virginia was the first state to ratify the amendment when a joint resolution was passed March 4, 1932, although the State Department resolutions were not mailed until March 8, 1932. The amendment was ratified on January 23, 1933, by Georgia, Missouri, Ohio and Utah (the thirty-sixth state) and certified by the Secretary of State on February 6, 1933; but in accordance with section 5, the amendment did not take effect until October 15, 1933. By October 15, 1933, the amendment had been ratified by all the states.

The Amendment follows:

SECTION 1. The terms of the President and Vice President shall end at noon on the 20th day of January, and the terms of Senators and Representatives at noon on the 3rd day of January, of the years in which such terms would have ended if this article had not been ratified; and the terms of their successors shall then begin.

SECTION 2. The Congress shall assemble at least once in every year, and such meeting shall begin at noon on the 3rd day of January, unless they shall by law appoint a different day.

SECTION 3. If, at the time fixed for the beginning of the term of the President, the President elect shall have died, the Vice President elect shall become President. If a President shall not have been chosen before the time fixed for the beginning of his term, or if the President elect shall have failed to qualify, then the Vice President elect shall act as President until a President shall have qualified; and the Congress may by law provide for the case wherein neither a President elect nor a Vice President elect shall have qualified, declaring who shall then act as President, or the manner in which one who is to act shall be selected, and such person shall act accordingly until a President or Vice President shall have qualified.

SECTION 4. The Congress may by law provide for the case of the death of any of the persons from whom the House of Representatives may choose a President whenever the right of choice shall have devolved upon them, and for the case of the death of any of the persons from whom the Senate may choose a Vice President whenever the right of choice shall have devolved upon them.

SECTION 5. Sections 1 and 2 shall take effect on the 15th day of October following the ratification of this article.

SECTION 6. This article shall be inoperative unless it shall have been ratified as an amendment to the Constitution by the legislatures of three-fourths of the several States within seven years from the date of its submission.

THE FIRST LADY

Lou Henry Hoover lived in Washington while Herbert Hoover was secretary of commerce under Presidents Harding and Coolidge from 1921 to 1928. She had numerous personal friends in the city when they moved into the White House, and as a result social functions were more friendly than formal.

HOOVER HONORED

President Hoover was one of the most honored Presidents in our history. He received over fifty honorary degrees from American universities, over twenty-five honorary degrees from foreign universities, the freedom of more than a dozen cities, and over seventy medals and awards, in addition to about a hundred miscellaneous honors.

On January 13, 1958, General Mark Wayne Clark, president of the Citadel, South Carolina State Military College, bestowed the honorary degree of doctor of laws on the former President at the Citadel. It was the eighty-third degree that he received, one for each year of his life. He was honored as "engineer, humanitarian and statesman."

On April 25, 1958, the University of the State of New York, at the 89th convocation of the Board of Regents, awarded him an honorary degree, which he received in absentia while recovering from a gall-bladder operation.

HOOVER, ENGINEER

A survey conducted in 1964 as part of the one hundredth anniversary of the School of Engineering and Applied Science of Columbia University named Herbert Clark Hoover and Thomas Alva Edison as the two greatest engineers in the history of the United States.

HOOVER LIVED THIRTY-ONE YEARS AFTER TERM

Herbert Clark Hoover lived longer after his term of office than any other President—31 years and 231 days. He was not, however, the oldest former President at the time of his death, nor was he the oldest upon completion of his presidential term.

HOOVER NATIONAL HISTORIC SITE

On August 12, 1965, Congress enacted a law (79 Stat. L. 119) "to establish the Herbert Hoover National Historical Site" near West Branch, Iowa (President Hoover's birthplace) and appropriated $1,650,000 for land acquisition and development.

FRANKLIN DELANO ROOSEVELT

32nd PRESIDENT

Born–Jan. 30, 1882

Birthplace–Hyde Park, N.Y.

College attended–Harvard College, Cambridge, Mass.

Date of graduation–June 24, 1903, four-year course, Bachelor of Arts

Religion–Episcopalian

Ancestry–Dutch

Occupation–Governor, lawyer

Date and place of marriage–Mar. 17, 1905, New York, N.Y.

Age at marriage–23 years, 46 days

Years married–40 years, 26 days

Political party–Democratic

State represented–New York

Term of office–Mar. 4, 1933-Apr. 12, 1945

Term served–12 years, 39 days

Administration–37th, 38th, 39th, 40th

Congresses–73rd, 74th, 75th, 76th, 77th, 78th, 79th

Age at inauguration–51 years, 33 days

Lived after term–Died in office

Date of death–Apr. 12, 1945

Age at death–63 years, 72 days

Place of death–Warm Springs, Ga.

Burial place–Family plot, Hyde Park, N.Y.

PARENTS

Father–James Roosevelt

Born–July 16, 1828, Hyde Park, N.Y.

Married (1)–Rebecca Brien Howland

Married (2)–Sara Delano

Occupation–Vice president of Delaware and Hudson Railroad, lawyer, financier

Died–Dec. 8, 1900, New York, N.Y.

Age at death–72 years, 145 days

First wife of father–Rebecca Brien Howland Roosevelt

Born–Jan. 15, 1831

Married–1853

Died–Aug. 21, 1876

Age at death–45 years, 218 days

Mother–Sara Delano Roosevelt

Born–Sept. 21, 1854, Newburgh, N.Y.

Married–Oct. 7, 1880, Hyde Park, N.Y.

Died–Sept. 7, 1941, Hyde Park, N.Y.

Age at death–86 years, 351 days

BROTHER

Franklin Delano Roosevelt was a second son, the only child of his father's second marriage.

Children of James Roosevelt and Rebecca Brien Howland Roosevelt

James Roosevelt, b. Mar. 27, 1854; d. May 7, 1927

Children of James Roosevelt and Sara Delano Roosevelt

Franklin Delano Roosevelt, b. Jan. 30, 1882; d. Apr. 12, 1945

CHILDREN

Anna Eleanor Roosevelt, b. May 3, 1906, New York, N.Y.; m. June 5, 1926, Curtis Bean Dall, Hyde Park, N.Y.; m. Jan. 18, 1935, John Boettiger, New

For additional data see the end of this section and also specific subject headings in the index.

York, N.Y.; m. Nov. 11, 1952, James Addison Halsted, Malibu, Calif.; d. Dec. 1, 1975, New York, N.Y.

James Roosevelt, b. Dec. 23, 1907, New York, N.Y.; m. June 4, 1930, Betsy Cushing, Brookline, Mass.; m. Apr. 14, 1941, Romelle Theresa Schneider, Beverly Hills, Calif.; m. July 1, 1956, Gladys Irene Owens, Los Angeles, Calif.

Franklin Roosevelt, b. Mar. 18, 1909; d. Nov. 8, 1909

Elliott Roosevelt, b. Sept. 23, 1910, New York, N.Y.; m. Jan. 16, 1932, Elizabeth Browning Donner, Bryn Mawr, Pa.; m. July 22, 1933, Ruth Josephine Googins, Burlington, Iowa; m. Dec. 3, 1944, Faye Emerson, Grand Canyon, Ariz.; m. Mar. 15, 1951, Minnewa Bell Ross, Miami Beach, Fla.

Franklin Delano Roosevelt, Jr., b. Aug. 17, 1914, Campobello, New Brunswick, Canada; m. June 30, 1937, Ethel Du Pont, Wilmington, Del.; m. Aug. 31, 1949, Suzanne Perrin, New York, N. Y.; m. July 1, 1970, Felicia Schiff Warburg Sarnoff, New York, N.Y.

John Aspinwall Roosevelt, b. Mar. 13, 1916, Washington, D.C.; m. June 18, 1938, Anne Lindsay Clark, Nahant, Mass.; m. Oct. 22, 1965, Irene Boyd McAlpin

MRS. FRANKLIN DELANO ROOSEVELT

Name–(Anna) Eleanor Roosevelt Roosevelt

Date of birth–Oct. 11, 1884

Birthplace–New York, N.Y.

Age at marriage–20 years, 157 days

Children–5 sons, 1 daughter

Mother–Anna Livingston Hall Roosevelt

Father–Elliott Roosevelt

His occupation–Sportsman

Date of death–Nov. 7, 1962

Age at death–78 years, 27 days

Place of death–New York, N.Y.

Burial place–Family plot, Hyde Park, N.Y.

Years younger than the President–2 years, 254 days

Years she survived the President–17 years, 209 days

THE ELECTION OF 1932

NOMINATIONS FOR TERM 1933-1937

Democratic Party Convention (26th)

June 27-July 2, 1932, Chicago Stadium, Chicago, Ill.

Nominated for President—Franklin Delano Roosevelt, N.Y.

Nominated for Vice President—John Nance Garner, Tex.

Roosevelt was nominated on the fourth ballot. Candidates for nomination and the votes they received on the first and fourth ballots:

Franklin Delano Roosevelt, N.Y., 666^1/$_4$, 945

Alfred Emanuel Smith, N.Y., 201^3/$_4$, 190^1/$_2$

John Nance Garner, Tex., 90^1/$_4$, 0

George White, Ohio, 52, 3

Melvin Alvah Traylor, Ill., 42^1/$_4$, 0

Harry Flood Byrd, Va., 25, 0

James Alexander Reed, Mo., 24, 0

William Henry Murray, Okla., 23, 0

Albert Cabell Ritchie, Md., 21, 3^1/$_2$

Newton Diehl Baker, Ohio, $8^1/_2$, $5^1/_2$
James Middleton Cox, Ohio, 0, 1
Total number of votes:
  First ballot: 1,154
  Fourth ballot: $1,148^1/_2$
Number necessary for nomination: 766

Republican Party Convention (20th)

June 14-16, 1932, Chicago Stadium, Chicago, Ill.
Nominated for President—Herbert Clark Hoover, Calif.
Nominated for Vice President—Charles Curtis, Kan.
  Hoover was nominated on the first ballot. Candidates for nomination and the votes they received:
Herbert Clark Hoover, Calif., $1,126^1/_2$
John James Blaine, Wis., 13
Calvin Coolidge, Mass., $4^1/_2$
Joseph Irwin France, Md., 4
Charles Gates Dawes, Ill., 1
James Wolcott Wadsworth, N.Y., 1
Total number of votes: 1,150
Nomination made unanimous

Socialist Party Convention

May 20-24, 1932, Municipal Auditorium, Milwaukee, Wis.
Nominated for President—Norman Mattoon Thomas, N.Y.
Nominated for Vice President—James Hudson Maurer, Pa.

Communist Party Convention

May 28, 1932, People's Auditorium, Chicago, Ill.
Nominated for President—William Zebulon Foster, Ill.
Nominated for Vice President—James William Ford, N.Y.

Prohibition Party Convention (16th)

July 5-7, 1932 at Indianapolis, Ind.
Nominated for President—William David Upshaw, Ga.
Nominated for Vice President—Frank Stewart Regan, Ill.

Liberty Party Convention

Aug. 17, 1932, St. Louis, Mo.
Nominated for President—William Hope Harvey, Ark.
Nominated for Vice President—Frank B. Hemenway, Wash.

Socialist Labor Party Convention

Apr. 30-May 2, 1932, Cornish Arms Hotel, New York, N.Y.
Nominated for President—Verne L. Reynolds, N.Y.
Nominated for Vice President—John W. Aiden, Mass.
Eric Hass of New York, nominated for President, was too young to qualify and declined.

Farmer Labor Party Convention

Apr. 26-27, 1932, Omaha, Neb.

Nominated for President—Frank Elbridge Webb, Calif.
Nominated for Vice President—Jacob Sechler Coxey, Ohio
The executive committee replaced Webb with Coxey on July 10, 1932, Julius J. Reiter of Minnesota was named for Vice President.

Jobless Party Convention

Aug. 17, 1932, Crevecoeur Speedway, St. Louis, Mo.
Nominated for President—James Renshaw Cox, Pa.
Nominated for Vice President—V. C. Tisdal, Okla.
Nominated by acclamation

National Party Convention

June 26, 1932, Indianapolis, Ind.
Nominated for President—Seymour E. Allen, Mass.
Allen declined the nomination

ELECTION RESULTS, NOV. 8, 1932—PRESIDENTIAL AND VICE PRESIDENTAL CANDIDATES

Democratic Party (22,821,857 votes)

Franklin Delano Roosevelt, N.Y.
John Nance Garner, Tex.

Republican Party (15,761,845 votes)

Herbert Clark Hoover, Calif.
Charles Curtis, Kan.

Socialist Party (881,951 votes)

Norman Mattoon Thomas, N.Y.
James Hudson Maurer, Pa.

Communist Party (102,785 votes)

William Zebulon Foster, Ill.
James William Ford, N.Y.

Prohibition Party (81,869 votes)

William David Upshaw, Ga.
Frank Stewart Regan, Ill.

Liberty Party (53,425 votes)

William Hope Harvey, Ark.
Frank B. Hemenway, Wash.

Socialist Labor Party (33,276 votes)

Verne L. Reynolds, N.Y.
John W. Aiken, Mass.

Farmer Labor Party (7,309 votes)

Jacob Sechler Coxey, Ohio
Julius J. Reiter, Minn.

ELECTORAL VOTES (531—48 states)

Roosevelt received 88.89 per cent (472 votes—42 states) as follows:

Ala. 11; Ariz. 3; Ark. 9; Calif. 22; Colo. 6; Fla. 7; Ga. 12; Idaho 4; Ill. 29; Ind. 14; Iowa 11; Kan. 9; Ky. 11; La. 10; Md. 8; Mass. 17; Mich. 19; Minn. 11; Miss. 9; Mo. 15; Mont. 4; Neb. 7; Nev. 3; N.J. 16; N.M. 3; N.Y. 47; N.C. 13; N.D. 4; Ohio 26; Okla. 11; Ore. 5; R.I. 4; S.C. 8; S.D. 4; Tenn. 11; Tex. 23; Utah 4; Va. 11; Wash. 8; W.Va. 8; Wis. 12; Wyo. 3.

Hoover received 11.11 per cent (59 votes—6 states) as follows: Conn. 8; Del. 3; Me. 5; Nev. 4; Pa. 36; Vt. 3.

THE ELECTION OF 1936
NOMINATIONS FOR TERM 1937-1941
Democratic Party Convention (27th)

June 23-27, 1936, Convention Hall, Philadelphia, Pa.
Nominated for President—Franklin Delano Roosevelt, N.Y.
Nominated for Vice President—John Nance Garner, Tex.
  Franklin Delano Roosevelt was renominated by acclamation and no vote was taken.

Republican Party Convention (21st)

June 9-12, 1936, Municipal Auditorium, Cleveland, Ohio
Nominated for President—Alfred Mossman Landon, Kan.
Nominated for Vice President—Frank Knox, Ill.
  Landon was nominated on the first ballot. Candidates for nomination and the votes they received:
Alfred Mossman Landon, Kan., 984
William Edgar Borah, Idaho, 19
Total number of votes: 1,003
Number necessary for nomination: 502

Union Party Convention

June 19, 1936
Nominated for President—William Lemke, N.D.
Nominated for Vice President—Thomas Charles O'Brien, Mass.

Socialist Party Convention

May 22-26, 1936, Municipal Auditorium, Cleveland, Ohio
Nominated for President—Norman Mattoon Thomas, N.Y.
Nominated for Vice President—George A. Nelson, Wis.

Communist Party Convention

June 24-28, 1936, New York, N.Y.
Nominated for President—Earl Russell Browder, Kan.
Nominated for Vice President—James William Ford, N.Y.

Prohibition Party Convention (17th)

May 5-7, 1936, Niagara Falls, N.Y.
Nominated for President—David Leigh Colvin, N.Y.
Nominated for Vice President—Alvin York, Tenn.
  York declined the nomination and the executive committee nominated Claude A. Watson of California.

Socialist Labor Party Convention

Apr. 25-28, 1936, Cornish Arms Hotel, New York, N.Y.
Nominated for President—John W. Aiken, Mass.
Nominated for Vice President—Emil F. Teichert, N.Y.

National Greenback Party (formerly the National Independent Party; renamed in 1934)

Apr. 6, 1936, Indianapolis, Ind.
Nominated for President—John Zahnd, Ind.
Nominated for Vice President—Florence Garvin, R.I.

ELECTION RESULTS, NOV. 3, 1936—PRESIDENTIAL AND VICE PRESIDENTIAL CANDIDATES

Democratic Party (27,476,673 votes)

Franklin Delano Roosevelt, N.Y.
John Nance Garner, Tex.

Republican Party (16,679,583 votes)

Alfred Mossman Landon, Kan.
Frank Knox, Ill.

Union Party (892,793 votes)

William Lemke, N.D.
Thomas Charles O'Brien, Mass.

Socialist Party (187,720 votes)

Norman Mattoon Thomas, N.Y.
George A. Nelson, Wis.

Socialist Party (187,720 votes)

Norman Mattoon Thomas, N.Y.
George A. Nelson, Wis.

Communist Party (80,159 votes)

Earl Russell Browder, Kan.
James Willam Ford, N.Y.

Prohibition Party (37,847 votes)

David Leigh Colvin, N.Y.
Claude A. Watson, Calif.

Socialist Labor Party (12,777 votes)

John W. Aiken, Mass.
Emil F. Teichert, N.Y.

ELECTORAL VOTES (531—48 states)

Roosevelt received 98.49 per cent (523 votes-—46 states—all states except Maine and Vermont).

Landon received 1.51 per cent (8 votes—2 states) as follows: Me. 5; Vt. 3.

THE ELECTION OF 1940

NOMINATIONS FOR TERM 1941-1945

Democratic Party Convention (28th)

July 15-18, 1940, Chicago Stadium, Chicago, Ill.
Nominated for President—Franklin Delano Roosevelt, N.Y.
Nominated for Vice President—Henry Agard Wallace, Iowa
   Roosevelt was nominated on the first ballot. Candidates for nomination and the votes they received:
Franklin Delano Roosevelt, N.Y., 946 $^{13}/_{30}$
James Aloysius Farley, N.Y., 72 $^{9}/_{10}$
John Nance Garner, Tex., 61
Millard Evelyn Tydings, Md., 9$^{1}/_{2}$
Cordell Hull, Tenn., 5$^{2}/_{3}$
Number necessary for nomination:551
Roosevelt nominated by acclamation

Republican Party Convention (22nd)

June 24-28, 1940, Convention Hall, Philadelphia, Pa.
Nominated for President—Wendell Lewis Willkie, N.Y.
Nominated for Vice President—Charles Linza McNary, Ore.
   Wilkie was nominated unanimously on the sixth ballot. Candidates for nomination and the votes they received on the first ballot:
Thomas Edmund Dewey, N.Y., 360
Robert Alphonso Taft, Ohio, 189
Wendell Lewis Willkie, N.Y., 105
Arthur Hendrick Vandenberg, Mich., 76
Arthur Horace James, Pa., 74
Joseph William Martin, Mass., 44
Frank Ernest Gannett, N.Y., 33
Henry Styles Bridges, N.H., 28
Arthur Capper, Kan., 18
Herbert Clark Hoover, Calif., 17
Charles Linza McNary, Ore., 13
Harlan John Bushfeld, S.D., 9
Total number of votes:
   First ballot: 1,000
   Sixth ballot: 998
Number necessary for nomination: 501

Socialist Party Convention

Apr. 6-8, 1940, National Press Club Auditorium, Washington, D.C.
Nominated for President—Norman Mattoon Thomas, N.Y.
Nominated for Vice President—Maynard C. Krueger, Ill.
   Thomas was nominated unanimously on the first ballot.

Prohibition Party Convention (18th)

May 8-10, 1940, Chicago, Ill.

   Nominated for President—Roger Ward Babson, Mass.
   Nominated for Vice President—Edgar V. Moorman, Ill.

Communist Party Convention (Workers Party)

May 30, June 1-2, 1940, Royal Windsor Hotel, New York, N.Y.
Nominated for President—Earl Russell Browder, Kan.
Nominated for Vice President—James William Ford, N.Y.

Socialist Labor Party Convention

Apr. 27-30, 1940, Chelsea Arms Hotel, New York, N.Y.
Nominated for President—John W. Aiden, Mass.
Nominated for Vice President—Aaron M. Orange, N.Y.

Greenback Party Convention

July 4, 1940, Indianapolis, Ind.
Nominated for President—John Zahnd, Ind.
Nominated for Vice President—James Elmer Yates, Ariz.
   Anna Milburn of Washington was nominated for the presidency but declined.

ELECTION RESULTS, NOV. 5, 1940—PRESIDENTIAL AND VICE PRESIDENTIAL CANDIDATES

Democratic Party (27,243,466 votes)

Franklin Delano Roosevelt, N.Y.
Henry Agard Wallace, Iowa

Republican Party (22,304,755 votes)

Wendell Lewis Willkie, N.Y.
Charles Linza McNary, Ore.

Socialist Party (99,557 votes)

Norman Mattoon Thomas, N.Y.
Maynard C. Krueger, Ill.

Prohibition Party (57,812 votes)

Roger Ward Babson, Mass.
Edgar V. Moorman, Ill.

Communist Party (Workers Party) (46,251 votes)

Earl Russell Browder, Kan.
James William Ford, N.Y.

Socialist Labor Party (9,458 votes)

John W. Aiken, Mass.
Aaron M. Orange, N.Y.

Additional Votes

Georgia, Independent Democrats, 22,428
California, Progressives, 16,506
Mississippi, Independent Republicans, 4,550
Minnesota, Industrial, 2,553
Pennsylvania, Independent Government, 1,518
Maryland, Labor Party of Maryland, 657
Miscellaneous, 5,701

ELECTORAL VOTES (531—48 states)

Roosevelt received 84.56 per cent (449 votes—38 states) as follows: Ala. 11; Ariz. 3; Ark. 9; Calif. 22; Conn. 8; Del. 3; Fla. 7; Ga. 12; Idaho 4; Ill. 29; Ky. 11; La. 10; Md. 8; Mass. 17; Minn. 11; Miss. 9; Mo. 15; Mont. 4; Nev. 3; N.H. 4; N.J. 16; N.M. 3; N.Y. 47; N.C. 13; Ohio 26; Okla. 11; Ore. 5; Pa. 36; R.I. 4; S.C. 8; Tenn. 11; Tex. 23; Utah 4; Va. 11; Wash. 8; W.Va. 8; Wis. 12; Wyo. 3.

Willkie received 15.44 per cent (82 votes—10 states) as follows: Colo. 6; Ind. 14; Iowa 11; Kan. 9; Me. 5; Mich. 19; Neb. 7; N.D. 4; S.D. 4; Vt. 3.

THE ELECTION OF 1944

NOMINATIONS FOR TERM 1945-1949

Democratic Party Convention (29th)

July 19-21, 1944, Chicago Stadium, Chicago, Ill.
Nominated for President—Franklin Delano Roosevelt, N.Y.
Nominated for Vice President—Harry S. Truman, Mo.

Roosevelt was nominated on the first ballot. Candidates for nomination and the votes they received:
Franklin Delano Roosevelt, N.Y., 1,086
Harry Flood Byrd, Va., 89
James Aloysius Farley, N.Y., 1
Total number of votes: 1,176
Number necessary for nomination: 589

Republican Party Convention (23rd)

June 26-28, 1944, Chicago Stadium, Chicago, Ill.
Nominated for President—Thomas Edmund Dewey, N.Y.
Nominated for Vice President—John William Bricker, Ohio

Dewey was nominated on the first ballot. Candidates for nomination and the votes they received:
Thomas Edmund Dewey, N.Y., 1,056
Douglas MacArthur, Wis., 1
Total number of votes: 1,057
Number necessary for nomination: 529

Socialist Party Convention

June 2-4, 1944, Berkshire Hotel, Reading, Pa.
Nominated for President—Norman Mattoon Thomas, N.Y.
Nominated for Vice President—Darlington Hoopes, Pa.

Prohibition Party Convention (19th)

Nov. 12, 1943, Indianapolis, Ind.
Nominated for President—Claude A. Watson, Calif.
Nominated for Vice President—Andrew Johnson, Ky.

F. C. Carrer of Maryland was chosen as vice presidential nominee but did not accept.

Socialist Labor Party Convention

Apr. 29-May 2, 1944, Cornish Arms Hotel, New York, N.Y.
Nominated for President—Edward A. Teichert, Pa.

Nominated for Vice President—Arla A. Albaugh, Ohio

America First Party Convention

Aug. 30, 1944, Detroit, Mich.
Nominated for President—Gerald Lyman Kenneth Smith, Mich.
Nominated for Vice President—Henry A. Romer, Ohio

Communist Party Convention

May 19-22, 1944, Riverside Plaza Hotel, New York, N.Y.
   No candidates were nominated though Roosevelt was favored.

ELECTION RESULTS, NOV. 7, 1944—PRESIDENTIAL AND VICE PRESIDENTIAL CANDIDATES

Democratic Party (25,602,505 votes)

Franklin Delano Roosevelt, N.Y.
Harry S. Truman, Mo.

Republican Party (22,006,278 votes)

Thomas Edmund Dewey, N.Y.
John William Bricker, Ohio

Socialist Party (80,518 votes)

Norman Mattoon Thomas, N.Y.
Darlington Hoopes, Pa.

Prohibition Party (74,758 votes)

Claude A. Watson, Calif.
Andrew Johnson, Ky.

Socialist Labor Party (45,336 votes)

Edward A. Teichert, Pa.
Arla A. Albaugh, Ohio

Additional Votes

Texas, Texas Regulars, 135,439
Massachusetts, blank votes, 49,328
Mississippi, Regular Democrats, 9,964
Mississippi, Independent Republicans, 7,859
South Carolina, Southern Democrats, 7,799
Georgia, Independent Democrats, 3,373
Miscellaneous, 2,527

ELECTORAL VOTES (531—48 states)

Roosevelt received 81.36 per cent (432 votes—36 states) as follows: Ala. 11; Ariz. 4; Ark. 9; Calif. 25; Conn. 8; Del. 3; Fla. 8; Ga. 12; Idaho 4; Ill. 28; Ky. 11; La. 10; Md. 8; Mass. 16; Mich. 19; Minn. 11; Miss. 9; Mo. 15; Mont. 4; Nev. 3; N.H. 4; N.J. 16; N.M. 4; N.Y. 47; N.C. 14; Okla. 10; Ore. 6; Pa. 35; R.I. 4; S.C. 8; Tenn. 12; Tex. 23; Utah 4; Va. 11; Wash. 8; W. Va. 8.

Dewey received 18.64 per cent (99 votes—12 states) as follows: Colo. 6; Ind. 13; Iowa 10; Kan. 8; Me. 5; Neb. 6; N.D. 4; Okla. 25; S.D. 4; Vt. 3; Wis. 12; Wyo. 3.

FIRST TERM

CABINET

March 4, 1933-January 20, 1937

State–Cordell Hull, Tenn., Mar. 4, 1933

Treasury–William Hartman Woodin, N.Y., Mar. 4, 1933; Henry Morgenthau, Jr., N.Y. (under secretary), ad interim Jan. 1, 1934-Jan. 8, 1934; Henry Morgenthau, Jr., N.Y., Jan. 8, 1934

War–George Henry Dern, Utah, Mar. 4, 1933

Attorney General–Homer Stille Cummings, Conn., Mar. 4, 1933

Postmaster General–James Aloysius Farley, N.Y., Mar. 4, 1933

Navy–Claude Augustus Swanson, Va., Mar. 4, 1933

Interior–Harold Le Claire Ickes, Ill., Mar. 4, 1933

Agriculture–Henry Agard Wallace, Iowa, Mar. 4, 1933

Commerce–Daniel Calhoun Roper, S.C., Mar. 4, 1933

Labor–Frances Perkins, N.Y., Mar. 4, 1933

SECOND TERM

CABINET

January 20, 1937-January 20, 1941

State–Cordell Hull, Tenn., continued from preceding administration

Treasury–Henry Morgenthau, Jr., N.Y., continued from preceding administration

War–George Henry Dern, Utah, continued from preceding administration; died Aug. 27, 1936; Harry Hines Woodring, Kan. (assistant secretary), ad interim Sept. 25, 1936-May 6, 1937; Harry Hines Woodring, Kan., May 6, 1937; Henry Lewis Stimson, N.Y., July 10, 1940

Attorney General–Homer Stille Cummings, Conn., continued from preceding administration; Frank Murphy, Mich., ad interim Jan. 2, 1939-Jan. 17, 1939; Frank Murphy, Mich., Jan. 17, 1939; Robert Houghwout Jackson, N.Y., Jan. 18, 1940

Postmaster General–James Aloysius Farley, N.Y., continued from preceding administration; recommissioned Jan. 22, 1937; Frank Comerford Walker, Pa., Sept. 10, 1940

Navy–Claude Augustus Swanson, Va., continued from preceding administration; died July 7, 1939; Charles Edison, N.J. (acting secretary), Aug. 5, 1939-Dec. 30, 1939; (assistant secretary) ad interim Dec. 30, 1939-Jan. 11, 1940; Charles Edison, N.J., Jan. 11, 1940; Frank Knox, Ill., July 10, 1940

Interior–Harold Le Claire Ickes, Ill., continued from preceding administration

Agriculture–Henry Agard Wallace, Iowa, continued from preceding administration; Claude Raymond Wickard, Ind., Aug. 27, 1940; entered upon duties Sept. 5, 1940

Commerce–Daniel Calhoun Roper, S.C., continued from preceding administration; Harry Lloyd Hopkins, N.Y., ad interim Dec. 24, 1938-Jan. 23, 1939; Harry Lloyd Hopkins, N.Y., Jan. 23, 1939; Jesse

Holman Jones, Tex., Sept. 16, 1940; entered upon duties Sept. 19, 1940

Labor–Frances Perkins, N.Y., continued from preceding administration

THIRD TERM

CABINET

January 20, 1941-January 20, 2945

State–Cordell Hull, Tenn., continued from preceding administration; Edward Riley Stettinius, Va., Nov. 30, 1944; entered upon duties Dec. 1, 1944

Treasury–Henry Morgenthau, Jr., N.Y., continued from preceding administration

War–Henry Lewis Stimson, N.Y., continued from preceding administration

Attorney General–Robert Houghwout Jackson, N.Y., continued from preceding administration; Francis Biddle, Pa., Sept. 5, 1941

Postmaster General–Frank Comerford Walker, Pa., continued from preceding administration; recommissioned Jan. 27, 1941

Navy–Frank Knox, Ill., continued from preceding administration; died Apr. 28, 1944; James Vincent Forrestal, N.Y., May 18, 1944

Interior–Harold Le Claire Ickes, Ill., continued from preceding administration

Agriculture–Claude Raymond Wickard, Ind., continued from preceding administration

Commerce–Jesse Holman Jones, Tex., continued from preceding administration

Labor–Frances Perkins, N.Y., continued from preceding administration

FOURTH TERM

CABINET

January 20, 1945-April 12, 1945

State–Edward Riley Stettinius, Va., continued from preceding administration

Treasury–Henry Morgenthau, Jr., N.Y., continued from preceding administration

War–Henry Lewis Stimson, N.Y., continued from preceding administration

Attorney General–Francis Biddle, Pa., continued from preceding administration

Postmaster General–Frank Comerford Walker, Pa., continued from preceding administration; recommissioned Feb. 6, 1945

Navy–James Vincent Forrestal, N.Y., continued from preceding administration

Interior–Harold Le Claire Ickes, Ill., continued from preceding administration

Agriculture–Claude Raymond Wickard, Ind., continued from preceding administration

Commerce–Jesse Holman Jones, Tex., continued from preceding administration; Henry Agard Wallace, Iowa, Mar. 1, 1945; entered upon duties Mar. 2, 1945

Labor–Francis Perkins, N.Y., continued from preceding administration

FIRST TERM

SEVENTY-THIRD CONGRESS

March 4, 1933-January 3, 1935

First session–March. 9, 1933-June 15, 1933 (99 days)
Second session–Jan. 3, 1934-June 18, 1934 (167 days)
Special session of the Senate–Mar. 4, 1933-Mar. 6, 1933 (3 days)
Vice President–John Nance Garner, Tex.
President pro tempore of the Senate–Key Pittman, Nev., elected Mar. 9, 1933
Secretary of the Senate–Edwin Alexander Halsey, Va., elected Mar. 9, 1933
Speaker of the House–Henry Thomas Rainey, Ill., elected Mar. 9, 1933, died Aug. 19, 1934
Clerk of the House–South Trimble, Ky., re-elected Mar. 9, 1933

SEVENTY-FOURTH CONGRESS

January 3, 1935-January 3, 1937

First session–Jan. 3, 1935-Aug. 26, 1935 (236 days)
Second session–Jan. 3, 1936-June 20, 1936 (170 days)
Vice President–John Nance Garner, Tex.
President pro tempore of the Senate–Key Pittman, Nev., reelected Jan. 7, 1935
Secretary of the Senate–Edwin Alexander Halsey, Va.
Speaker of the House–Joseph Wellington Byrns, Tenn., elected Jan. 3, 1935, died June 4, 1936; William Brockman Bankhead, Ala., elected June 4, 1936
Clerk of the House–South Trimble, Ky., reelected Jan. 3, 1935

SECOND TERM

SEVENTY-FIFTH CONGRESS

January 3, 1937-January 3, 1939

First session–Jan. 5, 1937-Aug. 21, 1937 (229 days)
Second session–Nov. 15, 1937-Dec. 21, 1937 (37 days)
Third session–Jan. 3, 1938-June 16, 1938 (165 days)
Vice President–John Nance Garner, Tex.
President pro tempore of the Senate–Key Pittman, Nev.
Secretary of the Senate–Edwin Alexander Halsey, Va.
Speaker of the House–William Brockman Bankhead, Ala., reelected Jan. 5, 1937
Clerk of the House–South Trimble, Ky., reelected Jan. 5, 1937

SEVENTY-SIXTH CONGRESS

January 3, 1939-January 3, 1941
First session—Jan. 3, 1939-Aug. 5, 1939 (215 days)
Second session—Sept. 21, 1939-Nov. 3, 1939 (44 days)
Third session—Jan. 3, 1940-Jan. 3, 1941 (366 days)
Vice President—John Nance Garner, Tex.
President pro tempore of the Senate—Key Pittman, Nev., died Nov. 10, 1940; William Henry King, Utah, elected Nov. 19, 1940
Secretary of the Senate—Edwin Alexander Halsey, Va.
Speaker of the House—William Brockman Bankhead, Ala., reelected Jan. 3, 1939, died Sept. 15, 1940; Sam [Samuel Taliaferro] Rayburn, Tex., elected Sept. 16, 1940
Clerk of the House—South Trimble, Ky., reelected Jan. 3, 1939

THIRD TERM

SEVENTY-SEVENTH CONGRESS

January 3, 1941-January 3, 1943
First session—Jan. 3, 1941-Jan. 2, 1942 (365 days)
Second session—Jan. 5, 1942-Dec. 16, 1942 (346 days)
Vice Presidents—John Nance Garner, Tex.; Henry Agard Wallace, Iowa, Jan. 20, 1941
President pro tempore of the Senate—Pat Harrison, Miss., elected Jan. 6, 1941, died June 22, 1941; Carter Glass, Va., elected July 10, 1941
Secretary of the Senate—Edwin Alexander Halsey, Va.
Speaker of the House—Sam [Samuel Taliaferro] Rayburn, Tex., reelected Jan. 3, 1941
Clerk of the House—South Trimble, Ky., reelected Jan. 3, 1941

SEVENTY-EIGHTH CONGRESS

January 3, 1943-January 3, 1945
First session—Jan. 6, 1943-Dec. 21, 1943 (350 days; in recess July 8-Sept. 14)
Second session—Jan. 10, 1944-Dec. 19, 1944 (345 days; in recess Apr. 1-Apr. 12, June 23-Aug. 1, Sept. 21-Nov. 14)
Vice President—Henry Agard Wallace, Iowa
President pro tempore of the Senate—Carter Glass, Va.
Secretary of the Senate—Edwin Alexander Halsey, Va.
Speaker of the House—Sam [Samuel Taliaferro] Rayburn, Tex., reelected Jan. 6, 1943
Clerk of the House—South Trimble, Ky., reelected Jan. 6, 1943

FOURTH TERM

SEVENTY-NINTH CONGRESS

January 3, 1945-January 3, 1947
First session—Jan. 3, 1945-Dec. 21, 1945 (353 days) (The House was in recess July 21-Sept. 5. The Senate was in recess Aug. 1-Sept. 5.)

Second session–Jan. 14, 1946—Aug. 2, 1946 (201 days) (The House was in recess Apr. 18-Apr. 30.)

Vice Presidents–Henry Agard Wallace, Iowa; Harry S. Truman, Mo., Jan. 20, 1945, succeeded to the presidency on the death of Franklin Delano Roosevelt on Apr. 12, 1945

President pro tempore of the Senate–Kenneth McKellar, Tenn., elected Jan. 6, 1945

Secretary of the Senate–Edwin Alexander Halsey, Va., died Jan. 29, 1945; Leslie L. Biffle, Ark., elected Feb. 8, 1945

Speaker of the House–Sam [Samuel Taliaferro] Rayburn, Tex., reelected Jan. 3, 1945

Clerk of the House–South Trimble, Ky., reelected Jan. 3, 1945, died Nov. 23, 1946

APPOINTMENTS TO THE SUPREME COURT

Chief Justice
Harlan Fiske Stone, N.Y., July 3, 1941

Associate Justices
Hugo LaFayette Black, Ala., Oct. 4, 1937
Stanley Forman Reed, Ky., Jan. 31, 1938
Felix Frankfurter, Mass., Jan. 20, 1939
William Orville Douglas, Conn., Apr. 17, 1939
Frank Murphy, Mich., Jan. 18, 1940
James Francis Byrnes, S.C., July 8, 1941
Robert Houghwout Jackson, N.Y. July 11, 1941
William Blount Rutledge, Iowa, Feb. 15, 1943

ADMINISTRATION—IMPORTANT DATES

Mar. 4, 1933, Good Neighbor policy in Latin American relations announced

Mar. 5-13, 1933, bank holiday

Mar. 9-June 16, 1933, "Hundred Days" congressional session in which New Deal recovery measures were enacted

Mar. 31, 1933, Civilian Conservation Corps created

May 12, 1933, Agricultural Adjustment Act passed

May 12, 1933, Federal Emergency Relief Act approved

May 18, 1933, Tennessee Valley Authority established

May 27, 1933, opening of Century of Progress Exposition, Chicago

June 5, 1933, gold repeal joint resolution canceled clauses in debts, taking United States completely off gold standard

June 13, 1933, Home Owners Loan Corporation created

June 16, 1933, Federal Deposit Insurance Corporation created

June 16, 1933, Farm Credit Administration authorized

June 16, 1933, National Recovery Administration and Public Works Administration created by National Industrial Recovery Act

July 1933, Wiley Post made solo world flight

Nov. 16, 1933, United States recognized U.S.S.R.

Dec. 5, 1933, Twenty-first Amendment to the Constitution ratified (repeal of Prohibition)

Jan. 30, 1934, Gold Reserve Act devaluated the dollar

G Washington

John Adams

Th Jefferson

James Madison

James Monroe

J. Q. Adams

Andrew Jackson

M Van Buren

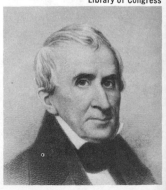

W. H. Harrison

John Tyler

James K. Polk

Zachary Taylor

Millard Fillmore

Frank Pierce

James Buchanan

R. B. Hayes

J. A. Garfield

Chester A. Arthur

Theodore Roosevelt

Wm H Taft

Woodrow Wilson

W.G. Harding

Calvin Coolidge

Herbert Hoover

ay 10, 1940, Churchill became Prime Minister of England

ay 28, 1940, King Leopold surrendered Belgian army

ne 27, 1940, national emergency declared

ne 28, 1940, Alien Registration Act passed

ept. 3, 1940, Roosevelt announced trade of fifty over-age destroyers
to Great Britain in exchange for air bases

Sept. 16, 1940, Selective Training and Service Act approved

Oct. 16, 1940, registration for selective service, ages 21 to 35

Oct. 28, 1940, Italy invaded Greece

Jan. 6, 1941, "Four Freedoms" enunciated

Mar. 11, 1941, Lend-Lease Act passed

June 22, 1941, Germany invaded Russia

July 7, 1941, Roosevelt announced occupation of Iceland by U.S.
troops on invitation of Icelandic government

July 26, 1941, General MacArthur appointed commander of U.S. forces
the Philippines

ly 30, 1941, United States recognized Czechoslovak govern-
ment-in-exile located in London and headed by Dr. Eduard Beneš

Aug. 9, 1941, Pres. Roosevelt and Prime Minister Churchill held three-
day conference off Newfoundland coast

Aug. 14, 1941, Atlantic Charter—eight-point statement of principles
for peace—issued jointly by United States and Great Britain

Sept. 29, 1941, three power Moscow conference; United States and
Great Britain agreed to send U.S.S.R. large supplies of war material

Dec. 7, 1941, Japan attacked Hawaii, Guam, and the Philippines

Dec. 8, 1941, United States declared war against Japan

Dec. 11, 1941, Germany and Italy declared war against the United
States

Dec. 12, 1941, Guam captured (first American possession to fall into
enemy hands)

Dec. 17, 1941, Rear Admiral Nimitz replaced Admiral Kimmel as commander-in-chief of U.S. Pacific fleet

Dec. 20, 1941, Admiral King designated commander-in-chief of U.S.
naval forces

Dec. 22, 1941, Prime Minister Churchill arrived in the United States
on a battleship; returned by airplane Jan. 14, 1942

Jan. 1, 1942, United Nations declaration signed by twenty-six nations
at Washington, D.C., affirming principles of Atlantic Charter

Jan. 2, 1942, fall of Manila, P.I.

Jan. 26, 1942, first American Expeditionary Force landed in Ulster,
Northern Ireland

Mar. 17, 1942, General MacArthur in command of Allied forces in
Australia and the southwest Pacific

Apr. 9, 1942, fall of Bataan, P.I.

Apr. 18, 1942, Kobe, Nagoya, Tokyo, and Yokohama bombed by
American airplanes from carrier *Hornet*

May 14, 1942, Women's Auxiliary Army Corps authorized

June 18, 1942, Churchill conferred with Roosevelt at Washington, D.C.

Oct.-Dec. 1942, Allied invasion of North Africa

Mar. 24, 1934, Philippine Independence Act, providing for dence in 1946

May 31, 1934, Platt Amendment repealed with ratification of treaty

June 6, 1934, Securities and Exchange Commission authorized

June 12, 1934, Reciprocal Tariff Act passed

June 19, 1934, Federal Communications Commission created

June 27, 1934, Railway Pension Act passed

June 28, 1934, Federal Housing Administration authorized

Apr. 8, 1935, Works Progress Administration established

May 27, 1935, National Industrial Recovery Act declared unconst tional

July 5, 1935, Wagner Labor Relations Act passed

Aug. 1935, Neutrality Act passed

Aug. 14, 1935, Social Security Act passed

Aug. 26, 1935, Federal Power Commission established under Pu Utility Holding Act

Jan. 6, 1936, Agricultural Adjustment Act declared unconstitution

Feb. 29, 1936, Soil Conservation and Domestic Allotment Act pas

June 26, 1936, Merchant Marine Act passed, providing for Marit Commission and ship subsidies

Dec. 1936, Inter-American Conference, Buenos Aires, Argentina

Jan.-June 1937, CIO sit-down strikes

Feb. 5, 1937, Supreme Court controversy started with Roosev "court packing" recommendations

Apr. 12, 1937, Supreme Court sanctioned power of Congress to r late labor relations of persons engaged in interstate commerce

May 24, 1937, Supreme Court held Social Security Act of Aug 1935 constitutional

July 22, 1937, Senate rejected President's Supreme Court "pacl plan by vote of 70 to 20

Sept. 2, 1937, Wagner-Steagall Housing Act passed

Oct.-Nov. 1937, business recession

Feb. 16, 1938, second Agricultural Adjustment Act passed

June 24, 1938, Food, Drug and Cosmetic Act passed

June 25, 1938, Fair Labor Standards Act passed

July 1938, Howard Hughes made world flight in three days and teen hours

Dec. 1938, Pan-American Conference on hemispheric solidarity, Peru

Feb. 18, 1939, opening of Golden Gate International Expositio Francisco, Calif.

Apr. 3, 1939, Administrative Reorganization Act passed

Apr. 30, 1939, opening of New York World's Fair

June 1939, visit of King George VI and Queen Elizabeth of En

Sept. 1, 1939, Germany invaded Poland

Sept. 3, 1939, Britain and France declared war on Germany War II started

Sept. 5, 1939, United States proclaimed its neutrality in Europ

Nov. 3, 1942, United States severed relations with Vichy government of France

Nov. 13, 1942, American naval victory at Guadalcanal

Dec. 2, 1942, self-sustained nuclear chain reaction demonstration, Chicago, Ill.

Jan. 14-24, 1943, Churchill and Roosevelt conferred in North Africa

Jan. 28, 1943, Roosevelt and President Vargas of Brazil conferred at Natal, Brazil

May-June 1943, United Nations Conference on Food and Agriculture, Hot Springs, Va., established United Nations Food and Agriculture Organization

Sept.-Dec. 1943, invasion of Italy

Nov. 9, 1943, United Nations Relief and Rehabilitation Administration established with signing of agreement by forty-four nations at Washington, D.C.

Nov. 28-Dec. 1, 1943, Churchill, Stalin, and Roosevelt conferred at Teheran, Iran

Dec. 8, 1943, American carriers raided the Marshall Islands

Mar. 4, 1944, first American bomber attacked Berlin

June 6, 1944, D-Day invasion of France by Allies

June 22, 1944, Servicemen's Readjustment Act (G.I. Bill of Rights) approved

July 1944, United Nations Monetary and Financial Conference, Bretton Woods, N.H.

Aug.-Oct. 1944, Dumbarton Oaks conference on a postwar international organization; proposals served as basis for United Nations charter

Feb. 4-11, 1945, Churchill, Stalin, Roosevelt conferred at Yalta in the Crimea

IMPORTANT DATES IN HIS LIFE

1896-1900, student at Groton School, Groton, Mass.

1900-1904, student at Harvard

1904-1907, student at Columbia Law School

1907, admitted to the bar

1907-1019, practiced in New York City with firm of Carter, Ledyard and Milburn

Nov. 8, 1910, elected to N.Y. Senate

Jan. 1, 1911-Mar. 17, 1913, first public office—New York State Senate (from Dutchess County)

Nov. 5, 1912, reelected to N.Y. Senate

1913-1920, assistant secretary of the Navy

1914, unsuccessful in Democratic primaries for U.S. Senate (from New York)

July-Sept. 1918, in Europe on army inspection

Jan. 1919, in Europe in charge of demobilization

July 1920, received Democratic nomination for the vice presidency at San Francisco convention as running mate of James M. Cox

Nov. 1920, defeated for the vice presidency

1920, returned to New York law practice with firm of Emmet, Marvin and Roosevelt

1920-1928, vice president of Fidelity and Deposit Company

Aug. 1921, stricken with infantile paralysis at summer home, Campobello, New Brunswick, Canada

1924, member of law firm of Roosevelt and O'Connor

1929-1933, governor of New York

Mar. 4, 1933-Jan. 19, 1937, President (first term)

Jan. 20, 1937-Jan. 19, 1941, President (second term) (first President to take office on the new date specified by the Twentieth Amendment)

Jan. 20, 1941-Jan. 19, 1945, President (third term)

Jan. 20, 1945-Apr. 12, 1945, President (fourth term)

FRANKLIN DELANO ROOSEVELT

_____was the fourth President born in New York.

_____was the seventh President to die in office.

_____was the eighth President whose mother was alive when he was inaugurated.

_____was the first President whose mother could have voted for him for the presidency.

_____was the third Democratic President since the Civil War.

_____was the fourth President to die a natural death in office.

_____was the first President elected for a third term (and also a fourth term).

_____was the first and only President inaugurated twice on Saturday (March 4, 1933 and Jan. 20, 1945).

_____was the first defeated vice presidential nominee to win election as President.

ROOSEVELT'S VICE PRESIDENTS

FIRST AND SECOND TERMS

Vice President–John Nance Garner (32nd V.P.)

Date of birth–Nov. 22, 1868

Birthplace–near Detroit, Red River County, Tex.

Political party–Democratic

State represented–Texas

Term of office–Mar. 4, 1933-Jan. 19, 1941

Age at inauguration–64 years, 102 days

Occupation after term–Retired, farmer

Date of death–Nov. 7, 1967

Age at death–98 years, 351 days

Place of death–Uvalde, Tex.
Burial place–Uvalde, Tex.
Additional data on Garner

    1890, admitted to bar; practiced in Uvalde County, Tex.
    1893-1896, judge, Uvalde County, Tex.
    1898-1902, Texas House of Representatives
    March 4, 1903-Mar. 3, 1933, U.S. House of Representatives (from Texas)
    Dec. 7, 1931, elected Speaker of U.S. House of Representatives
    Nov. 8, 1932, reelected to 73rd Congress and elected Vice President
    1941, retired to private life

THIRD TERM

Vice President–Henry Agard Wallace (33rd V.P.)

Date of birth–Oct. 7, 1888
Birthplace–Adair County, Iowa
Political Party–Democratic
State represented–Iowa
Term of office–Jan. 20, 1941-Jan. 19, 1945
Age at inauguration–52 years, 105 days
Occupation after term–Editor, plant breeder
Date of death–Nov. 18, 1965
Age at death–77 years, 42 days
Place of death–Danbury, Conn.
Burial place–Glendale Cemetery, Des Moines, Iowa
Additional data on Wallace

    1910, graduated from Iowa State College, Ames
    1910-1924, editorial staff, *Wallace's Farmer*
    1913-1933, bred high-yielding strains of corn
    1924-1929, editor, *Wallace's Farmer*
    1927, chairman, Agricultural Round Table, Williamsburg, Va.
    1929-1933, editor, *Iowa Homestead* and *Wallace's Farmer*
    1929, delegate, International Conference of Agricultural Economists, South Devon, England
    Mar. 4, 1933-Sept. 2, 1940, secretary of agriculture
    1944, failed to receive Democratic nomination for second term as Vice President
    Mar. 2, 1945-Sept. 20, 1946, secretary of commerce
    1948, unsuccessful candidate for the presidency on Progressive Party ticket

FOURTH TERM

Vice President–Harry S. Truman (34th V.P.)

Date of birth–May 8, 1884
Birthplace–Lamar, Mo.
Political party–Democratic
State represented–Missouri
Term of office–Jan. 20, 1945-Apr.
   12, 1945 (82 days)
Age at inauguration–60 years,
   257 days
Occupation after term–President
For further biographical information see Harry S. Truman, 34th President.

ADDITIONAL DATA ON ROOSEVELT

F.D.R. RELATED TO ELEVEN FORMER PRESIDENTS

Genealogists have shown that President Franklin Delano Roosevelt was related by blood or through marriage to eleven former Presidents: Washington, John Adams, Madison, John Quincy Adams, Van Buren, William Henry Harrison, Taylor, Grant, Benjamin Harrison, Theodore Roosevelt, and Taft.

ROOSEVELT FLEW TO ACCEPT NOMINATION AT CONVENTION

The first nominating convention at which a presidential nominee made a speech of acceptance was the Democratic convention held at Chicago, Ill., July 1932, when Governor Franklin Delano Roosevelt of New York accepted the nomination and addressed the delegates.

Roosevelt was also the first presidential candidate to fly to a political convention to make his acceptance speech. He chartered a ten-passenger tri-motor airplane for his party and flew from Albany, N.Y., to Chicago on July 2.

GARNER ELECTED TO TWO OFFICES

On November 8, 1932, John Nance Garner was elected as a representative to the 73rd Congress and also Vice President under President Roosevelt. Garner had been elected as a Democrat to the 58th Congress and the fifteen succeeding Congresses and served from March 4, 1903, to March 3, 1933. He resigned from the 73rd Congress on March 3, 1933, the day before his inauguration as Vice President.

ASSASSINATION OF ROOSEVELT ATTEMPTED

An attempt on the life of President Roosevelt was made on February 15, 1933, at Miami, Fla., by Giuseppe Zangara, a bricklayer, whose shot killed Anton Joseph Cermak, Mayor of Chicago, Ill., who was with the President. Cermak died on March 2, 1933. Zangara's shots wounded five other persons. Zangara was electrocuted on March 20, 1933, at the Florida State Prison, Raiford, Fla.

FIRST INAUGURATION

Franklin Delano Roosevelt took the oath of office on Saturday, March 4, 1933, on the east portico of the Capitol. Chief Justice Charles

Evans Hughes administered the oath.

A reception was held for about fifty diplomatic missions and a stand-up luncheon for about two thousand persons. The inaugural ball was held at the Washington Auditorium, Washington, D.C. Rosa Ponselle sang "The Star-Spangled Banner." The ball was attended by Mrs. Roosevelt but not by the President.

ELECTORS INVITED TO INAUGURAL

Presidential electors generally became forgotten people after they cast their ballots. The 531 electors, of whom all but 59 were Democrats, were invited by President-elect Roosevelt to attend his inaugural at Washington, D.C., on March 4, 1933. This was the first time the Eelectoral College was invited to witness an inaugural.

WOMAN APPOINTED TO CABINET

Roosevelt established a precedent when he appointed a woman to the presidential cabinet. He appointed Frances Perkins (Mrs. Paul Wilson) Secretary of Labor. She served from March 4, 1933, to June 30, 1945. Prior to the appointment Frances Perkins had been industrial commissioner for New York.

ROOSEVELT APPOINTED WOMAN MINISTER

On April 12, 1933, President Roosevelt appointed the first woman to represent the United States as a minister to a foreign country. The appointee was Ruth Bryan Owen, the eldest daughter of William Jennings Bryan, who was appointed Envoy Extraordinary and Minister Plenipotentiary to Denmark and Iceland. Her nomination was confirmed by the Senate without even the customary formality of reference to a committee.

U.S.S.R. RECOGNIZED

Recognition of the Union of Soviet Socialist Republics was effected November 16, 1933, between President Roosevelt and Maksim Maksimovich Litvinov, the Soviet People's Commissar for Foreign Affairs. The first Soviet representative to the United States was Alexander Antonovich Troyanovsky, who was accredited as Russian ambassador from January 8, 1934, to June 22, 1938. The first ambassador from the United States to the Union of Soviet Socialist Republics was William Christian Bullitt, who was appointed by President Roosevelt and who served from November 21, 1933, until August 25, 1936.

TWENTY-FIRST AMENDMENT ENACTED

The Twenty-first Amendment was the first amendment ratified by conventions in the several states. The first twenty amendments were ratified by state legislatures.

This amendment, which repealed the eighteenth, was proposed by the 72nd Congress on February 20, 1933. Ratification was completed on December 5, 1933, when the thirty-sixth state, Utah, approved the amendment. On this date the secretary of state announced that it had been adopted by the necessary number of states.

ROOSEVELT CONDUCTED RELIGIOUS SERVICES

The first President to conduct divine services as commander-in-chief of the U.S. Navy was President Franklin Delano Roosevelt, on Easter Sunday, April 1, 1934. He read from the Book of Common Prayer of the Episcopal Church, while on the quarter deck of the *Nourmahal,* east of Key West, Fla. The services were attended by the crew of the U.S.S. *Nourmahal* and the U.S.S. *Ellis* destroyer.

PRESIDENT ROOSEVELT RECORD TRAVELER

Franklin Delano Roosevelt established numerous precedents in the field of traveling while he was President of the United States.

He was the first President to visit South America while in office. On July 10, 1934, he stopped at Cartagena, Colombia. Prior to this visit, President Enrique Olaya Herrara of Colombia had visited President Roosevelt on board the cruiser U.S.S. *Houston.*

He was also the first President to go through the Panama Canal, passing through it on July 11, 1934, on the U.S.S. *Houston.* He was greeted at Balboa, Panama, by President Harmodio Arias and Foreign Secretary Arosemena of Panama.

Roosevelt was also the first President to visit Hawaii. He landed on July 25, 1934, at Hilo, Hawaii, where he was greeted by Governor Joseph Poindexter.

These three "firsts" took place while Roosevelt was President. Other Presidents had made similar trips either before or after their terms of office.

ROOSEVELT BROADCAST FROM A FOREIGN COUNTRY

The first President to broadcast from a foreign country was Franklin Delano Roosevelt, whose speech on July 10, 1934, from Cartagena, Colombia, South America, was relayed to New York and transmitted over the combined WEAF, WJZ, and WABC networks.

F.D.R. ORIGINATED A MYSTERY STORY

President Roosevelt was an avid reader of detective stories and contemplated writing one, but was stymied when he sought the solution. He propounded the question, "How can a man disappear with five million dollars in negotiable form and not be traced?"

Six writers submitted solutions, each constituting a separate chapter in the 202-page book, "The President's Mystery Story," published in 1935, by Farrar & Rinehart. The preface was written by Fulton Oursler and the various chapters by Anthony Abbot (pseudonym of Fulton Oursler), Samuel Hopkins Adams, John Erskine, Rupert Hughes, S. S. Van Dyne (pseudonym of Willard Huntington Wright), and Rita Weiman. The story was also published in the November 1935 issue of *Liberty* magazine.

PRESIDENT AND VICE PRESIDENT OUT OF THE COUNTRY

While President Roosevelt was aboard the U.S.S. *Houston* on his vacation, Vice President John Nance Garner sailed for Japan from Seattle, Wash., on October 16, 1936, on the *President Grant.* This was the first time that both President and Vice President were simultaneously out of the country. Under the act of succession of January 19, 1886, Cordell Hull, secretary of state, acted as President. Technically, President Roosevelt was on United States soil as he was on a United States naval ship.

VETO READ TO CONGRESS

The first veto message read directly by a President was the Patman bonus bill veto, read May 22, 1935, by President Roosevelt to a joint session of Congress. The bill provided for the immediate payment to veterans of the payable 1945 face value of their adjusted service certificates. Within an hour after the veto, the House voted 322 to 98 to override it. The original vote on the measure had been 318 to 90. The following day the Senate voted 54 to 40 to override the veto. The original vote had been 55 to 33. The 54 to 40 vote was short of the two-thirds vote needed to override the veto.

OFFICIAL FLAG FOR VICE PRESIDENT

The first flag for a Vice President was established February 7, 1936, by Executive Order No. 7,285, signed by President Roosevelt. The flag was designed with the seal of the United States and a blue star in each corner on a field of white. The Navy had previously created a flag for the Vice President, but its use by other governmental departments was optional.

PENSIONS TO PRIVATE WORKERS

The first pension payments by the United States Government to workers in private industry were mailed on July 13, 1936, when checks totaling $901.56 were sent to eighteen retired railroad employees, in accordance with the Railroad Retirement Act of August 29, 1935 (49 Stat. L. 967), which appropriated $46,685,000 "to establish a retirement system for employees of carriers subject to the Interstate Commerce Act, and for other purposes."

WORST REPUBLICAN DEFEAT

The worst defeat in recent times was suffered in 1936 by the Republican candidate, Alfred Mossman Landon of Kansas, who carried only two states, Maine and Vermont. He received 8 electoral votes. Franklin Delano Roosevelt carried forty-six states, receiving 523 electoral votes.

In 1912, William Howard Taft received only 8 electoral votes. The other 523 electoral votes were divided between Woodrow Wilson (435 votes) and Theodore Roosevelt (88 votes).

SECOND INAUGURATION

Franklin Delano Roosevelt took his second oath of office on Wednesday, January 20, 1937. The oath was administered by Chief Justice Charles Evans Hughes. This was the first inauguration held on January 20. The day was seasonably cold. Electric pads were used to keep the President and the Chief Justice warm.

ROOSEVELT RODE ON DIESEL

President Roosevelt was the first President to ride on a Diesel train. On October 23, 1937, he rode on a Diesel train on the Baltimore and Ohio Railroad from Washington, D.C., to New York City. He was en route to his home at Hyde Park, N.Y.

ROOSEVELT HONORED BY FOREIGN POSTAGE STAMP

Although the United States Postal Laws and Regulations forbid placing the picture of a living President on postage stamps, these laws do not apply outside the United States. In 1938, Guatemala issued a souvenir sheet of four stamps to commemorate the second term of President Jorge Ubico. One of the stamps, a four-cent carmine-and-sepia stamp, bore a picture of Franklin Delano Roosevelt.

ROOSEVELT ON TELEVISION

The first President to appear on television was Franklin Delano Roosevelt, who spoke on April 30, 1939, at the opening ceremonies of the New York World's Fair from the Federal Building on the Exposition Grounds overlooking the Court of Peace. The proceedings were telecast by the National Broadcasting Company.

ROOSEVELT RECEIVED KING AND QUEEN OF ENGLAND

The first King and Queen of England to visit the United States were King George VI and Queen Elizabeth, who arrived by way of Canada, crossing the international border on the night of June 7, 1939, at the Suspension Bridge Station, Niagara Falls, N.Y. At an outdoor picnic arranged by President Roosevelt, the King and Queen were served hot dogs. They visited New York City and Washington, D.C., and recrossed the border on the morning of June 12, 1939, bound for Halifax, Nova Scotia, whence they sailed on June 15, 1939.

FIRST THIRD-TERM PRESIDENT

Franklin Delano Roosevelt was the first and only President to be elected for a third term. He received 27,243,466 of the 49,815,312 votes cast on November 5, 1940, carrying 38 of the 48 states and winning 449 of the 531 electoral votes. His opponent, Wendell Lewis Willkie, the Republican candidate, received 22,304,755 votes and 82 electoral votes.

Roosevelt was reelected for a fourth term in 1944, definitely shattering the two-term tradition of all former Presidents. The ratification of the Twenty-second Amendment in 1951, however, limited the office of President to two terms.

THIRD INAUGURATION

Franklin Delano Roosevelt took his third oath of office on Monday, January 20, 1941. The oath was administered by Chief Justice Charles Evans Hughes. A buffet luncheon was served to invited guests. Despite the cold weather, there was an impressive parade.

Mrs. Sara Delano Roosevelt, who had been the first mother of a President to witness her son's second inauguration, also witnessed the third. Because of the two-term limitation set by the Twenty-second

Amendment, no other mother will have that distinction.

ROOSEVELT GODFATHER TO PRINCE GEORGE

The first President to become a godfather to a member of the British royal family was President Roosevelt. On August 4, 1942, the Duke of Kent, youngest brother of King George VI, served as proxy for President Roosevelt at the christening of his son, Michael George Charles Franklin, Prince George of Kent, who was born July 4, 1942.

ROOSEVELT BROADCAST IN FRENCH

Franklin Delano Roosevelt was the first President to broadcast in a foreign language. On November 7, 1942, he addressed the French people in their own language from Washington, D.C., at the same time that the American Army was taking part in the invasion of French territorial possessions in Africa.

ROOSEVELT LEFT THE UNITED STATES IN WARTIME

President Roosevelt was the first President to leave the confines of the United States in war time. His itinerary on a 16,965-mile trip follows: January 9, 1943, left Washington, D.C., by train; January 10, 1943, arrived at Miami, Fla., and flew to Trinidad, B.W.I.; January 11, flew from Trinidad to Belem, Brazil; January 12-13, flew to Bathurst, Gambia; January 14, arrived at Casablanca; January 21, drove to Rabat and Port Lyautey and back to Casablanca; January 24, drove from Casablanca to Marrakech; January 25, flew from Marrakech to Bathurst; January 27, flew from Bathurst to Roberts Field, Liberia, and back to Bathurst before taking off for Brazil; January 28, arrived at Natal; January 29, flew from Natal to Trinidad; January 30, flew from Trinidad to Miami; left Miami by train and arrived at Washington, D.C., January 31, 1943.

PRESIDENTS OF NEGRO COUNTRIES VISITIED THE UNITED STATES

The first president of a Negro country to visit the United States was President Edwin Barclay of Liberia, who addressed the United States Senate on May 27, 1943, the day following his arrival.

On October 14, 1943, President Elie Lescot of Haiti, former Minister to the United States, arrived for a brief visit.

ROOSEVELT PRESENTED MEDAL

On June 21, 1943, President Roosevelt presented the first Medal of Honor to a soldier who had already received a Distinguished Service Cross in World War II. It was awarded to Gerry Kisters of Bloomington, Ind., for heroism in the Sicily campaign. In May 1943 General George Catlett Marshall had awarded him the Distinguished Service Cross for bravery in Africa.

ROOSEVELT VISITED OTTAWA

On August 25, 1943, President Franklin Delano Roosevelt arrived at Ottawa, Ontario, the capital of Canada, by train from Quebec, where he had conferred with Winston Churchill. Roosevelt was the first President of the United States to make an official visit to the

Canadian capital while in office.

The Earl of Athlone, Governor-General of Canada, acting as Chancellor of the University of London, conferred an honorary doctor of laws degree (LL.D.) on Roosevelt at Government House, Ottawa, on August 25, 1943.

CABINET MEMBER ADDRESSED CONGRESS

Secretary of State Cordell Hull, who reported to President Roosevelt on the tripartite conference at Moscow for the maintenance of peace and security in the postwar world, established a precedent by making a further report to Congress on November 18, 1943. The two houses of Congress, being in recess, assembled to hear him. Technically, it was not a joint session.

DEMOCRATIC VICTORIES

Franklin Delano Roosevelt won four consecutive elections, as many as the Democrats had won between the time of Abraham Lincoln and Herbert Hoover.

In 1884 Grover Cleveland defeated James Gillespie Blaine.
In 1892 Grover Cleveland defeated Benjamin Harrison.
In 1912 Woodrow Wilson defeated William Howard Taft.
In 1916 Woodrow Wilson defeated Charles Evans Hughes.

FOURTH INAUGURATION

Franklin Delano Roosevelt took his fourth oath of office on Saturday, January 20, 1945. The oath was administered by Chief Justice Harlan Fiske Stone on the south portico of the White House, a location used for the third time since 1829. President Roosevelt, bareheaded and without an overcoat, delivered a six-minute address.

A light snow had fallen on the night preceding the inauguration, and on inauguration day the thermometer registered one degree above freezing. The sky was overcast and one of the smallest crowds in recent times witnessed the ceremonies. A canvas mat was spread on the lawn for the diplomats, high government officials, and the press. A crowd of about two thousand spectators gathered beyond the south fence. Roosevelt's thirteen grandchildren were present.

ENTIRE DIVISION CITED

The first presidential citation to an entire division was made on March 15, 1945, to the 101st Airborne Division, the heroes of Bastogne, by General Dwight David Eisenhower. For ten days—December 18-27, 1944—the men had withstood overwhelming odds. When the Germans demanded their surrender, General Anthony McAuliffe replied in one word: "Nuts!"

THE FIRST LADY

Mrs. Franklin Delano Roosevelt, born Anna Eleanor Roosevelt, daughter of Elliott Roosevelt, President Theodore Roosevelt's younger brother, was active in civic affairs. As a young girl she worked as a volunteer in a settlement house, and after her marriage she assisted her husband in his rising political career.

During her husband's administration she established a precedent as a first lady famous in her own right, through not without subjecting herself to much controversy and criticism. Engaging actively in public life, she traveled considerably, making numerous speeches and reporting her observations in the press. The first news conference held in the White House by a President's wife was held March 6, 1933, by Eleanor Roosevelt in the Red Room. It was attended by thirty-five newspaper women.

After the death of her husband, Eleanor Roosevelt continued to travel widely at home and abroad, to write about her experiences, and to devote herself to humanitarian interests both national and international. From 1949 to 1952 she served as a United States delegate to the United Nations General Assembly. Known almost as well in foreign countries as in her own, she was often referred to as "the first lady of the world."

FIRST PRESIDENT'S WIFE TO TRAVEL IN AN AIRPLANE

The first President's wife to travel in an airplane to a foreign country was Mrs. Franklin Delano Roosevelt. On March 6, 1934, she left Miami, Fla., in a commercial airplane, to visit Puerto Rico and the Virgin Islands in a 2,836-mile trip. Stops were also made at Port au Prince, Haiti, and Nuevitas, Cuba. Mrs. Roosevelt returned to the United States on March 1, 1934.

HARRY S. TRUMAN

33rd PRESIDENT

Born–May 8, 1884

Birthplace–Lamar, Mo.

College attended–None

Religion–Baptist

Ancestry–English-Scotch-Irish

Occupation–Farmer, haberdasher, judge, senator, Vice President

Date of marriage–June 28, 1919, Independence, Mo.

Age at marriage–35 years, 51 days

Years married–53 years, 181 days

Political party–Democratic

State represented–Missouri

Term of office–Apr. 12, 1945-Jan. 20, 1953 (Truman succeeded to the presidency on the death of Franklin Delano Roosevelt.)

Term served–7 years, 283 days

Administration–40th, 41st

Congresses–79th, 80th, 81st, 82nd

Age at inauguration–60 years, 339 days

Lived after term–19 years, 340 days

Occupation after term–Retired; writer

Date of death–Dec. 26, 1972

Age at death–88 years, 232 days

Place of death–Kansas City, Mo.

Burial place–Independence, Mo.

PARENTS

Father–John Anderson Truman

Born–Dec. 5, 1851, Jackson County, Mo.

Married–Dec. 28, 1881, Grandview, Mo.

Occupation–Farmer, livestock dealer

Died–Nov. 3, 1914, Kansas City, Mo.

Age at death–62 years, 333 days

Mother–Martha Ellen Young Truman

Born–Nov. 25, 1852, Jackson County, Mo.

Died–July 26, 1947, Grandview, Mo.

Age at death–94 years, 243 days

BROTHERS AND SISTERS

Harry S. Truman was the oldest of three children.

Children of John Anderson Truman and Martha Ellen Young Truman

Harry S. Truman, b. May 8, 1884; d. Dec. 26, 1972

Vivian Truman, b. Apr. 25, 1886

Mary Jane Truman, b. Aug. 12, 1889

CHILDREN

(Mary) Margaret Truman, b. Feb. 17, 1924, Independence, Mo.; m. Apr. 21, 1956, Clifton Daniel, Independence, Mo.

MRS. HARRY S. TRUMAN

Name–Bess (Elizabeth Virginia) Wallace Truman

Date of birth–Feb. 13, 1885

Birthplace–Independence, Mo.

Age at marriage–34 years, 135 days

Children–1 daughter

Mother–Madge Gates Wallace

Father–David Willock Wallace

His occupation–Farmer

Years younger than the President–281 days

For additional data see the end of this section and also specific subject headings in the index.

THE ELECTION OF 1948

NOMINATIONS FOR TERM 1949-1953

Democratic Party Convention (30th)

July 12-14, 1948, Convention Hall, Philadelphia, Pa.
Nominated for President—Harry S. Truman, Mo.
Nominated for Vice President—Alben William Barkley, Ky.
  Truman was nominated on the first ballot. Candidates for nomination and the votes they received:
Harry S. Truman, Mo., 947$\frac{1}{2}$
Richard Brevard Russell, Ga., 263
Paul Vories McNutt, Ind., $\frac{1}{2}$
Total number of votes: 1,211
Number necessary for nomination: 606

Republican Party Convention (24th)

June 21-25, 1948, Convention Hall, Philadelphia, Pa.
Nominated for President—Thomas Edmund Dewey, N.Y.
Nominated for Vice President—Earl Warren, Calif.
  Dewey was nominated unanimously on the third ballot. Candidates for nomination and the votes they received on the first ballot:
Thomas Edmund Dewey, N.Y., 434
Robert Alphonso Taft, Ohio, 224
Harold Edward Stassen, Minn., 157
Arthur Hendrick Vandenberg, Mich., 62
Earl Warren, Calif., 59
Dwight Herbert Green, Ill., 56
Alfred Herbert Driscoll, N.J., 35
Raymond Earl Baldwin, Conn., 19
Joseph William Martin, Mass., 18
Carroll Reece, Tenn., 15
Douglas MacArthur, Wis., 11
Everett McKinley Dirksen, Ill., 1
Total number of votes: 1,091
Number necessary for nomination: 548

States' Rights Democratic Party Convention ("Dixiecrat" Party)

July 17, 1948, Birmingham, Ala.
Nominated for President—James Strom Thurmond, S.C.
Nominated for Vice President—Fielding Lewis Wright, Miss.
  Thurmond was nominated by acclamation on the first ballot. This party was organized by Southern dissidents who opposed Truman's civil rights program.

Progressive Party Convention

July 23-25, 1948, Convention Hall, Philadelphia, Pa.
Nominated for President—Henry Agard Wallace, Iowa
Nominated for Vice President—Glen Hearst Taylor, Idaho
  This newly organized party adopted the same name as the political

party organized in 1912 to support the candidacy of Theodore Roosevelt. Wallace attracted the support of left-wing Democrats and others who favored negotiations with the U.S.S.R. to settle the cold war, and his party was charged with domination by Communists.

Socialist Party Convention

May 7-9, 1948, Knights of Malta Hall and Berkshire Hall, Reading, Pa.
Nominated for President—Norman Mattoon Thomas, N.Y.
Nominated for Vice President—Tucker Powell Smith, Mich.

Prohibition Party Convention (20th)

June 26-28, 1947, Winona Lake, Ind.
Nominated for President—Claude A. Watson, Calif.
Nominated for Vice President—Dale Learn, Pa.

Socialist Labor Party Convention

May 1-3, 1948, Cornish Arms Hotel, New York, N.Y.
Nominated for President—Edward A. Teichert, Pa.
Nominated for Vice President—Stephen Emery, N.Y.
   This party was listed in Minnesota, New York, and Pennsylvania as the Industrial Government Party.

Socialist Workers Party Convention (Trotskyites)

July 2-3, 1948, Irving Plaza Hall, New York, N.Y.
Nominated for President—Farrell Dobbs, N.Y.
Nominated for Vice President—Grace Carlson, Minn.
   This party was founded December 31, 1937 at Chicago, Ill. No presidential ticket was named until March 3, 1948. The thirteenth annual convention ratified the selection of the candidates.

Christian Nationalist Party Convention

Aug. 20-22, 1948, Keil Auditorium, St. Louis, Mo.
Nominated for President—Gerald Lyman Kenneth Smith, Mo.
Nominated for Vice President—Henry A. Romer, Ohio

Greenback Party

Indianapolis, Ind.
Nominated for President—John G. Scott, N.Y.
Nominated for Vice President—Granville B. Leeke, Ind.
   The nominations were made by mail referendum vote.

Vegetarian Party Convention

July 7, 1948, Hotel Commodore, New York, N.Y.
Nominated for President—John Maxwell, Ill.
Nominated for Vice President—Symon Gould, N.Y.
   This was the first convention of the American Vegetarian Party.
   John Maxwell was born in Kent, England, and was therefore constitutionally barred from becoming President.

ELECTION RESULTS, NOV. 2, 1948—PRESIDENTIAL AND VICE PRESIDENTIAL CANDIDATES

Democratic Party   (24,105,695 votes)

Harry S. Truman, Mo.
Alben William Barkley, Ky.

Republican Party   (21,969,170 votes)

Thomas Edmund Dewey, N.Y.
Earl Warren, Calif.

States' Rights Democratic Party ("Dixiecrat" Party)   (1,169,021 votes)

James Strom Thurmond, S.C.
Fielding Lewis Wright, Miss.

Progressive Party   (1,156,103 votes)

Henry Agard Wallace, Iowa
Glen Hearst Taylor, Idaho

Socialist Party   (139,009 votes)

Norman Mattoon Thomas, N.Y.
Tucker Powell Smith, Mich.

Prohibition Party   (103,216 votes)

Claude A. Watson, Calif.
Dale Learn, Pa.

Socialist Labor Party   (29,061 votes)

Edward A. Teichert, Pa.
Stephen Emery, N.Y.

Socialist Workers Party   (13,613 votes)

Farrell Dobbs, N.Y.
Grace Carlson, Minn.

ELECTORAL VOTES   (531—48 states)

Truman received 57.06 per cent (303 votes—28 states) as follows: Ariz. 4; Ark. 9; Calif. 25; Colo. 6; Fla. 8; Ga. 12; Idaho 4; Ill. 28; Iowa 10; Ky. 11; Mass. 16; Minn. 11; Mo. 15; Mont. 4; Nev. 3; N.M. 4; N.C. 14; Ohio 25; Okla. 10; R.I. 4; Tenn. 11 (of the 12 votes); Tex. 23; Utah 4; Va. 11; Wash. 8; W.Va. 8; Wis. 12; Wyo. 3.

Dewey received 35.59 per cent (189 votes—16 states) as follows: Conn. 8; Del. 3; Ind. 13; Kan. 8; Me. 5; Md. 8; Mich. 19; Neb. 6; N.H. 4; N.J. 16; N.Y. 47; N.D. 4; Ore. 6; Penn. 35; S.D. 4; Vt. 3.

Thurmond received 7.35 per cent (39 votes—4 states) as follows: Ala. 11; La. 10; Miss. 9; S.C. 8; Tenn. 1 (of the 12 votes).

FIRST TERM
CABINET

April 12, 1945-January 20, 1949

State–Edward Riley Stettinius, Va., continued from preceding administration; James Francis Byrnes, S.C., July 2, 1945; entered upon duties July 3, 1945; George Catlett Marshall, Pa., Jan. 8, 1947, entered upon duties Jan. 21, 1947

Treasury–Henry Morgenthau, Jr., N.Y., continued from preceding administration; Frederick Moore Vinson, Ky., July 18, 1945; entered upon duties July 23, 1945; John Wesley Snyder, Mo., June 12, 1946; entered upon duties June 25, 1946

Defense–James Vincent Forrestal, N.Y., July 26, 1947; entered upon duties Sept. 17, 1947

War–Henry Lewis Stimson, N.Y., continued from preceding administration; Robert Porter Patterson, N.Y., Sept. 26, 1945; entered upon duties Sept. 27, 1945; Kenneth Claiborne Royall, N.C., July 21, 1947; entered upon duties July 25, 1947; served until Sept. 17, 1947

Attorney General–Francis Biddle, Pa., continued from preceding administration; Thomas Campbell Clark, Tex., June 15, 1945; entered upon duties July 1, 1945

Postmaster General–Frank Comerford Walker, Pa., continued from preceding administration; Robert Emmet Hannegan, Mo., May 8, 1945; entered upon duties July 1, 1945; Jesse Monroe Donaldson, Mo., Dec. 16, 1947

Navy–James Vincent Forrestal, N.Y., continued from preceding administration; served until Sept. 17, 1947

Interior–Harold Le Claire Ickes, Ill., continued from preceding administration; Julius Albert Krug, Wis., Mar. 6, 1946, entered upon duties Mar. 18, 1946

Agriculture–Claude Raymond Wickard, Ind., continued from preceding administration; Clinton Presba Anderson, N.M., June 2, 1945; entered upon duties June 30, 1945; Charles Franklin Brannan, Colo., May 29, 1948; entered upon duties June 2, 1948

Commerce–Henry Agard Wallace, Iowa, continued from preceding administration; William Averell Harriman, N.Y., ad interim Sept. 28, 1946-Jan. 28, 1947; William Averell Harriman, Jan. 28, 1947; Charles Sawyer, Ohio, May 6, 1948

Labor–Frances Perkins, N.Y., continued from preceding administration; Lewis Baxter Schwellenbach, Wash., June 1, 1945; entered upon duties July 1, 1945; died June 10, 1948; Maurice Joseph Tobin, Mass., ad interim Aug. 13, 1948

SECOND TERM
CABINET

January 20, 1949-January 20, 1953

State–Dean Gooderham Acheson, Conn., Jan. 21, 1949

Treasury–John Wesley Snyder, Mo., continued from preceding administration

Defense—James Vincent Forrestal, N.Y., continued from preceding administration; Louis Arthur Johnson, W.Va., Mar. 28, 1949; George Catlett Marshall, Pa., Sept. 21, 1950; Robert Abercrombie Lovett, N.Y., Sept. 17, 1951

Attorney General—Thomas Campbell Clark, Tex., continued from preceding administration; James Howard McGrath, R.I., Aug. 19, 1949; entered upon duties Aug. 24, 1949

Postmaster General—Jesse Monroe Donaldson, Mo., continued from preceding administration; recommissioned Feb. 8, 1949

Interior—Julius Albert Krug, Wis., continued from preceding administration; Oscar Littleton Chapman, Colo. (under secretary), ad interim Dec. 1, 1949-Jan. 19, 1950; Oscar Littleton Chapman, Jan. 19, 1950

Agriculture—Charles Franklin Brannan, Colo., continued from preceding administration

Commerce—Charles Sawyer, Ohio, continued from preceding administration

Labor—Maurice Joseph Tobin, Mass., ad interim, continued from preceding administration

FIRST TERM

EIGHTIETH CONGRESS

January 3, 1947-January 3, 1949

First session—Jan. 3, 1947-Dec. 19, 1947 (351 days) (in recess July 27-Nov. 17)

Second session—Jan. 6, 1948-Dec. 31, 1948 (361 days) (in recess June 20-July 26, Aug. 7-Dec. 31)

Vice President—Vice President Harry S. Truman succeeded to the presidency on the death of Franklin Delano Roosevelt on Apr. 12, 1945

President pro tempore of the Senate—Arthur Hendrick Vandenberg, Mich., elected Jan. 4, 1947

Secretary of the Senate—Carl August Loeffler, Pa., elected Jan. 4, 1947

Speaker of the House—Joseph William Martin, Jr., Mass., elected Jan. 3, 1947

Clerk of the House—John Andrews, Mass., elected Jan. 3, 1947

SECOND TERM

EIGHTY-FIRST CONGRESS

January 3, 1949-January 3, 1951

First session—Jan. 3, 1949-Oct. 19, 1949 (290 days)

Second session—Jan. 3, 1950-Jan. 2, 1951 (365 days) (The House was in recess Apr. 6-Apr. 18. Both the House and the Senate were in recess Sept. 23-Nov. 27.)

Vice President—Alben William Barkley, Ky.

President pro tempore of the Senate—Kenneth Douglas McKellar, Tenn., elected Jan. 3, 1949

Secretary of the Senate—Leslie L. Biffle, Ark., elected Jan. 3, 1949

Speaker of the House–Sam [Samuel Taliaferro] Rayburn, Tex., elected Jan. 3, 1949
Clerk of the House–Ralph R. Roberts, Ind., elected Jan. 3, 1949

EIGHTY-SECOND CONGRESS

January 3, 1951-January 3, 1953

First session–Jan. 3, 1951-Oct. 20, 1951 (291 days) (The House was in recess Apr. 18-Apr. 29. The Senate was in recess Mar. 22-Apr. 2 and Aug. 23-Sept. 12.)
Second session–Jan. 8, 1952-July 7, 1952 (182 days)
Vice President–Alben William Barkley, Ky.
President pro tempore of the Senate–Kenneth Douglas McKellar, Tenn., elected Jan. 3, 1951
Secretary of the Senate–Leslie L. Biffle, Ark., elected Jan. 3, 1951
Speaker of the House–Sam [Samuel Taliaferro] Rayburn, Tex., elected Jan. 3, 1951
Clerk of the House–Ralph R. Roberts, Ind., elected Jan. 3, 1951

APPOINTMENTS TO THE SUPREME COURT

Chief Justice
Frederick Moore Vinson, Ky., June 21, 1946

Associate Justices
Harold Hitz Burton, Ohio, Oct. 1, 1945
Thomas Campbell Clark, Tex., Aug. 24, 1949
Sherman Minton, Ind., Oct. 12, 1949

ADMINISTRATION—IMPORTANT DATES

May 7, 1945, V-E Day—Germans unconditionally surrendered to Allied forces
June 26, 1945, United Nations charter signed at San Francisco
July 16, 1945, first atomic bomb detonated, Alamogordo, N.M.
July 17-Aug. 2, 1945, President Truman attended tripartite conference near Potsdam, Germany, establishing a Council of Foreign Ministers representing the United States, France, Great Britain, China, and the U.S.S.R.
July 28, 1945, United Nations charter ratified
Aug. 6, 1945, U.S. Air Force dropped atomic bomb on Hiroshima, Japan, first use of atomic energy in war
Aug. 9, 1945, second atomic bomb dropped on Nagasaki, Japan
Aug. 14, 1945, Japan surrendered
Sept. 2, 1945, V-J Day—Japanese accepted surrender terms aboard U.S.S. *Missouri*
Feb. 20, 1946, "full employment act" created Council of Economic Advisers
July 4, 1946, Philippine Republic established
Aug. 1, 1946, Atomic Energy Commission created
Aug. 2, 1946, Legislative Reorganization Act passed
Dec. 31, 1946, cessation of World War II hostilities proclaimed
Feb. 10, 1947, Big Four treaty signed after New York meeting of foreign

ministers, Dec. 1946

Apr. 12, 1947, United Nations granted United States trusteeship of Pacific Islands formerly held by Japan

May 15, 1947, Congress approved "Truman Doctrine"—aid to Greece and Turkey to combat communism

May-June 1947, Congress passed Labor-Management Relations Act (Taft-Hartley Law) and overrode presidential veto

June 10-12, 1947, President Truman in Ottawa as guest of Governor General Viscount Alexander of Tunis (first state visit to Canada by any President)

June 14, 1947, peace treaties with Bulgaria, Hungary, Italy, and Rumania ratified by the Senate

July 18, 1947, Presidential Succession Act passed

July 26, 1947, National Military Establishment created, with services integrated under secretary of defense

Sept. 2-19, 1947, President Truman flew to closing session of the Inter-American Defense Conference at Petrópolis, Brazil, and the signing of the hemispheric mutual defense treaty

Feb. 21-25, 1948, President Truman visited Puerto, the Virgin Islands, and U.S. naval base at Guantánamo, Cuba

Apr. 1, 1948, Soviets began Berlin blockade; United States and Great Britain set up airlift of food and coal to West Berlin

Apr. 2, 1948, Congress passed foreign aid bill establishing Economic Cooperation Administration (known as European Recovery Program or Marshall Plan)

Apr. 30, 1948, Organization of American States formed at the ninth International Conference of American States at Bogotá, Colombia, by twenty-one member countries

May 25, 1948, first union contract with sliding wage scale negotiated by General Motors and United Auto Workers

Jan. 19, 1949, President's salary raised to $100,000

Apr. 4, 1949, North Atlantic treaty signed by twelve nations, Washington, D.C.

Apr. 8, 1949, United States, Great Britain, and France agreed to establish West German republic

Apr. 20, 1949, discovery of cortisone announced

June 20, 1949, Big Four Paris Conference on Germany ended with only minor agreements

July 25, 1949, President signed NATO Pact (effective Aug. 24); asked for arms for Europe

Aug. 5, 1949, United States issued White Paper on China; aid to Chiang Kai-shek stopped

Sept. 19, 1949, soft-coal strike called by John L. Lewis

Sept. 28, 1949, Congress passed arms aid program for NATO Pact partners

Sept. 30, 1949, Berlin blockade ended

Oct. 1, 1949, United Steel Workers began strike against steel industry

Oct. 14, 1949, Communist leaders convicted of violation of Smith act

Oct. 26, 1949, minimum wage bill raised salaries to 75 cents an hour

Jan. 31, 1950, President Truman announced plans for production of hydrogen bomb

June 25, 1950, North Korean Communists crossed 38th Parallel, invading Republic of Korea; United Nations requested support for South Korea

July 1, 1950, first U.S. ground troops in Korea

July 3, 1950, U.S. troops and North Koreans in battle

July 8, 1950, General MacArthur named commander-in-chief of United Nations troops in Korea

Aug. 27, 1950, Army seized railroads to prevent strike

Oct. 7, 1950, U.S. First Cavalry made first crossing of the 38th Parallel in Korea

Nov. 1, 1950, attempted assassination of President Truman by two Puerto Rican nationalists

Nov. 26, 1950, Red Chinese entered Korean War; forced U.S. troops back

Dec. 8, 1950, United States banned shipments to Communist China

Dec. 16, 1950, President proclaimed state of national emergency

Feb. 26, 1951, Twenty-second Amendment ratified (limiting Presidents to two terms)

Apr. 2, 1951, General Eisenhower opened Supreme Headquarters Allied Powers, Europe (SHAPE) in Paris

Apr. 11, 1951, General MacArthur relieved of Far Eastern command because of failure to heed presidential directives

Sept. 1, 1951, Tripartite Security Treaty signed at San Francisco, Calif. (United States, Australia, and New Zealand)

Sept. 4, 1951, first transcontinental television broadcast

Sept. 8, 1951, Japanese peace treaty signed, San Francisco, Calif.

Oct. 19, 1951, war between United States and Germany formally ended

Dec. 31, 1951, Mutual Security Administration established to replace Economic Cooperation Administration

Mar. 20, 1952, Japanese Peace Treaty ratified by the Senate

Apr. 8, 1952, President Truman ordered seizure of steel mills to prevent a strike

May 23, 1952, railroads under army control since Aug. 27, 1950, restored to owners after signing of union contract

May 25, 1952, atomic artillery shell fired in Nevada

May 26, 1952, peace contract signed in Bonn by United States, Great Britain, France and West Germany

June 2, 1952, seizure of steel mills declared illegal by Supreme Court

July 25, 1952, Puerto Rico became a U.S. commonwealth

Nov. 1, 1952, first U.S. hydrogen bomb detonated, Eniwetok, Marshall Islands

IMPORTANT DATES IN HIS LIFE

1886, moved to Harrisonville, Mo.

1888, moved to farm at Grandview, Mo.

Dec. 28, 1890, moved to Independence, Mo.

1892, attended public school, Independence, Mo.

1895, worked at Clinton Drug Store, earning three dollars a week

1901, graduated from high school

1901, worked in mail room of Kansas City *Star*

1902, timekeeper for contractor working for Santa Fe Railroad

1903-1905, worked at National Bank of Commerce, Kansas City, Mo.

1905, worked at Union National Bank, Kansas City, Mo.

June 14, 1905, joined National Guard of Missouri as charter member of Battery B

1906-1917, worked as partner on his father's farm

1917, helped organize 2nd Missouri Field Artillery, and later 129th Field Artillery, 35th Division

June 22, 1917, commissioned a first lieutenant

Sept. 26, 1917, first lieutenant, Field Artillery

1917, went to School of Fire; did regular battery duty and ran the regimental canteen

Mar. 1918, recommended for promotion

Mar. 30, 1918, overseas with the Division School Detail; sailed on S.S. *George Washington*

Apr. 20-June 18, 1918, Second Corps Artillery School at Chantillon-sur-Seine

June 1918, rejoined regiment as a captain; made adjutant, Second Battalion

July 5, 1918, regiment sent to Artillery School at Coëtquidan

July 11, 1918, ordered to command Battery D, 129th Field Artillery

Aug. 15, 1918, ordered to front

Aug. 18, 1918, arrived in Vosges Mountains in Alsace

Sept. 12-16, 1918, at St. Mihiel

Sept. 26-Oct. 3, 1918, at Meuse-Argonne

Oct. 8-Nov. 7, 1918, at Sommedieu

Nov. 7-11, 1918, at second phase of Meuse-Argonne offensive

Apr. 20, 1919, returned to New York

May 6, 1919, discharged, as major

1919-1921, haberdashery business, Kansas City, Mo.

1922-1924, judge, County Court, Jackson County, Mo. (administrative, not judicial, position)

1923-1925, studied law at Kansas City Law School

1924, unsuccessful candidate for reelection as judge

1926-1934, presiding judge, County Court, Jackson County, Mo.

Jan. 3, 1935-Jan. 17, 1945, U.S. Senate (from Missouri)

1941-1944, chairman of Special Senate Committee to Investigate the National Defense Program ("Truman Committee")

Nov. 1944, nominated as vice presidential candidate on Democratic ticket

Jan. 20, 1945, inaugurated Vice President

Apr. 12, 1945, succeeded to the presidency on the death of President Roosevelt

July 1948, nominated for another term as President on Democratic ticket

Nov. 1948, won election, upsetting all polls predicting certain Republican victory

Jan. 20, 1949-Jan. 19, 1953, President (second term)

HARRY S. TRUMAN

____was the first President born in Missouri.

____was the ninth President whose mother was alive when he was inaugurated.

____was the fourth Democratic President since the Civil War.

TRUMAN'S VICE PRESIDENT

Vice President–Alben William Barkley (35th V.P.)

Date of birth–Nov. 24, 1877

Birthplace–near Lowes, Graves County, Ky.

Political party–Democratic

State represented–Kentucky

Term of office–Jan. 20, 1949-Jan 20, 1953

Age at inauguration–71 years, 57 days

Occupation after term–Senator

Date of death–Apr. 30, 1956

Age at death–78 years, 157 days

Place of death–Lexington, Va.

Burial place–Paducah, Ky.

Additional data on Barkley

1897, graduated from Marvin College, Clinton, Ky.

1901, admitted to bar; practiced in Paducah, Ky.

1905-1909, prosecuting attorney, McCracken County, Ky.

1909-1913, judge, McCracken County Court

Mar. 4, 1913-Mar. 3, 1927, U.S. House of Representatives (from Kentucky)

Mar. 4, 1927-Jan. 19, 1949, U.S. Senate (from Kentucky)

1937-1947, Democratic majority leader of Senate

1947-1948, Democratic minority leader of Senate

Jan. 3, 1955-Apr. 30, 1956, U.S. Senate (from Kentucky)

ADDITIONAL DATA ON TRUMAN

HARRY "S" TRUMAN

The initial "S" in President Harry S. Truman's name has no special significance and is not an abbreviation of any name. It is said to have been chosen by his parents to avoid a display of favoritism, since his paternal grandfather's name was Shippe (Anderson Shippe Truman) and his maternal grandfather's name was Solomon Young.

FIRST OATH OF OFFICE

Harry S. Truman took the oath of office on Thursday, April 12, 1945, at 7:09 P.M., in the Cabinet Room at the White House. The oath was administered by Chief Justice Harlan Fiske Stone.

TRUMAN WITNESSED OATH-TAKING OF SUPREME COURT JUDGE

President Truman was the first President to witness the swearing in of one of his Supreme Court appointees. On October 1, 1945, he attended the swearing-in ceremony of Harold Hitz Burton in the Supreme Court Chamber.

TRUMAN PRESENTED MEDAL TO CONSCIENTIOUS OBJECTOR

A unique medal presentation ceremony was held on October 12, 1945, when President Truman presented a medal of honor to a conscientious objector, the first time such an award was made. The recipient was Private Desmond T. Doss of Lynchburg, Va., whose acts of heroism and outstanding bravery as a medical corpsman on Okinawa between April 29 and May 21, 1943, earned him this signal distinction.

TRUMAN 33° MASON

Truman was the only President to attain the thirty-third and last degree of the Supreme Council of the Scottish Rite for the Southern jurisdiction which honor was accorded him on October 19, 1945, at the House of the Temple, Washington, D.C. Harding was nominated but died before the degree was conferred.

TRUMAN TRAVELED IN SUBMARINE

President Truman was the first President to travel underwater in a modern submarine. He embarked at Key West, Fla., on November 21, 1946, in the U-2513, a captured German submarine. The submarine submerged off Key West during naval exercises. (President Theodore Roosevelt went underwater in the *Plunger* on August 25, 1905, off Oyster Bay, N.Y.)

TWENTY-SECOND AMENDMENT

The Twenty-second Amendment, which limited the presidential term to two four-year terms, was proposed by Congress on March 26, 1947. It became effective on February 26, 1951, when the thirty-sixth state, Nevada, ratified it.

The amendment follows:

No person shall be elected to the office of the President more than twice, and no person who has held the office of President, or acted as President, for more than two years of a term to which some other person was elected President shall be elected to the office of the President more than once. But this article shall not apply to any person holding the office of President when this Article was proposed by the Congress, and shall not prevent any person who may be holding the office of President, or acting as President, during the term within which this article becomes operative from holding the office of President or acting as President during the remainder of such term.

TRUMAN TELECAST ADDRESS FROM WHITE HOUSE

The first presidential address telecast from the White House was delivered on October 5, 1947, by President Truman. He spoke about food conservation and the world food crisis, proposing meatless Tuesdays and eggless and poultryless Thurdays. The speech was relayed to New York City, Schenectady, and Philadelphia.

INAUGURATION IN 1949

Harry S. Truman took the oath of office on Thursday, January 20, 1949. It was administered by Chief Justice Frederick Moore Vinson. This was the first presidential inauguration in which a rabbi participated. Rabbi Samuel Thurman of the United Hebrew Temple of St. Louis, who had been Grand Chaplain of the Missouri Grand Lodge of Masons when Truman was Grand Master, delivered a prayer.

There was a brilliant and cloudless sky and the air was clear and crisp. The thermometer hovered between 30° and 40°. About 44,000 persons in the specially constructed grandstand witnessed the three-hour parade, which was seven and a half miles long. The ceremonies and parade were viewed by about a million persons in Washington. This was the first televised presidential inaugural, and it was estimated that ten million persons watched the ceremony on television. An estimated 100,000,000 listeners heard the proceedings on radio. The honor guard was Battery D, the unit in which the President had served during World War I. Over seven hundred airplanes, led by five B-36's, participated in a display of aerial power.

A reception was held at the National Gallery of Art for 7,500 to 10,000 guests, and an inaugural ball was held at the National Guard Armory.

As the White House was undergoing repairs, the President temporarily occupied Blair House.

ASSASSINATION ATTEMPT MADE ON TRUMAN

President Truman escaped assassination on November 1, 1950, when at 2:15 P.M. Oscar Collazo and Griselio Torresola, two Puerto Rican nationalists, tried to shoot their way into Blair House. Leslie Coffelt of Arlington, Va., a White House guard, was killed and two others wounded. Torresola was killed and Collazo was wounded.

One hour after the shooting, President Truman dedicated a memorial to British Field Marshal Sir John Dill at the Arlington National Cemetery.

On July 24, 1952, Collazo was sentenced to die on August 1, 1952, but his sentence was commuted to life imprisonment.

PRESS CONFERENCE TAPED

The first presidential press conference recorded on tape was held at the White House on January 25, 1951. It was recorded for the White House archives by the United States Army Signal Corps unit permanently attached to the White House to handle communications. Portions were released by consent of President Truman.

TRUMAN RECEIVED FIRST WOMAN AMBASSADOR

President Truman was the first President to receive officially a woman ambassador from a foreign country. On May 12, 1952, he received the letter of credence from Her Excellency Shrimati Vijaya Lakshmi Pandit, ambassador of India.

FORMER PRESIDENT ADDRESSED THE SENATE

Senator Claiborne Pell (Democrat, Rhode Island) introduced a resolution in the Senate which was enacted October 1, 1963. (*Congressional Quarterly Almanac,* 19:378, 1963) The Pell resolution stated that "former Presidents of the United States shall be entitled to address the Senate upon giving appropriate notice of their intentions to the Presiding Officer."

The first President to address the Senate was former President Harry S. Truman, whose presence in the Senate was acknowledged on May 8, 1964, his eightieth birthday. Truman replied in a brief sixty-eight word speech.

THE FIRST LADY

During her husband's administration Bess Wallace Truman, in contrast to her predecessor, was very retiring and endeavored to keep out of the public eye as much as possible. Mrs. Truman was well known to an intimate group of friends in Washington, however, as she had been her husband's secretary while he was a senator. The Trumans' daughter, Margaret, made frequent appearances as a concert singer and a television performer.

DWIGHT DAVID EISENHOWER

34th PRESIDENT

Born–Oct. 14, 1890 (Given name
—David Dwight)

Birthplace–Denison, Tex.

College attended–United States
Military Academy, West Point,
N.Y.

Date of graduation–June 12,
1915, four-year course

Religion–Presbyterian

Ancestry–Swiss-German

Occupation–Army officer

Date and place of marriage–July
1, 1916, Denver, Col.

Age at marriage–25 years, 260
days

Years married–52 years, 270 days

Political party–Republican

State represented–New York

Term of office–Jan. 20, 1953-Jan.
20, 1961

Term served–8 years

Administration–42nd, 43rd

Congresses–83rd, 84th, 85th,
86th

Age at inauguration–62 years, 98
days

Lived after term–8 years, 67 days

Occupation after term–Retired;
author

Date of death–Mar. 28, 1969

Age at death–79 years, 165 days

Place of death–Washington,
D.C.

Burial place–Abilene, Kan.

PARENTS

Father–David Jacob Eisenhower

Born–Sept. 23, 1863, Elizabeth-
ville, Pa.

Married–Sept. 23, 1885, Hope,
Kan.

Occupation–Mechanic, manager
of gas company, director of
employee savings for group of
public utilities

Died–Mar. 10, 1942, Abilene,
Kan.

Age at death–79 years, 168 days

Mother–Ida Elizabeth Stoever (or
Stover) Eisenhower

Born–May 1, 1862, Mount Sidney, Va.

Died–Sept. 11, 1946, Abilene,
Kans.

Age at death–84 years, 133 days

BROTHERS

David Dwight Eisenhower was
the third of seven sons.

*Children of David Jacob Eisen-
hower and Ida Elizabeth Stoever
Eisenhower*

Arthur Bradford Eisenhower, b.
Nov. 11, 1886; d. Jan. 26, 1958

Edgar Newton Eisenhower, b.
Jan. 19, 1889; d. July 12, 1971

Dwight David Eisenhower, b.
Oct. 14, 1890; d. Mar. 28, 1969

Roy Jacob Eisenhower, b. Aug.
9, 1892; d. June 17, 1942

Paul A. Eisenhower, b. May 12,
1894; d. Mar. 16, 1895

Earl Dewey Eisenhower, b. Feb.
1, 1898; d. Dec. 18, 1968

Milton Stover Eisenhower, b.
Sept. 15, 1899

CHILDREN

David Dwight Eisenhower, b.
Sept. 24, 1917, Denver, Colo.;
d. Jan. 2, 1921, Camp Meade,
Md.

For additional data see the end of this section and also specific
subject headings in the index.

John Sheldon Doud Eisenhower,
b. Aug. 3, 1923, Denver, Colo.;
m. June 10, 1947, Barbara Jean
Thompson, Fort Monroe, Va.
**MRS. DWIGHT DAVID EISEN-
HOWER**
Name–(Mamie) Geneva Doud
Eisenhower
Born–Nov. 14, 1896

Birthplace–Boone, Iowa
Age at marriage–19 years, 229
days
Children–2 sons
Mother–Elivera Carlson Doud
Father–John Sheldon Doud
His occupation–Meat packer
**Years younger than the Pres-
ident**–6 years, 30 days

THE ELECTION OF 1952
NOMINATIONS FOR TERM 1953-1957
Republican Party Convention (25th)

July 7-11, 1952, International Amphitheatre, Chicago, Ill.
Nominated for President—Dwight David Eisenhower, N.Y.
Nominated for Vice President—Richard Milhous Nixon, Calif.
Eisenhower was nominated on the first ballot.
Candidates for nomination and the votes they received:
Dwight David Eisenhower, N.Y., 845
Robert Alphonso Taft, Ohio, 280
Earl Warren, Calif., 77
Douglas MacArthur, Wis., 4
Total number of votes: 1,206
Number necessary for nomination: 604
Nomination made unanimous

Democratic Party Convention (31st)

July 21-26, 1952, International Amphitheatre, Chicago, Ill.
Nominated for President—Adlai Ewing Stevenson, Ill.
Nominated for Vice President—John Jackson Sparkman, Ala.
Stevenson was nominated on the third ballot. Candidates for nomin-
ation and the votes they received on the first and third ballots:
Estes Kefauver, Tenn., 340, 275$^1/_2$
Adlai Ewing Stevenson, Ill., 273, 617$^1/_2$
Richard Brevard Russell, Ga., 268, 261
William Averell Harriman, N.Y., 123$^1/_2$, 0
Robert Samuel Kerr, Okla., 65, 0
Alben William Barkley, Ky., 48$^1/_2$, 67$^1/_2$
Paul Andrew Dever, Mass., 37$^1/_2$, $^1/_2$
Hubert Horatio Humphrey, Minn., 26, 0
James William Fulbright, Ark., 22, 0
James Edward Murray, Mont., 12, 0
Harry S. Truman, Mo., 6, 0
Oscar Ross Ewing, Ind., 4, 3
Paul Howard Douglas, Ill., 3, 3
William Orville Douglas, Va., $^1/_2$, 0
Total number of votes:
First ballot: 1,229
Third ballot: 1,228

Number necessary for nomination: 616
Nomination made unanimous

Progressive Party Convention

July 4-6, 1952, International Amphitheatre, Chicago, Ill.
Nominated for President—Vincent William Hallinan, Calif.
Nominated for Vice President—Charlotta A. Bass, N.Y.

Prohibition Party Convention (21st)

Nov. 13-15, 1951, Indianapolis, Ind.
Nominated for President—Stuart Hamblen, Calif.
Nominated for Vice President—Enoch Arden Holtwick, Ill.

Socialist Labor Party Convention

May 3-5, 1952, Henry Hudson Hotel, New York, N.Y.
Nominated for President—Eric Hass, N.Y.
Nominated for Vice President—Stephen Emery, N.Y.

Socialist Party Convention

May 30, June 1-2, 1952, Hotel Hollenden, Cleveland, Ohio
Nominated for President—Darlington Hoopes, Pa.
Nominated for Vice President—Samuel Herman Friedman, N.Y.

Socialist Workers Party Convention

July 20, 1952, New York, N.Y.
Nominated for President—Farrell Dobbs, N.Y.
Nominated for Vice President—Myra Tanner Weiss, N.Y.

America First Party Convention

Aug. 25, 1952, Kansas City, Mo.
Nominated for Vice President—Harry Flood Byrd, Va.

American Labor Party Convention

Aug. 28, 1952, City Center Casino, New York, N.Y.
Nominated for President-Vincent William Hallinan, Calif.
Nominated for Vice President-Charlotta A. Bass, N.Y.
The party endorsed the candidates of the Progressive Party.

American Vegetarian Party

Nominated for President-Daniel J. Murphy, Calif.
Nominated for Vice President-Symon Gould, N.Y.

Church of God Party Convention

July 2-8, 1952, Moses Tabernacle, Nashville, Tenn.
Nominated for President-Homer Aubrey Tomlinson, N.Y.
Nominated for Vice President-Willie Isaac Bass, N.C.
    The Church of God Party was organized July 4, 1952, at the 46th annual general assembly of the Church of God, Nashville, Tenn.

Constitution Party Convention

Aug. 31, 1952, Philadelphia, Pa.
Nominated for President-Douglas MacArthur, Wis.
Nominated for Vice President-Harry Flood Byrd, Va.

Greenback Party

Nominated for President-Frederick C. Proehl, Wash.
Nominated for Vice President-Edward J. Bedell, Ind.
The candidates were nominated by referendum. Ballots were mailed to all dues-paying members.

Poor Man's Party

Nominated for President-Henry B Krajewski, N.J.
Nominated for Vice President-Frank Jenkins, N.J.

ELECTION RESULTS, NOV. 4, 1952—PRESIDENTIAL AND VICE PRESIDENTIAL CANDIDATES

Republican Party (33,778,963 votes)

Dwight David Eisenhower, N.Y.
Richard Milhous Nixon, Calif.

Democratic Party (27,314,992 votes)

Adlai Ewing Stevenson, Ill.
John Jackson Sparkman, Ala.

Progressive Party (135,007 votes)

Vincent William Hallinan, Calif.

Charlotta A. Bass, N.Y.

Prohibition Party (72,769 votes)

Stuart Hamblen, Calif.
Enoch Arden Holtwick, Ill.

Socialist Labor Party(30,376 votes)

Eric Haas, N.Y.
Enoch Arden Holtwick, Ill.

Socialist Party (19,685 votes)

Darlington Hoopes, Pa.
Samuel Herman Friedman, N.Y.

Socialist Workers Party (10,306 votes)

Farrell Dobbs, N.Y.
Myra Tanner Weiss, N.Y.

Other Parties

South Carolina Republicans (separate set of electors), 158,289
Christian Nationalists, 13,883
Poor Man's Party, 4,203
Oregon Independent votes, 3,665
Constitution Party, 3,089
People's Party of Connecticut, 1,466
Social Democrats, 504
America First Party, 233
Scattering, 4,489
Total: 189,821

ELECTORAL VOTES (531-48 states)

Eisenhower received 83.24 per cent (442 votes-39 states) as follows: Ariz. 4; Calif. 32; Colo. 6; Conn. 8; Del. 3; Fla. 10; Idaho 4; Ill. 27; Ind. 13; Iowa 10; Kan. 8; Me. 5; Md. 9; Mass. 16; Mich. 20; Minn. 11; Mo. 13; Mont. 4; Neb. 6; Nev. 3; N.H. 4; N.J. 16; N. M. 4; N.Y. 45; N.D. 4: Ohio 25; Okla. 8; Ore. 6; Pa. 32; R.I. 4; S.D. 4; Tenn. 11; Tex. 24; Utah 4; Vt. 3; Va. 12; Wash. 9; Wis. 12; Wyo. 3.

Stevenson received 16.76 per cent (89 votes-9 states) as follows: Ala. 11; Ark. 8; Ga. 12; Ky. 10; La. 10; Miss. 8; N.C. 14: S.C. 8; W. Va. 8.

THE ELECTION OF 1956

NOMINATIONS FOR TERM 1957-1961

Republican Party Convention (26th)

Aug. 20-23, 1956, the Cow Palace, San Francisco, Calif.
Nominated for President-Dwight David Eisenhower, N.Y.
Nominated for Vice President-Richard Milhous Nixon, Calif.
Eisenhower was nominated by acclamation on the first ballot.
Total number of votes: 1,323
Number necessary for nomination: 662

Democratic Party Convention (32nd)

Aug. 13-17, 1956, International Amphitheatre, Chicago, Ill.
Nominated for President-Adlai Ewing Stevenson, Ill.
Nominated for Vice President-Estes Kefauver, Tenn.
    Stevenson was nominated on the first ballot. Candidates for nomination and the votes they received:
Adlai Ewing Stevenson, Ill., 905$\frac{1}{2}$
William Averell Harriman, N.Y., 210
Lyndon Baines Johnson, Tex., 80
William Stuart Symington, Mo., 45$\frac{1}{2}$
Albert Benjamin Chandler, Ky., 36$\frac{1}{2}$
James Curran Davis, Ga., 33
John Stewart Battle, Va., 32$\frac{1}{2}$
George Bell Timmerman, Jr., S.C., 23$\frac{1}{2}$
Frank John Lausche, Ohio, 5$\frac{1}{2}$
Total number of votes: 1,372
Number necessary for nomination: 686$\frac{1}{2}$

Liberal Party Convention

Sept. 11, 1956, Manhattan Center, New York, N.Y.
Nominated for President-Adlai Ewing Stevenson, Ill.
Nominated for Vice President-Estes Kefauver, Tenn.

States' Rights Party Convention

Ooct. 15, 1956, Mosque Auditorium, Richmond, Va.
Nominated for President-Thomas Coleman Andrews, Va.
Nominated for Vice President-Thomas Harold Werdel, Calif.
The candidates were nominated by acclamation.

Prohibition Party Convention (22nd)

Sept. 4-6, 1955, Milford, Ind.
Nominated for President-Enoch Arden Holtwick, Ill.
Nominated for Vice President-Herbert Charles Holdridge, Calif.
  Holdridge resigned February 15, 1956, and the national committee substituted Edward M. Cooper of California.

Socialist Labor Party Convention

May 5-7, 1956, Henry Hudson Hotel, New York, N.Y.
Nominated for President-Eric Hass, N.Y.
Nominated for Vice President-Georgia Cozzini, Wis.

Texas Constitution Party

Nominated for President-William Ezra Jenner, Ind.
Nominated for Vice President-Joseph Bracken Lee, Utah

Socialist Workers Party Convention

Aug. 19, 1956, Adelphi Hall, New York, N.Y.
Nominated for President-Farrell Dobbs, N.Y.
Nominated for Vice President-Myra Tanner Weiss, N.Y.

American Third Party

Nominated for President-Henry Krajewski, N.J.
Nominated for Vice President-Anne Marie Yezo, N.J.

Socialist Party Convention

June 8-10, 1956, Chicago, Ill.
Nominated for President-Darlington Hoopes, Pa.
Nominated for Vice President-Samuel Herman Friedman, N.Y.

Pioneer Party Convention

Nov. 26-27, 1955, Milwaukee, Wis.
Nominated for President-William Langer, N.D.
Nominated for Vice President-Burr McCloskey, Ill.

American Vegetarian Party Convention

July 6, 1956, Los Angeles, Calif.
Nominated for President-Herbert M. Shelton, Calif.
Nominated for Vice President-Symon Gould, N.Y.

Greenback Party

Nominated for President-Frederick C. Proehl, Wash.
Nominated for Vice President-Edward Kirby Meador, Mass.
  The candidates were nominated by referendum. Ballots were mailed to all dues-paying members.

States' Rights Party of Kentucky

Nominated for President-Harry Flood Byrd, Va.
Nominated for Vice President-William Ezra Jenner, Ind.

South Carolinians for Independent Electors
Nominated for President-Harry Flood Byrd, Va.

Constitution Party Convention
Aug. 28, 1956, Fort Worth, Tex.
    Seventy-five delegates from seventeen states favored Thomas Coleman Andrews, Va., and Thomas Harold Werdel, Calif., who were to be nominated by the States' Rights party.

Christian National Party
Nominated for President-Gerald Lyman Kenneth Smith

ELECTION RESULTS, NOV. 6, 1956—PRESIDENTIAL AND VICE PRESIDENTIAL CANDIDATES

Republican Party (35,581,003 votes)
Dwight David Eisenhower, N.Y.
Richard Milhous Nixon, Calif.

Democratic Party (25,738,765 votes)
Adlai Ewing Stevenson, Ill.
Estes Kefauver, Tenn.

Liberal Party (292,557 votes)
Adlai Ewing Stevenson, Ill.
Estes Kefauver, Tenn.

States' Rights Party (109,961 votes)
Thomas Coleman Andrews, Va.
Thomas Harold Werdel, Calif.

Prohibition Party (41,937 votes)
Enoch Arden Holtwick, Ill.
Edward M. Cooper, Calif.

Socialist Labor Party (41,159 votes)
Eric Hass, N.Y.
Georgia Cozzini, Wis.

Texas Constitution Party (30,999 votes)
William Ezra Jenner, Ind.
Joseph Bracken Lee, Utah

Socialist Workers Party (5,549 votes)
Farrell Dobbs, N.Y.
Myra Tanner Weiss, N.Y.

American Third Party (1,829 votes)
Henry Krajewski, N.J.
Ann Marie Yezo, N.J.

Socialist Party (846 votes)

Darlington Hoopes, Pa.
Samuel Herman Friedman, N.Y.

Other Parties

Conservative Party (N.J.), 5,317
Black and Tan Grand Old Party (Miss.), 4,313
Industrial Government (N.Y.), 2,080
Militant Workers (Pa.), 2,035
American Party, 483
Virginia Social Democrats, 444
New Party (N.M.), 364

ELECTORAL VOTES (531—48 states)

Eisenhower received 86.06 per cent (457 votes—41 states) as follows:
Ariz. 4; Calif. 32; Colo. 6; Conn. 8; Del. 3; Fla. 10; Idaho 4; Ill.
27; Ind. 13; Iowa 10; Kan. 8; Ky. 10; La. 10; Me. 5; Md. 9; Mass.
16; Mich. 20; Minn. 11; Mont. 4; Neb. 6; Nev. 3; N.H. 4; N.J. 16;
N.M. 4; N.Y. 45; N.D. 4; Ohio 25; Okla. 8; Ore. 6; Pa. 32; R.I.
4; S.D. 4; Tenn. 11; Tex. 24; Utah 4; Vt. 3; Va. 12; Wash. 9; W.
Va. 8; Wis. 12; Wyo. 3.

Stevenson received 13.75 per cent (73 votes—7 states) as follows:
Ala. 10 (of the 11 votes); Ark. 8; Ga. 12; Miss. 8; Mo. 13; N.C.
14; S.C. 8.

Stevenson did not receive all 74 Democratic votes; one vote went
to Walter Burgwyn Jones of Alabama.

Jones received 00.19 per cent (1 of the 11 Ala. votes).

FIRST TERM
CABINET
Janurary 20, 1953-January 20, 1957

State–John Foster Dulles, D.C., Jan. 21, 1953
Treasury–George Magoffin Humphrey, Ohio, Jan. 21, 1953
Defense–Charles Erwin Wilson, Mich., Jan. 28, 1953
Attorney General–Herbert Brownell, Jr., N.Y., Jan. 21, 1953
Postmaster General–Arthur Ellsworth Summerfield, Mich., Jan. 21,
1953
Interior–Douglas McKay, Ore., Jan 21, 1953; Frederick Andrew Sea-
ton, Neb., June 8, 1956
Agriculture–Ezra Taft Benson, Utah, Jan. 21, 1953
Commerce–Sinclair Weeks, Mass., Jan. 21, 1953
Labor–Martin Patrick Durkin, Ill., Jan. 21, 1953; James Paul Mitchell,
N.J., Oct. 9, 1953
Health, Education, and Welfare–Oveta Culp Hobby, Tex., Apr. 11,
1953; Marion Bayard Folson, Ga., Aug. 1, 1955
SECOND TERM
CABINET
January 20, 1957-January 20, 1961

State–John Foster Dulles, D.C., continued from preceding administration; Christian Archibald Herter, Mass., Apr. 22, 1959

Treasury–George Magoffin Humphrey, Ohio, continued from preceding administration; Robert Bernerd Anderson, Tex., July 29, 1957

Defense–Charles Erwin Wilson, Mich., continued from preceding administration; Neil Hosler McElroy, Ohio, Oct. 9, 1957; Thomas Sovereign Gates, Jr., Pa., Dec. 2, 1959

Attorney General–Herbert Brownell, Jr., N.Y., continued from preceding administration; William Pierce Rogers, N.Y., Jan. 27, 1958

Postmaster General–Arthur Ellsworth Summerfield, Mich., continued from preceding administration

Interior–Frederick Andrew Seaton, Neb., continued from preceding administration

Agriculture–Ezra Taft Benson, Utah, continued from preceding administration

Commerce–Sinclair Weeks, Mass., continued from preceding administration; Lewis Lichtenstein Strauss, N.Y., Nov. 13, 1958, not confirmed, Senate rejected appointment June 18, 1959; Frederick Henry Mueller, Mich., Aug. 10, 1959

Labor–James Paul Mitchell, N.J., continued from preceding administration

Health, Education, and Welfare–Marion Bayard Folsom, Ga., continued from preceding administration; Arthur Sherwood Flemming, Ohio, Aug. 1, 1958

FIRST TERM
EIGHTY-THIRD CONGRESS
January 3, 1953-January 3, 1955

First session–Jan. 3, 1953-Aug. 3, 1953 (213 days)

Second session–Jan. 6, 1954-Dec. 2, 1954 (331 days)

Vice President–Richard Milhous Nixon, Calif.

President pro tempore of the Senate–Styles Bridges, N.H., elected Jan. 3, 1953

Secretary of the Senate–Felton McLellan Johnston, Miss., elected Jan. 3, 1953

Speaker of the House–Joseph William Martin, Mass., elected Jan. 3, 1953

Clerk of the House–Lyle O. Snader, Ill., elected Jan. 3, 1953

EIGHTY-FOURTH CONGRESS

January 3, 1955-January 3, 1957

First session–Jan. 5, 1955-Aug. 2, 1955 (210 days)

Second session–Jan. 3, 1956-July 27, 1956 (207 days)

Vice President–Richard Milhous Nixon, Calif.

President pro tempore of the Senate–Walter Franklin George, Ga., elected Jan. 5, 1955

Secretary of the Senate–Felton McLellan Johnston, Miss., elected Jan. 5, 1955

Speaker of the House–Sam [Samuel Taliaferro] Rayburn, Tex., elected Jan. 5, 1955

Clerk of the House–Ralph R. Roberts, Ind., elected Jan. 5, 1955
SECOND TERM

EIGHTY-FIFTH CONGRESS

January 3, 1957-January 3, 1959

First session–Jan. 3, 1957-Aug. 30, 1957 (239 days) (in recess Apr. 18-Apr. 29)

Second session–Jan. 7, 1958-Aug. 24, 1958 (230 days) (in recess Apr. 3-Apr. 14)

Vice President–Richard Milhous Nixon, Calif.

President pro tempore of the Senate–Carl Hayden, Ariz., elected Jan. 3, 1957

Secetary of the Senate–Felton McLellan Johnston, Miss., elected Jan. 5, 1957

Speaker of the House–Sam [Samuel Taliaferro]Rayburn, Tex., elected Jan. 3, 1957

Clerk of the House–Ralph R. Roberts, Ind., elected Jan. 3, 1957

EIGHTY-SIXTH CONGRESS

January 3, 1959-January 3, 1961

First session–Jan. 7, 1959-Sept. 15, 1959 (252 days) (in recess Mar. 26-Apr. 7)

Second session–Jan. 6, 1960-Sept. 1, 1960 (240 days) (The House was in recess Apr. 14-Apr. 18; May 27-May 31; July 3-Aug. 15. The Senate was in recess Apr. 14-Apr. 18; May 27-May 31; July 3–Aug. 8)

Vice President–Richard Milhous Nixon, Calif.

President pro tempore of the Senate–Carl Hayden, Ariz., elected Jan. 3, 1959

Secretary of the Senate–Felton McLellan Johnston, Miss., elected Jan. 5, 1959

Speaker of the House–Sam [Samuel Taliaferro] Rayburn, Tex., elected Jan. 7, 1959

Clerk of the House–Ralph R. Roberts, Ind., elected Jan. 7, 1959

APPOINTMENTS TO THE SUPREME COURT

Chief Justice
Earl Warren, Calif. Oct. 5, 1953

Associate Justices
John Marshall Harlan, N.Y., Mar. 28, 1955
William Joseph Brennan, Jr., N.J., Oct. 16, 1956
Charles Evans Whittaker, Mo., Mar. 25, 1957
Potter Stewart, Ohio, Oct. 14, 1958

ADMINISTRATION—IMPORTANT DATES

Jan. 1953, neutralization of Formosa by Seventh Fleet ended

May 22, 1953, tidelands oil law enacted, giving states title to offshore oil

June 19, 1953, execution of atomic spies Julius and Ethel Rosenberg, first spies sentenced to death by a U.S. civil court and the first executed for treason in peacetime.

July 27, 1953, Korean war ended with signing of armistice calling for demilitarized zone and voluntary repatriation of prisoners

Aug-Sept. 1953, American prisoners of war in Korea repatriated

Dec. 4-8, 1953, President Eisenhower conferred at Bermuda with prime ministers of Britain and France on exchange of atomic information

Jan. 21, 1954, first atomic submarine, *Nautilus,* launched, Groton, Conn.

Mar. 1, 1954, five representatives wounded in House of Representatives by shots fired by Puerto Rican nationalists

Apr. 22-June 17, 1954, Army-McCarthy hearings arising out of Senator McCarthy's charges of subversive activities

May 13, 1954, St. Lawrence Seaway bill authorized joint construction by the United States and Canada

May 17, 1954, Supreme Court declared racial segregation in schools unconstitutional

June 25-29, 1954, President and Prime Minister Churchill conferred at Washington, D.C. on world peace

July 21, 1954, Geneva agreement signed to end war in Indochina after French withdrawal

Aug. 24, 1954, Communist party outlawed, but party membership not made a crime

Sept. 1, 1954, social security coverage extended to 10 million additional persons (farmers, professional people, etc.)

Sept. 3, 1954, death penalty for peacetime espionage authorized

Sept. 6, 1954, world atomic pool without Soviet Union established

Sept. 8, 1954, Southeast Asia defense treaty (SEATO) signed

Oct. 25, 1954, first telecast of a cabinet meeting

Dec. 2, 1954, Senate voted condemnation of Senator McCarthy for conduct during Senate hearings

Jan. 24, 1955, President asked Congress for free hand in use of U.S. Forces to defend Formosa

Jan. 28, 1955, Congress approved presidential request to allow U.S. forces to defend Formosa against Communist aggression

Feb. 7, 1955, U.S. Seventh fleet helped evacuation of Communist-threatened Tachen Islands, near Formosa

Mar. 16, 1955, secret Yalta Conference papers released by State Department

Apr. 12, 1955, Salk vaccine declared "safe, effective and potent"

Apr. 21, 1955, U.S. occupation of Germany ended; troops remained on contractual basis

May 15, 1955, Big Four foreign ministers signed treaty restoring sovereignty of Austria

May 31, 1955, Supreme Court reaffirmed principle of school integration, ordering gradual compliance by local authorities

July 18-23, 1955, Geneva summit conference of Big Four heads of state

Aug. 1, 1955, U.S. and Chinese Communists opened talks in Geneva

Sept. 24, 1955, President suffered heart attack

Nov. 16, 1955, Big Four foreign ministers conference in Geneva ended in deadlock

Dec. 5, 1955, AFL-CIO merger

Jan. 30, 1956, British Prime Minister Eden conferred with President at Washington, D.C.

Mar. 12, 1956, manifesto issued by southern senators and representatives pledging use of all legal means to reverse Supreme Court integration ruling

June 9, 1956, President underwent emergency ileitis operation

July 19, 1956, United States withdrew offers to finance construction of Aswan Dam in Egypt, precipitating Egyptian seizure of Suez canal

July 22, 1956, Panama Declaration, affirming principles of Organization of American States, signed by President Eisenhower and eighteen other heads of state

Oct. 31, 1956, President, deploring Anglo French-Israeli attack on Egypt, promised that United States would not be involved

Nov. 8, 1956, United States offered to admit Hungarian refugees of anti-Soviet revolt

Mar. 9, 1957, Eisenhower Doctrine bill signed, authorizing use of U.S. forces to assist Middle East nations threatened by Communist aggression

Apr. 29, 1957, Secretary of the Army Brucker dedicated Army's first nuclear power reactor at Fort Belvoir, Va.

May 14, 1957, United States resumed military aid to Yugoslavia, halted during Tito's reconciliation with U.S.S.R.

June 1957, controversial Supreme Court decisions on civil rights, limiting powers of legislative and executive branches of government

June 1957, Prime Minister Kishi of Japan visited Washington, D.C.; joint American-Japanese communiqué issued announcing withdrawal of American ground combat forces in Japan

July 1957, United States proposed ban on nuclear tests after establishment of inspection system

July 29, 1957, United States ratified International Atomic Energy Agency (proposed by President in 1953) to pool atomic resources for peaceful use

Sept. 9, 1957, Congress approved establishment of Civil Rights Commission

Sept. 19, 1957, first underground nuclear explosion, Nevada proving grounds

Sept. 24, 1957, President sent federal troops to Little Rock, Ark., high school to enforce integration of Negro students

Oct. 4, 1957, launching of first Soviet Sputnik set off demand for greater American efforts in defense and technology

Nov. 25, 1957, President suffered mild stroke, but recovered rapidly

1957-1958, business recession; over 5 million unemployed before reversal of downward trend

Jan. 31, 1958, launching of Explorer I, first American satellite

May 13, 1958, Vice President Nixon, on Latin American tour, attacked by anti-U.S. demonstrators

May 30, 1958, American Unknown Soldier of World War II buried in Arlington National Cemetery

July-Oct. 1958, U.S. troops in Lebanon at request of Lebanese government threatened by United Arab Republic infiltration

July-Aug. 1958, polar voyages of atomic submarines *Nautilus* and *Skate*

July 29, 1958, National Aeronautics and Space Administration established

Sept. 1958, closing of schools in which integration had been ordered in Arkansas and Virginia

Jan. 3, 1959, Alaska proclaimed 49th state

Feb. 18-19, 1959, President and Mexican President López Mateos conferred at Acapulco, Mexico, announcing agreement to build dam on Rio Grande

Mar. 18, 1959, President signed act admitting Hawaii as the 50th state

Apr. 25, 1959, St. Lawrence Seaway opened

Aug. 25-Sept. 7, 1959, President visited Germany, England, and France

Oct. 13, 1959, President broke ground for Dwight D. Eisenhower Library, Abilene, Kan.

Dec. 3-22, 1959, President visited eleven nations in Europe, Asia, and Africa

May 7, 1960, United States admitted that U-2 plane shot down in U.S.S.R. had been on intelligence mission

May 16, 1960, collapse of East-West summit conference in Paris after U-2 incident

June 22, 1960, U.S.-Japanese security treaty ratified by Senate (ratified by Japan on June 19 after anti-American riots that caused cancellation of President's visit)

July 7, 1960, nearly all Cuban sugar imports prohibited

Sept. 20, 1960, opening of UN General Assembly in New York attended by world leaders

Nov. 16, 1960, President ordered naval and air patrol of Caribbean to prevent possible Communist invasion from Cuba

Jan. 3, 1961, President severed diplomatic relations with Cuba

Jan. 6, 1961, seven executives of electrical manufacturing companies jailed for antitrust violations

IMPORTANT DATES IN HIS LIFE

1909, graduated from Abilene High School, Abilene, Kan.

June 14, 1911, entered U.S. Military Academy (61st in class of 164, 95th in deportment); commissioned second lieutenant of infantry; assigned to 19th Infantry, San Antonio, Tex.

May 15, 1917, promoted to captain

1918, commanded 6,000 men at Tank Training Center at Camp Colt, near Gettysburg, Pa.; served at army training post in World War I, but did not go overseas

Oct. 14, 1918, lieutenant colonel (temporary rank) in Tank Corps

July 2, 1920, promoted to permanent rank of major; ordered to Fort Meade, Md., graduated from Infantry Tank School

1922-1924, executive officer, Camp Gaillard, Panama Canal Zone

1925-1926, Command and General Staff School, Fort Leavenworth, Kan.; graduated first in class of 275

1928, Army War College, Washington, D.C.

Nov. 8, 1929-Feb. 20, 1933, assistant executive, Office of Assistant Secretary of War

1933, Army Industrial college

1935-1939, major; assistant to General MacArthur in the Philippines

1940, returned to the United States; joined Fifteenth Infantry

1941, chief of staff, Third Army; brigadier general (temporary rank)

Feb. 1942, chief, War Plans Division of War Department General Staff

Apr. 1942; assistant chief of staff in charge of Operations Division of War Department General Staff; major general (temporary rank)

June 25, 1942, appointed commanding general, European Theatre of Operations

July 1942, lieutenant general (temporary rank); in London for strategy discussions with British

Nov. 8, 1942, appointed commander in chief of Allied forces in North Africa

Feb. 1943, full general (temporary rank)

July-Dec. 1943, directed invasions of Sicily and Italy

Dec. 24, 1943, appointed supreme commander, Allied Expeditionary Force

June 6, 1944, led D-Day invasion of Normandy

Dec. 20, 1944, General of the Army (temporary rank)

May 7, 1945, accepted surrender of German Army at Rheims (V-E Day)

May-Nov. 1945, commander of U.S. occupation forces in Europe

Nov. 19, 1945-Feb. 7, 1948, chief of staff, U.S. Army; first chief of staff under unification of armed services in 1947

Feb. 7, 1948, retired from active duty in the Army

June 7, 1948, appointed president of Columbia University

July 1948, declined to run for the presidency of the United States

Dec. 16, 1950, granted indefinite leave of absence from Columbia University to serve as commander of NATO forces in Europe

Jan. 1952, name entered in first Republican presidential primaries

May 30, 1952, turned over command of Allied forces in Europe to General Ridgway

June 1952, resigned from the Army

July 1952, received Republican presidential nomination

Nov. 4, 1952, elected President

Nov. 17, 1952, resigned from Columbia University, effective Jan. 19, 1953

Dec. 1952, made 22,000-mile preinauguration air trip to Korea to fulfill campaign pledge

Jan. 20, 1953-Jan. 20, 1957, President (first term)

Sept. 24, 1955, suffered heart attack at Denver, Colo.

Feb. 29, 1956, announced his availability for second term

June 9, 1956, underwent emergency ileitis operation

Aug. 22, 1956, renominated by Republicans

Nov. 6, 1956, elected President for second term

Jan. 21, 1957, inaugurated for second term (took oath of office in private ceremony on Sunday, Jan. 20)

Nov. 25, 1957, suffered mild stroke, but recovered rapidly

1961, retired to Gettysburg farm

Mar. 22, 1961, rank as General of the Army restored

1963, published *Mandate for Change,* 1953-1956

1965, published *Waging Peace,* 1956-1961

1967, published *At Ease*

DWIGHT DAVID EISENHOWER

____was the first President born in Texas.

____was the fourteenth President who was a resident of a state other than his native state.

____was the first President to serve a constitutionally limited term (as provided by the Twenty-second Amendment)

____was the first Republican in the twentieth century to win two successive presidential elections.

____was the first President of forty-nine (and later fifty) states.

____was the first President to serve with three congresses in which both chambers were controlled by an opposing political party.

EISENHOWER'S VICE PRESIDENT

Vice President–Richard Milhous Nixon (36th V.P.)

Date of birth–Jan. 9, 1913

Birthplace–Yorba Linda, Calif.

Polical party–Republican

State represented–California

Term of office–Jan. 20, 1953-Jan. 20, 1961

Age at inauguration–40 years, 11 days

Occupation after term–Lawyer

Additional data on Nixon

19—, worked in father's gas station

1934, graduated from Whittier College, Whittier, Calif.

1937, graduated from Duke University Law School

1937, admitted to the bar; practiced at Whittier, Calif.

Jan.-Aug. 1942, attorney with Office of Emergency Management, Washington, D.C.

1942-1946, lieutenant, j.g., U.S. Navy; served in South Pacific as aviation ground officer on Bougainville, Vella Lavella and Green Islands; won two battle stars

Jan. 3, 1947-Nov. 31, 1950, U.S. House of Representatives (from California)

Nov. 7, 1950, elected to U.S. Senate (from California)

Dec. 1, 1950, received interim appointment, after his own election, to replace senator who resigned several weeks before expiration of term

Jan. 3, 1951-Jan. 20, 1953, U.S. Senate

For further biographical information see Richard Milhous Nixon, 37th President.

ADDITIONAL DATA ON EISENHOWER
EISENHOWER CHANGED NAME

The Eisenhower family Bible records the birth of President Eisenhower's mother and father and his two brothers, Arthur and Edgar. The entry for a third son is "D. Dwight Eisenhower," the "D" an abbreviation for David. Later, David Dwight Eisenhower reversed his names.

EISENHOWER WON HIS WINGS

President Eisenhower learned to pilot an airplane when he was a lieutenant colonel in the Philippines on the staff of General Douglas MacArthur. His first solo flight was made on May 19, 1937. On November 30, 1939, he received pilot's license number 93,258. He was the first President licensed to pilot an airplane.

EISENHOWER RESIGNED AS GENERAL

On July 18, 1952, about a week after his nomination as the presidential candidate on the Republican ticket, General Eisenhower resigned as General of the Army, forfeiting an annual pension of $19,542 (later increased to $22,943), an office at government expense, and a staff of eight aides including a colonel, a lieutenant colonel, a major, and five enlisted men.

FIRST INAUGURATION

Dwight David Eisenhower took the oath of office on Tuesday, January 20, 1953. The oath was administered by Chief Justice Frederick Moore Vinson.

Before delivering his inaugural address, the President offered a prayer, the text of which follows:

My friends, before I begin the expression of these thoughts that I deem appropriate to this moment, would you permit me the privilege of uttering a little private prayer of my own. And I ask that you bow your heads.

Almighty God, as we stand here at this moment my future associates in the Executive branch of Government join me in beseeching that Thou will make full and complete our dedication to the service of the people in this throng, and their fellow citizens everywhere.

Give us, we pray, the power to discern clearly right from wrong and allow all our words and actions to be governed thereby, and by the laws of this land. Especially we pray that our concern shall be for all the people regardless of station, race or calling.

May cooperation be permitted and be the mutual aim of those who, under the concepts of our Constitution, hold to different political faiths; so that all may work for the good of our beloved country and Thy glory. Amen.

The two-and-a-half-hour inaugural parade was witnessed by an estimated 1 million persons, of whom 60,000 were in the grandstand in seats ranging in price from $3 to $15, according to location. About 22,000 service men and women and 5,000 civilians were in the parade, which included 50 state and organization floats costing $100,000. There were also 65 musical units, 350 horses, 3 elephants, an Alaskan dog team, and the 280-millimeter atomic cannon. It was the most elaborate inaugural pageant ever held.

In addition to a governors' reception for 3,000 invited guests, there were two inaugural festivals, one at the Uline Arena for 11,000 persons, and one at the Capitol Theater for 3,500 persons. Tickets ranged in price from $3 to $12. Forty stars of stage, screen, and TV participated in the celebration.

In the evening two inaugural balls were held, one at the National Guard Armory and the other at the gymnasium of McDonough Hall at Georgetown University.

INCOMING STAFF ATTENDED CHURCH SERVICE

The first occasion on which an entire official family attended church services with an incoming President took place on January 20, 1953, when President-elect Eisenhower and his staff attended a preinaugural service at the National Presbyterian Church on Connecticut Avenue, Washington, D.C. The Reverend Edward L. R. Elson, pastor of the church, conducted the service.

EISENHOWER BECAME COMMUNICANT

President Eisenhower was the first President to take the complete action from baptism to confirmation and full communicant membership in a church subsequent to his inauguration.

The President was received into the membership of the National Presbyterian Church of Washington, D.C., by baptism and confession of faith before the session of the church early on Sunday morning February 1, 1953, and thereafter on the same day participated as a church member in the service of Holy Communion.

EISENHOWER APPOINTED GRANDSONS TO POSITIONS HELD BY THEIR GRANDFATHERS

John Foster Dulles of New York, who served as Secretary of State under President Eisenhower from January 21, 1953, until April 1959, was the grandson of John Watson Foster of Indiana, who served as Secretary of State under Benjamin Harrison from June 29, 1892, to February 22, 1893.

John Marshall Harlan, who took office on March 28, 1955, as an Associate Justice of the Supreme Court, is a grandson of John Marshall Harlan, who served in the same capacity from November 29, 1877, to October 14, 1911.

NEW CABINET POST CREATED

Legislation enacted March 12, 1953 (67 Stat. L. 631), effective April 11, 1953, provided for a new cabinet department, the Department of

Health, Education, and Welfare. The first secretary was Oveta Culp Hobby (Mrs. William Pettus Hobby of Houston, Tex.). No provision was made to include the secretary in the presidential succession.

DIRECT QUOTATIONS PERMITTED

The first presidential press conference in which direct quotations were allowed to be used was attended by 161 reporters on December 16, 1953, at the White House. The thirty-five minute press conference with President Eisenhower was held from 10:31 A.M. to 11:05 A.M. The entire conference was printed in some newspapers, and it was also broadcast. The White House also released a tape recording for use on radio and television.

PRESIDENTIAL NEWS CONFERENCE TELEVISED

The first presidential news conference to be recorded by both newsreels and television was held January 19, 1955, when reporters questioned President Eisenhower about Red China and Formosa, national security, the imprisonment of American fliers, trade with the Communists, and other subjects. The conference was filmed by Fox Movietone News and the National Broadcasting Company, which pooled the telecast with the other networks. The program was held until officially released.

PAY OF VICE PRESIDENT AND OTHER OFFICIALS INCREASED

On March 2, 1955, President Eisenhower signed the congressional-judicial pay bill granting federal employees the highest salaries ever paid to government officials. The pay of congressmen was increased from $15,000 to $22,500 a year, and the pay of the Vice President and Speaker of the House from $30,000 to $35,000.

The salary of the chief justice was raised from $25,500 to $35,000; associate justices, from $25,500 to $35,000; higher court judges, from $17,500 to $25,000; lower court judges, from $15,000 to $22,500; deputy attorney generals, from $17,500 to $21,000; solicitor general, from $17,500 to $20,500 a year.

EISENHOWER TELECAST IN COLOR

President Dwight David Eisenhower was the first President telecast in color. He addressed the fortieth class reunion of the class of 1915 of the United States Military Academy at West Point, N.Y., on June 6, 1955. The film was shown, June 7, 1955, from 11 A.M. to 12 A.M. on NBC's "Home Show."

EISENHOWER STRICKEN WITH HEART ATTACK AND OTHER ILLNESSES

The first presidential candidate who had suffered a heart attack was President Eisenhower. The attack occurred on September 24, 1955, while the President was on vacation at Denver, Colo. His first steps after the illness were taken on October 25, 1955, at the Fitzsimons Army Hospital at Denver. On February 29, 1956, he announced that he would be available for a second term.

During his administration, President Eisenhower was operated upon for ileitis and also suffered a very slight stroke.

PRESIDENTIAL INAUGURAL CEREMONIES ACT

The presidential inaugural ceremonies act was an act "to provide for the maintenance of public order and the protection of life and property in connection with the presidential inaugural ceremonies," passed by joint resolution on August 6, 1956 (70 Stat. L. 1049). The act empowered the inaugural committee to make arrangements and plans for the inauguration.

SECOND INAUGURATION

As January 20, 1957, fell on a Sunday, President Eisenhower took the oath of office in a private White House ceremony.

On Monday, January 21, 1957, he repeated the oath at the inaugural ceremonies held on the east portico of the White House. The oath was administered by Chief Justice Earl Warren.

In the afternoon 750,000 spectators watched a three-and-a-half-hour parade over a three-mile route. Marching in the parade were 17,000 people, including 11,757 in military service. There were 47 marching units, 52 bands, and 10 drum and bugle corps. The highlight of the parade was a mammoth float—408 feet long and mounted on 164 wheels—which introduced the theme "Liberty and Strength Through Consent of the Governed."

Four inaugural balls were held in the evening at the Armory, the Mayflower Hotel, the Statler Hotel, and the Sheraton-Park Hotel.

EISENHOWER SUBMERGED IN ATOMIC SUBMARINE

President Eisenhower was the first President to submerge in an atomic-powered submarine. He was aboard the *Seawolf* on September 26, 1957, when the submarine submerged five miles southwest of Brentons Reef, off Newport, R.I., and remained sixty feet below the surface for about fifteen minutes. (Eisenhower had submerged twice before in a submarine—at Panama after World War I.)

EISENHOWER MAKES HOLE-ON-ONE

Former President Eisenhower made a hole-in-one on the 104-yard par-three thirteenth hole at the Seven Lake Country Club, Palm Springs, Calif., on February 6, 1968, in a foursome with Lee Freeman Gosden, George Allen and Leigh Battson.

THE OLDEST PRESIDENT

President Eisenhower, who was 70 years and 98 days old at the conclusion of his second term on Jan. 20, 1961, was the oldest President to leave office.

The oldest President at the time of his inauguration was William Henry Harrison, who was 68 years and 23 days old. He did not complete his term, dying 32 days after his inauguration.

EISENHOWER'S COMMISSION RESTORED

Legislation was enacted by Congress on March 14, 1961, to restore the five-star rank of General of the Army to former President Dwight

David Eisenhower, retroactive to December 20, 1944, the day he was first promoted to that rank. The legislation was approved by voice vote and signed by President John Fitzgerald Kennedy on March 24, 1961.

Eisenhower did not go on the military payroll, for he drew the annual presidential pension of $25,000, plus $50,000 for office expenses and staff.

THE FIRST LADY

Mary (Mamie) Geneva Doud Eisenhower was reserved, dignified, and unassuming, avoiding unnecessary publicity. Before her husband's administration, as an army wife for thirty-seven years, she grew accustomed to meeting groups of influential people.

JOHN FITZGERALD KENNEDY

35th PRESIDENT

Born–May 29, 1917
Birthplace–Brookline, Mass.
College attended–Harvard College, Cambridge, Mass.
Date of graduation–June 21, 1940, B.S. cum laude
Religion–Roman Catholic
Ancestry–Irish
Occupation–Author, congressman, senator
Date and place of marriage–Sept. 12, 1953, Newport, R.I.
Age at marriage–36 years, 106 days
Years married–10 years, 71 days
Political party–Democratic
State represented–Massachusetts
Term of office–Jan. 20, 1961-Nov. 22, 1963
Term served–2 years, 306 days
Administration–44th
Congresses–87th, 88th
Age at inauguration–43 years, 236 days
Lived after term–Died in office
Date of death–Nov. 22, 1963
Age at death–46 years, 177 days
Place of death–Dallas, Tex.
Burial place–Arlington National Cemetery, Va.

PARENTS

Father–Joseph Patrick Kennedy
Born–Sept. 6, 1888, East Boston, Mass.
Married–Oct. 7, 1914
Occupation–Banking, finance, real estate, Ambassador to Great Britain, 1937-1941
Died–Nov. 18, 1969, Hyannis Port, Mass.

Age at death–81 years, 73 days
Moth–Rose Elizabeth Fitzgerald Kennedy
Born–July 22, 1890, Boston, Mass.

BROTHERS AND SISTERS

John Fitzgerald Kennedy was the second child in a family of nine.

Children of Joseph Patrick Kennedy and Rose Fitzgerald Kennedy

Joseph Patrick Kennedy, Jr., b. July 25, 1915; d. August 12, 1944

John Fitzgerald Kennedy, b. May 29, 1917; d. Nov. 22, 1963

Rosemary Kennedy, b. Sept. 13, 1918

Kathleen Kennedy, b. Feb. 20, 1920; d. May 14, 1948

Eunice Mary Kennedy, b. July 10, 1921

Patricia Kennedy, b. May 6, 1924

Robert Francis Kennedy, b. Nov. 20, 1925; d. June 6, 1968

Jean Ann Kennedy, b. Feb. 20, 1928

Edward Moore Kennedy, b. February 22, 1932

CHILDREN

Caroline Bouvier Kennedy, b. Nov. 27, 1957, New York City

John Fitzgerald Kennedy, Jr., b. Nov. 25, 1960, Washington, D.C.

Patrick Bouvier Kennedy, b. Aug. 7, 1963, Otis Air Force Base, Mass.; d. Aug. 9, 1963, Boston,

For additional data see the end of this section and also specific subject headings in the index.

Mass. (Buried in Kennedy family plot in Hollywood Cemetery, Brookline, Mass.; reinterred Dec. 3, 1963, Arlington National Cemetery, Va.)

MRS. JOHN FITZGERALD KENNEDY

Name–Jacqueline Lee Bouvier Kennedy

Date of birth–July 28, 1929

Birthplace–Southampton, N.Y.

Age at marriage–24 years, 46 days

Children–1 daughter, 2 sons

Mother–Janet Norton Lee Bouvier

Father–John Vernou Bouvier III

His occupation–Lawyer, stockbroker

Stepfather–Hugh D. Auchincloss

His occupation–Stockbroker

Years younger than the President–12 years, 60 days

THE ELECTION OF 1960

NOMINATIONS FOR TERM 1961-1965

Democratic Party Convention (33rd)

July 11-15, 1960, Los Angeles Memorial Sports Arena and the Coliseum, Los Angeles, Calif.

Nominated for President—John Fitzgerald Kennedy, Mass.

Nominated for Vice President—Lyndon Baines Johnson, Tex.

Kennedy was nominated on the first ballot. Candidates for nomination and the votes they received:

John Fitzgerald Kennedy, Mass., 806

Lyndon Baines Johnson, Tex., 409

(William) Stuart Symington, Mo., 86

Adlai Ewing Stevenson, Ill., 79$^1/_2$

Robert Baumle Meyner, N.J., 43

Hubert Horatio Humphrey, Minn., 41$^1/_2$

George Armistead Smathers, Fla., 30

Ross Barnett, Miss., 23

Herschel Gellel Loveless, Iowa, 1$^1/_2$

Edmund Gerald Brown, Calif., $^1/_2$

Orval Eugene Faubus, Ark., $^1/_2$

Albert Dean Rossellini, Wash., $^1/_2$

Total number of votes: 1,521

Number necessary for nomination: 761

Republican Party Convention (27th)

July 25-28, 1960, International Amphitheatre, Chicago, Ill.

Nominated for President—Richard Milhous Nixon, Calif.

Nominated for Vice President—Henry Cabot Lodge, Mass.

Total number of votes: 1,331

Number necessary for nomination: 666

Nixon was nominated by acclamation.

National States' Rights Party Convention

Mar. 19-20, 1960, Dayton, Ohio

Nominated for President—Orval Eugene Faubus, Ark.

Nominated for Vice President—John Geraerdt Crommelin, Ala.
　Faubus was nominated against his wishes.

Socialist Labor Party Convention
May 7-9, 1960, Henry Hudson Hotel, New York, N.Y.
Nominated for President-Eric Hass, N.Y.
Nominated for Vice President-Georgia Cozzini, Wis.

Prohibition Party Convention
Sept. 1-3, 1959, Winona Lake, Ind.
Nominated for President—Rutherford Losey Decker, Mo.
Nominated for Vice President—Earle Harold Munn, Mich.

Socialist Workers Party
Nominated for President—Farrell Dobbs, N.Y.
Nominated for Vice President—Myra Tanner Weiss, N.Y.

Conservative Party of New Jersey
Nominated for President—Joseph Bracken Lee, Utah
Nominated for Vice President—Kent H. Courtney, La.
　Barry Morris Goldwater of Arizona declined the nomination.

Conservative Party of Virginia
Nominated for President—C. Benton Coiner, Va.
Nominated for Vice President—Edward M. Silverman, Va.

Constitution Party (Texas)
Nominated for President—Charles Loten Sullivan, Miss.

Constitution Party (Washington) Convention
Apr. 20-21, 1960, Indianapolis, Ind.
Nominated for President—Merritt Barton Curtis, Washington, D.C.

Greenback Party
Nominated for President—Whitney Hart Slocomb, Calif.
Nominated for Vice President—Edward Kirby Meador, Mass.
　The candidates were selected by mail referendum.

Independent Afro-American Party
Nominated for President—Clennon King, Ga.

Socialist Party Convention
May 28-30, 1960, Washington, D.C.
No candidates named

Tax Cut Party (America First Party; American Party)
Nominated for President—Lar Daly, Ill.
Nominated for Vice President—Merritt Barton Curtis, Washington,
　D.C.

Theocratic Party Convention

May 21, 1960, Fulton, Mo.
Nominated for President—Homer Aubrey Tomlinson, N.Y.
Nominated for Vice President—Raymond L. Teague, Alaska
    The Theocratic Party was organized March 21, 1960, at the Church of God, Fulton, Mo.

Vegetarian Party

Nominated for President—Symon Gould, N.Y.
Nominated for Vice President—Christopher Gian-Cursio, Fla.

ELECTION RESULTS, NOV. 8, 1960—PRESIDENTIAL AND VICE PRESIDENTIAL CANDIDATES

Democratic Party (34,227,096 votes)

John Fitzgerald Kennedy, Mass.
Lyndon Baines Johnson, Tex.

Republican Party (34,107,646 votes)

Richard Milhous Nixon, Calif.
Henry Cabot Lodge, Mass.

National States' Rights Party (214,195 votes)

Orval Eugene Faubus, Ark.
John Geraerdt Crommelin, Ala.

Socialist Labor Party (46,478 votes)

Eric Hass, N.Y.
Georgia Cozzini, Wis.

Prohibition Party (45,919 votes)

Rutherford Losey Decker, Mo.
Earle Harold Munn, Mich.

Socialist Workers Party (39,541 votes)

Farrell Dobbs, N.Y.
Myra Tanner Weiss, N.Y.

Conservative Party of New Jersey (8,708 votes)

Joseph Bracken Lee, Utah
Kent H. Courtney, La.

Conservative Party of Virginia (4,204 votes)

C. Benton Coiner, Va.

Edward M. Silverman, Va.

Additional Votes (142,598)

Byrd unpledged Democrats (Miss.), 116,248
Constitution Party (Tex.), Charles L. Sullivan and Merritt Barton Curtis, 18,169
Constitution Party (Wash.), Merritt Barton Curtis and B. N. Miller, 1,401

Tax Cut Party (Mich.), Lar Daly and B. N. Miller, 1,767

Independent Afro-American Party (Ala.), Clennon King and Reginald Carter, 1,485

Industrial Government Party (Minn.), 962

Write-in votes, 1,064

Scattering, 963

ELECTORAL VOTES (537—50 states)

Kennedy received 56.43 per cent (303 votes—22 states) as follows: Ala. 5 (of the 11 votes); Ark. 8; Conn. 8; Del. 3; Ga. 12; Hawaii 3; Ill. 27; La. 10; Md. 9; Mass. 16; Mich. 20; Minn. 11; Mo. 13; Nev. 3; N.J. 16; N.M. 4; N.Y. 45; N.C. 14; Pa. 32; R.I. 4; S.C. 8; Tex. 24; W.Va. 8.

Nixon received 40.78 per cent (219 votes—26 states) as follows: Alaska 3; Ariz. 4; Calif. 32; Colo. 6; Fla. 10; Idaho 4; Ind. 13; Iowa 10; Kan. 8; Ky. 10; Me. 5; Mont. 4; Neb. 6; N.H. 4; N.D. 4; Ohio 25; Okla. 7 (of the 8 votes); Ore. 6; S.D. 4; Tenn. 11; Utah 4; Vt. 3; Va. 12; Wash. 9; Wis. 12; Wyo. 3.

Byrd received 2.79 per cent (15 votes—2 states) as follows: Ala. 6 (of the 11 votes); Miss. 8; Okla. 1 (of the 8 votes)

CABINET

January 20, 1961-Nov. 22, 1963

State–(David) Dean Rusk, N.Y., Jan. 21, 1961

Treasury–C. (Clarence) Douglas Dillon, N.J., Jan. 21, 1961

Defense–Robert Strange McNamara, Mich., Jan. 21, 1961

Attorney General–Robert Francis Kennedy, Mass., Jan. 21, 1961

Postmaster General–J. (James) Edward Day, Calif., Jan. 21, 1961; John A. Gronouski, Wis., Sept. 30, 1963

Interior–Stewart Lee Udall, Ariz., Jan. 21, 1961

Agriculture–Orville Lothrop Freeman, Minn., Jan. 21, 1961

Commerce–Luther Hartwell Hodges, N.C., Jan. 21, 1961

Labor–Arthur Joseph Goldberg, Ill., Jan. 21, 1961; W. (William) Willard Wirtz, Ill., Sept. 25, 1962

Health, Education, and Welfare–Abraham Alexander Ribicoff, Conn., Jan. 21, 1961; Anthony Joseph Celebreze, Ohio, July 31, 1962

EIGHTY-SEVENTH CONGRESS

January 3, 1961-January 3, 1963

First session–Jan. 3, 1961-Sept. 27, 1961 (268 days) (The House was in recess Mar. 30-Apr. 10.)

Second session–Jan. 10, 1962-Oct. 13, 1962 (277 days) (The House was in recess Apr. 19-Apr. 30.)

Vice President–Lyndon Baines Johnson, Tex.

President protempore of the Senate–Carl Hayden, Ariz.

Secretary of the Senate–Felton McLellan Johnston, Miss

Speaker of the House–Sam (Samuel Taliaferro) Rayburn, Tex. (died Nov. 16, 1961); John William McCormack, Mass.

Clerk of the House–Ralph R. Roberts, Ind.

EIGHTY-EIGHTH CONGRESS

January 3, 1963-January 3, 1965
First session—Jan. 9, 1963-Dec. 30, 1963 (356 days) (The House was in recess Apr. 11-23)
Second session—Jan. 7, 1964-Oct. 3, 1964 (270 days) (The House was in recess Mar. 26-Apr. 6; July 2-20; Aug. 21-31. The Senate was in recess July 10-20; Aug. 1-31)
Vice President—Lyndon Baines Johnson, Tex., succeeded to the presidency on the death of John Fitzgerald Kennedy on Nov. 22, 1963
President pro tempore of the Senate—Carl Hayden, Ariz.
Secretary of the Senate—Felton McLellan Johnston, Miss.
Speaker of the House—John William McCormack, Mass.
Clerk of the House—Ralph R. Roberts, Ind.

APPOINTMENTS TO THE SUPREME COURT

Associate Justices
Byron Raymond White, Colo., Apr. 16, 1962
Arthur Joseph Goldberg, Ill., Oct. 1, 1962

ADMINISTRATION—IMPORTANT DATES

Jan. 20, 1961, President Kennedy's Inaugural Address called for dedication to "a struggle against the common enemies of man: tyranny, poverty, disease, and war itself"
Jan. 25, 1961, first live television press conference
Mar. 1, 1961, Peace Corps created by executive order
Mar. 6, 1961, President established a Committee on Equal Employment Opportunity, with Vice President Johnson as chairman
Mar. 23, 1961, President warned Communists that U.S. would not tolerate conquest of Laos
Mar. 26, 1961, President conferred with British Prime Minister Macmillan at Key West, Fla., regarding Laos crisis
Mar. 29, 1961, residents of District of Columbia granted the right to vote for President by the 23rd amendment
Apr. 12, 1961, first man in space, Soviet Major Yuri Gagarin, orbited earth
Apr. 17-20, 1961, failure of Bay of Pigs invasion, Cuba
May 1961, "Freedom riders"—biracial groups sponsored by the Committee on Racial Equality—boarded southbound buses to challenge segregation in interstate bus facilities
May 5, 1961, first U.S. astronaut, Commander Alan Bartlett Shepard, reached 116.5 mile altitude in space
May 5, 1961, minimum-wage bill raised hourly rate from $1.00 to $1.25 over a two-year period
May 16-18, 1961, President visited Ottawa, Canada
May 31-June 2, 1961, President conferred with President de Gaulle in Paris
June 3-4, 1961, President conferred with Premier Khrushchev in Vienna
June 4-5, 1961, President conferred with Prime Minister Macmillan

in London

June 5, 1961, Communist party ordered to register as agent of a foreign power by Supreme Court

June 21, 1961, President opened plant in Freeport, Tex., to convert salt water to fresh water

July 24, 1961, United States warned that interference with West Berlin access would be considered an aggressive act

Aug. 1, 1961, President signed bill to call up to 250,000 reservists for not more than one year

Aug. 5-17, 1961, charter of the Alliance for Progress, for Latin American economic aid and development, drafted and approved by Inter-American Economic and Social Council at Punta del Este, Uruguay

Aug. 10, 1961, President and Vice President Johnson agreed upon conditions under which latter should assume office upon disability of the President

Aug. 12-13, 1961, East Germany built wall to close border between East and West Berlin

Sept. 3, 1961, United States and Great Britain proposed to Soviet Union that all aboveground nuclear tests be banned

Sept. 4, 1961, President signed Foreign Assistance Act of 1961, setting up the Agency for International Development as the chief U.S. aid agency

Sept. 5, 1961, hijacking of airplanes made federal offense

Sept. 14, 1961, Berlin crisis discussed by Big Four foreign ministers at Washington, D.C.

Sept. 22, 1961, President signed the Peace Corps Act, giving statutory basis to the Corps

Sept. 23, 1961, President urged United States Steel Corporation to hold line on steel prices

Oct. 11, 1961, President advocated national program to combat mental retardation

Dec. 15-18, 1961, President visited Puerto Rico, Venezuela, Colombia

Dec. 21-22, 1961, President visited Bermuda

Jan. 25, 1962, President called for reciprocal tariff reductions in new trade expansion act

Feb. 7, 1962, almost total embargo placed on trade with Cuba

Feb. 10, 1962, Francis Gary Powers, U-2 pilot convicted of espionage in Soviet Union, freed in exchange for Soviet spy Rudolf Abel

Feb. 20, 1962, first U.S. astronaut in orbit; Lieutenant Colonel John Herschel Glenn, Jr., orbited earth three times

Mar. 2, 1962, President announced resumption of nuclear testing in atmosphere unless all tests were banned by April

Mar. 26, 1962, Supreme Court restricted rural domination of state legislatures

Apr. 11, 1962, President denounced rise in steel prices

Apr. 13, 1962, steel price rise rescinded

May 12, 1962, U.S. naval and ground forces ordered to Laos

May 28, 1962, worst one-day market slide since 1929, but sharp recovery on following day

June 25, 1962, Supreme Court declared public school prayers unconstitutional

June 29-July 1, 1962, Kennedy conferred with Mexican President Adolfo López Mateos in Mexico City

July 12, 1962, missile-borne thermonuclear device exploded over central Pacific

Aug. 27, 1962, Mariner II, unmanned spacecraft, sent aloft to probe space around Venus; passed Venus at distance of about 21,600 miles, Dec. 14, 1962

Sept. 30-Oct. 1, 1962, segregationists staged fifteen-hour riot on University of Mississippi campus to prevent enrollment of Negro student; two persons killed

Oct. 22, 1962, President announced imposition of "quarantine" on Cuba because of construction by Russians of offensive missile bases

Oct. 28, 1962, Soviet Premier Khrushchev agreed to halt construction of missile bases in Cuba and to remove Soviet rockets under United Nations supervision

Nov. 20, 1962, President issued executive order against racial discrimination in federally aided housing

Nov. 21, 1962, blockade of Cuba lifted

Dec. 17, 1962, radio and television broadcast of interview with three commentators in which President discussed nature of the presidency and reviewed first two years in office

Dec. 18, 1962, President in Nassau to confer with Prime Minister Macmillan on NATO fleet

Dec. 23-24, 1962, 1,113 prisoners captured in the Bay of Pigs invasion of Cuba released by Premier Castro and flown to United States, in exchange for $53 million worth of baby food and medicine supplied by U.S. citizens and business organizations

Jan. 7, 1963, higher postal rates in effect: 5 cents for first-class mail, 4 cents for postcards, etc.

Jan. 14, 1963, tax cuts to bolster economy recommended in President's State of the Union message

Jan. 29, 1963, President proposed omnibus education bill

Feb. 6, 1963, trade with Cuba restricted

Feb. 8, 1963, underground nuclear testing resumed

Feb. 14, 1963, Syncom I, communications satellite, launched

Feb. 28, 1963, President delivered special message on civil rights to Congress

Mar. 19, 1963, Declaration of San Jose pledging efforts to halt Soviet aggression in Western Hemisphere signed at San Jose, Costa Rica, by the presidents of Costa Rica, Guatemala, Honduras, Nicaragua, Panama, El Salvador, and the United States

Mar. 26, 1963, United States and U.S.S.R. resumed Berlin talks

Apr. 9, 1963, Winston Churchill granted honorary U.S. citizenship

Apr. 10, 1963, atomic submarine, U.S.S. *Thresher*, sank in North Atlantic with 129 men aboard

Apr. 11, 1963, first secret session in twenty years of U.S. Senate; discussion of $196 million appropriation for antimissile batteries

Apr. 23, 1963, Organization of American States meeting in Washington, D.C., voted to investigate Communist subversion in the Western Hemisphere

May 7, 1963, Telstar II, communications satellite, launched

June 11, 1963, Governor Wallace of Alabama, faced by National Guard troops, allowed two Negroes to enter University of Alabama

June 12, 1963, President's Advisory Council on the Arts established by executive order

June 17, 1963, Supreme Court decision declared required reading of Bible verses in public schools unconstitutional

June 19, 1963, strong civil rights legislation urged by President

June 20, 1963, agreement for a direct communication link with Soviet Union ("hot line") signed at Geneva

June 22, 1963, President visited Western Europe, conferring with heads of state

July 9, 1963, United States banned nearly all financial transactions with Cuba in effort to isolate Castro

July 18, 1963, President appealed to Congress for tax legislation to curb foreign purchases and reduce balance of payments deficit

July 25, 1963, United States, Great Britain, and Soviet Union agreed on limited nuclear test treaty, effective Oct. 10

Aug. 16, 1963, United States and Canada completed agreement to arm Canadian air defense systems with nuclear warheads under United States control

Aug. 27, 1963, Congress approved legislation barring national railroad strike by imposing compulsory arbitration

Aug. 28, 1963, civil rights march on Washington, D.C., by 200,000 persons, mostly Negroes

Sept. 20, 1963, President in UN speech asked for better U.S.-Soviet cooperation and a joint expedition to the moon

Sept. 22, 1963, Senate ratified treaty banning nuclear weapons tests in atmosphere, in outer space, and under water (but not underground tests)

Sept. 24-28, 1963, President visited eleven western states

Oct. 9, 1963, President approved sale of 150 million bushels of wheat to Soviet Union

Oct. 16, 1963, two nuclear detection satellites launched

Oct. 22-24, 1963, Second Armored Division, U.S.A., airlifted from Fort Hood, Tex. to West Germany in test flight

Nov. 1, 1963, President Diem and brother Ngo Dinh Nhu assassinated in Vietnam coup

Nov. 5, 1963, Federal Reserve Board raised margin requirements for stock exchange holdings from 50 per cent to 70 per cent

Nov. 16, 1963, President obtained release of Frederick Barghoorn, American professor arrested in Moscow on espionage charges

Nov. 22, 1963, President assassinated in Dallas, Tex.

IMPORTANT DATES IN HIS LIFE

1923-1935, attended public and private schools in Massachusetts, New

York, and Connecticut

Summer 1935, at London School of Economics

Fall 1936, entered Harvard

May 29, 1938, at age of twenty-one received $1 million trust fund established by his father

1939, on six months' leave from Harvard; worked in U.S. embassies in Paris and London

June 21, 1940, graduated from Harvard College, B.S. cum laude

Fall 1940, at Stanford University

Sept. 1941, Lt. j.g. U.S. Navy

Aug. 2, 1943, his torpedo boat, PT-109, rammed by Japanese destroyer *Amagiri*

Dec. 1943, returned from the Pacific area

Apr. 1945, honorable discharge from U.S. Navy

1945, awarded Navy and Marine Corps Medal and Purple Heart

1945, newspaper correspondent (covered UN Conference at San Francisco, British elections, Potsdam meeting, etc.)

Nov. 5, 1946, elected to U.S. House of Representatives (from Massachusetts); reelected in 1948 and 1950

1949, visited France, Poland, Russia, Turkey, Palestine, Balkans

1951, visited Britain, France, Italy, Spain, West Germany, Yugoslavia

Nov. 4, 1952, elected to U.S. Senate (from Massachusetts)

Oct. 21, 1954, spinal operation

Aug. 17, 1956, defeated for Democratic vice presidential nomination by Estes Kefauver

May 6, 1957, awarded Pulitzer Prize for biography *Profiles in Courage*

Nov. 4, 1958, reelected to U.S. Senate

July 13, 1960, nominated for presidency on first ballot at Democratic convention

Nov. 8, 1960, elected President, defeating Richard M. Nixon

Jan. 20, 1961, inaugurated President

Nov. 22, 1963, assassinated in Dallas, Tex.

JOHN FITZGERALD KENNEDY

____was the first President born in the twentieth century.

____was the first President who was a Roman Catholic.

____was the first President inaugurated on the new east front of the U.S. Capitol.

____was the first President whose parents survived him.

____was the first President whose inauguration was celebrated with five inaugural balls.

____was the first President whose inauguration was shown on color television.

____was the first President who had served in the U.S. Navy.

____was the second President buried in Arlington National Cemetery, Va.

____was the fourth President assassinated.

____was the eighth President to die in office.

KENNEDY's VICE PRESIDENT

Vice President–Lyndon Baines Johnson (37th V.P.)
Date of birth–Aug. 27, 1908
Birthplace–Near Stonewall, Tex.
Political party–Democratic
State represented–Texas
Term of office–Jan. 20, 1961-Nov. 22, 1963
Age at inauguration–52 years, 146 days
Occupation after term–President

For further biographical information see Lyndon Baines Johnson, 36th President.

ADDITIONAL DATA ON KENNEDY

FIFTH HARVARD COLLEGE GRADUATE PRESIDENT

John Fitzgerald Kennedy was the fifth President of the United States who was a graduate of Harvard College (June 21, 1940). Other chief executives of the United States who were Harvard alumni were John Adams (July 16, 1755), John Quincy Adams (July 13, 1787), Theodore Roosevelt (June 30, 1880), and Franklin Delano Roosevelt (June 24, 1903).

Rutherford Birchard Hayes, who graduated from Kenyon College, received his law degree in 1845 from the Harvard Law School.

KENNEDY, AUTHOR AND PULITZER PRIZE WINNER

John Fitzgerald Kennedy achieved distinction as a commentator on public affairs with his book *Why England Slept,* an account of England's slowness to rearm in the 1930's in the face of growing Nazi aggressiveness. It was published in 1940 when Kennedy was twenty-three years old and won acclaim as a thoughtful and penetrating study.

In 1945, working as a newspaper correspondent, he covered the UN Conference in San Francisco for the Chicago *Herald-American* and the Potsdam Conference and the British elections for International News Service.

While convalescing in a hospital from a spinal operation, Kennedy wrote *Profiles in Courage,* which was published in 1956 and for which he received the Pulitzer Prize for biography on May 7, 1957. It is a biographical work chronicling decisive moments in the lives of John Quincy Adams, Daniel Webster, Sam Houston, George Norris, and other political figures.

Many of Kennedy's speeches have been printed in collections—*The Strategy of Peace, To Turn the Tide,* etc.

KENNEDY A HERO IN NAVAL ACTION

John Fitzgerald Kennedy, who enlisted in the U.S. Navy in September 1941, assumed command on April 25, 1943, of PT-109, a gasoline-engine torpedo boat, 80 feet long with a beam of 20 feet 8 inches. The 38-ton boat had a draft of 5 feet, carried a complement of 17 men, and made the speed of 41 knots. Its armament consisted of four 21-inch torpedoes.

While attached to a convoy in the Blackett Strait in the Solomon Islands, the PT boat was rammed and cut in half by the Japanese destroyer *Amagiri* on August 2, 1943.

For his heroism in rescuing members of his crew, he was presented with the Navy and Marine Corps Medal in 1945 by Captain Frederick L. Conklin, the citation being signed by Admiral William Frederick Halsey:

> For heroism in the rescue of three men following the ramming and sinking of his motor torpedo boat while attempting a torpedo attack on a Japanese destroyer in the Solomon Islands area on the night of August 1-2, 1943. Lieutenant Kennedy, captain of the boat, directed the rescue of the crew and personally rescued three men, one of whom was seriously injured. During the following six days, he succeeded in getting his crew ashore, and after swimming many hours attempting to secure aid and food, finally effected the rescue of the men. His courage, endurance and excellent leadership contributed to the saving of several lives and was in keeping with the highest traditions in the United States Naval Service.

A youngster in Ashland, Wis., asked Kennedy how he had become a war hero. He replied, "It was involuntary; they sank my boat."

KENNEDY-NIXON DEBATES

The first presidential candidate debate series on television was the Nixon-Kennedy debate series during the 1960 presidential campaign which gave the voting public a closer look at the two major candidates and the issues. The first of four debates was held September 26, 1960, in a Chicago studio; the second, October 7, 1960, in a Washington, D.C. studio; the third, October 13, 1960 (Kennedy in New York City, Nixon in Hollywood, Calif.); and the fourth, October 21, 1960, in a New York studio.

SMALL POPULAR VOTE MARGIN

On November 8, 1960, the total vote cast was 68,836,385 votes: 34,227,096 votes or 49.71 per cent for Kennedy, 34,107,646 votes or 49.55 per cent for Nixon, and 501,643 votes or .74 per cent for all others.

This was the closest popular vote in United States history.

THE YOUNGEST ELECTED PRESIDENT

John Fitzgerald Kennedy was the youngest presidential nominee elected, and the youngest man elected to the office, but he was not the youngest President.

Kennedy was 43 years and 236 days old when he was inaugurated President. He was 2 years and 257 days younger than Theodore Roosevelt was when he was inaugurated for his second term, but Roosevelt was 279 days younger when he became President through succession.

Theodore Roosevelt, who was inaugurated Vice President of the United States, succeeded to the presidency on September 14, 1901, after the assassination of President William McKinley. Roosevelt was 42 years and 322 days old when he became President. He became a candidate for a second term and was sworn in March 4, 1905, when he was 46 years and 128 days old.

OLDEST AND YOUNGEST PRESIDENTS RIDE TOGETHER

During the inauguration ceremony on January 20, 1961, both the oldest retiring President and youngest elected President rode together in the same automobile. The retiring President Dwight David Eisenhower, born October 14, 1890 (70 years and 98 days) and the incoming President John Fitzgerald Kennedy, born May 29, 1917 (43 years and 236 days) participated in the inaugural ceremony.

INAUGURATION

At noon, on January 20, 1961, John Fitzgerald Kennedy took the oath of office as the thirty-fifth President of the United States on a platform erected on the newly renovated east front of the United States Capitol. The oath was administered by Chief Justice Earl Warren.

The ceremonies began at 11:30 A.M. with an invocation by Richard Cardinal Cushing of Boston. Prayers were also offered by Archbishop Iakovos, Primate of the Greek Orthodox Church of North and South America; the Reverend John Barclay of the Central Christian Church; and Rabbi Nelson Glueck, president of the Hebrew Union College, Cincinnati, Ohio. Marian Anderson sang "The Star-Spangled Banner," and Robert Frost read one of his poems, "The Gift Outright."

The President's 1,355-word inaugural address was very well received. Among the more eloquent passages was the memorable appeal:

And so, my fellow Americans, ask not what your country can do for you—ask what you can do for your country.

My fellow citizens of the world: ask not what America will do for you, but what together we can do for the freedom of man.

The day was cold (22°), clear, and sunny, with occasional blasts of icy wind. Washington was covered with eight inches of snow, which had fallen the previous night, but the inaugural route was cleared for the parade led by the President. Over 32,000 marchers participated. Included in the procession were an array of missiles and a truck bearing a PT boat with eight surviving members of the eleven-man crew which Kennedy had commanded in the Pacific during World War II.

Five inaugural balls were held in the evening at the Mayflower Hotel, the Statler Hotel, the Shoreham Hotel, the Sheraton Park Hotel, and the National Guard Armory.

Over four thousand Secret Service agents, policemen, plainclothesmen, and troops were assigned to protect the incoming and outgoing Presidents.

HOUSE SPEAKER ADMINISTERED OATH

The first Speaker of the House of Representatives to administer the oath of office of a Vice President of the United States was Sam

Rayburn, who on January 20, 1961, administered the oath of office to Vice President Lyndon Baines Johnson.

NEW CONGRESSIONAL APPORTIONMENT

A new apportionment of the 435 seats in the House of Representatives was made on the basis of the decennial census of the population (1960).

In the new apportionment, 9 states gained a total of 19 seats: Arizona, Hawaii, Maryland, Michigan, New Jersey, Ohio, and Texas each gained 1 seat; Florida gained 4 seats; California gained 8 seats. Sixteen states lost a total of 21 seats: Alabama, Illinois, Iowa, Kansas, Kentucky, Maine, Minnesota, Mississippi, Missouri, Nebraska, North Carolina, and West Virginia each lost 1 seat; Arkansas, Massachusetts, and New York each lost 2 seats; Pennsylvania lost 3 seats.

The present apportionment is as follows: Alabama 8, Alaska 1, Arizona 3, Arkansas 4, California 38, Colorado 4, Connecticut 6, Delaware 1, Florida 12, Georgia 10, Hawaii 2, Idaho 2, Illinois 24, Indiana 11, Iowa 7, Kansas 5, Kentucky 7, Louisiana 8, Maine 2, Maryland 8, Massachusetts 12, Michigan 19, Minnesota 8, Mississippi 5, Missouri 10, Montana 2, Nebraska 3, Nevada 1, New Hampshire 2, New Jersey 15, New Mexico 2, New York 41, North Carolina 11, North Dakota 2, Ohio 24, Oklahoma 6, Oregon 4, Pennsylvania 27, Rhode Island 2, South Carolina 6, South Dakota 2, Tennessee 9, Texas 23, Utah 2, Vermont 1, Virginia 10, Washington 7, West Virginia 5, Wisconsin 10, Wyoming 1.

TWENTY-THIRD AMENDMENT RATIFIED

The Twenty-third Amendment, granting the citizens of the District of Columbia the right to vote in presidential elections, was enacted by the 86th Congress and sent to the states for ratification on June 16, 1960. The first state to ratify was Hawaii, on June 23, 1960. The required number of votes (38) was reached on March 29, 1961, when New Hampshire, Kansas, and Ohio ratified. The Secretary of State formally declared the amendment a part of the Constitution on April 3, 1961.

Section 1 of the amendment follows:

The District constituting the seat of Government of the United States shall appoint in such manner as the Congress may direct:

A number of electors of President and Vice President equal to the whole number of Senators and Representatives in Congress to which the District would be entitled if it were a State, but in no event more than the least populous State; they shall be in addition to those appointed by the States, but they shall be considered, for the purpose of the election of President and Vice President, to be electors appointed by a State; and they shall meet in the District and perform such duties as provided by the twelfth article of amendment.

The first primary election was held May 5, 1964.

BROTHER APPOINTED TO CABINET

President Kennedy was the first President to appoint a brother to cabinet rank. On January 21, 1961, Robert Francis Kennedy was sworn in as Attorney General of the United States.

STATE DINNER AT MOUNT VERNON

The first state dinner held outside the White House since the erection of the building was tendered to Mohammed Ayub Khan, the President of Pakistan, on July 11, 1961, by President Kennedy at Mount Vernon, George Washington's Virginia home, which is maintained by the Mount Vernon Ladies' Association of the Union. (A luncheon—not a state dinner—was held at Mount Vernon on October 19, 1926, for Queen Marie of Rumania.)

BROTHER SERVED IN SENATE

President Kennedy was the first President to have a brother in the Senate. His brother Edward Moore Kennedy was elected November 6, 1962, to fill the unexpired senatorial term of the President. (After the election of John Fitzgerald Kennedy to the presidency in 1960, Benjamin A. Smith 2nd was appointed to occupy his senatorial seat on an interim basis until the 1962 election.) Edward Moore Kennedy was reelected November 3, 1964.

PRESIDENTS MAY ATTEND SENATE SESSIONS

The standing rules of the Senate admitting the President of the United States and his private secretary, the President-elect and Vice President-elect of the United States, and former Presidents and former Vice Presidents of the United States to the floor of the Senate while that body is in session have been amended by adding at the end of rule 33 the following: "Former Presidents of the United States shall be entitled to address the Senate upon appropriate notice to the Presiding Officer who shall thereupon make the necessary arrangements." This resolution "admitting former Presidents of the United States to a seat in the Senate as Senators-at-large with certain privileges" was considered and agreed to on October 1, 1963.

Before the adoption of this amendment, Presidents did not have the privilege of addressing the Senate.

WHITE HOUSE PATRONAGE OF THE ARTS

In their few years in the White House both President Kennedy and his wife did much to foster public interest in literature and the arts. Their own interest was shown at the very outset by the participation of the poet Robert Frost in the inaugural services. At the request of the President and Mrs. Kennedy a company of actors performed at the White House in scenes from Shakespeare, and the cellist Pablo Casals and other musicians performed string quartets at the White House on several occasions. The published lists of invited guests at the White House, including many distinguished writers, artists, and musicians, betokened the same interest in cultural matters. It was largely through the interest shown by President and Mrs. Kennedy that the French authorities consented to lend Leonardo da Vinci's "Mona Lisa," one of the treasures of the Louvre, for display in Washington, D.C., New York, and other major cities. The President's cultural interest was shown at the governmental level by his appointment of August Heckscher as Special Consultant on the Arts and by the executive order establishing the President's Advisory Council on the Arts, comprising heads of federal departments and agencies concerned with the arts, as well as thirty private citizens.

PRESIDENTIAL MEDAL OF FREEDOM

On February 22, 1963, President Kennedy changed the name of the Medal of Freedom, originated by President Truman in 1945, to the Presidential Medal of Freedom and announced that it would be conferred annually as the highest civilian honor on persons "who have contributed to the quality of American life." The medal, redesigned by President and Mrs. Kennedy, is a white star with gold eagles and thirteen silver stars on a blue field. The names of the twenty-nine Americans and two foreigners (Jean Monnet and Pablo Casals) who were to receive the medal in 1963 were announced by President Kennedy on July 4, 1963, but he did not live to make the presentations. (The medals were presented by President Johnson on December 6, 1963. President Johnson made two additional awards posthumously, one to the late President John Fitzgerald Kennedy and the other to the late Pope John XXIII.)

KENNEDY WITNESSED POLARIS FIRING

The first President to witness the firing of a Polaris missile was President John Fitzgerald Kennedy. On November 16, 1963, aboard the U.S.S. *Observation Island,* 32 miles off Cape Canaveral, Fla., Kennedy watched the firing from the submerged nuclear submarine, the U.S.S. *Andrew Jackson.* The Polaris A-2 missile broke through the surface of the water and headed on a 1,500 mile flight into the Caribbean.

KENNEDY ASSASSINATED

On November 22, 1963, while riding in an automobile procession from Love Field to the Trade Mart, Dallas, Tex., along streets lined with cheering spectators, President Kennedy was struck in the back of the right shoulder near the neck and in the back of the head by two rifle shots fired from a sixth-floor window in a building overlooking the route of the procession. The wounds caused immediate unconsciousness and despite the efforts of a team of surgeons at Parkland Memorial Hospital, he was pronounced dead within less than an hour.

Another shot, believed to be the second of the three that were fired, severely wounded the Governor of Texas, John Bowden Connally, Jr., who was sitting on a jump seat directly in front of the President. Mrs. Kennedy, Mrs. Connally, and a Secret Service agent were also in the automobile, in addition to the chauffeur. Vice President and Mrs. Johnson were in another automobile in the motorcade.

The accused assassin of the President, Lee Harvey Oswald, was shot and killed two days later in the Dallas Police Station by Jack Ruby (Rubenstein), a Dallas night-club owner.

KENNEDY COFFIN DISPLAYED IN CAPITOL ROTUNDA

John Fitzgerald Kennedy was the sixth President to lie in state in the Capitol Rotunda. The others were Lincoln, Garfield, McKinley, Harding, and Taft. The black-draped catafalque used to support the coffin of Abraham Lincoln was used for the Kennedy coffin.

THE GREATEST SIMULTANEOUS EXPERIENCE IN AMERICAN HISTORY

The assassination of President Kennedy and the events that followed until his interment in Arlington Cemetery have been described by the historian of the assassination as "the greatest simultaneous experience in American history." The events of the four days were witnessed on television by what was probably the largest mass audience in history, and the television coverage was extraordinarily full, including the reproduction of a film taken by a bystander showing the fatally wounded President slump into his wife's lap, views of the automobiles in the procession racing to the hospital, the swearing in of President Johnson in the presidential plane, the removal of the late President's coffin from the plane in Washington, the lying in state in the Capitol Rotunda, and the funeral services, procession, and burial at Arlington.

FUNERAL AND BURIAL

One of the greatest assemblages of foreign dignitaries to attend funeral services in the United States met at St. Matthew's Cathedral, Washington, D.C., on November 25, 1963, to pay their respects at the funeral of President Kennedy.

The President was interred at Arlington National Cemetery with full military honors as befitted a war hero and Commander in Chief of the United States Armed Forces. (William Howard Taft had been the only President previously buried in this national shrine.)

The foreign dignitaries who attended the funeral represented 102 countries. Among the many distinguished mourners were Prince Philip, representing Queen Elizabeth of Great Britain; Frederika, Queen of the Hellenes; Crown Princess Beatrix of The Netherlands; Baudouin I, King of the Belgians; Haile Selassie I, Emperor of Ethiopia; President Charles de Gaulle of France; and President Eamon de Valera of Eire. Other dignitaries who attended were from the United Nations, the European Coal and Steel Community, the European Atomic Energy Commission, and the Organization of American States.

In the funeral procession, precedence was established by alphabetical order of countries.

THE KENNEDY MEMORIAL LIBRARY

Harvard University set aside two acres in Boston, Mass., for the John F. Kennedy Memorial Library "that will belong to all the people."

On October 21, 1963, President Kennedy inspected the site, which was within view of Winthrop House, his residence in his undergraduate days. In accordance with his original intention, the library will hold not only President Kennedy's government papers but also those of other members of his administration. A fund of $10 million is to be raised by public contributions. The land and building will eventually be turned over to the United States Government to be administered by the Bureau of Archives.

CENTER FOR THE PERFORMING ARTS

A joint resolution of Congress, enacted January 23, 1964 (78 Stat. L. 4), renamed the National Cultural Center the John F. Kennedy Center for the Performing Arts.

CARRIER NAMED FOR KENNEDY

A contract for building an attack aircraft carrier to be named for President Kennedy was awarded in April 1964 to the Newport News Shipbuilding and Dry Dock Company, Newport News, Va. The U.S.S. *John F. Kennedy* (CVA-67) was laid down October 22, 1964. She was launched on April 1, 1967, and christened by Caroline Kennedy on May 27, 1967, at Newport News, Va. The carrier which was 1,057.5 feet long and had an 83,000-ton displacement was commissioned September 7, 1968. The complement consisted of 2,600 enlisted men and 120 officers. The first captain was Earl Preston Yates.

PRESIDENT'S BROTHER ASSASSINATED

On June 5, 1968, Senator Robert Francis Kennedy was shot by Sirhan Bishara Sirhan at the Ambassador Hotel, Los Angeles, Calif., and died the following day, June 6, 1968.

THE FIRST LADY

When she was in the White House Jacqueline Bouvier Kennedy, a painter, art collector, and linguist, had a marked influence on American taste. After attending several fashionable private schools, she made her debut in Newport, Rhode Island, and later studied at Vassar College, the Sorbonne in Paris, and George Washington University in Washington, D.C. For a year she was the Washington *Times-Herald's* "Inquiring Camera Girl"—a position involving both photography and reporting—and she also wrote feature stories for the paper.

As first lady, Mrs. Kennedy restored the interior of the White House with authentic art and furnishings of America's past, and when the restoration was complete she appeared on a nationwide televised tour of the White House, displaying and discussing its art treasures. This televised tour had an effect upon American decorating fashions. Mrs. Kennedy's hair and dress styles, too, were copied by many women.

Mrs. Kennedy also accompanied the President on official trips to Europe and to Latin America in 1961. On both tours she was acclaimed by her hosts for her charm and her command of foreign languages.

PRESIDENT'S WIFE RECEIVED BY POPE

Mrs. Kennedy, a Roman Catholic, was the first wife of an incumbent President of the United States to be received in private audience by the Pope. She was received by His Holiness Pope John XXIII on March 11, 1962.

Although she was the first to be received in private audience, Mrs. Kennedy was not the first wife of a President to call upon a Pope. President Grant's wife was received by Pope Leo XIII in March 1878. Mrs. Taft was received by Pope Leo XIII on July 21, 1902, before her husband became President. Mrs. Truman was received by Pope Pius XII on May 20, 1951, while her husband was in office, and Mrs. Eisenhower was received on October 17, 1951, before her husband became President.

MRS. KENNEDY VOTED SPECIAL FUNDS

On December 11, 1963 (77 Stat. L. 348), Congress voted Mrs. Kennedy office space for one year and a staff of her own choice for the same period at a combined salary of not more than $50,000, as well as funds to defray funeral expenses.

In addition, she was entitled to receive the yearly pension of $10,000 granted to widows of Presidents for life or until they remarry, and free mailing privileges for life. She and her children were also provided with Secret Service protection for a period of two years.

PRESIDENT'S WIDOW REMARRIED

On October 20, 1968, Jacqueline Kennedy married Aristotle Socrates Onassis in a Greek Orthodox ceremony in the chapel of the Little Virgin, on the island of Skorpios, off the Greek coast.

LYNDON BAINES JOHNSON
36th PRESIDENT

Born–Aug. 27, 1908
Birthplace–Near Stonewall, Tex.
College attended–Southwest Texas State College, San Marcos
Date of graduation–Aug. 19, 1930, B.S. degree
Religion–Disciples of Christ (International Convention of Christian Churches)
Ancestry–British
Occupation–Senator, rancher
Date and place of marriage–Nov. 17, 1934, San Antonio, Tex.
Age at marriage–26 years, 82 days
Years married–39 years, 66 days
Political party–Democratic
State represented–Texas
Term of office–Nov. 22, 1963-Jan. 20, 1969 (Johnson succeeded to the presidency on the death of John Fitzgerald Kennedy.)
Term served–5 years, 59 days
Administration–44th, 45th
Congresses–88th, 89th, 90th
Age at inauguration–55 years, 87 days
Lived after term–4 years, 2 days
Date of death–Jan. 22, 1973
Age at death–65 years, 148 days
Place of death–San Antonio, Tex.
Burial place–Johnson City, Tex.

PARENTS

Father–Sam Ealy Johnson, Jr.
Born–Oct. 11, 1877, Buda, Tex.
Married–Aug. 20, 1907, Fredericksburg, Tex.
Occupation–State legislator, school teacher, rancher
Died–Oct. 22, 1937, Austin, Tex.
Age at death–60 years, 11 days
Mother–Rebekah Baines Johnson
Born–June 26, 1881, McKinney, Tex.
Died–Sept. 12, 1958, Austin, Tex.
Age at death–77 years, 78 days

BROTHERS AND SISTERS

Lyndon Baines Johnson was the oldest of five children, two boys and three girls.

Children of Sam Ealy Johnson, Jr., and Rebekah Baines Johnson

Lyndon Baines Johnson, b. Aug. 27, 1908; d. Jan. 22, 1973
Rebekah Luruth Johnson, b. Sept. 12, 1910
Josefa Hermine Johnson, b. May 16, 1912; d. Dec. 25, 1961
Sam Houston Johnson, b. Jan. 31, 1914
Lucia Huffman Johnson, b. June 20, 1916

CHILDREN

Lynda Bird Johnson, b. Mar. 19, 1944, Washington, D.C.; m. Charles S. Robb, Dec. 9, 1967, at the White House, Washington, D.C.
Luci (originally Lucy) Baines Johnson, b. July 2, 1947, Washington, D.C.; m. Patrick John Nugent, Aug. 6, 1966, Washington, D.C.

For additional data see the end of this section and also specific subject headings in the index.

MRS. LYNDON BAINES JOHNSON

Name–Claudia Alta (Lady Bird) Taylor Johnson
Date of birth–Dec. 22, 1912
Birthplace–Karnack, Tex.
Age at marriage–21 years, 330 days

Children–2 daughters
Mother–Minnie Lee Pattillo Taylor
Father–Thomas Jefferson Taylor
His occupation–Planter, merchant
Years younger than the President–4 years, 107 days

THE ELECTION OF 1964

NOMINATIONS FOR TERM 1965-1969

Democratic Party Convention (34th)

Aug. 24-27, 1964, Convention Hall, Atlantic City, N.J.
Nominated for President—Lyndon Baines Johnson, Tex.
Nominated for Vice President—Hubert Horatio Humphrey, Minn.
    Johnson was nominated unanimously on the first ballot. Humphrey was nominated unanimously for the vice presidency on the first ballot.

Republican Party Convention (28th)

July 13-16, 1964, Grand National Livestock Pavilion (Cow Palace), San Francisco, Calif.
Nominated for President—Barry Morris Goldwater, Ariz.
Nominated for Vice President—William Edward Miller, N.Y.
    Goldwater was nominated on the first ballot. Candidates for nomination and the votes they received:
Barry Morris Goldwater, Ariz., 883
William Warren Scranton, Pa., 214
Nelson Aldrich Rockefeller, N.Y., 114
George Wilcken Romney, Mich., 41
Margaret Chase Smith, Me., 27
Walter Henry Judd, Minn., 22
Hiram Leong Fong, Hawaii, 5
Henry Cabot Lodge, Mass., 2
Total number of votes: 1,308
Number necessary for nomination: 655
Nomination made unanimous

Liberal Party of New York State

Nominated for President—Lyndon Baines Johnson, Tex.
Nominated for Vice President—Hubert Horatio Humphrey, Minn.
    The nominations were made Sept. 1, 1964, by the State Committee meeting in New York City.

Socialist Labor Party Convention

May 2-3, 1964, Henry Hudson Hotel, New York, N.Y.
Nominated for President—Eric Hass, N.Y.
Nominated for Vice President—Henning A. Blomen, Mass.

Prohibition Party Convention

Aug. 26-27, 1964, Chicago, Ill.
Nominated for President—Earle Harold Munn, Mich.
Nominated for Vice President—Mark Shaw, Mass.

Socialist Workers Party Convention

Dec. 28, 1963, New York, N.Y.
Nominated for President—Clifton De Berry, N.Y.
Nominated for Vice President—Edward Shaw, N.Y.

National States' Rights Party Convention

Mar. 2, 1964, Louisville, Ky.
Nominated for President—John Kasper, Tenn.
Nominated for Vice President—J. B. Stoner, Ga.

Constitution Party Convention

July 23-25, 1964, Houston, Tex.
Nominated for President—Joseph B. Lightburn, W.Va.
Nominated for Vice President—Theodore C. Billings, Colo. (54 delegates from 12 states)

Independent States' Rights Party Convention

Oct. 15, 1964, Richmond, Va.
Nominated for President—Thomas Coleman Andrews, Va.
Nominated for Vice President—Thomas H. Werdel, Calif.

Theocratic Party Convention

May 21, 1964, Fulton, Mo.
Nominated for President—Homer Aubrey Tomlinson, N.Y.
Nominated for Vice President—William R. Rogers, Mo.

Universal Party Convention

Aug. 8, 1964, Oakland, Calif.
Nominated for President—Kirby James Hensley, Calif.
Nominated for Vice President—John O. Hopkins, Iowa

ELECTION RESULTS, NOV. 3, 1964—PRESIDENTIAL AND VICE PRESIDENTIAL CANDIDATES

Democratic Party (42,825,463 votes)

Lyndon Baines Johnson, Tex.
Hubert Horatio Humphrey, Minn.

Republican Party (27,175,770 votes)

Barry Morris Goldwater, Ariz.
William Edward Miller, N.Y.

Liberal Party of New York State (342,432 votes)

Lyndon Baines Johnson, Tex.
Hubert Horatio Humphrey, Minn.

Socialist Labor Party (42,642 votes)

Eric Hass, N.Y.
Henning A. Blomen, Mass.

Prohibition Party (23,267 votes)

Earle Harold Munn, Mich.
Mark Shaw, Mass.

Socialist Workers Party (22,249 votes)

Clifton De Berry, N.Y.
Edward Shaw, N.Y.

National States' Rights Party (6,957 votes)

John Kasper, Tenn.
Jesse B. Stoner, Ga.

Additional votes

Blank and void, 199,675
Others, 20,692
Scattering, 9,696

ELECTORAL VOTES (538—50 states and District of Columbia)

Johnson received 90.34 per cent (486 votes—44 states and D.C.) as follows: Alaska 3; Ark. 6; Calif. 40; Colo. 6; Conn. 8; Del. 3; D.C. 3; Fla. 14; Hawaii 4; Idaho 4; Ill. 26; Ind. 13; Iowa 9; Kan. 7; Ky. 9; Me. 4; Md. 10; Mass. 14; Mich. 21; Minn. 10; Mo. 12; Mont. 4; Neb. 5; Nev. 3; N.H. 4; N.J. 17; N.M. 4; N.Y. 43; N.C. 13; N.D. 4; Ohio 26; Okla. 8; Ore. 6; Pa. 29; R.I. 4; S.D. 4; Tenn. 11; Tex. 25; Utah 4; Vt. 3; Va. 12; Wash. 9; W.Va. 7; Wis. 12; Wyo. 3.

Goldwater received 9.66 per cent (52 votes—6 states) as follows: Ala. 10; Ariz. 5; Ga. 12; La. 10; Miss. 7; S.C. 8

FIRST TERM
CABINET

November 22, 1963-January 20, 1965

State–(David) Dean Rusk, N.Y., continued from preceding administration

Treasury–C. (Clarence) Douglas Dillon, N.J., continued from preceding administration

Defense–Robert Strange McNamara, Mich., continued from preceding administration

Attorney General–Robert Francis Kennedy, Mass., continued from preceding administration

Postmaster General–John A. Gronouski, Wis., continued from preceding administration

Interior–Stewart Lee Udall, Ariz., continued from preceding administration

Agriculture–Orville Lothrop Freeman, Minn., continued from preceding administration

Commerce–Luther Hartwell Hodges, N.C., continued from preceding administration

Labor–W. (William) Willard Wirtz, Ill., continued from preceding administration

Health, Education, and Welfare–Anthony Joseph Celebrezze, Ohio, continued from preceding administration

SECOND TERM
CABINET

January 20, 1965-January 20, 1969

State–(David) Dean Rusk, N.Y., continued from preceding administration

Treasury–C. (Clarence) Douglas Dillon, N.J., continued from preceding administration; Henry Hamill Fowler, Va., Apr. 1, 1965; Joseph Walker Barr, Ind., Dec. 23, 1968

Defense–Robert Strange McNamara, Mich., continued from preceding administration; Clark McAdams Clifford, Md., Mar. 1, 1968

Attorney General–Robert Francis Kennedy, Mass., continued from preceding administration; Nicholas deBelleville Katzenbach, D.C., Feb. 13, 1965; William Ramsey Clark, Tex., Mar. 10, 1967

Postmaster General–John A. Gronouski, Wis., continued from preceding administration; Lawrence Francis O'Brien, Mass., Nov. 3, 1965; William Marvin Watson, Tex., Apr. 26, 1968

Interior–Stewart Lee Udall, Ariz., continued from preceding administration

Agriculture–Orville Lothrop Freeman, Minn., continued from preceding administration

Commerce–Luther Hartwell Hodges, N.C., continued from preceding administration; John Thomas Connor, N.J., Jan. 18, 1965; Alexander Buel Trowbridge, N.Y., June 14, 1967; Cyrus Rowlett Smith, N.Y., Mar. 6, 1968

Labor–W. (William) Willard Wirtz, Ill., continued from preceding administration

Health, Education, and Welfare–Anthony Joseph Celebrezze, Ohio, continued from preceding administration; John William Gardner, N.Y., Aug. 18, 1965; Wilbur Joseph Cohen, Wis., May 9, 1968

Housing and Urban Development–Robert Clifton Weaver, N.Y., Jan. 18, 1966; Robert Coldwell Wood, Mass., Jan. 7, 1969

Transportation–Alan Stephenson Boyd, Fla., Jan. 16, 1967

SECOND TERM
EIGHTY-NINTH CONGRESS

January 3, 1965-January 3, 1967

First session–Jan. 4, 1965-Oct. 23, 1965 (293 days)

Second session–Jan. 10, 1966-Oct. 22, 1966 (286 days) (The House was in recess Apr. 7-Apr. 18; June 30-July 11. The Senate was in recess Apr. 7-Apr. 13; June 30-July 11)

Vice President–Hubert Horatio Humphrey, Minn.

President pro tempore of the Senate–Carl Hayden, Ariz.
Secretary of the Senate–Felton McLellan Johnston, Miss.; Francis Ralph Valeo, N.Y., elected Oct. 1, 1966
Speaker of the House–John William McCormack, Mass.
Clerk of the House–Ralph R. Roberts, Ind.

NINETIETH CONGRESS

January 3, 1967-January 3, 1969

First session–Jan. 10, 1967-Dec. 15, 1967 (340 days)
Second session–Jan. 15, 1968-Oct. 14, 1968 (274 days)
Vice President–Hubert Horatio Humphrey, Minn.
President pro tempore of the Senate–Carl Hayden, Ariz.
Secretary of the Senate–Francis Ralph Valeo, N.Y.
Speaker of the House–John William McCormack, Mass.
Clerk of the House–William Pat Jennings, Va.

NINETY-FIRST CONGRESS

Jan. 3, 1969-Jan. 2, 1971

First session–Jan. 3, 1969-Dec. 23, 1969 (355 days)
Second session–Jan. 19, 1970-Jan. 2, 1971 (349 days)
Vice President of the United States–Hubert Horatio Humphrey, Minn.
President pro tempore of the Senate–Richard Brevard Russell, Ga.
Secretary of the Senate–Francis Ralph Valeo, N.Y.
Speaker of the House–John William McCormack, Mass.
Clerk of the House–William Pat Jennings, Va.

APPOINTMENTS TO THE SUPREME COURT

Associate Justices
Abe Fortas, Tex., Oct. 4, 1965
Thurgood Marshall, Md., Oct. 2, 1967 (private ceremony Sept. 1, 1967)

ADMINISTRATION—IMPORTANT DATES

Nov. 25-26, 1963, President Johnson conferred with President de Gaulle of France and other heads of state following funeral of President Kennedy

Nov. 27, 1963, President, in address to Congress, pledged to continue President Kennedy's policies and urged action on civil rights and tax cuts

Nov. 29, 1963, President appointed seven-man commission headed by Chief Justice Earl Warren to investigate assassination of President Kennedy

Dec. 2, 1963, President presented the Enrico Fermi Award to Dr. J. Robert Oppenheimer, nuclear physicist

Dec. 5, 1963, President announced terms of an agreement with Speaker of the House John William McCormack on temporary succession to the presidency

Dec. 6, 1963, thirty-three Presidential Medals of Freedom awarded

Dec. 9, 1963, President assigned responsibility for determining national oil policy to Department of the Interior

Dec. 12, 1963, Secretary of Defense Robert S. McNamara announced plans to discontinue or curtail activities at thirty-three military installations as an economy measure

Dec. 16, 1963, President signed a bill setting up a $1.2 billion construction program for college classrooms, laboratories, and libraries

Dec. 17, 1963, in address before the UN General Assembly, President stressed continuity of U.S. policy and called for an end to the cold war

Dec. 28-29, 1963, President conferred with Chancellor Erhard of West Germany at Texas ranch

Dec. 30, 1963, Congress enacted $3 billion foreign aid billing allowing President discretion on credit to Communist nations

Jan. 8, 1964, President, in State of the Union message to Congress, announced reduction of the federal budget and urged action against poverty and racial discrimination

Jan. 9-10, 1964, riots in Canal Zone brought on by dispute over flying of American flag; Panama demanded revision of Canal Zone treaty and suspended relations with United States

Jan. 11, 1964, U.S. Public Health Service issued report on cigarette smoking and cancer

Jan. 22, 1964, Columbia River power and flood control agreement signed by United States and Canada

Jan. 23, 1964, ratification of Twenty-fourth Amendment to Constitution, banning poll taxes in federal elections

Jan. 23, 1964, President signed bill authorizing federal participation in construction of John F. Kennedy Center for the Performing Arts

Feb. 12, 1964, British Prime Minister Sir Alec Douglas-Home conferred with President in Washington

Feb. 17, 1964, Supreme Court ruled that congressional districts should be equal in population

Feb. 21, 1964, President conferred with Mexican President López Mateos in Los Angeles

Feb. 21, 1964, arrival of first shipment of U.S. wheat sold to Soviet Union

Feb. 22, 1964, U.S.-U.S.S.R. two-year cultural agreement signed

Mar. 13, 1964, President flew over Ohio Valley flood area, promising aid

Mar. 16, 1964, President sent antipoverty program to Congress

Mar. 27, 1964, severe earthquake in Alaska

Apr. 3, 1964, U.S.-Panama relations restored

Apr. 22, 1964, New York City World's Fair opened

Apr. 24, 1964, President toured five states in poverty areas

May 7, 1964, President toured six Appalachian states in antipoverty drive

May 18, 1964, President asked Congress for $125 million additional aid to South Vietnam

June 1, 1964, U.S.-Rumanian trade agreement reached

June 15, 1964, Supreme Court ruled that state legislatures must have districts substantially equal in population in both houses.

June 28, 1964, President declared United States would risk war to preserve peace in Southeast Asia

July 2, 1964, President signed Civil Rights Act

July 18-21, 1964, racial violence in Harlem and Bedford-Stuyvesant sections of New York City; outbreaks in Rochester, N.Y. (July 24-26)

July 31, 1964, Ranger 7, U.S. spacecraft, relayed close-up pictures of the moon

Aug. 7, 1964, Congressional resolution gave advance approval to President Johnson for any actions in Southeast Asia following U.S. raids on North Vietnamese bases in retaliation for attacks on U.S. destroyers in Gulf of Tonkin

Aug. 20, 1964, $974.5 million antipoverty bill signed by President

Sept. 27, 1964, release of Warren Commission report on Kennedy assassination, with conclusion that Oswald was sole assassin

Oct. 3, 1964, hurricane killed 36 in Louisiana

Nov. 3, 1964, President defeated Barry Goldwater in landslide presidential election

Jan. 4, 1965, "Great Society" program proposed by President in State of the Union message

Feb. 7, 1965, U.S. planes bombed North Vietnamese bases after Vietcong attack on U.S. base

Feb. 17, 1965, Ranger 8 launched; crashed onto moon Feb. 20 after televising 7,000 photographs

Feb. 27, 1965, U.S. accused North Vietnam of increasing aggression against South Vietnam and reaffirmed support of South Vietnam

Mar. 3, 1965, Congress enacted $1.1 billion Appalachia aid bill

Mar. 8-9, 1965, U.S. Marines landed in South Vietnam (first American combat troops there)

Mar. 20, 1965 Alabama National Guard called out to protect Selma-Montgomery Freedom March

Mar. 23, 1965, Major Virgil I. Grissom and Lieutenant Commander John W. Young in first U.S. two-man space flight (Gemini 3)

Apr. 6, 1965, Early Bird, world's first commercial satellite, launched

Apr. 7, 1965, President announced readiness to begin Vietnamese peace discussions and proposed Southeast Asia development program

Apr. 11, 1965, tornadoes killed 250 and injured 2,500 in Middle West

Apr. 11, 1965, President signed $1.3 billion elementary and secondary school aid bill

Apr. 13, 1965, U.S. Marines landed in Dominican Republic after clashes between rebels and army

May 6, 1965, Congress appropriated $700 million for Vietnam conflict

May 18, 1965, U.S. raids on North Vietnam resumed after lull had failed to bring about negotiations

May 26, 1965, U.S. Marines in Dominican Republic replaced by patrols of Organization of American States

June 3, 1965, Major Edward H. White first American to walk in space (Gemini 4 flight)

June 17, 1965, Congress enacted legislation cutting excise taxes

June 30, 1965, tourists' duty-free limit reduced to $100 in retail value

July 14, 1965, Mariner 4 space flight past Mars

July 30, 1965, President signed Medicare bill

Aug. 6, 1965, President signed voting rights bill

Aug. 10, 1965, President signed $7.5 billion housing bill with rent subsidy provision

Aug. 11-16, 1965, 35 killed, 883 injured in six days of rioting, looting, and burning in Watts, black section of Los Angeles

Aug. 21-29, 1965, new records set in eight-day Gemini 5 space flight by Lieutenant Colonel L. Gordon Cooper and Lieutenant Commander Charles Conrad, Jr.

Aug. 31, 1965, Housing and Urban Affairs cabinet post created

Sept. 7-11, 1965, high death toll and widespread damage caused by hurricane in South

Oct. 3, 1965, President signed immigration bill eliminating national origins quotas

Oct. 4, 1965, Pope Paul VI in New York to deliver peace message at United Nations General Assembly; conferred with President

Oct. 6, 1965, President signed bill appropriating $300 million to combat heart disease, cancer, and stroke

Oct. 8, 1965, President underwent gall bladder surgery

Oct. 9, 1965, President signed $1.785 billion antipoverty bill, doubling previous appropriation

Oct. 15-16, 1965, antiwar rallies in Berkeley, Calif., New York City, and elsewhere; other rallies supporting U.S. policy

Nov. 8, 1965, President signed Higher Education Act, authorizing federal aid and National Teacher Corps

Nov. 9-10, 1965, electric power failure affecting 25 million persons in Northeast

Nov. 10, 1965, aluminum price increase rescinded under Administration pressure; copper price increase rescinded Nov. 19

Nov. 27, 1965, Vietnamese peace march on Washington by 15,000 demonstrators

Dec. 5, 1965, Federal Reserve Board raised discount rate to 4.5 per cent to tighten credit and stabilize prices

Dec. 9, 1965, President pledged continuation of Vietnamese peace efforts

Dec. 14-21, 1965, President conferred in Washington with foreign leaders (Pakistani President Ayub Khan, Dec. 14-15; British Prime Minister Wilson, Dec. 16-17; West German Chancellor Erhard, Dec. 20-21)

Dec. 15, 1965, successful rendezvous in space of two separately launched manned capsules (Gemini 6 and Gemini 7)

Dec. 24, 1965, beginning of holiday truce and thirty-seven-day suspension of U.S. bombing of North Vietnam

Dec. 29, 1965, U.S. emissaries sent to various capitals to explore peace negotiation possibilities

Jan. 5, 1966, steel industry compromised on price increase under Administration pressure

Jan. 12, 1966, President's State of the Union message televised in color

Feb. 1, 1966, President outlined $3.3 billion foreign aid program, stressing self-help and population control

Feb. 3, 1966, White House report on automation recommended subsidized minimum income

Feb. 4, 1966, President authorized grain shipment to famine-threatened India

Feb. 6-8, 1966, President and four Cabinet officers conferred in Honolulu with South Vietnamese leaders

Feb. 10, 1966, President proposed Food for Freedom program

Feb. 10-23, 1966, Vice President Humphrey on Asian tour

Mar. 16, 1966, first "docking" of two orbiting space vehicles (Gemini 8 and Agena target)

Mar. 18, 1966, support of NATO by United States and thirteen other nations reaffirmed despite withdrawal of France from defense system

Mar. 21, 1966, President submitted consumer protection program

Mar. 31, 1966, President asked for cutbacks in spending to offset sharp increase in prices

Apr. 7, 1966, 15,000 Army specialists withdrawn from Europe to train units for duty in Vietnam

Apr. 7, 1966, missing U.S. H-bomb recovered off Spanish Mediterranean coast after midair collision of bomber and refueling plane

Apr. 14-15, 1966, President visited Mexico City to dedicate statue of Lincoln; reaffirmed support of Alliance for Progress

Apr. 21, 1966, artificial heart pump successfully implanted

Apr. 26, 1966, automobile industry announced willingness to abide by federal safety standards; reported recall of 8.7 million cars to check possible flaws

May 1966, controversies over draft and Administration policy in Vietnam; President appealed for national unity May 17

May 20, 1966, Atomic Energy Commission reported that China had probably achieved thermonuclear reaction in May 9 test

May 26, 1966, President denounced white supremacist regimes in Africa and pledged assistance to developing African nations

May 30, 1966, soft landing on moon by Surveyor 1

June 1-2, 1966, White House Conference on Civil Rights attended by 2,400 participants

June 13, 1966, Supreme Court ruled that Fifth Amendment protection against self-incrimination limits interrogation of suspects and use of confessions and guarantees right to have counsel

June 22, 1966, House Armed Services Committee began hearings on alleged inequities in Selective Service System

July 1966, racial unrest in a number of cities

July 4-9, 1966, convention of National Association for the Advancement of Colored People rejected "black power" doctrine advocated by other black organizations

July 7-Aug. 19, 1966, strike of machinists halted major U.S. airlines

July 12, 1966, President declared that United States sought "peace of conciliation," not conquest, in Asia; major political purge reported in China

July 30, 1966, U.S. planes attacked Communist base in demilitarized zone of South Vietnam

Aug. 15-Sept. 1, 1966, Senate hearings on "crisis in America's cities"

Aug. 16-19, 1966, disorder at congressional hearings on activities of Americans who aided Vietcong

Aug. 21, 1966, President met Prime Minister Pearson of Canada at Campobello, N.B.

Aug. 24, 1966, President agreed to proposals for all-Asian Vietnamese peace conference

Sept. 1966, racial disorder in Atlanta, Ga.

Sept. 8, 1966, President urged suspension of business tax credit for new investment as anti-inflationary measure

Sept. 9, 1966, President signed bill establishing federal automobile safety standards

Sept. 19, 1966, President signed $3.5 billion foreign aid bill

Sept. 23, 1966, President signed bill increasing minimum hourly wage to $1.60 and expanding coverage

Oct. 7, 1966, President called for improved relations with Eastern Europe

Oct. 13, 1966, President rejected plea for unilateral suspension of bombing of North Vietnam

Oct. 15, 1966, Department of Transportation established as Cabinet office

Oct. 17-Nov. 2, 1966, President toured six Asian and Pacific nations; attended summit conference in Manila and visited troops in Vietnam

Nov. 3, 1966, President signed $3.9 billion water pollution control bill

Nov. 4, 1966, U.S.-Soviet agreement signed on direct New York-Moscow air service

Nov. 8, 1966, Guinea ousted members of Peace Corps and other U.S. personnel in retaliation for alleged U.S. involvement in dispute between Guinea and Ghana

Nov. 16, 1966, President underwent abdominal and laryngeal surgery

Nov. 18, 1966, sharply detailed photographs of moon's surface transmitted by Lunar Orbiter 2

Nov. 29, 1966, United Nations rejected resolution to admit Communist China; another proposal, favoring "two Chinas" in the UN, rejected by United States

Dec. 3, 1966, President met President Díaz Ordaz of Mexico on trip to inspect Amistad Dam across Rio Grande

Dec. 14, 1966, nuclear planning group created by members of NATO (except France)

Dec. 19, 1966, United Nations General Assembly unanimously accepted draft treaty prohibiting nuclear weapons in space

Jan. 2, 1967, New Year truce ended in Vietnam

Jan. 10, 1967, President asked Congress to enact 6 per cent surcharge on income taxes to support war and domestic programs

Jan. 24, 1967, President submitted $169.2 billion budget for fiscal 1968

Jan. 27, 1967, three astronauts killed in fire in spacecraft at Cape Kennedy, Fla., while conducting tests for scheduled launching

Jan. 30, 1967, President urged Congress to enact air pollution control program

Feb. 1967, disclosures of financial backing of numerous private foundations by U.S. Central Intelligence Agency

Feb. 6, 1967, President submitted crime control message to Congress

Feb. 9-10, 1967, King Hassan II of Morocco visited President

Feb. 10, 1967, Twenty-fifth Amendment, dealing with presidential disability, ratified

Feb. 15, 1967, President submitted civil rights proposals to Congress

Feb. 16, 1967, President proposed consumer protection measures

Mar. 1, 1967, House of Representatives voted to exclude Representative Adam Clayton Powell of New York on charges of improper expenditures of government funds

Mar. 16, 1967, Senate approved U.S.-Soviet consular treaty

Mar. 20-21, 1967, President conferred with South Vietnamese leaders in Guam

Mar. 21, 1967, President's proposals for peace talks rejected by Ho Chi Minh

Apr. 1967, bombing of North Vietnam intensified

Apr. 11, 1967, Representative Adam Clayton Powell reelected

Apr. 12-14, 1967, President met at Punta del Este, Uruguay, with chiefs of state of 18 members of Organization of American States

Apr. 15, 1967, peace marches staged in New York and San Francisco to protest war in Vietnam

Apr. 23-26, 1967, President attended funeral of Konrad Adenaur

May 1967, demilitarized zone between North and South Vietnam invaded by U.S.-led forces; Hanoi bombed by U.S. planes

May 11, 1967, Senate approved four-year extension of military draft

June 1967, U.S. pledged neutrality in Middle East war between Arab states and Israel

June 8, 1967, 34 Americans killed in accidental Israeli bombing of U.S. Navy ship in Mediterranean

June 13, 1967, House approved $70 billion defense bill—largest single appropriations bill ever passed by either house

June 23, 25, 1967, President conferred with Soviet Premier Kosygin at Glassboro, N.J.

June 23, 1967, Senate voted (92 to 5) to censure Senator Thomas J. Dodd of Connecticut for using political funds for personal benefit

July 1967, prolonged riots in black slums of Newark, N.J., and Detroit exacted heavy toll of life and property; numerous outbreaks of racial violence in other ghetto areas

Aug. 24, 1967, draft treaty to ban atomic proliferation submitted by U.S. and U.S.S.R. to UN Disarmament Committee

Sept. 3, 1967, $1.60 minimum wage established

Sept. 29, 1967, President at San Antonio, Tex., reaffirmed American readiness to stop bombing of North Vietnam when that would lead promptly to productive discussions during which North Vietnam would not take advantage of halt

Jan. 23, 1968, U.S.S. *Pueblo* and 83-man crew seized in Sea of Japan by North Koreans

Mar. 31, 1968, President announced a partial halt to bombing of North Vietnam

Apr. 4, 1968, Dr. Martin Luther King assassinated, Memphis, Tenn.; riots in Washington, D.C., forced President to call out troops

Apr. 11, 1968, President signed Civil Rights Act prohibiting discrimination in sale or rental of housing

Apr. 14, 1968, outbreaks of racial violence had already occurred in many cities in the United States

June 5-6, 1968, Senator Robert F. Kennedy shot and killed in Los Angeles, while celebrating his California presidential primary victory

Aug. 1968, violence erupted in Chicago at Democratic National Convention with confrontation of antiwar demonstrators and Chicago police

Oct. 31, 1968, President announced complete halt to bombing of North Vietnam

Dec. 22, 1968, U.S.S. *Pueblo* crew released

Jan. 15, 1969, Budget message to Congress

IMPORTANT DATES IN HIS LIFE

1913, moved to Johnson City, Tex.

1924, graduated from Johnson City High School

1928-1929, taught grade school in Cotulla, Tex.

Aug. 19, 1930, graduated from Southwest Texas State Teachers College, San Marcos, with B.S. degree

1930, received permanent high school teacher's certificate; majored in history and minored in English and social science

1930-1931, taught public speaking and debate at Sam Houston High School, Houston, Tex.

1932-1935, secretary to Representative Richard Mifflin Kleberg (Democrat, Texas)

1935, studied at Georgetown University Law School, Washington, D.C.

1935-1937, state director of National Youth Administration for Texas

Apr. 10, 1937, won special election for seat in U.S. House of Representatives to fill vacancy caused by death of James Paul Buchanan (Democrat, Texas); reelected five times and served until Dec. 31, 1948

June 21, 1940, special duty officer, naval intelligence, U.S. Naval Reserve

June 28, 1941, defeated in special election for U.S. Senate

Dec. 1941, obtained consent of the House of Representatives for a leave of absence to enter service in U.S. Naval Reserve (first member of Congress in World War II to enter active duty); commissioned lieutenant commander

July 1942, received Silver Star for gallantry under fire when patrol bomber in which he was flying was attacked by Japanese

June 1, 1948, commissioned commander, U.S.N.R.

Nov. 2, 1948, elected to U.S. Senate (from Texas)

Jan. 2, 1951, Democratic whip (served until 1953)

Jan. 3, 1953, Democratic leader (served until 1961)

Nov. 2, 1954, reelected to U.S. Senate

July 2, 1955, suffered heart attack

July 13, 1960, nominated for the presidency by Speaker Sam Rayburn at Democratic convention; received 409 votes; defeated by John F. Kennedy

July 14, 1960, nominated for vice presidency by unanimous vote

Nov. 8, 1960, defeated John G. Tower, Republican, in election for U.S. Senate

Nov. 8, 1960, elected Vice President of the United States

Jan. 3, 1961, sworn in as senator from Texas for third term; resigned three minutes after being sworn in

Jan. 20, 1961, sworn in as Vice President of the United States

Aug. 23-Sept. 7, 1962, visited Near East, Greece, and Italy; had audience with Pope John XXIII

Sept. 3-17, 1963, visited Scandinavian countries

Nov. 22, 1963, in presidential motorcade in Dallas, Tex., at time of President Kennedy's assassination; sworn in as President of the United States after President Kennedy's death

Aug. 24, 1964, nominated for President on Democratic ticket

Nov. 3, 1964, elected President of the United States

Jan. 20, 1965, inaugurated 36th President of the United States

Oct. 8, 1965, underwent gall bladder surgery

Nov. 16, 1966, underwent surgery for repair of ventral incisional hernia and removal of nonmalignant polyp from vocal cord

Mar. 31, 1968, President informed the nation in a televised speech that he would not accept the nomination of the Democratic Party for President; decision influenced by country's split over Vietnam war, and strong race run by Senator Eugene McCarthy (Democrat, S.D.), opponent of the war, in the crucial New Hampshire presidential primary

Jan. 20, 1969, first day in 34 years as a private citizen

Apr. 8, 1972, heart attack, Charlottesville, Pa.

LYNDON BAINES JOHNSON

_____was the first President from a southern state since Zachary Taylor.

_____was the first President to ride in an armored automobile at his inauguration.

_____was the first President to review an inaugural parade in a heated reviewing stand.

_____was the first President sworn in behind a three-sided bullet-proof glass enclosure.

_____was the first President to take the oath of office in an airplane.

_____was the first President sworn in by a woman.

_____was the first President who took his oath on a Bible held by his wife.

_____was the first President to bring his dog (the beagle named Him) to an inaugural parade.

_____was the first President inaugurated in a business suit.

_____was the first Vice President to witness the assassination of the President whom he succeeded in office.

_____was the first Democratic President to carry Vermont.

_____was the first Democratic President to carry Maine since 1912.

_____was the first President to hold an inaugural luncheon in the old Supreme Court of the Capitol.

_____was the first President to have an inaugural parade in which the Air Force paraded.

_____was the second President born in Texas.

_____was the second President named Johnson to succeed to the presidency on the death of the incumbent.

_____was the third Vice President named Johnson.

_____was the fourth President to become President as the result of assassination.

_____was the eighth President to become President as the result of the death of his predecessor.

JOHNSON'S VICE PRESIDENT

Vice President–Hubert Horatio Humphrey (38th V.P.)
Date of birth–May 27, 1911
Birthplace–Wallace, S.D.
Political party–Democratic—Farmer Labor
State represented–Minnesota
Term of office–Jan. 20, 1965,-Jan. 20, 1969
Age at inauguration–53 years, 238 days

Additional data on Humphrey

1929, graduated from Doland, S.D., high school

1929-1930, University of Minnesota; left to work in father's drug store

1932-1933, six-month course at Denver College of Pharmacy; graduated with degree

1933-1937, pharmacist, Humphrey Drug Co., Huron, S.D.

1937-1939, University of Minnesota; graduated with A.B. degree; Phi Beta Kappa

1939, M.A., University of Louisiana

1939-1940, assistant instructor, political science, University of Louisiana

1940-1941, graduate work at University of Minnesota

1941, administrative staff of Works Progress Administration, later head of Minnesota state division

1942-1943, assistant state supervisor adult education, Minnesota; chief of war services section; director of training reemployment division

1943, assistant regional director, War Manpower Commission

1943-1944, visiting professor of political science, Macalester College

June 11, 1945, elected mayor of Minneapolis; reelected June 9, 1947

Nov. 2, 1948, elected to U.S. Senate from Minnesota; reelected 1954
and 1960

July 1952, received 134 votes for nomination for presidency at Democratic Party convention

July 14, 1960, received $41^1/_2$ votes in Deomocatic Party convention
(Kennedy with 806 votes nominated)

1961-1964, Senate majority whip

Aug. 27, 1964, named vice presidential candidate at Democratic Party
convention

Nov. 3, 1964, elected Vice President

Dec. 29, 1964, resigned from Senate

Jan. 20, 1965, inaugurated Vice President

Aug. 1968, chosen on first ballot at Chicago convention as presidential
nominee of Democratic Party

Nov. 5, 1968, defeated by Richard M. Nixon in a close race for the
presidency

ADDITIONAL DATA ON JOHNSON

JOHNSON WELL PREPARED FOR PRESIDENCY

Lyndon Baines Johnson was exceptionally well prepared to succed
to the presidency. As Vice President he had served on the National
Security Council and was chairman of the National Aeronautics and
Space Council, and he was consulted by President Kennedy on all
major policy matters. As chairman of the President's Committee on
Equal Employment Opportunity, he was in close touch with two major
domestic issues-civil rights and employment. On his trips abroad as
Vice President he had conferred with Chancellor Konrad Adenauer
of West Germany, President Charles de Gaulle of France, and other
leading world figures. An added advantage was his long experience
in Congress-nearly twelve years in the House of Representatives and
twelve years in the Senate, including seven years as the Senate Democratic leader, a post in which he served with great effectiveness.

JOHNSON SWORN IN

Lyndon Baines Johnson took the oath of office as President of the
United States on November 22, 1963. The oath was administered by
Judge Sarah Tilghman Hughes, District Judge of the North District
of Texas, in the jet airplane "Air Force One" at Love Field, Dallas,
Tex. Mrs. Johnson, Mrs. Kennedy, and twenty-five others witnessed
the ceremony.

JOHNSON'S FIRST PROCLAMATION

President Johnson's first proclamation, on November 23, 1963, was
a declaration of a day of national mourning (November 25) as a tribute
to his predecessor, John Fitzgerald Kennedy. An extract from the proclamation follows:

He upheld the faith of our Fathers, which is freedom for all
men. He broadened the frontiers of that faith, and backed it with
the energy and the courage which are the mark of the Nation

he led, A man of wisdom, strength and peace, he molded and moved the power of our Nation in the service of a world of growing liberty and order. All who love freedom will mourn his death. As he did not shrink from his responsibilities, but welcomed them, so he would not have us shrink from carrying on his work beyond this hour of national tragedy. He said it himself: "The energy, the faith, the devotion which we bring to this endeavor will light our country and all who serve it—and the glow from that fire can truly light the world."

JOHNSON DECRIED FEAR

Replying to the Secret Service guards who urged President Johnson to ride from the White House to St. Matthew's Cathedral, instead of walking with the world's great leaders to attend the Kennedy funeral services, Johnson said, "I'd rather give my life than be afraid to give it."

SECRET SERVICE AGENTS HONORED

One of President Johnson's first acts was to pay high tribute on December 4, 1963, to Rufus Youngblood, who at the time of President Kennedy's assassination "volunteered his life to save mine." The citation read: "Upon hearing the first shot, Mr. Youngblood instantly vaulted across the front seat of the car, pushed the Vice President to the floor and shielded the Vice President's body with his own." The previous day, another Secret Service Agent, Clinton J. Hill, was awarded the Treasury Department Medal for "exceptional bravery." In similar manner, he had shielded Mrs. Kennedy with his own body.

TWENTY-FOURTH AMENDMENT RATIFIED

The Twenty-fourth Amendment to the Constitution, banning the use of poll taxes as a requirement for voting in federal elections, was acted upon by the House of Representatives on August 27, 1962, when it approved Senate Joint Resolution No. 29, passed March 27, 1962.

The first state to ratify the proposed amendment was Illinois, on November 14, 1962. The required number of votes (38) was reached on January 23, 1964, when South Dakota voted its approval.

Section 1 of the Amendment follows:

The right of citizens of the United States to vote in any primary or other election for President or Vice President, for electors for President or Vice President, or for Senator or Representative in Congress, shall not be denied or abridged by the United States or any state by reason of failure to pay any poll tax or other tax.

HONORARY DEGREES

The first President and his wife to receive honorary degrees simultaneously were President and Mrs. Lyndon Baines Johnson. On May 30, 1964, the University of Texas at Austin awarded the President a Doctor of Laws degree and Mrs. Johnson a Doctor of Letters degree.

WARREN COMMISSION REPORT

A commission to investigate and report on the Kennedy assassination was authorized December 13, 1963, by Senate Joint Resolution 137. The commission consisted of Chief Justice Earl Warren of California, Senator Richard Brevard Russell (Democrat, Georgia), Senator John Sherman Cooper (Republican, Kentucky), Representative Hale Boggs (Democrat, Louisiana), Representative Gerald Rudolph Ford (Republican, Michigan), Allen Welsh Dulles, former director of the Central Intelligence Agency, and John Jay McCloy, former U.S. Military Governor and High Commissioner for Germany.

The report was released September 28, 1964. It contained the following statement: "On the basis of the evidence before the Commission it concludes that Oswald acted alone."

WOMAN CONSIDERED FOR PRESIDENTIAL NOMINATION

The first woman considered for nomination for the presidency by a major political party was Senator Margaret Chase Smith of Maine, whose name was placed in nomination by Senator George David Aiken of Vermont on July 15, 1964, at the Republican National Convention, San Francisco, Calif. She received 27 votes on the first roll call, which was later declared a unanimous vote for Senator Barry Morris Goldwater.

LARGEST POPULAR VOTE

The total number of votes cast in the election on November 8, 1960, was 68,836,385 votes. In the election of November 3, 1964, the number of votes cast was 70,668,839, an increase of 1,832,454 votes.

Lyndon Baines Johnson received 42,825,463 votes. This was a little more than 61 per cent of all the votes cast, the highest percentage received in any election, including that of 1936, when Franklin Delano Roosevelt defeated Alfred Mossman Landon.

President Johnson did not receive the greatest percentage of electoral votes, however. He received 486 of the 538 votes, 90.34 per cent. In the 1936 election, President Roosevelt received 523 of the 531 votes cast, or about 98.5 per cent.

INAUGURATION IN 1965

The weather was clear and cold on inauguration day, Wednesday, January 20, 1965, and the bright sun made the temperature rise from 38° to 45° by 3 P.M. The oaths of office were administered to Vice President Hubert Horatio Humphrey by Speaker John William McCormack and to President Lyndon Baines Johnson by Chief Justice Earl Warren. The President's twelve-hundred-word speech, lasting twenty-two minutes, was spoken softly and deliberately, drawing applause eleven times. A bullet-proof glass protected the President.

The Congressional Inaugural Committee sponsored a luncheon in the old Supreme Court chamber in the Capitol. The guests sat at ten circular tables.

The President led the motorcade from the Capitol down Pennsylvania Avenue to the White House, where he and his family and guests watched the fifty-two bands, fifteen thousand marchers, and numerous floats pass by until 5:08 P.M. About a million persons lined the streets to watch the two-and-a-half-hour inaugural parade.

At 9:18 P.M., wearing black tie, the President left the White House to attend the five inaugural balls at the Mayflower Hotel, Statler-Hilton Hotel, National Guard Armory, Shoreham Hotel, and Sheraton Park Hotel. (Twenty-eight thousand persons paid twenty-five dollars each for admission to the balls.) The President was accompanied by his wife and the Vice President and his wife. He returned to the White House at 12:21 A.M.

OATH TAKEN ON MOTHER'S BIBLE

Lyndon Baines Johnson took his oath of office with his hand upon the Bible given him by his mother many years earlier. The Bible was held by Mrs. Johnson. The occasion was the first on which a wife held the Bible upon which her husband took the oath and obligation of the presidency. It was the same Bible upon which he took his oath as Vice President of the United States. It was inscribed "To Lyndon and Lady Bird. Love, Mother."

PLANS FOR JOHNSON'S PAPERS

Congress enacted legislation on September 6, 1965 (79 Stat. L. 648), to authorize the Administrator of General Services to enter into an agreement with the University of Texas for the Lyndon Baines Johnson Presidential Archival Depository. The university will maintain, operate, and protect the depository as a part of the National Archives system. The Lyndon Baines Johnson Library and School of Public Affairs, Austin, Tex., was dedicated May 22, 1971.

NEW CABINET POSTS CREATED

The Department of Housing and Urban Development was authorized September 9, 1965 (79 Stat. L. 667). The first secretary was Robert Clifton Weaver of New York, who was sworn in January 18, 1966.

The Department of Transportation was authorized October 15, 1966 (80 Stat. L. 931) to deal with air, rail, and highway transportation. It comprises thirty-four federal agencies, including the Federal Aviation Agency, the Coast Guard, the Civil Aeronautics Board, the Bureau of Public Roads, and the Interstate Commerce Commission. The first secretary was Alan Stephenson Boyd of Florida, who was appointed in November 1966 and sworn in January 16, 1967.

PAPAL VISIT

The first President to confer in the United States with a Pope was Lyndon Baines Johnson, who called upon Pope Paul VI at the Waldorf Astoria Hotel, New York City, on October 4, 1965, while the Pope was in New York to address the United Nations. As Vice President he had had an audience with Pope John XXIII in Rome.

TWENTY-FIFTH AMENDMENT RATIFIED

The Twenty-fifth Amendment was introduced by Senator Birch

Bayh of Indiana on December 12, 1963. It was ratified on February 10, 1967, when the thirty-eighth state voted for its adoption. There is some dispute as to whether North Dakota, Minnesota, or Nevada was the thirty-eighth state, for North Dakota withdrew its original ratifying resolution after discovering it was only the thirty-seventh. The text of the amendment follows:

SECTION I. In case of the removal of the President from office or his death or resignation, the Vice President shall become President.

SECTION II. Whenever there is a vacancy in the office of the Vice President, the President shall nominate a Vice President who shall take the office upon confirmation by a majority vote of both houses of Congress.

SECTION III. Whenever the President transmits to the President pro tempore of the Senate and the Speaker of the House of Representatives his written declaration that he is unable to discharge the powers and duties of his office, and until he transmits to them a written declaration to the contrary, such powers and duties shall be discharged by the Vice President as Acting President.

SECTION IV. Whenever the vice President and a majority of either the principal officers of the executive departments, or of such other body as Congress may by law provide, transmit to the President pro tempore of the Senate and the Speaker of the House of Representatives, their written declaration that the President is unable to discharge the powers and duties of his office, the Vice President shall immediately assume the powers and duties of the office as Acting President.

Thereafter, when the President transmits to the President pro tempore of the Senate and the Speaker of the House of Representatives his written declartion that no inability exists, he shall resume the powers and duties of his office unless the Vice President and a majority of either the principal officers of the executive department, or of such other body as Congress may by law provide, transmit within four days to the President pro tempore of the Senate and the Speaker of the House of Representatives their written declaration that the President is unable to discharge the powers and duties of his office. Thereupon Congress shall decide the issue, assembling within 48 hours for that purpose if not in session. If the Congress, within 21 days after receipt of the latter written declaration, or, if Congress is not in session, within 21 days after Congress is required to assemble, determines by two-thirds vote of both houses that the President is unable to discharge the powers and duties of his office, the Vice President shall continue to discharge the same as Acting President; otherwise, the President shall resume the powers and duties of his office.

MARSHALL APPOINTED TO SUPREME COURT

The first black appointed to the United States Supreme Court was Thurgood Marshall of Maryland, age 59, the son of a Pullman car steward and great-grandson of a slave. He was appointed June 13, 1967, by President Johnson to succeed Justice Tom C. Clark. On July 13, 1965, Marshall had been appointed United States Solicitor General and on October 6, 1961, judge of the United States Second Circuit Court of Appeals.

L.B.J.

The monogram and initials L.B.J. are closely associated with President Johnson. They are the initials of Lyndon Baines Johnson; of Mrs. Johnson, whose nickname is Lady Bird; and of his two daughters, Lynda Bird and Luci Baines. The initials provide the name of his ranch, the LBJ, and were also used for one of his dogs, Little Beagle Johnson.

JOHNSON ANALYZED HIMSELF

In an article reprinted from the *Texas Quarterly* in the April 1959 issue of the *Reader's Digest* Vice President Lyndon Johnson wrote:

I am a free man, an American, a United States Senator, and a Democrat, in that order. I am also a liberal, a conservative, a consumer, a parent, a voter, and not as young as I used to be nor as old as I expect to be—and I am all those things in no fixed order.

THE FIRST LADY

Claudia Alta Taylor Johnson brought to the White House a rich background of experience in political and business activities. A well-known figure in the public and social life of the capital, she had aided and encouraged her husband in his campaigns for office and had also helped to manage their broadcasting and ranching interests.

The nickname "Lady Bird" was first applied to Mrs. Johnson when she was two years old by the family cook, who said that she was "purty as a lady bird."

RICHARD MILHOUS NIXON
37th PRESIDENT

Born–Jan. 9, 1913
Birthplace–Yorba Linda, Calif.
College attended–Whittier College
Date of graduation–June 9, 1934, four-year course, Bachelor of Arts degree
Religion–Quaker
Ancestry–English, Scotch-Irish
Occupation–Lawyer, representative senator
Date and place of marriage–June 21, 1940, Riverside, Calif.
Age at marriage–27 years, 163 days
Political party–Republican
State represented–New York
Term of office–Jan. 20, 1969-Aug. 9, 1974
Administration–46th, 47th
Congresses–91st, 92nd, 93rd
Age at inauguration–56 years, 11 days

PARENTS

Father–Francis Anthony Nixon
Born–Dec. 3, 1878, McArthur, Vinton County, Ohio
Married–June 25, 1908
Occupation–Oil field worker, street car motorman, service station owner
Died–Sept. 4, 1956, Whittier, Calif.
Age at death–78 years, 274 days
Mother–Hannah Milhous Nixon
Born–Mar. 7, 1885, Butlersville, Jennings County, Ind.
Died–Sept. 30, 1967, Whittier, Calif.
Age at death–82 years, 207 days

BROTHERS AND SISTERS

Richard Milhous Nixon was the second of five sons.

Children of Francis Anthony Nixon and Hannah Milhous Nixon

Harold Samuel Nixon–b. June 1, 1909; d. Mar. 7, 1933
Richard Milhous Nixon—b. Jan. 9, 1913
Francis Donald Nixon—b. Nov. 23, 1914
Arthur Burdg Nixon—b. May 26, 1918; d. Aug. 10, 1925
Edward Calvert Nixon—b. May 3, 1930

CHILDREN

Patricia (Tricia) Nixon, b. Feb. 21, 1946, San Francisco, Calif.; m. Edward Finch Cox, June 12, 1971, at the White House, Washington, D.C.
Julie Nixon, b. July 5, 1948, Washington, D.C.; m. Dwight David Eisenhower II, Dec. 22, 1968, New York City

MRS. RICHARD MILHOUS NIXON

Name–Thelma Catherine (Patricia) Ryan Nixon
Date of birth–Mar. 16, 1912
Birthplace–Ely, Nev.
Age at marriage–28 years, 97 days
Children–2 daughters
Mother–Katharina (Halberstadt) Bender Ryan
Father–William Ryan
Years older than the President–299 days

For additional data see the end of this section and also specific subject headings in the index.

THE ELECTION OF 1968

NOMINATIONS FOR TERM 1969-1973

Republican Party Convention (29th)

Aug. 5-8, 1968, Convention Hall, Miami Beach, Fla.

Nominated for President—Richard Milhous Nixon

Nominated for Vice President—Spiro Theodore Agnew, Md.

Nixon was nominated on the first ballot. Candidates for nomination and the votes they received:

Richard Milhous Nixon, N.Y., 692
Nelson Aldrich Rockefeller, N.Y., 277
Ronald Reagan, Calif., 182
James Allen Rhodes, Ohio, 55
George Romney, Mich., 50
Clifford Philip Case, N.J., 22
Frank Carlson, Kan., 20
Winthrop Rockefeller, Ark., 18
Hiram Leong Fong, Hawaii, 14
Harold Edward Stassen, Pa., 2
John Vliet Lindsay, N.Y., 1
Total number of votes: 1,333
Number necessary for nomination: 667

Democratic Party Convention (35th)

Aug. 26-29, 1968, International Amphitheater, Chicago, Ill.

Nominated for President—Hubert Horatio Humphrey, Minn.

Nominated for Vice President—Edmund Sixtus Muskie, Me.

Humphrey was nominated on the first ballot. Candidates for nomination and the votes they received:

Hubert Horatio Humphrey, Minn., $1,761^3/_4$
Eugene Joseph McCarthy, Minn., 601
George Stanley McGovern, S.D., $146^1/_2$
Channing Emery Phillips, D.C., $67^1/_2$
Daniel Killian Moore, N.C., $17^1/_2$
Edward Moore Kennedy, Mass., $12^3/_4$
Paul E. Bryant, $1^1/_2$
George Corley Wallace, Ala., 1
James H. Gray, Ga., $^1/_2$
Total number of votes: 2,622
Number necessary for nomination: 1,312

American Independent Party (Courage Party in New York) Convention

Nominated for President—George Corley Wallace, Ala.

Nominated for Vice President—Curtis Emerson LeMay, Ohio

Samuel Marvin Griffin, Ga., was originally selected (Feb. 14, 1968), as the vice presidential candidate until Curtis Emerson LeMay was named on Oct. 3, 1968.

Liberal Party Convention

Sept. 24, 1968, Hotel Roosevelt, New York, N.Y.
Nominated for President—Hubert Horatio Humphrey, Minn.
Nominated for Vice President—Edmund Sixtus Muskie, Me.
   The Liberal Party endorsed the candidates of the Democratic Party.

Peace and Freedom Party Convention

Aug. 18, 1968, Ann Arbor, Mich.
Nominated for President—Eldridge Cleaver
Nominated for Vice President—Judith Mage, N.Y.
   On the first ballot Cleaver received $161^1/_2$ votes, Dick Gregory 54.

Socialist Labor Party Convention

May 5, 1968, Towers Hotel, Brooklyn, N.Y.
Nominated for President—Henning A. Blomen, Mass.
Nominated for Vice President—George Sam Taylor, Pa.

Socialist Workers Party Convention

Aug. 28, 1968, New York, N.Y.
Nominated for President—Fred Halstead, N.Y.
Nominated for Vice President—Paul Boutelle, N.J.

Prohibition Party Convention

June 28-29, 1967, Young Women's Christian Association, Detroit, Mich.
Nominated for President—Earle Harold Munn, Sr., Mich.
Nominated for Vice President—Rolland E. Fisher, Kan.

Communist Party (USA) Convention

July 3-7, 1968, Diplomat Hotel, New York, N.Y.
Nominated for President—Charlene Mitchell, Calif.
Nominated for Vice President—Michael Zagarell, N.Y.
   First national slate since 1940.

Constitution Party Convention

July 18-21, 1968, Denver, Colo.
Nominated for President—Richard K. Troxell, Tex.
Nominated for Vice President—Merle Thayer, Iowa

Freedom and Peace Party

Nominated for President—Dick Gregory (Richard Claxton Gregory), Ill.

Patriotic Party Convention

July 2-4, 1967
Nominated for President—George Corley Wallace, Ala.
Nominated for Vice President—William Penn Patrick, Calif.

Theocratic Party Convention

Nominated for President—Bishop William R. (Bill) Rogers, Mo.

Universal Party Convention

Denver, Colo.
Nominated for President—The Rev. Kirby James Hensley, Calif.
Nominated for Vice President—Roscoe B. MacKenna

ELECTION RESULTS, NOV. 5, 1968—PRESIDENTIAL AND VICE PRESIDENTIAL CANDIDATES

Republican Party (31,710,470 votes)

Richard Milhous Nixon, N.Y.
Spiro Theodore Agnew, Md.

Democratic Party (30,898,055 votes)

Hubert Horatio Humphrey, Minn.
Edmund Sixtus Muskie, Me.

American Independent Party (9,446,167 votes)

George Corley Wallace, Ala.
Curtis Emerson LeMay, Ohio

Liberal Party (311,622 votes)

Hubert Horatio Humphrey, Minn.
Edmund Sixtus Muskie, Me.

Conservative Party of Kansas (88,921 votes)

George Corley Wallace, Ala.
Curtis Emerson LeMay, Ohio

Peace and Freedom Party (74,014 votes)

Eldridge Cleaver
Judith Mage, N.Y.

Socialist Labor Party (51,962 votes)

Henning Albert Blomen, Mass.
George Sam Taylor, Pa.

Socialist Workers Party (38,011 votes)

Fred Wolf Halstead, N.Y.
Paul Benjamin Boutelle, N.J.

Prohibition Party (14,787 votes)

Earle Harold Munn, Sr., Mich.
Rolland E. Fisher, Kan.

Additional Votes (386,195)

Courage Party (N.Y.), 358,864
Independent Party (Ala.), 10,960
New Party (Ariz., 2,751; Colo., 1,393; N,H., 421; Vt., 579), 5,144
New Politics Party (Mich.), 4,585
Petition Party (Iowa), 3,377
People's Constitutional Party (N.M.), 1,519
New Reform Party (Mont.), 470

Communist Party (Minn. 415; Ohio, 23), 438
Free Ballot Party (Wash.), 377
Industrial Government Party (Minn.), 285
Universal Party (Iowa), 142
Constitution Party (N.D.), 34
Write-in votes, 2,645
Scattering 3,982

ELECTORAL VOTES (538 votes—50 states and District of Columbia)

Nixon received 55.94 per cent (301 votes—32 states) as follows: Alaska 3; Ariz. 5; Calif. 40; Colo. 6; Del. 3; Fla. 14; Idaho 4; Ill. 26; Ind. 13; Iowa 9; Kan. 7; Ky. 9; Mo. 12; Mont. 4; Neb. 5; Nev. 3; N.H. 4; N.J. 17; N.M. 4; N.C. 12; N.D. 4; Ohio 26; Okla. 8; Ore. 6; S.C. 8; S.D. 4; Tenn. 11; Utah 4; Vt. 3; Va. 12; Wis. 12; Wyo. 3.

Humphrey received 35.50 per cent (191 votes—13 states and D.C.,) as follows: Conn. 8; Hawaii 4; Me. 4; Md. 10; Mass. 14; Mich. 21; Minn. 10; N.Y. 43; Pa. 29; R.I. 4; Tex. 25; Wash. 9; W.Va. 7; D.C. 3.

Wallace received 8.55 per cent (46 votes—5 states) as follows: Ala. 10; Ark. 6; Ga. 12; La. 10; Miss. 7; N.C. 1.

THE ELECTION OF 1972

NOMINATIONS FOR TERM 1973-1977

Republican Party Convention (30th)

Aug. 21-23, 1972, Convention Hall, Miami Beach, Fla.
Nominated for President—Richard Milhous Nixon, Calif.
Nominated for Vice President—Spiro Theodore Agnew, Md.

Nixon was nominated on the first ballot. Candidates for nomination and the votes they received:
Richard Milhous Nixon, Calif., 1,347
Paul Norton McCloskey, Jr., Calif., 1
Total number of votes: 1,348
Number necessary for nomination: 675

Democratic Party Convention (36th)

July 10-13, 1972, Convention Hall, Miami Beach, Fla.
Nominated for President—George Stanley McGovern, S.D.
Nominated for Vice President—Thomas Francis Eagleton, Mo.

Eagleton resigned 19 days later and was replaced on August 8, 1972, by Robert Sargent Shriver, Md., selected by the Democratic National Committee.

McGovern was nominated on the first ballot. Candidates for nomination and the votes they received:
George Stanley McGovern, S.D., 1,864.95
Henry Martin Jackson, Wash., 485.65
George Corley Wallace, Ala., 377.5
Shirley Anita St. Hill Chisholm, N.Y., 101.45
Terry Sanford, N.C., 69.5

Hubert Horatio Humphrey, Minn., 35.0
Wilbur Daigh Mills, Ark., 32.8
Edmund Sixtus Muskie, Me., 20.8
Edward Moore Kennedy, Mass., 10.65
Wayne Levere Hays, Ohio, 5.0
Eugene Joseph McCarthy, Minn., 2.0
Walter Frederick Mondale, Minn., 1.0
Abstentions, 9.7
Total number of votes: 3,016
Number necessary for nomination: 1,509

American Independent Party Convention (Courage Party in New York)

Aug. 3-5, 1972, Freedom Hall, Louisville, Ky.
Nominated for President—John George Schmitz, Calif.
Nominated for Vice President—Thomas Jefferson Anderson, Tenn.
  Schmitz was nominated on the first ballot. Candidates for nomination and the votes they received:
John George Schmitz, Calif., 329.75
George Lester Garfield, Ga., 55.65
Allen Greer, Fla., 25.5
Thomas Jefferson Anderson, Tenn., 23.6
Richard B. Kay, 16.0

Socialist Workers Party Convention

Detroit, Mich.
Nominated for President—Linda Jenness, Ga.
Nominated for Vice President—Andrew Pulley, Ill.
  Both candidates were ineligible as they were under the statutory age.

Socialist Labor Party Convention

Apr. 8-10, 1972, Detroit-Hilton, Detroit, Mich.
Nominated for President—Louis Fisher, Ill.
Nominated for Vice President—Genevieve Gunderson, Minn.

Communist Party Convention (20th)

Feb. 18, 1972, New York, N.Y.
Nominated for President—Gus Hall, N.Y.
Nominated for Vice President—Jarvis Tyner
  Present at the convention were 275 delegates from 34 states.

Prohibition Party Convention

Nominated for President—Earle Harold Munn, Sr., Mich.
Nominated for Vice President—Marshall Inchapher

Libertarian Party Convention

Nominated for President—John Hospers, Calif.
Nominated for Vice President—Theodora Nathan, Ore.

People's Party Convention

July 27-30, 1972, St. Louis, Mo.
Nominated for President—Dr. Benjamin McLane Spock
Nominated for Vice President—Julius Hobson, Washington, D.C.

America First Party Convention

Nominated for President—John V. Mahalchik
Nominated for Vice President—Irving Homer

Universal Party Convention

Nominated for President—Gabriel Green
Nominated for Vice President—Daniel Fry

ELECTION RESULTS, NOV. 7, 1972—PRESIDENTIAL AND VICE PRESIDENTIAL CANDIDATES

Republican Party (46,740,323 votes)

Richard Milhous Nixon, Calif.
Spiro Theodore Agnew, Md.

Democratic Party (28,901,598 votes)

George Stanley McGovern, S.D.
Robert Sargent Shriver, Md. .

American Independent Party (993,199 votes)

John George Schmitz, Calif.
Thomas Jefferson Anderson, Tenn.

Conservative Party of New York (368,136 votes)

Richard Milhous Nixon, Calif.
Spiro Theodore Agnew, Md.

Socialist Workers Party (96,176 votes)

Linda Jenness, Ga.
Andrew Pulley, Ill.

Socialist Labor Party (53,617 votes)

Louis Fisher, Ill.
Genevieve Gunderson, Minn.

Communist Party (25,222 votes)

Gus Hall, N.Y.
Jarvis Tyner

Prohibition Party (13,444 votes)

Earle Harold Munn, Sr., Mich.
Marshall Inchapher

Libertarian Party (2,691 votes)

John Hospers, Calif.
Theodora Nathan, Ore.

Additional Votes (309,231)

Liberal Party (N.Y.), 183,128
Constitutional Party (Pa.), 70,593
Peace and Freedom Party, 64,098
National Democratic Party (Alaska), 37,815
People's Party (N.J.), 5,355
Independent Government Party (Minn.), 2,855
United Citizen's Party (S.C.), 2,265
People's Party (Wash.), 2,644
America First Party (N.J.), 1,743
People's Party (Ky.), 1,118
Liberty Union Party (Vt.), 1,010
Independent Party (Wis.), 506
Universal Party (Iowa), 199
Write-in votes, 10,776
Scattering, 12,915

ELECTORAL VOTES (538—50 states and District of Columbia)

Nixon received 96.6 per cent (520 votes—49 states) as follows: Ala. 9; Alaska 3; Ariz. 6; Ark. 6; Calif. 45; Colo. 7; Conn. 8; Del. 3; Fla. 17; Ga. 12; Hawaii 4; Idaho 4; Ill. 26; Ind. 13; Iowa 8; Kan. 7; Ky. 9; La. 10; Me. 4; Md. 10; Mich. 21; Minn. 10; Miss. 7; Mo. 12; Mont. 4; Neb. 5; Nev. 3; N.H. 4; N.J. 17; N.M. 4; N.Y. 41; N.C. 13; N.D. 3; Ohio 25; Okla. 8; Ore. 6; Pa. 27; R.I. 4; S.C. 8; S.D. 4; Tenn. 10; Tex. 26; Utah 4; Vt. 3; Va. 11; Wash. 9; W.Va. 6; Wis. 11; Wyo. 3.

McGovern received 3.4 per cent (17 votes—1 state and D.C.) as follows: Mass. 14; D.C. 3.

One delegate from Virginia cast his one vote for John Hospers, Libertarian Party.

FIRST TERM

CABINET

January 20, 1969-January 20, 1973

State–William Pierce Rogers, Md., Jan. 22, 1969

Treasury–David Matthew Kennedy, Ill., Jan. 22, 1969-Feb. 1, 1971; John Bowden Connally, Jr., Tex. , Feb. 11, 1971; George Pratt Shultz, Ill., June 12, 1972

Defense–Melvin Robert Laird, Wis., Jan. 22, 1969

Attorney General–John Newton Mitchell, N.Y., Jan. 22, 1969; Richard Gordon Kleindienst, Ariz., June 12, 1972

Postmaster General–Winton Malcolm Blount, Ala., Jan. 22, 1969-July 1, 1971

Interior–Walter Joseph Hickel, Alaska, Jan. 24, 1969-Nov. 25, 1970; Rogers Clark Ballard Morton, Md., Jan. 29, 1971

Agriculture–Clifford Morris Hardin, Neb., Jan. 22, 1969-Nov. 11, 1971; Earl Lauer Butz, Ind., Dec. 2, 1971

Commerce–Maurice Hubert Stans, N.Y., Jan. 22, 1969; Peter George Peterson, Ill., Feb. 21, 1972

Labor–George Pratt Shultz, Ill., Jan. 22, 1969-July 2, 1970; James Day Hodgson, Minn., July 2, 1970

Health, Education, and Welfare–Robert Hutchinson Finch, Calif., Jan. 22, 1969-June 23, 1970; Elliot Lee Richardson, Mass., June 24, 1970

Housing and Urban Development–George Wilcken Romney, Mich., Jan. 22, 1969

Transportation–John Anthony Volpe, Mass., Jan. 22, 1969

SECOND TERM

Term of office–January 20, 1973-August 9, 1974

Term served–1 year, 201 days

CABINET

State–William Pierce Rogers, Md., continued from preceding administration, resigned Sept. 3, 1973; Henry Alfred Kissinger, Sept. 22, 1973

Treasury–George Pratt Shultz, Ill., continued from preceding administration

Defense–Melvin Robert Laird, Wis., continued from preceding administration; Elliot Lee Richardson, Mass., Feb. 2, 1973; James Rodney Schlesinger, Va., July 2, 1973

Attorney General–Richard Gordon Kleindienst, Ariz., continued from preceding administration, resigned Apr. 30, 1973; Elliot Lee Richardson, Mass., May 25, 1973, resigned Oct. 20, 1973; Robert H. Bork (acting), Oct. 21, 1973; William Bart Saxbe, Ohio, Jan. 4, 1974

Interior–Rogers Clark Ballard Morton, Md., continued from preceding administration

Agriculture–Earl Lauer Butz, Ind., continued from preceding administration

Commerce–Peter George Peterson, Ill, continued from preceding administration; Frederick Baily Dent, S.C., Feb. 2, 1973

Labor–James Day Hodgson, Minn., continued from preceding administration; Peter Joseph Brennan, N.Y., Feb. 2, 1973

Health, Education, and Welfare–Elliot Lee Richardson, Mass., continued from preceding administration; Caspar Willard Weinberger, Calif., Feb. 12, 1973

Housing and Urban Development–George Wilcken Romney, Mich., continued from preceding administration; James Thomas Lynn, Ohio, Feb. 2, 1973

Transportation–John Anthony Volpe, Mass., continued from preceding administration; Claude Stout Brinegar, Calif., Feb. 2, 1973

Treasury–William Edward Simon, N.J., sworn in May 8, 1974

FIRST TERM

NINETY-FIRST CONGRESS

January 3, 1969-January 2, 1971

First session–Jan. 3, 1969-Dec. 23, 1969 (355 days)

Second session–Jan. 19, 1970-Jan. 2, 1971 (349 days)

Vice President–Spiro Theodore Agnew, Md.

President pro tempore of the Senate–Richard Brevard Russell, Ga.
Secretary of the Senate–Francis Ralph Valeo, N.Y.
Speaker of the House–John William McCormack, Mass.
Clerk of the House–William Pat Jennings, Va.

NINETY-SECOND CONGRESS

January 21, 1971-January 21-1973
First session–Jan. 21, 1971-Dec. 17, 1971 (331 days)
Second session–Jan. 18, 1972-Oct. 18, 1972 (275 days)
Vice President–Spiro Theodore Agnew, Md.
President pro tempore of the Senate–Richard Brevard Russell, Ga.,
    d. Jan. 21, 1971; Allen Joseph Ellender, Sr., La., elected Jan. 23,
    1971
Secretary of the Senate–Francis Ralph Valeo, N.Y.
Speaker of the House–Carl Bert Albert, Okla.
Clerk of the House–William Pat Jennings, Va.

SECOND TERM

NINETY-THIRD CONGRESS

January 3, 1973-January 3, 1975
First session–Jan. 3, 1973-Dec. 22, 1973
Second session–Jan. 21, 1974-Dec. 20, 1974
Vice President–Spiro Theodore Agnew, Md., resigned Oct. 10, 1973;
    Gerald Rudolph Ford, Mich., sworn in Dec. 6, 1973, succeeded to
    the presidency on the resignation of President Nixon, Aug. 9, 1974
President pro tempore of the Senate–James Oliver Eastland, Miss.
Secretary of the Senate–Francis Ralph Valeo, N.Y.
Speaker of the House–Carl Bert Albert, Okla.
Clerk of the House–William Pat Jennings, Va.

APPOINTMENTS TO THE SUPREME COURT

Chief Justice
Warren Earl Burger, Minn., June 23, 1969

Associate Justices
Harry Andrew Blackman, Minn., June 9, 1970
Lewis Franklin Powell, Jr., Va., Jan. 7, 1972
William Hubbs Rehnquist, Wis., Jan. 7, 1972

ADMINISTRATION — IMPORTANT DATES

Mar. 2, 1969, Pentagon admitted to Congress that it had been spend-
    ing $350 million annually for the research and development of bio-
    logical and chemical weapons
July 20, 1969, first men landed on moon (Apollo 11 astronauts Neil
    A. Armstrong and Edwin E. Aldrin, Jr.)
Aug. 14, 1969, world's largest mint opened in Philadelphia
Nov. 24, 1969, United States signed non-proliferation treaty on nuclear
    weapons
Jan. 1, 1970, President signed bill creating Council on Environmental
    Quality

Mar. 17, 1970, United States cast first veto in United Nations Security Council

Mar. 20, 1970, postal workers' strike for higher wages spread throughout country

Apr. 8, 1970, Senate rejected nomination of G. Harrold Carswell to Supreme Court (second rejection of southern conservative; first nominee, Clement F. Haynsworth, Jr., rejected Nov. 21, 1969)

Apr. 10, 1970, Senate Foreign Relations Committee voted to repeal the 1964 Gulf of Tonkin resolution

Apr. 13, 1970, critical loss of power and oxygen in command module of Apollo 13 forced crew to transfer to lunar module and return to Earth

Apr. 20, 1970, President announced withdrawal of 150,000 American troops from Vietnam within a year

Apr. 21, 1970, Americans observed first Earth Day, demonstrating against environmental pollution

Apr. 30, 1970, President announced sending of U.S. troops to Cambodia

May 1, 1970, death of four students killed by gunfire of National Guardsmen at Kent State University (Ohio) during antiwar demonstration touched off nationwide protests

May 14, 1970, two students killed in police gunfire at Jackson State College (Miss.)

June 3, 1970, President declared incursion into Cambodia successful

June 22, 1970, President signed extension of 1965 Voting Rights Act lowering voting age to eighteen

June 29, 1970, American ground troops left Cambodia

July 1, 1970, NASA revealed Skylab program for construction of laboratory in space by 1972

July 9, 1970, President proposed creation of independent Environmental Protection Agency

Aug. 12, 1970, postal reform bill signed

Sept. 25, 1970, military guards placed on commercial planes to discourage hijacking

Oct. 7, 1970, Nixon asked for cease-fire in Southeast Asia

Dec. 2, 1970, Senate vetoed supersonic transport aircraft (SST)

Dec. 18, 1970, Army destroyed biological weapons

Jan 21, 1971, U.S. and Soviet space officials agreed to cooperate in research

Feb. 11, 1971, 63 nations signed treaty banning nuclear weapons from the ocean

Mar. 4, 1971, President declared South Vietnamese drive into Laos successful and promised continued withdrawal of American forces

Mar. 7, 1971, American planes bombed Laos and Cambodia in support of South Vietnamese action

Mar. 29, 1971, First Lieutenant William L. Calley found guilty of premeditated murder of 22 South Vietnamese civilians at Songmy (My Lai) in 1968

Apr. 7, 1971, President announced withdrawal of 100,000 American soldiers from South Vietnam by Dec. 1, 1971

Apr. 20, 1971, Supreme Court ruled that busing could be used to achieve desegregation in dual school systems of South

Apr. 26, 1971, presidential commission recommended that Communist China be admitted to the United Nations without expelling Nationalist China (Taiwan)

May 1, 1971, Amtrak took over intercity passenger rail lines

May 2-5, 1971, antiwar demonstrators protested Vietnamese War in Washington, D.C.; several thousands arrested

June 10, 1971, President lifted twenty-one-year embargo on trade with Communist China

June 13, 1971, New York *Times* printed excerpts from "Pentagon Papers," classified report on history of U.S. involvement in Vietnam; right to publish material later upheld by Supreme Court

June 28, 1971, Daniel Ellsberg, Defense Department staff member in Johnson Administration, admitted turning over copy of Pentagon Papers to New York *Times;* arraigned on charges of possessing classified material

July 1, 1971, United States Postal Service inaugurated as semi-independent agency

July 5, 1971, President certified Twenty-sixth Amendment lowering voting age from 21 to 18

Aug. 5, 1971, Astronaut Major Alfred M. Worden of Apollo 15 took first deep space walk

Aug. 15, 1971, President announced drastic monetary and fiscal program; 90-day wage, price, and rent freeze; "floating" dollar no longer tied to gold; other measures to achieve economic stability

Sept. 3, 1971, secret undercover operation directed by White House aides (later exposed as the "plumbers") broke into the office of the psychiatrist of Daniel Ellsberg seeking evidence against Ellsberg

Oct. 23, 1971, UN General Assembly voted to seat Communist China and to expel Nationalist China

Nov. 13, 1971, Phase II of economic stabilization program went into effect with mandatory, flexible controls

Dec. 1971, presidential adviser Henry Kissinger made two trips to Communist China to pave way for President's proposed trip in 1972

Dec. 18, 1971, United States devalued dollar in ten-nation agreement restructuring currency exchange rates; 10 per cent import surtax lifted; Pay Board and Price Commission established

Jan. 5, 1972, President approved plans for development of space shuttle

Feb. 7, 1972, President signed Federal Election Campaign Act requiring all campaign contributions to be reported

Feb. 14, 1972, President order relaxation of restrictions of U.S. trade with Communist China

Feb. 22, 1972, President conferred with Premier Chou En-Lai in Peking

Mar. 22, 1972, Senate approved constitutional amendment banning sex discrimination (subsequent ratification by 38 states required)

Apr. 3, 1972, President devalued dollar 8.57 per cent and raised gold price from $35 to $38 an ounce

May 15, 1972, Governor George Corley Wallace of Alabama, contender for Democratic presidential nomination, wounded in assassination attempt at Laurel, Md., rally

May 15, 1972, island of Okinawa returned to Japan

May 22, 1972, President conferred with Communist Party Secretary Leonid I. Brezhnev in Moscow

May 24, 1972, space exploration agreement with Soviet Union signed, ensuring compatibility of spacecraft docking systems

May 26, 1972, U.S.-Soviet strategic arms control agreements signed

June 15-16, 1972, President Luis Echeverría Álvarez of Mexico addressed joint session of Congress and conferred with President Nixon on problems of migrant workers

June 17, 1972, five men arrested in burglary of Democratic National Committee headquarters at the Watergate complex, Washington, D.C.

June 19, 1972, Justice Department announced that FBI would investigate Watergate break-in

June 29, 1972, Supreme Court declared death penalty unconstitutional

July 8, 1972, President announced $750 million sale of grain to Soviet Union

Aug. 12, 1972, U.S. combat ground troops departed from Vietnam

Sept. 1, 1972, President ended two days of summit talks with Japanese prime minister in Hawaii; Japanese agreed to reduce U.S. trade deficit by importing American goods

Oct. 19, 1972, President announced impoundment of funds appropriated by Congress in order to limit Federal spending to $250 billion for fiscal 1973

Nov. 2, 1972, five hundred American Indians invaded Bureau of Indian Affairs Building, Washington, D.C., to protest Bureau policies

Dec. 30, 1972, U.S. bombing of Hanoi-Haiphong area halted; resumption of peace talks announced

Jan. 5, 1973, President announced reorganization plan for Executive departments (consolidation of authority and reduction of White House staff)

Jan. 11, 1973, Phase III of economic stabilization program begun; voluntary and self-administered controls placed upon wages and prices

Jan. 15, 1973, President ordered halt to military action against North Vietnam

Jan. 27, 1973, United States, North Vietnam, South Vietnam, and Viet Cong provisional government signed cease-fire agreement in Paris; end of military draft announced

Feb. 7, 1973, Senate established Select Committee headed by Sam J. Ervin (Democrat, N.C.) to investigate Watergate affair

Feb. 12, 1973, first war prisoners released at Hanoi

Feb. 12, 1973, 10 per cent devaluation of American dollar (second devaluation in fourteen months)

Feb. 27, 1973, 200 members of American Indian Movement seized Wounded Knee on Oglala Sioux reservation in South Dakota

Mar. 29, 1973, U.S. troops completed withdrawal from South Vietnam

Apr. 1, 1973, week-long boycott of meat begun by consumers to protest rising prices

Apr. 2-3, 1973, President conferred with South Vietnamese President Nguyen Van Thieu at San Clemente, Calif.

April 12, 1973, U.S. Court of Appeals forbade Federal impoundment of funds appropriated by Congress for Missouri highways

Apr. 30, 1973, President announced three Watergate-connected resignations (Attorney General Richard G. Kleindienst and chief White House aides John D. Ehrlichman and H. R. Haldeman) and one dismissal (John W. Dean, counsel to President)

May 8, 1973, seventy-day occupation of Wounded Knee ended

May 11, 1973, charges against Daniel Ellsberg dismissed because of "conduct of the Government" in the case

May 18, 1973, Archibald Cox named special Watergate prosecutor

June 13, 1973, second temporary freeze on wages and prices in effect

June 16-25, 1973, Soviet leader Brezhnev visited United States, holding summit talks with President and signing nine agreements

June 27, 1973, Senate confirmed Clarence Kelley as new director of FBI

July 16, 1973, Alexander P. Butterfield, former presidential appointments secretary, revealed that President had taped all discussions and phone calls in his offices

July 17, 1973, Pentagon revealed that President and Defense Secretary Melvin R. Laird had authorized secret bombing of Cambodia and subsequent falsification of reports

July 31, 1973, Representative Robert F. Drinan (Democrat, Mass.) introduced first impeachment resolution against President for "high crimes and misdemeanors"

Aug. 13, 1973, Phase IV of economic stabilization program effected; mandatory economic controls established

Oct. 2, 1973, energy shortage reached crisis proportions; mandatory fuel allocation announced

Oct. 6, 1973, fourth Arab-Israeli war broke out

Oct. 10, 1973, Vice President Spiro T. Agnew resigned

Oct. 12, 1973, President nominated Gerald R. Ford as Vice President; Ford later confirmed and sworn in (Dec. 6, 1973)

Oct. 14, 1973, President, ordered by Court of Appeals to relinquish tapes to U.S. District Court Judge John J. Sirica, proposed compromise summary of tapes

Oct. 18-21, 1973, Arab countries embargoed oil deliveries in effort to curtail U.S. support to Israel

Oct. 20, 1973, Attorney General Elliot L. Richardson resigned rather than enforce President's order to dismiss special Watergate prosecutor Cox, who had rejected President's compromise on tapes; Assistant Attorney General William Ruckelshaus also resigned

Nov. 1973, wholesale price index hit peak; controls reached point of diminishing return; program of decontrols begun

Nov. 5, 1973, Leon Jaworski appointed new special Watergate prosecutor

Nov. 7, 1973, war powers bill enacted by Congress over presidential veto

Nov. 25, 1973, President announced program to conserve energy by reducing speed limits, banning Sunday gasoline sales, and reducing nonessential lighting

Nov. 26, 1973, President turned over seven tapes to Judge Sirica

Dec. 1973, Cost of Living Council ended price and wage controls in automobile industry

Dec. 3, 1973, William E. Simon appointed director of newly created Federal Energy Office

Dec. 8, 1973, President released accounting of his personal finances and tax returns from 1969 through 1972 (first large-scale accounting by a President)

Jan. 2, 1974, President signed bill to limit highway speed to fifty-five miles per hour as a fuel-conservation measure

Jan. 4, 1974, President refused to comply with subpoena of Watergate tapes and documents issued by Senate Select [Ervin] Committee

Jan. 24, 1974, Egil Krogh, Jr., of White House "plumbers" unit, sentenced after conviction on conspiracy charge relating to burglary of office of Daniel Ellsberg's psychiatrist (first major presidential aide to be sentenced)

Jan. 30, 1974, State of the Union message offered ten-point program to check inflation, deal with the energy crisis, promote peace and bring about domestic reform

Feb. 1974, President pledged continued aid as Cambodian rebels renewed Pnom Penh attacks

Feb. 1, 1974, President, in economic message to Congress, predicted severe inflation

Feb. 6, 1974, House of Representatives authorized Judiciary Committee impeachment inquiry

Feb. 8, 1974, astronauts of Skylab 3 returned after record space flight of eighty-four days

Feb. 25, 1974, Herbert W. Kalmbach, President's lawyer and fundraiser, allowed to plead guilty to charges of campaign irregularities in return for cooperation with special prosecutor

March 1, 1974, seven former presidential aides indicted in Watergate cover-up conspiracy: John N. Mitchell, H. R. Haldeman, John D. Ehrlichman, Charles W. Colson (charges dropped June 3, 1974), Robert C. Mardian, Kenneth W. Parkinson (acquitted Jan. 1, 1975), Gordon Strachan (charges dismissed Mar. 10, 1975); separate sealed report, delivered to House Judiciary Committee, named President as unindicted co-conspirator (disclosure made June 5, 1974)

Mar. 7, 1974, six men indicted on conspiracy charges related to break-in at office of Daniel Ellsberg's psychiatrist

Apr. 3, 1974, tornadoes in southern states caused over 300 deaths and 1,200 injuries and damage exceeding $1 billion

Apr. 8, 1974, President signed bill raising minimum wage to $2 per hour

Apr. 11, 1974, House Judiciary Committee subpoenaed tapes and records of White House conversations relating to Watergate

Apr. 14, 1974, Westar 1, domestic communication satellite, launched

Apr. 28, 1974, former Attorney General Mitchell and former Secretary of Commerce Stans acquitted of charge of obstructing an investigation of financier Robert L. Vesco in return for 1972 campaign contribution

Apr. 30, 1974, edited transcripts of selected White House tapes released to the public

May 2, 1974, former Vice President Agnew disbarred by Maryland Court of Appeals as a result of his *nolo contendere* plea (Oct. 10, 1973) on tax-evasion charge

May 4, 1974, Expo '74 opened in Spokane, Wash.

May 7, 1974, Federal Energy Administration created, replacing Federal Energy Office

May 9, 1974, House Judiciary Committee opened hearings on impeachment

May 15, 1974, Dwight L. Chapin, former presidential appointments secretary, sentenced after conviction on charges of lying to grand jury investigating Watergate break-in

May 16, 1974, former Attorney General Kleindienst pleaded guilty to misdemeanor charge based on inaccurate and incomplete testimony before Senate committee investigating antitrust settlement (first attorney general convicted of criminal offense); felony charges of perjury dropped in return for misdemeanor plea

May 21, 1974, Jeb Stuart Magruder, former deputy director of the Committee to Reelect the President, sentenced on charges related to Watergate break-in and cover-up

June 3, 1974, Supreme Court ruled in 5 to 3 decision that women must receive equal pay for equal work

June 10-19, 1974, President on nine-day tour conferred with Arab and Israeli leaders (first incumbent President to visit Middle East)

June 17, 1974, Cost of Living Council abolished

June 20, 1974, transcripts of Watergate tapes released to House Judiciary Committee

June 21, 1974, Charles W. Colson, former White House special counsel, sentenced after guilty plea on charges of obstructing justice in trial of Daniel Ellsberg

July 1, 1974, Turkey announced decision to rescind ban on opium cultivation despite threat of U.S. military aid cutoff

July 3, 1974, President signed limited nuclear agreements in Moscow

July 12, 1974, President signed bill curbing executive impoundment of appropriated funds

July 12, 1974, Senate Select Committee issued 2,217-page final report on Watergate

July 24, 1974, Supreme Court upheld order that presidential tapes and documents be surrendered to the Watergate special prosecutor (first Supreme Court deliberation on criminal case in which President was named as co-conspirator)

July 25, 1974, Supreme Court overruled cross-district busing in decision on Detroit school desegregation plan

July 27-30, 1974, House Judiciary Committee, after months of investigation and nationwide television hearings (July 24-30), recommended to the full House three articles of impeachment: obstruction of justice in the Watergate cover-up, abuse of presidential powers, and contempt of Congress in refusing to supply subpoenaed papers

July 29, 1974, former Secretary of Treasury Connally indicted in milk-support bribery scandal (acquitted Apr. 27, 1975)

July 30, 1974, President surrendered to Judge Sirica eleven subpoenaed tapes that Supreme Court had ordered turned over July 24

July 31, 1974, John D. Ehrlichman, former chief domestic adviser to the President, sentenced after conviction on charges relating to "plumbers" burglary and cover-up

Aug. 2, 1974, former presidential counsel John W. Dean III sentenced on charges related to his admitted part in Watergate cover-up

Aug. 5, 1974, transcripts of June 23, 1972, White House conversations released, revealing that President had directed FBI to end investigation of Watergate break-in

Aug. 9, 1974, President resigned

IMPORTANT DATES IN HIS LIFE

June 7, 1937, graduated from Duke University Law School

1946, joined law firm of Wingert & Bewley in Whittier, Calif. (firm name changed to Wingert, Bewley & Nixon; later to Bewley, Knoop & Nixon)

Nov. 6, 1946, elected to U.S. House of Representatives (from California); reelected in 1948

Nov. 7, 1950, elected to U.S. Senate (from California)

Dec. 1, 1950, appointed to fill unexpired term of Senator Sheridan Downey of California

July 10, 1952, nominated for vice presidency by Republican Party (Eisenhower ticket)

Sept. 23, 1952, delivered "Checkers" speech on nationwide television; defended acceptance of $18,000 fund from supporters with business interests by maintaining that only political expenses were paid from fund; cited personal gift to Nixon family—cocker spaniel, Checkers

Nov. 4, 1952, elected Vice President of the United States

Nov. 6, 1956, reelected Vice President

May 1958, visited South America on goodwill tour; attacked by anti-U.S. demonstrators in Caracas, Venezuela

July 24, 1959, engaged in sharp discussion with Soviet Premier Nikita S. Khrushchev in Moscow during visit to U.S.S.R. ("kitchen debate" in showroom of American exhibition)

July 28, 1960, nominated for presidency by Republican Party

Nov. 8, 1960, lost presidential election to John Fitzgerald Kennedy by 118,574 votes (two tenths of 1 per cent of total 69 million votes)

1961, returned to California law practice

1962, nominated for governorship of California; defeated in election

Mar. 29, 1962, Six Crises published

Jan. 1963, joined New York City law firm of Mudge, Stern, Baldwin & Todd (later Nixon, Mudge, Rose, Alexander, Guthrie & Stern)

RICHARD MILHOUS NIXON 457

Apr. 27, 1966, argued first U.S. Supreme Court case (in behalf of James S. Hill against *Life* magazine)

Aug. 8, 1968, nominated for presidency by Republican Party

Nov. 5, 1968, elected President of the United States

Jan. 20, 1969, inaugurated 37th President of the United States

Feb. 23, 1969, left on European tour

Feb. 1972, visited Communist China

Aug. 23, 1972, nominated for second term

Nov. 7, 1972, reelected President of the United States

Jan. 20, 1973, inaugurated for second term

Apr. 3, 1974, announced intention of paying $432,787 to cover underpayment of federal taxes

June 5, 1974, disclosure that President had been named unindicted co-conspirator in sealed report by grand jury in Watergate cover-up case (Mar. 1, 1974)

June 24, 1974, White House announced after Middle East trip that President had suffered from phlebitis

July 27-30, 1974, House Judiciary Committee voted to recommend impeachment on grounds of obstruction of justice, abuse of power, and contempt of Congress

Aug. 8, 1974, in televised address announced intention to resign

Aug. 9, 1974, retired to his residence in San Clemente, Calif.

Sept. 18, 1974, accepted pardon from President Ford for all federal offenses that he "committed or may have committed"

Oct. 29, 1974, underwent surgery to prevent blood clot in leg from entering lung

Apr. 20, 1975, announced plan for presidential library at University of Southern California

RICHARD MILHOUS NIXON

____was the first President to nominate a Vice President under the Twenty-fifth Amendment.

____was the second President against whom articles of impeachment were drawn up.

____was the first President to resign.

____was the first President to be pardoned by his successor for possible offenses against the United States.

NIXON'S VICE PRESIDENTS
FIRST AND SECOND TERMS

Vice President–Spiro Theodore Agnew (Anagnostopoulos)

Date of birth–Nov. 9, 1918

Birthplace–Baltimore, Md.

Political party–Republican

State represented–Maryland

Term of office–Jan. 20, 1969–Oct. 10, 1973

Age at inauguration–51 years, 72 days

Additional data on Agnew

1942-1946, World War II company commander with Tenth Armored Division in Europe; recalled for one year during Korean conflict

1947, night school law degree, University of Baltimore Law School
1947-1962, law practice, Baltimore, Md.
1958-1961, chairman, county board of zoning appeals, Baltimore County
1960, ran last in five-way race for circuit judge, Baltimore County
1962, became Baltimore County executive (four-year term)
Nov. 8, 1966, elected governor of Maryland (four-year term; fifth Republican governor in 180 years)
Jan. 25, 1967, inaugurated as governor of Maryland
Jan. 7, 1969, resigned as governor of Maryland
Jan. 20, 1969, inaugurated as Vice President of the United States
Dec. 26, 1969-Jan. 19, 1970, traveled to Philippines, South Vietnam, Taiwan, Nepal, Afghanistan, Malaysia, Singapore, Indonesia, Australia, New Zealand
Aug. 22-Sept. 1, 1970, visited South Korea, Taiwan, South Vietnam, Cambodia, Thailand
Apr. 30-May 3, 1971, visited Jamaica
June 27-28, 1971, visited South Korea, Singapore, India, Kuwait, Saudi Arabia, Ethiopia, Kenya, the Congo, Spain, Morocco, Portugal
Oct. 10-23, 1971, visited Turkey, Iran, Greece
May 9-19, 1972, visited Japan, Thailand, South Vietnam
Nov. 7, 1972, reelected Vice President of the United States
Jan. 20, 1973, inaugurated for second term
Oct. 10, 1973, resigned as Vice President of the United States; pleaded no contest to charges of income tax evasion before U.S. District Court, Baltimore, Md.; received $10,000 fine and accepted three years unsupervised probation

SECOND TERM

Vice President–Gerald Rudolph Ford
Date of birth–July 14, 1913
Birthplace–Omaha, Neb.
Political party–Republican
State represented–Michigan
Term of office–Dec. 6, 1973-Aug. 9, 1974
Age at inauguration–61 years, 145 days

Additional data on Ford

1931, graduated from Grand Rapids, Mich., South High School
1935, graduated from University of Michigan, B.A. degree
1941, law degree, Yale University Law School
1942-1946, served in World War II
Jan. 3, 1949-Dec. 6, 1973, U.S. House of Representatives (from Michigan)
Jan. 4, 1965, elected minority leader, House of Representatives
Dec. 6, 1973, confirmed by Congress as Vice President of the United States to fill vacancy left by resignation of Spiro T. Agnew

VICE PRESIDENTIAL VACANCY

The Twenty-fifth Amendment to the Constitution, ratified on February 10, 1967, provides that "whenever there is a vacancy in the office of the Vice President, the President shall nominate a Vice President who shall take office upon confirmation by a vote of both Houses of Congress."

The resignation of Vice President Agnew on October 10, 1973, left the position vacant. President Nixon nominated Gerald Rudolph Ford, House Republican leader from Michigan, in accord with the provisions of the Twenty-fifth Amendment. The nomination was confirmed by the Senate in a vote of 92 to 3, on November 27, 1973, and by the House of Representatives in a vote of 387 to 35, on December 6, 1973.

Ford was sworn in by Chief Justice Warren E. Burger, on December 6, 1973, in the 116-year-old House chamber, as the fortieth Vice President of the United States.

ADDITIONAL DATA ON NIXON

FIRST INAUGURATION

Nixon was inaugurated Monday, January 20, 1969, at 12:15 P.M. The oath of office was administered by Chief Justice Earl Warren. The rain held off, but the air was heavily overcast, and the temperature ranged from 33 to 38 degrees. Nixon made a seventeen-minute inaugural address. About 38,000 reserved seats were sold along the parade route.

FIRST PRESIDENT TO ATTEND LAUNCHING OF A MANNED SPACE FLIGHT

The first President in office to attend the launching of a manned space flight was Richard Milhous Nixon, who viewed the launching of Apollo 12 at 11:22 A.M., on November 14, 1969, from Pad A at Cape Kennedy, Fla. The crew consisted of Commander Charles Conrad, Jr., Richard Francis Gordon, Jr., in command of the module pilot, and Alan LaVern Bean. The total flight time was 244 hours, 36 minutes and 25 seconds. All mission objectives were successfully accomplished.

TWENTY-SIXTH AMENDMENT RATIFIED

The Twenty-sixth Amendment to the Constitution enabling individuals eighteen years or older to vote was passed by the Senate (94 to 0) on March 10, 1971, and by the House of Representatives (400 to 19) on March 23, 1971. It was enacted June 30, 1971, when it was passed by Alabama, North Carolina, and Ohio, who were the 36th, 37th, and 38th states to ratify. The first state to ratify was Minnesota, on March 23, 1971. President Richard Milhous Nixon certified the amendment on July 5, 1971.

NIXON VISITED COMMUNIST CHINA

The first President to visit a nation not recognized by the United

States was Richard Milhous Nixon, who left the United States on February 17, 1972, and arrived in the People's Republic of China on February 21, 1972, where he conferred with Chairman Mao Tse-tung and Premier Chou En-lai.

NIXON'S SUPERCABINET

On January 5, 1973, President Nixon elevated three cabinet members to the rank of White House counselors. They were Secretary of Health, Education, and Welfare Caspar Willard Weinberger, who was placed in charge of human resources; Secretary of Housing and Urban Development James Thomas Lynn, placed in charge of community development; and Secretary of Agriculture Earl Lauer Butz, placed in charge of natural resources. The supercabinet was dismantled May 10, 1973.

SECOND INAUGURATION

There was a stiff breeze blowing, with the temperature in the low forties, when Nixon was sworn in for his second term on Saturday, January 20, 1973. He was the thirteenth President sworn in for a second term. The oath was administered by Chief Justice Warren Earl Burger. The theme of the parade was "The Spirit of '76" and the costs exceeded four million dollars. Many protestors expressed disapproval.

THE WATERGATE SCANDAL

On June 17, 1972, five men were arrested for breaking into the Democratic National Committee headquarters at the Watergate hotel and office building complex on the Potomac, in Washington, D.C. At the time of their capture, they were found to be in possession of electronic surveillance devices and cameras, all part of an elaborate bugging scheme—devised, it transpired, by agents of the Committee to Re-elect the President.

The break-in was followed by various attempts to cover up the incident on the part of important government officials and chief aides in the Nixon Administration. The full impact of the situation was not felt immediately, but by the end of 1972 the Senate and the press had begun to probe into the Watergate incident. A series of accusations followed, some formal, some implied, concerning covert and illegal activities dealing with campaign sabotage. These activities were said to have been sanctioned directly by White House aides and members of the President's campaign committee.

In total, seven men were indicted by a Federal Grand Jury, on September 15, 1972, on charges related to the bugging and break-in of the Democratic National Committee's offices at Watergate. One conspirator told U.S. District Court Judge John J. Sirica, who presided over the trial of the Watergate Seven, that high-ranking officials were involved in the cover-up.

It became apparent that further examination of the Watergate break-in and cover-up was necessary. On April 17, 1973, President Nixon authorized a new investigation with the appointment of a special Watergate prosecutor, Archibald Cox of Harvard Law School. (He was later dismissed by President Nixon, on October 20, 1973, to be replaced by Leon Jaworski; refusal to dismiss Cox led to the resignations of Attorney General Elliot L. Richardson and Deputy Attorney General William D. Ruckelshaus.)

On May 17, 1973, the seven-man Senate Select Committee on Presidential Campaign Activities (better known as the Watergate Committee), headed by Senator Samuel J. Ervin, Jr. (Democrat, N.C.), reconvened and began a nationally televised inquiry into the events leading up to and following the Watergate incident. The testimony given to the Watergate Committee, by those involved, seriously impaired the credibility of the President. This led to many demands for his impeachment or resignation, and the House Judiciary Committee began an inquiry into possible grounds for impeachment. At the same time, the FBI was investigating an unexplained erasure in a White House tape recording of a conversation on Watergate.

More than twenty-five individuals and many important corporations were involved in court actions stemming from the Watergate affair, from illegal corporation campaign contributions, and from the September 3, 1971, break-in at the California office of the psychiatrist of Daniel Ellsberg, who had made public the classified Pentagon Papers. Two former Cabinet members and campaign committee officials—John N. Mitchell, former Attorney General, and Maurice H. Stans, former Secretary of Commerce—and the President's closest aides—H. R. Haldeman, former White House chief of staff, and John D. Ehrlichman, former chief domestic adviser—were among those indicted.

From the testimony of party and governmental aides—including all those who resigned their posts or were dismissed—the public became aware of the ramifications of an episode widely regarded as the worst high-level political scandal in the nation's history.

THE WATERGATE CRISIS

The tangled web of scandals collectively known as Watergate continued to dominate the attention of the country during the first seven months of 1974. Constitutional clashes between the Executive and Legislative branches and between the Executive and Judicial branches were given exhaustive coverage by the mass media. Confrontations were reported with accelerating frequency: charges and denials, subpoenas and claims of executive privilege and confidentiality, indictments and sentencings of Cabinet members and presidential aides. Senate and House probes ground on; prosecutors argued their cases in court. Edited transcripts of taped White House conversations, then the tapes themselves—with unexplained gaps—were made public. Each day brought revelations of political immorality on a scale unprecedented in the American experience.

The increasing clamor for resignation or impeachment reflected the turning tide of opinion against the President reelected with the second largest electoral sweep in history. His Vice President had been forced to resign, pleading no contest to tax-evasion charges. What brought about his own downfall was not merely the tapes of the conversations after the Watergate burglary, but a complex of schemes and misconduct at the highest levels. Some of the events predated the June 1972 break-in, some ensued, and all were damaging; the attempt to conceal staff responsibility for the theft; the earlier break-in at the office of Dr. Lewis J. Fielding (psychiatrist of Daniel Ellsberg, who had released the Pentagon Papers); the use of domestic surveillance and intelligence operations against political adversaries; the use of the Internal Revenue Service for political benefit; huge undisclosed campaign contributions by large corporations; the secret bombing of Cambodia; the President's questioned income-tax returns; unwarranted federal expenditures for personal homes; the failure to cooperate with congressional investigators and special prosecutors. Two years of "Watergate," of intensifying erosion of popular and congressional support, led to the first resignation from office of a President of the United States.

THE RESIGNATION

On Thursday, August 8, 1974, at 9:00 P.M., Richard Milhous Nixon, the thirty-seventh President of the United States, announced in a nationally televised speech that he would resign, effective at noon on August 9. Referring to his earlier repeated declarations that he would not leave office before his term expired, the President explained his decision:

Throughout the long and difficult period of Watergate, I have felt it was my duty to persevere, to make every possible effort to complete the term of office to which you elected me.

In the past few days, however, it has become evident to me that I no longer have a strong enough political base in the Congress to justify continuing that effort. . . .

I would have preferred to carry through to the finish whatever the personal agony it would have involved. . . .

I have never been a quitter.

To leave office before my term is completed is opposed to every instinct in my body. But as President I must put the interests of America first.

America needs a full-time President and a full-time Congress.

. . .

To continue to fight through the months ahead for my personal vindication would almost totally absorb the time and attention of both the President and the Congress in a period when our entire focus should be on the great issues of peace abroad and prosperity without inflation at home.

Therefore, I shall resign the presidency effective at noon tomorrow.

On the morning of August 9, the President bade farewell to his

Cabinet and staff. The Nixon family left immediately for San Clemente, Calif., and did not attend the noon swearing-in of Gerald Rudolph Ford as thirty-eighth President.

ACCEPTANCE OF THE PARDON

In San Clemente, Calif., former President Nixon accepted the pardon granted on September 8, 1974, by President Ford. The unconditional pardon for all federal offenses that he "committed or may have committed or taken part in" while in office precluded any indictment. A statement issued from San Clemente revealed his perspective and mood:

In accepting this pardon, I hope that his compassionate act will contribute to lifting the burden of Watergate from our country. . . .

Looking back on what is still in my mind a complex and confusing maze of events, decisions, pressures and personalities, one thing I can see clearly now is that I was wrong in not acting more decisively and more forthrightly in dealing with Watergate, particularly when it reached the stage of judicial proceedings and grew from a political scandal into a national tragedy.

No words can describe the depth of my regret and pain at the anguish my mistakes over Watergate have caused the nation and the presidency—a nation I so deeply love and an institution I so greatly respect.

I know many fair-minded people believe that my motivations and action in the Watergate affair were intentionally self-serving and illegal. I now understand how my own mistakes and misjudgments have contributed to that belief and seemed to support it. This burden is the heaviest one of all to bear.

That the way I tried to deal with Watergate was the wrong way is a burden I shall bear for every day of the life that is left to me.

THE FIRST LADY

Thelma Catherine Ryan Nixon (better known as Patricia or Pat Nixon) has been active in politics since her husband's congressional campaigns in California. During his vice presidency, Mrs. Nixon accompanied her husband on diplomatic and goodwill tours; during his presidency, she accompanied him on his trip to the Soviet Union and on his historic visit to Communist China.

In her youth Mrs. Nixon worked at various jobs to earn money to attend the University of Southern California, from which she graduated with honors in 1937. She taught commercial subjects in Whittier, Calif., and during World War II, while her husband was in the Navy, she was employed as an economist in the Office of Price Administration in San Francisco.

As first lady, Mrs. Nixon has shown interest in educational programs and self-help projects and has traveled widely on a number of public missions.

GERALD RUDOLPH FORD
38th PRESIDENT

Born–July 14, 1913 (original name: Leslie Lynch King, Jr.)

Birthplace–Omaha, Neb.

College attended–University of Michigan, Ann Arbor

Date of Graduation–June 17, 1935, four-year course, B.A. degree

Postgraduate education–Yale University, New Haven, Conn.

Date of graduation–June 18, 1941, LL.B. degree

Religion–Episcopalian

Ancestry–English

Occupation–Lawyer, Representative, Vice President

Date and place of marriage–Oct. 15, 1948, Grand Rapids, Mich.

Age at marriage–35 years, 93 days

Political party–Republican

State represented–Michigan

Term of office–Aug. 9, 1974-

Administration–47th

Congresses–93rd, 94th

Age at inauguration–61 years, 26 days

PARENTS

Father–Leslie Lynch King

Born–July 25, 1882, Riverton, Wyo.

Married (1)–Dorothy Ayer Gardner, 1912

Married (2)–Margaret Atwood, Jan. 5, 1919, Yuma, Ariz.

Occupation–Wool trader

Died–Feb. 18, 1941, Tucson, Ariz.

Age at death–59 years, 208 days

Mother–Dorothy Ayer Gardner King Ford

Born–Feb. 28, 1892, Harvard, Ill.

Married (1)–Leslie Lynch King, 1912

Married (2)–Gerald Rudolff Ford, Feb. 1, 1916, Grand Rapids, Mich.

Died–September 17, 1967, Grand Rapids, Mich.

Age at death–75 years, 201 days

Second husband of mother–Gerald Rudolff Ford

Born–Dec. 9, 1889, Grand Rapids, Mich.

Occupation–Paint company owner

Died–Jan. 26, 1962, Grand Rapids, Mich.

Age at death–72 years, 48 days

Second wife of father–Margaret Atwood

Born–1891

Married (1)–Leslie Lynch King, Jan. 5, 1919, Yuma, Ariz.

Married (2)–Roy Mather, 1949

Gerald Rudolph Ford (originally named Leslie Lynch King, Jr.) was the only child of Leslie Lynch King and Dorothy Ayer Gardner King, whose marriage ended in divorce in 1915. She moved from Omaha to Grand Rapids and there married Gerald Rudolff Ford, who adopted her son and renamed him Gerald R. Ford, Jr. The younger Ford changed the spelling of his middle name to *Rudolph*.

Children of Gerald Rudolff Ford and Dorothy Ayer Gardner King Ford (half-brothers of Gerald Rudolph Ford)

Thomas Gardner Ford, b. July 15, 1918, Grand Rapids, Mich.; m.

For additional data see the end of this section and also specific subject headings in the index.

Janet Packer, Sept. 12, 1942

Richard Addison Ford, b. June 3, 1924, Grand Rapids, Mich.; m. Ellen Platte, June 12, 1947

James Francis Ford, b. Aug. 11, 1927, Grand Rapids, Mich.; m. Barbara Brunner, May 28, 1949

Children of Leslie Lynch King and Margaret Atwood King (half-sisters and half-brother of Gerald Rudolph Ford)

Marjorie King, b. 1921; m. Alton Werner

Leslie (Bud) Henry King, b. 1923

Patricia King, b. 1925

CHILDREN

Michael Gerald Ford, b. Mar. 14, 1950, Washington, D.C.; m. Gayle Ann Brumbaugh, July 5, 1974, Catonsville, Md.

John (Jack) Gardner Ford, b. Mar. 16, 1952, Washington, D.C.

Steven Meigs Ford, b. May 19,

1956, Washington, D.C.

Susan Elizabeth Ford, b. July 6, 1957, Washington, D.C.

MRS. GERALD RUDOLPH FORD

Name–Elizabeth (Betty) Bloomer Warren Ford

Date of birth–Apr. 8, 1918

Birthplace–Chicago, Ill.

Age at marriage (to Gerald Rudolph Ford, Oct. 15, 1948)–30 years, 190 days

Children–3 sons, 1 daughter

Mother–Hortense Nehr Bloomer

Father–William Stephenson Bloomer

His occupation–Machinery salesman

Years younger than the President–4 years, 278 days

Elizabeth Bloomer's first marriage was to William C. Warren in 1942. They were divorced on September 22, 1947.

CABINET

August 9, 1974-

State–Henry Alfred Kissinger, Mass., continued from preceding administration

Treasury–William Edward Simon, N.J., continued from preceding administration

Defense–James Rodney Schlesinger, Va., continued from preceding administration; Donald Rumsfield, Ill., Nov. 19, 1975

Attorney General–William Bart Saxbe, Ohio, continued from preceding administration; Edward Hirsch Levi, Ill., Feb. 7, 1975

Interior–Rogers Clark Ballard Morton, Jr., Md., continued from preceding administration; Stanley Knapp Hathaway, Wyo., June 13, 1975; Thomas Kleppe, N.D., Oct. 17, 1975

Agriculture–Earl Lauer Butz, Ind., continued from preceding administration

Commerce–Frederick Baily Dent, S.C., continued from preceding administration; Rogers Clark Ballard Morton, Jr., Md., May 1, 1975; Elliott Lee Richardson, Mass., confirmed Dec. 1975

Labor–Peter Joseph Brennan, N.Y., continued from preceding administration; John Thomas Dunlop, Mass., Mar. 18, 1975

Health, Education, and Welfare–Caspar Willard Weinberger, Calif., continued from preceding administration; Forrest David Mathews, Ala., Aug. 8, 1975

Housing and Urban Development–James Thomas Lynn, Ohio, continued from preceding administration; Carla Anderson Hills, Calif., Mar. 10, 1975

Transportation–Claude Stout Brinegar, Calif., continued from preceding administration; William Thaddeus Coleman, Jr., Pa., Mar. 7, 1975

NINETY-THIRD CONGRESS

January 3, 1973-January 3, 1975

First session–Jan. 3, 1973-Dec. 22, 1973
Second session–Jan. 21, 1974-Dec. 20, 1974
Vice President–Vice President Ford succeeded to the presidency on the resignation of President Nixon, Aug. 9, 1974; Nelson Aldrich Rockefeller, N.Y., sworn in Dec. 19, 1974
President pro tempore of the Senate–James Oliver Eastland, Miss.
Secretary of the Senate–Francis Ralph Valeo, N.Y.
Speaker of the House–Carl Bert Albert, Okla.
Clerk of the House–William Pat Jennings, Va.

NINETY-FOURTH CONGRESS

January 3, 1975-January 3, 1977

First session–Jan. 14, 1975-
Vice President–Nelson Aldrich Rockefeller, N.Y.
President pro tempore of the Senate–James Oliver Eastland, Miss.
Secretary of the Senate–Francis Ralph Valeo, N.Y.
Speaker of the House–Carl Bert Albert, Okla.
Clerk of the House–William Pat Jennings, Va.

ADMINISTRATION — IMPORTANT DATES

Aug. 12, 1974, President addressed Congress, calling for measures to fight inflation, "public enemy number one"

Aug. 14, 1974, forty-year ban on private gold transactions lifted

Aug. 20, 1974, House of Representatives accepted judiciary Committee's impeachment report (action would have initiated impeachment proceedings and trial had President Nixon not resigned)

Aug. 21, 1974, $25.2 billion education bill enacted, placing limitations on busing

Aug. 24, 1974, Council of Wage and Price Stability established

Sept. 2, 1974, federal standards for private pension plans adopted

Sept. 4, 1974, diplomatic relations established with East Germany

Sept. 8, 1974, President granted unconditional pardon to former President Nixon

Sept. 16, 1974, President offered plan granting conditional amnesty to draft evaders and military deserters

Sept. 27-28, 1974, President held national economic conference, renewing commitment to fight inflation and recession

Sept. 30-Oct. 4, 1974, international conference on oil-price crisis held in Washington

Oct. 1, 1974, Watergate cover-up trial of seven former presidential aides began

Oct. 8, 1974, President, in televised address, outlined anti-inflation tax program, proposing temporary 5 per cent surcharge on corporate and upper-level incomes, small reduction of taxes on lower-level incomes, investment tax credit, and liberalization of capital gains tax

Oct. 15, 1974, campaign reform legislation enacted, providing for public funding of presidential campaigns

Oct. 17, 1974, compromise legislation on military aid to Turkey passed by Congress

Oct. 19, 1974, limited Soviet grain purchases authorized

Oct. 29, 1974, federal savings insurance limit increased from $20,000 to $40,000

Nov. 1974, mass cutbacks and layoffs announced by automobile manufacturers

Nov. 4, 1974, Watergate prosecutors released document in which defendant E. Howard Hunt refuted contention that burglars had been given money solely for humanitarian reasons

Nov. 5, 1974, Democratic landslide in congressional elections

Nov. 19, 1974, President conferred in Tokyo with prime minister and emperor of Japan (first incumbent President to visit Japan and first to visit a foreign country without a Vice President in office)

Nov. 20, 1974, Department of Justice filed civil antitrust suit against American Telephone and Telegraph Corporation

Nov. 21, 1974, $11.8 billion mass transit bill enacted

Nov. 23-24, 1974, President Ford and Soviet leader Leonid Brezhnev conferred in Vladivostok on nuclear weapons agreement

Dec. 15-16, 1974, President Ford and French President Valéry Giscard d'Estaing met on island of Martinique to discuss energy and gold policies

Dec. 19, 1974, Nelson Aldrich Rockefeller confirmed and sworn in as Vice President

Dec. 20, 1974, Congress passed foreign trade bill with Soviet emigration provisions despite Soviet rejection of conditions

Jan. 1, 1975, John N. Mitchell, H. R. Haldeman, John D. Ehrlichman, and Robert C. Mardian convicted in Watergate cover-up trial; Kenneth W. Parkinson acquitted

Jan. 4, 1975, President announced establishment of commission to investigate charges of illegal domestic surveillance by the CIA

Jan 15, 1975, President's State of the Union address proposed economic and energy-conservation measures, including income-tax cuts and increased taxes on crude oil

Jan. 16, 1975, Department of Commerce reported steep drop in gross national product and continuing inflation

Jan. 20, 1975, President appointed twenty-five members to American Revolutionary Bicentennial Advisory Council

Jan. 23, 1975, import fee on petroleum increased by one dollar per barrel

Jan. 28, 1975, President requested $522 million in aid for South Vietnam as military situation worsened

Feb. 3, 1975, President submitted $349.4 billion federal budget, predicting slow recovery from serious recession (11.3 per cent inflation and 8.1 per cent unemployment)

Feb. 12, 1975) U.S. military aid to Cambodia doubled as Communist rebels intensified attacks

Mar. 1975, military situation in Cambodia and South Vietnam rapidly deteriorated

Mar. 7, 1975, Senate adopted new filibuster rule, changing requirements for cloture from two-thirds to three-fifths vote

Mar. 9, 1975, Alaskan oil pipeline construction started

Mar. 17, 1975, Supreme Court ruled that federal government has exclusive rights to oil and gas resources on continental shelf beyond the three-mile limit

Mar. 19, 1975, disclosure of multimillion-dollar CIA-backed operation to recover nuclear missiles from Soviet submarine lost in Pacific Ocean

Mar. 23, 1975, breakdown of Arab-Israeli negotiations led by Secretary of State Kissinger

Mar. 29, 1975, President signed $22.8 billion tax-cut and tax-rebate legislation

Apr. 3, 1975, start of airlift of Vietnamese children to adoptive parents in the United States

Apr. 10, 1975, President appealed to Congress for military and humanitarian aid to South Vietnam as thousands of refugees fled areas lost by Saigon

Apr. 16, 1975, Cambodian government surrendered to Communist rebel forces

Apr. 17, 1975, former Secretary of the Treasury Connally acquitted in milk-price bribery trial

Apr. 19, 1975, ceremonies honoring bicentennial anniversary of battles of Concord and Lexington

Apr. 21, 1975, President Nguyen Van Thieu of South Vietnam resigned

Apr. 24, 1975, evacuation of thousands of South Vietnamese to Guam; tentative congressional agreement on evacuation and humanitarian aid, but not military aid

Apr. 27, 1975, Saigon shelled and imperiled by approaching Communist forces; President Ford ordered helicopter evacuation of remaining Americans

Apr. 29, 1975, U.S. involvement in South Vietnam ended with evacuation of 1,000 Americans and 5,500 South Vietnamese

Apr. 30, 1975, South Vietnam government announced unconditional surrender to the Vietcong

IMPORTANT DATES IN HIS LIFE

June 1931, graduated from South High School, Grand Rapids, Mich.

1932-1933, member of University of Michigan's national championship football teams

1934, voted most valuable player

1935-1940, assistant varsity football coach, Yale University

July 1936, worked as ranger in Yellowstone National Park

June 7, 1941, admitted to Michigan bar; practiced in Grand Rapids

June 18, 1941, graduated from Yale Law School, LL.B. degree

Apr. 20, 1942, enlisted as ensign in U.S. Naval Reserve

Jan. 1946, discharged as lieutenant commander; resumed law practice in Grand Rapids

Sept. 14, 1948, won Republican nomination for U.S. House of Representatives, defeating four-term incumbent in primary

Nov. 2, 1948, elected to Congress

Jan. 3, 1949-Dec. 6, 1973, served in U.S. House of Representatives (Fifth District, Michigan)

1965, co-author (with John R. Stiles) of *Portrait of the Assassin* (Lee Harvey Oswald)

Jan. 4, 1965, elected House minority leader

Dec. 6, 1973, confirmed as Vice President (nominated by President Nixon, under provisions of the Twenty-fifth Amendment, after resignation of Vice President Agnew)

Aug. 9, 1974, succeeded to presidency following resignation of President Nixon

GERALD RUDOLPH FORD

____was the first President to succeed to the presidency under the Twenty-fifth Amendment.

____was the first President to succeed to the presidency as a result of the resignation of his predecessor.

____was the first President to pardon his predecessor for possible offenses against the United States.

____was the ninth President to succeed to the presidency without being elected to the office.

FORD'S VICE PRESIDENT

Vice President–Nelson Aldrich Rockefeller (41st V.P.)

Date of birth–July 8, 1908

Birthplace–Bar Harbor, Me.

Political party–Republican

State represented–New York

Term of office–December 19, 1974-

Age at inauguration–66 years, 165 days

Additional data on Rockefeller

June 17, 1930, graduated from Dartmouth College, A.B., cum laude

1931-1938, director, Rockefeller Center, Inc. (president, 1938-1945, 1948-1951; chairman, 1945-1953, 1956-1958)

1939-1941, 1946-1953, president, Museum of Modern Art

Aug. 1940, appointed coordinator of Inter-American Affairs by President Roosevelt

1944-1945, assistant secretary of state for American republic affairs

Nov. 1950, appointed chairman of Development Advisory Board, Point IV program, by President Truman

Nov. 1952, appointed chairman of President's Advisory Committee on Government Organization by President Eisenhower

1953-1954, under secretary, Department of Health, Education, and Welfare

1954, founded Museum of Primitive Art

1954-1955, special assistant to the President for foreign affairs

1956-1958, chairman, Rockefeller Brothers Fund special studies project, "America at Mid Century"

1956-1959, headed studies of New York State constitution

1958-1973, governor of New York (resigned Dec. 18, 1973)

1972-1974, chairman, National Commission on Water Quality

1973-1974, chairman, Commission on Critical Choices for America

Aug. 20, 1974, nominated as Vice President by President Ford under provisions of the Twenty-fifth Amendment

ADDITIONAL DATA ON FORD

OATH OF OFFICE

Gerald Rudolph Ford was sworn in as the thirty-eighth President on August 9, 1974, at 12:03 P.M. The oath of office was administered by Chief Justice Warren E. Burger in the East Room of the White House. In his inaugural comments to a nation saddened and stunned by the tumultuous events of the preceding months, he took note of the unprecedented circumstances under which he had succeeded to the presidency:

The oath I have taken is the same oath that was taken by George Washington and by every President under the Constitution. But I assume the presidency under extraordinary circumstances, never before experienced by Americans. This is an hour of history that troubles our minds and hurts our hearts.

Therefore, I feel it is my first duty to make an unprecedented compact with my countrymen. Not an inaugural speech, not a fireside chat, not a campaign speech, just a little straight talk among friends. And I intend it to be the first of many.

I am acutely aware that you have not elected me as your President by your ballots. So I ask you to confirm me as your President with your prayers. And I hope that such prayers will also be the first of many.

If you have not chosen me by secret ballot, neither have I gained office by any secret promises. I have not campaigned either for the presidency or the vice presidency. I have not subscribed to any partisan platform, I am indebted to no man and only to one woman—my dear wife—as I begin the most difficult job in the world.

I have not sought this enormous responsibility, but I will not shirk it. . . .

My fellow Americans, our long national nightmare is over.

Our Constitution works; our great republic is a government of laws and not of men.

THE NIXON PARDON

On Sunday morning, September 8, 1974, President Ford startled the nation with his announcement that he had decided to grant his predecessor "a full, free and absolute pardon," explaining his decision as an act of conscience to promote the healing of a troubled nation and to spare the former President and his family further suffering. Public response to the pardon was heated, with many outraged by the President's action and much talk of secret "deals." The pardon was irrevocable, however, and the protest abated. The text of the proclamation concludes:

Now, therefore, I, Gerald R. Ford, President of the United States, pursuant to the pardon power conferred upon me by Article II, Section 2, of the Constitution, have granted and by these presents do grant a full, free and absolute pardon unto Richard Nixon for all offenses against the United States which he, Richard Nixon, has committed or may have committed or taken part in during the period from January 20, 1969, through August 9, 1974.

In witness whereof, I have hereunto set my hand this 8th day of September in the year of Our Lord Nineteen Hundred Seventy-four, and of the independence of the United States of America the 199th.

FIRST PRESIDENTIAL TEAM IN OFFICE WITHOUT NATIONAL ELECTION

The first President and Vice President to serve together without being elected to their respective offices were President Gerald Rudolph Ford and Vice President Nelson Aldrich Rockefeller. Both reached office under the provisions of the Twenty-fifth Amendment.

Ford was nominated Vice President by President Nixon on October 12, 1973, two days after the resignation of Spiro Theodore Agnew; on December 6, 1973, Ford was confirmed and sworn in. With the resignation of Nixon on August 9, 1974, Ford succeeded to the presidency.

Rockefeller was nominated Vice President by President Ford on August 20, 1974; on December 19, 1974, after protracted hearings, he was confirmed and sworn in.

Nixon served 56 days without a Vice President; Ford served 132 days without a Vice President.

COMMISSION ESTABLISHED TO INVESTIGATE CIA ACTIVITIES

On January 4, 1975, President Ford announced the establishment of a "blue ribbon" panel to investigate repeated charges of illegal domestic espionage by the Central Intelligence Agency. In an earlier statement, on December 22, 1974, he had declared that he would not tolerate domestic operations by the CIA in violation of its charter.

The President, on January 5, 1975, named Vice President Rockefeller to head the panel and appointed seven other members: John Thomas Connor, a corporate executive and former Secretary of Commerce;

Clarence Douglas Dillon, an investment banker and former Secretary of the Treasury; Erwin Nathaniel Griswold, former Solicitor General of the United States and former dean of Harvard Law School; Joseph Lane Kirkland, secretary-treasurer of the AFL-CIO; Lyman Louis Lemnitzer, retired army general and once chairman of the Joint Chiefs of Staff; Ronald Reagan, former governor of California; and Edgar Finley Shannon, former president of the University of Virginia.

PRESIDENT'S STATEMENT ON VIETNAM EVACUATION

With the military collapse of the Thieu regime in April 1975, President Ford ordered the evacuation of all remaining American personnel in South Vietnam. Reporting on his actions to the nation on April 29, he declared:

During the past week, I had ordered the reduction of American personnel in the United States mission in Saigon to levels that could be quickly evacuated during emergency, while enabling that mission to continue to fulfill its duties.

During the day on Monday, Washington time, the airport at Saigon came under persistent rocket as well as artillery fire and was effectively closed. The military situation in the area deteriorated rapidly.

I therefore ordered the evacuation of all personnel remaining in South Vietnam. The evacuation has been completed. . . .

This action closes a chapter in the American experience. I ask all Americans to close ranks, to avoid recrimination about the past, to look ahead to the many goals we share and to work together on the great tasks that remain to be accomplished.

PRESIDENT AND STEPFATHER BOTH THIRTY-THIRD-DEGREE MASONS

The thirty-third and highest degree of the Ancient Accepted Scottish Rite of Freemasonry was conferred on Gerald Rudolff Ford, Sr., on September 30, 1949. The same honorary membership was conferred on Gerald Rudolph Ford, his stepson, on September 26, 1962 (in the Supreme Council for the Northern Masonic Jurisdiction of the United States of America).

THE FIRST LADY

Elizabeth (Betty) Bloomer Warren Ford was suddenly and dramatically thrust into her position as First Lady in August 1974, just eight months after her husband had assumed office as Vice President.

Before her marriage to Gerald Ford, she had pursued a number of activities. A teenage model at a store in Grand Rapids, she was later a dance instructor and a student of Martha Graham. After attending the Bennington School of the Dance in Vermont, she moved to New York City to work with the Graham dance group; then, back in Grand Rapids, she became a fashion coordinator and a volunteer teacher of dance to underprivileged children.

As the wife of a member of Congress, Mrs. Ford took no direct part in politics, concentrating her efforts on providing a strong and devoted family background for her husband and children. As the President's wife, she became more active; one public stand was her endorsement of the Equal Rights Amendment.

Part II
COMPARATIVE DATA
Begins on Page 474

THE PRESIDENTS
CHRONOLOGY, FAMILY HISTORY, AND NAMES

PRESIDENTS OF THE UNITED STATES—YEARS SERVED

1. George Washington–1789-1797
2. John Adams–1797-1801
3. Thomas Jefferson–1801-1809
4. James Madison–1809-1817
5. James Monroe–1817-1825
6. John Quincy Adams–1825-1829
7. Andrew Jackson–1829-1837
8. Martin Van Buren–1837-1841
9. William Henry Harrison–1841
10. John Tyler–1841-1845
11. James Knox Polk–1845-1849
12. Zachary Taylor–1849-1850
13. Millard Fillmore–1850-1853
14. Franklin Pierce–1853-1857
15. James Buchanan–1857-1861
16. Abraham Lincoln–1861-1865
17. Andrew Johnson–1865-1869
18. Ulysses Simpson Grant–1869-1877
19. Rutherford Birchard Hayes–1877-1881
20. James Abram Garfield–1881
21. Chester Alan Arthur–1881-1885
22. Grover Cleveland–1885-1889
23. Benjamin Harrison–1889-1893
24. Grover Cleveland–1893-1897
25. William McKinley–1897-1901
26. Theodore Roosevelt–1901-1909
27. William Howard Taft–1909-1913
28. Woodrow Wilson–1913-1921
29. Warren Gamaliel Harding–1921-1923
30. Calvin Coolidge–1923-1929
31. Herbert Clark Hoover–1929-1933
32. Franklin Delano Roosevelt–1933-1945
33. Harry S. Truman–1945-1953
34. Dwight David Eisenhower–1953-1961
35. John Fitzgerald Kennedy–1961-1963
36. Lyndon Baines Johnson–1963-1969
37. Richard Milhous Nixon–1969-1974

BIRTH AND DEATH DATES

Washington–1732-1799
J. Adams–1735-1826
Jefferson–1743-1826
Madison–1751-1836
Monroe–1758-1831

J. Q. Adams–1767-1848
Jackson–1767-1845
Van Buren–1782-1862
W. H. Harrison–1773-1841
Tyler–1790-1862
Polk–1795-1849
Taylor–1784-1850
Fillmore–1800-1874
Pierce–1804-1869
Buchanan–1791-1868
Lincoln–1809-1865
A. Johnson–1808-1875
Grant–1822-1885
Hayes–1822-1893
Garfield–1831-1881
Arthur–1830-1886
Cleveland–1837-1908
B. Harrison–1833-1901
McKinley–1843-1901
T. Roosevelt–1858-1919
Taft–1857-1930
Wilson–1856-1924
Harding–1865-1923
Coolidge–1872-1933
Hoover–1874-1964
F.D. Roosevelt–1882-1945
Truman–1884-1972
Eisenhower–1890-1969
Kennedy–1917-1963
L. B. Johnson–1908-1973
Nixon–1913-

STATES REPRESENTED AND PARTY AFFILIATIONS

Washington–Virginia, Federalist
J. Adams–Massachusetts, Federalist
Jefferson–Virginia, Democratic-Republican
Madison–Virginia, Democratic-Republican
Monroe–Virginia, Democratic-Republican
J. Q. Adams–Massachusetts, Democratic-Republican
Jackson–Tennessee, Democrat (Democratic-Republican)
Van Buren–New York, Democrat (Democratic-Republican)
W. H. Harrison–Ohio, Whig
Tyler–Virginia, Whig
Polk–Tennessee, Democrat
Taylor–Louisiana, Whig
Fillmore–New York, Whig
Pierce–New Hampshire, Democrat
Buchanan–Pennsylvania, Democrat
Lincoln–Illinois, Republican

A. Johnson–Tennessee, Democrat (but nominated and elected with Lincoln on Republican ticket)
Grant–Illinois, Republican
Hayes–Ohio, Republican
Garfield–Ohio, Republican
Arthur–New York, Republican
Cleveland–New York, Democrat
B. Harrison–Indiana, Republican
McKinley–Ohio, Republican
T. Roosevelt–New York, Republican
Taft–Ohio, Republican
Wilson–New Jersey, Democrat
Harding–Ohio, Republican
Coolidge–Massachusetts, Republican
Hoover–California, Republican
F. D. Roosevelt–New York, Democrat
Truman–Missouri, Democrat
Eisenhower–New York, Republican
Kennedy–Massachusetts, Democrat
L. B. Johnson–Texas, Democrat
Nixon–New York, Republican

DATES AND PLACES OF BIRTH

Washington–Feb. 22, 1732, Westmoreland County, Va.
J. Adams–Oct. 30, 1735, Braintree (now Quincy) Mass.
Jefferson–Apr. 13, 1743, Shadwell, Va.
Madison–Mar. 16, 1751, Port Conway, Va.
Monroe–Apr. 28, 1758, Westmoreland County, Va.
J. Q. Adams–July 11, 1767, Braintree, Mass.
Jackson–Mar. 15, 1767, Waxhaw, S.C.
Van Buren–Dec. 5, 1782, Kinderhook, N.Y.
W. H. Harrison–Feb. 9, 1773, Berkeley, Va.
Tyler–Mar. 29, 1790, Greenway, Va.
Polk–Nov. 2, 1795, Mecklenburg County, N.C.
Taylor–Nov. 24, 1784, Orange County, Va.
Fillmore–Jan. 7, 1800, Cayuga County, N.Y.
Pierce–Nov. 23, 1804, Hillsborough, N.H.
Buchanan–Apr. 23, 1791, Cove Gap, Pa.
Lincoln–Feb. 12, 1809, Hardin County, Ky.
A. Johnson–Dec. 29, 1808, Raleigh, N.C.
Grant–Apr. 27, 1822, Point Pleasant, Ohio
Hayes–Oct. 4, 1822, Delaware, Ohio
Garfield–Nov. 19, 1831, Orange, Ohio
Arthur–Oct. 5, 1830, Fairfield, Vt.
Cleveland–Mar. 18, 1837, Caldwell, N.J.
B. Harrison–Aug. 20, 1833, North Bend, Ohio
McKinley–Jan. 29, 1843, Niles, Ohio
T. Roosevelt–Oct. 27, 1858, New York, N.Y.
Taft–Sept. 15, 1857, Cincinnati, Ohio

Wilson–Dec. 28, 1856, Staunton, Va.
Harding–Nov. 2, 1865, Corsica, Ohio
Coolidge–July 4, 1872, Plymouth, Vt.
Hoover–Aug. 10, 1874, West Branch, Iowa
F. D. Roosevelt–Jan. 30, 1882, Hyde Park, N.Y.
Truman–May 8, 1884, Lamar, Mo.
Eisenhower–Oct. 14, 1890, Denison, Tex.
Kennedy–May 29, 1917, Brookline, Mass.
L. B. Johnson–Aug. 27, 1908, near Stonewall, Tex.
Nixon–Jan. 9, 1913, Yorba Linda, Calif.

Two Presidents were born in 1767, Jackson (March 15) and John Quincy Adams (July 11). Two also were born in 1822, Grant (April 27) and Hayes (October 4).

Two Presidents were born on November 2, Polk in 1795 and Harding in 1865.

No Presidents were born in June.

The first President born outside the original thirteen states was Lincoln.

The first President born west of the Mississippi River was Hoover.

The President born farthest north was Arthur, born in Fairfield, Vt.

The Presidents born farthest east were John Adams and John Quincy Adams, born in Braintree (now Quincy), Mass.

The President born farthest south was Lyndon Baines Johnson, born near Stonewall, Tex.

The President born farthest west was Richard Milhous Nixon, born in Yorba Linda, Calif.

Only two Presidents were born in large cities: Taft, born in Cincinnati, Ohio, and Theodore Roosevelt, born in New York City.

PRESIDENTS BORN BRITISH SUBJECTS

Eight Presidents were British subjects even though they were born in North America: Washington, John Adams, Jefferson, Madison, Monroe, John Quincy Adams, Jackson, and William Henry Harrison. The first President not born a British subject was Van Buren.

THE PRESIDENTS OF CHARLES CITY COUNTY

Charles City County, Va., is noted as the birthplace of two men who were simultaneously elected President and Vice President of the United States. They were William Henry Harrison and John Tyler, elected November 3, 1840, and inaugurated March 3, 1841.

The careers of the two men who became the ninth and the tenth Presidents had much in common. Both had been members of the Virginia legislature and both had been state governors. Harrison of Indiana and Tyler of Virginia. Each had served in the House of Representatives and the Senate.

THREE SUCCESSIVE OHIO PRESIDENTS

The 18th, 19th, and 20th Presidents—Grant, Hayes, and Garfield—were Republicans, born in Ohio, and generals in the Union Army.

FIVE OF LAST SEVEN PRESIDENTS BORN WEST OF THE MISSISSIPPI RIVER

Herbert Clark Hoover, the 31st President, born August 10, 1874, in West Branch, Iowa, was the first President born west of the Mississippi River. Harry S. Truman, the 33rd President, was born May 8, 1884, in Lamar, Mo.; Dwight David Eisenhower, the 34th President, was born October 14, 1890, in Denison, Tex.; Lyndon Baines Johnson, the 36th President, was born August 27, 1908, near Stonewall, Tex.; and Richard Milhous Nixon, the 37th President was born Jan. 9, 1913, in Yorba Linda, Calif.

BIRTHDAYS

January

    7, 1800, Fillmore
    9, 1913, Nixon
  29, 1843, McKinley
  30, 1882, F.D. Roosevelt

February

    9, 1773, W. H. Harrison
  12, 1809, Lincoln
  22, 1732, Washington

March

  15, 1767, Jackson
  16, 1751, Madison
  18, 1837, Cleveland
  29, 1790, Tyler

April

  13, 1743, Jefferson
  23, 1791, Buchanan
  27, 1822, Grant
  28, 1758, Monroe

May

    8, 1884, Truman
  29, 1917, Kennedy

July

    4, 1872, Coolidge
  11, 1767, J. Q. Adams

August

  10, 1874, Hoover
  20, 1833, B. Harrison
  27, 1908, L. B. Johnson

September

  15, 1857, Taft

October

4, 1822, Hayes
5, 1830, Arthur
14, 1890, Eisenhower
27, 1858, T. Roosevelt
30, 1735, J. Adams

November

2, 1795, Polk
2, 1865, Harding
19, 1831, Garfield
23, 1804, Pierce
24, 1784, Taylor

December

5, 1782, Van Buren
28, 1856, Wilson
29, 1808, A. Johnson

BIRTHPLACES

Virginia (8)

Washington
Jefferson
Madison
Monroe
W. H. Harrison
Tyler
Taylor
Wilson

Ohio (7)

Grant
Hayes
Garfield
B. Harrison
McKinley
Taft
Harding

New York (4)

Van Buren
Fillmore
T. Roosevelt
F. D. Roosevelt

Massachusetts (3)

J. Adams
J. Q. Adams
Kennedy

Bush, Geo. H. W. #41

North Carolina (2)
Polk,
A. Johnson

Texas (2)
Eisenhower
L. B. Johnson

Vermont (2)
Arthur
Coolidge

California (1) *2*
Nixon *Reagan*

Iowa (1)
Hoover

Kentucky (1)
Lincoln

Michigan
Ford

Missouri (1)
Truman

New Hampshire (1)
Pierce

Georgia
Carter

New Jersey (1)
Cleveland

Pennsylvania (1)
Buchanan

California
Reagan

South Carolina (1)
Jackson

ANCESTRY
Washington–English
J. Adams–English
Jefferson–Welsh
Madison–English
Monroe–Scotch
J. Q. Adams–English
Jackson–Scotch-Irish
Van Buren–Dutch
W. H. Harrison–English
Tyler–English
Polk–Scotch-Irish
Taylor–English
Fillmore–English
Pierce–English
Buchanan–Scotch-Irish

Arkansas
Clinton

Bush .GeoW. II 43

Lincoln–English
A. Johnson–English
Grant–English-Scotch
Hayes–Scotch
Garfield–English
Arthur–Scotch-Irish
Cleveland–English-Irish
B. Harrison–English
McKinley–Scotch-Irish
T. Roosevelt–Dutch
Taft–English
Wilson–Scotch-Irish
Harding–English-Scotch-Irish
Coolidge–English
Hoover–Swiss-German
F. D. Roosevelt–Dutch
Truman–English-Scotch-Irish
Eisenhower–Swiss-German
Kennedy–Irish
L. B. Johnson–English
Nixon–Scotch-Irish

ANCESTRY (ARRANGED BY NATIONAL ORIGINS)

Dutch

Van Buren
T. Roosevelt
F. D. Roosevelt

English

Washington
J. Adams
Madison
J. Q. Adams
W. H. Harrison
Tyler
Taylor
Fillmore
Pierce
Lincoln
A. Johnson
Garfield
B. Harrison
Taft
Coolidge
L. B. Johnson

English-Irish

Cleveland

English-Scotch

Grant

English-Scotch-Irish

Harding
Truman

Irish

Kennedy

Scotch

Monroe
Hayes

Scotch-Irish

Jackson
Polk
Buchanan
Arthur
McKinley
Wilson
Nixon

Swiss-German

Hoover
Eisenhower

Welsh

Jefferson

PRESIDENTS WHO WERE RELATED

John Adams and John Quincy Adams, father and son, were the most closely related Presidents.

William Henry Harrison was the grandfather of Benjamin Harrison.

James Madison and Zachary Taylor were second cousins.

Franklin Delano Roosevelt, genealogists have shown, was remotely related to eleven former Presidents, five by blood and six by marriage. He was a fifth cousin of Theodore Roosevelt.

NAMES OF PRESIDENTS' PARENTS

Given names of fathers and full maiden names of mothers are listed below:

Washington

Augustine and Mary Ball

J. Adams

John and Susanna Boylston

Jefferson

Peter and Jane Randolph

Madison
James and Eleanor ("Nellie") Rose Conway

Monroe
Spence and Elizabeth Jones

J. Q. Adams
John and Abigail Smith

Jackson
Andrew and Elizabeth Hutchinson

Van Buren
Abraham and Maria Goes Hose Van Alen

W. H. Harrison
Benjamin and Elizabeth Bassett

Tyler
John and Mary Armistead

Polk
Samuel and Jane Knox

Taylor
Richard and Sarah Strother

Fillmore
Nathaniel and Phoebe Millard

Pierce
Benjamin and Anna Kendrick

Buchanan
James and Elizabeth Speer

Lincoln
Thomas and Nancy Hanks

A. Johnson
Jacob and Mary McDonough

Grant
Jesse Root and Hannah Simpson

Hayes
Rutherford and Sophia Birchard

Garfield
Abram and Eliza Ballou

Arthur
William and Malvina Stone

Cleveland
Richard Falley and Anne Neal

B. Harrison
John Scott and Elizabeth Ramsey Irwin

McKinley
William and Nancy Campbell Allison

T. Roosevelt
Theodore and Martha Bulloch

Taft
Alphonso and Louise Maria Torrey

Wilson
Joseph Ruggles and Jessie Woodrow

Harding
George Tryon and Phoebe Dickerson

Coolidge
John Calvin and Victoria Josephine Moor

Hoover
Jesse Clark and Hulda Minthorn

F. D. Roosevelt
James and Sara Delano

Truman
John Anderson and Martha Ellen Young

Eisenhower
David Jacob and Ida Elizabeth Stover

Kennedy
Joseph Patrick and Rose Fitzgerald

L. B. Johnson
Sam Ealy and Rebekah Baines

Nixon
Francis Anthony and Hannah Milhous

OCCUPATIONS OF PRESIDENTS' FATHERS

At various times the fathers of the Presidents were engaged in different occupations—in some cases two or more at the same time.

Washington
Augustine Washington, farmer, planter

J. Adams
John Adams, farmer, shoemaker (cordwainer)

Jefferson
Peter Jefferson, farmer, planter, surveyor, professor

Madison
James Madison, farmer, landowner, vestryman, justice of the peace

Monroe
Spence Monroe, farmer, circuit judge

J. Q. Adams
John Adams, statesman (President of the United States), farmer, lawyer

Jackson
Andrew Jackson, farmer, linen weaver

Van Buren
Abraham Van Buren, farmer, innkeeper, captain in the militia

W. H. Harrison
Benjamin Harrison, statesman

Tyler
John Tyler, lawyer, judge, governor

Polk
Samuel Polk, farmer, planter

Taylor
Richard Taylor, farmer, soldier

Fillmore
Nathaniel Fillmore, farmer, magistrate

Pierce
Benjamin Pierce, farmer, soldier, tavern owner, governor

Buchanan
James Buchanan, farmer, merchant

Lincoln
Thomas Lincoln, farmer, carpenter, wheelwright

A. Johnson
Jacob Johnson, sexton, porter, constable

Grant
Jesse Root Grant, leather tanner, factory manager

Hayes
Rutherford Hayes, storekeeper

Garfield
Abram Garfield, farmer, canal constructor

Arthur
William Arthur, Baptist minister

Cleveland
Richard Falley Cleveland, Congregational minister

B. Harrison
John Scott Harrison, farmer, congressman

McKinley
William McKinley, iron manufacturer

T. Roosevelt
Theodore Roosevelt, glass importer, merchant

Taft
Alphonso Taft, lawyer, U.S. Secretary of War

Wilson
Joseph Ruggles Wilson, Presbyterian minister

Harding
George Tryon Harding, physician

Coolidge
John Calvin Coolidge, farmer, storekeeper, notary public

Hoover
Jesse Clark Hoover, farm implement business, blacksmith

F. D. Roosevelt
James Roosevelt, lawyer, financier, railroad vice president

Truman
John Anderson Truman, farmer, livestock dealer

Eisenhower
David Jacob Eisenhower, mechanic, gas company manager

Kennedy
Joseph Patrick Kennedy, banker, financier, real estate executive,
United States ambassador to Great Britain

L. B. Johnson
Sam Ealy Johnson, Jr., state legislator, school teacher, rancher

Nixon
Francis Anthony Nixon, citrus worker, grocer and gasoline station
owner

Twenty of the thirty-six Presidents were sons of farmers or planters.
Eight of the fathers were members of the learned professions: four
lawyers, three clergymen, and one physician.
Nine of the fathers were salaried or engaged in their own business.

Only three Presidents were sons of statesmen of national prominence: William Henry Harrison, whose father was one of the signers of the Declaration of Independence; John Quincy Adams, whose father, a lawyer, had been a President of the United States; and John Fitzgerald Kennedy, whose father had served as ambassador to Great Britain. Benjamin Harrison's grandfather was W. H. Harrison, the ninth President.

THREE MINISTERS' SONS ELECTED TO THE PRESIDENCY

The fathers of Chester Alan Arthur, Grover Cleveland, and Woodrow Wilson were ministers. William Arthur was a Baptist clergymen; Richard Falley Cleveland was a Congregational clergyman; and Joseph Ruggles Wilson was a Presbyterian clergyman.

THREE GOVERNORS' SONS ELECTED TO THE PRESIDENCY

The fathers of three Presidents had served their respective states as governors.

William Henry Harrison's father, Benjamin Harrison, served as governor of Virginia from November 30, 1781, to November 30, 1784.

John Tyler's father, John Tyler, also served as governor of Virginia. He served from December 12, 1808, to January 15, 1811.

Franklin Pierce's father, Benjamin Pierce, served two terms as the constitutional executive of New Hampshire, 1827-1828 and 1829-1830.

NUMBER OF CHILDREN IN THE PRESIDENTS' FAMILIES

No President was an only child; most came from large families.

Nineteen Presidents came from families of 6 or more children:

Seven came from families of 10 or more children: Benjamin Harrison (13), Madison (12), Buchanan (11), Washington (10), Jefferson (10), Polk (10), and Taft (10).

Seven came from families of 9 children: Taylor, Fillmore, Pierce, Arthur, Cleveland, McKinley, and Kennedy.

Two came from families of 8 children: Tyler and Harding.

Two came from families of 7 children: William Henry Harrison and Eisenhower.

One came from a family of 6 children: Grant.

Seven Presidents came from families of 5 children: Monroe, John Quincy Adams, Van Buren, Hayes, Garfield, Lyndon Baines Johnson, and Nixon.

Two Presidents came from families of 4 children: Theodore Roosevelt and Wilson.

Five Presidents came from families of 3 children: John Adams, Jackson, Lincoln, Hoover, and Truman.

Three Presidents came from families of 2 children: Andrew Johnson, Coolidge, and Franklin Delano Roosevelt.

Summing up, the parents of the thirty-six Presidents had a total of 239 children.

POSITION IN FAMILY AND NUMBER OF BROTHERS AND SISTERS

Each of the following nine Presidents was not only the oldest child in the family but the oldest son: John Adams, Madison, Monroe, Polk, Grant, Harding, Coolidge, Truman, and Lyndon Baines Johnson.

Each of the following nine Presidents was the second child in the family: John Quincy Adams, Fillmore, Buchanan, Lincoln, and Theodore Roosevelt (each the oldest son); and Andrew Johnson, Hoover, Franklin Delano Roosevelt, Kennedy, and Nixon (each the second son).

Six Presidents occupied the position of third child in the family.

Six Presidents occupied the position of fifth child in the family.

One President occupied the position of sixth child in the family.

Four Presidents occupied the position of seventh child in the family.

Washington was the fourth son, the fifth child in a family of 10 (7 boys and 3 girls).

John Adams was the first son, the first child in a family of 3 boys.

Jefferson was the first son, the third child in a family of 10 (4 boys and 6 girls).

Madison was the first son, the first child in a family of 12 (8 boys and 4 girls).

Monroe was the first son, the first child in a family of 5 (4 boys and 1 girl).

John Quincy Adams was the first son, the second child in a family of 5 (3 boys and 2 girls).

Jackson was the third son, the third child in a family of 3 boys.

Van Buren was the second son, the third child in a family of 5 (4 boys and 1 girl).

William Henry Harrison was the third son, the seventh child in a family of 7 (3 boys and 4 girls).

Tyler was the second son, the sixth child in a family of 8 (3 boys and 5 girls).

Polk was the first son, the first child in a family of 10 (6 boys and 4 girls).

Taylor was the third son, the third child in a family of 9 (6 boys and 3 girls).

Fillmore was the first son, the second child in a family of 9 (6 boys and 3 girls).

Pierce was the first son, the second child in a family of 9 (5 boys and 4 girls).

Buchanan was the first son, the second child in a family of 11 (5 boys and 6 girls).

Lincoln was the first son, the second child in a family of 3 (2 boys and 1 girl).

Andrew Johnson was the second son, the third child in a family of 3 (2 boys and 1 girl).

Grant was the first son, the first child in a family of 6 (3 boys and 3 girls).

Hayes was the third son, the fifth child in a family of 5 (3 boys and 2 girls).

Garfield was the third son, the fifth child in a family of 5 (3 boys and 2 girls).

Arthur was the first son, the fifth child in a family of 9 (3 boys and 6 girls).

Cleveland was the third son, the fifth child in a family of 9 (4 boys and 5 girls).

Benjamin Harrison was the third son, the fifth child in a family of 13 (8 boys and 5 girls).

McKinley was the third son, the seventh child in a family of 9 (4 boys and 5 girls).

Theodore Roosevelt was the first son, the second child in a family of 4 (2 boys and 2 girls).

Taft was the sixth son, the seventh child in a family of 10 (8 boys and 2 girls).

Wilson was the first son, the third child in a family of 4 (2 boys and 2 girls).

Harding was the first son, the first child in a family of 8 (3 boys and 5 girls).

Coolidge was the first son, the first child in a family of 2 (1 boy and 1 girl).

Hoover was the second son, the second child in a family of 3 (2 boys and 1 girl).

Franklin Delano Roosevelt was the second son, the second child in a family of 2 boys.

Truman was the first son, the first child in a family of 3 (2 girls and 1 boy).

Eisenhower was the third son, the third child in a family of 7 boys.

Kennedy was the second son, the second child in a family of 9 (4 boys and 5 girls).

Lyndon Baines Johnson was the first son, the first child in a family of 5 (2 boys and 3 girls).

Nixon was the second son, the second child in a family of 5 boys.

AGE OF PRESIDENTS AT DEATH OF FATHER AND DEATH OF MOTHER

In the following list the name of each President is followed by (1) his age when his father died and (2) his age when his mother died.

Washington–11 years, 49 days; 57 years, 184 days

J. Adams–25 years, 207 days; 61 years, 169 days

Jefferson–14 years, 126 days; 32 years, 352 days

Madison–49 years, 348 days; 77 years, 301 days

Monroe–about 16 years; about 68 years

J. Q. Adams–59 years, 358 days; 51 years, 109 days

Jackson–born posthumously; about 13 years

Van Buren–34 years, 124 days; 34 years, 73 days

W. H. Harrison–18 years, 74 days; about 19 years

Tyler–22 years, 283 days; about 7 years

Polk–32 years, 3 days; survived by mother

Taylor–41 years, 56 days; 38 years, 19 days
Fillmore–63 years, 80 days; 31 years, 115 days
Pierce–34 years, 129 days; about 34 years
Buchanan–30 years, 49 days; 42 years, 21 days
Lincoln–41 years, 339 days; 9 years, 235 days
A. Johnson–3 years, 6 days; 47 years, 46 days
Grant–51 years, 63 days; 61 years, 14 days
Hayes–born posthumously; 44 years, 26 days
Garfield–1 year, 170 days; survived by mother
Arthur–45 years, 22 days; 38 years, 103 days
Cleveland–16 years, 197 days; 45 years, 123 days
B. Harrison–44 years, 278 days; 16 years, 360 days
McKinley–49 years, 299 days; 54 years, 317 days
T. Roosevelt–19 years, 105 days; 25 years, 110 days
Taft–33 years, 248 days; 50 years, 84 days
Wilson–46 years, 24 days; 31 years, 108 days
Harding–survived by father; 44 years, 199 days
Coolidge–53 years, 257 days; 12 years, 253 days
Hoover–6 years, 124 days; 9 years, 196 days
F. D. Roosevelt–18 years, 312 days; 59 years, 220 days
Truman–30 years, 179 days; 63 years, 79 days
Eisenhower–51 years, 147 days; 55 years, 332 days
Kennedy–survived by father and mother
L. B. Johnson–29 years, 56 days; 50 years, 16 days
Nixon–43 years, 239 days; 54 years, 264 days

AGE OF PRESIDENTS AT DEATH OF MOTHER

Three Presidents were less than ten years of age when their mothers died.

Seven Presidents were under twenty-one when their mothers died.

Eighteen Presidents were over forty when their mothers died.

Thirteen Presidents were over fifty when their mothers died.

Four Presidents were over sixty when their mothers died.

Only three Presidents were survived by their mothers.

The following is a comparative list:

Tyler—7 years
Hoover—9 years, 196 days
Lincoln—9 years, 235 days
Coolidge—12 years, 253 days
Jackson—13 years
B. Harrison—16 years, 360 days
W. H. Harrison—19 years
T. Roosevelt—25 years, 110 days
Wilson—31 years, 108 days
Fillmore—31 years, 115 days
Jefferson—32 years, 352 days
Pierce—34 years
Van Buren—34 years, 73 days
Taylor—38 years, 19 days
Arthur—38 years, 103 days

Buchanan—42 years, 21 days
Hayes—44 years, 26 days
Harding—44 years, 199 days
Cleveland—45 years, 123 days
A. Johnson—47 years, 46 days
L. B. Johnson—50 years, 16 days
Taft—50 years, 84 days
J. Q. Adams. —51 years, 109 days
Nixon—54 years, 264 days
McKinley—54 years, 317 days
Eisenhower—55 years, 332 days
Washington—57 years, 184 days
F. D. Roosevelt—59 years, 220 days
Grant—61 years, 14 days
J. Adams—61 years, 169 days
Truman—63 years, 79 days
Monroe—68 years
Madison—77 years, 332 days
Polk—survived by mother
Garfield—survived by mother
Kennedy—survived by mother

AGE OF PRESIDENTS AT DEATH OF FATHER

Two Presidents were born posthumously, Jackson and Hayes.

Two Presidents were survived by their fathers, Harding and Kennedy.

The following is a comparative list:

Jackson—born posthumously
Hayes—born posthumously
Garfield—1 year, 170 days
A. Johnson—3 years, 6 days
Hoover—6 years, 124 days
Washington—11 years, 49 days
Jefferson—14 years, 126 days
Monroe—16 years
Cleveland—16 years, 197 days
W. H. Harrison—18 years, 74 days
F. D. Roosevelt—18 years, 312 days
T. Roosevelt—19 years, 105 days
Tyler—22 years, 283 days
J. Adams—25 years, 207 days
L. B. Johnson—29 years, 56 days
Buchanan—30 years, 49 days
Truman—30 years, 179 days
Polk—32 years, 3 days
Taft—33 years, 248 days
Van Buren—34 years, 124 days
Pierce—34 years, 129 days
Taylor—41 years, 56 days

Lincoln—41 years, 339 days
Nixon—43 years, 239 days
B. Harrison—44 years, 278 days
Arthur—45 years, 22 days
Wilson—46 years, 24 days
McKinley—49 years, 299 days
Madison—49 years, 348 days
Grant—51 years, 63 days
Eisenhower—51 years, 147 days
Coolidge—53 years, 257 days
J. Q. Adams—59 years, 358 days
Fillmore—63 years, 80 days

PRESIDENTS SURVIVED BY PARENTS

The only President survived by both parents was Kennedy.

Two Presidents—Harding and Kennedy—were survived by their fathers.

Three Presidents—Polk, Garfield, and Kennedy—were survived by their mothers.

PARENTS OF PRESIDENTS ALIVE AT INAUGURATION

Both parents at inauguration

Both parents of two Presidents were living when their sons took office:

Ulysses Simpson Grant was inaugurated March 4, 1869; his father, Jesse Root Grant, died June 29, 1873; his mother, Hannah Simpson Grant, died May 11, 1883.

John Fitzgerald Kennedy was inaugurated January 20, 1961; his father, Joseph Patrick Kennedy, and his mother, Rose Fitzgerald Kennedy, both attended the ceremony.

Father at inauguration

Four fathers, in addition to those of Grant and Kennedy, lived to see their sons take office as President:

John Quincy Adams was inaugurated March 4, 1825; his father, John Adams, died July 4, 1826.

Millard Fillmore took office July 10, 1850; his father, Nathaniel Fillmore, died May 2, 1863.

Warren Gamaliel Harding was inaugurated March 4, 1921; his father, George Tryon Harding, died November 19, 1928.

Calvin Coolidge took office August 3, 1923; his father, John Calvin Coolidge, died March 18, 1926.

Mother at inauguration

Eight mothers, in addition to those of Grant and Kennedy, lived to see their sons take office as President:

George Washington was inaugurated April 30, 1789; his mother, Mary Ball Washington, died August 25, 1789.

John Adams was inaugurated March 4, 1797; his mother, Susanna Boylston Adams, died April 17, 1797.

James Madison was inaugurated March 4, 1809; his mother, Eleanor Rose Conway Madison, died February 11, 1829.

James Knox Polk was inaugurated March 4, 1845; his mother, Jane Knox Polk, died January 11, 1852.

James Abram Garfield was inaugurated March 4, 1881; his mother, Eliza Ballou Garfield, died January 21, 1888.

William McKinley was inaugurated March 4, 1897; his mother, Nancy Allison McKinley, died December 12, 1897.

Franklin Delano Roosevelt was inaugurated March 4, 1933; his mother, Sara Delano Roosevelt, died September 7, 1941.

Harry S. Truman took office April 12, 1945; his mother, Martha Ellen Young Truman, died July 25, 1947.

NINE PRESIDENTS' FATHERS REMARRIED

The fathers of nine Presidents remarried. Four of them remarried after the birth of their President-sons.

Millard Fillmore was 31 years and 114 days old when his mother, Phoebe Millard Fillmore, died on May 2, 1831. His father married Eunice Love on May 2, 1834.

Abraham Lincoln was 9 years and 235 days old when his mother, Nancy Hanks Lincoln, died on October 5, 1818. His father married Sarah Bush Johnston on December 2, 1819.

Warren Gamaliel Harding was 44 years and 198 days old when his mother, Phoebe Elizabeth Dickerson Harding, died on May 29, 1910. His father married Aline Severns on August 11, 1921.

Calvin Coolidge was 12 years and 253 days old when his mother, Victoria Josephine Moor Coolidge, died on March 14, 1885. His father married Caroline A. Brown on September 9, 1891.

Five Presidents were the sons of their fathers' second marriages. They were Washington, Pierce, Benjamin Harrison, Taft, and Franklin Delano Roosevelt.

WIVES OF THE PRESIDENTS—DATES OF BIRTH, MARRIAGE, AND DEATH

Washington

Martha Dandridge Custis, b. June 21, 1731; m. Jan. 6, 1759; d. May 22, 1802

J. Adams

Abigail Smith, b. Nov. 11, 1744; m. Oct. 25, 1764; d. Oct. 28, 1818

Jefferson

Martha Wayles Skelton, b. Oct. 19, 1748; m. Jan. 1, 1772; d. Sept. 6, 1782

Madison

Dolley (Dorothea) Dandridge Payne Todd, b. May 20, 1768; m. Sept. 15, 1794; d. July 12, 1849

Monroe

Elizabeth Kortright, b. June 30, 1768; m. Feb. 16, 1786; d. Sept. 23, 1830

J. Q. Adams

Louisa Catherine Johnson, b. Feb. 12, 1775; m. July 26, 1797; d. May 14, 1852

Jackson

Rachel Donelson Robards, b. June 15 (?), 1767; m. Jan. 17, 1794; d. Dec. 22, 1828

Van Buren

Hannah Hoes, b. Mar. 8, 1783; m. Feb. 21, 1807; d. Feb. 5, 1819

W. H. Harrison

Anna Symmes, b. July 25, 1775; m. Nov. 25, 1795; d. Feb. 25, 1864

Tyler

Letitia Christian, b. Nov. 12, 1790; m. Mar. 29, 1813; d. Sept. 10, 1842
Julia Gardiner, b. May 4, 1820; m. June 26, 1844, d. July 10, 1889

Polk

Sarah Childress, b. Sept. 4, 1803; m. Jan. 1, 1824; d. Aug. 14, 1891

Taylor

Margaret Smith, b. Sept. 21, 1788; m. June 21, 1810; d. Aug. 18, 1852

Fillmore

Abigail Powers, b. Mar. 13, 1798; m. Feb. 5, 1826; d. Mar. 30, 1853
Caroline Carmichael McIntosh, b. Oct. 21, 1813; m. Feb. 10, 1858; d. Aug. 11, 1881

Pierce

Jane Means Appleton, b. Mar. 12, 1806; m. Nov. 10, 1834; d. Dec. 2, 1863

Lincoln

Mary Todd, b. Dec. 13, 1818; m. Nov. 4, 1842; d. July 16, 1882

A. Johnson

Eliza McCardle, b. Oct. 4, 1810; m. May 5, 1827; d. Jan. 15, 1876

Grant

Julia Dent, b. Jan. 26, 1826; m. Aug. 22, 1848; d. Dec. 14, 1902

Hayes

Lucy Ware Webb, b. Aug. 28, 1831; m. Dec. 30, 1852; d. June 25, 1889

Garfield

Lucretia Rudolph, b. Apr. 19, 1832; m. Nov. 11, 1858; d. Mar. 14, 1918

Arthur

Ellen Lewis Herndon, b. Aug. 30, 1837; m. Oct. 25, 1859; d. Jan.

12, 1880

Cleveland

Frances Folsom, b. July 21, 1864; m. June 2, 1886; d. Oct. 29, 1947

B. Harrison

Caroline Lavinia Scott, b. Oct. 1, 1832; m. Oct. 20, 1853; d. Oct. 25, 1892

Mary Scott Lord Dimmick, b. Apr. 30, 1858; m. Apr. 6, 1896; d. Jan. 5, 1948

McKinley

Ida Saxton, b. June 8, 1847; m. Jan. 25, 1871; d. May 26, 1907

T. Roosevelt

Alice Hathaway Lee, b. July 29, 1861; m. Oct. 27, 1880; d. Feb. 14, 1884

Edith Kermit Carow, b. Aug. 6, 1861; m. Dec. 2, 1886; d. Sept. 30, 1948

Taft

Helen Herron, b. Jan. 2, 1861; m. June 19, 1886; d. May 22, 1943

Wilson

Ellen Louise Axson, b. May 15, 1860; m. June 24, 1885; d. Aug. 6, 1914

Edith Bolling Galt, b. Oct. 15, 1872; m. Dec. 18, 1915; d. Dec. 28, 1961

Harding

Florence Kling De Wolfe, b. Aug. 15, 1860; m. July 8, 1891; d. Nov. 21, 1924

Coolidge

Grace Anna Goodhue, b. Jan. 3, 1879, m. Oct. 4, 1905, d. July 8, 1957

Hoover

Lou Henry, b. Mar. 29, 1875; m. Feb. 10, 1899; d. Jan. 7, 1944

F. D. Roosevelt

(Anna) Eleanor Roosevelt, b. Oct. 11, 1884; m. Mar. 17, 1905; d. Nov. 7, 1962

Truman

Bess (Elizabeth) Virginia Wallace, b. Feb. 13, 1885; m. June 28, 1919

Eisenhower

Mamie Geneva Doud, b. Nov. 14, 1896; m. July 1, 1916

Kennedy

Jacqueline Lee Bouvier, b. July 28, 1929; m. Sept. 12, 1953

L. B. Johnson

Claudia Alta (Lady Bird) Taylor, b. Dec. 22, 1912; m. Nov. 17, . 1934

Nixon

(Thelma Catherine) Patricia Ryan, b. Mar. 16, 1912; m. June 21, 1940

BIRTHPLACES OF PRESIDENTS' WIVES

Martha Washington–New Kent County, Va.
Abigail Adams–Weymouth, Mass.
Martha Jefferson–Charles City County, Va.
Dolley Madison–Guilford County, N.C.
Elizabeth Monroe–New York, N.Y.
Louisa Adams–London, England
Rachel Jackson–Halifax County, N.C.
Hannah Van Buren–Kinderhook, N.Y.
Anna Harrison–Morristown, N.J.
Letitia Tyler–New Kent County, Va.
Julia Tyler–Gardiners Island, N.Y.
Sarah Polk–Murfreesboro, Tenn.
Margaret Taylor–Calvert County, Md.
Abigail Fillmore–Stillwater, N.Y.
Caroline Fillmore–Morristown, N.J.
Jane Pierce–Hampton, N.H.
Mary Lincoln–Lexington, Ky.
Eliza Johnson–Leesburg, Tenn.
Julia Grant–St. Louis, Mo.
Lucy Hayes–Chillicothe, Ohio
Lucretia Garfield–Hiram, Ohio
Ellen Arthur–Fredericksburg, Va.
Frances Cleveland–Buffalo, N.Y.
Caroline Harrison–Oxford, Ohio
Mary Harrison–Honesdale, Pa.
Ida McKinley–Canton, Ohio
Alice Roosevelt–Chestnut Hill, Mass.
Edith Roosevelt–Norwich, Conn.
Helen Taft–Cincinnati, Ohio
Ellen Wilson–Savannah, Ga.
Edith Wilson–Wytheville, Va.
Florence Harding–Marion, Ohio
Grace Coolidge–Burlington, Vt.
Lou Hoover–Waterloo, Iowa
Eleanor Roosevelt–New York, N.Y.
Bess Truman–Independence, Mo.
Mamie Eisenhower–Boone, Iowa
Jacqueline Kennedy–Southampton, N.Y.
Claudia Johnson–Karnack, Tex.
Patricia Nixon–Ely, Nev.

BIRTHPLACES OF PRESIDENTS' WIVES (ARRANGED BY LOCATION)

New York (7)

Elizabeth Monroe

Hannah Van Buren
Julia Tyler
Abigail Fillmore
Frances Cleveland
Eleanor Roosevelt
Jacqueline Kennedy

Ohio (6)

Lucy Hayes
Lucretia Garfield
Caroline Harrison
Ida McKinley
Helen Taft
Florence Harding

Virginia (5)

Martha Washington
Martha Jefferson
Letitia Tyler
Ellen Arthur
Edith Wilson

Iowa (2)

Lou Hoover
Mamie Eisenhower

Massachusetts (2)

Abigail Adams
Alice Roosevelt

Missouri (2)

Julia Grant
Bess Truman

New Jersey (2)

Anna Harrison
Caroline Fillmore

North Carolina (2)

Dolley Madison
Rachel Jackson

Tennessee (2)

Sarah Polk
Eliza Johnson

Connecticut (1)

Edith Roosevelt

Georgia (1)

Ellen Wilson

Kentucky (1)
Mary Lincoln

Maryland (1)
Margaret Taylor

Nevada (1)
Patricia Nixon

New Hampshire (1)
Jane Pierce

Pennsylvania (1)
Mary Harrison

Texas (1)
Claudia Johnson

Vermont (1)
Grace Coolidge

London, England (1)
Louisa Adams

NAMES OF WIVES' PARENTS

Further data may be found under the names of the Presidents' wives in Part I.

Martha Washington
John and Frances Jones Dandridge

Abigail Adams
William and Elizabeth Quincy Smith

Martha Jefferson
John and Martha Eppes Wayles

Dolley Madison
John and Mary Coles Payne

Elizabeth Monroe
Lawrence and Hannah Aspinwall Kortright

Louisa Adams
Joshua and Catherine Nuth Johnson

Rachel Jackson
John and Rachel Stockley Donelson

Hannah Van Buren
John and Maria Quackenboss Hoes

Anna Harrison
John Cleves and Susan Livingston Symmes

Letitia Tyler
Robert and Mary Brown Christian

Julia Tyler
David and Juliana McLachlan Gardiner

Sarah Polk
Joel and Elizabeth Childress

Margaret Taylor
Walter and Ann Mackall Smith

Abigail Fillmore
Lemuel and Abigail Newland Powers

Caroline Fillmore
Charles and Temperance Blachley Carmichael

Jane Pierce
Jesse and Elizabeth Appleton

Mary Lincoln
Robert Smith and Eliza Ann Parker Todd

Eliza Johnson
John and Sarah Phillips McCardle

Julia Grant
Frederick and Ellen Wrenshall Dent

Lucy Hayes
James and Maria Cook Webb

Lucretia Garfield
Zebulon and Arabella Green Mason Rudolph

Ellen Arthur
William Lewis and Frances Elizabeth Hansbrough Herndon

Frances Cleveland
Oscar and Emma Cornelia Harmon Folsom

Caroline Harrison
John Witherspoon and Mary Potts Neal Scott

Mary Harrison
Russell Farnham and Elizabeth Scott Lord

Ida McKinley
James Asbury and Catherine Dewalt Saxton

Alice Roosevelt
George Cabot and Caroline Haskell Lee

Edith Roosevelt
Charles and Gertrude Elizabeth Tyler Carow

Helen Taft
John Williamson and Harriet Collins Herron

Ellen Wilson
Samuel Edward and Margaret Hoyt Axson

Edith Wilson
William Holcombe and Sallie White Bolling

Florence Harding
Amos H. and Louisa M. Bouton Kling

Grace Coolidge
Andrew Issachar and Lemira Barnett Goodhue

Lou Hoover
Charles Delano and Florence Weed Henry

Eleanor Roosevelt
Elliott and Anna Hall Roosevelt

Bess Truman
David Willock and Madge Gates Wallace

Mamie Eisenhower
John Sheldon and Elivera Carlson Doud

Jacqueline Kennedy
John Vernou and Janet Lee Bouvier

Claudia Johnson
Thomas Jefferson and Minnie Lee Pattillo Taylor

Patricia Nixon
William and Katharina Halberstadt Ryan

OCCUPATIONS OF WIVES' FATHERS

The names of wives whose fathers' occupations are not definitely known are omitted.

Martha Washington
Colonel John Dandridge, planter

Abigail Adams
William Smith, Congregational minister

Martha Jefferson
John Wayles, planter, lawyer

Dolley Madison
John Payne, farmer, planter

Elizabeth Monroe
Captain Lawrence Kortright, former British army officer

Louisa Adams
Joshua Johnson, U.S. consul

Rachel Jackson
Colonel John Donelson, surveyor

Anna Harrison
John Cleves Symmes, judge

Letitia Tyler
Colonel Robert Christian, planter

Julia Tyler
David Gardiner, senator

Sarah Polk
Captain Joel Childress, planter

Margaret Taylor
Walter Smith, planter

Abigail Fillmore
Lemuel Powers, Baptist minister

Jane Pierce
Jesse Appleton, Congregational minister

Mary Lincoln
Robert Smith Todd, banker

Julia Grant
Frederick Dent, judge

Lucy Hayes
Dr. James Webb, physician

Lucretia Garfield
Zeb Rudolph, farmer

Ellen Arthur
Captain William Lewis Herndon, U.S. naval officer

Frances Cleveland
Oscar Folsom, lawyer

Caroline Harrison
John Witherspoon Scott, Presbyterian minister

Mary Harrison
Russell Farnham Lord, canal engineer

Ida McKinley
James Asbury Saxton, banker

Helen Taft
John Williamson Herron, judge

Ellen Wilson
Samuel Edward Axson, Presbyterian minister

Edith Wilson
William Holcombe Bolling, judge

Florence Harding
Amos Kling, banker

Lou Hoover
Charles Delano Henry, banker

Eleanor Roosevelt
Elliott Roosevelt, coal mining interests

Bess Truman
David Willock Wallace, farmer

Mamie Eisenhower
John Sheldon Doud, meat packer

Jacqueline Kennedy
John Vernou Bouvier, lawyer, stockbroker

Claudia Johnson
Thomas Jefferson Taylor, planter, merchant

Patricia Nixon
William Ryan, miner

FIVE PRESIDENTS MARRIED MINISTERS' DAUGHTERS

Five Presidents married the daughters of ministers. They were John Adams, Millard Fillmore, Franklin Pierce, Benjamin Harrison, and Woodrow Wilson.

John Adams married Abigail Smith, daughter of William Smith, a Congregational minister, who was ordained a minister of the gospel on November 4, 1729, at Norwich, Conn.

Millard Fillmore married Abigail Powers, daughter of Lemuel Powers, a Baptist clergyman.

Franklin Pierce married Jane Means Appleton, daughter of Jesse Appleton, a Congregational minister.

Benjamin Harrison married Caroline Scott, daughter of John Witherspoon Scott, ordained a clergyman in 1830 in the Presbyterian church. Scott was also a professor and served at Washington College, Miami University, and Oxford Female College.

Woodrow Wilson married Ellen Louise Axson, daughter of Samuel Edward Axson, a Presbyterian minister.

EDUCATION OF THE PRESIDENTS' WIVES

It is difficult to appraise the education of the wives of the Presidents as most of the earlier first ladies had no formal schooling. Since the requirements and the standards of the institutions they did attend varied considerably, and since the curricula are not known in most instances, it is possible to give only a brief résumé.

The first wife of a President who regularly attended school was Anna Harrison (Mrs. William Henry Harrison); she attended the Clinton Academy at Easthampton, L.I., and Mrs. Graham's Boarding School for Young Ladies at No. 1 Broadway, New York City.

Julia Tyler went to Chegary Institute, New York City.

Sarah Polk attended the Moravian Female Academy, Salem, N.C.

Mary Lincoln studied at the academy conducted by John Ward, and at Mme. Mentelle's school, Lexington, Ky., where she studied French.

Julia Grant attended a boarding school.

Lucretial Garfield was a pupil at Geauga Seminary and at Hiram College at Hiram, Ohio.

Caroline Harrison, the first wife of Benjamin Harrison, attended the Oxford Female Seminary.

Mary Harrison, the second wife of Benjamin Harrison, attended Mrs. Moffat's School at Princeton, N.J., and Elmira College, Elmira, N.Y.

Ida McKinley went to Brook Hall Seminary, Media, Pa.

Edith Roosevelt attended Miss Comstock's private school at New York City.

Helen Taft went to Miss Nourse's private school at Cincinnati, Ohio, and the University of Cincinnati.

Ellen Wilson went to private schools and the Female Seminary at Rome, Ga.; she also took courses at the Art Students' League, New York City.

Edith Bolling Wilson attended Martha Washington College, Abington, Va., and Powell's School, Richmond, Va.

Florence Harding took courses at the Cincinnati Conservatory of Music.

Eleanor Roosevelt studied abroad; she received an honorary D.H.L. degree from Russell Sage College in 1929.

Bess Truman graduated from high school at Independence, Mo., and attended the Barstow School for Girls, Kansas City, Mo.

The first wife of a President to graduate from college was Lucy Hayes, who graduated from Ohio Wesleyan University, Delaware, Ohio, in 1850.

Frances Cleveland graduated from Wells College, Aurora, N.Y., in June 1885, receiving a B.A. degree.

Grace Coolidge graduated from the University of Vermont in 1902, receiving a bachelor of philosophy degree.

Lou Hoover received a B.A. degree in 1898 from Leland Stanford Junior University, Stanford, Calif.

Jacqueline Kennedy attended the Holton-Arms School, Washington, D.C., 1942-1944, and Miss Porter's School, Farmington, Conn., 1944-1947. She entered Vassar College in 1947, spent her junior year at the Sorbonne in Paris, and received a B.A. degree from George Washington University in 1951.

Claudia Johnson graduated from Marshall High School and St. Mary's Episcopal School for Girls. She received a B.A. degree in 1933 from the University of Texas.

Patricia Nixon graduated from the University of Southern California in 1937.

Many of the Presidents' wives went abroad to further their education.

PRESIDENTS' MARRIAGES

Noted under the name of each President in the following list are (1) his age at marriage; (2) his wife's age at marriage; and (3) the duration of the marriage.

Washington

26 years, 318 days
27 years, 199 days
40 years, 342 days

J. Adams

28 years, 360 days
19 years, 348 days
54 years,   3 days

Jefferson

28 years, 263 days
23 years, 74 days
10 years, 248 days

Madison

43 years, 183 days
26 years, 118 days
41 years, 286 days

Monroe

27 years, 294 days
17 years, 231 days
44 years, 219 days

J. Q. Adams

30 years, 15 days
22 years, 164 days
50 years, 212 days

Jackson

about 24 years
about 24 years
about 37 years

Van Buren

24 years, 78 days
23 years, 350 days
11 years, 349 days

W. H. Harrison

22 years, 289 days
20 years, 123 days
45 years, 130 days

Tyler (first wife)

23 years
22 years, 137 days
29 years, 165 days

Tyler (second wife)

54 years, 89 days
24 years, 53 days
17 years, 206 days

Polk

28 years, 60 days
20 years, 119 days
25 years, 165 days

Taylor

25 years, 209 days
21 years, 273 days
40 years, 18 days

Fillmore (first wife)

26 years, 29 days
27 years, 329 days
27 years, 53 days

Fillmore (second wife)

58 years, 34 days
44 years, 112 days
16 years, 36 days

Pierce

29 years, 352 days
28 years, 243 days
29 years, 22 days

Lincoln

33 years, 265 days
23 years, 326 days
22 years, 162 days

A. Johnson

18 years, 127 days
16 years, 213 days
48 years, 87 days

Grant

26 years, 117 days
22 years, 208 days
36 years, 335 days

Hayes

30 years, 87 days
21 years, 124 days
40 years, 18 days

Garfield

26 years, 357 days
26 years, 206 days
22 years, 312 days

Arthur

29 years, 20 days
22 years, 56 days
20 years, 79 days

Cleveland

49 years, 76 days
21 years, 316 days
22 years, 22 days

B. Harrison (first wife)

20 years, 61 days
21 years, 19 days
39 years,   5 days

B. Harrison (second wife)

62 years, 229 days
37 years, 341 days
 4 years, 341 days

McKinley

27 years, 361 days
23 years, 231 days
30 years, 232 days

T. Roosevelt (first wife)

22 years

19 years, 82 days
3 years, 110 days

T. Roosevelt (second wife)

28 years, 36 days
25 years, 118 days
32 years, 35 days

Taft

28 years, 277 days
25 years, 168 days
43 years, 262 days

Wilson (first wife)

28 years, 178 days
25 years, 40 days
29 years, 43 days

Wilson (second wife)

58 years, 355 days
43 years, 64 days
8 years, 47 days

Harding

25 years, 248 days
30 years, 327 days
32 years, 25 days

Coolidge

33 years, 92 days
26 years, 274 days
27 years, 93 days

Hoover

24 years, 184 days
23 years, 318 days
44 years, 331 days

F. D. Roosevelt

23 years, 46 days
20 years, 157 days
40 years, 26 days

Truman

35 years, 51 days
34 years, 135 days
53 years, 181 days

Eisenhower

25 years, 260 days
19 years, 229 days
52 years, 270 days

Kennedy

36 years, 106 days
24 years, 46 days
10 years, 71 days

L. B. Johnson

26 years, 82 days
21 years, 330 days
39 years, 66 days

Nixon

27 years, 163 days
28 years, 97 days

MARRIAGE TO WIDOWS

Six Presidents married widows, including three of the first four Presidents.

George Washington married Martha Dandridge Custis, the widow of Colonel Daniel Parke Custis, on January 6, 1759. In June 1749, at the age of seventeen, she had married Custis, who was twenty years her senior. He died in 1757 of tuberculosis and she became a widow at the age of twenty-five.

Thomas Jefferson married Martha Wayles Skelton, widow of Bathurst Skelton, on January 1, 1772. She had married Skelton on November 20, 1766. He died on September 30, 1768.

James Madison married Dolley (Dorothea) Payne Todd, widow of John Todd, Sr., on September 15, 1794. She had married Todd on January 7, 1790, in the Friends Meeting House, Pine Street, Philadelphia, Pa.

The other three Presidents who married widows were widowers:

Millard Fillmore married Caroline Carmichael McIntosh, the widow of Ezekiel C. McIntosh.

Benjamin Harrison married Mary Scott Lord Dimmick, the widow of Walter Erskine Dimmick, a New York lawyer.

Woodrow Wilson married Edith Bolling Galt, the widow of Norman Galt, a Washington, D.C., jeweler. She had married Galt on April 30, 1896. Galt died on January 28, 1908.

MARRIAGE TO DIVORCEES

Andrew Jackson married Rachel Donelson Robards, who had been married to Captain Lewis Robards. Robards had sued for divorce, but technically the status of the divorce was in question—a fact the Jacksons were not aware of at the time of their marriage. Jackson had a second wedding ceremony performed three years after the first to eliminate all possible doubts concerning the legality of his marriage.

Warren Gamaliel Harding married Florence Kling De Wolfe, who had been married to Henry De Wolfe. Her marriage to Harding took place after the death of her former husband.

WIVES WITH CHILDREN BY FORMER HUSBANDS

Martha Washington was the mother of four children by her marriage to Daniel Parke Custis. The children were Patsy and Jackey Custis, who had died in infancy; Martha Parke Custis, who died in 1774 at the age of sixteen; and John Parke Custis, who died in 1781 at the age of twenty-five, leaving two children.

Martha Jefferson was the mother of one son by her marriage to Bathurst Skelton, who had died before she was twenty. Her son, John Skelton, born November 7, 1767, had died June 10, 1771.

Dolley Madison was the mother of two sons by her marriage to John Todd. Her sons were John Payne Todd, born February 29, 1792, and William Payne Todd, who had died in infancy in 1793.

Florence Harding was the mother of one son by her marriage in 1880 to Henry De Wolfe—a marriage which had ended in divorce. Her son, Marshall Eugene De Wolfe, died of tuberculosis.

LIFE SPAN OF PRESIDENTS' WIVES

Five wives died before their husbands became President:
Martha Jefferson
Rachel Jackson
Hannah Van Buren
Ellen Arthur
Alice Roosevelt (1st wife)
Three wives died while their husbands were in office:
Letitia Tyler (1st wife)
Caroline Harrison (1st wife)
Ellen Wilson (1st wife)
Twenty-seven wives died after their husbands' terms:
Martha Washington
Abigail Adams
Dolley Madison
Elizabeth Monroe
Louisa Adams
Anna Harrison
Julia Tyler (2nd wife)
Sarah Polk
Margaret Taylor
Abigail Fillmore (1st wife)
Caroline Fillmore (2nd wife)
Jane Pierce
Mary Lincoln
Eliza Johnson
Julia Grant
Lucy Hayes
Lucretia Garfield
Frances Cleveland
Mary Harrison (2nd wife)
Ida McKinley
Edith Roosevelt (2nd wife)

Edith Wilson (2nd wife)
Helen Taft
Florence Harding
Grace Coolidge
Lou Hoover
Eleanor Roosevelt

AGE OF WIVES AT DEATH

Mary Harrison–89 years, 250 days
Edith Wilson–89 years, 64 days
Anna Harrison–88 years, 215 days
Sarah Polk–87 years, 344 days
Edith Roosevelt–87 years, 45 days
Lucretia Garfield–85 years, 329 days
Frances Cleveland–83 years, 100 days
Helen Taft–82 years, 140 days
Dolley Madison–81 years, 53 days
Grace Coolidge–78 years, 186 days
Eleanor Roosevelt–78 years, 27 days
Louisa Adams–77 years, 91 days
Julia Grant–76 years, 322 days
Abigail Adams–73 years, 351 days
Martha Washington–70 years, 355 days
Julia Tyler–69 years, 67 days
Lou Hoover–68 years, 284 days
Caroline Fillmore–67 years, 294 days
Eliza Johnson–65 years, 103 days
Florence Harding–64 years, 98 days
Margaret Taylor–63 years, 331 days
Mary Lincoln–63 years, 215 days
Elizabeth Monroe–62 years, 85 days
Rachel Jackson–61 years, 190 days
Caroline Harrison–60 years, 24 days
Ida McKinley–59 years, 352 days
Lucy Hayes–57 years, 301 days
Jane Pierce–57 years, 265 days
Abigail Fillmore–55 years, 17 days
Ellen Wilson–54 years, 83 days
Letitia Tyler–51 years, 302 days
Ellen Arthur–42 years, 135 days
Hannah Van Buren–35 years, 334 days
Martha Jefferson–33 years, 322 days
Alice Roosevelt–22 years, 192 days.

LONGEVITY OF THE PRESIDENTS' WIVES

Of the forty Presidents' wives, five are living (1973): Bess Truman, Mamie Eisenhower, Jacqueline Kennedy Onassis, Claudia Johnson, and Patricia Nixon.

Nine of the thirty-five wives no longer living were 81 years of age or older when they died: Dolley Madison, Anna Harrison, Sarah Polk,

Lucretia Garfield, Frances Cleveland, Mary Harrison (2nd wife), Edith Roosevelt (2nd wife), Helen Taft, and Edith Wilson (2nd wife).

Fourteen of the thirty-five wives were 70 or older when they died. In addition to the nine mentioned above, they were Martha Washington, Abigail Adams, Louisa Adams, Julia Grant, Grace Coolidge, and Eleanor Roosevelt.

Twenty-six of the thirty-five wives were 60 or older when they died.

Thirty-one of the thirty-five wives were 50 or older when they died.

The wife who died at the most advanced age was the second wife of Benjamin Harrison, who was 89 years and 250 days old when she died.

The wife who died at the earliest age was the first wife of Theodore Roosevelt, who was only 22 years and 192 days old when she died.

PLACES OF DEATH AND BURIAL OF PRESIDENTS' WIVES

Martha Washington
Mount Vernon, Va.; Mount Vernon, Va.

Abigail Adams
Quincy, Mass.; Quincy, Mass.

Martha Jefferson
Monticello, Va.; Monticello, Va.

Dolley Madison
Washington, D.C., Montpelier, Va.

Elizabeth Monroe
Oak Hill, Va.; Richmond, Va.

Louisa Adams
Washington, D.C.; Quincy, Mass.

Rachel Jackson
Nashville, Tenn.; Nashville, Tenn.

Hannah Van Buren
Albany, N.Y.; Kinderhook, N.Y.

Anna Harrison
North Bend, Ohio; North Bend, Ohio

Letitia Tyler
Washington, D.C.; Cedar Grove, Va.

Julia Tyler
Richmond, Va.; Richmond, Va.

Sarah Polk
Nashville, Tenn.; Nashville, Tenn.

Margaret Taylor
Pascagoula, Miss.; Springfield, Ky.

Abigail Fillmore
Washington, D.C.; Buffalo, N.Y.

Caroline Fillmore
Buffalo, N.Y.; Buffalo, N.Y.

Jane Pierce
Andover, Mass.; Concord, N.H.

Mary Lincoln
Springfield, Ill.; Springfield, Ill.

Eliza Johnson
Greene County, Tenn.; Greeneville, Tenn.

Julia Grant
Washington, D.C.; New York, N.Y.

Lucy Hayes
Fremont, Ohio; Fremont, Ohio

Lucretia Garfield
Pasadena, Calif.; Cleveland, Ohio

Ellen Arthur
Albany, N.Y.; Albany, N.Y.

Frances Cleveland
Baltimore, Md.; Princeton, N.J.

Caroline Harrison
Washington, D.C.; Indianapolis, Ind.

Mary Harrison
New York, N.Y.; Indianapolis, Ind.

Ida McKinley
Canton, Ohio; Canton, Ohio

Alice Roosevelt
New York, N.Y.; Cambridge, Mass.

Edith Roosevelt
Oyster Bay, N.Y.; Oyster Bay, N.Y.

Helen Taft
Washington, D.C.; Arlington, Va.

Ellen Wilson
Washington, D.C.; Rome, Ga.

Edith Wilson
Washington, D.C.; Washington, D.C.

Florence Harding

Marion, Ohio; Marion, Ohio

Grace Coolidge

Northampton, Mass.; Plymouth, Vt.

Lou Hoover

New York, N.Y.; Palo Alto, Calif.

Eleanor Roosevelt

New York, N.Y.; Hyde Park, N.Y.

WIDOWS OF PRESIDENTS GRANTED FREE USE OF THE MAILS

An act of Congress of April 3, 1800—"an act to extend the privilege of franking letters and packages to Martha Washington" (2 Stat. L. 19)—granted the widow of George Washington the free use of the mails for her natural life. Other presidential widows to whom the franking privilege was extended by acts of Congress were the following:

Dolley Madison, July 2, 1836
Anna Harrison, September 9, 1841
Louisa Adams, March 9, 1848
Sarah Polk, January 10, 1850
Margaret Taylor, July 18, 1850
Mary Lincoln, February 10, 1866
Lucretia Garfield, December 20, 1881
Julia Grant, June 28, 1886
Ida McKinley, January 22, 1902
Mary Harrison, February 1, 1909
Frances Cleveland, February 1, 1909
Edith Roosevelt, October 27, 1919
Florence Harding, January 25, 1924
Edith Wilson, March 4, 1924
Helen Taft, June 14, 1930
Grace Coolidge, June 16, 1934
Eleanor Roosevelt, May 7, 1945
Jacqueline Kennedy, December 11, 1963
Mamie Eisenhower, Apr. 25, 1969

PENSIONS TO PRESIDENTIAL WIDOWS

Pensions of varying amounts were paid to presidential widows by specific acts of Congress. The first to receive a pension was Anna Harrison (Mrs. William Henry Harrison). On June 30, 1841, Congress passed "an act for the relief of Mrs. Harrison, widow of the late President of the United States." She was granted $25,000, equivalent to a year's salary for a President.

A similar award of $25,000 was made to Mary Lincoln on December 21, 1865, and on July 14, 1870, Congress passed "an act granting a pension to Mary Lincoln" which provided "that the Secretary of the Interior be, and is hereby authorized to place the name of Mary Lincoln, widow of Abraham Lincoln, deceased, late President of the

United States, on the pension roll." It authorized a pension of $3,000 a year. An act of February 2, 1882, awarded her an annual pension of $5,000.

An act of March 31, 1882—"an act granting pensions to Lucretia R. Garfield, Sarah Childress Polk and Julia Gardiner Tyler"—directed the Secretary of the Interior to place their names "on the pension roll and pay each of them a pension during their respective natural lives at the rate of $5,000 a year from and after the 19th day of September 1881." It also specified that the pension of $5,000 granted by this act to Julia Tyler should be in lieu of the pension previously granted her by Congress.

On July 27, 1882, Congress passed an act awarding Lucretia Garfield the sum of $50,000.

Annual pensions of $5,000 were also awarded to the following:

Julia Grant, December 26, 1885 (24 Stat. L. 653)
Ida McKinley, April 17, 1902 (32 Stat. L. 1328)
Edith Roosevelt, February 25, 1919 (40 Stat. L. 1530)
Edith Wilson, February 28, 1929 (45 Stat. L. 2338)
Grace Coolidge, January 14, 1937 (50 Stat. L. 923)
Helen H. Taft, May 22, 1937 (50 Stat. L. 973)
Mary Harrison, May 24, 1938 (52 Stat. L. 1318)
Frances Folsom Cleveland Preston, November 25, 1940 (50 Stat. L. 1396) (Mrs. Cleveland had remarried in 1913.)

On August 25, 1958 (72 Stat. L. 838) Congress passed an act granting annual pensions of $10,000 to the widows of Presidents. Entitled to this pension have been Edith Wilson, Eleanor Roosevelt, and Jacqueline Kennedy.

On January 8, 1971 (84 Stat. L. 1963) the pension to widows of Presidents was increased to $20,000. The pension terminated if the widow remarried before becoming 60 years of age.

PRESIDENT'S WIDOW IN EXECUTIVE CAPACITY

The first president's widow to serve the Federal Government in an executive capacity was Anna Eleanor Roosevelt, who was appointed on December 19, 1945, by President Harry S. Truman, to the United States delegation to the United Nations General Assembly. (The other delegates appointed at the same time were Edward Riley Stettinius and Senators Tom Connally and Arthur Hendrick Vandenberg.) On April 29, 1946, she was elected to lead the preliminary United Nations Human Rights Commission, which upon its establishment on January 27, 1947, again elected her as its leader.

"FIRST LADY"

The term "first lady" as a synonym for the wife of a President is believed to have been used for the first time in 1877 by Mary Clemmer Ames in an article in the *Independent* describing the inauguration of President Rutherford Birchard Hayes on Monday, March 5, 1877.

The term became popular when a comedy about Dolley Madison by Charles Nirdlinger entitled *The First Lady in the Land* was produced by Henry B. Harris at the Gaiety Theatre, New York City, on December 4, 1911. It featured Elsie Ferguson, Clarence Handyside, Luke Martin, David Todd, and Beatrice Noyes.

MARRIAGE STATISTICS

Thirty-five of the thirty-six Presidents married. (James Buchanan was the only President who did not marry.) Five Presidents remarried after the death of their first wives.

The President who married at the earliest age was Andrew Johnson, who married Eliza McCardle when he was 18 years and 127 days old.

The President who married for the first time at the most advanced age was Grover Cleveland, who married Frances Folsom when he was 49 years and 76 days old.

Benjamin Harrison was married for a second time when he was 62 years and 229 days old, a little more than three years after he retired from the presidency.

The youngest of the five Presidents to remarry was Theodore Roosevelt, who married Edith Kermit Carow when he was 28 years and 36 days old.

The greatest age difference between a President and his wife was that of John Tyler, who was 54 years and 89 days old at marriage, and his second wife, Julia Gardiner, who was 24 years and 53 days old.

The next greatest age difference between a President and his wife was that of Grover Cleveland, who was 49 years and 76 days old at marriage, and Frances Folsom, who was 21 years and 316 days old.

The President who was married the longest was John Adams who was married 54 years and 3 days.

Presidents who celebrated golden anniversaries were John Adams, his son John Quincy Adams, Harry S. Truman, and Dwight David Eisenhower. John Adams was married 54 years and 3 days and John Quincy Adams was married 50 years and 112 days. Truman was married 53 years and 180 days and Eisenhower was married 52 years and 270 days.

The shortest marriage was that of Theodore Roosevelt and his first wife, Alice Hathaway Lee, who had been married only 3 years and 110 days when she died.

The wife who married at the earliest age was Eliza McCardle, who married Andrew Johnson when she was 16 years and 213 days old.

The oldest to marry a President was Caroline Carmichael McIntosh, who married Millard Fillmore, her second husband, when she was 44 years and 112 days old.

The oldest to marry for the first time was Bess Wallace, who married Harry S. Truman when she was 34 years and 135 days old.

Five Presidents married women older than they: Washington, Harding, Fillmore, Benjamin Harrison, and Nixon. Washington was 246 days younger than his wife, and Harding was 5 years and 79 days younger. Both Mrs. Washington and Mrs. Harding survived their husbands. Fillmore and Benjamin Harrison also married slightly older women. Fillmore was 1 year and 300 days younger than his wife, and Harrison was 323 days younger. Both Fillmore and Harrison survived their wives and remarried. Nixon was 1 year and 66 days younger than his wife.

TWO PRESIDENTS MARRIED ON THEIR BIRTHDAYS

Two Presidents were married on their birthdays. John Tyler married Letitia Christian, his first wife, on March 29, 1813, his twenty-third birthday. Theodore Roosevelt married Alice Hathaway Lee, his first wife, on October 27, 1880, his twenty-second birthday.

WIDOWERS IN THE WHITE HOUSE

Two widowers were elected President: Thomas Jefferson, whose wife had died on September 6, 1782, almost nineteen years before his inauguration on March 4, 1801, and Martin Van Buren, whose wife had died on February 5, 1819, more than eighteen years before his inauguration on March 4, 1837.

Andrew Jackson's wife died on December 22, 1828. She lived to see him elected but died before he was inaugurated on March 4, 1829.

Chester Alan Arthur was a widower when he succeeded to the presidency. His wife had died on January 12, 1880, before he was elected Vice President in November 1880.

When Theodore Roosevelt was elected Vice President in 1900, he was married to his second wife, his first wife having died in 1884.

SECOND MARRIAGES

Theodore Roosevelt remarried before he became President. Tyler and Wilson remarried while they were in office. Fillmore and Benjamin Harrison remarried after their terms as President.

With the exception of Theodore Roosevelt, who was 2 years and 293 days older than his second wife, these Presidents married women considerably younger than they were. Fillmore was 13 years and 287 days older than his wife, Wilson was 15 years and 291 days older, Harrison was 24 years and 253 days older, and Tyler was 30 years and 26 days older.

Three of the five Presidents who remarried had children by both wives: John Tyler, Benjamin Harrison, and Theodore Roosevelt.

Millard Fillmore and Woodrow Wilson had children by their first marriages but none by their second.

Three of the five wives, Mrs. Fillmore, Mrs. Harrison, and Mrs. Wilson, were widows when they married.

All of the five wives survived their husbands.

PRESIDENTS' WIDOWS REMARRIED

The widows of two former Presidents remarried after the death of the Presidents.

Frances Folsom Cleveland, widow of Grover Cleveland, married Professor Thomas Jex Preston, Jr., in Princeton, N.J., on February 10, 1913. Cleveland died June 24, 1908.

Jacqueline Lee Bouvier Kennedy, widow of John Fitzgerald Kennedy, married Aristotle Socrates Onassis on the island of Skorpios,

Greece, on October 20, 1968. Kennedy died November 22, 1963.

CHILDREN OF THE PRESIDENTS

Washington–None
J. Adams–3 boys, 2 girls
Jefferson–1 boy, 5 girls
Madison–None
Monroe–1 boy, 2 girls
J. Q. Adams–3 boys, 1 girl
Jackson–None
Van Buren–4 boys
W. H. Harrison–6 boys, 4 girls
Tyler (by first wife)–3 boys, 5 girls
Tyler (by second wife)–5 boys, 2 girls
Polk–None
Taylor–1 boy, 5 girls
Fillmore (by first wife)–1 boy, 1 girl
Fillmore (by second wife)–None
Pierce–3 boys
Buchanan–None
Lincoln–4 boys
A. Johnson–3 boys, 2 girls
Grant–3 boys, 1 girl
Hayes–7 boys, 1 girl
Garfield–5 boys, 2 girls
Arthur–2 boys, 1 girl
Cleveland–2 boys, 3 girls
B. Harrison (by first wife)–1 boy, 1 girl
B. Harrison (by second wife)–1 girl
McKinley–2 girls
T. Roosevelt (by first wife)–1 girl
T. Roosevelt (by second wife)–4 boys, 1 girl
Taft–2 boys, 1 girl
Wilson (by first wife)–3 girls
Wilson (by second wife)–None
Harding–None
Coolidge–2 boys
Hoover–2 boys
F. D. Roosevelt–5 boys, 1 girl
Truman–1 girl
Eisenhower–2 boys
Kennedy–2 boys, 1 girl
L. B. Johnson–2 girls
Nixon–2 girls
Total number of boys: 77
Total number of girls: 54

Six of the thirty-six Presidents had no children. They were Washington, Madison, Jackson, Polk, Harding, and Buchanan, who was a bachelor.

The thirty Presidents who had children had a total of 131 children, 77 boys and 54 girls. Only four of them did not have boys—McKinley, Wilson, Truman, and Lyndon Baines Johnson. Six of them had boys and no girls— Van Buren, Pierce, Lincoln, Coolidge, Hoover, and Eisenhower.

The President who had the greatest number of children was John Tyler, the father of fifteen. He had three sons and five daughters by his first wife, Letitia Christian. He married Julia Gardiner while he was President. After leaving the White House, they had seven children, five sons and two daughters.

The President who had the greatest number of children prior to his election was William Henry Harrison, who had ten children, four of whom were alive when he became President.

CHILDREN BORN IN FOREIGN COUNTRIES

George Washington Adams, the son of John Quincy Adams, was the first child of a President born in a foreign country. He was born April 13, 1801, in Berlin, Germany. His youngest sister, Louisa Catherine Adams, was born ten years later in St. Petersburg, Russia. Their father was serving the United States abroad on diplomatic assignments.

Both of President Hoover's sons were born in London, England. Herbert Clark Hoover, Jr., was born August 4, 1903, and Allan Henry Hoover, July 17, 1907.

Franklin Delano Roosevelt, Jr., was born at Campobello, New Brunswick, Canada, on August 17, 1914.

CHILDREN WHO DIED WHILE THEIR FATHERS WERE IN OFFICE

Charles Adams, son of John Adams, 20 years old, died Nov. 30,1800
Mary Jefferson, 26 years old, died April 17, 1804
William Wallace (Tad) Lincoln, 11 years old, died Feb. 29, 1862
Calvin Coolidge, Jr., 16 years old, died July 7, 1924
Patrick Bouvier Kennedy, 2 days old, died Aug. 9, 1963.

PRESIDENTS' SONS AT THE UNITED STATES MILITARY ACADEMY, WEST POINT, N.Y.

Frederick Dent Grant, graduated June 12, 1871; 37th in a class of 41
John Sheldon Doud Eisenhower, graduated June 6, 1944; 138th in a class of 474

PRESIDENTS' SONS IN MILITARY SERVICE

Spanish-American War

James Webb Cook Hayes, won Medal of Honor in the Philippines campaign (Dec. 4, 1899, Vigan action)

World War I

Quentin Roosevelt, son of Theodore Roosevelt, shot down in aerial combat in France, died July 14, 1918

World War II

Theodore Roosevelt, Jr., died of a heart attack July 12, 1944, in Normandy, France

Sons of Franklin Delano Roosevelt
James Roosevelt
Elliot Roosevelt
Franklin Delano Roosevelt, Jr.
John Aspinwall Roosevelt

Korean War

John Sheldon Doud Eisenhower

PRESIDENTS' SONS WHO SERVED IN PRESIDENTIAL CABINETS

Robert Todd Lincoln, Secretary of War (Garfield)
James Rudolph Garfield, Secretary of the Interior (T. Roosevelt)
Herbert Clark Hoover, Jr., Under Secretary of State (Eisenhower)
Franklin Delano Roosevelt, Jr., Under Secretary of Commerce (L. B. Johnson)

PRESIDENTS' SONS WHO SOUGHT THE PRESIDENCY

John Scott Harrison, son of William Henry Harrison, proposed by the Whigs, but declined in 1856. (His own son, Benjamin Harrison, was elected President in 1888.)

John Van Buren, proposed by the Free Soil Democrats in 1848, but declined in favor of his father, Martin Van Buren, who was defeated in the election by Zachary Taylor

Robert Todd Lincoln, a contender for the nomination at the Republican conventions in 1884 and 1888

Robert Alphonso Taft, a leading contender at the 1940, 1948, and 1952 Republican conventions

PRESIDENTS' SONS WHO SERVED IN CONGRESS

Senate and House of Representatives

John Quincy Adams, Mass. (son of John Adams) Senate, Mar. 4, 1803-June 6, 1808
  House of Representatives, (22nd-30th Congresses, Mar. 4, 1831-Feb. 23, 1848)

Senate

Robert Alphonso Taft, Ohio (son of William Howard Taft) Jan. 3, 1939-July 31, 1953

House of Representatives

Charles Francis Adams, Mass. (son of John Quincy Adams)
  36th-37th Congresses, Mar. 4, 1859-May 1, 1861
John Scott Harrison, Ohio (son of William Henry Harrison)
  33rd-34th Congresses, Mar. 4, 1853-Mar. 3, 1857
David Gardiner Tyler, Va. (son of John Tyler)
  53rd-54th Congresses, Mar. 4, 1893-Mar. 3, 1897

Franklin Delano Roosevelt, Jr., N.Y. (son of Franklin Delano Roosevelt)
   81st-82nd-83rd Congresses, June 14, 1949-Jan. 2, 1955
James Roosevelt, Calif. (son of Franklin Delano Roosevelt)
   84th-85th-86th Congresses, Jan. 3, 1955-Sept. 30, 1965

WHITE HOUSE WEDDINGS

1812
Mar. 29, Mrs. Lucy Payne Washington, sister of Mrs. James Madison and widow of George Steptoe Washington, a nephew of George Washington, to Thomas Todd, Associate Justice, U.S. Supreme Court; the Reverend Mr. McCormick officiated

1820
Mar. 9, Maria Hester Monroe, youngest daughter of President James Monroe, to Samuel Lawrence Gouverneur; the Reverend Mr. Hawley officiated

1828
Feb. 25, Mary Catherine Hellen, niece of Mrs. John Quincy Adams, to John Adams, son of President John Quincy Adams; the Reverend Mr. Hawley officiated

1832
Apr. 10, Mary A. Eastin, niece of President Andrew Jackson, to Lucien J. Polk; the Reverend Mr. Hawley officiated

Nov. 29, Delia Lewis, daughter of William B. Lewis of President Jackson's "kitchen cabinet" to Alphonse Joseph Pageot, secretary of the French legation

1842
Jan. 31, Elizabeth Tyler, daughter of President John Tyler, to William Nevison Waller; the Reverend Mr. Hawley officiated

1874
May 21, Nellie Grant, daughter of President Ulysses Simpson Grant, to Algernon Charles Frederick Sartoris of the British legation, the Reverend Dr. Tiffany officiated

1878
June 19, Emily Platt, niece of President Rutherford Birchard Hayes, to Colonel Russell Hastings; Bishop Jagger officiated

1886
June 2, Frances Folsom to President Grover Cleveland; the Reverend Dr. Sunderland officiated

1906
Feb. 17, Alice Roosevelt, daughter of President Theodore Roosevelt, to Representative Nicholas Longworth; the Right Reverend Mr. Satterlee officiated

1913
Nov. 25, Jessie Woodrow Wilson, daughter of President Woodrow Wilson, to Francis Bowes Sayre; the Reverend Dr. Beach officiated

1914
May 7, Eleanor Wilson, daughter of President Woodrow Wilson,

to William Gibbs McAdoo, Secretary of the Treasury in President
Wilson's cabinet; the Reverend Dr. Beach officiated

1918

Aug. 7, Alice Wilson, niece of President Woodrow Wilson, to the
Reverend Isaac Stuart McElroy, Jr.; the Reverend Isaac Stuart
McElroy, Sr., officiated

1942

July 30, Mrs. Louise Gill Macy to Harry L. Hopkins, Secretary of
Commerce in President Franklin Delano Roosevelt's second administration; the Reverend Mr. Clinchy officiated

1967

Dec. 9, Lynda Bird Johnson, daughter of President Lyndon Baines
Johnson, to Charles Spittal Robb; the Reverend Gerald McAllister
officiated

1971

June 12, Patricia Tricia Nixon, daughter of President Richard Milhous Nixon, to Edward Ridley Finch Cox; the Reverend Edward
Gardiner Latch officiated

THE PRESIDENTS' DESCENDANTS

The direct lineage of the Presidents extends to the ninth and tenth
generations in the case of John Adams and Jefferson. Jefferson's descendants number over 1,225; Adams' descendants over 735.

The President with the greatest number of children was John Tyler,
who had fifteen children by his two wives. William Henry Harrison
led with the greatest number of grandchildren and great-grandchildren. He had 48 grandchildren and 106 great-grandchildren.

With the deaths of Presidents Washington, Madison, Polk, Buchanan, and Harding, their respective lines ceased.

ALPHABETICAL LIST OF PRESIDENTS

Adams, John
Adams, John Quincy
Arthur, Chester Alan
Buchanan, James
Cleveland, Grover
Coolidge, Calvin
Eisenhower, Dwight David
Fillmore, Millard
Garfield, James Abram
Grant, Ulysses Simpson
Harding, Warren Gamaliel
Harrison, Benjamin
Harrison, William Henry
Hayes, Rutherford Birchard
Hoover, Herbert Clark
Jackson, Andrew
Jefferson, Thomas
Johnson, Andrew
Johnson, Lyndon Baines

Kennedy, John Fitzgerald
Lincoln, Abraham
McKinley, William
Madison, James
Monroe, James
Nixon, Richard Milhous
Pierce, Franklin
Polk, James Knox
Roosevelt, Franklin Delano
Roosevelt, Theodore
Taft, William Howard
Taylor, Zachary
Truman, Harry S.
Tyler, John·
Van Buren, Martin
Washington, George
Wilson, Woodrow

THE PRESIDENTS' NAMES

Seven Presidents bore the same given names as their fathers: John Adams, James Madison, Andrew Jackson, John Tyler, James Buchanan, William McKinley, and Theodore Roosevelt.

Eight Presidents had family names ending in *son:* Jefferson, Madison, Jackson, William Henry Harrison, Andrew Johnson, Benjamin Harrison, Wilson, and Lyndon Baines Johnson.

Three Presidents had the same family names as the three earlier Presidents to whom they were related: John Quincy Adams, son of John Adams; Benjamin Harrison, grandson of William Henry Harrison; and Franklin Delano Roosevelt, a fifth cousin of Theodore Roosevelt.

Andrew Johnson and Lyndon Baines Johnson bore the same family name but were not related.

Seventeen of the thirty-six Presidents were not given a middle initial or name. They were George Washington, John Adams, Thomas Jefferson, James Madison, James Monroe, Andrew Jackson, Martin Van Buren, John Tyler, Zachary Taylor, Millard Fillmore, Franklin Pierce, James Buchanan, Abraham Lincoln, Andrew Johnson, Benjamin Harrison, William McKinley, and Theodore Roosevelt. (Harry Truman gave himself the middle initial "S.")

Twenty-one of the thirty-six Presidents were given biblical names. Five were named James—the name most frequently given: Madison, Monroe, Polk, Buchanan, and Garfield (whose middle name, Abram, was also biblical). Five were named John: John Adams, John Quincy Adams, Tyler, Coolidge (originally John Calvin), and Kennedy. Two were named Andrew: Jackson and Johnson. Two were named Thomas: Jefferson and Wilson (originally Thomas Woodrow). One—Lincoln—was named Abraham. One—Harrison—was named Benjamin. Also given biblical names were Harding, whose middle name was Gamaliel; Eisenhower, who transposed his names from David

Dwight to Dwight David; Taylor, whose first name, Zachary, was an adaptation of Zachariah; Grant, who dropped his original first name, Hiram; and Cleveland, who dropped his original first name, Stephen.

Five Presidents were given at birth first names that they later changed. Hiram Ulysses Grant became Ulysses Simpson Grant, Stephen Grover Cleveland became Grover Cleveland, Thomas Woodrow Wilson became Woodrow Wilson, John Calvin Coolidge became Calvin Coolidge, and David Dwight Eisenhower became Dwight David Eisenhower.

The last names of five Presidents began with the letter *H:* William Henry Harrison, Rutherford Birchard Hayes, Benjamin Harrison, Warren Gamaliel Harding, and Herbert Clark Hoover.

NICKNAMES AND SOBRIQUETS

Many of the Presidents have been known by nicknames and sobriquets, a few of which are given below. In some instances, malcontents have applied epithets to those whom they disliked intensely.

Washington

American Fabius
Atlas of America
Cincinnatus of the West
Deliverer of America
Farmer President
Father of His Country
Father of Pittsburgh
Old Fox
Sage of Mount Vernon
Savior of His Country
Stepfather of His Country
Surveyor President
Sword of the Revolution

J. Adams

Atlas of Independence
Colossus of Debate
Colossus of Independence
Duke of Braintree
Father of American Independence
Father of the American Navy
His Rotundity
Old Sink or Swim
Partisan of Independence

Jefferson

Father of the Declaration of Independence
Father of the University of Virginia
Long Tom
Man of the People

Pen of the Revolution
Philosopher of Democracy
Red Fox
Sage of Monticello
Scribe of the Revolution

Madison

Father of the Constitution
Sage of Montpelier

Monroe

Era of Good Feeling President
Last of the Cocked Hats

J. Q. Adams

Accidental President
Old Man Eloquent
Second John

Jackson

Duel Fighter
Hero of New Orleans
King Andrew the First
Land Hero of 1812
Mischievous Andy
Old Hickory
People's President
Pointed Arrow
Sage of the Hermitage
Sharp Knife

Van Buren

American Talleyrand
Enchanter
Fox
Kinderhook Fox
King Martin the First
Little Magician
Little Van
Machiavellian Belshazzar
Mistletoe Politician
Petticoat Pet
Red Fox of Kinderhook
Sage of Kinderhook
Sage of Lindenwald
Whiskey Van
Wizard of Kinderhook
Wizard of the Albany Regency

W. H. Harrison

Farmer President

Hero of Tippecanoe
Log Cabin President
Old Granny
Old Tip
Old Tippecanoe
Tippecanoe
Washington of the West

Tyler

Accidental President
His Accidency
Young Hickory

Polk

First Dark Horse
Napoleon of the Stump
Young Hickory

Taylor

Old Buena Vista
Old Rough and Ready
Old Zach

Fillmore

Accidental President
American Louis Philippe
His Accidency
Wool-Carder President

Pierce

Handsome Frank
Purse
Young Hickory

Buchanan

Bachelor President
Old Buck
Old Public Functionary
Sage of Wheatland
Ten-cent Jimmy

Lincoln

Ancient
Buffoon
Caesar
Father Abraham
Flatboat Man
Grand Wrestler
Great Emancipator
Honest Abe
Illinois Baboon

Jester
Long 'Un
Man of the People
Martyr President
Railsplitter
Sage of Springfield
Sectional President
Tycoon
Tyrant
Uncle Abe

A. Johnson

Daddy of the Baby
Father of the Homestead Act
His Accidency
King Andy the First
Old Andy
Old Veto
Sir Veto
Tennessee Tailor
Veto President

Grant

American Casear
Butcher from Galena
Butcher Grant
Galena Tanner
Great Hammerer
Great Peacemaker
Hero of Appomattox
Hero of Fort Donelson
Old Three Stars
Silent Man
Tanner President
Texas
Uncle Sam
Unconditional Surrender
Union Safeguard
United States
Unprecedented Strategist
Unquestionably Skilled
Useless Grant

Hayes

Dark Horse President
Fraud President
Granny Hayes
Hero of '77
His Fraudulency
Old Eight to Seven

President De Facto

Garfield

Canal Boy
Martyr President
Preacher President
Teacher President

Arthur

America's First Gentlemen
Arthur the Gentleman
Dude President
Elegant Arthur
First Gentleman of the Land
His Accidency
Our Chet
Prince Arthur

Cleveland

Buffalo Hangman
Buffalo Sheriff
Claimant
Dumb Prophet
Grover the Good
Hangman of Buffalo
Man of Destiny
Old Grover
Old Veto
People's President
Perpetual Candidate
Pretender
Reform Governor
Sage of Princeton
Stubborn Old Grover
Stuffed Prophet
Uncle Jumbo
Veto Governor
Veto Mayor
Veto President

B. Harrison

Centennial President
Chinese Harrison
Grandfather's Hat
Grandpa's Grandson
Kid Gloves Harrison
Little Ben
Son of His Grandfather

McKinley

Idol of Ohio
Napoleon of Protection
Prosperity's Advance Agent
Stocking-foot Orator
Wobbly Willie

T. Roosevelt

Bull Moose
Driving Force
Dynamo of Power
Four Eyes
Great White Chief
Happy Warrior
Haroun-al-Roosevelt
Hero of San Juan Hill
Man on Horseback
Meddler
Old Lion
Rough Rider
T.R.
Teddy
Telescope Teddy
Trust Buster
Typical American

Wilson

Coiner of Weasel Words
Phrasemaker
Professor
Schoolmaster in Politics

Coolidge

Red
Silent Cal

Hoover

Chief
Friend of Helpless Children
Grand Old Man
Hermit Author of Palo Alto
Man of Great Heart

F. D. Roosevelt

Boss
F.D.R.
Houdini in the White House
Sphinx
Squire of Hyde Park
That Man in the White House

Truman

Give 'Em Hell Harry
Haberdasher Harry
High Tax Harry
Man from Missouri
Man of Independence

Eisenhower

General Ike
Ike

Kennedy

J.F.K.
Jack

L. B. Johnson

L.B.J.
Landslide Lyndon
Light Bulb Johnson

Nixon

Tricky Dick
Richard the Chicken-hearted

CULTURAL AND VOCATIONAL BACKGROUND

PRESIDENTS WHO ATTENDED COLLEGE

The following is a list of Presidents who attended college, the institutions attended, and the dates of graduation:

J. Adams–Harvard, July 16, 1755
Jefferson–William and Mary, Apr. 25, 1762
Madison–Princeton, Sept. 25, 1771
Monroe–William and Mary, 1776
J. Q. Adams–Harvard, July 18, 1787
W. H. Harrison–Hampden-Sydney, left before graduation
Tyler–William and Mary, July 4, 1807
Polk–North Carolina, June 4, 1818
Pierce–Bowdoin, Sept. 1, 1824
Buchanan–Dickinson, Sept. 27, 1809
Grant–U.S. Military Academy, July 1, 1843
Hayes–Kenyon, Aug. 3, 1842
Garfield–Williams, Aug. 6, 1856
Arthur–Union, July 1848
B. Harrison–Miami, June 24, 1852
McKinley–Allegheny, left before graduation
T. Roosevelt–Harvard, June 30, 1880
Taft–Yale, June 27, 1878
Wilson–Princeton, June 18, 1879
Harding–Ohio Central, left before graduation
Coolidge–Amherst, June 26, 1895

Hoover–Stanford, May 29, 1895
F. D. Roosevelt–Harvard, June 24, 1903
Eisenhower–U.S. Military Academy, June 12, 1915
Kennedy–Harvard, June 21, 1940
L. B. Johnson–Southwest Texas State, Aug. 19, 1930
Nixon–Whittier, June 9, 1934

COLLEGES OF THE PRESIDENTS

Allegheny–McKinley
Amherst–Coolidge
Bowdoin–Pierce
Dickinson–Buchanan
Hampden-Sydney–W. H. Harrison
Harvard–J. Adams, J. Q. Adams, T. Roosevelt, F. D. Roosevelt, Kennedy
Kenyon–Hayes
Miami–B. Harrison
North Carolina–Polk
Ohio Central–Harding
Princeton–Madison, Wilson
Southwest Texas State–L. B. Johnson
Stanford–Hoover
Union–Arthur
U.S. Military Academy–Grant, Eisenhower
Whittier–Nixon
William and Mary–Jefferson, Monroe, Tyler
Williams–Garfield
Yale–Taft

PRESIDENTS WHO DID NOT ATTEND COLLEGE

Washington
Jackson
Van Buren
Taylor
Fillmore
Lincoln
A. Johnson
Cleveland
Truman

EARLY OCCUPATIONS

Washington–Surveyor, farmer
J. Adams–Lawyer, teacher
Jefferson–Lawyer
Madison–Lawyer
Monroe–Lawyer, soldier
J. Q. Adams–Lawyer, private secretary
Jackson–Lawyer, saddler
Van Buren–Lawyer
W. H. Harrison–Soldier

Tyler–Lawyer
Polk–Lawyer, clerk
Taylor–Farmer, soldier
Fillmore–Lawyer, wool comber
Pierce–Lawyer
Buchanan–Lawyer
Lincoln–Lawyer, farm worker
A. Johnson–Tailor, public official
Grant–Farmer, soldier
Hayes–Lawyer
Garfield–Lawyer, canal driver
Arthur–Lawyer, teacher
Cleveland–Clerk, teacher
B. Harrison–Lawyer
McKinley–Lawyer, teacher
T. Roosevelt–Public official
Taft–Lawyer
Wilson–Lawyer, teacher
Harding–Journalist
Coolidge–Lawyer
Hoover–Engineer
F. D. Roosevelt–Lawyer
Truman–Farmer, haberdasher, judge
Eisenhower–Soldier
Kennedy–Student, legislator
L. B. Johnson–Teacher, rancher
Nixon–Lawyer

OCCUPATIONS OF THE PRESIDENTS

Twenty-four of the thirty-six Presidents were admitted to the bar as attorneys, having fulfilled the legal requirements. However, they were not all graduates of law schools.

The twelve Presidents not lawyers were Washington and William Henry Harrison, who were farmers and soldiers; Harding, a publisher and editor; Hoover, an engineer; Taylor, Grant, and Eisenhower, professional soldiers; Andrew Johnson, Theodore Roosevelt, Truman, Kennedy, and Lyndon Baines Johnson, public officials.

OCCUPATIONS AFTER TERMS

Three Presidents engaged in governmental activities after completing their terms: John Quincy Adams became a representative, Andrew Johnson became a senator, and Hoover was active on various government commissions.

Grant and Hoover devoted considerable time to writing; Hoover was also active as a public speaker. Truman and Eisenhower have likewise been active as writers and speakers.

John Adams, Pierce, and Buchanan retired from public life and avoided public appearances.

Five Presidents were active as farmers or planters: Washington, Jefferson, Madison, Jackson, and Hayes. Washington was also active as commander-in-chief of the army.

Benjamin Harrison was a professor of international law at Leland Stanford University.

Six Presidents traveled extensively after their terms: Van Buren, Fillmore, Polk, Pierce, Grant, and Theodore Roosevelt.

Truman, Eisenhower, and L. B. Johnson devoted much time to writing and to developing the libraries named for them.

POLITICAL EXPERIENCE

Presidents who had not revealed administrative ability prior to election or proved their vote-getting power were those famed for their military exploits, namely Washington, Grant, and Eisenhower. Grant, however, had served in Andrew Johnson's cabinet as secretary of war ad interim.

The following is a list of the various capacities in which Presidents served and the number of Presidents who served in each:

Mayors of home towns—3
Ministers to foreign countries—7
Governors of states—13
Vice Presidents—12
Members of presidential cabinets—9
U.S. Representatives—17
U.S. Senators—16
Members of both the House and Senate—10
Some Presidents served in more than one capacity.

MAYORS OF HOME TOWNS

Andrew Johnson–Greeneville, Tenn., 1830-1834
Grover Cleveland–Buffalo, N.Y., 1882
Calvin Coolidge–Northampton, Mass., 1910-1911

MINISTERS TO FOREIGN COUNTRIES

J. Adams–Great Britain
Jefferson–France
Monroe–France
J. Q. Adams–The Netherlands, Portugal, Prussia, Russia, Great Britain
Van Buren–Great Britain
W. H. Harrison–Columbia
Buchanan–Great Britain

STATE GOVERNORS

Jefferson–Virginia
Monroe–Virginia
Van Buren–New York
Tyler–Virginia
Polk–Tennessee
Hayes–Ohio
A. Johnson–Tennessee
Cleveland–New York
McKinley–Ohio

T. Roosevelt–New York
Wilson–New Jersey
Coolidge–Massachusetts
F. D. Roosevelt–New York

TERRITORIAL GOVERNORS

Jackson–Florida
W. H. Harrison–Indiana

PRESIDENTS WHO SERVED IN PRESIDENTIAL CABINETS

Secretary of State

Jefferson (under Washington), Sept. 26, 1789-Mar. 3, 1797 (entered upon duties Mar. 22, 1790)

Madison (under Jefferson), Mar. 5, 1801-Mar. 3, 1809 (entered upon duties May 2, 1801)

Monroe (under Madison), Apr. 2, 1811-Mar. 3, 1817 (entered upon duties Apr. 6, 1811)

J. Q. Adams (under Monroe), Mar. 5, 1817-Mar. 3, 1825 (entered upon duties Sept. 22, 1817)

Van Buren (under Jackson), Mar. 6, 1829-May 23, 1831 (entered upon duties Mar. 28, 1829)

Buchanan (under Polk), Mar. 6, 1845-Mar. 3, 1849 (entered upon duties Mar. 10, 1845)

Buchanan (under Taylor), Mar. 4, 1849-Mar. 6, 1849

Secretary of War

Monroe (under Madison), ad interim Jan. 1, 1813-Jan. 13, 1813

Monroe (under Madison), ad interim Aug. 30, 1814-Mar. 14, 1815

Grant (under Johnson), ad interim Aug. 12, 1867-Jan. 13, 1868

Taft (under T. Roosevelt), Jan. 11, 1904-June 29, 1908 (to take effect Feb. 1, 1904)

Secretary of Commerce

Hoover (under Harding), Mar. 5, 1921-Aug. 2, 1923

Hoover (under Coolidge), Aug. 3, 1923-Aug. 21, 1928

PRESIDENTS WHO SERVED IN CONGRESS—STATES REPRESENTED AND TERMS OF OFFICE

Washington–Virginia
Continental Congress, 1774-1775
J. Adams–Massachusetts
Continental Congress, 1774-1778
Jefferson–Virginia
Continental Congress, 1775-1776; 1783-1785
Madison–Virginia
Continental Congress, 1780-1783; 1786-1788
U.S. House of Representatives, 1st-4th Congresses, Mar. 4, 1789-Mar. 3, 1797
Monroe–Virginia
Continental Congress, 1783-1786

U.S. Senate, Nov. 9, 1790-May 27, 1794

J. Q. Adams–Massachusetts

U.S. Senate, Mar. 4, 1803-June 8, 1808

U.S. House of Representatives, 22nd-30th Congresses, Mar. 4, 1831-Feb. 23, 1848

Jackson–Tennessee

U.S. House of Representatives, 4th Congress, Dec. 5, 1796-Mar. 3, 1797

U.S. Senate, elected for the term commencing Mar. 4, 1797, and served Sept. 26, 1797-Apr. 1798; Mar. 4, 1823-Oct. 14, 1825

Van Buren–New York

U.S. Senate, Mar. 4, 1821-Dec. 20, 1828

W. H. Harrison–Ohio

U.S. House of Representatives, a delegate from the Territory Northwest of the River Ohio, Mar. 4, 1799-May 14, 1800

U.S. House of Representatives, 14th Congress, Oct. 8, 1816-Mar. 3, 1819, took his seat Dec. 2, 1816

U.S. Senate, Mar. 4, 1825-May 20, 1828

Tyler–Virginia

U.S. House of Representatives, 16th Congress, Dec. 16, 1817-Mar. 3, 1821

U.S. Senate, Mar. 4, 1827-Feb. 29, 1836

Polk–Tennessee

U.S. House of Representatives, 19th-25th Congresses, Mar. 4, 1825-Mar. 3, 1839

Fillmore–New York

U.S. House of Representatives, 23rd Congress, Mar. 4, 1833-Mar. 3, 1835; 25th-27th Congresses, Mar. 4, 1837-Mar. 3, 1843

Pierce–New Hampshire

U.S. House of Representatives, 23rd-24th Congresses, Mar. 4, 1833-Mar. 3, 1837

U.S. Senate, Mar. 4, 1837-Feb. 28, 1842

Buchanan–Pennsylvania

U.S. House of Representatives, 17th-21st Congresses, Mar. 4, 1821-Mar. 3, 1831

U.S. Senate, Dec. 6, 1834-Mar. 5, 1845

Lincoln–Illinois

U.S. House of Representatives, 30th Congress, Mar. 4, 1847-Mar. 3, 1849

A. Johnson–Tennessee

U.S. House of Representatives, 28th-32nd Congresses, Mar. 4, 1843-Mar. 3, 1853

U.S. Senate, Oct. 8, 1857-Mar. 4, 1862; Mar. 4, 1875-July 31, 1875

Hayes–Ohio

U.S. House of Representatives, 39th-40th Congresses, Mar. 4, 1865-July 20, 1867

Garfield–Ohio

U.S. House of Representatives, 38th-46th Congresses, Mar. 4, 1863-Nov. 8, 1880

U.S. Senate (elected to the Senate, but declined Dec. 23, 1880, having been elected President of the United States)

B. Harrison–Indiana
U.S. Senate, Mar. 4, 1881-Mar. 3, 1887

McKinley–Ohio
U.S. House of Representatives, 45th-47th Congresses, Mar. 4, 1877-Mar. 3, 1883; 48th Congress, Mar. 4, 1883-May 27, 1884; 49th-51st Congresses, Mar. 4, 1885-Mar. 3, 1891

Harding–Ohio
U.S. Senate, Mar. 4, 1915-Jan. 13, 1921

Truman–Missouri
U.S. Senate, Jan. 3, 1935-Jan. 17, 1945

Kennedy–Massachusetts
U.S. House of Representatives, 80th-82nd Congresses, Jan. 3, 1947-Jan. 3, 1953
U.S. Senate, Jan. 3, 1953-Dec. 22, 1960

L. B. Johnson–Texas
U.S. House of Representatives, 75th-80th Congresses, Apr. 10, 1937-Jan. 3, 1949
U.S. Senate, Jan. 3, 1949-Jan. 3, 1961

Nixon–New York
U.S. House of Representatives, 80th-81st Congresses, Jan. 3, 1947-Jan. 2, 1951
U.S. Senate, Jan. 3, 1951-Jan. 3, 1953

PRESIDENTS ELECTED TO BOTH HOUSES OF CONGRESS (11)

J. Q. Adams
Jackson
W. H. Harrison
Tyler
Pierce
Buchanan
A. Johnson
Garfield (elected, but did not serve)
Kennedy
L. B. Johnson
Nixon

PRESIDENTS WHO SERVED ONLY IN THE HOUSE OF REPRESENTATIVES (6)

Madison
Polk
Fillmore
Lincoln
Hayes
McKinley

PRESIDENTS WHO SERVED ONLY IN THE SENATE (5)

Monroe
Van Buren

B. Harrison
Harding
Truman

PRESIDENTS WHO DID NOT SERVE IN CONGRESS (14)

Washington
J. Adams
Jefferson
Taylor
Grant
Arthur
Cleveland
T. Roosevelt
Taft
Wilson
Coolidge
Hoover
F. D. Roosevelt
Eisenhower

MILITARY SERVICE

The Constitution (Article II, section 2) provides that "the President shall be Commander in Chief of the Army and Navy of the United States, and of the Militia of the several states, when called into the actual Service of the United States."

Twenty-two of the thirty-six Presidents were in actual military service. They are listed below under the wars in which they served, with an asterisk preceding the name of each of the Presidents who served in two or more wars. The dates of service are listed in the individual biographies in Part I.

Revolutionary War

Washington
Monroe
*Jackson

War of 1812

*Jackson
W. H. Harrison
*Taylor

Black Hawk War

*Taylor
Lincoln

Mexican War

*Taylor
Pierce
Buchanan
*Grant

Civil War

A. Johnson
*Grant
Hayes
Garfield
Arthur
B. Harrison
McKinley

Spanish-American War

T. Roosevelt

World War I

Truman
*Eisenhower

World War II

*Eisenhower
Kennedy
L. B. Johnson

Korean War

Eisenhower
Kennedy
L.B. Johnson
Nixon

The following had no military service:
J. Adams
Jefferson
Madison
J. Q. Adams
Van Buren
Polk
Fillmore
Cleveland
Taft
Wilson
Harding
Coolidge
Hoover
F. D. Roosevelt

PRESIDENTS WOUNDED IN ACTION

James Monroe was wounded in the shoulder at the battle of Trenton, N.J., on December 26, 1776, in the Revolutionary War.

Rutherford Birchard Hayes was wounded four times while serving in the Union army. On May 10, 1862, a shell wounded his right knee at Giles Court House, Va. He was wounded in the left arm by a musket ball on September 14, 1862, at the battle of South Mountain, Md. On September 19, 1864, while at Winchester, Va., he was wounded in his head and shoulder by a musket ball. At the battle of Cedar

Creek, Va., October 19, 1864, he was wounded in the ankle, his horse was shot from under him, and he was erroneously reported dead. The following day, he was promoted to brigadier general.

John Fitzgerald Kennedy received the Purple Heart for injuries sustained in action off the Solomon Islands on August 2, 1943. Following the ramming and sinking of his PT boat, he personally rescued three of his men, one of whom was seriously wounded.

TWO FUTURE PRESIDENTS IN SAME REGIMENT DURING CIVIL WAR

The 23rd Ohio Regiment, which was organized in June 1861, had on its roster the names of two soldiers who later became Presidents of the United States. On June 23, 1861, William McKinley, age 18, was enrolled as a private. He was promoted to commissary sergeant on April 15, 1862, and commissioned as a second lieutenant on September 23, 1862, and as a first lieutenant on February 7, 1863. He became a captain on July 25, 1864. On March 13, 1865, he was brevetted a major of volunteers for gallantry and meritorious service during the campaign in West Virginia and in the Shenandoah Valley. He was mustered out July 26, 1865.

Rutherford Birchard Hayes, age 38, was commissioned a major on June 27, 1861; he advanced to lieutenant colonel on October 24, 1861, and to colonel on October 24, 1862. He was made a brigadier general of volunteers on October 19, 1864, and was brevetted major general of volunteers on March 13, 1865, for gallantry and distinguished service during the campaign of 1864 in West Virginia, and particularly at the battles of Fisher's Hill and Cedar Creek, Va. He resigned June 8, 1865.

RELIGIOUS AFFILIATIONS

Episcopalian (9)

Washington
Madison
Monroe
W. H. Harrison
Tyler
Taylor
Pierce
Arthur
F. D. Roosevelt

Presbyterian (7)

Jackson
Polk
Buchanan
Cleveland
B. Harrison
Wilson
Eisenhower

Unitarian (4)

J. Adams
J. Q. Adams
Fillmore
Taft

Methodist (3)

Grant
Hayes
McKinley

Baptist (2)

Harding
Truman

Disciples of Christ (2)

Garfield
L. B. Johnson

Dutch Reformed (2)

Van Buren
T. Roosevelt

Congregationalist (1)

Coolidge

Roman Catholic (1)

Kennedy

Society of Friends (Quaker) (2)

Hoover
Nixon

No specific denomination (3)

Jefferson
Lincoln
A. Johnson

The religious affiliations of Presidents often differed from that of their parents, since some of them adopted other religious faiths.

MEMBERS OF PHI BETA KAPPA—YEAR OF ELECTION, CHAPTER, AND TYPE OF MEMBERSHIP

J. Q. Adams–1787, Harvard, in course
Van Buren–1830, Union, honorary
Pierce–1825, Bowdoin, alumnus
Hayes–1880, Kenyon, alumnus
Garfield–1864, Williams, alumnus
Arthur–1848, Union, in course
Cleveland–1907, Princeton, honorary
T. Roosevelt–1880, Harvard, in course
Wilson–1889, Wesleyan, honorary

Coolidge–1921, Amherst, alumnus
F. D. Roosevelt–1929, Harvard, alumnus; 1929, Hobart, honorary
   Members in course are elected from candidates for degrees in liberal arts and sciences, generally from the upper tenth of the graduating class.

   Alumni members are elected from the alumni body of the sheltering institution; ordinarily they have been graduated at least ten years and are thought to merit recognition for scholarly accomplishment.

   Honorary members are elected from outside the student and alumni bodies of the sheltering institution, and are chosen on substantially the same basis as alumni members. Of honorary members the chapters now elect severally an average of not more than one in each triennium.

PRESIDENTS WHO WERE MASONS

Washington–Aug. 4, 1753, Fredericksburg Lodge No. 4, Fredericksburg, Va.
Monore–1775, Williamsburg Lodge No. 6, Williamsburg, Va.
Jackson–1800, Harmony Lodge No. 1, Nashville, Tenn.
Polk–Sept. 4, 1820, Columbia Lodge No. 31, Columbia, Tenn.
Buchanan–Jan. 24, 1817, Lodge No. 43, Lancaster, Pa.
A. Johnson–1851, Greeneville Lodge No. 119, Greeneville, Tenn.
Garfield–Nov. 22, 1864, Magnolia Lodge No. 20, Columbus, Ohio
McKinley–May 3, 1865, Hiram Lodge No. 21, Winchester, Va.
T. Roosevelt–Apr. 24, 1901, Matinecock Lodge No. 806, Oyster Bay, N.Y.
Taft–Feb. 18, 1909, affiliated with Kilwinning Lodge No. 356, Cincinnati, Ohio
Harding–Aug. 27, 1920, Marion Lodge No. 70, Marion, Ohio
F. D. Roosevelt–Nov. 28, 1911, Holland Lodge No. 8, Hyde Park, N.Y.
Truman–Mar. 9, 1909, Belton Lodge No. 450, Belton, Mo.
L. B. Johnson–Oct. 30, 1937, Johnson City Lodge No. 561, Johnson City, Tex.

BOOKS WRITTEN BY THE PRESIDENTS

   Practically all of the Presidents distinguished themselves as writers. Perhaps the most prolific were John Quincy Adams, Theodore Roosevelt, and Herbert Hoover.

   Many of the books contained addresses and speeches and were compiled by editors. Others were extracts from famous speeches and addresses. Many of the famous speeches were published separately in de luxe editions. Many were not written for publication, but eventually were published.

   The following list contains most of the books (of 36 or more pages) written by the Presidents. Posthumous collections of letters, speeches, and papers are listed after works prepared specifically for publication by the Presidents themselves. Many collected works containing letters, papers, messages, etc. have also been printed.

George Washington

The letters and papers of George Washington have been published
in many collections.

John Adams

Thoughts on Government, 1776
History of the Dispute with America from Its Origin in 1754, 1784
*Defence of the Constitutions of Government of the United States of
America* (3 volumes), 1787-1788
Discourses on Davila, 1805
*Correspondence Between the Hon. John Adams and the Late William
Cunningham,* 1823
*Familiar Letters of John Adams and His Wife Abigail Adams During
the Revolution,* 1876

Thomas Jefferson

Notes on the State of Virginia, 1785
Manual of Parliamentary Practice, 1801
*Proceedings of the Government of the United States in Maintaining the
Public Right to the Beach of the Mississippi,* 1812
Essay Towards Facilitating Instruction. . . . 1851
Writings of Thomas Jefferson (9 volumes), 1853-54
Calendar of Correspondence of Thomas Jefferson (3 volumes), 1894-1903
Jeffersonian Cyclopedia, 1900
Jefferson's Germantown Letters, 1906
Autobiography of Thomas Jefferson, 1914

James Madison

Letters of Helvidius, 1796
Examination of the British Doctrine, 1806
Papers of James Madison (3 volumes), 1840
Letters and Other Writings of James Madison (4 volumes), 1865
Calendar of the Correspondence of James Madison, 1894
Writings of James Madison (9 volumes), 1900-1910

James Monroe

*View of the Conduct of the Executive in the Foreign Affairs of the United
States,* 1798
Calendar of the Correspondence of James Monroe, 1891
Writings of James Monroe (7 volumes), 1898-1903

John Quincy Adams

Jubilee of the Constitution, 1789
An answer to Paine's Rights of Man, 1793
Letters on Silesia, 1804
Letter to Hon. Harrison Gray Otis, 1808
Lectures on Rhetoric and Oratory, 1810
*Duplicate Letters, the Fisheries and the Mississippi. Documents Relating
to Transactions at the Negotiation of Ghent,* 1822

Eulogy on the Life and Character of James Monroe, 1831
Dermot MacMorrogh, or the Conquest of Ireland, 1834
Oration on the Life and Character of Gilbert Motier de La Fayette, 1835
Eulogy on the Life and Character of James Madison, 1836
Letters from John Quincy Adams to His Constituents of the Twelfth Congressional District in Massachusetts, 1837
Oration Before the Inhabitants of Newburyport, 1837
Discourse on Education, 1840
Social Compact, 1842
New England Confederacy of 1648, 1843
Life of General Lafayette, 1847
Letters of John Quincy Adams to His Son on the Bible, 1850
Lives of James Madison and James Monroe, 1850
Letters and Opinions of the Masonic Fraternity, 1851
Poems of Religion and Society, 1854
Memoirs of John Quincy Adams (12 volumes), 1874-1877
Letters and Addresses on Freemasonry, 1875
Life in a New England Town (diary of J.Q.A.), 1903
Diary of John Quincy Adams, 1929

Andrew Jackson

Correspondence of Andrew Jackson (7 volumes), 1926-1935

Martin Van Buren

Inquiry into the Origin and Course of Political Parties in the United States, 1867
Autobiography of Martin Van Buren, 1920

William Henry Harrison

Discourse on the Aborigines of the Valley of Ohio, 1839

John Tyler

Lecture Delivered Before the Maryland Institute for the Promotion of the Mechanic Arts, 1855

James Knox Polk

Diary of James Knox Polk (4 volumes), 1910
Letters of James K. Polk to Cave Johnson, 1915

Zachary Taylor

Letters of Zachary Taylor, 1908

Millard Fillmore

Early Life of Hon. Millard Fillmore (by Fillmore), 1880
Millard Fillmore Papers (2 volumes), 1907

James Buchanan

The Administration on the Eve of the Rebellion, 1865
Works of James Buchanan (12 volumes), 1908-1911

Abraham Lincoln

Legacy of Fun, 1865

Lincoln's Anecdotes, 1867
Abraham Lincoln's Complete Works (2 volumes), 1894
Autobiography of Abraham Lincoln, 1905
Writings of Abraham Lincoln (8 volumes), 1905-1906
Life and Works of Abraham Lincoln (9 volumes), 1907
Uncollected Letters of Abraham Lincoln, 1917
Abraham Lincoln's Don'ts, 1918

Andrew Johnson

Speeches of Andrew Johnson, 1866

Ulysses Simpson Grant

Personal Memoirs (2 volumes), 1885-1886
General Grant's Letters to a Friend, 1897

Rutherford Birchard Hayes

Diary and Letters of R. B. Hayes (5 volumes), 1922

James Abram Garfield

Great Speeches of James Abram Garfield, 1881

Grover Cleveland

Principles and Purposes of Our Form of Government, 1892
Writings and Speeches of Grover Cleveland, 1892
Self Made Man in American Life, 1897
Independence of the Executive, 1900
Presidential Problems, 1904
Fishing and Shooting Sketches, 1906
Good Citizenship, 1908
Addresses—State Papers, 1909
Venezuelan Boundary Controversy, 1913
Letters of Grover Cleveland, 1933

Benjamin Harrison

Constitution and Administration of the U.S.A., 1897
This Country of Ours, 1897
Views of an Ex-President, 1901

William McKinley

Life and Speeches of William McKinley, 1896
The Tariff, 1904

Theodore Roosevelt

Naval War of 1812, 1882
Hunting Trip of a Ranchman, 1885
Thomas Hart Benton, 1887
Ranch Life and the Hunting-Trail, 1888
Winning of the West, 1889
History of New York City, 1891
The Wilderness Hunter, 1893
Hero Tales from American History (with Henry Cabot Lodge), 1895

Gouverneur Morris, 1896
American Ideals and Other Essays, 1897
Rough Riders, 1899
Oliver Cromwell, 1900
Strenuous Life, 1900
Outdoor Pastimes of an American Hunter, 1905
Good Hunting, 1907
True Americanism, 1907
African and European Addresses, 1910
African Game Trails, 1910
New Nationalism, 1910
Conservation of Womanhood and Childhood, 1912
Realizable Ideals, 1912
History as Literature and Other Essays, 1913
Progressive Principles, 1913
Theodore Roosevelt, An Autobiography, 1913
Life-Histories of African Game Animals (with Edmund Heller), 1914
Through the Brazilian Wilderness, 1914
America and the World War, 1915
Book-Lover's Holiday in the Open, 1916
Fear God and Take Your Own Part (articles from the *Metropolitan*), 1916
The Foes of Our Own Household, 1917
Great Adventure, 1918
National Strength and International Duty, 1918
Theodore Roosevelt's Letters to His Children, 1919
Letters to Anna Roosevelt Cowles, 1870-1918, 1924
Who Should Go West, 1927
Theodore Roosevelt's Diaries of Boyhood and Youth, 1928
Letters to Kermit Roosevelt, 1902-1908, 1946

William Howard Taft

Four Aspects of Civic Duty, 1906,
Present Day Problems, Addresses 1908
Political Issues and Outlooks, 1909
Popular Government, 1913
Anti-Trust Act and the Supreme Court, 1914
United States and Peace, 1914
Ethics in Service, 1915
Our Chief Magistrate and His Powers 1916
Liberty Under Law, 1922

Woodrow Wilson

Congressional Government, 1885
The State, 1889
State and Federal Governments of the United States, 1889
Division and Re-union, 1893
George Washington, 1896
Mere Literature and Other Essays, 1896

When a Man Comes to Himself, 1901
History of the American People (5 volumes), 1902
Constitutional Government, 1911
New Freedom, 1913
Robert E. Lee, an Interpretation, 1924
Public Papers of Woodrow Wilson (6 volumes), 1925-1927

Warren Gamaliel Harding

Rededicating America, 1920
Our Common Country, 1921

Calvin Coolidge

Have Faith in Massachusetts, 1919
Price of Freedom, 1924
America's Need for Education, 1925
Autobiography of Calvin Coolidge, 1929

Herbert Clark Hoover

Principles of Mining, 1909
American Individualism, 1922
New Day, 1928
Boyhood in Iowa, 1931
Hoover After Dinner, 1933
Challenge to Liberty, 1934
Addresses Upon the American Road (8 volumes), 1938-1961
America's Way Forward, 1939
Shall We Send Our Youth to War? 1939
America's First Crusade, 1942
Problems of Lasting Peace, 1942
Memoirs—Volume I, *Years of Adventure, 1874-1920,* 1951; Volume II,
   The Cabinet and the Presidency, 1920-1933, 1952; Volume III, *The
   Great Depression, 1929-1941,* 1952
Ordeal of Woodrow Wilson, 1958

Franklin Delano Roosevelt

Happy Warrior, Alfred E. Smith, 1928
Records of the Town of Hyde Park, 1928
Government, Not Politics, 1932
Looking Forward, 1933
On Our Way, 1934
Public Papers and Addresses of F. D. Roosevelt (13 volumes), 1938-1950
Records of Crum Elbow Precinct, Dutchess County, 1940

Harry S. Truman

Memoirs—Volume I, *Year of Decision,* 1955; Volume II, *Years of Trial
   and Hope,* 1956

Dwight David Eisenhower

Crusade in Europe, 1951
The White House Years—Volume I, *Mandate for Change, 1953-1956,*
   1963; Volume II, *Waging Peace, 1956-1961,* 1965

At Ease, Stories I Tell to Friends, 1967
In Review: Pictures I've Kept, 1969

John Fitzgerald Kennedy

Why England Slept, 1940
Profiles in Courage, 1956 (Pulitzer Prize for biography, 1957)
A Nation of Immigrants, 1959
The Strategy of Peace, 1960
To Turn the Tide, 1962
The Burden and the Glory, 1964

Lyndon Baines Johnson

My Hope for America, 1964
A Time for Action, 1964
This America, 1966
The Vantage Point, Perspectives of the Presidency, 1971

Richard Milhous Nixon

Six Crises, 1962

PRESIDENTS' SPORTS AND HOBBIES

Sports or games indulged in by Presidents while in office are listed below. Some Presidents were real enthusiasts, others participated mildly.

Billiards—J. Q. Adams, Garfield
Boxing—T. Roosevelt
Bridge—Eisenhower
Croquet—Hayes
Driving—Hayes
Fishing—Washington, Jefferson, Arthur, Cleveland, Coolidge, Hoover, F. D. Roosevelt, Truman, Eisenhower
Golf—Taft, Wilson, Harding, Coolidge, Eisenhower, Nixon
Hunting—B. Harrison, T. Roosevelt, Eisenhower
Indian clubs—Coolidge
Jujitsu—T. Roosevelt
Mechanical horse—Coolidge
Medicine ball—Hoover
Painting—Eisenhower
Pitching hay—Coolidge
Poker—Harding, Truman
Riding—Washington, Jefferson, Jackson, Van Buren, Taylor, McKinley, T. Roosevelt, Taft, Wilson, Harding, L. B. Johnson
Sailing—F. D. Roosevelt, Kennedy
Shooting—Hayes, T. Roosevelt
Swimming—J. Q. Adams, McKinley, F. D. Roosevelt, Kennedy
Tennis—T. Roosevelt
Touch football—Kennedy
Walking—J. Q. Adams, Lincoln, McKinley, Wilson, Truman
Wrestling—T. Roosevelt

PRESIDENTS' MUSICAL ACCOMPLISHMENTS

Very few Presidents had musical training or the ability to play instruments. Jefferson and Tyler played the violin, Truman and Nixon the piano, and Coolidge the harmonica. As a young man, Harding palyed the alto horn and the cornet.

RESIDENCE

RESIDENT STATES OF THE PRESIDENTS

The Presidents, when inaugurated, were residents (though not necessarily natives) of the states listed below.

New York (8)

Van Buren
Fillmore
Arthur
Cleveland
T. Roosevelt
F. D. Roosevelt
Eisenhower
Nixon

Ohio (6)

W. H. Harrison
Hayes
Garfield
McKinley
Taft
Harding

Virginia (5)

Washington
Jefferson
Madison
Monroe
Tyler

Massachusetts (4)

J. Adams
J. Q. Adams
Coolidge
Kennedy

Tennessee

Jackson
Polk
A. Johnson

Illinois (2)

Lincoln
Grant

California (1)
Hoover

Indiana (1)
B. Harrison

Louisiana (1)
Taylor

Missouri (1)
Truman

New Hampshire (1)
Pierce

New Jersey (1)
Wilson

Pennsylvania (1)
Buchanan

Texas (1)
L. B. Johnson

PRESIDENTS WHO RESIDED IN STATES OTHER THAN THEIR BIRTHPLACES

The fifteen Presidents listed below were residents of states other than their native states. The name of each is followed by (1) the state in which he resided and (2) the state in which he was born.

Jackson–Tennessee, South Carolina
W. H. Harrison–Ohio, Virginia
Polk–Tennessee, North Carolina
Taylor–Louisiana, Virginia
Lincoln–Illinois, Kentucky
A. Johnson–Tennessee, North Carolina
Grant–Illinois, Ohio
Arthur–New York, Vermont
Cleveland–New York, New Jersey
B. Harrison–Indiana, Ohio
Wilson–New Jersey, Virginia
Coolidge–Massachusetts, Vermont
Hoover–California, Iowa
Eisenhower–New York, Texas
Nixon–New York, California

FAMOUS PRESIDENTIAL HOMES

Many of the Presidents were born in or lived in homes which have become famous. Some of the more famous homes or estates follow:

Washington

Mount Vernon, Mount Vernon, Va.

Jefferson
Monticello, Charlottesville, Va.

Madison
Montpelier, Va.

Monroe
Ash Lawn, Oak Hill, Va.

Jackson
The Hermitage, Nashville, Tenn.

Van Buren
Lindenwald, Kinderhook, N.Y.

Tyler
Sherwood Forest, Charles City County, Va.

Buchanan
Wheatland, Pa.

Hayes
Spiegel Grove, near Fremont, Ohio

T. Roosevelt
Sagamore Hill, Oyster Bay, N.Y.

Coolidge
The Beeches, Northampton, Mass.

L. B. Johnson
The LBJ ranch, near Johnson City, Tex.
There are other well-known residences, such as the F. D. Roosevelt Home at Hyde Park, N.Y., and the Eisenhower farm at Gettysburg, Pa., but they are not known by any special names.

AGE AND PHYSICAL CHARACTERISTICS

AGES OF PRESIDENTS IN OFFICE

Andrew Jackson was 69 years and 354 days old when he completed his eight years as President.

James Buchanan was 69 years and 315 days old when he left office, but he served only four years. He was four years older than Jackson when inaugurated.

The oldest President inaugurated was William Henry Harrison, who was 68 years and 23 days old when he was inaugurated. He served only 31 days before he died.

President Eisenhower was 62 years and 98 days old when he was inaugurated. Upon completion of his eight years in office he was 70 years and 98 days old, 109 days older than Jackson.

The youngest President elected to office was John Fitzgerald Kennedy, who was 43 years and 236 days old when he was inaugurated.

Theodore Roosevelt was 42 years and 322 days old when he succeeded to the presidency.

PHYSICAL APPEARANCE

There is much interest in comparing the physical characteristics of the Presidents at the time when they were inaugurated or assumed office.

As contemporary reports vary and as writers interpret according to their own impressions, many conflicting reports exist. The description of a Republican President by a Democrat may differ from one by a Republican, and even without bias due to politics, personal appraisals by different people may vary.

The following is a list of known characteristics:

Washington

Height, 6 feet 2 inches; weight, 175 pounds; brown sandy hair, powdered, under powdered wig; blue eyes; high brow, scar on left cheek, black mole under right ear, pockmarks on nose and cheeks; strongly pointed chin; false teeth; powerful physique; broad sloping shoulders

J. Adams

Height, 5 feet 7 inches; corpulent; bald; expanded eyebrows

Jefferson

Height, 6 feet $2\frac{1}{2}$ inches; sandy, reddish hair; prominent cheekbones and chin; large hands and feet

Madison

Height, 5 feet 4 inches (smallest President in stature); weight, about 100 pounds; blond hair; blue eyes; weak speaking voice

Monroe

Height, 6 feet; rugged physique; blue-gray eyes, well-shaped nose, broad forehead; stooped shoulders

J. Q. Adams

Height, 5 feet 7 inches; bald

Jackson

Height, 6 feet 1 inch; thin; weight, 140 pounds; bushy iron-gray hair, brushed high above forehead; clear, dark blue eyes; prominent eyebrows

Van Buren

Height, 5 feet 6 inches; small, erect, slender; red and graying hair, bald spot, deep wrinkles

W. H. Harrison

Height, 5 feet 8 inches; long, thin face, irregular features

Tyler

Height, 6 feet; thin; light brown hair; blue eyes; light complexion; high-bridged nose

Polk

Height, 5 feet 8 inches; nearly white hair, worn long; sharp gray eyes; high forehead, thin, angular brow

Taylor

Height, 5 feet 8 inches; weight, 170 pounds; black hair; gray eyes, squint; ruddy complexion; short legs in proportion to body

Fillmore

Height, 5 feet 9 inches; finely proportioned body; thin, grayish hair; blue eyes; light complexion; smooth forehead; well-developed chest

Pierce

Height, 5 feet 10 inches; erect bearing; penetrating dark gray eyes; small but strong features; stiff military carriage

Buchanan

Height, 6 feet; imperfect vision; light complexion; protruding chin; short neck; muscular appearance

Lincoln

Height, 6 feet 4 inches (tallest President); weight, 180 pounds; beard; black hair; gray eyes

A. Johnson

Height, 5 feet 10 inches; stocky; brown hair, worn long; light eyes; high forehead

Grant

Height, 5 feet $8^1/_2$ inches; beard; square, straight brows; large head; heavy nostrils; firm-set mouth

Hayes

Height, 5 feet $8^1/_2$ inches; weight, 170 pounds; dark brown hair; sandy red beard; deeply set blue eyes; large head, high forehead, straight nose, circling brows; mild but very audible voice

Garfield

Height, 6 feet; light brown, graying hair, receding hair line; beard; blue eyes; large head, high forehead; strong frame, broad shoulders; left-handed

Arthur

Height, 6 feet 2 inches; full side whiskers and mustache; handsome appearance; well-proportioned body

Cleveland

Height, 5 feet 11 inches; weight, 260 pounds, corpulent; graying hair, growing bald; heavy, drooping mustache; short neck

B. Harrison

Height, 5 feet 6 inches; blond, graying hair; full beard; small, bright blue eyes; short neck; short legs

McKinley

Height, 5 feet 7 inches; high forehead, receding hair line; prominent chin; broad forehead

T. Roosevelt

Height, 5 feet 10 inches; pince-nez eyeglasses with thick lenses; prominent teeth; bushy eyebrows; drooping mustache; high voice

Taft

Height, 6 feet; huge frame; weight, 300-332 pounds; deep-set eyes; ruddy complexion; turned-up mustache

Wilson

Height, 5 feet 11 inches; weight, 170 pounds; eyeglasses; clean-cut, ascetic face

Harding

Height, 6 feet; high forehead; graying hair; bushy eyebrows

Coolidge

Height, 5 feet 10 inches; large, clear forehead; thin nose; tightly set lips

Hoover

Height, 5 feet 11 inches; square-faced; ruddy complexion

F. D. Roosevelt

Height, 6 feet 2 inches; weight, 188 pounds; high forehead; graying hair; occasionally wore eyeglasses; wore braces on his legs

Truman

Height, 5 feet 9 inches; weight, 167 pounds; receding steel gray hair, parted on left; hazel eyes; eyeglasses with thick lenses

Eisenhower

Height, 5 feet 10½ inches; weight, 168-173 pounds; bald, with fringe of sandy, graying hair; blue eyes; ruddy complexion, engaging smile

Kennedy

Height, 6 feet; weight, 170-175 pounds; dark red hair, handsome appearance

L. B. Johnson

Height, 6 feet 3 inches; weight, 200 pounds; eyeglasses occasionally

Nixon

Height, 5 feet 11½ inches; receding hair line; bushy eyebrows; up-swept nose; jutting jaw

DEATH AND BURIAL

DATE OF DEATH, AGE AT DEATH, PLACE OF DEATH, AND PLACE OF BURIAL OF THE PRESIDENTS

Washington

Dec. 14, 1799; 67 years, 295 days; Mount Vernon, Va.

J. Adams

July 4, 1826; 90 years, 247 days; Quincy, Mass.

Jefferson

July 4, 1826; 83 years, 82 days; Charlottesville, Va.

Madison

June 28, 1836; 85 years, 104 days; Montpelier, Va.

Monroe

July 4, 1831; 73 years, 67 days; New York, N.Y.; buried at Richmond, Va.

J. Q. Adams

Feb. 23, 1848; 80 years, 227 days; Washington, D.C.; buried at Quincy, Mass.

Jackson

June 8, 1845; 78 years, 85 days; Nashville, Tenn.

Van Buren

July 24, 1862; 79 years, 231 days; Kinderhook, N.Y.

W. H. Harrison

Apr. 4, 1841; 68 years, 54 days; Washington, D.C.; buried at North Bend, Ohio

Tyler

Jan. 18, 1862; 71 years, 295 days; Richmond, Va.

Polk

June 15, 1849; 53 years, 225 days; Nashville, Tenn.

Taylor

July 9, 1850; 65 years, 227 days; Washington, D.C.; buried at Spring-field, Ky.

Fillmore

Mar. 8, 1874; 74 years, 60 days; Buffalo, N.Y.

Pierce

Oct. 8, 1869; 64 years, 319 days; Concord, N.H.

Buchanan

June 1, 1868; 77 years, 39 days; Lancaster, Pa.

Lincoln

Apr. 15, 1865; 56 years, 62 days; Washington, D.C.; buried at Springfield, Ill.

A. Johnson

July 31, 1875; 66 years, 214 days; Carter's Station, Tenn.; buried at Greeneville, Tenn.

Grant

July 23, 1885; 63 years, 87 days; Mt. McGregor, N.Y.; buried at New York, N.Y.

Hayes

Jan. 17, 1893; 70 years, 105 days; Fremont, Ohio

Garfield

Sept. 19, 1881; 49 years, 304 days; Elberon, N.J.; buried at Cleveland, Ohio

Arthur

Nov. 18, 1886; 56 years, 44 days; New York, N.Y.; buried at Albany, N.Y.

Cleveland

June 24, 1908; 71 years, 98 days; Princeton, N.J.

B. Harrison

Mar. 13, 1901; 67 years, 205 days; Indianapolis, Ind.

McKinley

Sept. 14, 1901; 58 years, 228 days; Buffalo, N.Y.; buried at Canton, Ohio

T. Roosevelt

Jan. 6, 1919; 60 years, 71 days; Oyster Bay, N.Y.

Taft

Mar. 8, 1930; 72 years, 174 days; Washington, D.C.; buried at Arlington National Cemetery, Arlington, Va.

Wilson

Feb. 3, 1924; 67 years, 37 days; Washington, D.C.

Harding

Aug. 2, 1923; 57 years, 273 days; San Francisco, Calif.; buried at Marion, Ohio

Coolidge

Jan. 5, 1933; 60 years, 185 days; Northampton, Mass.; buried at Plymouth, Vt.

Hoover

Oct. 20, 1964; 90 years, 71 days; New York, N.Y.; buried at West Branch, Iowa

F. D. Roosevelt

Apr. 12, 1945; 63 years, 72 days; Warm Springs, Ga.; buried at Hyde Park, N.Y.

Truman

Dec. 26, 1972; 88 years, 232 days; Kansas City, Mo.; buried at Independence, Mo.

Eisenhower

Mar. 28, 1969; 79 years, 165 days; Washington, D.C.; buried at Abilene, Kan.

Kennedy

Nov. 22, 1963; 46 years, 177 days; Dallas, Tex.; buried at Arlington National Cemetery, Arlington, Va.

L. B. Johnson

Jan. 22, 1973; 65 years, 148 days; San Antonio, Tex.; buried at Johnson City, Tex.

DEATH DATES ARRANGED BY MONTHS OF THE YEAR

January

5 1933—Coolidge
6 1919—T. Roosevelt
17 1893—Hayes
18 1862—Tyler
22 1973—L. B. Johnson

February

3 1924—Wilson
23 1848—J. Q. Adams

March

8 1874—Fillmore
8 1930—Taft
13 1901—B. Harrison
28 1969—Eisenhower

April

4 1841—W. H. Harrison
12 1945—F. D. Roosevelt
15 1865—Lincoln

June

    1 1868—Buchanan
    8 1845—Jackson
   15 1849—Polk
   24 1908—Cleveland
   28 1836—Madison

July

    4 1826—J. Adams
    4 1826—Jefferson
    4 1831—Monroe
    9 1850—Taylor
   23 1885—Grant
   24 1862—Van Buren
   31 1865—A. Johnson

August

    2 1923—Harding

September

   14 1901—McKinley
   19 1881—Garfield

October

    8 1869—Pierce
   20 1964—Hoover

November

   18 1886—Arthur
   22 1963—Kennedy

December

   14 1799—Washington
   26 1972—Truman

PRESIDENTS' DEATHS

Of the thirty-five Presidents no longer living in 1973, eight died in office and twenty-seven survived their terms.

No President died in the month of May.

Seven of the thirty-five Presidents died in July.

Two Presidents, John Adams and Thomas Jefferson, died on the same day, July 4, 1826.

The Whig Party nominated four presidential candidates; the two who were elected, William Henry Harrison and Zachary Taylor, died in office.

Two Democratic Presidents died in office: Franklin Delano Roosevelt, who died during his fourth term, and John Fitzgerald Kennedy, who was assassinated.

PRESIDENTS WHO DIED IN OFFICE

Eight Presidents died in office:

William Henry Harrison–died Apr. 4, 1841, Washington, D.C.; served 1 month; unexpired term of 3 years and 11 months filled by John Tyler

Zachary Taylor–died July 9, 1850, Washington, D.C.; served 1 year, 4 months, and 5 days; unexpired term of 2 years, 7 months, and 26 days filled by Millard Fillmore

Abraham Lincoln–died Apr. 15, 1865, Washington, D.C.; served 1 month and 10 days of second term; unexpired term of 3 years, 10 months, and 20 days filled by Andrew Johnson

James Abram Garfield–died Sept. 19, 1881, Elberon, N.J.; served 6 months and 15 days; unexpired term of 3 years, 5 months, and 15 days filled by Chester Alan Arthur

William McKinley–died Sept. 14, 1901, Buffalo, N.Y.; served 6 months and 10 days of second term; unexpired term of 3 years, 5 months; and 20 days filled by Theodore Roosevelt

Warren Gamaliel Harding–died Aug. 2, 1923, San Francisco, Calif.; served 2 years, 4 months, and 29 days; unexpired term of 1 year, 7 months, and 2 days filled by Calvin Coolidge

Franklin Delano Roosevelt–died Apr. 12, 1945, Warm Springs, Ga.; served 2 months and 23 days of fourth term; unexpired term of 3 years, 9 months, and 7 days filled by Harry S. Truman

John Fitzgerald Kennedy–died Nov. 22, 1963, Dallas, Tex.; served 2 years, 306 days; unexpired term of 1 year, 1 month, and 29 days filled by Lyndon Baines Johnson

The presidency of the United States has been held for a total of 23 years and 11 months by men who were not elected to the office but who obtained it through the death of the incumbent.

LENGTH OF LIFE AFTER COMPLETION OF TERM

Of the thirty-five Presidents who are no longer living, twenty-seven survived their terms of office. The following list shows the number of years lived after retirement from the presidency:

Polk–103 days
Arthur–1 year, 260 days
Washington–2 years, 285 days
Wilson– 2 years, 337 days
Coolidge–3 years, 308 days
L. B. Johnson–4 years, 2 days
Monroe–6 years, 122 days
A. Johnson–6 years, 149 days
Buchanan–7 years, 89 days
B. Harrison–8 years, 9 days
Eisenhower–8 years, 67 days
Jackson–8 years, 96 days
Grant–8 years, 141 days
T. Roosevelt–9 years, 309 days
Cleveland–11 years, 112 days (after second term)

Hayes–11 years, 319 days
Pierce–12 years, 218 days
Tyler–16 years, 320 days
Jefferson–17 years, 122 days
Taft–17 years, 4 days
J. Q. Adams–18 years, 356 days
Cleveland–19 years, 112 days (after first term)
Madison–19 years, 116 days
Truman–19 years, 340 days
Fillmore–21 years, 4 days
Van Buren–21 years, 142 days
J. Adams–25 years, 122 days
Hoover–31 years, 231 days

AGE AT DEATH

The average life span of the thirty-five Presidents who are no longer living was 69 years and 105 days. The following list shows the relative longevity of the Presidents:

J. Adams–90 years, 247 days
Hoover–90 years, 71 days
Truman–88 years, 232 days
Madison–85 years, 104 days
Jefferson–83 years, 82 days
J. Q. Adams–80 years, 227 days
Van Buren–79 years, 231 days
Eisenhower–79 years, 165 days
Jackson–78 years, 85 days
Buchanan–77 years, 39 days
Fillmore–74 years, 60 days
Monroe–73 years, 67 days
Taft–72 years, 174 days
Tyler–71 years, 295 days
Cleveland–71 years, 98 days
Hayes–70 years, 105 days
W. H. Harrison–68 years, 54 days
Washington–67 years, 295 days
B. Harrison–67 years, 205 days
Wilson–67 years, 37 days
A. Johnson–66 years, 214 days
Taylor–65 years, 227 days
L. B. Johnson–65 years, 148 days
Pierce–64 years, 319 days
Grant–63 years, 87 days
F. D. Roosevelt–63 years, 72 days
Coolidge–60 years, 185 days
T. Roosevelt–60 years, 71 days
McKinley–58 years, 228 days
Harding–57 years, 273 days
Lincoln–56 years, 62 days

Arthur–56 years, 44 days
Polk–53 years, 225 days
Garfield–49 years, 304 days
Kennedy–46 years, 177 days

RELATIVE LONGEVITY OF THE PRESIDENTS AND THEIR PARENTS

The following list notes the age at death (1) of each President, (2) of his father, and (3) of his mother:

Washington

67 years, 295 days; about 49 years; 59 years, 148 days

J. Adams

90 years, 247 days; 70 years, 106 days; 98 years, 43 days

Jefferson

83 years, 82 days; 49 years, 170 days; 56 years, 50 days

Madison

85 years, 104 days; 77 years, 337 days; 98 years, 33 days

Monroe

73 years, 67 days; _____; _____

J. Q. Adams

80 years, 227 days; 90 years, 247 days; 73 years, 351 days

Jackson

78 years, 85 days; _____; _____

Van Buren

79 years, 231 days; 80 years, 40 days; about 70 years

W. H. Harrison

68 years, 54 days; 65 years, 19 days; about 62 years

Tyler

71 years, 295 days; 65 years, 312 days; about 36 years

Polk

53 years, 225 days; 55 years, 123 days; 75 years, 57 days

Taylor

65 years, 227 days; 84 years, 291 days; 61 years, 364 days

Fillmore

74 years, 60 days; 91 years, 343 days; about 51 years

Pierce

64 years, 319 days, 81 years, 97 days; about 70 years

Buchanan

77 years, 39 days; about 60 years; about 66 years

Lincoln
56 years, 62 days; 73 years, 11 days; 34 years, 242 days

A. Johnson
66 years, 214 days; about 33 years; 72 years, 211 days

Grant
63 years, 87 days; 79 years, 157 days; 84 years, 169 days

Hayes
70 years, 105 days; 35 years, 197 days; 74 years, 198 days

Garfield
49 years, 304 days; 33 years, 126 days; 86 years, 122 days

Arthur
56 years, 44 days; 78 years, 326 days; 66 years, 262 days

Cleveland
71 years, 98 days; 49 years, 104 days; 76 years, 165 days

B. Harrison
67 years, 205 days; 73 years, 233 days; 40 years, 28 days

McKinley
58 years, 228 days; 85 years, 9 days; 88 years, 234 days

T. Roosevelt
60 years, 71 days; 46 years, 140 days; 49 years, 221 days

Taft
72 years, 174 days; 80 years, 197 days; 80 years, 88 days

Wilson
67 years, 37 days; 80 years, 327 days; 61 years, 116 days

Harding
57 years, 273 days; 84 years, 160 days; 66 years, 159 days

Coolidge
60 years, 185 days; 80 years, 352 days; 39 years

Hoover
90 years, 71 days; 34 years, 99 days; 34 years, 296 days

F. D. Roosevelt
63 years, 72 days; 72 years, 145 days; 86 years, 351 days

Truman
88 years, 232 days; 78 years, 274 days; 82 years, 207 days

Eisenhower
79 years, 165 days; 79 years, 168 days; 84 years, 133 days

L. B. Johnson
  65 years, 148 days; 60 years, 11 days; 77 years, 78 days

RELATIVE LONGEVITY OF THE PRESIDENTS AND THEIR WIVES

It is often stated that the presidency is a killing job, but over half of the Presidents who are no longer living had greater life spans than their respective wives (though they did not necessarily survive their wives). The following list shows the number of years by which the President's life span exceeded that of his wife:

J. Adams–16 years, 261 days
Jefferson–49 years, 125 days
Madison–4 years, 51 days
Monroe–10 years, 347 days
J. Q. Adams–3 years, 136 days
Jackson–16 years, 260 days
Van Buren–43 years, 262 days
Tyler (first wife)–19 years, 358 days
Tyler (second wife)–2 years, 228 days
Taylor–1 year, 261 days
Fillmore (first wife)–19 years, 43 days
Fillmore (second wife)–6 years, 131 days
Pierce–7 years, 54 days
A. Johnson–1 year, 111 days
Hayes–12 years, 169 days
Arthur–13 years, 274 days
B. Harrison (first wife)–7 years, 181 days
T. Roosevelt (first wife)–37 years, 244 days
Wilson (first wife)–12 years, 319 days
Hoover–21 years, 152 days

The following is a list of wives whose life spans were greater than those of their husbands:

Mrs. Washington–3 years, 40 days
Mrs. W. H. Harrison–20 years, 161 days
Mrs. Polk–34 years, 119 days
Mrs. Lincoln–7 years, 153 days
Mrs. Grant–13 years, 235 days
Mrs. Garfield–36 years, 25 days
Mrs. Cleveland–12 years, 12 days
Mrs. B. Harrison (second wife)–22 years, 45 days
Mrs. McKinley–1 year, 124 days
Mrs. T. Roosevelt (second wife)–26 years, 339 days
Mrs. Taft–9 years, 331 days
Mrs. Wilson (second wife)–22 years, 27 days
Mrs. Harding–3 years, 190 days
Mrs. Coolidge–18 years, 1 day
Mrs. F. D. Roosevelt–24 years, 320 days

PRESIDENTS WHO SURVIVED THEIR WIVES

Of the thirty-five Presidents who are no longer living, thirteen became widowers. The following list shows the number of years each lived after the death of his wife:

J. Adams–7 years, 249 days
Jefferson–43 years, 301 days
Monroe–284 days
Jackson–16 years, 168 days
Van Buren–43 years, 169 days
Tyler (first wife)–19 years, 130 days
Fillmore (first wife)–20 years, 343 days
Pierce–5 years, 310 days
Hayes–3 years, 206 days
Arthur–6 years, 310 days
B. Harrison (first wife)–8 years, 139 days
T. Roosevelt (first wife)–34 years, 326 days
Wilson (first wife)–9 years, 181 days
Hoover–20 years, 286 days

PRESIDENTS' WIVES WHO SURVIVED THEIR HUSBANDS

Of the wives who are no longer living, nineteen became widows. The following list shows the number of years each lived after the death of her husband:

Mrs. Washington–2 years, 159 days
Mrs. Madison–13 years, 14 days
Mrs. J. Q. Adams–4 years, 80 days
Mrs. W. H. Harrison–22 years, 327 days
Mrs. Tyler (second wife)–27 years, 173 days
Mrs. Polk–42 years, 60 days
Mrs. Taylor–2 years, 40 days
Mrs. Fillmore (second wife)–7 years, 156 days
Mrs. Lincoln–17 years, 92 days
Mrs. A. Johnson–168 days
Mrs. Grant–17 years, 144 days
Mrs. Garfield–36 years, 176 days
Mrs. Cleveland–39 years, 127 days
Mrs. B. Harrison (second wife)–46 years, 298 days
Mrs. McKinley–5 years, 254 days
Mrs. T. Roosevelt (second wife)–29 years, 267 days
Mrs. Taft–13 years, 75 days
Mrs. Wilson (second wife)–37 years, 328 days
Mrs. Harding–1 year, 111 days
Mrs. Coolidge–24 years, 184 days
Mrs. F. D. Roosevelt–17 days, 209 days

CAUSES OF DEATH

The exact causes of death of many Presidents are not known, since medical and death certificates were not always filed. Furthermore, in many instances there were complications, and the direct causes of death could not be ascertained. There may also be differences in terminology; in the past, illnesses were grouped under generic headings, whereas today the same illnesses would be described by specific terms.

Washington–Pneumonia

J. Adams–Debility

Jefferson–Diarrhea

Madison–Debility

Monroe–Debility

J. Q. Adams–Paralysis

Jackson–Consumption, dropsy

Van Buren–Asthma

W. H. Harrison–Pleurisy, pneumonia

Tyler–Bilious fever

Polk–Diarrhea

Taylor–Bilious fever, typhoid fever, cholera morbus

Fillmore–Debility, paralysis

Pierce–Stomach inflammation

Buchanan–Rheumatic gout

Lincoln–Assassination

A. Johnson–Paralysis

Grant–Cancer (carcinoma of the tongue and tonsils)

Hayes–Heart disease

Garfield–Assassination

Arthur–Bright's disease, apoplexy (cerebral hemorrhage)

Cleveland–Debility, coronary sclerosis

B. Harrison–Pneumonia

McKinley–Assassination

T. Roosevelt–Inflammatory rheumatism

Taft–Debility

Harding–Apoplexy (rupture of brain artery), pneumonia, enlargement of the heart, high blood pressure

Wilson–Apoplexy, paralysis

Coolidge–Heart failure (coronary thrombosis)

Hoover–Bleeding from upper gastrointestinal tract; strained vascular system

F. D. Roosevelt–Cerebral hemorrhage

Truman–Minor lung congestion; complexity of organic failures; collapse of cardiovascular system

Eisenhower–Heart disease

Kennedy–Assassination

L. B. Johnson–Heart failure

ASSASSINATIONS AND ATTEMPTED ASSASSINATIONS

Four Presidents—Lincoln, Garfield, McKinley, and Kennedy—were assassinated while in office.

Attempts were made against the lives of Presidents Jackson, Theodore Roosevelt, and Truman. Attempts were made also against Lincoln and Franklin Delano Roosevelt before they assumed the presidency.

Details are given in the respective biographical chapters in Part I.

On August 25, 1965, Congress enacted a law (79 Stat. L. 580) making it a federal crime to kill, kidnap, or assault the President, Vice President, or President-elect.

LAST WORDS

Since emotions and grief are important factors in death scenes, there is variance in the reported accounts. The generally accepted last words of the Presidents follow:

Washington–"It is well."

J. Adams–"Thomas Jefferson still survives." "Independence forever."

Jefferson–"Is it the fourth?" (A reference to the Fourth of July) "I resign my spirit to God, my daughter to my country."

Madison–"I always talk better lying down."

J. Q. Adams–"This is the last of earth. I am content."

Jackson–"I hope to meet each of you in heaven. Be good children, all of you, and strive to be ready when the change comes."

Van Buren–"There is but one reliance."

W. H. Harrison–"Sir, I wish you to understand the true principles of government. I wish them carried out. I ask nothing more." (Spoken in delirium to Vice President Tyler)

Tyler–"Doctor, I am going. . . . perhaps it is best."

Polk–"I love you, Sarah, for all eternity, I love you."

Taylor–"I am about to die. I expect the summons very soon. I have tried to discharge all my duties faithfully. I regret nothing, but am sorry that I am about to leave my friends."

Fillmore–"The nourishment (food) is palatable."

Buchanan–"O Lord, God Almighty, as Thou wilt."

A. Johnson–"Oh, do not cry. Be good children and we shall all meet in Heaven."

Grant–"Water."

Hayes–"I know that I am going where Lucy is." (His wife)

Garfield–"The people my trust." "Oh, Swaim, there is a pain here. . . . oh, oh, Swaim." (Spoken to David Gaskill Swaim, his chief of staff)

Cleveland–"I have tried so hard to do right."

B. Harrison–"Are the doctors here?" "Doctor . . . my lungs."

McKinley–"It is God's way. His will be done, not ours." "We are all going, we are all going, we are all going. Oh, dear."

T. Roosevelt–"Please put out the light."

Wilson–"Edith." (His wife) "I'm a broken machine, but I'm ready."

Harding–"That's good. Go on, read some more." (Spoken to his wife, who was reading to him)

F. D. Roosevelt–"I have a terrific headache

Eisenhower–"I've always loved my wife. I've always loved my children. I've always loved my grandchildren. And I have always loved my country."

Kennedy–"My God, I've been hit."

BURIAL SITES

Washington
Mount Vernon, Va., family vault

J. Adams
Quincy, Mass., First Unitarian Church

Jefferson
"Monticello," Charlottesville, Va., family plot

Madison
Montpelier, Va., family plot

Monroe
Richmond, Va., Hollywood Cemetery

J. Q. Adams
Quincy, Mass., First Unitarian Church

Jackson
Nashville, Tenn., Hermitage estate

Van Buren
Kinderhook, N.Y., Kinderhook Cemetery

W. H. Harrison
North Bend, Ohio, William Henry Harrison Memorial State Park

Tyler
Richmond, Va., Hollywood Cemetery

Polk
Nashville, Tenn., State Capitol grounds

Taylor
Springfield, Ky., family plot

Fillmore
Buffalo, N.Y., Forest Lawn Cemetery

Pierce
Concord, N.H., Old North Cemetery

Buchanan
Lancaster, Pa., Woodward Hill Cemetery

Lincoln
Springfield, Ill., Oak Ridge Cemetery

A. Johnson
Greeneville, Tenn., Andrew Johnson National Cemetery

Grant
New York, N.Y., Grant's Tomb

Hayes
Fremont, Ohio, Spiegel Grove State Park

Garfield
Cleveland, Ohio, Lake View Cemetery

Arthur
Albany, N.Y., Rural Cemetery

Cleveland
Princeton, N.J., Princeton Cemetery

B. Harrison
Indianapolis, Ind., Crown Hill Cemetery

McKinley
Canton, Ohio, near Westlawn Cemetery

T. Roosevelt
Oyster Bay, N.Y., Young's Memorial Cemetery

Taft
Arlington, Va., Arlington National Cemetery

Wilson
Washington, D.C., National Cemetery

Harding
Marion, Ohio, Marion Cemetery

Coolidge
Plymouth, Vt., Notch Cemetery

Hoover
West Branch, Iowa

F. D. Roosevelt
Hyde Park, N.Y., family plot

Truman
Independence, Mo., Harry S. Truman Library Institute

Eisenhower
Abilene, Kan.

Kennedy
Arlington, Va., Arlington National Cemetery

L. B. Johnson
Johnson City, Tex., family plot at LBJ ranch

PRESIDENTS BURIED AT ARLINGTON

The first President buried in the National Cemetery at Arlington, Va., was William Howard Taft, interred March 11, 1930. On November

25, 1963, President John Fitzgerald Kennedy was buried at Arlington.

THE PRESIDENTS' ESTATES

There has always been interest in comparing the estates of Presidents. In order not to obtain an inaccurate impression, there are certain basic facts to consider.

First, there is a variance between the appraisal of the same estate by different people, especially concerning real property and personal possessions. Unless a piece of property is actually sold, values range from high to low according to different appraisers.

When comparing the monetary value of Presidents' estates, one must consider the purchasing power of the dollar in the years under consideration. For example, it might now take about $20 million to acquire Washington's real estate, which was valued at $530,000. (It may be noted that Washington was "land poor." Although his land holdings were worth a great deal, he was sometimes hard pressed for cash.)

Even if the figures given are exact to the penny, they are not always accurate estimates of the Presidents' wealth because many Presidents, while living, made appreciable gifts and donations to their families. Often estates were divided and distributed before death to avoid the imposition of excise and inheritance taxes.

The figures below indicate the total value of the estates, not solely cash and securities. They are estimates and are likely to vary with the final amounts reported by the administrators or filed with the surrogates.

Washington–$530,000 ("land poor")

J. Adams–$30,000

Jefferson–owed $40,000

Madison–value unknown

Monroe–none

J. Q. Adams–$60,000

Jackson–value unknown ("land poor")

Van Buren–value unknown

W. H. Harrison–in debt

Tyler–value unknown

Polk–$100,000 to $150,000

Taylor–$142,000

Fillmore–value unknown

Pierce–$70,000

Buchanan–value unknown

Lincoln–$83,000 (net estate of $83,343 increased by the administrators to $110,974)

A. Johnson–$50,000

Grant–none (left manuscript of book which brought in approximately $500,000)

Hayes–value unknown

Garfield–value unknown

Arthur–value unknown

Cleveland–$250,000
B. Harrison–$375,000
McKinley–$215,000
T. Roosevelt–$811,000
Taft–$475,000
Harding–$487,000
Wilson–$600,000
Coolidge–$500,000
Hoover–value unknown (in the millions)
F. D. Roosevelt–$1,085,500
Truman–exact value unknown
Eisenhower–exact value unknown
Kennedy–value unknown (in the millions)
Johnson–exact value unknown

PRESIDENTS PAST AND FUTURE

Between the years 1822 and 1826, there were eighteen men living who had held the office of President, were in office, or were destined to hold office—the greatest number alive at any one period in history. The following is a list of those eighteen Presidents, with dates of birth and death:

J. Adams–1735-1826
Jefferson–1743-1826
Madison–1751-1836
Monroe–1758-1831
J. Q. Adams–1767-1848
Jackson–1767-1845
Van Buren–1782-1862
W. H. Harrison–1773-1841
Tyler–1790-1862
Polk–1795-1849
Taylor–1784-1850
Fillmore–1800-1874
Pierce–1804-1869
Buchanan–1791-1868
Lincoln–1809-1865
A. Johnson–1808-1875
Grant–1822-1885
Hayes–1822-1893

A similar compilation of Vice Presidents past and future appears on page 665.

FORMER PRESIDENTS ALIVE WHEN NEW PRESIDENT TOOK OFFICE

J. Adams–1797—Washington
Jefferson–1801—J. Adams
Madison–1809—J. Adams, Jefferson
Monroe–1817—J. Adams, Jefferson, Madison
J. Q. Adams–1825—J. Adams, Jefferson, Madison, Monroe

Jackson–1829—Madison, Monroe, J. Q. Adams; 1833 (second term)— Madison, J. Q. Adams

Van Buren–1837—J. Q.Adams, Jackson

W. H. Harrison–1841—J. Q. Adams, Jackson, Van Buren

Tyler–1841—J. Q. Adams, Jackson, Van Buren

Polk–1845—J. Q. Adams, Jackson, Van Buren, Tyler

Taylor–1849—Van Buren, Tyler, Polk

Fillmore–1850—Van Buren, Tyler

Pierce–1853—Van Buren, Tyler, Fillmore

Buchanan–1857—Van Buren, Tyler, Fillmore, Pierce

Lincoln–1861—Van Buren, Tyler, Fillmore, Pierce, Buchanan

A. Johnson–1865—Fillmore, Pierce, Buchanan

Grant–1869—Fillmore, Pierce, A. Johnson

Hayes–1877—Grant

Garfield–1881—Grant, Hayes

Arthur–1881—Grant, Hayes

Cleveland–1885—Grant, Hayes, Arthur

B. Harrison–1889—Hayes, Cleveland

Cleveland–1893—B. Harrison

McKinley–1897—Cleveland, B. Harrison

T. Roosevelt–1901—Cleveland

Taft–1909—T. Roosevelt

Wilson–1913—T. Roosevelt, Taft

Harding–1921—Taft, Wilson

Coolidge–1923—Taft, Wilson

Hoover–1929—Taft, Coolidge

F. D. Roosevelt–1933—Hoover

Truman–1945—Hoover

Eisenhower–1953—Hoover, Truman

Kennedy–1961—Hoover, Truman, Eisenhower

L. B. Johnson–1963—Hoover, Truman, Eisenhower; 1965 (second term)—Truman, Eisenhower

Nixon–1969—Truman, Eisenhower, Johnson; 1973 (second term)— Johnson

PERIODS IN WHICH THERE WERE NO FORMER PRESIDENTS LIVING

There were five periods during which no former Presidents of the United States were living.

The first period was December 14, 1799-March 3, 1801, during the administration of John Adams. George Washington, the first and only living former President, died on December 14, 1799.

The second period was July 31, 1875-March 3, 1877, during the administration of Ulysses S. Grant. Andrew Johnson died on July 31, 1875.

The third period was June 24, 1908-March 3, 1909, during the administration of Theodore Roosevelt. Grover Cleveland died on June 24, 1908.

The fourth period was January 5, 1933-March 3, 1933, during the administration of Herbert Hoover. Calvin Coolidge died on January 5, 1933.

The fifth period began January 20, 1973, during the second term of Richard Milhous Nixon. Harry S. Truman died December 26, 1972, and L. B. Johnson died on January 22, 1973.

COMMEMORATIVES

PRESIDENTS DEPICTED ON COINS

The first President depicted on a U.S. coin (excluding commemorative currency) was Abraham Lincoln, shown on the bronze penny commemorating the centennial of his birth. The new design for the bronze one-cent piece was adopted in April 1909, and the coinage began in May 1909, at the mint in Philadelphia, Pa. The first delivery of the coins was made June 30, 1909, to the Cashier of the Mint. No coins were paid out until after the close of the fiscal year, the distribution beginning on August 2, 1909.

The second President depicted on a U.S. coin was George Washington, shown on a twenty-five-cent silver coin, the bicentennial quarter commemorating the bicentennial of his birth. The first coins were struck June 4, 1932, at the Philadelphia mint.

The third President depicted on a U.S. coin was Thomas Jefferson, shown on the five-cent piece of 1938. The first coins were ordered cast on October 1, 1938, and released to the public on November 15, 1938. They were coined at the mints at Philadelphia, Pa., Denver, Colo., and San Francisco, Calif.

The fourth President depicted on a U.S. coin was Franklin Delano Roosevelt, shown on a ten-cent silver piece. Production of the coins commenced January 16, 1946. They were coined at Denver and San Francisco and were issued on January 30, 1946, Roosevelt's birthday.

The fifth President depicted on a U.S. coin was John Fitzgerald Kennedy, shown on a fifty-cent piece. The coins were authorized by Congress on December 30, 1963 (77 Stat. L. 843) to replace the Franklin half-dollars. They were minted at Denver and Philadelphia and first offered for public distribution on March 24, 1964. About 70 million coins were minted.

The sixth President depicted on a U.S. coin was Dwight David Eisenhower, shown on a silver dollar.

PRESIDENTS DEPICTED ON PAPER CURRENCY

Portraits of Presidents appear on U.S. paper currency on the following denominations: Washington, one dollar; Jefferson, two dollars; Lincoln, five dollars; Jackson, twenty dollars; Grant, fifty dollars; McKinley, five hundred dollars; Cleveland, one thousand dollars; Madison, five thousand dollars; Wilson, one hundred thousand dollars.

PRESIDENTS DEPICTED ON POSTAGE STAMPS

The Presidents have served as subjects on postage stamps since the first issue in 1847, but it was not until 1938 that one issue depicted all the Presidents.

The 1938 issue of ordinary postage stamps showed likenesses of all the Presidents from Washington to Coolidge arranged in accordance with their tenure of office. The following list names the President, the denomination and color of the stamp, and the date of issue in 1938:

Washington–1 cent green, Apr. 25
J. Adams–2 cent red, June 3
Jefferson–3 cent purple, June 16
Madison–4 cent pink, July 1
Monroe–5 cent blue, July 21
J. Q. Adams–6 cent red orange, July 28
Jackson–7 cent sepia, Aug. 4
Van Buren–8 cent olive, Aug. 11
W. H. Harrison–9 cent pink, Aug. 18
J. Tyler–10 cent salmon, Sept. 2
Polk–11 cent blue, Sept. 8
Taylor–12 cent lavender, Sept. 14
Fillmore–13 cent green, Sept. 22
Pierce–14 cent blue, Oct. 6
Buchanan–15 cent gray, Oct. 13
Lincoln–16 cent black, Oct. 20
Johnson–17 cent crimson, Oct. 27
Grant–18 cent brown, Nov. 3
Hayes–19 cent lilac, Nov. 10
Garfield–20 cent green, Nov. 10
Arthur–21 cent steel blue, Nov. 22
Cleveland–22 cent copper red, Nov. 22
B. Harrison–24 cent gray, Dec. 2
McKinley–25 cent burgundy, Dec. 2
T. Roosevelt–30 cent blue, Dec. 8
Taft–50 cent lavender, Dec. 8
Wilson–$1 lavender and black, Aug. 29
Harding–$2 green and black, Sept. 29
Coolidge–$5 red and black, Nov. 17

Other commemorative stamps depicting Presidents were issues commemorating Franklin Delano Roosevelt, Hoover, Kennedy, Truman, and L. B. Johnson.

THE KENNEDY POSTAGE STAMPS

The five-cent John F. Kennedy memorial stamp was first placed on sale May 29, 1964, at Boston, Mass. There were 2,003,096 first-day covers canceled. The printing order was 500 million stamps. The likeness was based on a photograph taken by William S. Murphy of the Los Angeles *Times*.

On May 29, 1965, an eleven-cent aerogramme was first placed on sale at Boston, Mass. An initial printing of 20 million of the lightweight "make-it-yourself" envelope was authorized. The aerogramme, based on a photograph taken by Douglas Jones of *Look* magazine, was printed in gold, purple, and black. The total run was 112 million of which 337,422 were first-day cancellations.

On May 29, 1967, a thirteen-cent brown stamp, the rate for surface mail to any part of the world, was issued at Brookline, Mass., on the fiftieth anniversary of Kennedy's birthday. The design of this vertical issue was based on a photograph by Jacques Lowe in the book *The Kennedy Years*.

TRUMAN STAMP ISSUED

A vertical eight-cent Truman memorial stamp was first issued May 8, 1973, at Independence, Mo. It was printed on the Giori press in black, red, and blue and was designed by Bradbury Thompson based on a photograph taken by Leo Stein.

JOHNSON STAMP ISSUED

An eight-cent vertical jumbo-size Lyndon B. Johnson memorial stamp was released August 27, 1973, at Austin, Tex., on the sixty-fifth anniversary of his birth. It was designed by Bradbury Thompson based on a portrait by Madame Elizabeth Shoumatoff. It was printed by gravure on the Andreotti press in six inks, buff, yellow, red, blue, and two blacks of different consistency.

THE PRESIDENTIAL MEDALS

The thirty-six Presidents of the United States have been commemorated by bronze medals, three inches in diameter. These medals are sold by the Superintendent, United States Mint, Philadelphia, Pa., for $5.00 each with the understanding that they are not to be resold at a profit.

The Washington medal was designed by DuVivier; the Jefferson and Madison medals by Reich; the Monroe, John Quincy Adams, Jackson and Van Buren medals by Furst; the William Henry Harrison, Lincoln, Hayes, Wilson, and Harding medals by Morgan; the Garfield, Arthur, Benjamin Harrison, McKinley, Theodore Roosevelt, and Taft medals by C. Barber and Morgan; the Fillmore, Pierce, and Buchanan medals by Ellis and Wilson; the Andrew Johnson medal by Pacquet; the Grant and Cleveland medals by W. Barber; the Coolidge, Hoover, and Franklin Delano Roosevelt medals by Sinnock; the Truman medal (first term) by Sinnock and Roberts, (second term) by Roberts and von Hebel; the Eisenhower medal (first term) and the Kennedy and L. B. Johnson medals by Roberts and Gasparro. The Nixon medal was also designed by Frank Gasparro.

The designers of the John Adams, Tyler, Polk, and Taylor medals are unknown.

PRESIDENTS IN THE HALL OF FAME

The Hall of Fame for Great Americans on the New York University campus, New York City, has honored twelve Presidents.

At the first Hall of Fame election in 1900, five Presidents were elected: Washington, John Adams, Jefferson, Lincoln, and Grant.

In 1905, two more Presidents were elected: Madison and John Quincy Adams.

Five years later, Jackson was elected. In 1930, Monroe was elected, and in 1935, Cleveland. Both Wilson and Theodore Roosevelt were elected in 1950.

One of the qualifications for election is that twenty-five years must have passed between the death of the nominee and the election.

PRESIDENTS IN STATUARY HALL

Statuary Hall, established by act of July 2, 1864, permits each state to place in Statuary Hall, in the House of Representatives, two statues honoring their distinguished citizens. The statues of three Presidents have been placed in the rotunda; Garfield by Ohio, Jackson by Tennessee, and Washington by Virginia.

PLACES NAMED FOR PRESIDENTS

Only one state, Washington, bears the name of a President. The capital cities of four states were named for Presidents: Jackson, Miss., Jefferson City, Mo., Lincoln, Neb., and Madison, Wis.

COUNTIES NAMED FOR PRESIDENTS

The following is a list of counties named for Presidents. (A number of similarly named counties commemorate other individuals who bore the same names as certain Presidents.)

Washington–31
Ala., Ark., Colo., Fla., Ga., Idaho, Ill., Ind., Iowa, Kan., Ky., La., Me., Md., Minn., Miss., Mo., Neb., N.Y., N.C., Ohio, Okla., Ore., Pa., R.I., Tenn., Tex., Utah, Vt , Va., Wis.

Jefferson–26
Ala., Ark., Colo., Fla., Ga., Idaho, Ill., Ind., Iowa, Kan., Ky., La., Miss., Mo., Mont., Neb., N.Y., Ohio, Okla., Ore., Pa., Tenn., Tex., Wash., W.Va., Wis.

Jackson–22
Ala., Ark., Colo., Fla., Ill., Ind., Iowa, Kan., Ky., La., Mich., Miss., Mo., N.C., Ohio, Okla., Ore., S.D., Tenn., Tex., W.Va., Wis.

Madison–19
Ala., Ark., Fla., Ga., Idaho, Ill., Ind., Iowa, Ky., La., Miss., Mo., Mont., N.Y., N.C., Ohio, Tenn., Tex., Va.

Lincoln–16
Ark., Colo., Idaho, Kan., La., Minn., Miss., Neb., Nev., N.M., Okla., Ore., S.D., Wash., W.Va., Wyo.

Grant–12
Ark., Kan., La., Minn., Neb., N.M., N.D., Okla., Ore., S.D., Wash., W.Va.

Polk–11
Ark., Fla., Ga., Iowa, Minn., Mo., Neb., Ore., Tenn., Tex., Wis.

J. Adams–8
Idaho, Iowa, Miss., Neb., Ohio, Pa., Wash., Wis.

Garfield–6
Colo., Mont., Neb., Okla., Utah, Wash.

Van Buren–4
Ark., Iowa, Mich., Tenn.
W. H. Harrison–4
Ind., Iowa, Miss., Ohio
Taylor–4
Fla., Ga., Iowa, Ky.
Pierce–4
Ga., Neb., Wash., Wis.
J. Q. Adams–3
Ill., Ind., N.D.
Buchanan–3
Iowa, Mo., Va.
Tyler–2
Texas, W.Va.
Fillmore–2
Minn., Neb.
Cleveland–2
Ark., Okla.
T. Roosevelt–2
Mont., N.M.
Hayes–1
Neb.
McKinley–1
N.M.
B. Harrison–1
Ky.
Arthur–1
Neb.
Harding–1
N.M.

No counties have been named for Andrew Johnson, Taft, or Wilson, or for the Presidents following Harding.

THE PRESIDENTIAL MOUNTAIN RANGE

The Presidential Range of the White Mountains in New Hampshire includes a group of peaks named for Presidents: Mount Washington, 6,288 feet; Mount Adams, 5,798 feet; Mount Jefferson, 5,715 feet; Mount Monroe, 5,385 feet; Mount Madison, 5,363 feet; Mount Pierce, 4,312 feet; and Mount Jackson, 4,052 feet. Mount Quincy Adams, a spur of Mount Adams, is 5,470 feet.

Other mountains in New Hampshire named for Presidents but not in the presidential range are Mount Garfield, 4,488 feet; and Mount Lincoln, 5,108 feet.

GENERAL STATISTICS

Births

8 of 36 were born in Virginia

19 of 36 were born in New York, Ohio or Virginia
 5 of 36 were born in November

PARENTS AND ANCESTORS OF THE PRESIDENTS

20 of 36 were of English ancestry
20 of 36 had fathers who were farmers or planters
 4 of 36 had fathers who were lawyers
 3 of 36 had fathers who were ministers
 3 of 36 had fathers who were state governors
 1 of 36 had a father who was a physician
 2 of 36 were posthumous children
11 of 36 lost their fathers before they were 21
 6 of 36 lost their fathers while in their teens
 9 of 36 had fathers who married twice
 2 of 36 were survived by their fathers
 6 of 36 had fathers living at their inaugurations
 1 of 36 had a father who was President
 1 of 36 had a grandfather who was President
 3 of 36 were survived by their mothers
10 of 36 had mothers living at their inaugurations
 2 of 36 had both parents living at their inaugurations

SIBLINGS OF THE PRESIDENTS

 7 of 36 had 9 or more brothers and sisters
14 of 36 had 8 or more brothers and sisters
15 of 36 had 7 or more brothers and sisters
17 of 36 had 6 or more brothers and sisters
18 of 36 had 5 or more brothers and sisters
10 of 36 were the first-born in their families
 5 of 36 were the second-born, the first sons in their families
 4 of 36 were the second-born, the second sons, in their families
18 of 36 were the first-born sons in their families
31 of 36 had sisters
No President was an only child

MARRIAGE AND WIVES OF THE PRESIDENTS

35 of 36 Presidents married
 6 of 36 Presidents married widows
 2 of 36 Presidents married divorcees
 2 of 36 Presidents married on their birthdays
 4 of 36 Presidents celebrated golden wedding anniversaries
 3 of 36 Presidents lost their wives before they were inaugurated
 3 of 36 Presidents lost their wives while in office
 5 of 36 Presidents remarried
 1 of 40 wives was not born in the United States
19 of 40 wives were born in New York, Ohio or Virginia
 7 of 40 wives were college graduates
 5 of 40 wives were older than their husbands

4 of 40 wives had children by former husbands
14 of 35 wives lived to be over 70
9 of 35 wives lived to be over 80
9 of 35 wives died in Washington, D.C.

CHILDREN OF THE PRESIDENTS

6 of 36 were childless
12 of 36 had no daughters
11 of 36 had no sons
1 of 36 had fifteen children
1 of 36 had a son who became President
2 of 36 had sons who became senators
7 of 36 had sons who became representatives
1 of 36 had a son who served in both houses of Congress.

LIFE AND DEATH OF THE PRESIDENTS

30 of 36 lived to be over 60
7 of 36 died in July
3 of 36 died on July 4
8 of 36 died in office
4 of 36 were assassinated
31 of 36 died a natural death

CULTURAL, VOCATIONAL, AND GEOGRAPHICAL BACK-GROUND OF THE PRESIDENTS

11 of 36 were Episcopalians
26 of 36 were college graduates
12 of 36 were members of Phi Beta Kappa
14 of 36 were Masons
23 of 36 had military service
25 of 36 were lawyers
5 of 36 served as secretaries of state
8 of 36 served in presidential cabinets
12 of 36 served as Vice Presidents
22 of 36 were elected to Congress
16 of 36 served as senators
17 of 36 served as representatives
11 of 36 served in both houses of Congress
7 of 36 served as ambassadors
13 of 36 served as state governors
5 of 36 were residents of Virginia
18 of 36 were residents of New York, Ohio, or Virginia
15 of 36 were residents of states other than their native states

COMMEMORATIVES

13 of 36 were elected to the Hall of Fame
3 of 36 are honored by statues in Statuary Hall
24 of 36 had counties named for them
4 of 36 had capital cities named for them
1 of 36 had a state named for him

ELECTIONS, TENURE, AND AGES OF THE PRESIDENTS

11 of 36 were Democrats
13 of 36 were Republicans
 1 of 36 was elected for a 4th term
 1 of 36 was elected for a 3rd term
12 of 36 were elected for a 2nd term
 9 of 36 served full second terms
10 of 36 were elected for one term
 5 of 36 served less than one term
 9 of 36 succeeded to the presidency
 3 of 36 who succeeded to the presidency were subsequently elected
in their own right
15 of 36 did not receive a majority of popular votes
 6 of 36 were in their forties when they took office
30 of 36 were over 50 when they took office
 7 of 36 were over 60 when they took office

THE PRESIDENCY
ELECTIONS

CONSTITUTIONAL PROVISIONS

The following constitutional provisions apply to presidential elections:

ARTICLE II, SECTION 1. The executive Power shall be vested in a President of the United States of America. He shall hold his Office during the Term of four Years, and, together with the Vice-President, chosen for the same Term, be elected, as follows:

Each State shall appoint, in such Manner as the Legislature thereof may direct, a Number of Electors, equal to the whole Number of Senators and Representatives to which the State may be entitled in the Congress: but no Senator or Representative, or Person holding an Office of Trust or Profit under the United States, shall be appointed an Elector.

[The Electors shall meet in their respective States, and vote by Ballot for two persons, of whom one at least shall not be an Inhabitant of the same State with themselves. And they shall make a List of all the persons voted for, and of the Number of Votes for each; which List they shall sign and certify, and transmit sealed to the Seat of the Government of the United States, directed to the President of the Senate. The President of the Senate shall, in the Presence of the Senate and House of Representatives, open all the Certificates, and the Votes shall then be counted. The Person having the greatest Number of Votes shall be the President, if such Number be a Majority of the whole Number of Electors appointed; and if there be more than one who have such Majority, and have an equal Number of Votes, then the House of Representatives shall immediately chuse by Ballot one of them for President; and if no Person have a Majority, then from the five highest on the List the said House shall in like Manner chuse the President. But in chusing the President, the Votes shall be taken by States, the Representation from each State having one Vote; A quorum for this purpose shall consist of a Member or Members from two-thirds of the States, and a Majority of all the States shall be necessary to a Choice. In every Case, after the Choice of the President, the Person having the greatest Number of Votes of the Electors shall be the Vice-President. But if there should remain two or more who have equal Votes, the Senate shall chuse from them by Ballot the Vice-President.][1]

The Congress may determine the Time of chusing the Electors, and the Day on which they shall give their Votes; which Day shall be the same throughout the United States. (*Constitution ratified Sept. 17, 1787.*)

[1]Superseded by Amendment XII

AMENDMENT XII. The electors shall meet in their respective states and vote by ballot for President and Vice-President, one of whom, at least, shall not be an inhabitant of the same state with themselves; they shall name in their ballots the person voted for as President, and in distinct ballots the person voted for as Vice-President, and they shall make distinct lists of all persons voted for as President, and of all persons voted for as Vice-President, and of the number of votes for each, which lists they shall sign and certify, and transmit sealed to the seat of the government of the United States, directed to the President of the Senate;—The President of the Senate shall, in presence of the Senate and House of Representatives, open all the certificates and the votes shall then be counted;—The person having the greatest number of votes for President, shall be the President, if such number be a majority of the whole number of Electors appointed; and if no person have such majority, then from the persons having the highest numbers not exceeding three on the list of those voted for as President, the House of Representatives shall choose immediately, by ballot, the President. But in choosing the President, the votes shall be taken by states, the representation from each state having one vote; a quorum for this purpose shall consist of a member or members from two-thirds of the states, and a majority of all the states shall be necessary to a choice. And if the House of Representatives shall not choose a President whenever the right of choice shall devolve upon them, [before the fourth day of March next following][2] then the Vice-President shall act as President, as in the case of the death or other constitutional disability of the President. The person having the greatest number of votes as Vice-President, shall be the Vice-President, if such number be a majority of the whole number of Electors appointed, and if no person have a majority, then from the two highest numbers on the list, the Senate shall choose the Vice-President; a quorum for the purpose shall consist of two-thirds of the whole number of Senators, and a majority of the whole number shall be necessary to a choice. But no person constitutionally ineligible to the office of President shall be eligible to that of Vice-President of the United States. (*Amendment XII ratified 1804.*)

Amendment XX. Section 1. The terms of the President and Vice-President shall end at noon on the 20th day of January, and the terms of Senators and Representatives at noon on the 3rd day of January, of the years in which such terms would have ended if this article had not been ratified; and the terms of their successors shall then begin.

²Superseded by Amendment XX

Section 3. If, at the time fixed for the beginning of the term of the President, the President elect shall have died, the Vice-President elect shall become President. If a President shall not have been chosen before the time fixed for the beginning of his term, or if the President elect shall have failed to qualify, then the Vice-President elect shall act as President until a President shall have qualified; and the Congress may by law provide for the case wherein neither a President elect nor a Vice-President elect shall have qualified, declaring who shall then act as President, or the manner in which one who is to act shall be selected, and such person shall act accordingly until a President or Vice-President shall have qualified.

Section 4. The Congress may by law provide for the case of the death of any of the persons from whom the House of Representatives may choose a President whenever the right of choice shall have devolved upon them, and for the case of the death of any of the persons from whom the Senate may choose a Vice-President whenever the right of choice shall have devolved upon them. (*Amendment XX ratified Jan. 23, 1933.*)

Amendment XXII. Section 1. No person shall be elected to the office of the President more than twice, and no person who has held the office of President, or acted as President, for more than two years of a term to which some other person was elected President shall be elected to the office of the President more than once. But this Article shall not apply to any person holding the office of President when this Article was proposed by the Congress, and shall not prevent any person who may be holding the office of President, or acting as President, during the term within which this Article becomes operative from holding the office of President or acting as President during the remainder of such term. *(Amendment XXII ratified Feb. 27, 1951.)*

NOMINATING CONVENTIONS FIRST HELD BY ANTI-MA-SONIC PARTY

Until 1832, candidates for the presidency and the vice presidency were selected by caucuses generally held in secret by the various political parties.

The first national nominating convention at which delegates from various states selected their candidates was held by the newly formed Anti-Masonic Party, which held its first convention at Philadelphia, Pa., in 1830.

The first convention at which national nominating was the feature was held on September 26, 1831, at the Athenaeum, Baltimore, Md. The presiding officer at this convention was John Spencer of New York. Two tellers—Abner Phelps of Massachusetts and Thaddeus Stevens of Pennsylvania—were appointed. They sat in the center of the hall where the delegates, when their names were called, deposited their ballots in an open box. The first ballot for the presidency showed 111 votes cast, of which 108 were for William Wirt of Maryland, 1 for Richard Rush of Pennsylvania, and two blanks. As only 84 votes were necessary for the choice, it was moved that the nomination be made unanimous. Wirt thus became the first presidential candidate nominated by a national nominating convention.

CONVENTIONS OF 1832

In 1832, both the National Republicans and the Democrats held their first nominating conventions at Baltimore, Md. The Democrats unanimously nominated Andrew Jackson of Tennessee on the first ballot, and the National Republicans unanimously nominated Henry Clay of Kentucky on the first ballot.

THE TWO-THIRDS RULE

The two-thirds rule requiring presidential and vice presidential nominees to obtain two thirds of the votes cast at the nominating convention was first adopted May 22, 1832, at the Democratic National Convention held at Baltimore, Md. The rule was an extension of a provision adopted in 1831:

> Resolved: That each state be entitled, in the nomination to be made of a candidate for the vice presidency, to a number of votes equal to the number to which they will be entitled in the electoral college, under the new apportionment, in voting for the President and the Vice President; and that two thirds of the whole number of the votes in the convention shall be necessary to constitute a choice.

THE TWO-THIRDS RULE ABROGATED

On June 25, 1936, at the sixth session of the Democratic National Convention in Philadelphia, Pa., Bennett Champ Clark of Missouri brought in the Report of the Committee on Rules and Order of Business. The report stated that "all questions, including the question of nomination of candidates for President of the United States and Vice President of the United States, shall be determined by a majority vote of the delegates to the convention, and the rule heretofore existing in Democratic conventions requiring a two-thirds vote in such cases is hereby abrogated."

PRESIDENTS NOMINATED IN CHURCHES

Two Presidents were nominated by their parties at conventions held in churches. Three unsuccessful presidential candidates were also nominated in churches.

Martin Van Buren was nominated on May 20, 1835, by the Democrats at a convention held in the First Presbyterian Church, Baltimore, Md. William Henry Harrison was nominated on December 4, 1839, by the Whigs at a convention held at the First Lutheran (or Zion) Church, Baltimore, Md.

The three unsuccessful candidates nominated in churches were Henry Clay, nominated on May 1, 1844, by the Whigs in convention at the Universalist Church, Baltimore, Md.; Lewis Cass, nominated on May 22, 1848, by the Democrats at the Universalist Church, Baltimore, Md.; and John Bell, nominated by the Constitutional Union Party on May 9, 1860, in the First Presbyterian Church, Baltimore, Md.

NATIONAL POLITICAL CONVENTIONS HELD BY MAJOR PARTIES

The following is a list of conventions from 1856 through 1972. The date on which each convention started is followed by the duration, the city in which the convention was held, and the presidential nominee. The winning party is listed above the defeated party.

1856

Democratic, June 2, 5 days, Cincinnati, Ohio, James Buchanan
Republican, June 17, 3 days, Philadelphia, Pa., John Charles Fremont

1860

Republican, May 16, 3 days, Chicago, Ill., Abraham Lincoln
Democratic, Apr. 23, 10 days, Charleston, S.C. (adjourned to Baltimore)
Democratic, June 18, 6 days, Baltimore, Md., Stephen Arnold Douglas

1864

Republican, June 7, 2 days, Baltimore, Md., Abraham Lincoln
Democratic, Aug. 29, 3 days, Chicago, Ill., George Brinton McClellan

1868

Republican, May 20, 2 days, Chicago, Ill., Ulysses Simpson Grant
Democratic, July 4, 6 days, New York, N.Y., Horatio Seymour

1872

Republican, June 5, 2 days, Philadelphia, Pa., Ulysses Simpson Grant
Democratic, June 9, 2 days, Baltimore, Md., Horace Greeley

1876

Republican, June 14, 3 days, Cincinnati, Ohio, Rutherford Birchard Hayes
Democratic, June 27, 3 days, St. Louis, Mo., Samuel Jones Tilden

1880

Republican, June 2, 6 days, Chicago, Ill., James Abram Garfield
Democratic, June 22, 3 days, Cincinnati, Ohio, Winfield Scott Hancock

1884

Democratic, July 8, 4 days, Chicago, Ill., Grover Cleveland
Republican, June 3, 4 days, Chicago, Ill., James Gillespie Blaine

1888

Republican, June 19, 6 days, Chicago, Ill., Benjamin Harrison
Democratic, June 5, 3 days, St. Louis, Mo., Grover Cleveland

1892

Democratic, June 21, 3 days, Chicago, Ill., Grover Cleveland
Republican, June 7, 4 days, Minneapolis, Minn., Benjamin Harrison

1896

Republican, June 16, 3 days, St. Louis, Mo., William McKinley
Democratic, July 7, 5 days, Chicago, Ill., William Jennings Bryan

1900

Republican, June 19, 3 days, Philadelphia, Pa., William McKinley
Democratic, July 4, 3 days, Kansas City, Mo., William Jennings Bryan

1904

Republican, June 21, 3 days, Chicago, Ill., Theodore Roosevelt
Democratic, July 6, 4 days, St. Louis, Mo., Alton Brooks Parker

1908

Republican, June 16, 4 days, Chicago, Ill., William Howard Taft
Democratic, July 8, 3 days, Denver, Colo., William Jennings Bryan

1912

Democratic, June 25, 7 days, Baltimore, Md., Woodrow Wilson
Republican, June 18, 5 days, Chicago, Ill., William Howard Taft

1916

Democratic, June 14, 3 days, St. Louis, Mo., Woodrow Wilson
Republican, June 7, 4 days, Chicago, Ill., Charles Evans Hughes

1920

Republican, June 8, 5 days, Chicago, Ill., Warren Gamaliel Harding
Democratic, June 28, 8 days, San Francisco, Calif., James Middleton Cox

1924

Republican, June 10, 3 days, Cleveland, Ohio, Calvin Coolidge
Democratic, June 24, 14 days, New York, N.Y., John William Davis

1928

Republican, June 12, 4 days, Kansas City, Mo., Herbert Hoover
Democratic, June 26, 4 days, Houston, Tex., Alfred Emanuel Smith

1932

Democratic, June 27, 3 days, Chicago, Ill., Franklin Delano Roosevelt
Republican, June 14, 3 days, Chicago, Ill., Herbert Hoover

1936

Democratic, June 23, 5 days, Philadelphia, Pa., Franklin Delano Roosevelt
Republican, June 9, 4 days, Cleveland, Ohio, Alfred Mossman Landon

1940

Democratic, July 15, 4 days, Chicago, Ill., Franklin Delano Roosevelt
Republican, June 24, 5 days, Philadelphia, Pa., Wendell Lewis Willkie

1944

Democratic, July 19, 3 days, Chicago, Ill., Franklin Delano Roosevelt
Republican, June 26, 3 days, Chicago, Ill., Thomas Edmund Dewey

1948

Democratic, July 12, 3 days, Philadelphia, Pa., Harry S. Truman
Republican, June 21, 5 days, Philadelphia, Pa., Thomas Edmund Dewey

1952

Republican, July 7, 5 days, Chicago, Ill., Dwight David Eisenhower
Democratic, July 21, 6 days, Chicago, Ill., Adlai Ewing Stevenson

1956

Republican, Aug. 20, 4 days, San Francisco, Calif., Dwight David Eisenhower
Democratic, Aug. 13, 4 days, Chicago, Ill., Adlai Ewing Stevenson

1960

Democratic, July 11, 5 days, Los Angeles, Calif., John Fitzgerald Kennedy
Republican, July 25, 4 days, Chicago, Ill., Richard Milhous Nixon

1964

Democratic, Aug. 24, 4 days, Atlantic City, N.J., Lyndon Baines Johnson
Republican, July 13, 4 days, San Francisco, Calif., Barry Morris Goldwater

1968

Republican, Aug. 5, 4 days, Miami Beach, Fla., Richard Milhous Nixon
Democratic, Aug. 26, 4 days, Chicago, Ill., Hubert Horatio Humphrey

1972

Republican, Aug. 21, 3 days, Miami Beach, Fla., Richard Milhous Nixon

Democratic, July 10, 4 days, Miami Beach, Fla., George Stanley McGovern

CONVENTION CITIES (1856-1972)

The following lists show the number of conventions held in each city. Dates in boldface indicate years in which the party was victorious.

Republican Convention

Chicago, Ill., 14—**1860**, **1868**, **1880**, 1884, **1888**, **1904**, **1908**, 1912, 1916, **1920**, 1932, 1944, **1952**, 1960

Philadelphia, Pa., 5—1856, **1872**, **1900**, 1940, 1948

Cleveland, Ohio, 2—**1924**, 1936

Miami Beach, Fla., 2—**1968**, **1972**

San Francisco, Calif., 2—**1956**, 1964

Baltimore, Md., 1—**1864**

Cincinnati, Ohio, 1—**1876**

Kansas City, Mo., 1—**1928**

Minneapolis, Minn., 1—1892

St. Louis, Mo., 1—**1896**

Democratic Conventions

Chicago, Ill., 10—1864, **1884**, **1892**, 1896, **1932**, **1940**, **1944**, 1952, 1956, 1968

St. Louis, Mo., 4—1876, 1888, 1904, **1916**

Baltimore, Md., 3—1860, 1872, **1912**

Cincinnati, Ohio, 2—**1856**, 1880

New York, N.Y., 2—1868, 1924

Philadelphia, Pa., 2—**1936**, **1948**

Atlantic City, N.J., 1—**1964**

Charleston, S.C., 1—1860

Denver, Colo., 1—1908

Houston, Tex., 1—1928

Kansas City, Mo., 1—1900

Los Angeles, Calif., 1—**1960**

Miami Beach, Fla., 1—1972

San Francisco, Calif., 1—1920

PRESIDENTS NOMINATED IN CHICAGO

Ten of the thirty-six Presidents were nominated in Chicago, Ill.

The Republicans nominated fourteen candidates in Chicago. Eight were elected: Lincoln, 1860; Grant, 1868; Garfield, 1880; Benjamin Harrison, 1888; Theodore Roosevelt, 1904; Taft, 1908; Harding, 1920; and Eisenhower, 1952. Six were unsuccessful: Blaine, 1884; Taft, 1912; Hughes, 1916; Hoover, 1932; Dewey, 1944; and Nixon, 1960.

The Democrats at ten conventions in Chicago nominated six individuals as candidates. Two were elected: Cleveland, 1884 and 1892; Franklin D. Roosevelt, 1932, 1940, and 1944. Four were unsuccessful:

McClellan, 1864; Bryan, 1896; Stevenson, 1952 and 1956; Humphrey, 1968.

CONVENTION FAILED TO SELECT NOMINEES

The only nominating convention of a major party which did not decide upon a presidential candidate was the Democratic convention of 1860, which met at the Hall of the South Carolina Institute, Charleston, S.C., on April 23, 1860. After ten days in session, during which 57 indecisive ballots were taken, the convention adjourned to meet at Baltimore, Md., on June 18, 1860. In a six-day session at the Front Street Theatre in Baltimore, Stephen Arnold Douglas of Illinois was nominated on the second bllot.

ADMISSION CHARGED AT CONVENTION

The first political convention at which admission was charged was the Progressive Party Convetnion, held at Convention Hall, Philadelphia, Pa., July 23-25, 1948. The public also paid to hear the candidates' acceptance speeches at Shibe Park, the grounds of the Philadelphia Athletics baseball team. Approximately $15,000 was received to defray campaign expenses.

LONGEST NOMINATING CONVENTION

The Democratic convention of 1924, in session 14 days, required 103 ballots before a presidential nominee was agreed upon. On the first ballot, William Gibbs McAdoo of California had $431\frac{1}{2}$ votes, nearly twice as many as the next highest candidate, Alfred Emanuel Smith of New York, who had 241 votes. As 731 votes were necessary for choice, the balloting continued and 103 ballots were taken before one candidate received the necessary number. John William Davis of West Virginia, who had only 31 votes on the first ballot, won the nomination on the 103rd ballot, receiving 844 votes.

CONVENTION RULES

There is no set rule which governs every convention although there is more or less standard procedure. Conventions usually open with an invocation. Credentials and committee rules are reported upon. A temporary chairman is selected. The keynote speech is delivered. Accredited delegates vote for a permanet chairman. The reports of committees are voted upon and a platform is adopted. A presidential nominee is chosen. A vice presidential nominee is chosen. Committees are appointed to notify the selected nominees. A new national committee is selected to act for the party and carry on the campaign and the work of the party until the next convention.

CONVENTION DELEGATES

Each political party has the right and privilege to determine the qualifications and number of its delegates. Conventions adopt their own regulations and procedures, and these are subject to change.

The apportionment of delegates varies from convention to convention in accordance with the rules. The methods of selecting delegates vary according to the regulations of the state organizations.

Five states which hold primaries for district delegates also have delegates-at-large selected by state committeemen or chosen at state conventions.

APPORTIONMENT OF VOTES—1964 NATIONAL CONVENTIONS

In the following list the first figure refers to the Republican convention and the second to the Democratic convention.

Alabama—20, 38
Alaska—12, 12
Arizona—16, 19
Arkansas—12, 32
California—86, 154
Colorado—18, 23
Connecticut—16, 43
Delaware—12, 22
Florida—34, 51
Georgia—24, 53
Hawaii—8, 25
Idaho—14, 15
Illinois—58, 114
Indiana—32, 51
Iowa—24, 35
Kansas—20, 27
Kentucky—24, 34
Louisiana—20, 46
Maine—14, 16
Maryland—20, 48
Massachusetts—34, 69
Michigan—48, 92
Minnesota—26, 50
Mississippi—13, 24
Missouri—24, 58
Montana—14, 17
Nebraska—16, 19
Nevada—6, 22
New Hampshire—14, 15
New Jersey—40, 77
New Mexico—14, 26
New York—92, 179
North Carolina—26, 58
North Dakota—14, 15
Ohio—58, 99
Oklahoma—22, 30
Oregon—18, 24
Pennsylvania—64, 125
Rhode Island—14, 27
South Carolina—16, 38
South Dakota—14, 15

Tennessee—28, 40
Texas—56, 99
Utah—14, 16
Vermont—12, 12
Virginia—30, 42
Washington—24, 35
West Virginia—14, 37
Wisconsin—30, 46
Wyoming—30, 15
District of Columbia—9, 16
Puerto Rico—5, 8
Virgin Islands—3, 5
Canal Zone—0, 5
Guam—0, 3
Total number of delegates—1,308; 2,316

CONVENTION NOMINATIONS—1832-1972

Since the first nominating convention in 1832, there have been 72 conventions held by the major political parties. At these 72 conventions, 44 presidential nominations were made by acclamation or on the first ballot. (Franklin Delano Roosevelt was renominated in 1936 by acclamation and no vote was taken.) Of the 43 candidates nominated on the first ballot, 22 were elected—13 Republicans and 9 Democrats; of the 21 losers who were nominated on the first ballot, 11 were Democrats, 8 were Republicans, and 2 were Whigs.

The successful candidate who required the greatest number of ballots at a nominating convention was Franklin Pierce, Democrat, who did not receive the nomination until the 49th ballot. Woodrow Wilson, Democrat, was a runner-up, requiring 46 ballots before he was nominated in 1912. The Republican who required the greatest number of ballots in order to win a nomination was James Abram Garfield, who was nominated on the 36th ballot in 1880.

John William Davis, Democrat, ranks far out in the field of candidates requiring large numbers of ballots for nomination. In 1924 there were 103 ballots before Davis was selected as the Democratic Party's standard-bearer.

PRESIDENTIAL NOMINATIONS

The candidates and the people who propose them realize that at the nominating convention only one candidate for President and one for Vice President can be nominated. But that does not prevent others from competing. At the 1924 Democratic Party convention, for example, there were sixty nominations for the presidency. Sometimes a nomination is made as a courtesy or a mark of recognition to an individual or to a state. Often a state casts its vote for a "favorite son" or for a person who obviously has no chance of winning. This is often done to enable the state to bargain or make a deal with one of the other more logical candidates, and it generally happens when there are two leading contenders vying for the nomination.

Occasionally votes are cast for a contender who is not likely to win in order to play for time and prevent another candidate from winning the majority or plurality of votes. Sometimes votes are deliberately withheld on the early ballots and released gradually to show that a candidate is gaining strength. Once in a while a nomination is made with the hope that the leading candidate will be unable to secure the necessary number of votes and that there may be a switch to a dark-horse candidate.

Sometimes a candidate is proposed for nomination even though there is no intention of having him win the nomination. The action may enable someone to make a speech to show his oratory so that he in turn may later be nominated, or it may advance an individual who is being groomed for the vice presidency or some appointive office.

Often a candidate is nominated without opposition and receives a unanimous vote. Occasionally no tally of votes is made, the nomination being by acclamation. In many cases, after a vote is recorded, a motion is offered to make the nomination unamimous. Since this involves no change in the selection of candidates and since it shows a solid and united party, many nominations are declared unanimous even though the candidate does not receive all the votes on the earlier ballots. It often happens at conventions that after the vote has been tabulated and recorded, states change their votes from one candidate to another. For this reason, there is sometimes a disparity in the returns, and as a result the amended vote differs from the original vote.

DEMOCRATIC PRESIDENTIAL CANDIDATES NOMINATED ON THE FIRST BALLOT—1832-1972

(Elections won by Democrats are indicated by asterisks)

*1832–Andrew Jackson, Tenn.
*1836–Martin Van Buren, N.Y.
 1840–Martin Van Buren, N.Y.
 1864–George Brinton McClellan, N.J.
 1872–Horace Greeley, N.Y.
 1888–Grover Cleveland, N.Y.
*1892–Grover Cleveland, N.Y.
 1900–William Jennings Bryan, Neb.
 1904–Alton Brooks Parker, N.Y.
 1908–William Jennings Bryan, Neb.
*1916–Woodrow Wilson, N.J.
 1928–Alfred Emanuel Smith, N.Y.
*1936–Franklin Delano Roosevelt, N.Y.
*1940–Franklin Delano Roosevelt, N.Y.
*1944–Franklin Delano Roosevelt, N.Y.
*1948–Harry S. Truman, Mo.
 1956–Adlai Ewing Stevenson, Ill.
*1960–John Fitzgerald Kennedy, Mass.
*1964–Lyndon Baines Johnson, Tex.
 1968–Hubert Horatio Humphrey, Minn.
 1972–George Stanley McGovern, S.D.

REPUBLICAN PRESIDENTIAL CANDIDATES NOMINATED ON THE FIRST BALLOT—1856-1972

(Elections won by Republicans are indicated by asterisks.)

1856–John Charles Fremont, Calif.
*1864–Abraham Lincoln, Ill.
*1868–Ulysses Simpson Grant, Ill.
*1872–Ulysses Simpson Grant, Ill.
1892–Benjamin Harrison, Ind.
*1896–William McKinley, Ohio
*1900–William McKinley, Ohio
*1904–Theodore Roosevelt, N.Y.
*1908–William Howard Taft, Ohio
1912–William Howard Taft, Ohio
*1924–Calvin Coolidge, Mass.
*1928–Herbert Clark Hoover, Calif.
1932–Herbert Clark Hoover, Calif.
1936–Alfred Mossman Landon, Kan.
1944–Thomas Edmund Dewey, N.Y.
*1952–Dwight David Eisenhower, N.Y.
*1956–Dwight David Eisenhower, N.Y.
1960–Richard Milhous Nixon, Calif.
1964–Barry Morris Goldwater, Ariz.
*1968–Richard Milhous Nixon, N.Y.
*1972–Richard Milhous Nixon, Calif.

REPUBLICAN PRESIDENTIAL CANDIDATES

The Republican Party nominated 30 candidates for the presidency (1856-1972) of whom 18 were elected.

Five candidates were nominated twice and were elected both times. They were Lincoln, Grant, McKinley, Eisenhower, and Nixon.

One candidate was nominated twice and defeated both times. The candidate was Dewey.

Six candidates were nominated once and served one term. They were Hayes, Garfield, T. Roosevelt, Harding, and Coolidge.

Three candidates were elected for one term and defeated when they ran for reelection. They were B. Harrison, Taft, and Hoover.

Seven candidates were nominated but were not elected. They were Fremont, Blaine, Hughes, Landon, Willkie, Goldwater, and Nixon in 1960.

PRESIDENTIAL "DARK HORSES"

Numerous dark horses have made spectacular and unbelievable runs to secure nominations. The first dark horse to win was Polk, in 1844. Three other dark horses achieved victories: Pierce in 1852, Garfield in 1880, and Harding in 1920. Two dark horses made valiant attempts but were not elected: Seymour in 1868 and Bryan in 1896.

BROTHERS NOMINATED FOR THE PRESIDENCY

At the eighth Republican convention, held at Exposition Hall, June 3-6, 1884, the names of two brothers were placed in nomination for the presidency. One was John Sherman, United States Senator from Ohio, the other, General William Tecumseh Sherman. The former received thirty votes on the first ballot, the latter two votes.

William Tecumseh Sherman, who succeeded Grant as general and commander of the army, retired from military service in 1884. In a letter to his brother, Senator John Sherman, dated St. Louis, Mo., May 7, 1884, General Sherman wrote:

Why should I, at sixty-five years of age, with a reasonable provision for life, not a dollar of debt, and with the universal respect of my neighbors and countrymen, embark in the questionable game of politics? The country is in a state of absolute peace, and it would be a farce to declare that any man should sacrifice himself to a mere party necessity.

WOMEN PRESIDENTIAL AND VICE PRESIDENTIAL CANDIDATES

Only the minor political parties have nominated women as presidential or vice presidential candidates. The nominations follow:

1872–Victoria Claflin Woodhull, N.Y., presidential nominee of the People's Party (Equal Rights Party)

1884–Belva Ann Bennett Lockwood, D.C., presidential nominee of the Equal Rights Party

1888–Belva Ann Bennett Lockwood, D.C., presidential nominee of the Equal Rights Party

1924–Marie Caroline Brehm, Calif., vice presidential nominee of the Prohibition Party

1936–Florence Garvin, R.I., vice presidential nominee of the National Greenback Party

1948–Grace Carlson, Minn., vice presidential nominee of the Socialist Workers Party

1952–Charlotta A. Bass, N.Y., vice presidential nominee of the Progressive Party

1952–Myra Tanner Weiss, N.Y., vice presidential nominee of the Socialist Workers Party

1952–Charlotta A. Bass, N.Y., vice presidential nominee of the American Labor Party

1956–Georgia Cozzini, Wis., vice presidential nominee of the Socialist Labor Party

1956–Myra Tanner Weiss, N.Y., vice presidential nominee of the Socialist Workers Party

1956–Ann Marie Yezo, N.J., vice presidential nominee of the American Third Party

1960–Georgia Cozzini, Wis., vice presidential nominee of the Socialist Labor Party

1960–Myra Tanner Weiss, N.Y., vice presidential nominee of the Socialist Workers Party

1968–Charlene Mitchell, N.Y., presidential nominee of the Communist Party; the first black woman nominated for the presidency

1968–Judith Mage, N.Y., vice presidential nominee of the Peace and

Freedom Party

1972–Theodora Nathan, Ore., vice presidential nominee of the Libertarian Party

1972–Genevieve Gunderson, Minn., vice presidential nominee of the Socialist Labor Party

1972–Linda Jenness, presidential nominee of the Socialist Workers Party

BLACK PRESIDENTIAL AND VICE PRESIDENTIAL CANDIDATES

1932–James William Ford, N.Y., vice presidential nominee of the Communist Party

1936–James William Ford, N.Y., vice presidential nominee of the Communist Party

1940–James William Ford, N.Y., vice presidential nominee of the Communist Party

1952–Charlotta A. Bass, N.Y., vice presidential nominee of the American Labor Party

1952–Charlotta A. Bass, N.Y., vice presidential nominee of the Progressive Party

1964–Clifton De Berry, N.Y., presidential nominee of the Socialist Workers Party

1968–Paul Boutelle, N.J., vice presidential nominee of the Socialist Workers Party

1968–Eldridge Cleaver, presidential nominee of the Peace and Freedom Party

1968–Dick (Richard Claxton) Gregory, Ill., presidential nominee of the Freedom and Peace Party

1968–Charlene Mitchell, Calif., presidential nominee of the Communist Party

1972–Julius Hobson, D.C., vice presidential nominee of the People's Party

1972–Jarvis Tyner, vice presidential nominee of the Communist Party

GENERALS VERSUS ADMIRALS FOR THE PRESIDENCY

Despite the many sea battles in which United States naval heroes have been engaged, no admiral has been nominated for the presidency. The preference has been entirely in favor of the generals.

The Presidents who had been generals were Washington, Jackson, William Henry Harrison, Taylor, Pierce, Grant, Hayes, Garfield, Benjamin Harrison, and Eisenhower. Andrew Johnson and Arthur were military governors with the rank of general.

Nominated by their respective parties but unsuccessful in the contest for the presidency were Generals Winfield Scott, George B. McClellan, John Charles Fremont, and Winfield Scott Hancock.

Although Theodore Roosevelt was not a general, he had served with distinction in the Spanish-American War.

PRESIDENTIAL CANDIDATES FROM THE SAME STATES

Illinois presented two presidential candidates in 1860, Abraham Lincoln and Stephen Arnold Douglas. Lincoln received 180 electoral votes and Douglas 12 electoral votes.

Illinois had two presidential nominees in 1872. Ulysses Simpson Grant received 286 electoral votes and David Davis received 1 electoral vote.

In 1904, Theodore Roosevelt and Alton Brooks Parker were the candidates, both from New York. Roosevelt received 336 electoral votes, and Parker received 140 electoral votes.

Ohio had two candidates for the presidency in 1920, Warren Gamaliel Harding and James Middleton Cox, the former receiving 404 electoral votes, the latter 127 electoral votes.

In 1940 the two presidential candidates were Franklin Delano Roosevelt of New York and Wendell Lewis Willkie of New York. Roosevelt received 449 electoral votes and Willkie received 82 electoral votes.

New York again in 1944 presented two presidential candidates. Franklin Delano Roosevelt received 432 electoral votes and Thomas Edmund Dewey received 99 electoral votes.

DEFEATED PRESIDENTIAL CANDIDATES RENOMINATED

The first presidential candidate renominated by the Republicans after being defeated was Thomas Edmund Dewey of New York, who was defeated in the November 7, 1944, election by President Franklin Delano Roosevelt. Dewey, renominated at the June 21-25, 1948, convention in Philadelphia, Pa., was defeated by Harry S. Truman in the election of November 2, 1948. Richard Milhous Nixon was defeated in 1960 by John Fitzgerald Kennedy but was renominated and elected in 1968.

Grover Cleveland, a Democrat, was defeated in 1888 but was renominated and reelected in 1892.

DEFEATED PRESIDENTIAL CANDIDATES RETURNED TO THE SENATE

Senators who were returned to the Senate after being defeated as presidential candidates were: Henry Clay of Kentucky, Whig Party candidate defeated November 5, 1844, returned to Senate March 4, 1849; Barry Morris Goldwater of Arizona, Republican Party candidate defeated November 3, 1964, returned to Senate January 3, 1969; Hubert Horatio Humphrey of Minnesota, Democratic Party candidate defeated November 5, 1968, returned to Senate January 3, 1971.

OLDEST PRESIDENTIAL CANDIDATE

The oldest presidential candidate was Peter Cooper, born February 12, 1791, in New York City, who was 85-years-old when he was nominated on May 17, 1876, by the Greenback Party in convention at Indianapolis, Ind. He received 81,737 votes at the November 7, 1876 election.

PERSISTENT PRESIDENTIAL CANDIDATE

The most persistent of the presidential candidates was Norman Mattoon Thomas, who was nominated six times by the Socialist Party and defeated at each election. In 1928, he received 267,420 votes as a candidate against Herbert Hoover. As a contestant in the elections won by Franklin Delano Roosevelt he received 884,782 votes in 1932, 187,512 votes in 1936, 116,798 votes in 1940, and 74,757 votes in 1944. He was also a candidate in 1948, receiving 95,908 votes in the election won by Harry S. Truman.

FIRST WOMAN PRESIDENTIAL CANDIDATE

The first woman presidential candidate proposed at a major political party convention was Margaret Chase Smith of Maine, who was nominated by Senator George David Aiken of Vermont on July 15, 1964, at the Republican National Convention at San Francisco, Calif.

BLACK PRESIDENTIAL CANDIDATES

The first black presidential candidate porposed at a major political party convention was Rev. Channing Emery Phillips of Washington, D.C., who was proposed August 28, 1968, at the Democratic Convention, Chicago, Ill.

The first black woman presidential candidate was Mrs. Charlene Mitchell, who was nominated by the Communist Party on July 7, 1968, at the Diplomat Hotel, New York City.

CANDIDATES WHO WERE DIVORCED

Governor James Middleton Cox of Ohio, the Democratic nominee defeated by Warren Gamaliel Harding in 1920, had been divorced and had remarried.

Governor Adlai Ewing Stevenson of Illinois, the Democratic nominee defeated by Dwight David Eisenhower in 1952 and 1956, was the only other divorced candidate representing a major party.

AUTOMOBILE USED IN CAMPAIGN

The first presidential candidate to ride in an automobile was William Jennings Bryan, who, accompained by his wife, was given a ride in 1896 at Decatur, Ill., in an automobile made by the Mueller Manufacturing Company. There were only ten automobiles in the United States at that time.

PRESIDENTIAL CANDIDATES WHO SERVED PRISON TERMS

Eugene Victor Debs of Indiana, the Socialist candidate for the presidency in 1900, 1904, 1908, 1912, and 1920, was in jail when he was nominated on May 13, 1920. Sentenced to ten years in federal prison for violation of the Espionage Act, he had begun his sentence on April 13, 1919, and was in prison when he received over 917,000 votes in the November 2, 1920 election. He was pardoned December 25, 1921.

On August 28, 1952, the American Labor Party nominated as its presidential candidate Vincent Hallinan of California, who had been released from the McNeil Island Federal Penitentiary on August 17, 1952, after serving six months for contempt of court in connection with his defense of Harry Bridges, the labor leader.

Farrell Dobbs, presidential candidate of the Socialist Workers Party in 1948, 1952, 1956, and 1960, was sent to prison on December 31, 1943, having been convicted on December 8, 1941, on charges of advocating the overthrow of the government by force and violence.

John Kasper of Tennessee, presidential nominee of the National States' Rights Party in 1964, served three terms in jail on charges of having interfered with court-ordered desegregation in Tennessee.

PRESIDENTIAL CANDIDATE KILLED IN ATTEMPT TO RESCUE DROWNING BOY

Frank T. Johns, of Portland, Ore., Socialist Labor presidential candidate in 1924 and 1928, was campaigning at Bend, Ore., on the bank of the Deschutes River, on May 21, 1928, when his speech was interrupted by a cry for help. Charles Rhodes, an eleven-year-old, was being drawn into deep water about seventy-five feet from the shore. Johns rushed to the boy's rescue and brought him to about ten feet from the shore when he collapsed and they both drowned. Johns was thirty-nine years of age.

To fill the vacancy caused by the death of Johns, the party nominated Verne L. Reynolds.

PRESIDENTIAL CANDIDATE ASSASSINATED

Senator Robert Francis Kennedy of New York was assassinated by Sirhan Bishara Sirhan on June 5, 1968, at the Biltmore Hotel, Los Angeles, Calif., while campaigning for the Democratic presidential nomination. He died June 6, 1968.

PROVISIONS FOR DEATH OF CANDIDATE OR PRESIDENT-ELECT

If a presidential nominee should die before election day, his party would select a new candidate in his place. It could be anyone and would not necessarily be the vice presidential nominee. The Democrats require the choice to be made by the Democratic National Committee, each state having the same number of votes. The person with the majority would be nominated for the presidency. The Republicans allow the choice to be made eihter by the Republican National Committee (the committee members having the same number of votes as their states at the national convention) or by another convention if time permits.

If the President-elect should die after election day but before the meeting of the electoral college, the electors could vote as they desire. They are not obliged to select the Vice President-elect. If both President-elect and Vice President-elect should die, the electoral college could choose any two persons for the offices, with or without the consent of the political party.

If the President-elect should die after receiving the votes of the electoral college, the Vice President would be sworn in as President. If both the President and the Vice President should die, the rule of succession would be invoked: the Speaker of the House, the president pro tempore of the Senate, the Secretary of State, the Secretary of the Treasury, and so forth.

DEATH OF PRESIDENTIAL CANDIDATE GREELEY

Only once in the history of the United States has a presidential candidate died before inauguration day. Horace Greeley of New York, the Liberal Republican and Democratic candidate defeated by Ulysses Simpson Grant in 1872, died on November 29, after election day but before the electoral college assembled. His death released his 66 electors; with complete freedom of choice, they voted as follows: 42 for Thomas Andrews Hendricks of Indiana, 18 for Benjamin Gratz Brown of Missouri (Greeley's vice presidential running mate), 2 for Charles J. Jenkins of Georgia, 1 for David Davis of Illinois, and 3 for the deceased Greeley. By resolution of the House, the votes for Greeley were not counted.

Before his nomination, Greeley had held one legislative office. Filling a vacancy in the House of Representatives, he had served as a Whig congressman from New York from December 4, 1848, to March 3, 1849. In 1872 the Democrats accepted him as their candidate with great reluctance. Greeley, an abolitionist and one of the founders of the Republican Party, had never voted the Democratic ticket. (Grant, on the other hand, the Republican nominee, had never voted the Republican ticket; it is believed that Grant had voted only once before —casting his ballot for the Democrat Buchanan in the election of 1856.)

Greeley was the object of much abuse during the campaign. In a letter dated November 5, 1872, he complained: "I have been so bitterly assailed that I hardly know whether I am running for the presidency or the penitentiary." He was physically and mentally exhausted by the campaign, and lived only three weeks after his defeat.

DEATH OF DEFEATED PRESIDENTIAL AND VICE PRESIDENTIAL CANDIDATES

In 1940 the Republicans nominated Wendell Lewis Willkie for the presidency and Charles Linza McNary for the vice presidency at the twenty-second Republican convention held in Philadelphia, Pa., June 24-28. Both died before January 19, 1945, the last day of the term for which they sought election. Had they been elected, the United States would have been without a President and a Vice President for part of the term and the Speaker of the House of Representatives would have headed the country. McNary died February 25, 1944, at the age of 69 years and 258 days; Willkie died October 8, 1944, at the age of 52 years and 232 days.

POPULAR ELECTION RETURNS

Unlike the official electoral vote count, popular election return figures vary from source to source because there is no uniformity of selection in the tabulations. Many charts use estimated returns, preliminary returns, or incomplete returns, which are derived from newspapers, press associations, political parties, and the candidates themselves. These figures are subject to recount, to the addition of absentee ballots and the soldier vote, and to final revision. They are also subject to human error in recording and to the ever present possibility of typographical errors.

Since official figures are not always available from the secretary of state of each state, and since some official figures are interspersed with nonofficial figures, the popular election returns are not always 100 per cent correct. Most of the figures in this book have been obtained from an official federal publication, *Historical Statistics of the United States 1789-1945*.

PRESIDENTIAL ELECTORS

The Constitution, which went into effect on June 21, 1788, when it was ratified by New Hampshire, the ninth of the original thirteen states, provided for a President and Vice President and specified the manner in which they were to be elected. Article II, section 1, provided for election by electors and designated the number of electors, the method by which they were to be chosen, and their electoral function:

> Each State shall appoint, in such Manner as the Legislature thereof may direct, a Number of Electors, equal to the whole number of Senators and Representatives to which the State may be entitled in the Congress: but no Senator or Representative, or person holding an Office of Trust or Profit under the United States, shall be appointed an Elector.
>
> The Electors shall meet in their respective States, and vote by Ballot for two Persons, of whom one at least shall not be an inhabitant of the same State with themselves.

On September 13, 1788, the Continental Congress directed that each state choose its own electors in the manner it saw fit and that these electors be chosen on the first Wednesday in January (January 7) 1789. These electors were directed to cast their ballots on the first Wednesday in February (February 4) 1789.

Each elector was entitled to cast two ballots, one for the President and one for the Vice President. There was no distinction between the two offices on the ballot. According to the Constitution:

> The Person having the greatest number of Votes shall be the President, if such Number be a Majority of the whole Number of Electors appointed; and if there be more than one who have such Majority, and have an equal Number of Votes, then the House of Representatives shall immediately chuse by Ballot one of them for President; and if no Person have a Majority, then from the five highest on the List the said House shall in like Manner chuse the President. But in chusing the President, the votes shall be taken by States, the Representation from each State having one Vote; A quorum for this Purpose shall consist of a

Member or Members from two thirds of the States, and a Majority of all the States shall be necessary to a Choice. In every Case, after the Choice of the President, the Person having the greatest Number of Votes of the Electors shall be the Vice President. But if there should remain two or more who have equal Votes, the Senate shall chuse from them by Ballot the Vice President.

This method was found to have several objections and to meet them the Twelfth Amendment was drawn up. The Amendment, declared in force on September 25, 1804, made the following provision:

The Electors shall meet in their respective states, and vote by ballot for President and Vice President, one of whom, at least, shall not be an inhabitant of the same state with themselves; they shall name in their ballots the person voted for as President, and in distinct ballots the person voted for as Vice President, and they shall make distinct lists of all persons voted for as President, and of all persons voted for as Vice President, and of the number of votes for each, which lists they shall sign and certify, and transmit sealed to the seat of the government of the United States, directed to the President of the Senate;—The President of the Senate shall, in the presence of the Senate and the House of Representatives, open all the certificates and the votes shall then be counted;—The person having the greatest number of votes for President, shall be the President, if such number be a majority of the whole number of electors appointed. . . .

On March 1, 1792, an act of Congress (1 Stat. L. 239) fixed the meeting of electors within thirty-four days preceding the first Wednesday in December.

The act of February 3, 1887 (24 Stat. L. 373) provided that the electors should meet on the second Wednesday in February.

An act of Congress of June 5, 1934 (48 Stat. L. 879) fixed the time and place for the meeting of the presidential electors as the sixth day of January, when the votes are counted in the presence of the two houses.

The electors meet in their respective states (at their state capitals) on the first Monday after the second Wednesday in December.

As provided for in the Constitution, the electors are equal in number to the whole number of representatives and senators (531 in the election of 1956, 537 in the election of 1960, and 538 in the election of 1964-1972. The group is known as the "electoral college" and exists for the sole purpose of casting two ballots, one for President and one for Vice President.

The result is recorded in triplicate; one copy is sent to the President of the Senate by mail; one copy is sent to him by messenger; and one copy is deposited with the Federal judge of the district in which the electors meet.

THE ELECTORAL COLLEGE TODAY

With the emergence of political parties in the early nineteenth century, the electoral college began to function in the way it does now—a way quite different from that intended by the framers of the Constitution. The President is elected by the mechanism of *electoral votes* (derived from popular votes) rather than by the will of the *electors*. In accordance with the provisions of the Constitution, electors still choose the President. But the electors are chosen by means of the popular votes registered for the party candidates. By casting ballots for specified party candidates, voters choose the party electors, who in turn go through the formality of voting for the party candidates when the electoral college convenes. The machinery by which the electors are chosen varies from state to state—in many states the names of the electors do not even appear on the ballot—but in each state the party candidate with the highest number of popular votes receives all of the state's electoral votes.

Since the names of the electors are identified with party affiliations, they are morally committed to vote for the candidate endorsed by their party. They are not obliged to do so, however, and theoretically they can still vote as they please. (Over the years this prerogative has been exercised only by six electors.) In six states—Alabama, California, Idaho, Massachusetts, Mississippi, and Oregon—laws have been passed instructing the electors to vote for the candidates of their political parties. The first state law requiring presidential electors to cast their ballots for President and Vice President of the political party for which they were chosen was enacted by Maine on March 25, 1969.

The individuals who serve as electors are generally designated by political groups and usually are persons who have contributed heavily to the party coffers or who have served the party with distinction. The honor is available to all citizens except those excluded by the Constitution: senators and representatives and persons "holding an Office of Trust or Profit under the United States."

ELECTIONS DEVOLVING UPON THE HOUSE AND SENATE

In the event that a presidential candidate does not receive a majority of the electoral votes, the House of Representatives chooses a President from the three leading contenders. Each state is entitled to one vote, and the winning candidate must receive a majority. Should the House of Representatives fail to choose a President, the Vice President elect becomes President.

The House was called into action twice, in 1801 and in 1825, when Thomas Jefferson and John Quincy Adams were elected respectively.

If the vice presidential candidate does not receive a majority of the electoral votes, the Senate, voting as individuals, selects the Vice President from the two highest candidates. The only time the Senate was called upon to exercise this privilege was in 1837, when it elected Richard Mentor Johnson.

THE ELECTORAL VOTE FOR PRESIDENT

The following list shows the total number of electoral votes in each election from 1789 through 1973. The parenthetical are those comprising the totals—the number of representatives and the number of senators.

1789–69 (49, 20)
1793–132 (102, 30)
1797, 1801–138 (106, 32)
1805–176 (142, 34)
1809–175 (141, 34)
1813–217 (171, 36)
1817–217 (169, 38)
1821–235 (187, 48)
1825, 1829–261 (213, 48)
1833–286 (238, 48)
1837, 1841–294 (242, 52)
1845–275 (223, 52)
1849–290 (230, 60)
1853, 1857–296 (234, 62)
1861–303 (237, 66)
1865–233 (183, 50)
1869–294 (220, 74)
1873–352 (278, 74)
1877, 1881–369 (293, 76)
1885, 1889–401 (325, 76)
1893–444 (356, 88)
1897, 1901–447 (357, 90)
1905–476 (386, 90)
1909–483 (391, 92)
1913, 1957–531 (435, 96)
1961–537 (437, 100)
1965-1973–538 (438, 100)

In 1789, there were 69 electors each of whom had two votes, one for President and one for Vice President. The candidate with the greatest number of votes was elected President, the second highest became Vice President. George Washington of Virginia received 69 votes. Other votes were cast as follows: John Adams, Mass., 34; John Jay, N.Y., 9; Robert Hanson Harrison, Md., 6; John Rutledge, S.C., 6; John Hancock, Mass., 4; George Clinton, N.Y., 3; Samuel Huntington, Conn., 2; Homer Virgil Milton, Ga., 2; James Armstrong, Pa., 1; Benjamin Lincoln, Mass., 1; Edward Telfair, Ga., 1.

In 1792, the second term, George Washington of Virginia received 132 votes. Others for whom votes were cast were: John Adams, Mass., 77; George Clinton, N.Y., 60; Thomas Jefferson, Va., 4; Aaron Burr, N.Y., 1.

In 1796, the third term, votes were cast as follows: John Adams, Mass., 71; Thomas Jefferson, Va., 68; Thomas Pinckney, S.C., 59; Aaron Burr, N.Y., 30; Samuel Adams, Mass., 15; Oliver Ellsworth, Conn., 11; George Clinton, N.Y., 7; John Jay, N.Y., 5; James Iredell, N.C., 3; John Henry, Md., 2; Samuel Johnston, N.C., 2; George Washington, Va., 2; Charles Cotesworth Pinckney, S.C., 1.

In 1800, the fourth term, votes were cast as follows: Thomas Jefferson, Va., 73; Aaron Burr, N.Y., 73; John Adams, Mass., 65; Charles Cotesworth Pinckney, S.C., 64; John Jay, N.Y., 1.

In 1804, the fifth term, votes were cast as follows: Thomas Jefferson, Va., 162; Charles Cotesworth Pinckney, S.C., 14.

In 1808, the sixth term, votes were cast as follows: James Madison, Va., 122; Charles Cotesworth Pinckney, S.C., 47; George Clinton, N.Y., 6.

In 1812, the seventh term, the votes were cast as follows: James Madison, Va., 128; De Witt Clinton, N.Y., 69.

In 1816, the eighth term, votes were cast as follows: James Monroe, Va., 183; Rufus King, N.Y., 34.

In 1820, the ninth term, votes were cast as follows: James Monroe, Va., 231; John Quincy Adams, Mass., 1. (Senator William Plumer, N.H., cast the vote for Adams.)

In 1824, the tenth term, votes were cast as follows: Andrew Jackson, Tenn., 99; John Quincy Adams, Mass., 84; William Harris Crawford, Ga., 41; Henry Clay, Ky., 37. (Three of New York's 36 electors deserted Henry Clay to vote for Jackson.)

In 1828, the eleventh term, votes were cast as follows: Andrew Jackson, Tenn., 178; John Quincy Adams, Mass., 83.

From 1789 thru 1973, the electors in the electoral college cast 17,592 votes. Every elector, however, was not able or did not cast a ballot. Thirty-six voters did not vote, the largest number being 17 in 1873 (1789, 4 votes; 1792, 3 votes; 1808, 1 votes; 1812, 1 vote; 1817, 4 votes; 1821, 3 votes; 1833, 2 votes; 1865, 1 vote; 1873, 17 votes).

Of the 17,592 votes cast, only 6 votes were cast contrary to "instructions."

In 1796, Samuel Miles, a Pennsylvania Federalist voted for John Adams instead of Thomas Jefferson.

In 1949, Preston Parks of Tennessee, one of the 12 electors from Tennessee, voted for James Strom Thurmond of South Carolina, the States Rights candidate, instead of Harry S. Truman.

In 1957, W. F. Turner of Montgomery, Ala., one of the 11 electors of Alabama, voted for Walter Burgwyn Jones, a circuit court judge of Montgomery, Ala., instead of Adlai Ewing Stevenson.

In 1961, Henry D. Irwin of Bartlesville, Okla., one of the electors of Oklahoma, cast his vote for Senator Harry Flood Byrd of Virginia.

In 1969, Dr. Lloyd W. Bailey of Rocky Mount, N.C., one of the 13 Republican electors from North Carolina, voted for George Corley Wallace, instead of Richard Milhous Nixon.

In 1973, Roger L. McBride of Charlottesville, Va., voted for John Hospers of Oregon, candidate of the Libertarian Party, instead of Richard Milhous Nixon.

ELECTORAL ODDITIES

It would have been possible for a presidential candidate to win any election from 1912 through 1964 without receiving a single vote in thirty-six states.

A presidential candidate with the electoral votes of only 12 states could have won the election. The combined electoral vote of New York (45), Pennsylvania (32), California (32), Illinois (27), Ohio (25),

Texas (24) Michigan (20), Massachusetts (16), New Jersey (16), North Carolina (14), Indiana (13), and Missouri (13) amounted to 277 votes, whereas only 266 votes were required for victory.

In 1956, for example, the total vote cast in the 12 states mentioned above was 39,768,470. Under the unit or block system by which the candidate with the highest vote receives the entire electoral vote of a state, a candidate with 20,000,000 votes could have carried the twelve vital states. Thus a candidate with the votes of only 12.5 per cent of the population of the United States (over 200,000,000) could conceivably have been elected President of the United States.

Only 3 Presidents were elected without carrying New York and Pennsylvania: Wilson in 1916, Truman in 1948, and Nixon in 1968.

FIRST ELECTORAL VOTE CAST FOR A WOMAN

The first electoral vote for a woman was cast by Roger L. McBride of Charlottesville, Va., whose vote for Theodora Nathan of Oregon, vice presidential candidate of the Libertarian Party was counted January 6, 1973.

PRESIDENTS ELECTED WITHOUT A POPULAR MAJORITY

Many presidents were elected without receiving a majority of the votes cast. Listed below are the 15 popular elections in which the winning candidates failed to receive a popular majority. The names of all candidates are followed by the percentage of popular votes received. Winning candidates in each election are listed first.

1824

John Quincy Adams, Dem.-Rep., 30.54
Andrew Jackson, Dem.-Rep., 43.13
Henry Clay, Dem.-Rep., 13.24
William Harris Crawford, Dem.-Rep., 13.09

1844

James Knox Polk, Dem., 49.56
Henry Clay, Whig, 48.13
James Gillespie Birney, Liberty, 2.31

1848

Zachary Taylor, Whig, 47.35
Lewis Cass, Dem., 42.52
Martin Van Buren, Free Soil, 10.13

1856

James Buchanan, Dem., 45.63
John Charles Fremont, Rep., 33.27
Millard Fillmore, American, 21.08
Others, .02

1860

Abraham Lincoln, Rep., 39.80

Stephen Arnold Douglas, Dem., 29.40
John Cabell Breckinridge, Nat. Dem., 18.20
John Bell, Constitutional, 12.60

1876

Rutherford Birchard Hayes, Rep., 48.04
Samuel Jones Tilden, Dem., 50.99
Peter Cooper, Greenback, .97

1880

James Abram Garfield, Rep., 48.32
Winfield Scott Hancock, Dem., 48.21
James Baird Weaver, Greenback Labor, 3.35
Others, .12

1884

Grover Cleveland, Dem., 48.53
James Gillespie Blaine, Rep., 48.24
Benjamin Franklin Butler, Anti-Monopoly, 1.74
John Pierre St. John, Prohibition, 1.49

1888

Benjamin Harrison, Rep., 47.86
Grover Cleveland, Dem., 48.66
Clinton Bowen Fisk, Prohibition, 2.19
Alson Jenness Streeter, Union Labor, 1.29

1892

Grover Cleveland, Dem., 46.04
Benjamin Harrison, Rep., 43.01
James Baird Weaver, People's, 8.53
Others, 2.42

1912

Woodrow Wilson, Dem., 41.85
Theodore Roosevelt, Progressive, 27.42
William Howard Taft, Rep., 23.15
Others, 7.58

1916

Woodrow Wilson, Dem., 49.26
Charles Evans Hughes, Rep., 46.12
Allan Louis Benson, Socialist, 3.16
Others, 1.46

1948

Harry S. Truman, Dem., 49.51
Thomas Edmund Dewey, Rep., 45.13
James Strom Thurmond, States' Rights, 2.40
Henry Agard Wallace, Progressive, 2.38
Others, .58

1960

John Fitzgerald Kennedy, Dem., 49.48
Richard Milhous Nixon, Rep., 49.32
Unpledged, .88
Others, .31

1968

Richard Milhous Nixon, Rep., 43.4
Hubert Horatio Humphrey, Dem., 42.7
George Corley Wallace, American Independent, 13.5
Others, .4

ELECTORAL VOTES CAST FOR BROTHERS IN 1796

In the election of 1796, before the President and the Vice President were separately voted upon, the electors voted for two brothers, Thomas and Charles Pinckney of South Carolina.

Thomas Pinckney received 59 of the electoral votes. (John Adams, who received 71 votes, was elected President, and Thomas Jefferson, who received 68 electoral votes, was elected Vice President.) Pinckney served as minister to Great Britain from 1792 to 1796 and in 1794-1795 was envoy extraordinary to Spain.

Charles Pinckney, governor of South Carolina, received one electoral vote in 1796. He also received 64 electoral votes in the election of 1800 and 14 in the election of 1804 (elections won by Jefferson). In the election of 1808 (won by Madison), he received 47 electoral votes.

VICE PRESIDENT DECLARED HIMSELF ELECTED

On Wednesday, February 8, 1797, John Adams, Vice President of the United States, acting as presiding officer of the Senate, at the joint session of the Senate and the House of Representatives, said after the tally of the votes of the electoral college, "In obedience to the Constitution and Law of the United States and to the commands of both Houses of Congress expressed in their resolution passed in the present session, I declare that John Adams is elected President of the United States for four years, to commence with the fourth day of March next; and that Thomas Jefferson is elected Vice President of the United States for four years to commence with the fourth of March next. And may the Sovereign of the Universe, the ordainer of civil government on earth, for the preservation of liberty, justice and peace, among men, enable both to discharge the duties of these offices conformably to the Constitution of the United States with conscientious diligence, punctuality and perseverance."

There were 138 electoral votes cast, a majority of 70 votes being required for election. No distinction was made as to the office of President and the Vice President. The candidate with the largest number of votes was elected President, the second largest was elected Vice President. (It was possible for the President and the Vice President to belong to different parties.)

POPULAR AND ELECTORAL VOTES

In 1960 the popular vote was almost equally divided between Kennedy and Nixon. Kennedy received 34,227,096 popular votes, and Nixon received 34,107,646 votes. The total vote cast in 1960 was 68,-836,385 including 44,623 votes for Byrd, and a scattering of votes for others. Of the 537 electoral votes, Kennedy received 303, Nixon 219, and Byrd 15.

In 1964, the total popular vote cast was 70,097,935, of which 42,825,-463 were for Johnson and 27,146,969 for Goldwater. Johnson received more than 61 per cent of all the popular votes cast, a higher percentage than that of any candidate in previous elections, including the election of 1936, in which Franklin Delano Roosevelt defeated Alfred Mossman Landon. Johnson's percentage of electoral votes, however, was smaller than that of Roosevelt. Johnson received 486 of the 538 votes, or 90.33 per cent. In 1936 Roosevelt received 523 of the 531 votes, or about 98.5 per cent.

"THIRD PARTY" ELECTORAL VOTES

In the 30 presidential elections since the organization of the Republican Party in 1856, the two-party system has been dominant. With one exception (the Progressive Party in 1912), the strength of third parties has been of little consequence.

Third parties have won electoral votes in only 6 elections. In 1856, Millard Fillmore, presidential candidate of the American Party, received 8 of the 296 electoral votes (2.7 per cent). In 1860, John Bell, presidential candidate of the Constitutional Union Party, received 39 of the 303 electoral votes (12.87 per cent). In 1892, James Baird Weaver, presidential candidate of the People's Party, received 22 of the 444 electoral votes (4.95 per cent). In 1912, Theodore Roosevelt, presidential candidate of the Progressive Party, received 88 of the 531 electoral votes (16.57 per cent). In 1924, Robert Marion La Follette, presidential candidate of the Progressive Party, received 13 of the 531 electoral votes (2.45 per cent). In 1948, James Strom Thurmond, presidential candidate of the States' Rights Democratic Party, received 39 of the 531 electoral votes (7.35 per cent). In 1968, George Corley Wallace, presidential candidate of the American Independent Party, received 46 of the 538 electoral votes (8.55 per cent).

DEFEATED CANDIDATES LATER ELECTED TO PRESIDENCY

Many candidates defeated at one election for the presidency or the vice presidency were later elected to the presidency.

In the election of 1792, Thomas Jefferson received 4 electoral votes for the vice presidency. John Adams received 77 electoral votes and was elected Vice President, George Washington being reelected for a second term.

In the election of 1796, Thomas Jefferson received 68 electoral votes and John Adams 71 electoral votes. Adams, who had the highest number of votes, was elected President, and Jefferson, who had the next highest number, was automatically elected Vice President.

In the election of 1808, James Madison was elected President. His Vice President was George Clinton of New York, who received 113 electoral votes. Others who received vice presidential electoral votes were James Monroe and James Madison, each of whom received 3 electoral votes.

In the election of 1820, James Monroe received 231 electoral votes and John Quincy Adams received 1 electoral vote.

In the election of 1824, Andrew Jackson was defeated for the presidency by John Quincy Adams. Jackson received a larger number of electoral votes, but not a majority. The House of Representatives voted by states and elected Adams. In the same year Jackson also received 13 electoral votes for the vice presidency and Martin Van Buren received 9 electoral votes. Calhoun was elected Vice President.

In the election of 1836, Martin Van Buren, with 170 electoral votes, was elected President. He defeated William Henry Harrison, who received 73 electoral votes. John Tyler, who received 47 electoral votes, was defeated for the vice presidency by Richard Mentor Johnson.

In the election of 1840, when Harrison won with 234 electoral votes, 1 electoral vote was cast for James Knox Polk.

In the election 1888, Grover Cleveland was defeated for reelection by Benjamin Harrison. In the election of 1892, however, Cleveland was successful in his attempt to regain the presidency.

In the election of 1920, Calvin Coolidge was elected Vice President under Harding, defeating Franklin Delano Roosevelt, who received 127 electoral votes.

In the election of 1964, Richard Milhous Nixon was defeated for the presidency by John Fitzgerald Kennedy. In the elections of 1968 and 1972, Nixon was successful in his attempts to gain the presidency.

ELECTIONS IN WHICH PRESIDENTS WERE RENOMINATED BUT NOT REELECTED

1797

George Washington (not a candidate for reelection), 2 electoral votes; John Adams elected, 71 electoral votes

1800

John Adams, 65 electoral votes; defeated by Thomas Jefferson, 73 electoral votes (election decided by House of Representatives because of Jefferson-Burr electoral tie)

1828

John Quincy Adams, 83 electoral votes; defeated by Andrew Jackson, 178 electoral votes

1840

Martin Van Buren, 60 electoral votes; defeated by William Henry Harrison, 234 electoral votes

1856

Millard Fillmore, 8 electoral votes; defeated by James Buchanan, 174 electoral votes

1888

Grover Cleveland, 168 electoral votes; defeated by Benjamin Harrison, 233 electoral votes

1892

Benjamin Harrison, 145 electoral votes; defeated by Grover Cleveland, 277 electoral votes

1912

Theodore Roosevelt, 88 electoral votes; William Howard Taft, 8 electoral votes; defeated by Woodrow Wilson, 435 electoral votes

1932

Herbert Clark Hoover, 59 electoral votes; defeated by Franklin Delano Roosevelt, 472 electoral votes

Some Presidents had also been defeated when they ran for office prior to their successful elections.

FIVE PRESIDENTS DENIED RENOMINATION

Four of the five Presidents denied renomination by their political party became President only through the death of the Chief Executive.

John Tyler, who became the tenth President after the death of William Henry Harrison, and served from April 6, 1841 to March 3, 1845, was not renominated by the Whig Party which convened May 1, 1844, in Baltimore, Md. Henry Clay was nominated for the presidency on the first ballot by acclamation.

Millard Fillmore became the thirteenth President on July 10, 1850, after the death of Zachary Taylor, and served until March 3, 1853. When the Whig Party convened at Baltimore, Md., June 17-20, 1852, Fillmore received 133 votes and Winfield Scott received 131 votes. On the fifty-third ballot, Scott received 159 votes and was declared the nominee of the Whig Party. Fillmore received 112 votes and Daniel Webster received 21 votes.

Andrew Johnson became the seventeenth President on April 15, 1865, after the assassination of Abraham Lincoln. Johnson served to March 3, 1869. The Democratic Party convention held in New York City, July 4-9, 1868, did not support Johnson. Instead, the nomination went to Horatio Seymour who was nominated on the twenty-second ballot.

Chester Alan Arthur, who served as the twenty-first President, from September 20, 1881 to March 3, 1885, due to the death of James Abram Garfield, was nominated for the presidency at the Republican Party convention in Chicago, Ill., June 3-6, 1884. James Gillespie Blaine who received 541 votes was elected, on the fourth ballot. Johnson received only 207 votes.

Tyler, Fillmore, A. Johnson, and Arthur were Vice Presidents who succeeded to the presidency due to the death of the incumbent.

Franklin Pierce was nominated for the presidency by the Democratic Party in convention in Baltimore, Md., June 1-5, 1852. Four years later, at the Democratic Party convention in Cincinnati, Ohio, June 2-6, 1856, Pierce was not renominated. On the seventeenth ballot, James Buchanan was nominated and later elected President.

POLITICAL PARTIES AND ELECTIONS

Federalists

Federalists won 3 (37.5 per cent) of 8 elections. (Elections won by Federalists are indicated by asterisks.)

*1788	Washington	1804	Pinckney
*1792	Washington	1808	Pinckney
*1796	J. Adams	1812	Clinton
1800	J. Adams	1816	King

Whigs

Whigs (originally known as National Republicans) won 2 (33.3 per cent) of 6 elections. (Elections won by Whigs are indicated by asterisks.)

1836	W. H. Harrison	*1848	Taylor
*1840	W. H. Harrison	1852	Scott
1844	Clay	1856	Fillmore

Democrats

Democrats (orginally called Democratic-Republicans) have won 24 (55.8 per cent) of 45 elections. (Elections won by Democrats are indicated by asterisks.)

1796	Jefferson	1876	Tilden
*1800	Jefferson	1880	Hancock
*1804	Jefferson	*1884	Cleveland
*1808	Madison	1888	Cleveland
*1812	Madison	*1892	Cleveland
*1816	Monroe	1896	Bryan
*1820	Monroe	1900	Bryan
*1824	J. Q. Adams	1904	Parker
*1828	Jackson	1908	Bryan
*1832	Jackson	*1912	Wilson
*1836	Van Buren	*1916	Wilson
1840	Van Buren	1920	Cox
*1844	Polk	1924	Davis
1848	Cass	1928	Smith
*1852	Pierce	*1932	F. D. Roosevelt
*1856	Buchanan	*1936	F. D. Roosevelt
1860	Douglas	*1940	F. D. Roosevelt
1864	McClellan	*1944	F. D. Roosevelt
1868	Seymour	*1948	Truman
1872	Greeley	1952	Stevenson

1956	Stevenson	1968	Humphrey
*1960	Kennedy	1972	McGovern
*1964	L. B. Johnson		

Republicans

Republicans have won 18 (60 per cent) of 30 elections from 1856 through 1972. (Elections won by Republicans are indicated by asterisks.)

1856	Fremont	1916	Hughes
*1860	Lincoln	*1920	Harding
*1864	Lincoln	*1924	Coolidge
*1868	Grant	*1928	Hoover
*1872	Grant	1932	Hoover
*1876	Hayes	1936	Landon
*1880	Garfield	1940	Willkie
1884	Blaine	1944	Dewey
*1888	B. Harrison	1948	Dewey
1892	B. Harrison	*1952	Eisenhower
*1896	McKinley	*1956	Eisenhower
*1900	McKinley	1960	Nixon
*1904	T. Roosevelt	1964	Goldwater
*1908	Taft	*1968	Nixon
1912	Taft	*1972	Nixon

NOMINATIONS AND ELECTIONS—1832-1972

In the 36 presidential elections from 1832 through 1972, the Republicans (and Whigs) nominated a total of 25 men; of these, 15 were successful in 20 of the 36 elections (Lincoln, Grant, McKinley, Eisenhower, and Nixon were elected twice).

In 16 unsuccessful elections, the Republicans and Whigs nominated a total of 15 candidates.

In the 36 elections, the Democrats similarly nominated a total of 26 men; of these, 11 were elected in 16 elections (Franklin Delano Roosevelt was elected 4 times, Cleveland and Wilson twice).

In 20 unsuccessful elections, the Democrats nominated a total of 15 candidates.

REPUBLICAN VERSUS DEMOCRATIC ADMINISTRATIONS

In the years 1856-1972 (the Republican Party ran John Charles Fremont as its first presidential candidate in 1856) the Republicans have elected 13 individuals for a total of 18 terms or 72 years.

The Republican administrations have been those of Lincoln (and Andrew Jackson), 8 years; Grant, 8 years; Hayes, 4 years; Garfield (and Arthur), 4 years; Benjamin Harrison, 4 years; McKinley (and Theodore Roosevelt), 8 years; Roosevelt, 4 years; Taft, 4 years; Harding (and Coolidge), 4 years; Coolidge, 4 years; Hoover, 4 years; Eisenhower, 8 years; Nixon, 8 years.

In the years 1856-1972 the Democrats have elected 7 individuals for a total of 12 terms or 48 years.

The Democratic administrations have been those of Buchanan, 4 years; Cleveland, 8 years (two non-consecutive terms); Wilson, 8 years; Franklin Delano Roosevelt (and Truman), 16 years; Truman, 4 years; Kennedy (and Lyndon Baines Johnson), 4 years; Johnson, 4 years.

ADMINISTRATION CHANGES

In the 47 presidential elections from 1789 through 1972, only 17 Presidents have succeeded Presidents of a different political party:

Thomas Jefferson (Dem.-Rep.) followed John Adams (Fed.)

Andrew Jackson (Dem.) followed John Quincy Adams (Dem.-Rep.)

William Henry Harrison (Whig) followed Martin Van Buren (Dem.)

James Knox Polk (Dem.) followed John Tyler (Whig)

Zachary Taylor (Whig) followed James Knox Polk (Dem.)

Franklin Pierce (Dem.) followed Millard Fillmore (Whig)

Abraham Lincoln (Rep.) followed James Buchanan (Dem.)

Grover Cleveland (Dem.) followed Chester Alan Arthur (Rep.)

Benjamin Harrison (Rep.) followed Grover Cleveland (Dem.)

Grover Cleveland (Dem.) followed Benjamin Harrison (Rep.)

William McKinley (Rep.) followed Grover Cleveland (Dem.)

Woodrow Wilson (Dem.) followed William Howard Taft (Rep.)

Warren Gamaliel Harding (Rep.) followed Woodrow Wilson (Dem.)

Franklin Delano Roosevelt (Dem.) followed Herbert Hoover (Rep.)

Dwight David Eisenhower (Rep.) followed Harry S. Truman (Dem.)

John Fitzgerald Kennedy (Dem.) followed Dwight David Eisenhower (Rep.)

Richard Milhous Nixon (Rep.) followed Lyndon Baines Johnson (Dem.)

THE LONGEST POLITICAL REGIME

The Democratic-Republicans, considered the forerunners of the present-day Democrats, had the longest uninterrupted term of office. On March 4, 1801, Thomas Jefferson took office and served 8 years. He was followed by James Madison, who served 8 years; James Monroe, who served 8 years; and John Quincy Adams, who served 4 years. The party had been in power 28 years, from March 4, 1801, to March 4, 1829, when Andrew Jackson (usually considered the first Democrat in the present sense) was inaugurated.

The longest Republican regime began on March 4, 1861, when Abraham Lincoln was inaugurated. Lincoln was reelected and after his death Andrew Johnson completed the remainder of the term. Grant was elected twice and served 8 years. Rutherford B. Hayes served 4 years. James A. Garfield was elected and after his death Chester A. Arthur completed the remainder of the term. The Republicans were in power 24 years, from March 4, 1861, to March 4, 1885, when Grover Cleveland, a Democrat, was inaugurated.

PRESIDENTS NOT NOTIFIED OF THEIR ELECTION

No provision has ever been made for notifying the President of his election. His first official notification takes place when he and the

Vice President-elect enter the Senate Chamber. After the notification, the President generally goes to the east portico of the Capitol, where he delivers his inaugural address and then takes the oath as President.

ALPHABETICAL LIST OF PRESIDENTIAL AND VICE PRESIDENTIAL CANDIDATES—1789-1824

The candidates on the following list ran for the presidency before a formal political party structure developed in the United States. Until 1804 each elector cast one vote for each of two individuals. The runner-up in the balloting became Vice President. Beginning in 1804, candidates were named separately for the vice presidency and voted for separately by the electors.

Adams, John–1789, 1792, 1796, 1800
Adams, John Quincy–1820, 1824
Adams, Samuel–1796
Armstrong, James–1789
Burr, Aaron–1792, 1796, 1800
Calhoun, John Caldwell–1824 and 1828, VP
Clay, Henry–1824
Clinton, DeWitt–1812
Clinton, George–1789, 1792, 1796; 1804 and 1808, VP
Crawford, William Harris–1816, 1824
Ellsworth, Oliver–1796
Gerry, Elbridge–1812, VP
Hancock, John–1789
Harper, Robert Goodloe–1816 and 1820 VP
Harrison, Robert Hanson–1789
Henry, John–1796
Howard, John Eager–1816, VP
Huntington, Samuel–1789
Ingersoll, Jared–1812, VP
Iredell, James–1796
Jackson, Andrew–1824
Jay, John–1789, 1796, 1800
Jefferson, Thomas–1792, 1796, 1800, 1804
Johnson, Samuel–1796
King, Rufus–1804 and 1808, VP; 1816
Langdon, John–1808, VP
Lincoln, Benjamin–1789
Macon, Nathaniel–1824, VP
Madison, James–1808, 1812
Marshall, John–1816, VP
Milton, John–1789
Monroe, James–1808, VP; 1816, 1820
Pinckney, Charles Cotesworth–1796, 1800, 1804, 1808
Pinckney, Thomas–1796
Rodney, Daniel–1816 and 1820, VP
Ross, James–1816, VP
Rush, Richard–1820, VP

Rutledge, John–1789
Sanford, Nathan–1824, VP
Stockton, Richard–1820, VP
Telfair, Edward–1789
Tompkins, Daniel D.–1816 and 1820, VP
Van Buren, Martin–1824, VP
Washington, George–1789, 1792, 1796

ALPHABETICAL LIST OF PRESIDENTIAL AND VICE PRESIDENTIAL CANDIDATES—1828-1972

The abbreviation VP following the year indicates a vice presidential candidacy for the year specified.

Adams, Charles Francis–1848, VP, Free Soil
Adams, Charles Francis, Jr.–1872, VP, Straight-Out Democratic
Adams, John Quincy–1828, Federalist
Agnew, Spiro Theodore–1968 and 1972, VP, Republican
Aiken, John W.–1932, VP, Socialist Labor; 1936, 1940, Socialist Labor
Albaugh, Arla A.–1944, VP, Socialist Labor
Allen, Seymour E.–1932, National
Anderson, Thomas Jefferson–1972, VP, American Independent
Andrews, Thomas Coleman–1956, American Vegetarian; 1964, Independent States' Rights
Arthur, Chester Alan–1880, VP, Republican
Babson, Roger Ward–1940, Prohibition
Banks, Nathaniel Prentice–1856, North American
Barker, Wharton–1900, People's
Barkley, Alben William–1948, VP, Democratic
Barnum, R.G.–1920, VP, Single Tax
Bass, Charlotta A.–1952, VP, American Labor, Progressive
Bass, Willia Isaac–1952, VP, Church of God
Bell, John–1860, Constitutional Union
Bennington, Wesley Henry–1928, VP, Greenback
Benson, Allan Louis–1916, Socialist
Bentley, Charles Eugene–1896, National
Bidwell, John–1892, Prohibition
Billings, Theodore C.–1964, VP, Constitution
Birney, James Gillespie–1840, 1844, Liberty
Black, James–1872, Prohibition
Blaine, James Gillespie–1884, Republican
Blair, Francis Preston–1868, VP, Democratic
Blomen, Henning A.–1964, VP, Socialist Labor; 1968, Socialist Labor
Bouck, William–1924, VP, Farmer Labor
Boutelle, Paul–1968, VP, Socialist Workers
Breckinridge, John Cabell–1856, VP, Democratic; 1860, Independent Democratic, Southern Democratic
Brehm, Marie Caroline–1924, VP, Prohibition
Bricker, John William–1944, VP, Republican
Brooks, John Anderson–1888, VP, Prohibition
Browder, Earl Russell–1936, 1940, Communist

Brown, Benjamin Gratz–1872, VP, Democratic, Liberal Republican, Liberal Republican Convention of Colored Men

Bryan, Charles Wayland–1924, VP, Democratic

Bryan, William Jennings–1896, Democratic, National Silver, Populist; 1900, Democratic, People's, Silver Republican; 1908 Democratic

Buchanan, James–1856, Democratic

Buckner, Simon–1896, VP, National Democratic

Butler, Benjamin Franklin–1884, Anti-Monopoly, Greenback

Butler, William Orlando–1848, VP, Democratic

Byrd, Harry Flood–1952, VP, America First, Constitution; 1956, States' Rights

Caffery, Donelson–1900, National

Calhoun, John Caldwell–1828, VP, Democratic

Carlson, Grace–1948, VP, Socialist Workers

Carroll, George W.–1904, VP, Prohibiiton

Cary, Samuel Fenton–1876, VP, Greenback

Cass, Lewis–1848, Democratic

Chafin, Eugene Wilder–1908, 1912, Prohibition

Chambers, Benjamin J.–1880, VP, Greenback Labor

Christensen, Parley Parker–1920, Farmer Labor

Clay, Henry–1832, National Republican; 1844, Whig

Cleaver, Eldridge–1968, Peace and Freedom

Cleveland, Grover–1884, 1888, 1892, Democratic

Cochrane, John–1864, VP, Independent Republican

Coffin, Lorenzo S.–1908, VP, United Christian

Coiner, C. Benton–1960, Conservative (Va.)

Colfax, Schuyler–1868, VP, Republican

Colvin, David Leigh–1920, VP, Prohibition; 1936, Prohibition

Colvin, John–1888, VP, Industrial Reform

Conant, John A.–1884, VP, American Prohibition

Coolidge, Calvin–1920, VP, Republican; 1924, Republican

Cooper, Peter–1876, Greenback

Corregan, Charles Hunter–1904, Socialist Labor

Courtney, Kent, H.–1960, VP, Conservative (N.J.)

Cowdrey, Robert Hall–1888, United Labor

Cox, James Middleton–1920, Democratic

Cox, James Renshaw–1932, Jobless

Cox, William Wesley–1904, VP, Socialist Labor; 1920, Socialist Labor

Coxey, Jacob Sechler–1932, VP, Farmer Labor

Cozzini, Georgia–1956 and 1960, VP, Socialist Labor

Cranfill, James Britton–1892, VP, Prohibition

Crommelin, John Geraerdt–1960, VP, National States' Rights

Crowley, Jeremiah D.–1928, VP, Socialist Labor

Cunningham, Charles E.–1888, VP, Union Labor

Curtis, Charles,–1928 and 1932, VP, Republican

Curtis, James Langdon–1888, American

Curtis, Merritt Barton–1960, Constitution (Wash.); 1960, VP, Tax Cut

Dallas, George Mifflin–1844, VP, Democratic

Daly, Lar–1960, Tax Cut

Daniel, William–1884, VP, Prohibition
Davis, David–1872, Labor Reform
Davis, Henry Gassaway–1904, VP, Democratic
Davis, John William–1924, Democratic
Dawes, Charles Gates–1924, VP, Republican
Dayton, William Lewis–1856, VP, Republican
De Berry, Clifton–1964, Socialist Workers
Debs, Eugene Victor–1900, Social-Democratic; 1904, 1908, 1912, 1920, Socialist
Decker, Rutherford Losey–1960, Prohibition
Dewey, Thomas Edmund–1944, 1948, Republican
Dobbs, Farrell–1948, 1952, 1956, 1960, Socialist Workers
Donelson, Andrew Jackson–1856, VP, American Whig
Donnelly, Ignatius–1900, VP, People's
Douglas, Stephen Arnold–1860, Democratic
Douglass, Frederick–1872, VP, Equal Rights
Dow, Neal–1880, Prohibition
Earle, Thomas–1840, VP, Liberty
Edgerton, James Arthur–1928, VP, Prohibition
Eisenhower, Dwight David–1952, 1956, Republican
Ellis, Seth Hockett–1900, Union Reform
Ellmaker, Amos–1832, VP, Anti-Masonic
Emery, Stephen–1948, VP, Socialist Labor
Everett, Edward–1860, VP, Constitution
Fairbanks, Charles Warren–1904, 1916, VP, Republican
Faris, Herman Preston–1924, Prohibition
Faubus, Orval Eugene–1960, National States' Rights
Ferguson, James Edward–1920, American
Field, James Gaven–1892, VP, People's
Fillmore, Millard–1848, VP, Whig; 1856, American, Whig
Fisher, Louis–1972, Socialist Labor
Fisher, Rolland E.–1968, VP, Prohibition
Fisk, Clinton Bowen–1888, Prohibition
Floyd, John–1832, Independent
Foote, Charles C.–1848, VP, National Liberty
Ford, James Willliam–1932, 1936, 1940, VP, Communist
Foster, William Zebulon–1924, 1928, 1932, Workers (Communist)
Frelinghuysen, Theodore–1844, VP, Whig
Fremont, John Charles–1856, Republican; 1864, Independent Republican
Friedman, Samuel Herman–1952 and 1956, VP, Socialist
Fry, Daniel–1972, VP, Universal
Garfield, James Abram–1880, Republican
Garner, John Nance–1932 and 1936, VP, Democratic
Garvin, Florence–1936, VP, National Greenback
Gian-Cursio, Christopher–1960, VP, Vegetarian
Gillhaus, August–1908, Socialist Labor; 1912 and 1920, VP, Socialist Labor
Gitlow, Benjamin–1924, 1928, VP, Workers (Communist)
Goldwater, Barry Morris–1964, Republican

Gould, Symon–1948 and 1952 and 1956, VP, American Vegetarian; 1960, Vegetarian

Graham, William Alexander–1852, VP, Whig

Granger, Francis–1836, VP, Whig

Grant, Ulysses Simpson–1868, Republican; 1872, National Working Men, Republican

Graves, John Temple–1908, VP, Independence

Greeley, Horace–1872, Democratic, Liberal Republican, Liberal Republican Convention of Colored Men

Green, Gabriel–1972, Universal

Gregory, Dick–1968, VP, Freedom and Peace

Groesbeck, William Slocum–1872, Independent Liberal Republican

Gunderson, Genevieve–1972, VP, Socialist Labor

Hale, John Parker–1848, Liberty; 1852, Free Soil

Hall, Gus–1972, Communist

Hallinan, Vincent William– 1952, American Labor, Progressive

Halstead, Fred–1968, Socialist Workers

Hamblen, Stuart–1952, Prohibition

Hamlin, Hannibal–1860, VP, Republican

Hancock, Winfield Scott–1880, Democratic

Hanford, Benjamin–1904 and 1908, VP, Socialist

Hanly, James Franklin–1916, Prohibition

Harding, Warren Gamaliel–1920, Republican

Harriman, Job–1900, VP, Social-Democratic

Harrison, Benjamin–1888, 1892, Republican

Harrison, Caleb–1916, VP, Socialist Labor

Harrison, William Henry–1836, 1840, Whig

Harrop, Roy M.–1924, VP, Greenback

Harvey, William Hope–1932, Liberty

Hass, Eric–1952, 1856, 1960, 1964, Socialist Labor

Hayes, Maximilian Sebastian–1920, VP, Farmer Labor

Hayes, Rutherford Birchard–1876, Republican

Hemenway, Frank B.–1932, VP, Liberty

Hendricks, Thomas Andrews–1876 and 1884, VP, Democratic

Hensley, Kirby James–1964, 1968, Universal

Hisgen, Thomas Louis–1908, Independence

Hobart, Garret Augustus–1896, VP, Republican

Hobson, Julius–1972, VP, People's

Holcomb, Austin–1904, Continental

Holdridge, Herbert Charles–1956, VP, Prohibition

Holtwick, Enock Arden–1952, VP, Prohibition; 1956, Prohibition

Homer, Irving–1972, VP, America First

Hoopes, Darlington–1944, VP, Socialist; 1952, Socialist

Hoover, Herbert Clark–1928, 1932, Republican

Hopkins, John O.–1964, VP, Universal

Hospers, John–1972, Libertarian

Howe, Archibald Murray–1900, VP, National

Hughes, Charles Evans–1916, Republican

Humphrey, Hubert Horatio–1964, VP, Democratic, Liberal (N.Y.);

1968, Democratic
Inchapher, Marshall–1972, VP, Prohibition
Jackson, Andrew–1828, 1832, Democratic
Jenner, William Ezra–1956, States' Rights
Jenness, Linda–1972, Socialist Workers
Johns, Frank T.–1924, Socialist Labor
Johnson, Andrew–1864, VP, Republican
Johnson, Andrew (Ky.)–1944, VP, Prohibition
Johnson, Hale–1896, VP, Prohibition
Johnson, Herschel Vespasian–1860, VP, Democratic
Johnson, Hiram Warren–1912, VP, Progressive
Johnson, Lyndon Baines–1960, VP, Democratic; 1964, Democratic, Liberal (N.Y.)
Johnson, Richard Mentor–1836 and 1840, VP, Democratic
Johnson, William Freame–1856, VP, North American
Julian, George Washington–1852, VP, Free Soil
Kasper, John–1964, National States' Rights
Kefauver, Estes–1956, VP, Democratic, Liberal
Kennedy, John Fitzgerald–1960, Democratic
Kern, John Worth–1908, VP, Democratic
King, A.–1904, VP, Continental
King, Clennon–1960, Independent Afro-American
King, Leicester–1848, Liberty
King, William Rufus De Vane–1852, VP, Democratic
Kirby, Edward–1956, VP, Greenback
Kirkpatrick, Donald–1876, VP, American National
Kirkpatrick, George Ross–1916, VP, Socialist
Knox, Frank–1936, VP, Republican
Krajewski, Henry–1956, American Third
Krueger, Maynard C.–1940, VP, Socialist
La Follette, Robert Marion–1924, Progressive, Socialist
Landon, Alfred Mossman–1936, Republican
Landrith, Ira–1916, VP, Prohibition
Lane, Joseph–1860, VP, Independent Democrat, Southern Democrat
Langer, William–1956, Pioneer
Learn, Dale–1948, VP, Prohibition
Lee, Henry–1832, VP, Independent
Lee, Joseph Bracken–1956, VP, Texas Constitution; 1960, Conservative (N.J.)
Leeke, Granville B.–1948, VP, Greenback
LeMay, Curtis Emerson–1968, VP, American Independent, Courage
Lemke, William–1936, Union
Leonard, Jonah Fitz Randolph–1900, United Christian
Levering, Joshua–1896, Prohibition
Lightburn, Joseph B.–1964, Constitution
Lincoln, Abraham–1860, 1864, Republican
Lincoln, John Cromwell–1924, VP, Commonwealth Land
Lockwood, Belva Ann Bennett– 1884, 1888, Equal Rights
Lodge, Henry Cabot–1960, VP, Republican

Logan, John Alexander–1884, VP, Republican
Love, Alfred Henry–1888, VP, Equal Rights
MacArthur, Douglas–1952, America First, Constitution
Macauley, Robert Colvin–1920, Single Tax
McClellan, George Brinton–1864, Democratic
McCloskey, Burr–1956, VP, Pioneer
McDonald, Duncan–1924, Farmer Labor
McGovern, George Stanley–1972, Democratic
MacKenna, Roscoe B.–1968, VP, Universal
McKinley, William–1896, 1900, Republican
McNary, Charles Linza–1940, VP, Republican
Mage, Judith–1968, VP, Peace and Freedom
Maguire, Matthew–1896, VP, Socialist Labor
Mahalchik, John V.–1972, America
Malloney, Joseph Francis–1900, Socialist Labor
Marshall, Thomas Riley–1912 and 1916, VP, Democratic
Martin, David H.–1900, VP, United Christian
Matchett, Charles Horatio–1896, Socialist Labor
Maurer, James Hudson–1928 and 1932, VP, Socialist
Maxwell, John–1948, Vegetarian
Meador, Edward Kirby–1956, VP, Greenback
Metcalf, Henry Brewer–1900, VP, Prohibition
Miller, William Edward–1964, VP, Republican
Mitchell, Charlene–1968, Communist
Moorman, Edgar V.–1940, VP, Prohibition
Morris, Thomas–1844, VP, Liberty
Morton, Levi Parsons–1888, VP, Republican
Munn, Earle Harold–1960, VP, Prohibition; 1964, 1968, 1972, Prohibition
Munro, Donald L.–1908, VP, Socialist Labor
Murphy, Daniel J.–1952, American Vegetarian
Muskie, Edmund Sixtus–1968, VP, Democratic
Nathan, Theodora–1972, VP, Libertarian
Nations, Gilbert Owen–1924, American
Nelson, George A.–1936, VP, Socialist
Nicholson, Samuel T.–1900, VP, Union Reform
Nixon, Richard Milhous–1952 and 1956, VP, Republican; 1960, 1968, 1972, Republican
O'Brien, Thomas Charles–1936, VP, Union
O'Conor, Charles–1872, Straight-Out Democratic
Olmstead, Frederick Law–1872, VP, Independent Liberal Republican
Orange, Aaron M.–1940, VP, Socialist Labor
Palmer, John McAuley–1896, National Democratic
Parker, Alton Brooks–1904, Democratic
Parker, Joel–1872, VP, Labor Reform
Parker, John Milliken–1916, VP, Progressive
Pendleton, George Hunt–1864, VP. Democratic
Phelps, John Wolcott–1880, American
Pierce, Franklin–1852, Democratic

Polk, James Knox–1844, Democratic
Pomeroy, Samuel Clarke–1880, VP, American; 1884, American Prohibition
Proehl, Frederick C.–1956, Greenback
Pulley, Andrew–1972, VP, Socialist Workers
Randall, Charles, Hiram–1924, VP, American
Redstone, Albert E.–1888, Industrial Reform
Regan, Frank Stewart–1932, VP, Prohibition
Reid, Whitelaw–1892, VP, Republican
Reimer, Arthur Elmer–1912, 1916, Socialist Labor
Remmel, Valentine–1900, VP, Socialist Labor
Reynolds, Verne L.–1924, VP, Socialist Labor; 1928, 1932, Socialist Labor
Robinson, Joseph Taylor–1928, VP, Democratic
Rogers, William R.–1964, VP, Theocratic; 1968, Theocratic
Romer, Henry A.–1944, VP, America First; 1948, VP, Christian Nationalist
Roosevelt, Franklin Delano–1920, VP, Democratic; 1932, 1936, 1940, 1944, Democratic
Roosevelt, Theodore–1900, VP, Republican; 1904, 1912, 1916, Republican, Progressive
Rush, Richard–1828, VP, Federalist
Russell, John–1872, VP, Prohibition
St. John, John Pierce–1884, Prohibition
Schmitz, John George–1972, American Independent
Scott, John G.–1948, Greenback
Scott, Winfield–1852, Whig
Seidel, Emil–1912, VP, Socialist
Sergeant, John–1832, VP, National Republican
Sewall, Arthur–1896, VP, Democratic, National Silver
Seymour, Horatio–1868, Democratic
Shaw, Edward–1964, VP, Socialist Workers
Shaw, Mark–1964, VP, Prohibition
Shelton, Herbert M.–1956, American Vegetarian
Sherman, James Schoolcraft–1908 and 1912, VP, Republican
Shriver, Robert Sargent–1972, VP, Democratic
Silverman, Edward M.–1960, VP, Conservative (Va.)
Slocomb, Whitney Hart–1960, Greenback
Smith, Alfred Emanuel–1928, Democratic
Smith, Geral Lyman Kenneth–1944, America First; 1948, Christian Nationalist
Smith, Gerrit–1848, National Liberty
Smith, Green Clay–1876, Prohibition
Smith, Tucker Powell–1948, VP, Socialist
Southgate, James Haywood–1896, VP, National
Sparkman, John Jackson–1952, VP, Democratic
Spock, Benjamin McLane–1972, People's
Stedman, Seymour–1920, VP, Socialist
Stevenson, Adlai Ewing–1892 and 1900 VP, Democratic; 1900, VP,

People's, Silver Republican
Stevenson, Adlai Ewing–1952, 1956, Democratic; 1956, Liberal
Stewart, Gideon Tabor–1876, VP, Prohibition
Stoner, J.B.–1964, VP, National States'- Rights
Streeter, Alson Jenness–1888, Union Labor
Sullivan, Charles Loten–1960, Constitution (Tex.)
Swallow, Silas Comfort–1904, Prohibition
Taft, William Howard–1908, 1912, Republican
Taylor, George Sam–1968, VP, Socialist Labor
Taylor, Glen Hearst–1948, VP, Progressive
Taylor, Zachary–1848, Whig
Teague, Raymond L.–1960, VP, Theocratic
Teichert, Edward A.–1944, 1948, Socialist Labor
Teichert, Emil F.–1936, VP, Socialist Labor
Thayer, Merle–1968, VP, Contitution
Thomas, Norman Mattoon–1928, 1932, 1936, 1940, 1944, 1948, Socialist
Thompson, Henry Adams–1880, VP, Prohibition
Thurman, Allen Granberry–1888, VP, Democraic
Thurmond, James Strom–1948, States' Rights
Tibbles, Thomas Henry–1904, VP, People's
Tilden, Samuel Jones–1876, Democratic
Tisdal, V. C.–1932, VP, Jobless
Tomlinson, Homer Aubrey–1952, Church of God; 1960, 1964, Theocratic
Troxell, Richard K.–1968, Constitution
Truman, Harry S.–1944, VP, Democratic; 1948, Democratic
Turner, Daniel Braxton–1908, United Christian
Tyler, John–1840, VP, Whig; 1844, National Democratic
Tyner, Jarvis–1972, VP, Communist
Upshaw, William David–1932, Prohibition
Van Buren, Martin–1832, VP, Democratic; 1836, 1840, Democratic; 1848, Free Soil
Varney, William Frederick–1928, Prohibition
Verseen, Will–1928, VP, Farmer Labor
Wakefield, William H. T.–1888, VP, United Labor
Walker, James B.–1876, American National
Wallace, George Corley–1968, American Independent, Courage (N.Y.)
Wallace, Henry Agard–1940, VP, Democratic; 1948, Progressive
Wallace, William J.–1824, Commonwealth Land
Warren, Earl–1948, VP, Republican
Watkins, Aaron Sherman–1908 and 1912, VP, Prohibition; 1920, Prohibition
Watson, Claude A.–1944, 1948, Prohibition
Watson, Thomas Edward–1896, VP, Populist; 1904, 1908, People's
Weaver, James Baird–1880, Greenback labor; 1892, People's
Webb, Frank Elbridge–1928, 1932, Farmer Labor
Weiss, Myra Tanner–1952 and 1956 and 1960, VP, Socialist Workers
Werdel, Thomas Harold–1964, VP, Independent States' Rights

West, Absolom Madden–1884, VP, Anti-Monopoly, Greenback
Wheeler, Burton Kendall–1924, VP, Progressive, Socialist
Wheeler, William Almon–1876, VP, Republican
Wigginton, Peter Dinwiddie–1888, VP, American
Willkie, Wendell Lewis–1940, Republican
Williams, Samuel–1908, VP, People's
Wilson, Henry–1872, VP, Republican, National Working Men
Wilson, Woodrow–1912, 1916, Democratic
Wing, Simon–1892, Socialist Labor
Wirt, William–1832, Anti-Masonic
Woodhull, Victoria Claflin–1872, Equal Rights
Woolley, John Granville–1900, Prohibition
Wright, Fielding Lewis–1948, VP, States' Rights
Yates, James Elmer–1940, VP, Greenback
York, Alvin–1936, VP, Prohibition
Zargarell, Michael–1968, VP, Communist
Zahnd, John–1924, 1928, 1936, 1940, Greenback

THE OFFICE

PRESIDENTIAL OATH OF OFFICE

The presidential oath of office was administered 47 times by 14 men to Presidents-elect from 1789 to 1972, and 8 times by 6 men and 1 woman to Vice Presidents who succeeded to the presidency due to death of the incumbent.

The following oath of office is prescribed by Article II, section 1 of the Constitution:

I do solemnly swear (or affirm) that I will faithfully execute the Office of President of the United States, and will to the best of my ability, preserve, protect and defend the Constitution of the United States.

PRESIDENTIAL INAUGURAL OATHS ADMINISTERED BY CHIEF JUSTICES OF THE UNITED STATES

Chief Justice John Marshall administered the oath nine times to five Presidents: Jefferson twice, Madison twice, Monroe twice, J. Q. Adams once, and Jackson twice.

Chief Justice Roger Brooke Taney administered the oath to more Presidents than anyone—seven times to seven men—once each to Van Buren, W. H. Harrison, Polk, Taylor, Pierce, Buchanan, and Lincoln.

Chief Justice Melville Weston Fuller swore in six Presidents: B. Harrison, Cleveland, T. Roosevelt, Taft, and McKinley twice.

Chief Justice Earl Warren administered the oath four times, once each to Eisenhower, Kennedy, L. B. Johnson, and Nixon.

Chief Justices who administered the inaugural oath three times each were Salmon Portland Chase, Charles Evan Hughes, Morrison Remick Waite, and Edward Douglass White. Chase swore in Lincoln once and Grant twice. Hughes administered the oath to F. D. Roosevelt three times. White swore in Wilson twice and Harding once.

Those Chief Justices who administered the oath twice were William Howard Taft and Frederick Moore Vinson. Taft swore in Coolidge and Hoover. Vinson swore in Truman and Eisenhower.

Other Chief Justices who administered the oath were Oliver Ellsworth to John Adams, Harlan Fiske Stone to F. D. Roosevelt and Truman, and Warren Earl Burger to Nixon.

Only two of the eight men who succeeded to the presidency because of a President's death had the inaugural oath administered by Chief Justice of the United States. Salmon Portland Chase gave the oath to Andrew Johnson and Harlan Fiske Stone to Harry S. Truman.

ADMINISTRATION OF OATHS

The presidential oath of office is not required to be administered by the Chief Justice of the United States. The following Presidents of the United States were not sworn in by the Chief Justice:

George Washington, Apr. 30, 1789, oath administered by Robert R. Livingston, Chancellor of New York State

George Washington, Mar. 4, 1793, by William Cushing, Associate Justice of the Supreme Court

John Tyler, Apr. 6, 1841, by William Cranch, Chief Justice of the United States Circuit Court of the District of Columbia

Millard Fillmore, July 10, 1850, by William Cranch, Chief Justice of the United States Circuit Court of the District of Columbia

Chester Alan Arthur, Sept. 20, 1881, by John R. Brady, Justice of the New York Supreme Court (Arthur was sworn in two days later by Chief Justice Morrison Remick Waite.)

Theodore Roosevelt, Sept. 14, 1901, by John R. Hazel, of the United States District Court

Calvin Coolidge, Aug. 3, 1923, by his father, John Calvin Coolidge, a notary public and justice of the peace. (The oath was repeated Aug. 21, 1923, before Adolph August Hoehling of the District of Columbia Supreme Court.)

Lyndon Baines Johnson, Nov. 22, 1963, by Sarah Tilghman Hughes, District Judge of the North District of Texas

No specific requirements exist as to the place where the oath must be administered. The following Presidents took their oaths in cities other than Washington, D.C.:

George Washington, 1789, New York City

George Washington, 1793, Philadelphia, Pa.

Chester Alan Arthur, 1881, New York City

Theodore Roosevelt, 1901, Buffalo, N.Y.

Calvin Coolidge, 1923, Plymouth, Vt.

Lyndon Baines Johnson, 1963, Dallas, Tex.

INAUGURAL OATHS

Listed below under the names of the Presidents elected to office are the dates on which the oaths were taken and the names of the administering officials (Chief Justice of the United States unless otherwise identified).

Washington

Thurs., Apr. 30, 1789; Robert R. Livingston, Chancellor of New York State

Mon. Mar. 4, 1793; William Cushing, Associate Justice of the Supreme Court

J. Adams

Sat., Mar. 4, 1797; Oliver Ellsworth

Jefferson

Wed., Mar. 4, 1801; John Marshall
Mon., Mar. 4, 1805; Marshall

Madison

Sat., Mar. 4, 1809; Marshall
Thurs., Mar. 4, 1813; Marshall

Monroe

Tues., Mar. 4, 1817; Marshall
Mon., Mar. 5, 1821; Marshall

J. Q. Adams

Fri., Mar. 4, 1825; Marshall

Jackson

Wed., Mar. 4, 1829; Marshall
Mon., Mar. 4, 1833; Marshall

Van Buren

Sat., Mar. 4, 1837; Roger Brooke Taney

W. H. Harrison

Thurs., Mar. 4, 1841; Taney

Polk

Tues., Mar. 4, 1845; Taney

Taylor

Mon., Mar. 5, 1849, Taney

Pierce

Fri., Mar. 4, 1853; Taney

Buchanan

Wed., Mar. 4, 1857; Taney

Lincoln

Mon., Mar. 4, 1861; Taney
Sat., Mar. 4, 1865; Salmon Portland Chase

Grant

Thurs., Mar. 4, 1869; Chase
Tues., Mar. 4, 1873; Chase

Hayes
Mon., Mar. 5, 1877; Morrison Remick Waite

Garfield
Fri., Mar. 4, 1881; Waite

Cleveland
Wed., Mar. 4, 1885; Waite

B. Harrison
Mon., Mar. 4, 1889; Melville Weston Fuller

Cleveland
Sat., Mar. 4, 1893; Fuller

McKinley
Thurs., Mar. 4, 1897; Fuller
Mon., Mar. 4, 1901; Fuller

T. Roosevelt
Sat., Mar. 4, 1905; Fuller

Taft
Thurs., Mar. 4, 1909; Fuller

Wilson
Tues., Mar. 4, 1913; Edward Douglass White
Mon., Mar. 5, 1917; White

Harding
Fri., Mar. 4, 1921; White

Coolidge
Wed., Mar. 4, 1925; William Howard Taft

Hoover
Mon., Mar. 4, 1929; Taft

F. D. Roosevelt
Sat., Mar. 4, 1933; Charles Evans Hughes
Wed., Jan. 20, 1937; Hughes
Mon., Jan. 20, 1941; Hughes
Sat., Jan. 20, 1945; Harlan Fiske Stone

Truman
Thurs., Jan. 20, 1949; Frederick Moore Vinson

Eisenhower
Tues., Jan. 20, 1953; Vinson
Mon., Jan. 21, 1957; Earl Warren

Kennedy
Fri., Jan. 20, 1961; Warren

L. B. Johnson

Wed., Jan. 20, 1965; Warren

Nixon

Mon., Jan. 20, 1969; Warren

Sat., Jan. 20, 1973; Warren Earl Burger

   The following took their oaths after succeeding to the presidency on the death of their predecessors:

Tyler

Tues., Apr. 6, 1841; William Cranch, Chief Justice, U.S. Circuit Court, District of Columbia

Fillmore

Wed., July 10, 1850; Cranch

A. Johnson

Sat., Apr. 15, 1865; Salmon Portland Chase

Arthur

Tues., Sept. 20, 1881; John R. Brady, Justice, New York Supreme Court

Thurs., Sept. 22, 1881; Morrison Remick Waite

T. Roosevelt

Sat., Sept. 14, 1901; John R. Hazel, Justice, U.S. District Court

Coolidge

Fri., Aug. 3, 1923; John Calvin Coolidge, notary public and justice of the peace

Tues., Aug. 21, 1923; Adolph August Hoehling, Justice, District of Columbia Supreme Court

Truman

Thurs., Apr. 12, 1945; Harlan Fiske Stone

L. B. Johnson

Fri., Nov. 22, 1963; Sarah Tilghman Hughes, District Judge of the North District of Texas

SUNDAY INAUGURATION DATES

   Only four of the thirty-seven March inaugurations fell on Sunday— in 1821, 1849, 1877, and 1917. In those years the public ceremonies were postponed until the following day.

   James Monroe, the fifth President, postponed taking his oath of office for his second term until Monday, March 5, 1821.

   Zachary Taylor, the twelfth President, did not take his oath of office until Monday, March 5, 1849 (a circumstance which has caused many to assert that David Rice Atchison, president pro tempore of the Senate, was President for one day between the outgoing James Knox Polk and the incoming Zachary Taylor).

Rutherford Birchard Hayes, the nineteenth President, came into office following a bitter election dispute. He took the oath of office twice: once on Saturday, March 3, 1877, at a private ceremony, and again on Monday, March 5, at a public ceremony.

Woodrow Wilson, the twnety-eighth President, postponed taking his second oath of office until Monday, March 5, 1917.

Only one of the ten January inaugurations has fallen on Sunday. Dwight David Eisenhower, the thirty-fourth President, was inaugurated on Sunday, January 20, 1957, at a private ceremony, and again on Monday, January 21, at a public ceremony.

January 20 will fall on Sunday only three times in the next hundred years: in 1985, 2013, and 2041.

INAUGURAL SITES

Thirty-five of the forty-seven inaugurations of the elected presidents were held on the east portico of the Capitol. The other twelve inaugurations were held at the following places:

Federal Hall, Wall Street, New York, N.Y.

    1789—George Washington

Congress Hall, Sixth and Chestnut Streets, Philadelphia, Pa.

    1793—George Washington

    1797—John Adams

Senate chamber, Washington, D.C.

    1801—Thomas Jefferson

    1805—Thomas Jefferson

    1909—William Howard Taft

House of Representatives, Washington, D.C.

    1809—James Madison

    1813—James Madison

    1821—James Monroe

    1825—John Quincy Adams

    1833—Andrew Jackson

South portico, White House, Washington, D.C.

    1945—Franklin Delano Roosevelt

INAUGURAL WEATHER

Of the 47 presidential inaugurations between 1789 and 1973, there were 30 held in clear weather, 10 in rain, and 7 in snow, the weather reported being the weather at noon.

Contemporary reports on the weather often disagree as the weather was not always the same during the entire day. For example, when Hayes was inaugurated in 1877, it rained until 7 A.M. on March 5 (inauguration day) but it was clear the rest of the day. On the day Garfield was inaugurated, March 4, 1881, it snowed and rained until 10 A.M., and then it cleared, much of the snow having disappeared by the time of the inaugural parade. When Taft was inaugurated in 1909, temperatures were about freezing; over nine inches of snow had fallen on March 3 and until 12:30 P.M. on March 4, and the afternoon of March 4 was windy and cloudy.

The rainy days were in 1845, 1865, 1869, 1873, 1889, 1901, 1929, 1933, 1937, and 1957.

The snowy days were in 1817, 1821, 1833, 1841, 1853, 1893, and 1909.

Details of the weather at the January 20 inaugurations follow: 1937, raining, 33°; 1941, clear, 29°; 1945, cloudy, 35°; 1949, clear, 38°; 1953, partly cloudy, 49°; 1957, overcast, 43°; 1961, crisp, cold, 28°; 1965, clear, 38°.

RETIRING PRESIDENTS AT INAUGURATIONS OF SUCCESSORS

All but three retiring Presidents have attended the inaugurations of their successors. John Adams was not present at Thomas Jefferson's inauguration, John Quincy Adams was not present at Andrew Jackson's, and Andrew Johnson was not present at Ulysses Simpson Grant's.

PRESIDENTIAL TRANSITION ACT

"To promote the orderly transfer of the executive power in connection with the expiration of the term of office of a President and the inauguration of a new President" is the full title of the Presidential Transition Act of 1963 (78 Stat. L. 153), enacted March 7, 1964. The act provides funds and authority for the new President.

AGE AT INAUGURATION OR SUCCESSION

The average age at which the 37 Presidents were inducted into office was 54 years and 299 days. (Cleveland's non-consecutive inaugurations are counted separately.)

The oldest at the time of his inauguration or succession was William Henry Harrison, who took office when he was 68 years and 23 days old; the youngest was Theodore Roosevelt, who became President when he was 42 years and 322 days old.

Seven Presidents were over sixty when they took office: William Henry Harrison, Buchanan, Taylor, Eisenhower, Jackson, John Adams, and Truman.

Seven Presidents were under fifty when they became chief executive: Polk, Garfield, Pierce, Cleveland (first term), Grant, Theodore Roosevelt, and Kennedy.

The range in age, from oldest to youngest, is indicated in the following list:

W. H. Harrison–68 years, 23 days
Buchanan–65 years, 315 days
Taylor–64 years, 100 days
Eisenhower–62 years, 98 days
Jackson–61 years, 354 days
J. Adams–61 years, 125 days
Truman–60 years, 309 days
Monroe–58 years, 310 days
Madison–57 years, 353 days
Jefferson–57 years, 325 days
J. Q. Adams–57 years, 236 days
Washington–57 years, 67 days

A. Johnson–56 years, 107 days
Wilson–56 years, 66 days
Nixon–56 years, 11 days
Cleveland (second term)–55 years, 351 days
B. Harrison–55 years, 196 days
Harding–55 years, 122 days
L. B. Johnson–55 years, 87 days
Hoover–54 years, 206 days
Hayes–54 years, 151 days
Van Buren–54 years, 89 days
McKinley–54 years, 34 days
Lincoln–52 years, 20 days
Taft–51 years, 170 days
F. D. Roosevelt–51 years, 33 days
Coolidge–51 years, 30 days
Tyler–51 years, 8 days
Arthur–50 years, 350 days
Fillmore–50 years, 184 days
Polk–49 years, 122 days
Garfield–49 years, 105 days
Pierce–48 years, 101 days
Cleveland (first term)–47 years, 351 days
Grant–46 years, 311 days
Kennedy–43 years, 236 days
T. Roosevelt–42 years, 322 days

INAUGURAL ADDRESSES

George Washington, who was inaugurated for a second term on March 4, 1793, at Philadephia, Pa., used only 135 words in his inaugural address. The longest inaugural address was delivered during a snowfall by William Henry Harrison, who employed 8,445 words, almost twice as many as any other president. He used the personal pronoun "I" forty-five times, a record use. The only president who did not use "I" in his inaugural address was Theodore Roosevelt. The average number of words in the 47 inaugurals is 2,425, the first-person pronoun being used an average of 15 times, about once every 142 words.

The following list shows the number of words used by the Presidents in their inaugural addresses:

Washington
  1,425 (first)
  135 (second)

J. Adams
  2,308

Jefferson
  1,729 (first)
  2,158 (second)

Madison
  1,175 (first)
  1,209 (second)

Monroe
  3,217 (first)
  4,467 (second)

J. Q. Adams
  2,906

Jackson
1,125 (first)
1,172 (second)

Van Buren
3,838

W. H. Harrison
8,445

Polk
4,776

Taylor
996

Pierce
3,334

Buchanan
2,821

Lincoln
3,634 (first)
698 (second)

Grant
1,128 (first)
1,337 (second)

Hayes
2,480

Garfield
2,978

Cleveland
1,681 (first)

B. Harrison
4,388

Cleveland
2,015 (second)

McKinley
3,967 (first)
2,217 (second)

T. Roosevelt
985

Taft
5,433

Wilson
1,802 (first)
1,526 (second)

Harding
3,318

Coolidge
4,059

Hoover
3,801

F. D. Roosevelt
1,883 (first)
1,807 (second)
1,340 (third)
559 (fourth)

Truman
2,242

Eisenhower
2,446 (first)
2,449 (second)

Kennedy
1,355

L. B. Johnson
1,437

Nixon
2,130 (first)
1,668 (second)

PRESIDENTIAL REQUIREMENTS

There are no legal requirements for the presidency except for one paragraph in Article II, section 1 of the Constitution:

No Person except a natural born Citizen, or a Citizen of the United States, at the time of the adoption of this Constitution, shall be eligible to the Office of President; neither shall any Person be eligible to that Office who shall not have attained to the Age of thirty five Years, and been fourteen Years a Resident within the United States.

PRESIDENTIAL DUTIES AND POWERS

The duties and powers of the President are specifically enumerated in the Constitution:

ARTICLE II, SECTION 2. The President shall be Commander in Chief of the Army and Navy of the United States, and of the Militia of the several States, when called into the actual Service of the United States; he may require the Opinion, in writing, of the principal Officer in each of the Executive Departments, upon any Subject relating to the Duties of their respective Offices, and he shall have the Power to grant Reprieves and Pardons for Offences against the United States, except in Cases of Impeachment.

He shall have Power, by and with the Advice and Consent of the Senate, to make Treaties, provided two thirds of the Senators present concur; and he shall nominate, and by and with the Advice and Consent of the Senate, shall appoint Ambassadors, other public Ministers and Consuls, Judges of the Supreme Court, and all other Officers of the United States, whose Appointments are not herein otherwise provided for, and which shall be established by Law; but the Congress may by Law vest the Appointment of such inferior Officers, as they think proper, in the President alone, in the Courts of Law, or in the Heads of Departments.

The President shall have Power to fill up all Vacancies that may happen during the Recess of the Senate, by granting Commissions which shall expire at the End of their next Session.

SECTION 3. He shall from time to time give to the Congress Information of the State of the Union, and recommend to their Consideration such Measures as he shall judge necessary and expedient; he may, on extraordinary Occasions, convene both Houses, or either of them, and in Case of Disagreement between them, with Respect to the Time of Adjournment, he may adjourn them to such Time as he shall think proper; he shall receive Ambassadors and other public Ministers; he shall take Care that the Laws be faithfully executed, and shall Commission all the Officers of the United States.

PRESIDENTIAL MESSAGES

Presidential messages are not required in any specific form or at any specified time. The annual State of the Union messages are either read to Congress or delivered by the President in person. Presumably, they fulfill the requirement of Article 2, section 3 of the Constitution, which provides that the President "shall from time to time give to the Congress Information of the State of the Union."

William Henry Harrison and James Abram Garfield did not prepare State of the Union messages. Harrison served only 32 days and Garfield only 199 days.

George Washington did not prepare a message during the calender year 1789, but delivered two messages in 1790, one on January 8 and one on December 8.

Until the administration of Franklin Delano Roosevelt in 1933, there were 141 messages. Of these 125 were delivered in December, 1 in January, 1 in September, 3 in October, and 11 in November.

Since the inauguration date was changed to January, 41 messages have been made in January and 2 in February.

The longest State of the Union message was sent to Congress in 1946 by President Harry S. Truman and consisted of more than 25,000 words.

It is generally conceded that most presidential speeches are prepared by writers, presumably carrying out the wishes and thoughts of the executives. It is estimated that President Lyndon Baines Johnson's speech of January 8, 1964, consisting of 3,059 words, required the services of about twenty-four writers, who took about six weeks to draft the speech, with ten to sixteen major revisions.

STATE OF THE UNION MESSAGES

Washington

Jan. 8, 1790
Dec. 8, 1790
Oct. 25, 1791
Nov. 6, 1792
Dec. 3, 1793
Nov. 19, 1794
Dec. 8, 1795
Dec. 7, 1796

J. Adams

Nov. 22, 1797
Dec. 8, 1798
Dec. 3, 1799
Nov. 22, 1800

Jefferson

Dec. 8, 1801
Dec. 15, 1802
Oct. 17, 1803
Nov. 8, 1804
Dec. 3, 1805
Dec. 2, 1806
Oct. 27, 1807
Nov. 8, 1808

Madison

Nov. 29, 1809
Dec. 5, 1810
Nov. 5, 1811
Nov. 4, 1812
Dec. 7, 1813
Sept. 20, 1814
Dec. 5, 1815

Dec. 3, 1816

Monroe

Dec. 2, 1817
Nov. 16, 1818
Dec. 7, 1819
Nov. 14, 1820
Dec. 3, 1821
Dec. 3, 1822
Dec. 2, 1823
Dec. 7, 1824

J. Q. Adams

Dec. 6, 1825
Dec. 5, 1826
Dec. 4, 1827
Dec. 2, 1828

Jackson

Dec. 8, 1829
Dec. 6, 1830
Dec. 6, 1831
Dec. 4, 1832
Dec. 3, 1833
Dec. 1, 1834
Dec. 7, 1835
Dec. 5, 1836

Van Buren

Dec. 5, 1837
Dec. 3, 1838
Dec. 2, 1839
Dec. 5, 1840

Tyler

Dec. 7, 1841
Dec. 6, 1842
Dec. 5, 1843
Dec. 3, 1844

Polk

Dec. 2, 1845
Dec. 8, 1846
Dec. 7, 1847
Dec. 5, 1848

Taylor

Dec. 4, 1849

Fillmore

Dec. 2, 1850
Dec. 2, 1851
Dec. 6, 1852

Pierce

Dec. 5, 1853
Dec. 4, 1854
Dec. 31, 1855
Dec. 2, 1856

Buchanan

Dec. 8, 1857
Dec. 6, 1858
Dec. 19, 1859
Dec. 3, 1860

Lincoln

Dec. 3, 1861
Dec. 1, 1862
Dec. 8, 1863
Dec. 6, 1864

A. Johnson

Dec. 4, 1865
Dec. 3, 1866
Dec. 3, 1867
Dec. 9, 1868

Grant

Dec. 6, 1869
Dec. 5, 1870
Dec. 4, 1871
Dec. 2, 1872
Dec. 1, 1873
Dec. 7, 1874

Dec. 7, 1875
Dec. 5, 1876

Hayes

Dec. 3, 1877
Dec. 2, 1878
Dec. 1, 1879
Dec. 6, 1880

Arthur

Dec. 6, 1881
Dec. 4, 1882
Dec. 4, 1883
Dec. 1, 1884

Cleveland—1st Administration

Dec. 8, 1885
Dec. 6, 1886
Dec. 6, 1887
Dec. 3, 1888

B. Harrison

Dec. 3, 1889
Dec. 1, 1890
Dec. 9, 1891
Dec. 6, 1892

Cleveland—2nd Administration

Dec. 4, 1893
Dec. 3, 1894
Dec. 2, 1895
Dec. 7, 1896

McKinley

Dec. 6, 1897
Dec. 5, 1898
Dec. 5, 1899
Dec. 3, 1900

T. Roosevelt

Dec. 3, 1901
Dec. 2, 1902
Dec. 7, 1903
Dec. 6, 1904
Dec. 5, 1905
Dec. 3, 1906
Dec. 3, 1907
Dec. 8, 1908

Taft

Dec. 7, 1909

Dec. 6, 1910
Dec. 5, 1911
Dec. 3, 1912

Wilson

Dec. 2, 1913
Dec. 8, 1914
Dec. 7, 1915
Dec. 5, 1916
Dec. 4, 1917
Dec. 2, 1918
Dec. 2, 1919
Dec. 7, 1920

Harding

Dec. 4, 1921
Dec. 8, 1922

Coolidge

Dec. 6, 1923
Dec. 3, 1924
Dec. 8, 1925
Dec. 7, 1926
Dec. 6, 1927
Dec. 4, 1928

Hoover

Dec. 3, 1929
Dec. 2, 1930
Dec. 8, 1931
Dec. 6, 1932

F. D. Roosevelt

Jan. 3, 1934
Jan. 4, 1935
Jan. 3, 1936
Jan. 6, 1937
Jan. 3, 1938
Jan. 4, 1939
Jan. 3, 1940
Jan. 6, 1941
Jan. 6, 1942
Jan. 7, 1943

Jan. 11, 1944
Jan. 6, 1945

Truman

Jan. 22, 1946
Jan. 6, 1947
Jan. 7, 1948
Jan. 5, 1949
Jan. 4, 1950
Jan. 8, 1951
Jan. 9, 1952
Jan. 7, 1953

Eisenhower

Feb. 2, 1953
Jan. 7, 1954
Jan. 6, 1955
Jan. 5, 1956
Jan. 10, 1957
Jan. 9, 1958
Jan. 9, 1959
Jan. 7, 1960
Jan. 12, 1961

Kennedy

Jan. 30, 1961
Jan. 11, 1962
Jan. 14, 1963

L. B. Johnson

Jan. 8, 1964
Jan. 4, 1965
Jan. 12, 1966
Jan. 10, 1967
Jan. 17, 1968
Jan. 14, 1969

Nixon

Jan. 22, 1970
Jan. 22, 1971
Jan. 20, 1972
Feb. 2, 1973
Jan. 30, 1974

THE PRESIDENTIAL VETO

Article I, section 7 of the Constitution contains the following provisions:

Every Bill which shall have passed the House of Representatives and the Senate, shall, before it becomes a Law, be presented to the President of the United States; if he approve he shall sign it, but if not he shall return it, with his Objections to that House in which it shall have originated, who shall enter the Objections at large on their Journal, and proceed to reconsider it. If after such Reconsideration two thirds of that House shall agree to pass the bill, it shall be sent, together with the Objections, to the other House, by which it shall likewise be reconsidered, and if approved by two thirds of that House, it shall become a Law. . . . If any bill shall not be returned by the President within ten Days (Sundays excepted) after it shall have been presented to him, the Same shall be a Law, in like Manner as if he had signed it, unless the Congress by their Adjournment prevent its Return, in which case it shall not be a Law.

Every Order, Resolution, or Vote to which the Concurrence of the Senate and House of Representatives may be necessary (except on a question of Adjournment) shall be presented to the President of the United States; and before the Same shall take Effect, shall be approved by him, or being disapproved by him, shall be repassed by two thirds of the Senate and House of Representatives, according to the Rules and Limitations prescribed in the Case of a Bill.

The Constitution thus provides not only for a regular veto, which Congress may override by a two-thirds majority of both Houses, but also for a "pocket veto"—if the President opposes a bill sent to him ten days before the adjournment of Congress, he can, instead of vetoing it, merely ignore it, or "pocket" it, and prevent it from becoming a law.

The following list shows the number of bills vetoed by each President. Noted in parenthesis after each total are the figures comprising the total: first, the number of regular vetoes; second, the number of pocket vetoes; third, the number of vetoes sustained by Congress; and fourth, the number passed over his veto.

Washington–2 (2, 0; 2, 0)
J. Adams–0
Jefferson–0
Madison–7 (5, 2: 7, 0)
Monroe–2 (1, 1; 1, 1)
J. Q. Adams–0
Jackson–12 (5, 7; 12, 0)
Van Buren–0
W. H. Harrison–0
Tyler–10 (6, 4; 9, 1)
Polk–3 (2, 1; 3, 0)
Taylor–0
Fillmore–0
Pierce–9 (9, 0; 4, 5)
Buchanan–7 (4, 3; 7, 0)
Lincoln–6 (2, 4; 6, 0)
A. Johnson–28 (21, 7; 13, 15)

Grant–92 (44, 48; 88, 4)
Hayes–13 (12, 1; 12, 1)
Garfield–0
Arthur–12 (4, 8; 11, 1)
Cleveland (first term)–414 (304, 110; 412, 2)
B. Harrison–44 (19, 25; 43, 1)
Cleveland (second term)–170 (42, 128; 165, 5)
McKinley–42 (6, 36; 42, 0)
T. Roosevelt–82 (42, 40; 81, 1)
Taft–39 (30, 9; 38, 1)
Wilson–44 (33, 11; 38, 6)
Harding– 6 (5, 1; 6, 0)
Coolidge–50 (20, 30; 46, 4)
Hoover–37 (21, 16; 34, 3)
F. D. Roosevelt–631 (371, 260; 622, 9)
Truman–250 (180, 70; 238, 12)
Eisenhower–181 (73, 108; 179, 2)
Kennedy–21 (12, 9; 21, 0)
L. B. Johnson–30 (16, 14; 30, 0)
Nixon (1969-1972)–31 (14, 17; 27, 4)
Total–2,275 (1,305, 970; 2,197, 78)

Franklin Delano Roosevelt holds the record for having vetoed the greatest number of bills—631—but this embraced a twelve-year period. During a two-term period, Grover Cleveland vetoed 584 bills.

The President who had the largest number of vetoes overridden—15—was Andrew Johnson.

PRESIDENTIAL AND VICE PRESIDENTIAL SALARIES

Article II, section 1 of the Constitution contains the following provision:

> The President shall, at stated Times, receive for his Services, a Compensation, which shall neither be encreased nor diminished during the Period for which he shall have been elected, and he shall not receive within that period any other Emolument from the United States, or any of them.

The First Congress fixed the salary of the President of the United States at $25,000 a year, to be paid quarterly, in full consideration for his respective service with the use of the furniture and other effects now in his possession. This act of September 24, 1789 (1 Stat. L. 72) also fixed the salary of the Vice President at $5,000 a year.

The act of March 3, 1873 (17 Stat. L. 486) raised the salary of the President to $50,000 and that of the Vice President to $10,000. The law became effective with the new term which followed the next day. Consequently, President Grant served his first term at a salary of $25,-000, and his second term at $50,000.

The act of June 23, 1906 (34 Stat. L. 454) authorized an additional sum not exceeding $25,000 for the traveling expenses of the President, "such sum when appropriated to be expended in the discretion of the President and accounted for on his certificate solely."

The act of March 4, 1909 (35 Stat. L. 859) raised the salary of the President to $75,000, and that of the Vice President to $12,000. The first President to receive $75,000 was Taft.

The act of June 25, 1948 (62 Stat. L. 678) increased the President's traveling expenses to $40,000 a year.

The act of January 19, 1949 (63 Stat. L. 4) increased the rates of compensation of the President, the Vice President and the Speaker of the House of Representatives. The act authorized a salary of $100,-000 a year for the President to be paid monthly and an additional expense allowance of $50,000 a year "to assist in defraying expenses relating to or resulting from the discharge of his official duties, for which expense allowance no tax liability shall accrue and for which no accounting shall be made by him."

President Truman was the first President to received the $100,000 yearly salary.

An act approved October 20, 1951, subjected the expense allowances to income taxes.

In recent years, the salary of the Vice President has more than doubled.

The act of January 19, 1943 (63 Stat. L. 4) provided that the Vice President's salary be increased from $20,000 to $30,000, plus an expense allowance of $10,000 for which no tax liability shall occur or accounting be made by him.

The act of March 2, 1955 (69 Stat. L. 11), effective as of March 1, 1955, "to adjust the salaries of judges of United States courts, United States attorneys, Members of Congress, and for other purposes," increased the salary of the Vice President from $30,000 to $35,000.

The Federal Employees Salary Act of 1964, August 14, 1964 (78 Stat. L. 422), raised the salary of the Vice President from $35,000 to $43,000.

The act of January 17, 1969 (83 Stat. L. 3), effective January 20, 1969, raised the salary of the President to $200,000.

The act of September 15, 1969 (83 Stat. L. 107) raised the Vice President's salary from $43,000 to $62,500.

PRESIDENTS' PENSIONS

A presidential pension was authorized by act of August 25, 1958 (72 Stat. L. 838). Under the act former Presidents receive a monetary allowance of $25,000 a year for life; adequate office space, appropriately furnished and equipped; a sum not to exceed $50,000 a year for office help; and unlimited free mailing privileges. A pension of $10,000 a year is authorized for widows of former Presidents.

PRESIDENTS' SECRETARIES

The salary of the secretaries of the Presidents was paid by the Presidents from their private funds until 1857.

On March 3, 1857, the 34th Congress enacted a law (11 Stat. L. 228) which provided "that the President of the United States be and is hereby authorized to appoint or employ, in his official household, one private secretary at an annual salary of $2,500."

The first private secretary to a President to be recognized as such and to be paid a salary was James Buchanan Henry, who served as secretary of President James Buchanan from 1857 to 1859.

The first "Secretary to the President" was authorized by the 56th Congress on April 17, 1900 (31 Stat. L. 97). The salary of the secretary was set at $5,000 and that of each of two assistant secretaries at $2,800.

An act of June 25, 1948 (62 Stat. L. 672) provided that the Secretary to the President receive $10,000 a year and authorized six administrative assistants whose salaries were not to exceed $10,000 each.

OTHER PERQUISITES OF THE PRESIDENCY

In addition to his salary, a President is the beneficiary of many perquisites, which may vary from time to time. He and his family live rent-free at the White House; a fleet of automobiles is at his disposal; and a squad of about twenty-five Secret Service men, paid by the Treasury Department, guard him. A yacht, belonging to the Navy and maintained by regular Navy appropriations, is assigned to his use, as well as a presidential airplane owned by the Air Force. Horses for riding are supplied by the Army and a private Pullman car that is armor-plated with bullet-proof windows is at his disposal. He is attended by a personal physician supplied by the armed forces and has access to any of the Army and Navy hospitals. A library, supplied by booksellers, is at his disposal in the White House. A separate police force of over one hundred is assigned to guard the White House and its grounds. The President is served by domestic servants (but must supply them with food).

THE PRESIDENTS, THE COURTS, AND ARRESTS

A misconception prevails that the President may not be summoned to court and is immune from arrest. Actually, the President may be summoned to court and is liable to arrest. There is nothing in the Constitution which grants him immunity.

Thomas Jefferson was summoned on June 10, 1807, to appear as a witness in the trial of Aaron Burr for treason, but refused to attend. (See page 57.) This action established a precedent but did not bind future Presidents.

In 1853, Franklin Pierce, driving home by carriage from the home of William Morgan in southeast Washington, D.C., ran down an aged woman, Mrs. Nathan Lewis. Pierce was arrested by Constable Stanley Edelin, but the case was dropped as Pierce was not proved guilty.

Ulysses Simpson Grant, driving his carriage west on M Street, between 11th and 12th streets, Washington, D.C., was stopped for speeding by a black police officer. When the officer learned the identity of the driver, he hesitated before issuing a ticket. Grant told him to do his duty and accepted the ticket. He put up twenty dollars collateral, which he forfeited when he failed to appear for trial. Grant later wrote a letter to the officer's superior, commending his obedience to duty.

Since the advent of the automobile, police officers have frequently stopped automobiles carrying Presidents, but no arrests have been made.

PROTECTION AGAINST THREATS

On June 25, 1948, Congress enacted a law (62 Stat. L. 740) which made threats by mail against the President punishable by a thousand-dollar fine or imprisonment for not more than five years or both. On June 1, 1955 (69 Stat. L. 80), this protection was extended to the President-elect and to the Vice President.

Legislation providing "penalties for the assassination of the President or the Vice President" was enacted August 28, 1965 (79 Stat. L. 580). It provided that "whoever kills any individual who is the President of the United States, the President-elect, the Vice-President. . . . whoever kidnaps any individual as designated above shall be punished by imprisonment for any term of years or for life. . . . or by death or imprisonment for any term of years or for life if death results to such individual. . . . whoever attempts to kill or kidnap any individual. . . . shall be punished by imprisonment for any term of years or for life. . . . " The Attorney General of the United States is authorized to pay an amount not to exceed $100,000 for information and services concerning a violation of this section." Assistance may be requested from any Federal, State or local agency, including the Army, Navy and Air Force."

Legislation "to provide continuing authority for the protection of former Presidents and their wives or widows" was enacted September 15, 1965 (79 Stat. L. 791). The Secret Service was authorized "to protect the person of a former President and his wife during his lifetime and the person of a widow and minor children of a former President for a period of four years after he leaves or dies in office, unless such protection is declined." This law was amended October 21, 1968 (82 Stat. L. 1198) "to protect the person of a former President and his wife during his lifetime, the person of the widow of a former President until her death or remarriage, and minor children of a former President until they reach sixteen years of age, unless such protection is declined."

On June 6, 1968, Congress enacted legislation (82 Stat. L. 170) which appropriated $400,000 "to authorize the United States Secret Service to furnish protection to major presidential or vice presidential candidates."

THE PRESIDENT'S FLAG

Before 1916 several Presidents had flags, but these were not official and were really nothing but emblems.

The official President's flag—the President's seal in bronze upon a blue background with a large white star in each corner—was adopted on May 29, 1916, by President Wilson's executive order No. 2,390.

President Truman, by executive order No. 9,646, dated October 25, 1945, made several further changes and increased the number of stars to forty-eight, one for each state.

Legislation altering the number of stars to provide for Alaska and Hawaii was enacted February 6, 1960, effective July 4, 1960.

President Eisenhower's executive order No. 10,798, dated January 3, 1959, increased the number of stars on the flag to 49 to provide for Alaska. On August 21, 1959, the President revoked this order and increased the number of stars to 50 to provide for Hawaii (executive order No. 10,834).

SALUTE TO THE PRESIDENT

The President is customarily honored with a twenty-one-gun salute. The twenty-one-gun salute is given also to former Presidents, sovereigns, members of a royal family, and Presidents of other republics. It is claimed that the twenty-one-gun salute commemorates the year 1776, and for that reason salutes are often fired thus: one-seven-seven-six.

THE PRESIDENTIAL YACHTS

The gunboat U.S.S. *Mayflower* (length, 275 feet; beam, 36 feet; draft, 17 feet; displacement, 2,690 tons) was assigned to duty as the President's yacht in 1902. She was built at Clydebank, Scotland, in 1896 for Ogden Goelet and was purchased for $1,250,000 by the United States. She was used in 1898 in war service in Cuba. The yacht was used by Presidents Theodore Roosevelt, Taft, Harding, and Coolidge until March 22, 1929. President Hoover ordered her to be laid up in the interest of economy. She caught fire and sank on January 24, 1931, at League Island Navy Yard, Philadelphia, Pa. The hulk was sold October 19, 1931.

Other U.S. naval vessels used by Presidents were the U.S.S. *Despatch, Dolphin* and *Sylph.*

The yachts used by President Franklin Delano Roosevelt were the U.S.S. *Sequoia* in 1933 and 1935, the U.S.S. *Potomac* in 1936, and the U.S.S. *Williamsburg* in 1935.

TERMS OF OFFICE

Nineteen Presidents served one term or part of one term.

Ten of these nineteen Presidents served a full four-year term: John Adams, John Quincy Adams, Van Buren, Polk, Pierce, Buchanan, Hayes, Benjamin Harrison, Taft, and Hoover.

Five died without completing their first term: William Henry Harrison, Taylor, Garfield, Harding, and Kennedy.

Five succeeded to the presidency and filled the unexpired portions of a first term: Tyler, Fillmore, Andrew Johnson, Arthur, and Lyndon Baines Johnson.

Seventeen Presidents served more than one term.

Nine of these seventeen Presidents served two full terms: Washington, Jefferson, Madison, Monroe, Jackson, Grant, Cleveland, Wilson, and Eisenhower.

One—Franklin Delano Roosevelt—served three full terms and part of a fourth term.

Two were reelected for a second term but died before completing it: Lincoln and McKinley.

Four who succeeded to the presidency and filled unexpired terms were also elected on their own and served a second term: Theodore Roosevelt, Coolidge, Truman, and Lyndon Baines Johnson.

The following list shows the length of service of past Presidents:

W. H. Harrison–32 days
Garfield–199 days
Taylor–1 year, 128 days
Harding–2 years, 151 days
Fillmore–2 years, 236 days
Kennedy–2 years, 306 days
Arthur–3 years, 166 days
A. Johnson–3 years, 322 days
Tyler–3 years, 332 days
J. Adams–4 years
J. Q. Adams–4 years
Van Buren–4 years
Polk–4 years
Pierce–4 years
Buchanan–4 years
Hayes–4 years
B. Harrison–4 years
Taft–4 years
Hoover–4 years
Lincoln–4 years, 43 days
McKinley–4 years, 194 days
L. B. Johnson–5 years, 59 days
Coolidge–5 years, 213 days
T. Roosevelt–7 years, 171 days
Truman–7 years, 283 days
Washington–7 years, 308 days (first term began Apr. 30 instead of Mar. 4)
Jefferson–8 years
Madison–8 years
Monroe–8 years
Jackson–8 years
Grant–8 years
Cleveland–8 years (two non-consecutive terms)
Wilson–8 years
Eisenhower–8 years
F. D. Roosevelt–12 years, 39 days (first term ended Jan. 20 instead of Mar. 3)

TERMS OF OFFICE—THE EARLY YEARS

In the first fifty years of United States history (1789-1839), three Presidents were not reelected for a second term: John Adams, John Quincy Adams, and Van Buren. The Presidents who were elected for two terms during this period were Washington, Jefferson, Madison,

Monroe, and Jackson.

THE ONE-TERM TRADITION

After Andrew Jackson's second term, which ended in 1837, a one-term presidential policy prevailed until 1865, when Abraham Lincoln was sworn in for a second term he did not live to complete.

Presidents who for various reasons served one term or less during this period were Van Buren, William Henry Harrison, Tyler, Polk, Taylor, Fillmore, Pierce, and Buchanan.

PRESIDENTS WHO SUCCEEDED THEMSELVES IN OFFICE

George Washington–Apr. 30, 1789-Mar. 3, 1793; Mar. 3, 1793-Mar. 3, 1797

Thomas Jefferson–Mar. 4, 1801-Mar. 3, 1809

James Madison–Mar. 4, 1809-Mar. 3, 1817

James Monroe–Mar. 4, 1817-Mar. 3, 1825

Andrew Jackson–Mar. 4, 1829-Mar. 3, 1837

Abraham Lincoln–Mar. 4, 1861-Mar. 3, 1865; Mar. 4, 1865-Apr. 15, 1865

Ulysses Simpson Grant–Mar. 4, 1869-Mar. 3, 1877

William McKinley–Mar. 4, 1897-Mar. 3, 1901; Mar. 4, 1901-Sept. 14, 1901

Theodore Roosevelt–Sept. 14, 1901-Mar. 3, 1905, succession; Mar. 4, 1905-Mar. 3, 1909

Woodrow Wilson–Mar. 4, 1913-Mar. 3, 1921

Calvin Coolidge–Aug. 3, 1924-Mar. 3, 1925; Mar. 4, 1925-Mar. 3, 1929

Franklin Delano Roosevelt–Mar. 4, 1933-Apr. 12, 1945

Harry S. Truman–Apr. 12, 1945-Jan. 19, 1949; Jan. 20, 1949-Jan. 20, 1953

Dwight David Eisenhower–Jan. 20. 1953-Jan. 20, 1961

Lyndon Baines Johnson–Nov. 22, 1963-Jan. 20, 1965, succession; Jan. 20, 1965-Jan. 20 1969

Richard Milhous Nixon–Jan. 20, 1969-Jan. 20, 1974; Jan. 20, 1974-Aug. 9, 1974

THE CABINET

The cabinet is an advisory body; the members hold office at the pleasure of the President. Although it is customary for cabinet members to submit their resignations when a new administration enters into power, cabinet members are not required to do so. They are appointed for fixed terms and remain in office until successors are appointed.

There is nothing in the Constitution which specifically provides for a cabinet, nor are there any laws regulating the qualifications or duties of those designated as members of the cabinet.

The first cabinet office of the newly formed government was authorized by act of Congress of July 27, 1789 (1 Stat. L. 28) "establishing an executive department to be denominated the Department of Foreign Affairs." Later, it was redesignated the Department of State. John Jay of New York was Secretary of Foreign Affairs under the Confederation, and continued to act, at the request of President Washington, until Thomas Jefferson of Virginia entered upon his duties on March

22, 1790.

The second department created was the War Department, authorized by act of August 7, 1789 (1 Stat. L. 49) "to establish an executive department to be denominated the Department of War." The first Secretary of War was Henry Knox of Massachusetts, who took office on September 12, 1789.

The third department was the Treasury Department, authorized by act of September 2, 1789 (1 Stat. L. 65) "to establish the Treasury Department." On September 11, 1789, Alexander Hamilton of New York assumed his duties as the first Secretary of the Treasury.

These three departments constituted the first cabinet. The annual salary for the Secretary of War was $3,000, and for the Secretary of State and the Secretary of the Treasury $3,500 each.

The Attorney General and the Postmaster General served as members of the cabinet although neither was the head of a department at that time. Their compensation was $1,500 a year (September 24, 1789, 1 Stat. L. 93). On September 26, 1789, Samuel Osgood of Massachusetts became the Postmaster General and on the same date Edmund Randolph of Virginia was appointed Attorney General, assuming his duties on February 2, 1790.

The sixth cabinet post was that of Secretary of the Navy. The act of April 30, 1789 (1 Stat. L. 553) established "an executive department to be denominated the Department of the Navy." The Secretary received an annual salary of $3,000. The first Secretary of the Navy was Benjamin Stoddert of Maryland, who entered upon his duties on June 18, 1798 during the administration of President John Adams.

These six posts constituted the cabinet from 1798 to 1849.

On March 3, 1849, "an act to establish the Home Department" was passed (9 Stat. L. 395). President Zachary Taylor appointed Thomas Ewing of Ohio as the first Secretary of the Home Department. He took office March 8, 1849. The name of the department was later changed to Department of the Interior.

Forty years later, on February 13, 1889, an eighth cabinet post was created. Norman Jay Colman of Missouri was appointed Secretary of Agriculture by President Grover Cleveland. He assumed his duties on February 13, 1889. (He had been Commissioner of Agriculture from April 4, 1885, to February 12, 1889.)

The Attorney General, one of the first cabinet group, was given departmental power on June 22, 1870, by "an act to establish the Department of Justice" (16 Stat. L. 162). This act placed the Attorney General at the head of the Department of Justice.

On June 8, 1872, the Post Office Department was created by "an act to revise, consolidate, and amend the statute relating to the Post Office Department" (17 Stat. L. 283). This act gave a department to the Postmaster General, who had been given equal cabinet status in 1829 by President Andrew Jackson.

The ninth cabinet post was that of Secretary of Commerce and Labor, established by an act of February 14, 1903 (32 Stat. L. 826), "to establish Department of Commerce and Labor." The first incumbent was George Bruce Cortelyou of New York, who took office on February 16, 1903, at a salary of $8,000 a year during the first term of President Theodore Roosevelt.

During President Taft's administration, the cabinet post of Secretary of Commerce and Labor was discontinued and in its stead two cabinet posts were created, the Department of Commerce and the Department of Labor, under authority of the act of March 4, 1913 (37 Stat. L. 736). The first Secretary of Commerce was William Cox Redfield of New York and the first Secretary of Labor was William Bauchop Wilson of Pennsylvania. They were appointed by President Woodrow Wilson and assumed office on March 5, 1913.

On July 26, 1947, the National Security Act of 1947 (61 Stat. L. 495) was passed "to promote the National Security by providing for a Secretary of Defense." The Secretary of Defense was to be head of the National Military Establishment, consisting of the Department of the Army, the Department of the Navy, and the Department of the Air Force, together with all other agencies created under Title II of the act. The first Secretary of Defense was James Vincent Forrestal of New York.

The next change in the organization of the cabinet was made in the administration of President Dwight David Eisenhower, who appointed Oveta Culp Hobby of Texas as the first Secretary of Health, Education, and Welfare. She took office on April 11, 1953.

Two new cabinet positions were created by President Lyndon Baines Johnson. The Department of Housing and Urban Development was authorized September 9, 1965 (79 Stat. L. 667). The first incumbent was Robert Clifton Weaver of New York, who was sworn in January 18, 1966. The Department of Transportation was authorized October 15, 1966 (80 Stat. L. 931) to deal with air, rail, and highway transportation. The first director was Alan Stephenson Boyd of Florida, who was sworn in January 16, 1967.

CABINET CHANGES DURING PRESIDENTIAL ADMINISTRATIONS

Three of the Presidents who did not live to complete their terms in the White House retained their original cabinets during their incumbency. They were William Henry Harrison, Taylor, and Garfield. Except for ad interim appointments and appointees carried over from the preceding administrations for a few days, these Presidents had only one cabinet officer for each post.

The only President to retain a cabinet for a full four-year period was Franklin Pierce. John Quincy Adams, with two different Secretaries of War, had the next closest retaining record.

The President who had the greatest number of changes in his administration was John Tyler, who succeeded to the presidency upon the death of William Henry Harrison. When Tyler became President in 1841, the consensus of the six-man cabinet was that he be designated "Acting President." This suggestion angered Tyler, and a few months after taking office he caused all of the members of his cabinet to resign, with the exception of Daniel Webster, who finally resigned in 1843. In less than four years in office, Tyler made 26 changes in his cabinet. In all fairness to him, however, it should be noted that 6 of the changes were made to replace appointees of Harrison, 11 were interim appointments, several others were occasioned by death, and still others were necessitated by the transfer of cabinet members to different departments. Tyler himself appointed 2 Secretaries of State, 3 Secretaries of the Treasury, 3 Secretaries of War, 2 Attorneys General, 1 Postmaster General, and 4 Secretaries of the Navy. His ad interim appointments included 4 Secretaries of State, 3 Secretaries of the Treasury, 1 Secretary of War, 2 Secretaries of the Navy, and 1 Postmaster General.

THE YOUNGEST CABINET OFFICERS

The list below shows the youngest person who served in cabinet offices. Under the name of each office is the name of the youngest incumbent, with his age upon assuming office, the President under whom he served, and his length of service.

State

Edmund Jennings Randolph—40 years, 176 days; under Washington, Feb. 2, 1794-Aug. 19, 1795

Treasury

Alexander Hamilton—32 years, 243 days; under Washington, Sept. 11, 1789-Feb. 1, 1795

War

John Caldwell Calhoun—35 years, 204 days; under Monroe, Oct. 8, 1817-Mar. 3, 1825

Attorney General

Richard Rush—33 years, 165 days; under Madison, Feb. 10, 1814-Oct. 30, 1817

Postmaster General

Gideon Granger—34 years, 134 days; under Jefferson, Nov. 28, 1801-Mar. 16, 1814

Navy

Samuel Lewis Southard—36 years, 99 days; under Monroe, Sept. 16, 1823-Mar. 3, 1829

Interior

Hoke Smith—37 years, 185 days; under Cleveland, Mar. 6, 1893-Aug. 31, 1896

Agriculture

Orville Lothrop Freeman—42 years, 195 days; under Kennedy and L. B. Johnson, Jan. 20, 1961-Jan. 20, 1969

Commerce and Labor

George Bruce Cortelyou—40 years, 205 days; under T. Roosevelt, Feb. 16, 1903-June 30, 1904

Commerce

Herbert Clark Hoover—46 years, 207 days; under Harding, Mar. 5, 1921-Aug. 20, 1928

Labor

James John Davis—47 years, 129 days; under Harding, Mar. 5, 1921-Dec. 7, 1930

Defense

Robert Strange McNamara—44 years, 225 days; under Kennedy and L. B. Johnson, Jan. 20, 1961-March 1, 1968

Health, Education, and Welfare

Oveta Culp Hobby—48 years, 81 days; under Eisenhower, Apr. 11, 1953-Aug. 1, 1955

CABINET OFFICERS WHO SERVED IN TWO OR MORE POSITIONS

Many cabinet members have held two or more different positions in presidential cabinets. The following list shows under the name of the appointing President (1) the name of the cabinet officer; (2) his position and the date of appointment; and (3) his prior position and the date of appointment (with the name of the earlier appointing President, if any).

Washington

Timothy Pickering—State, 1795; ad interim, War, 1795
Edmund Randolph—State, 1794; Attorney General, 1789

Adams

Samuel Dexter—War, 1801; Treasury, 1801

Jefferson

Henry Dearborn—ad interim, Navy, 1801; War, 1801
Levi Lincoln—Attorney General, 1801; ad interim, State, 1801

Madison

William Harris Crawford—Treasury, 1816; War, 1815
James Monroe—ad interim, War, 1814; State, 1811
Robert Smith—State, 1809; Navy, 1801 (appointed by Jefferson)

Monroe

Richard Rush—ad interim, State, 1817; Attorney General, 1814 (appointed by Madison)

J. Q. Adams

Samuel Lewis Southard—War, 1828; ad interim, Treasury, 1825; Navy, 1823 (appointed by Monroe)

Jackson

Benjamin Franklin Butler—ad interim, War, 1836; Attorney General, 1833

Louis McLane—State, 1833; Treasury, 1831

Roger Brooke Taney—Treasury, 1833; Attorney General, 1831; ad interim, Attorney General, 1831

Levi Woodbury—Treasury, 1834; Navy, 1831

Tyler

John Caldwell Calhoun—State, 1844; War, 1817 (appointed by Monroe)

John Nelson—ad interim, State, 1844; Attorney General, 1843

Abel Parker Upshur—State, 1843; Navy, 1841

Polk

John Young Mason—Attorney General, 1845; Navy, 1844 (appointed by Tyler)

Pierce

William Learned Marcy—State, 1853; War, 1845 (appointed by Polk)

Buchanan

Jeremiah Sullivan Black—State, 1860; Attorney General, 1857

Lewis Cass—State, 1857; War, 1831 (appointed by Jackson)

Joseph Holt—War, 1861; Postmaster General, 1859

Isaac Toucey—Treasury, 1860; Navy, 1857; Attorney General, 1848 (appointed by Polk)

Lincoln

Edwin McMasters Stanton—War, 1862; Attorney General, 1860 (appointed by Buchanan)

Grant

Alphonso Taft—War, 1876; Attorney General, 1876

Hayes

William Maxwell Evarts—State, 1877; Attorney General, 1868 (appointed by A. Johnson)

Arthur

Walter Quintin Gresham—Treasury, 1884; Postmaster General, 1883

Cleveland

Richard Olney—State, 1895; Attorney General, 1893

William Freeman Vilas—Interior, 1888; Postmaster General, 1885

McKinley

John Sherman—State, 1897; Treasury, 1877 (appointed by Hayes)

T. Roosevelt

Charles Joseph Bonaparte—Attorney General, 1906; Navy, 1905

George Bruce Cortelyou—Treasury, 1907; Postmaster General, 1905;

Commerce and Labor, 1903

Victor Howard Metcalf—Navy, 1906; Commerce and Labor, 1904

William Henry Moody—Attorney General, 1904; Navy, 1902

Elihu Root—State, 1905; War, 1899 (appointed by McKinley)

Taft

Philander Chase Knox—State, 1909; Attorney General, 1901 (appointed by McKinley)

George von Lengerke Meyer—Navy, 1909; Postmaster General, 1907 (appointed by T. Roosevelt)

Harding

Hubert Work—Interior, 1923; Postmaster General, 1922

Hoover

Henry Lewis Stimson—State, 1929; War, 1911 (appointed by Taft)

F. D. Roosevelt

Henry Agard Wallace—Commerce, 1945; Agriculture, 1933

Truman

James Vincent Forrestal—Defense, Sept. 17, 1947; Navy, May 18, 1944 (appointed by F. D. Roosevelt)

Nixon

Elliot Lee Richardson—Attorney General, May 1973; Defense, Feb. 1973; Health, Education, and Welfare, 1970

TENURE OF POSTMASTER GENERAL

The only cabinet member not appointed for an indefinite term is the Postmaster General. The act of June 8, 1872 (17 Stat. L. 284) provides that the term and office of the Postmaster General shall be for and during the term of the President by whom he is appointed, and for one month thereafter unless sooner removed.

On July 1, 1971, the cabinet position of Postmaster General was abolished. Winton Malcolm Blount was the last man to hold the post.

FIRST WOMAN IN CABINET POST

The first woman member of a cabinet was Frances Perkins (Mrs. Paul Wilson), who was appointed Secretary of Labor by President Franklin D. Roosevelt. She served from March 4, 1933, to June 30, 1945. She had been Industrial Commissioner for New York prior to this appointment.

FIRST SENATE REJECTION OF CABINET APPOINTEE

The first cabinet appointee rejected by the Senate was Roger Brooke Taney of Maryland, nominated by President Andrew Jackson on June 24, 1834, as Secretary of the Treasury.

LONGEST CABINET SERVICE

The cabinet officer with the longest tenure of office was James Wilson of Iowa, who took office March 5, 1897, as Secretary of Agriculture during President McKinley's first administration. He remained in office through McKinley's first and second administrations, through Theodore Roosevelt's two administrations, and through William Howard Taft's administration, serving until March 6, 1913, when Woodrow Wilson replaced him with David Franklin Houston. Wilson served one day longer than sixteen years.

WALLACE FAMILY IN CABINET POSTS

Henry Agard Wallace was a cabinet member before and after his term as Vice President. Prior to his term as Vice President under President Franklin Delano Roosevelt (January 20, 1941-January 19, 1945), he had served as Secretary of Agriculture (March 4, 1933-September 2, 1940). After his vice presidential term, he served as Secretary of Commerce under Roosevelt and Truman (March 2, 1945-September 27, 1946).

His father, Henry Cantwell Wallace, was Secretary of Agriculture under Presidents Harding and Coolidge, serving from March 5, 1921, to his death on October 25, 1924.

PRESIDENTIAL AND CONGRESSIONAL POLITICS

The following list shows the political alignment of each presidential administration and the strength of each party in Congress during the administration. (Abbreviations: D—Democrat; DR—Democratic-Republican; F—Federalist; NR—National Republican; Op—Opposition; R—Republican; W—Whig)

Washington

Administration—Federalist
1st Congress (1789-1791)
   Senate—F 17; Op 3
   House—F 38; Op 36
2nd Congress (1791-1793)
   Senate—F 16; DR 13
   House—DR 38; F 37
3rd Congress (1793-1795)
   Senate—F 17; DR 13
   House—DR 57; F 45
4th Congress (1795-1797)
   Senate—F 19; DR 13
   House—F 54; DR 52

J. Adams

Administration—Federalist
5th Congress (1797-1799)
   Senate—F 20; DR 12
   House—F 58; DR 48

6th Congress (1799-1801)
  Senate.-F 19; DR 13
  House—F 64; DR 42

Jefferson

Administration—Democratic-Republican
7th Congress (1801-1803)
  Senate—DR 18; F 14
  House—DR 69; F 36
8th Congress (1803-1805)
  Senate—DR 25; F 9
  House—DR 102; F 39
9th Congress (1805-1807)
  Senate—DR 27; F 7
  House—DR 116; F 25
10th Congress (1807-1809)
  Senate—DR 28; F 6
  House—DR 118; F 24

Madison

Administration—Democratic-Republican
11th Congress (1809-1811)
  Senate—DR 28; F 6
  House—DR 94; F 48
12th Congress (1811-1813)
  Senate—DR 30; F 6
  House—DR 108; F 36
13th Congress (1813-1815)
  Senate—DR 27; F 9
  House—DR 112; F 68
14th Congress (1815-1817)
  Senate—DR 25; F 11
  House—DR 117; F 65

Monroe

Administration—Democratic-Republican
15th Congress (1817-1819)
  Senate—DR 34; F 10
  House—DR 141; F 42
16th Congress (1819-1821)
  Senate—DR 35; F 7
  House—DR 156; F 27
17th Congress (1821-1823)
  Senate—DR 44; F 4
  House—DR 158; F 25
18th Congress (1823-1825)
  Senate—DR 44; F 4
  House—DR 187; F 26

J. Q. Adams

Administration—Democratic-Republican
19th Congress (1825-1827)
 Senate—DR 26; F 20
 House—DR 105; F 97
20th Congress (1827-1829)
 Senate—DR 28; F 20
 House—DR 119; F 94

Jackson

Administration—Democratic
21st Congress (1829-1831)
 Senate—D 26; NR 22
 House—D 139; NR 74
22nd Congress (1831-1833)
 Senate—D 25; NR 21
 House—D 141; NR 58; others 14
23rd Congress (1833-1835)
 Senate—D 20; NR 20
 House—D 147; others 118
24th Congress (1835-1837)
 Senate—D 27; W 25
 House—D 145; W 98

Van Buren

Administration—Democratic
25th Congress (1837-1839)
 Senate—D 30; W 18; others 4
 House—D 108; W 107; others 24
26th Congress (1839-1841)
 Senate—D 28; W 22
 House—D 124; W 118

W. H. Harrison (and Tyler)

Administration—Whig
27th Congress (1841-1843)
Senate—W 28; D 22; others 2
 House—W 133; D 102; others 6

Tyler

Administration—Whig
28th Congress (1843-1845)
 Senate—W 28; D 25; others 1
 House—D 142; W 79; others 1

Polk

Administration—Democratic
29th Congress (1845-1847)
 Senate—D 31; W 25
 House—D 143; W 77; others 1

30th Congress (1847-1849)
  Senate—D 36; W 21; others 1
  House—W 115; D 108; others 4

Taylor

Administration—Whig
31st Congress (1849-1851)
  Senate—D 35; W 25; others 2
  House—D 112; W 109; others 9

Taylor (and Fillmore)

Administration—Whig
32nd Congress (1851-1853)
  Senate—D 35; W 24; others 3
  House—D 140; W 88; others 5

Pierce

Administration—Democratic
33rd Congress (1853-1855)
  Senate—D 38; W 22; others 2
  House—D 159; W 71; others 4
34th Congress (1855-1857)
  Senate—D 42; R 15; others 5
  House—R 108; D 83; others 43

Buchanan

Administration—Democratic
35th Congress (1857-1859)
  Senate—D 39; R 20; others 5
  House—D 131; R 92; others 14
36th Congress (1859-1861)
  Senate—D 38; R 26; others 2
  House—R 113; D 101; others 23

Lincoln

Administration—Republican
37th Congress (1861-1863)
  Senate—R 31; D 11; others 7; vacant 1
  House—R 106; D 42; others 28; vacant 2
38th Congress (1863-1865)
  Senate—R 39; D 12
House—R 103; D 80

Lincoln (and Johnson)

Administration—Republican
39th Congress (1865-1867)
  Senate—R 42; D 10
  House—R 145; D 46
40th Congress (1867-1869)
  Senate—R 42; D 11

House—R 143; D 49; vacant 1

Grant

Administration—Republican
41st Congress (1869-1871)
  Senate—R 61; D 11; others 2
  House—R 170; D 73
42nd Congress (1871-1873)
  Senate—R 57; D 17
  House—R 139; D 104
43rd Congress (1873-1875)
  Senate—R 54; D 19; vacant 1
  House—R 203; D 88; vacant 2
44th Congress (1875-1877)
  Senate—R 46; D 29; vacant 1
  House—D 181; R 107; others 3; vacant 2

Hayes

Administration—Republican
45th Congress (1877-1879)
  Senate—R 39; D 36; others 1
  House—D 156; R 137
46th Congress (1879-1881)
  Senate—D 43; R 33
  House—D 150; R 128; others 14; vacant 1

Garfield (and Arthur)

Administration—Republican
47th Congress (1881-1883)
  Senate—R 37; D 37; others 2
  House—R 152; D 130; others 11

Arthur

Administration—Republican
48th Congress (1883-1885)
  Senate—R 40; D 36
  House—D 200; R 119; others 6

Cleveland

Administration—Democratic
49th Congress (1885-1887)
  Senate—R 41; D 34; vacant 1
  House—D 182; R 140; others 2; vacant 1
50th Congress (1887-1889)
  Senate—R 39; D 37
  House—D 170; R 151; others 4

B. Harrison

Administration—Republican
51st Congress (1889-1891)
  Senate—R 47; D 37

House—R 173; D 156; others 1
52nd Congress (1891-1893)
  Senate—R 47; D 39; others 2
  House—D 231; R 88; others 14

Cleveland

Administration—Democratic
  53rd Congress (1893-1895)
  Senate—D 44; R 38; others 3; vacant 3
  House—D 220; R 126; others 8
54th Congress (1895-1897)
  Senate—R 44; D 39; others 5
  House—R 246; D 104; others 7

McKinley

Administration—Republican
55th Congress (1897-1899)
  Senate—R 46; D 34; others 10
  House—R 206; D 134; others 16; vacant 1
56th Congress (1899-1901)
  Senate—R 53; D 26; others 11
  House—R 185; D 163; others 9

McKinley (and Roosevelt)

Administration—Republican
57th Congress (1901-1903)
  Senate—R 56; D 29; others 3; vacant 2
  House—R 198; D 153; others 5; vacant 1

T. Roosevelt

Administration—Republican
58th Congress (1903-1905)
  Senate—R 58; D 32
  House—R 207 D 178; vacant 1
59th Congress (1905-1907)
  Senate—R 58; D 32
  House—R 250; D 136
60th Congress (1907-1909)
  Senate—R 61: D 29; vacant 2
  House—R 222; D 164

Taft

Administration—Republican
61st Congress (1909-1911)
  Senate—R 59; D 32; vacant 1
  House—R 219; D 172
62nd Congress (1911-1913)
  Senate—R 49; D 42; Vacant 1
  House—D 228; R 162; others 1

Wilson

Administration—Democratic
63rd Congress (1913-1915)
  Senate—D 51; R 44; others 1
  House—D 290; R 127; others 18
64th Congress (1915-1917)
  Senate—D 56; R 39; others 1
  House—D 231; R 193; others 8; vacant 3
65th Congress (1917-1919)
  Senate—D 53; R 42; others 1
  House—R 216; D 210; others 9
66th Congress (1919-1921)
  Senate—R 48; D 47; others 1
  House—R 237; D 191; others 7

Harding

Administration—Republican
67th Congress (1921-1923)
  Senate—R 59; D 37
  House—R 300; D 132; others 1; vacant 2

Coolidge

Administration—Republican
68th Congress (1923-1925)
  Senate—R 51; D 43; others 2
  House—R 225; D 207; others 3
69th Congress (1925-1927)
  Senate—R 54; D 40; others 1; vacant 1
  House—R 247; D 183; others 5
70th Congress (1927-1929)
  Senate—R 48; D 47; others 1
  House—R 237; D 195; others 3

Hoover

Administration—Republican
71st Congress (1929-1931)
  Senate—R 56; D 39; others 1
  House.-R 267; D 163; others 1; vacant 4
72nd Congress (1931-1933)
  Senate—R 48; D 47; others 1
  House—R 218; R 216; others 1

F. D. Roosevelt

Administration—Democratic
73rd Congress (1933-1935)
  Senate—D 59; R 36; others 1
  House—D 313; R 117; others 5
74th Congress (1935-1937)
  Senate—D 69; R 25; others 2
  House—D 322; R 103; others 10

75th Congress (1937-1939)
   Senate—D 75; R 17; others 4
   House—D 333; R 89; others 13
76th Congress (1939-1941)
   Senate—D 69; R 23; others 4
   House—D 262; R 169; others 4
77th Congress (1941-1943)
   Senate—D 66; R 28; others 2
   House—D 267; R 162; others 6
78th Congress (1943-1945)
   Senate—D 57; R 38; others 1
   House—D 222; R 209; others 4

F. D. Roosevelt (and Truman)

Administration—Democratic
79th Congress (1945-1947)
   Senate—D 57; R 38; others 1
   House—D 243; R 190; others 2

Truman

Administration—Democratic
80th Congress (1947-1949)
   Senate—R 51; D 45
   House—R 246; D 188; others 1
81st Congress (1949-1951)
   Senate—D 54; R 42
   House—D 263; R 171; others 1
82nd Congress (1951-1953)
   Senate—D 48; R 47; others 1
   House—D 234; R 199; others 2

Eisenhower

Administration—Republican
83rd Congress (1953-1955)
   Senate—R 48; D 46; others 2
   House—R 221; D 213; others 1
84th Congress (1955-1957)
   Senate—D 48; R 47; others 1
   House—D 232; R 203
85th Congress (1957-1959)
   Senate—D 49; R 47
   House—D 234; R 201
86th Congress (1959-1961)
   Senate—D 64; R 34
   House—D 283; R 153

Kennedy

Administration—Democratic
87th Congress (1961-1963)
   Senate—D 65; R 35

House—D 261; R 176

Kennedy (and L. B. Johnson)

Administration—Democratic
88th Congress (1963-1965)
  Senate—D 67; R 33
  House—D 258; R 177

L. B. Johnson

Administration—Democratic
89th Congress (1965-1967)
  Senate—D 67; R 33
  House—D 295; R 140
90th Congress (1967-1969)
  Senate—D 64; R 36
  House—D 248; R 187

Nixon

Administration—Republican
91st Congress (1969-1971)
  Senate—D 57; R 43
  House—D 243; R 192
92nd Congress (1971-1973)
  Senate—D 54; R 45; vacant 1
  House—D 254; R 180; vacant 1
93rd Congress (1973-1975)
  Senate—D 56; R 42; others 2
  House—D 240; R 192; others 3

PRESIDENTS WITH OPPOSTION MAJORITIES IN CONGRESS

Each elected President since 1788 came to office with a Senate majority of his own party, with the exception of Eisenhower and Nixon.

Each elected President came to office with a House of Representatives majority of his own party, with five exceptions:
  Washington (1793—2nd term)
  Hayes (1876)
  Cleveland (1885)
  Eisenhower (1957—2nd term)
  Nixon (1968—1st term; 1972—2nd term)

REMOVAL FROM OFFICE

Provisions for removing the President from office are contained in Article II, section 4 of the Constitution:

> The President, Vice President and all civil Officers of the United States, shall be removed from Office on Impeachment for, and Conviction of, Treason, Bribery, or other high Crimes and Misdemeanors.

PRESIDENTIAL SUCCESSION

Article II, section 1 of the Constitution of the United States provided for presidential succession as follows:

In Case of the Removal of the President from Office, or of his Death, Resignation, or Inability to discharge the Powers and Duties of the said Office, the Same shall devolve on the Vice President, and the Congress may by Law provide for the Case of Removal, Death, Resignation or Inability, both of the President and Vice President, declaring what Officer shall then act as President, and such Officer shall act accordingly, until the Disability be removed, or a President shall be elected.

A law was enacted by Congress on March 1, 1792 (1 Stat. L 239) which provided that

in case of the removal, death, resignation, or disability of both the President and the Vice President of the United States, the President of the Senate pro tempore, and in case there shall be no President of the Senate, then the Speaker of the House of Representatives for the time being shall act as President of the United States until such disability be removed or until a President be elected.

Although the Twelfth Amendment, ratified in 1804, did not change the order of presidential succession, it provided that both the President and the Vice President be elected separately, voiding the system whereby the presidential candidate with the second largest vote became Vice President and thus eligible to succeed to the presidency.

No change was made in the order of succession from 1792 until the Presidential Succession Act of January 19, 1886 (24 Stat. L. 1) was passed during Grover Cleveland's administration. This act, entitled "An Act to provide for the performance of the duties of the office of President in case of the removal, resignation or inability both of the President and Vice President," provided that the succession should devolve upon the departmental secretaries according to the order of the creation of their respective departments. The order was State, Treasury, War, Attorney General, Postmaster General, Navy, Interior, Agriculture, Commerce and Labor (easily remembered by the mnemonic *St Wapniacl*). Actually, the order of succession was incorrect as the Department of War was established prior to the Treasury Department.

The Presidential Succession Act of July 18, 1947 (61 Stat. L. 380)— "to provide for the performance of the duties of the office of President in case of the removal, resignation, death or inability both of the President and the Vice President"—established the succession as follows: the Vice President, the Speaker of the House of Representatives, the President pro tempore of the Senate, the Secretary of State, the Secretary of the Treasury, the Secretary of War, the Attorney General, the Postmaster General, the Secretary of the Navy, the Secretary of the Interior, the Secretary of Agriculture, the Secretary of Commerce, and the Secretary of Labor.

The act of July 26, 1947 (61 Stat. L. 509) substituted the Secretary of Defense for the Secretary of War and eliminated the Secretary of the Navy.

In 1955 the succession was elaborated as follows: the Vice President, the Speaker of the House of Representatives, the President pro tempore of the Senate, the Secretary of State, the Secretary of the Treasury, the Secretary of Defense, the Attorney General, the Postmaster General, the Secretary of the Interior, the Secretary of Agriculture, the Secretary of Commerce, and the Secretary of Labor.

The Twenty-fifth Amendment, adopted February 10, 1967, was designed to assure a clear line of presidential succession, fill vice presidential vacancies, and provide for continuity in case of disability. The text follows:

SECTION 1. In case of the removal of the President from office or his death or resignation, the Vice President shall become President.

SECTION 2. Whenever there is a vacancy in the office of the Vice President, the President shall nominate a Vice President who shall take the office upon confirmation by a majority vote of both houses of Congress.

SECTION 3. Whenever the President transmits to the President pro tempore of the Senate and the Speaker of the House of Representatives his written declaration that he is unable to discharge the powers and duties of his office, and until he transmits to them a written declaration to the contrary, such powers and duties shall be discharged by the Vice President as Acting President.

SECTION 4. Whenever the Vice President and a majority of either the principal officers of the executive departments, or of such other body as Congress may by law provide, transmit to the President pro tempore of the Senate and the Speaker of the House of Representatives their written declaration that the President is unable to discharge the powers and duties of his office, the Vice President shall immediately assume the powers and duties of the office as Acting President.

Thereafter, when the President transmits to the President pro tempore of the Senate and the Speaker of the House of Representatives his written declaration that no inability exists, he shall resume the powers and duties of his office unless the Vice President and a majority of either the principal officers of the executive department, or of such other body as Congress may by law provide, transmit within four days to the President pro tempore of the Senate and the Speaker of the House of Representatives their written declaration that the President is unable to discharge the powers and duties of his office. Thereupon Congress shall decide the issue, assembling within 48 hours for that purpose if not in session. If the Congress, within 21 days after receipt of the latter written declaration, or, if Congress is not in session, within 21 days after Congress is required to assemble, determines by two-thirds vote of both houses that the President is unable to discharge the powers and duties of his office, the Vice President shall continue to discharge the same as Acting President; otherwise, the President shall resume the powers and duties of his office.

No President and Vice President have died during the same administration, and no cabinet officer has succeeded to the presidency as a result of death. Statisticians have calculated that the death from natural causes of both President and Vice President in the same administration is not likely to occur more than once in 840 years.

THE PRESIDENTS AND THEIR VICE PRESIDENTS

VICE PRESIDENT'S OATH

I do solemnly swear that I will support and defend the Constitution of the United States against all enemies, foreign and domestic, that I will bear true faith and allegiance to the same: that I take this obligation freely, without any mental reservation or purpose of evasion, and I will well and faithfully discharge the duties of the office on which I am about to enter. So help me God.

PRESIDENTS AND VICE PRESIDENTS

There have been 37 Presidents (36 individuals, with Grover Cleveland counted twice since his two terms were not consecutive), of whom only 33 had Vice Presidents. Four of these men who succeeded to the presidency were not subsequently elected in their own right and never had Vice Presidents. Since 9 of the 33 had two Vice Presidents and since one had 3 Vice Presidents, there have been 43 presidential-vice-presidential "teams." (Actually, only 41 individuals have held the office of Vice President, but 2 of the 40 each served under two different Presidents.)

The following is a list of the Presidents and their Vice Presidents. Biographical material on each Vice President may be found in Part I in the appropriate presidential section.

Washington
John Adams (first and second terms)

J. Adams
Thomas Jefferson

Jefferson
Aaron Burr (first term)
George Clinton (second term)

Madison
George Clinton (first term)
Elbridge Gerry (second term)

Monroe
Daniel D. Tompkins (first and second terms)

J. Q. Adams
John Caldwell Calhoun

Jackson
John Caldwell Calhoun (first term)
Martin Van Buren (second term)

Van Buren
Richard Mentor Johnson

W. H. Harrison
John Tyler

Tyler
———

Polk
George Mifflin Dallas

Taylor
Millard Fillmore

Fillmore
———

Pierce
William Rufus De Vane King

Buchanan
John Cabell Breckinridge

Lincoln
Hannibal Hamlin (first term)
Andrew Johnson (second term)

A. Johnson
———

Grant
Schuyler Colfax (first term)
Henry Wilson (second term)

Hayes
William Almon Wheeler

Garfield
Chester Alan Arthur

Arthur
———

Cleveland (first term)
Thomas Andrews Hendricks

B. Harrison
Levi Parsons Morton

Cleveland (second term)
Adlai Ewing Stevenson

McKinley
Garret Augustus Hobart (first term)
Theodore Roosevelt (second term)

T. Roosevelt
____(first term)
Charles Warren Fairbanks (second term)

Taft
James Schoolcraft Sherman

Wilson
Thomas Riley Marshall (first and second terms)

Harding
Calvin Coolidge

Coolidge
____(first term)
Charles Gates Dawes (second term)

Hoover
Charles Curtis

F. D. Roosevelt
John Nance Garner (first and second terms)
Henry Agard Wallace (third term)
Harry S. Truman (fourth term)

Truman
____(first term)
Alben William Barkley (second term)

Eisenhower
Richard Milhous Nixon (first and second terms)

Kennedy
Lyndon Baines Johnson

L. B. Johnson
Hubert Horatio Humphrey

Nixon
Spiro Theodore Agnew (first term; resigned October 10, 1973, after serving 10 months of his second term)
Gerald Rudolph Ford, Jr. (second term; December 6, 1973, sworn in, filling vacancy left by resignation of Spiro Agnew)

VICE PRESIDENTS — TERMS OF OFFICE AND PRESIDENTS SERVED

1. **John Adams**
   1789-1797, Washington

2. **Thomas Jefferson**
   1797-1801, J. Adams

3. **Aaron Burr**
   1801-1805, Jefferson

4. **George Clinton**
   1805-1809, Jefferson
   1809-1812, Madison

5. **Elbridge Gerry**
   1813-1814, Madison

6. **Daniel D. Tompkins**
   1817-1825, Monroe

7. **John Caldwell Calhoun**
   1825-1829, J. Q. Adams
   1829-1832, Jackson

8. **Martin Van Buren**
   1833-1837, Jackson

9. **Richard Mentor Johnson**
   1837-1841, Van Buren

10. **John Tyler**
    1841, W. H. Harrison

11. **George Mifflin Dallas**
    1845-1849, Polk

12. **Millard Fillmore**
    1849-1850, Taylor

13. **William Rufus De Vane King**
    1853, Pierce

14. **John Cabell Breckinridge**
    1857-1861, Buchanan

15. **Hannibal Hamlin**
    1861-1865, Lincoln

16. **Andrew Johnson**
    1865, Lincoln

17. **Schuyler Colfax**
    1869-1873, Grant

18. **Henry Wilson**
    1873-1875, Grant

19. **William Almon Wheeler**
    1877-1881, Hayes

20. **Chester Alan Arthur**
    1881, Garfield

21. **Thomas Andrews Hendricks**
    1885, Cleveland (first term)

22. **Levi Parsons Morton**
    1889-1893, B. Harrison

23. **Adlai Ewing Stevenson**
    1893-1897, Cleveland (second term)

24. **Garret Augustus Hobart**
    1897-1899, McKinley

25. **Theodore Roosevelt**
    1901, McKinley

26. **Charles Warren Fairbanks**
    1905-1909, T. Roosevelt

27. **James Schoolcraft Sherman**
    1909-1912, Taft

28. **Thomas Riley Marshall**
    1913-1921, Wilson

29. **Calvin Coolidge**
    1921-1923, Harding

30. **Charles Gates Dawes**
    1925-1929, Coolidge

31. **Charles Curtis**
    1929-1933, Hoover

32. **John Nance Garner**
    1933-1941, F. D. Roosevelt

33. **Henry Agard Wallace**
    1941-1945, F. D. Roosevelt

34. **Harry S. Truman**
    1945, F. D. Roosevelt

35. **Alben William Barkley**
    1949-1953, Truman

36. Richard Milhous Nixon
　　1953-1961, Eisenhower

37. Lyndon Baines Johnson
　　1961-1963, Kennedy

38. Hubert Horatio Humphrey
　　1965-1969, L. B. Johnson

39. Spiro Theodore Agnew
　　1969-1973, Nixon

40. Gerald Rudolph Ford, Jr.
　　1973-　　Nixon

PRESIDENTS AND VICE PRESIDENTS—NUMERICAL POSITION

Although the President and the Vice President are inaugurated at the same ceremony, it does not follow that their numerical position with regard to their offices is the same. As some Vice Presidents have served two Presidents and as some Presidents have had two Vice Presidents, and as some Vice Presidents have succeeded to the presidency without a corresponding Vice President, there is often little relationship in the numerical positions of the Presidents and their Vice Presidents.

The following list shows the numerical order of the Presidents and Vice Presidents whose numbers were the same.

1. Washington, Adams
2. J. Adams, Jefferson
3. Jefferson (first term), Burr
4. Madison, Clinton (second term)
7. Jackson (first term), Calhoun (second term)
11. Polk, Dallas
12. Taylor, Fillmore
16. Lincoln, A. Johnson
18. Grant (second term), Wilson
19. Hayes, Wheeler
20. Garfield, Arthur
25. McKinley (second term), T. Roosevelt
26. T. Roosevelt (second term), Fairbanks
27. Taft, Sherman
28. Wilson, Marshall
29. Harding, Coolidge
30. Coolidge (second term), Dawes
31. Hoover, Curtis
32. F. D. Roosevelt (first and second terms), Garner

VICE PRESIDENTS—STATES REPRESENTED AND PARTY AFFILIATIONS

Adams—Massachusetts, Federalist
Jefferson—Virginia, Democratic-Republican

Burr–New York, Democratic-Republican
Clinton–New York, Democratic-Republican
Gerry–Massachusetts, Democratic-Republican
Tompkins–New York, Democratic-Republican
Calhoun–South Carolina, Democratic-Republican
Van Buren–New York, Democrat
R. M. Johnson–Kentucky, Democrat
Tyler–Virginia, Whig
Dallas–Pennsylvania, Democrat
Fillmore–New York, Whig
King–Alabama, Democrat
Breckinridge–Kentucky, Democrat
Hamlin–Maine, Republican
A. Johnson–Tennessee, Democrat (but nominated and elected with Lincoln on Republican ticket)
Colfax–Indiana, Republican
Wilson–Massachusetts, Republican
Wheeler–New York, Republican
Arthur–New York, Republican
Hendricks–Indiana, Democrat
Morton–New York, Republican
Stevenson–Illinois, Democrat
Hobart–New Jersey, Republican
T. Roosevelt–New York, Republican
Fairbanks–Indiana, Republican
Sherman–New York, Republican
Marshall–Indiana, Democrat
Coolidge–Massachusetts, Republican
Dawes–Illinois, Republican
Curtis–Kansas, Republican
Garner–Texas, Democrat
Wallace–Iowa, Democrat
Truman–Missouri, Democrat
Barkley–Kentucky, Democrat
Nixon–California, Republican
L. B. Johnson–Texas, Democrat
Humphrey–Minnesota, Democrat
Agnew–Maryland, Republican
Ford–Michigan, Republican

VICE PRESIDENTS—DATES AND PLACES OF BIRTH

Adams–Oct. 30, 1735, Braintree (now Quincy), Mass.
Jefferson–Apr. 13, 1743, Shadwell, Va.
Burr–Feb. 6, 1756, Newark, N.J.
Clinton–July 26, 1739, Little Britain, N.Y.
Gerry–July 17, 1744, Marblehead, Mass.
Tompkins–June 21, 1774, Fox Meadows (now Scarsdale), N.Y.
Calhoun–Mar. 18, 1782, Abbeville District, S.C.
Van Buren–Dec. 5, 1782, Kinderhook, N.Y.

R. M. Johnson–Oct. 17, 1780, Floyd's Station, Ky.
Tyler–Mar. 29, 1790, Charles City County, Va.
Dallas–July 10, 1792, Philadelphia, Pa.
Fillmore–Jan. 7, 1800, Summerhill, N.Y.
King–Apr. 7, 1786, Sampson County, N.C.
Breckinridge–Jan. 21, 1821, Lexington, Ky.
Hamlin–Aug. 27, 1809, Paris, Me.
A. Johnson–Dec. 29, 1808, Raleigh, N.C.
Colfax–Mar. 23, 1823, New York, N.Y.
Wilson–Feb. 16, 1812, Farmington, N.H.
Wheeler–June 30, 1819, Malone, N.Y.
Arthur–Oct. 5, 1830, Fairfield, Vt.
Hendricks–Sept. 7, 1819, Muskingum County, Ohio
Morton–May 16, 1824, Shoreham, Vt.
Stevenson–Oct. 23, 1835, Christian County, Ky.
Hobart–June 3, 1844, Long Branch, N.J.
T. Roosevelt–Oct. 27, 1858, New York, N.Y.
Fairbanks–May 11, 1852, Unionville Center, Ohio
Sherman–Oct. 24, 1855, Utica, N.Y.
Marshall–Mar. 14, 1854, North Manchester, Ind.
Coolidge–July 4, 1872, Plymouth, Vt.
Dawes–Aug. 27, 1865, Marietta, Ohio
Curtis–Jan. 25, 1860, Topeka, Kan.
Garner–Nov. 22, 1868, Red River County, Tex.
Wallace–Oct. 7, 1888, Adair County, Iowa
Truman–May 8, 1884, Lamar, Mo.
Barkley–Nov. 24, 1877, Graves County, Ky.
Nixon–Jan. 9, 1913, Yorba Linda, Calif.
L. B. Johnson–Aug. 27, 1908, Stonewall, Tex.
Humphrey–May 27, 1911, Wallace, S.D.
Agnew–Nov. 9, 1918, Baltimore, Md.
Ford–July 14, 1913, Omaha, Neb.

VICE PRESIDENTS PAST AND FUTURE

As a rule there are not very many living Vice Presidents in any single year. In 1824, 1864, 1865, and 1868, however there were at least eighteen individuals who had held the office of Vice President, were in office, or were destined to be elected to the office.

The following is a list of the nineteen Vice Presidents alive in 1824, with dates of birth and death:

Adams–1735-1826
Jefferson–1743-1826
Burr–1756-1836
Tompkins–1774-1825
R. M. Johnson–1780-1850
Calhoun–1782-1850
Van Buren–1782-1862
King–1786-1853
Tyler–1790-1862

Dallas–1792-1864
Fillmore–1800-1874
A. Johnson–1808-1875
Hamlin–1809-1891
Wilson–1812-1875
Wheeler–1819-1887
Hendricks–1819-1885
Breckinridge–1821-1875
Colfax–1823-1885
Morton–1824-1920

The following is a list of the eighteen Vice Presidents alive in 1864, with dates of birth and death:

Dallas–1792-1864
Fillmore–1800-1874
A. Johnson–1808-1875
Hamlin–1809-1891
Wilson–1812-1875
Wheeler–1819-1887
Hendricks–1819-1885
Breckinridge–1821-1875
Colfax–1823-1885
Morton–1824-1920
Arthur–1830-1886
Stevenson–1835-1914
Hobart–1844-1899
Fairbanks–1852-1918
Marshall–1854-1925
Sherman–1855-1912
T. Roosevelt–1858-1919
Curtis–1860-1936

The death of Dallas in 1864 was offset by the birth of Dawes (1865-1951), and the number remained the same in 1865. The birth of Garner (1868-1967) brought the number to nineteen in 1868.

A similar compilation of Presidents past and future appears on page 568.

VICE PRESIDENTS — BIRTHPLACES

New York (8)

Clinton
Tompkins
Van Buren
Fillmore
Colfax
Wheeler
T. Roosevelt
Sherman

Kentucky (4)

R. M. Johnson
Breckinridge
Stevenson
Barkley

Ohio (3)

Hendricks
Fairbanks

Dawes

Vermont (3)

Arthur
Morton
Coolidge

Massachusetts (2)

Adams
Gerry

New Jersey (2)

Burr
Hobart

North Carolina (2)

King
A. Johnson

Texas (2)

Garner
L. B. Johnson

Virginia (2)

Jefferson
Tyler

California (1)

Nixon

Indiana (1)

Marshall

Iowa (1

Wallace

Kansas (1)

Curtis

Maine (1)

Hamlin

Maryland (1)

Agnew

Missouri (1)

Truman

Nebraska (1)

Ford

New Hampshire (1)

Wilson

Pennsylvania (1)

Dallas

South Carolina (1)

Calhoun

South Dakota (1)

Humphrey

NEW YORK STATE THE BIRTHPLACE OF EIGHT VICE PRESIDENTS

The number of Vice Presidents born in New York State has been greater than the number born in any two other states combined. The eight Vice Presidents born in New York were George Clinton (who served under Jefferson and Madison), Daniel D. Tompkins (under Monroe), Martin Van Buren (under Jackson), Millard Fillmore (under Taylor), Schuyler Colfax (under Grant), William Almon Wheeler (under Hayes), Theodore Roosevelt (under McKinley), and James Schoolcraft Sherman (under Taft). Three of the eight succeeded to the presidency: Van Buren, Fillmore, and Theodore Roosevelt.

YOUNGEST AND OLDEST VICE PRESIDENTS FROM KENTUCKY

The two Vice Presidents who were the youngest and the oldest at their respective inaugurations were both natives of Kentucky. The youngest was John Cabell Breckinridge, born at Lexington, Ky., who was 36 years and 42 days old when he was inaugurated Vice President under President James Buchanan in 1857. The oldest was Alben William Barkley, born near Lowes, in Graves County, Ky., who was 71 years and 57 days old when he was inaugurated Vice President under President Harry S. Truman in 1949.

RESIDENT STATES OF THE VICE PRESIDENTS

The Vice Presidents, when inaugurated, were residents (though not necessarily natives) of the following states:

New York (10)
Burr
Clinton
Tompkins
Van Buren
Fillmore
Wheeler
Arthur
Morton
T. Roosevelt
Sherman

Indiana (4)
Colfax
Hendricks
Fairbanks
Marshall

Massachusetts (4)
Adams
Gerry
Wilson
Coolidge

Kentucky (3)
R. M. Johnson
Breckinridge
Barkley

Illinois (2)
Stevenson
Dawes

Texas (2)
Garner
L. B. Johnson

Virginia (2)
Jefferson
Tyler

Alabama (1)
King

California (1)
Nixon

Iowa (1)
Wallace

Kansas (1)
Curtis

Maine (1)
Hamlin

Maryland (1)
Agnew

Michigan (1)
Ford

Minnesota (1)
Humphrey

Missouri (1)
Truman

New Jersey (1)
Hobart

Pennsylvania (1)
Dallas

South Carolina (1)
Calhoun

Tennessee (1)
A. Johnson

VICE PRESIDENTS ELECTED FROM STATES OTHER THAN THEIR BIRTHPLACES

The ten Vice Presidents listed below were elected from states other than their native states. The name of each is followed by (1) the state from which he was elected and (2) the state in which he was born.

Burr–New York, New Jersey
King–Alabama, North Carolina
A. Johnson–Tennessee, North Carolina
Colfax–Indiana, New York
Wilson–Massachusetts, New Hampshire
Hendricks–Indiana, Ohio
Morton–New York, Vermont
Stevenson–Illinois, Kentucky
Fairbanks–Indiana, Ohio
Coolidge–Massachusetts, Vermont
Dawes–Illinois, Ohio
Humphrey–Minnesota, South Dakota
Ford–Michigan, Nebraska

JOHNSONS SOUGHT VICE PRESIDENTIAL OFFICE

Five unrelated men named Johnson were important contenders for the vice presidency. Three of the five were elected: Richard Mentor Johnson, who served under Van Buren; Andrew Johnson, who served during Lincoln's second term and succeeded to the presidency upon the death of Lincoln; and Lyndon Baines Johnson, who served under Kennedy, succeeded to the presidency upon the death of Kennedy, and was later elected to the presidency in his own right. The two defeated Johnsons were Herschel Vespasian Johnson of Georgia, who ran on the Democratic ticket in 1860 under Stephen Arnold Douglas, and Hiram Warren Johnson of California, who was the running mate of Theodore Roosevelt in 1912 on the Progressive ticket.

VICE PRESIDENT WILSON'S NAME

One Vice President, in addition to the Johnsons, bore the same name as a President. Henry Wilson, Vice President during Grant's second administration from March 4, 1873, to November 22, 1875, was not related to President Woodrow Wilson, nor was his name originally Wilson. He was born Jeremiah Jones Colbaith and legally changed his name to Wilson.

INDIAN ELECTED VICE PRESIDENT

Senator Charles Curtis of Kansas, whose mother was a full-blooded member of the Kaw tribe of Indians, was elected Vice President of the United States to serve from March 4, 1929, to March 3, 1933, under President Hoover.

UNSUCCESSFUL VICE PRESIDENTIAL ASPIRANT ELECTED PRESIDENT OF CONFEDERATE STATES

Jefferson Davis of Mississippi became president of the Confederate

States of America on February 18, 1861. Nine years earlier, he had been a contender for the vice presidential nomination at the Democratic national convention held at the Maryland Institute, Baltimore, Md., June 1-5, 1852. On the first ballot New York cast two votes for Davis; on the second ballot, Illinois cast eleven votes for him.

OCTOGENARIAN NOMINATED FOR VICE PRESIDENCY

The oldest nominee for the presidency or the vice presidency was Henry Gassaway Davis of West Virginia, a former senator, who was 80 years and 235 days old when he was nominated at the Democratic convention at St. Louis, Mo., in July 1904.

BLACK CONTENDER FOR THE VICE PRESIDENTIAL NOMINATION

At the Republican convention held at Chicago, Ill., in June 1880, Blanche Kelso Bruce, United States Senator from Mississippi, received eleven votes in the balloting for the vice presidency. He was the first black candidate for the vice presidential nomination of a major political party.

VICE PRESIDENTIAL TERMS

Eighteen of the forty Vice Presidents served full four-year terms. They were Thomas Jefferson, Aaron Burr, Martin Van Buren, Richard Mentor Johnson, George Mifflin Dallas, John Cabell Breckinridge, Hannibal Hamlin, Schuyler Colfax, William Almon Wheeler, Levi Parsons Morton, Adlai Ewing Stevenson, Charles Warren Fairbanks, Charles Gates Dawes, Charles Curtis, Henry Agard Wallace, Alben William Barkley, Richard Milhous Nixon, and Theodore Spiro Agnew.

Eight Vice Presidents did not complete their full four-year terms, for they succeeded to the presidency upon the death of their predecessors. They were John Tyler, Millard Fillmore, Andrew Johnson, Chester Alan Arthur, Theodore Roosevelt, Calvin Coolidge, Harry S. Truman, and Lyndon Baines Johnson. (Four of the eight—Roosevelt, Coolidge, Truman, and Johnson—were also elected to the presidency in their own right.)

Six Vice Presidents died before completing their four-year terms. They were William Rufus De Van King, who served 45 days; Thomas Andrews Hendricks, 266 days; Elbridge Gerry, 1 year and 264 days; Henry Wilson, 2 years and 263 days; Garret Augustus Hobart, 2 years and 262 days; and James Schoolcraft Sherman, 3 years and 240 days.

Eight Vice Presidents were reelected for second terms. They were John Adams, George Clinton, Daniel D. Tompkins, John Caldwell Calhoun, Thomas Riley Marshall, John Nance Garner, Richard Milhouse Nixon, and Theodore Spiro Agnew. Agnew resigned October 10, 1973, having served 263 days of his second term.

Of the eight who were reelected, two served their second terms under different Presidents: Clinton under Jefferson and Madison, and Calhoun under John Quincy Adams and Andrew Jackson. Neither Clinton nor Calhoun completed his second term. Clinton was reelected to serve under James Madison from 1809 to 1813, but he died April 20, 1812, leaving the nation without a Vice President for 318 days. Calhoun was reelected to serve under Jackson from 1829 to 1833, but he resigned December 28, 1832, after his election to the Senate to fill the vacancy caused by the resignation of Robert Young Hayne of South Carolina. Calhoun served 82 days less than eight full years.

Technically, only three of the forty Vice Presidents served eight full years in office. They were Tompkins, who served under Monroe; Marshall, who served under Wilson; and Nixon, who served under Eisenhower. Two other Vice Presidents served two full terms: Adams served 47 days less than eight full years because he did not assume office until April 21, 1789 (nine days before George Washington was inaugurated). Garner served 43 days less than eight full years because his second term under Franklin Delano Roosevelt expired on January 20, instead of the previous March 3 date.

RESIGNATION OF VICE PRESIDENT CALHOUN

John Caldwell Calhoun, of South Carolina, who served as Vice President under President John Quincy Adams from March 4, 1825, to March 3, 1829, was reelected Vice President to serve under Andrew Jackson from March 4, 1829, to March 3, 1833. He differed with Jackson on the tariff policy and resigned December 28, 1832, having been elected on December 12 to fill the vacant seat of Robert Y. Hayne, who had been elected governor of South Carolina. Calhoun served as senator from December 29, 1832, to March 3, 1843, in the 22nd and the seven succeeding congresses. He also served as senator from November 26, 1845, until his death on March 31, 1850.

RESIGNATION OF VICE PRESIDENT AGNEW

Theodore Spiro Agnew, of Maryland, who served as Vice President under President Richard Milhous Nixon from January 29, 1969, to October 10, 1973, resigned on October 10, 1973, because of charges brought against him by the Internal Revenue Service concerning the violation of income tax laws. He pleaded no contest and the other charges of bribery, extortion, and conspiracy were dismissed. Agnew was placed on probation and given a $10,000 fine.

RESIGNATION PROCEDURE

The only evidence of a refusal to accept, or of a resignation of the office of President or Vice President, shall be an instrument in writing, declaring the same, and subscribed by the person refusing to accept or resigning, as the case may be, and delivered into the office of the Secretary of State. (June 25, 1948, 62 Stat. L. 678, ch. 644)

PRESIDENTIAL AND VICE PRESIDENTIAL TEAMS SELDOM REELECTED

Only six of the forty-seven elections from 1789 through 1972 resulted in the reelection of a President and his Vice President. However, there were in all only twelve elections in which Presidents were reelected for a second consecutive term.

The six Presidents who carried their Vice Presidents into office for a second term were Washington (1789-1797), Monroe (1817-1825), Wilson (1913-1921), Franklin Delano Roosevelt (1933-1941), Eisenhower (1953-1961), and Nixon (1969-1973). The Vice Presidents elected with them were respectively Adams, Tompkins, Marshall, Garner, Nixon, and Agnew. (Roosevelt's Vice Presidents for his third and fourth terms were Wallace and Truman.)

In 1804, when Jefferson was elected for a second term, Burr was replaced by Clinton. At this election, the President and the Vice President were on separate ballots and it would have been possible to elect one and not the other.

Four Presidents had different Vice Presidents during their second terms because of the death or resignation of their Vice Presidents. Clinton, who had served as Vice President during the second term of Jefferson, died in office during the first term of Madison, and Gerry was elected to serve during Madison's second term. Hobart died during the first term of McKinley and Theodore Roosevelt was selected for the second term. Calhoun resigned during the first term of Jackson, and Van Buren served as Vice President during Jackson's second term. Agnew resigned during the second term of Nixon, and Nixon in accordance with the Twenty-fifth Amendment nominated Representative Gerald Rudolph Ford, Jr., to fill the vacancy. This nomination depended on confirmation by a majority vote of both houses of Congress. Ford was sworn in as the fortieth Vice President of the United States, on December 6, 1973.

Lincoln had two Vice Presidents, Hamlin and Andrew Johnson. Grant's Vice Presidents were Colfax and Wilson.

Cleveland was elected for two nonconsecutive terms (1885-1889 and 1893-1897), and he had a different Vice President each term. Hendricks died while in office during the first term, and Stevenson served during the second term.

PRESIDENTIAL AND VICE PRESIDENTIAL CANDIDATES

Two Republican presidential and vice presidential teams have been elected twice: Eisenhower and Nixon; Nixon and Agnew.

Two Democratic teams were elected for second terms: Wilson and Marshall and Franklin Delano Roosevelt and Garner.

The only Republican Vice Presidents elected to the presidency were Theodore Roosevelt, Coolidge, and Nixon. The only Democratic Vice Presidents elected to the presidency were Van Buren, Truman, and Lyndon Baines Johnson.

The only presidential and vice presidential teams defeated for a second term were Van Buren and Richard Mentor Johnson (1836) and Hoover and Curtis (1932). Several other Presidents were defeated for reelection, but each had a different vice presidential running mate.

VICE PRESIDENTIAL CANDIDATE RESIGNED

The first and only vice presidential candidate of a major political party to resign was Senator Thomas Francis Eagleton of Missouri, who was nominated July 13, 1972, at the Democratic National Convention held at Miami Beach, Florida. He submitted his resignation on August 1, 1972, and the National Democratic Committee nominated Robert Sargent Shriver of Maryland.

VACANCIES IN THE OFFICE OF VICE PRESIDENT

In the 183 years between 1789 and 1972, there was no Vice President for 37 years and 159 days, almost one fifth of the time.

Of the forty Vice Presidents, Lyndon Baines Johnson was the sixteenth who did not complete his four-year term as Vice President.

Seven Vice Presidents died in office and did not complete their terms:

George Clinton, the 4th Vice President, took office March 4, 1809, and died April 20, 1812. He served 3 years and 47 days, the office remaining vacant 318 days.

Elbridge Gerry, the 5th Vice President, took office March 4, 1813, and died November 23, 1814. He served 1 year and 264 days, the office remaining vacant 2 years and 101 days.

William Rufus De Vane King, the 13th Vice President, took office March 4, 1853, and died April 18, 1853. He served 45 days, the office remaining vacant 3 years and 320 days.

Henry Wilson, the 18th Vice President, took office March 4, 1873, and died November 22, 1875. He served 2 years and 263 days, the office remaining vacant 1 year and 2 days.

Thomas Andrews Hendricks, the 21st Vice President, took office March 4, 1885, and died November 25, 1885. He served 266 days, the office remaining vacant 3 years and 99 days.

Garret Augustus Hobart, the 24th Vice President, took office March 4, 1897, and died November 21, 1899. He served 2 years and 262 days, the office remaining vacant 1 year and 103 days.

James Schoolcraft Sherman, the 27th Vice President, took office March 4, 1909, and died October 30, 1912. He served 3 years and 240 days, the office remaining vacant 125 days.

Two Vice Presidents resigned:

John Caldwell Calhoun, the 7th Vice President, resigned on December 28, 1832. The office remained vacant 66 days.

Theodore Spiro Agnew, the 39th Vice President, resigned on October 10, 1973. The office remained vacant 58 days until Congress confirmed Gerald Rudolph Ford, Jr., on December 6, 1973, on which date he was sworn in.

Eight Vice Presidents succeeded to the presidency:

John Tyler, the 10th Vice President, succeeded William Henry Harrison, who died in office, and the office remained vacant 333 days.

Millard Fillmore, the 12th Vice President, succeeded Zachary Taylor, who died in office, and the office remained vacant 2 years and 238 days.

Andrew Johnson, the 16th Vice President, succeeded Abraham Lincoln, who was assassinated, and the office remained vacant 3 years and 323 days.

Chester Alan Arthur, the 20th Vice President, succeeded James Abram Garfield, who was assassinated, and the office remained vacant 3 years and 166 days.

Theodore Roosevelt, the 25th Vice President, succeeded William McKinley, who was assassinated, and the office remained vacant 3 years and 171 days.

Calvin Coolidge, the 29th Vice President, succeeded Warren Gamaliel Harding, who died in office, and the office remained vacant 1 year and 214 days.

Harry S. Truman, the 34th Vice President, succeeded Franklin Delano Roosevelt, who died in office, and the office remained vacant 3 years and 283 days.

Lyndon Baines Johnson, the 37th Vice President, succeeded John Fitzgerald Kennedy, who was assassinated, and the office remained vacant 1 year and 59 days.

The Twenty-fifth Amendment, adopted in 1967, will eliminate future vice presidential vacancies. Section 2 of the Amendment provides that whenever there is a vacancy, "the President shall nominate a Vice President who shall take office upon confirmation by a majority vote of both houses of Congress."

VICE PRESIDENTS — STATUS AFTER HOLDING OFFICE

Three Vice Presidents were elected to the presidency after completing their vice presidential terms: John Adams, Thomas Jefferson (who served as President for two terms), and Martin Van Buren.

Richard Milhous Nixon was the first Vice President elected President not directly after his vice presidential term. Nixon was Vice President from January 20, 1953, to January 20, 1961, under President Dwight David Eisenhower. Nixon was not in government service until January 20, 1969, when he was inaugurated President.

Eight Vice Presidents succeeded to the presidency upon the death of the Presidents under whom they had served: John Tyler, Millard Fillmore, Andrew Johnson, Chester Alan Arthur, Theodore Roosevelt, Calvin Coolidge, Harry S. Truman, and Lyndon Baines Johnson.

Four of the eight who succeeded to the presidency were elected for additional four-year terms: Theodore Roosevelt, Calvin Coolidge, Harry S. Truman, and Lyndon Baines Johnson.

Five Vice Presidents served in the Senate after their vice presidential terms: John Caldwell Calhoun (who resigned as Vice President to serve in the Senate), John Cabell Breckinridge, Hannibal Hamlin, Andrew Johnson (who was elected to the Senate after serving as President), and Alben William Barkley.

Seven Vice Presidents died in office: George Clinton (who died during his second term), Elbridge Gerry, William Rufus De Vane King, Henry Wilson, Thomas Andrews Hendricks, Garret Augustus Hobart, and James Schoolcraft Sherman.

VICE PRESIDENTS IN THE PRESIDENCY

Twelve men who were elevated to the vice presidency also served as chief executive.

The eight who succeeded to the presidency when their predecessors died served the unexpired terms as follows: Tyler, 3 years and 332 days; Fillmore, 2 years and 236 days; Andrew Johnson, 3 years and 323 days; Arthur, 3 years and 166 days; Theodore Roosevelt, 3 years and 171 days; Coolidge, 1 year and 214 days; Truman, 3 years and 283 days; Lyndon Baines Johnson, 1 year and 59 days—a total of 23 years and 324 days during which the country was run by men who had not been elected to presidential office.

Four of the eight were elected for additional four-year terms: Theodore Roosevelt, Coolidge, Truman, and Lyndon Baines Johnson.

Three others were elected to the presidency after the expiration of their vice presidential terms: John Adams, Jefferson (who served as President for two terms), and Van Buren.

Richard Milhous Nixon was a candidate for the presidency after his vice presidential term expired, but was defeated by Kennedy in 1960. Eight years later Nixon tried again and was elected.

EIGHTH AND TENTH VICE PRESIDENTS BECAME THE EIGHTH AND TENTH PRESIDENTS

Martin Van Buren, who was the eighth Vice President (March 4, 1833-March 3, 1837) was elected to the presidency and served as eighth President (March 4, 1837-March 3, 1841).

John Tyler, who was the tenth Vice President (March 4, 1841-April 4, 1841) succeeded to the presidency when William Henry Harrison died, and thus became the tenth President.

VICE PRESIDENTS — AGE AT INAUGURATION AND AGE AT DEATH

Adams
53 years, 174 days; 90 years, 247 days

Jefferson
53 years, 325 days; 83 years, 82 days

Burr
45 years, 26 days; 80 years, 220 days

Clinton
(under Jefferson) 65 years, 221 days; 72 years, 268 days
(under Madison) 69 years, 221 days; 72 years, 268 days

Gerry
68 years, 230 days; 70 years, 129 days

Tompkins
42 years, 256 days; 50 years, 355 days

Calhoun
(under J. Q. Adams) 42 years, 351 days; 68 years, 13 days
(under Jackson) 46 years, 351 days; 68 years, 13 days

Van Buren
50 years, 89 days; 79 years, 231 days

R. M. Johnson
56 years, 138 days; 70 years, 33 days

Tyler
50 years, 340 days; 71 years, 295 days;

Dallas
52 years, 237 days; 72 years, 174 days

Fillmore
49 years, 56 days; 74 years, 60 days

King
66 years, 331 days; 67 years, 11 days

Breckinridge
36 years, 42 days; 54 years, 116 days

Hamlin
51 years, 189 days; 81 years, 311 days

A. Johnson
56 years, 65 days; 66 years, 214 days

Colfax
45 years, 346 days; 61 years, 296 days

Wilson
61 years, 16 days; 63 years, 279 days

Wheeler
57 years, 247 days; 67 years, 339 days

Arthur
50 years, 150 days; 56 years, 44 days

Hendricks
65 years, 178 days; 66 years, 79 days

Morton
64 years, 292 days; 96 years

Stevenson
57 years, 132 days; 78 years, 234 days

Hobart
52 years, 274 days; 55 years, 171 days

T. Roosevelt
42 years, 128 days; 60 years, 71 days

Fairbanks

52 years, 297 days; 66 years, 24 days

Sherman

53 years, 131 days; 57 years, 6 days

Marshall

58 years, 355 days; 71 years, 79 days

Coolidge

48 years, 243 days; 60 years, 185 days

Dawes

59 years, 189 days; 85 years, 239 days

Curtis

69 years, 38 days; 76 years, 14 days

Garner

64 years, 102 days; 98 years, 351 days

Wallace

52 years, 105 days; 77 years, 42 days

Truman

60 years, 257 days; 88 years, 232 days

Barkley

71 years, 57 days; 78 years, 157 days

Nixon

40 years, 11 days

L. B. Johnson

52 years, 146 days; 65 years, 148 days

Humphrey

53 years, 238 days

Agnew

51 years, 72 days

Ford

61 years, 145 days (age at time of taking office)

The average age at inauguration was 57 years and 206 days. In this computation Clinton (who served as Vice President under Jefferson and Madison) and Calhoun (who served as Vice President under John Quincy Adams and Jackson) are each counted twice.

The oldest Vice President to succeed to the presidency upon the death of the President was Truman, who was 60 years and 339 days old when he became President after the death of Franklin Delano Roosevelt.

The youngest Vice President to succeed to the presidency upon the death of the President was Theodore Roosevelt, who was 42 years and 322 days old when he became President after the death of McKinley.

The average age at death of the 36 Vice Presidents who are no longer living was 71 years and 294 days.

COMPARATIVE AGES OF THE PRESIDENTS AND THEIR VICE PRESIDENTS ON INAUGURATION DAY

The following list shows the age at inauguration of each President and Vice President. Omitted from the list of Presidents are Tyler, Fillmore, Andrew Johnson, and Arthur, who had no Vice Presidents since they succeeded to the presidency but were not elected for additional terms in their own right, as were Theodore Roosevelt, Coolidge, Truman, and Lyndon Baines Johnson.

Seven Presidents had two Vice Presidents: Jefferson—Burr and Clinton; Madison—Clinton and Gerry; Jackson—Calhoun and Van Buren; Lincoln—Hamlin and Johnson; Grant—Colfax and Wilson; McKinley—Hobart and Roosevelt; Nixon—Agnew and Ford (Ford was not inaugurated with Nixon). Franklin Delano Roosevelt had three Vice Presidents—Garner, Wallace, and Truman.

Washington–57 years, 67 days; **J. Adams**–53 years, 174 days (at their first inauguration) (Adams inaugurated Apr. 21, 1789; Washington inaugurated Apr. 30, 1789)

J. Adams–61 years, 125 days; **Jefferson**–53 years, 325 days

Jefferson–57 years, 325 days; **Burr**–45 years, 26 days

Jefferson–61 years, 325 days; **Clinton**–65 years, 221 days

Madison–57 years, 353 days; **Clinton**–69 years, 221 days

Madison–61 years, 353 days; **Gerry**–68 years, 230 days

Monroe–58 years, 310 days; **Tompkins**–42 years, 256 days (at their first inauguration)

J. Q. Adams–57 years, 236 days; **Calhoun**–42 years, 351 days

Jackson–61 years, 354 days; **Calhoun**–46 years, 351 days

Jackson–65 years, 354 days; **Van Buren**–50 years, 89 days

Van Buren–54 years, 89 days; **R. M. Johnson**–56 years, 138 days

W. H. Harrison–68 years, 23 days; **Tyler**–50 years, 340 days

Polk–49 years, 122 days; **Dallas**–52 years, 237 days

Taylor–64 years, 100 days; **Fillmore**–49 years, 56 days

Pierce–48 years, 101 days; **King**–66 years, 331 days

Buchanan–65 years, 315 days; **Breckinridge**–36 years, 42 days

Lincoln–52 years, 20 days; **Hamlin**–51 years, 189 days

Lincoln–56 years, 20 days; **A. Johnson**–56 years, 65 days

Grant–46 years, 311 days; **Colfax**–45 years, 346 days

Grant–50 years, 311 days; **H. Wilson**–61 years, 16 days

Hayes–54 years, 151 days; **Wheeler**–57 years, 247 days

Garfield–49 years, 105 days; **Arthur**–50 years, 150 days

Cleveland–47 years, 351 days; **Hendricks**–65 years, 178 days

B. Harrison–55 years, 196 days; **Morton**–64 years, 292 days

Cleveland–55 years, 351 days; **Stevenson**–57 years, 132 days

McKinley–54 years, 34 days; **Hobart**–52 years, 274 days

McKinley–58 years, 34 days; **T. Roosevelt**–42 years, 128 days

T. Roosevelt–46 years, 128 days; **Fairbanks**–52 years, 297 days

Taft–51 years, 170 days; **Sherman**–53 years, 131 days

Wilson–56 years, 66 days; **Marshall**–58 years, 355 days (at their first inauguration)

Harding–55 years, 122 days; **Coolidge**–48 years, 243 days

Coolidge–52 years, 243 days; **Dawes**–59 years, 189 days

Hoover–54 years, 206 days; **Curtis**–69 years, 38 days

F. D. Roosevelt–51 years, 33 days; **Garner**–64 years, 102 days (at their first inauguration)

F. D. Roosevelt–58 years, 355 days; **Wallace**–52 years, 105 days

F. D. Roosevelt–62 years, 355 days; **Truman**–60 years, 257 days

Truman–64 years, 257 days; **Barkley**–71 years, 57 days

Eisenhower–62 years, 98 days; **Nixon**–40 years, 11 days (at their first inauguration)

Kennedy–43 years, 236 days; **L. B. Johnson**–52 years, 146 days

Johnson–56 years, 146 days; **Humphrey**–53 years, 238 days

Nixon–56 years, 11 days; **Agnew**–51 years, 72 days

The following Presidents were older than the Vice Presidents inaugurated with them: Washington, John Adams, Jefferson (first Vice President), Monroe, John Quincy Adams, Jackson (first and second Vice Presidents), William Henry Harrison, Taylor, Buchanan, Lincoln (first Vice President), Grant (first Vice President), McKinley (first and second Vice Presidents), Harding, Franklin Delano Roosevelt (second and third Vice Presidents), Eisenhower, Lyndon Baines Johnson, and Richard Milhous Nixon.

The following Presidents were younger than the Vice Presidents inaugurated with them: Jefferson (second Vice President), Madison (first and second Vice Presidents), Van Buren, Polk, Pierce, Lincoln (second Vice President), Hayes, Garfield, Cleveland (first and second Vice Presidents), Benjamin Harrison, Theodore Roosevelt, Taft, Wilson, Coolidge, Hoover, Franklin Delano Roosevelt (first Vice President), Truman, and Kennedy.

The average age of the Vice Presidents was 57 years and 206 days, that of the Presidents 54 years and 299 days.

VICE PRESIDENTS DECLARE THEIR OPPONENTS ELECTED PRESIDENT

On Wednesday, February 13, 1861, Vice President John Cabell Breckinridge of Kentucky under James Buchanan, announced in the House of Representatives' joint session assembled to count the electoral votes that "Abraham Lincoln, of Illinois, having received a majority of the whole number of electoral votes, is elected President of the United States for four years, commencing the fourth of March 1861. Hannibal Hamlin, of Maine, having received a majority of the whole number of electoral votes, is duly elected Vice President of the United States for four years commencing the fourth of March. The business for which the two Houses were assembled having been finished, the Senate will now return to its own Chamber."

The electoral votes for President were cast as follows; Abraham Lincoln of Illinois 180 votes, John Cabell Breckinridge of Kentucky 72 votes, John Bell of Tennessee 39 votes, and Stephen Arnold Douglas of Illinois 12 votes.

On January 6, 1961, Vice President Richard Milhous Nixon, Republican of California under President Eisenhower, announced at a joint session of Congress assembled in the House of Representatives' chamber for the counting of the electoral votes, that the tally stood 303 votes for John Fitzgerald Kennedy, Democrat of Massachusetts, 219 votes for Richard Milhous Nixon, and 15 votes for Harry Flood Byrd. (A majority of 269 of the 537 votes was necessary. After announcing that his opponent was elected, Nixon said, "In our campaigns, no matter how hard they may be, no matter how close the election may turn out to be, those who lose accept the verdict and support those who won."

In January 1969, Vice President Hubert Horatio Humphrey, Vice President under L. B. Johnson, was in Norway representing the United States at the funeral of former United Nations Secretary-General Trygve Lie. Senator Richard Brevard Russell presided during the counting of the electoral votes that elected Richard Milhous Nixon as President of the United States.

VICE PRESIDENTS IN CONGRESS

Twenty-seven of the forty Vice Presidents had served in Congress before becoming Vice President. Three others had served in the Continental Congress.

Twelve served in both the House of Representatives and the Senate: Calhoun, Richard Mentor Johnson, Tyler, King, Breckinridge, Hamlin, Andrew Johnson, Hendricks, Curtis, Barkley, Nixon, and Lyndon Baines Johnson.

Seven served only in the Senate: Burr, Van Buren, Dallas, Wilson, Fairbanks, Truman, and Humphrey.

Nine served only in the House of Representatives: Gerry, Fillmore, Colfax, Wheeler, Morton, Stevenson, Sherman, Garner, and Ford.

Twelve Vice Presidents never served in either house of Congress: John Adams, Jefferson, Clinton, Tompkins (who was elected to the House of Representatives but did not serve), Arthur, Hobart, Marshall, Theodore Roosevelt, Coolidge, Dawes, Wallace, and Agnew.

The following is a list of the Vice Presidents elected to Congress, with the states they represented and their terms of office:

J. Adams–Massachusetts
Continental Congress, 1774-1778
Jefferson–Virginia
Continental Congress, 1775-1776; 1783-1785
Burr–New York
U.S. Senate, Mar. 4, 1791-Mar. 3, 1797
Clinton–New York
Continental Congress, May 15, 1775-July 8, 1777

Gerry–Massachusetts
Continental Congress, 1776-1781; 1782-1785
U.S. House of Representatives, 1st-2nd Congresses, Mar. 4, 1789-Mar. 3, 1793

Tompkins–New York
U.S. House of Representatives, elected to 9th Congress, but resigned before term

Calhoun–South Carolina
U.S. House of Representatives, 12th-15th Congresses, Mar. 4, 1811-Nov. 3, 1817
U.S. Senate, Dec. 29, 1832-Mar. 3, 1843; Nov. 26, 1845-Mar. 31, 1850

Van Buren–New York
U.S. Senate, Mar. 4, 1821-Dec. 20, 1828

R. M. Johnson–Kentucky
U.S. House of Representatives, 10th-15th Congresses, Mar. 4, 1807-Mar. 3, 1819
U.S. Senate, Dec. 10, 1819-Mar. 3, 1829

Tyler–Virginia
U.S. House of Representatives, 14th-16th Congresses, Dec. 16, 1817-Mar. 3, 1821
U.S. Senate, Mar. 4, 1827-Feb. 29, 1836

King–North Carolina; Alabama
U.S. House of Representatives, 12th-14th Congresses, Mar. 4, 1811-Nov. 4, 1816
U.S. Senate, Dec. 14, 1819-Apr. 15, 1844; July 1, 1848-Dec. 20, 1852

Dallas–Pennsylvania
U.S. Senate, Dec. 13, 1831-Mar. 3, 1833

Fillmore–New York
U.S. House of Representatives, 23rd Congress, Mar. 4, 1833-Mar. 3, 1835; 25th-27th Congresses, Mar. 4, 1837-Mar. 3, 1843

Breckinridge–Kentucky
U.S. House of Representatives, 32nd-33rd Congresses, Mar. 4, 1851-Mar. 3, 1855
U.S. Senate, Mar. 4, 1861 (expelled by resolution of Dec. 4, 1861)

Hamlin–Maine
U.S. House of Representatives, 28th-29th Congresses, Mar. 4, 1843-Mar. 3, 1847
U.S. Senate, June 8, 1848-Jan. 7, 1857; Mar. 4, 1857-Jan. 17, 1861; Mar. 4, 1869-Mar. 3, 1881

A. Johnson–Tennessee
U.S. House of Representatives, 28th-32nd Congresses, Mar. 4, 1843-Mar. 3, 1853
U.S. Senate, Oct. 8, 1857-Mar. 4, 1862; Mar. 4, 1875-July 31, 1875

Colfax–Indiana
U.S. House of Representatives, 34th-40th Congresses, Mar. 4, 1855-Mar. 3, 1869

Wilson–Massachusetts
U.S. Senate, Jan. 31, 1855-Mar. 3, 1873

Wheeler–New York

U.S. House of Representatives, 37th Congress, Mar. 4, 1861-Mar. 3, 1863; 41st-44th Congresses, Mar. 4, 1869-Mar. 3, 1877

Hendricks–Indiana

U.S. House of Representatives, 32nd-33rd Congresses, Mar. 4, 1851-Mar. 3, 1855

U.S. Senate, Mar. 4, 1863-Mar. 3, 1869

Morton–New York

U.S. House of Representatives, 46th-47th Congresses, Mar. 4, 1879-Mar. 21, 1881

Stevenson–Illinois

U.S. House of Representatives, 44th Congress, Mar. 4, 1875-Mar. 3, 1877; 46th Congress, Mar. 4, 1879-Mar. 3, 1881

Fairbanks–Indiana

U.S. Senate, Mar. 4, 1897-Mar. 3, 1905

Sherman–New York

U.S. House of Representatives, 50th-51st Congresses, Mar. 4, 1887-Mar. 3, 1891; 53rd-60th Congresses, Mar. 4, 1893-Mar. 3, 1909

Curtis–Kansas

U.S. House of Representatives, 53rd-59th Congresses, Mar. 4, 1893-Jan. 28, 1907

U.S. Senate, Jan. 29, 1907-Mar. 3, 1913; Mar. 4, 1915-Mar. 3, 1929

Garner–Texas

U.S. House of Representatives, 58th-73rd Congresses, Mar. 4, 1903-Mar. 3, 1933

Truman–Missouri

U.S. Senate, Jan. 3, 1935-Jan. 17, 1945

Barkley–Kentucky

U.S. House of Representatives, 63rd-69th Congresses, Mar. 4, 1913-Mar. 3, 1927

U.S. Senate, Mar. 4, 1927-Jan. 19, 1949; Jan. 3, 1955-Apr. 30, 1956

Nixon–California

U.S. House of Representatives, 80th-81st Congresses, Jan. 3, 1947-Jan. 3, 1951

U.S. Senate, Jan. 3, 1951-Jan. 20, 1953

L. B. Johnson–Texas

U.S. House of Representatives, 75th-80th Congresses, Apr. 10, 1937-Jan. 3, 1949

U.S. Senate, Jan. 3, 1949-Jan. 3, 1961

Humphrey–Minnesota

U.S. Senate, Jan. 3, 1949-Dec. 29, 1964

Ford–Michigan

U.S. House of Representatives, 81st-93rd Congresses, Jan. 3, 1949-Dec. 6, 1973

VICE PRESIDENTS WHO WERE STATE GOVERNORS

The following Vice Presidents served as governors of their respective states: Jefferson, Va.; Clinton, N.Y.; Gerry, Mass.; Tompkins, N.Y.; Van Buren, N.Y.; Tyler, Va.; Hamlin, Me.; A. Johnson, Tenn.; Hendricks, Ind.; T. Roosevelt, N.Y.; Marshall, Ind.; Coolidge, Mass.;

F. D. Roosevelt, N.Y.; and Agnew, Md.

VICE PRESIDENTS — DATE OF DEATH, PLACE OF DEATH, AND PLACE OF BURIAL

J. Adams
July 4, 1826; Quincy, Mass.; Quincy, Mass.

Jefferson
July 4, 1826; Monticello, Va.; Monticello, Va.

Burr
Sept. 14, 1836; Staten Island, N.Y.; Princeton, N.J.

Clinton
Apr. 20, 1812; Washington,D.C.; Kingston, N.Y.

Gerry
Nov. 23, 1814; Washington, D.C.; Washington, D.C.

Tompkins
June 11, 1825; Staten Island, N.Y.; New York, N.Y.

Calhoun
Mar. 31, 1850; Washington, D.C.; Charleston, S.C.

Van Buren
July 24, 1862; Kinderhook, N.Y.; Kinderhook, N.Y.

R. M. Johnson
Nov. 19, 1850; Frankfort, Ky.; Frankfort, Ky.

Tyler
Jan. 18, 1862; Richmond, Va.; Richmond, Va.

Dallas
Dec. 31, 1864; Philadelphia, Pa.; Philadelphia, Pa.

Fillmore
Mar. 8, 1874; Buffalo, N.Y.; Buffalo, N.Y.

King
Apr. 18, 1853; Cahaba, Ala.; Selma, Ala.

Breckinridge
May 17, 1875; Lexington, Ky.; Lexington, Ky.

Hamlin
July 4, 1891; Bangor, Me.; Bangor, Me.

A. Johnson
July 31, 1875; Carter's Station, Tenn.; Greeneville, Tenn.

Colfax
Jan. 13, 1885; Mankato, Minn.; South Bend, Ind.

Wilson
Nov. 22, 1875; Washington, D.C.; Natick, Mass.
Wheeler
June 4, 1887; Malone, N.Y.; Malone, N.Y.
Arthur
Nov. 18, 1886; New York, N.Y.; Albany, N.Y.
Hendricks
Nov. 25, 1885; Indianapolis, Ind.; Indianapolis, Ind.

Morton
May 16, 1920; Rhinebeck, N.Y.; Rhinebeck, N.Y.
Stevenson
June 14, 1914; Chicago, Ill.; Bloomington, Ill.
Hobart
Nov. 21, 1899; Paterson, N.J.; Paterson, N.J.

T. Roosevelt
Jan. 6, 1919; Oyster Bay, N.Y.; Oyster Bay, N.Y.
Fairbanks
June 4, 1918; Indianapolis, Ind.; Indianapolis, Ind.
Sherman
Oct. 30, 1912; Utica, N.Y.; Utica, N.Y.

Marshall
June 1, 1925; Washington, D.C.; Indianapolis, Ind.
Coolidge
Jan. 5, 1933; Northampton, Mass.; Plymouth, Vt.
Dawes
Apr. 23, 1951; Evanston, Ill.; Chicago, Ill.

Curtis
Feb. 8, 1936; Washington, D.C.; Topeka, Kan.
Garner
Nov. 7, 1967; Uvalde, Tex.; Uvalde, Tex.
Barkley
Apr. 30, 1956; Lexington, Va.; Paducah, Ky.
Wallace
Nov. 18, 1965; Danbury, Conn.; Des Moines, Iowa

Truman

Dec. 26, 1972; Kansas City, Mo.; Independence, Mo.

L. B. Johnson

Jan. 22, 1973; San Antonio, Tex.; Johnson City, Tex.

EIGHT VICE PRESIDENTS DIED IN NOVEMBER

Eight of the forty men who served as Vice President died in November: Elbridge Gerry, Nov. 23, 1814; Richard Mentor Johnson, Nov. 19, 1850; Henry Wilson, Nov. 22, 1875; Chester Alan Arthur, Nov. 18, 1886; Thomas Andrews Hendricks, Nov. 25, 1885; Garret Augustus Hobart, Nov. 21, 1899; John Nance Garner, Nov. 7, 1967; and Henry Agard Wallace, Nov. 18, 1965. Four of the eight—Gerry, Wilson, Hendricks, and Hobart—died before the completion of their terms.

PENSION TO VICE PRESIDENT'S WIDOW

On January 25, 1929, Congress passed an act (45 Stat. L. 2041) awarding an annual pension of $3,000 to Lois I. Marshall, widow of Vice President Thomas Riley Marshall, who had served under President Wilson. This was the first pension awarded to the widow of a Vice President.

FIRST VICE PRESIDENT TO MARRY IN OFFICE

Alben William Barkley, Vice President under President Harry S. Truman, was the first Vice President to marry in office. He married Elizabeth Jane Rucker Hadley on November 18, 1949, in St. Louis, Mo. She was born in Keytesville, Mo., and died September 6, 1964, at Washington, D.C. She was formerly married to Carleton S. Hadley.

VICE PRESIDENT JOHNSON SWORN IN BY RAYBURN

Lyndon Baines Johnson was sworn in as Vice President of the United States on January 20, 1961, at 12:41 P.M., by Speaker of the House Sam Rayburn, the first Vice President sworn in by a Speaker of the House.

VICE PRESIDENT'S RESIDENCE

Legislation authorizing the planning, design, construction, furnishing, and maintenance of an official residence for the Vice President was enacted April 9, 1966 (80 Stat. L. 106). An appropriation of $750,-000 was authorized but construction was delayed for the sake of economy. The residence is expected to be erected on the ten-acre site of the United States Naval Observatory.

FIRST ELECTORAL VOTE CAST FOR WOMAN VICE PRESIDENTIAL CANDIDATE

The first electoral vote for a woman was cast by Roger L. McBride, of Charlottesville, Va., whose vote for Theodora Nathan of Oregon, vice presidential candidate of the Libertarian Party, was counted January 6, 1973.

TWENTY-SEVEN COUNTIES NAMED FOR VICE PRESIDENTS
Calhoun–11
Ala., Ark., Fla., Ga., Ill., Iowa, Mich., Miss., S.C., Tex.,W.Va.
R. M. Johnson–5
Ill., Iowa, Ky., Mo., Neb.
Dallas–4
Ark., Iowa, Mo., Tex.
Clinton–2
N.Y., Ohio
Colfax–2
Neb., N.M.
Tompkins–1
N.Y.
King–1
Wash.
Hamlin–1
S.D.

INDEX

Listed in this index are the names of the Presidents and Vice Presidents; the names of political parties represented in national elections; general topics relating to all Presidents (e.g., *Inaugurations*); and special subjects associated with a single President (e.g., *Emancipation Proclamation*).

To find detailed information about a specific President, see the entry noting the individual biographical chapter in Part I. (Each chapter is arranged as follows: general summary, family history, nomination and election, cabinet appointments, sessions of Congress, Supreme Court appointments, important dates, Vice President, additional data.)

To find information about the Presidents collectively, see the subject entries noting the comparative data in Part II.

Millions read these ace bestsellers —have you?

ENRICHMENT LIBRARY

The Adventure of Birth Bing $1.25	
Bachelor Fatherhood McFadden $1.50	
How to Find a Job Larson $1.95	
The Art of Vegetarian Cookery Wason $1.25	
The First Babyfood Cookbook Morris $1.50	
How to Stop Fighting with Your Kids Dreikurs $1.50	
Chuang Tzu: Genius of the Absurd Waltham $1.50	
I Ching Translated by C. Waltham 95c	
In A Darkness Wechsler $1.25	
Malpractice and You Barchilon $1.75	
Nine Months to Go Klein $1.25	
The Pills in Your Life Halberstam $1.50	
Positive Self Analysis Book I Singer $1.50	

AN Agatha Christie CHRONOLOGY

NANCY BLUE WYNNE

The only one volume listing of every Christie novel, short story and collection, including plot outlines of MURDER ON THE ORIENT EXPRESS and major and lesser known works.
